Animals of the Tidal Marsh

Franklin C. Daiber
Professor of Marine Biology and Biological Sciences
College of Marine Studies and
School of Life and Health Sciences
University of Delaware

VNR **VAN NOSTRAND REINHOLD COMPANY**
NEW YORK   CINCINNATI   TORONTO   LONDON   MELBOURNE

Van Nostrand Reinhold Company Regional Offices:
New York   Cincinnati   Atlanta   Dallas   San Francisco

Van Nostrand Reinhold Company International Offices:
London   Toronto   Melbourne

Copyright © 1982 by Van Nostrand Reinhold Company

Library of Congress Catalog Card Number: 80-26403
ISBN: 0-442-24854-7

Manufactured in the United States of America

Published by Van Nostrand Reinhold Company
135 West 50th Street, New York, N.Y.   10020

Published simultaneously in Canada by Van Nostrand Reinhold Ltd.

15 14 13 12 11 10 9 8 7 6 5 4 3 2 1

Library of Congress Cataloging in Publication Data

Daiber, Franklin C.
  Animals of the tidal marsh.

  Includes bibliographies and index.
  1. Tidemarsh fauna.   I. Title.
QL114.D34   591.52′636   80-26403
ISBN 0-442-24854-7

Preface

This book had its inception when, simultaneously, Dr. Robert Reimold and Dr. William Queen asked me to write a chapter in their publication, *The Ecology of Halophytes,* and Charles Lesser of the Fish and Game Division of the Department of Natural Resources and Environmental Control of the State of Delaware asked me to review work that had been done on Delaware's tidal marshes. A further inducement was provided by Dr. V. J. Chapman who asked me to prepare a chapter for the volume, *Wet Coastal Ecosystems.* More material was compiled than could be incorporated into these requests within the time and space restraints delineated. Subsequently the older literature has been more intensively reviewed and newer information incorporated into an expanded text.

The purpose of this book is to bring together the literature as it pertains to the biology and natural history of those animals characteristic of tidal marshes. The scope of coverage spans the protozoa through the mammals and, as one might surmise, the literature is scattered throughout a great diversity of journals and other publications. The amounts of information available for differing species varies tremendously. Medical concerns, reactions to pestiferous species, special interests of sportsmen, and economic factors have served as the stimuli for much of the early studies on the biology of particular species such as the insect pests, waterfowl, and muskrat. It has become increasingly apparent in the last decade, that there are many more and different kinds of animals inhabiting these marshes than had previously been thought to be the case. In order to ascertain how the tidal marsh ecosystem works, how to preserve or to manage such a resource for the most good and least amount of disruption, it has become imperative that more detailed knowledge be acquired: what species are present, how do they carry on their life functions, and how do they interact?

My purpose will have been accomplished if I can bring the literature together into a unit, call attention to the needs for more information, and suggest opportunities for future research.

Franklin/C. Daiber

Acknowledgments

I am indebted to many people over the years for the guidance and help that has culminated in this book. While they have been generous with their knowledge, time, and patience, proffering very good suggestions and extending justifiable criticism, I should make it clear at the outset that the responsibility for opinions expressed rests solely with me.

In particular, I am grateful to my parents who provided an atmosphere of learning and encouragement, and to Professor H. O. Burdick for extending my vision into new vistas and instilling an enthusiasm for the broad field of biology. I would like to thank Mr. Norman Wilder, formerly Director of the Delaware Fish and Game Division who, while seeking information to guide him in management decisions, induced me to examine tidal marshes. Special thanks are due to colleagues and associates who have taken on the task of reviewing various portions of the manuscript: Drs. E. Paul Catts, John Kraft, and Frank Murphey, Chapter 2; Dr. R. Reimold, Chapter 3; Drs. L. Hurd and W. Odum, Chapter 4; Drs. R. Axtell, J. Burger, M. Carriker, P. Catts, R. Chabreck, J. Christy, C. Epifanio, R. Lake, D. Maurer, R. Roth, M. Taylor, and J. Tietjen, Chapter 5; Drs. L. Hurd and M. Sullivan, Chapter 6; Drs. Hurd and Maurer, Chapter 7.

I want to thank all those students who have put up with the cold, the heat, the mud, the wet, the insects, and the long hours as they worked with me over the years. I am grateful for their enthusiasm and inquisitiveness which provided me with stimulation and a gratifying experience.

I want to thank my secretaries, Sandra Goodley and Ellen Tyrawski for being so patient and gracious in typing the innumerable drafts, and handling all the other chores associated with processing the manuscript.

Lastly, a big "thank you" to my wife, Joanne, a willing companion on numerous busman's holidays to tidal marshes, here and abroad. Once the writing was completed, she volunteered to examine the entire manuscript, use her scientific training and editorial skills to improve readability and to mold the various sections into a cohesive whole.

Contents

1
General Considerations

Tidal marshes mean different things to different people. Man has been manipulating tidal marsh lands for agricultural purposes for many centuries (Warren, 1911). By means of the Swamp Land Acts of 1849, 1850, and 1860, the Federal government of the United States encouraged the exploitation of wetlands for agricultural purposes (Shaw and Fredine, 1956). Penfound and Schneidau (1945) and Bourn and Cottam (1950) described what they considered to be detrimental results. Early in the century Smith (1902) characterized the role of these marshes in mosquito production, while Stearns *et al.* (1940) and Dozier *et al.* (1948) identified their economic contribution in muskrat production. Tidal marshes provide food, shelter, and nesting sites for waterfowl and other wildlife (Shaw and Fredine, 1956; Barske, 1961; Linduska, 1964). They can contribute to educational programs and serve as sites for scientific research (Niering, 1961). The tidal streams and the marsh surface provide a source of food, oysters, blue crabs, waterfowl, fish, and muskrats (Rankin, 1961) and in some areas act as a mineral resource (Sanders and Ellis, 1961); some serve as pasturage for domestic animals (Reimold, 1976). These many uses to which wetlands have been subjected often result in conflicts of interest (Daiber, 1959).

Odum (1961) called attention to the contribution tidal marshes make to estuarine and coastal waters' productivity. Since then there has been a plethora of research dealing with production, nutrient fluxes, and techniques (Teal, 1962; Nixon and Oviatt, 1973; Boon, 1975; Woodwell and Whitney, 1977; Hopkins *et al.* 1978; Linthurst and Reimold, 1978).

Pough (1961) reminded us of the natural beauty of these coastal marshes, of the near-sighted views of some people, and how through the use of easements, this muted beauty could be retained for the future. Goodwin (1961) suggested ways in which to use these coastal lands at a highly productive level. In the interim there have been numerous meetings and symposia directed at preservation or wise management of our coastal resources (Newsom, 1968; Chabreck, 1973; Odum and Skjei, 1974; Montanari and Kusler, 1978). Odum (1961) stated the need to consider: (1) a functional approach to both utilization and production; (2) the estuary as a whole; (3) the

1

great diversity inherent in the marsh ecosystem; and (4) ways to cope with man-made alterations which originate from other than biological motives. What followed were functionally oriented studies such as those of Teal (1962), Day *et al.* (1973), and Welsh (1975); rehabilitation studies by Woodhouse *et al.* (1974); and symposia and syntheses by Ranwell (1972), Reimold and Queen (1974), and Chapman (1977).

Through it all has been the underlying recognition that individual plant and animal species contribute to the marsh-estuarine ecosystem. There has been a growing realization that, in order to understand the ecosystem and how it functions, more information has to be garnered concerning distributions, life histories, ecological and physiological requirements, and behavior responses of the individual species comprising a coastal tidal marsh. Although there is an extensive literature pertaining to salt-marsh animal distributions, life histories, and ecology, it has been only partially compiled and reviewed (Daiber, 1974). Much of this literature relates to distinctive and varied plant-animal interaction.

Shanholtzer (1974) synthesized information concerning inter-relationships between marsh vertebrates and plants and identified two associations: direct and indirect. The direct interactions involve spatial and physical utilization of vegetation, providing a habitat volume and structural foundation for feeding, reproductive, and roosting activities. This also includes thermal effects and refuge from predation. The indirect effects involve nutrient cycling and seed dispersal and become evident some time after the actual contact between plant and animal.

Various workers have listed numerous marine invertebrate species associated with tidal marshes; Kraeuter and Wolf (1974) eliminated those found in the creeks, pools, and similar areas to leave only a few species as indigenous to the marsh surface. The direct effect of these few species on the vegetation appears minimal but the opposite interaction includes protection from predation, a stabilizing platform, or a food source. Kraeuter and Wolf also recognized indirect effects; those that ameliorate various environmental fluctuations such as wave action, current velocities, humidity, temperature, and light.

Nichol (1936) divided the fauna of the marsh surface in English salt marshes into two groups: (1) animals visiting the marsh to feed; and (2) animals living permanently on the marsh. Nichol found this latter group of particular interest in terms of respiration rather than the impact of salinity; most species being air-breathing Insecta. Ranwell (1974) described the terrestrial nature of the surface found in the marshes of the Fal Estuary of Cornwall whose populations are controlled by drowning from unexpected, though infrequent, tidal floodings. There is a characteristic fauna associated with the marsh surface and for those English marshes described by Nichol (1936) it consisted of such species as *Orchestia gammarella* (Crustacea),

Paragnathia maxillaris (Isopoda), *Poliera marina* (Insecta), and *Dichirotrichus pubescens* (Insecta). Nichol commented on the distinctive animals associated with tidal marsh pools. The fauna of these ponds with salinities lower than $5\%_{00}$ was dominated by various insects, *Aedes detritus, Helophorus viridicillis,* and *Agabus bipustulatus* and the crustacean *Gammarus duebeni*. Pools with higher salinities ($15-20\%_{00}$) were dominated by *Gobius microps* (Pisces), *Neomysis vulgaris* (Crustacea), *Corophium volutator* (Crustacea), and *Nereis diversicolor* (Polychaeta). Other species were found to be common in particular pools. Nichol spoke to what has become a well-established dictum: salt-marsh animals cannot escape changing salinities. They must tolerate the osmotic effect on body fluids brought on by variable salinities.

Half a world away, Paviour-Smith (1956) added to the explanation of marsh surface communities by reporting work done at Hoopers Inlet on the Otago Peninsula wherein animal zonations, food pyramids, and trophic categories of a New Zealand salt meadow were defined. There was a broad area under the water edge dominated by *Salicornia australis,* merging into a narrow band of salt meadow which in turn gave way to grass and herbs. Paviour-Smith identified the boundary between the salt and grass meadows as an ecotone characterized by tussocks of *Poa caespitosa* and *Scirpus nodasus.* The salt meadow possessed four plant species. *Samolus repens* was more abundant in the lower reaches of the *Salicornia* zone, *Selliera radicans* and *Scirpus cernuus* in the intermediate region while *Cotula bioica* did not appear until the salt meadow proper.

The wide overlap of marine and terrestrial animals was the most striking feature of the transect across the *Salicornia* zone, salt meadow and into the grass land. In the lower *Salicornia* area, Collembola, Coleoptera, cyclorraphous larvae, Hemiptera, lepidopterous larvae, mites, spiders, and oligochaetes occurred along with amphipods, polychaete worms, and crabs. In the salt-meadow ecotone, the amphipod *Orchestia chiliensis* was still present with a more completely terrestrial fauna. Paviour-Smith reiterated the fact that these animals must adapt to or tolerate varying conditions of water and salinity. The larger, surface arthropods had their maximum abundance in the drier grass meadow while the soil microfauna and arthropods were more evident in the transitional salt-meadow zone.

The mesofauna of the salt meadow were mostly full-time annual residents whose seasonal variations were due to breeding cycles. Temperature and population curves were similar with increases from October to April with a peak from January to March. While there were many irregularities in the microfauna, Paviour-Smith showed an overall tendency toward a larger soil population during the warmer winter and early spring months than in the cooler summer and early fall.

Generalities directed to salt-marsh vegetation and animal zonations have been put forth by Macnae (1957), Teal (1962), and Healy (1975). Macnae identified five vegetation zones in a South African salt marsh: (1) a *Zosteretum*, (2) a *Spartinetum atricta*, (3) an *Arthrocnemetum perenne*, (4) a *Limonietum*, and (5) an *Arthrocnemetum* of shrubby species. These were used as markers for animal zonations which Macnae considered to be more complex and less precise.

Healy described the aquatic fauna of pans and channels as brackish in nature and distributed along a salinity gradient with the greatest species numbers and highest densities in the lower zones. The majority of the species that are aerial in nature and associated with vegetation were found along the landward margins of the marsh and are not considered typical of salt marshes. The fauna of the marsh surface were described as being influenced by tidal frequency with the exception of infauna smaller than one centimeter which were the same throughout the marsh.

Teal characterized five regions consisting of (1) creek bank, a muddy or sandy region between low water and the lower limits of *Spartina*; (2) stream-side marsh, 1–3 meters wide comprising tall *Spartina* just above the bare bank; (3) levee marsh with intermediate *Spartina;* (4) short *Spartina*, a region consisting of short widely spaced plants; and (5) *Salicornia* marsh, sandy areas near land where *Salicornia* is conspicuous. Although Teal confined his observations to the Georgia marshes, these categories can be applied to most tidal marshes. These distinctions reflect the interaction of tidal inundation, drainage, salinity, substrate, and marsh height on vegetation zonation. Because these parameters come together in differing combinations, one should expect some variance in vegetational patterns from marsh to marsh. The animals associated with these five vegetation zones were placed into three general categories by Teal: (1a) terrestrial animals living in the marsh, (b) terrestrial or fresh-water species living on the landward edge; (2) aquatic species with their center of abundance in the estuary, (a) estuarine species limited to the marsh low-water level, (b) species in the stream-side marsh, (c) estuarine species found well into the marsh; (3) marsh species with aquatic ancestors, (a) species with planktonic larvae and (b) species living entirely within the marsh. Teal recorded 57 percent of the aquatic species (2a and 2b) occupying the lowest portions of the marsh where exposure at low tide is the shortest. Those on the marsh were living at one edge of their species distributions; their numbers maintained by migrations from the water and by adaptations and tolerance levels. Those living above the mud were subject to great environmental stress and those penetrating farthest onto the marsh have adopted burrowing habits. The remainder were either tolerant enough to inhabit the entire marsh or were most common on the marsh itself. The terrestrial species comprised almost half the marsh fauna, yet have made few adaptations for marsh living and were much less important in community energetics than the aquatic species (Teal, 1962).

MacDonald (1969b) and Phleger (1970) have examined marsh faunas from the perspective of ecological zoogeography. MacDonald collected a total of 76 molluscan species from the tidal creeks and *Spartina-Salicornia* salt marshes of the North American Pacific coast. The distributions of these various species could be separated into two zoogeographic provinces, the Californian extending southward from Point Conception to Cedros Island (27° 30′–34° 30′ N) and the Oregonian proceeding northward from Point Conception to Dixon Entrance (34° 30′–50° N). There were one or two widely distributed species while the remaining species were represented by small numbers of patchily distributed individuals. This organization was observed to be fairly uniform between different sites within the same faunal province, based on identity and numbers of species present and their relative abundance and size frequency. There were seven species restricted to the Oregonian province and thirteen restricted to the Californian province.

MacDonald reported a distinction between the marsh and creek faunas. The marsh fauna was very uniform in composition, so much so that groups of species that frequently recur together could be identified by inspection. Five species comprised 96.9 percent of living specimens collected from quantitative samples. *Assiminea californica* occurred at every site sampled. *Littorina newcombiana* and *Phytia myosotis* were found north of Point Conception while *Cerithidea californica* and *Melampus olivaceus* occurred only south of Point Conception. The remaining 3.1 percent of marsh fauna were frequently found in tidal creeks.

The tidal creek faunas usually contained more species and had a more variable species composition. Recurrent groups were identified by computer not by inspection as in the marshes. One or two species were numerically dominant. When more than one occurred, a recurrent group could be identified. Such groups reflected the local dispersion and relative abundance of different species. The remaining species functioned independently of each other. This greater variability has been attributed to infaunal-epifaunal relations and sediment types. All of the marsh fauna was identified as epibenthic and independent of sediment type while the creek species were mostly infauna (83.4 percent). The variable nature of sediments and species habitats could account for the absence of certain infaunal species at the various sampling sites.

Although MacDonald considered the salt-marsh molluscs to occupy similar types of niches (i.e., all epifaunal species feeding on algae and plant detritus), the standing crop of living animals increased considerably north to south, suggesting that resources available within each niche increased at lower latitudes. Within the creek environment, the number of niche types occupied by molluscan fauna did not change with latitude but species types did (infaunal and epifaunal species, and feeding types). The number of species found in successively larger salt marshes or tidal creeks were not significantly larger. This suggested to MacDonald that the increasing species diversity noted from increasingly larger units may reflect the presence of a greater variability of habitats rather than an enrichment of faunas.

Phleger (1970) has summarized his work on Foraminifera populations and factors influencing their distributions. The striking feature of the marsh environment is the great variation in values of parameters known to affect the occurrence and development of foraminiferal populations such as pH of the sediments, nature of sediments and particle size, extent of inundation, oxygen levels, salinity, temperatures, etc. The Gulf of Mexico foraminiferal assemblages differed between a low *Spartina* and a *Salicornia* high marsh. The standing stock was generally large but varied between 10–1500/10 millimeter surface sediment one centimeter thick. Samples from tidal flats had twice the average standing stock of a low marsh and four times the population of the high marsh. Fewer species were present in marsh samples than were found from the adjoining tidal flats.

In contrast, on the Pacific coast of North America, the standing stocks were described as being greater on a high marsh than from a tidal flat despite wide variations. There were distinctions in faunal assemblages between the tidal flats, marsh channels, and the marsh surface. Low- and high-marsh assemblages could be differentiated in some places.

It is evident from Phleger's observations of foraminiferal assemblages from the Gulf and Pacific coasts of North America and elsewhere, that marshes often contain mixtures of lagoon or bay assemblages along with endemic marsh species. The dominance of one group depends on the hydrology of the marsh and lagoon or estuary and the position of the fauna in the marsh. Some eleven species have been considered endemic to marshes but all are not found in any one marsh or in all geographic regions: *Ammoastuta inepta, Arenoparrella mexicana, Discorinopsis aquayoi, Haplophragmoides* spp., *Jadammina polystoma, Miliammina fusca, Protoschista findens, Pseudoponides andersoni, Tiphotrocha comprimata, Trochammina inflata,* and *Trochammina macrescens.* However, there are world-wide similarities in assemblages of marsh foraminifera. Phleger found *Trochammina inflata* present in every marsh examined while *Miliammina fusca, Jadammina polystoma* and *Trochammina macrescens* occurred in most marshes.

Another factor woven through the fabric of tidal marsh ecology is the considerable influence man has had on the vegetation and animals of tidal marshes, particularly through water level regulation. Marshes have been drained for insect control or agricultural use, or flooded for wildlife management purposes (summarized by Daiber, 1974). The apparent impact of drainage and lower water tables on marsh invertebrate faunas has been summarized in work carried out on the Mispillion marshes of Delaware (Bourn and Cottam, 1950). Dramatic reductions of all forms of macro-invertebrates were noted. The *Spartina alterniflora* zone showed reductions ranging from 39.3 percent to 82.2 percent. Populations in the *Spartina patens* region were decreased by 41.2 percent and 97.3 percent and those occurring in the *Scirpus robustus* area by 49.6 percent to 97.0 percent. Bourn and Cottam asserted that such reductions had direct effects on waterfowl by limiting available food supplies. Another example is the work of Stearns *et al.* (1940) who identified the decline in desirable muskrat foods and house-building materials in a brackish Delaware marsh following a lowering of the water table brought on by ditching. They reported a decline in the muskrat population in ditched marshes induced by the movement of the animals to un-ditched locales. It is evident from the foregoing that many discrete environmental factors, working independently or in concert, influence the distributions, abundance, and life cycles of tidal marsh animals. The succeeding chapters will review these various factors in detail.

2
Zonation and Distribution

INTRODUCTION

Numerous authors have discussed the influence of tidal flooding, salinity, soil characteristics, and other parameters on the distribution and zonation of marsh vegetation. Chapman (1960, 1974) and Ranwell (1972) have very ably summarized much of the existing work on the subject. There is an extensive literature on salt-marsh animal distributions, life histories, and ecology and much of it deals with an examination and evaluation of the various factors affecting animal zonations. Even a casual perusal of this literature points up the complexity and multiplicity of interactions affecting a great variety of marsh animals.

This literature is spotty. Certain animals such as the fiddler crabs attract considerable attention. Several authors have a special interest in a particular taxonomic group (Phleger-Foraminifera or Luxton-Acarinida) and examine salt marshes for the animals of their interest.

There is a very definite relationship between vegetation distribution and zonation, marsh height, and tidal flooding. Adams (1963) among others very specifically stated that vegetation characteristics are related to the driving force of tidal action and that such distributions can be segregated into a low- and high-marsh zone. Chapman (1960) defined the low marsh as an area that has more than 360 submergences a year, a maximum period of continuous exposure not to exceed nine days and more than 1.2 hours of submergence during daylight hours per diem. Accordingly, a high marsh is defined as having fewer than 360 submergences per year, a minimum period of continuous exposure exceeding ten days and less than one hour of submergence during daylight hours per diem. The line of demarcation is approximately mean high water. While Ranwell (1972) called attention to the inability to draw a sharp distinction, he recognized the presence of high- and low-marsh areas. Ranwell went on to say that marsh height is much more sensitive to tidal submergence toward the marsh seaward limits. The landward portion of the marsh is dominated by edaphic factors associated with emergence: total nitrogen levels, increases in organic content, soil water levels, sea water, soil type, potassium-calcium relationships, and shifts from calcium to sodium ion dominance (Gray and Bunce, 1972; Gray and Scott, 1977). On the basis of 0.25 m^2 quadrats spaced over a one-meter elevation gradient, Zedler (1977) was unable to discern any realistic vegetational zones or associations on a marsh in the Tijuana estuary, California. She considered elevation to be a good indicator of the changing environment, with lower elevations having higher salinity, more inundation, higher soil organic matter, and more clay than upper elevations. Vascular plant dominance changed gradually with elevations. *Spartina foliosa* dominated the lowest elevations, followed by *Salicornia bigelovii* and *Batis maritima, Jaumea carnosa, Suaeda californica, Frankenia grandifolia, Monanthochloe littoralis* and *Salicornia subterminalis. Salicornia virginica* was common at all but the highest elevations. As pointed out earlier, vegetational zonation can be used as markers for animal zonations which are considered to be more complex and less precise (Macnae, 1957 a and b). It would be interesting to examine the animal distributions in Zedler's study marsh.

RELATION TO VEGETATION, MARSH HEIGHT, TIDAL FLOODING, AND DRAINAGE

Protozoa

Each marsh environment has its own distinctive Foraminifera assemblages. Plant zonations reflect environmental differences and it could be expected that such differences would be reflected in foraminiferal distributions. Different plant assemblages could provide different food for such microorganisms (Phleger, 1965). Buzas (1969) suggested the amount and kind of food is important in determining Foraminifera species densities.

Phleger and Walton (1950) identified two major Foraminifera facies in the area of Barnstable, Massachusetts: one found within the harbor characterized by *Trochammina inflata;* and the second an adjacent nearshore Cape Cod Bay facies dominated by *Proteonina atlantica* and *Eggerella advena.* Temperature and salinity variation tended to separate these two groups. The authors distinguished three subfacies comprising the Barnstable Harbor fauna: the high marsh consisting of *Spartina patens* and *S. glabra* (=*S. alterniflora*), the intertidal flats and the channels. The greatest total populations of harbor Foraminifera were measured on the high marsh and were dominated by *Trochammina inflata* and *T. macrescens. Miliammina fusca* occurred here in greatest frequency while *Armorella sphaerica, Webbinella* sp. and *Valvulineria* sp. were confined to this zone suggesting an indigenous fauna. While total populations of Foraminifera were much smaller on the intertidal flats, the recognition of *Elphidium incertum* made the intertidal zone a distinctive habitat. The presence of small populations at the channel

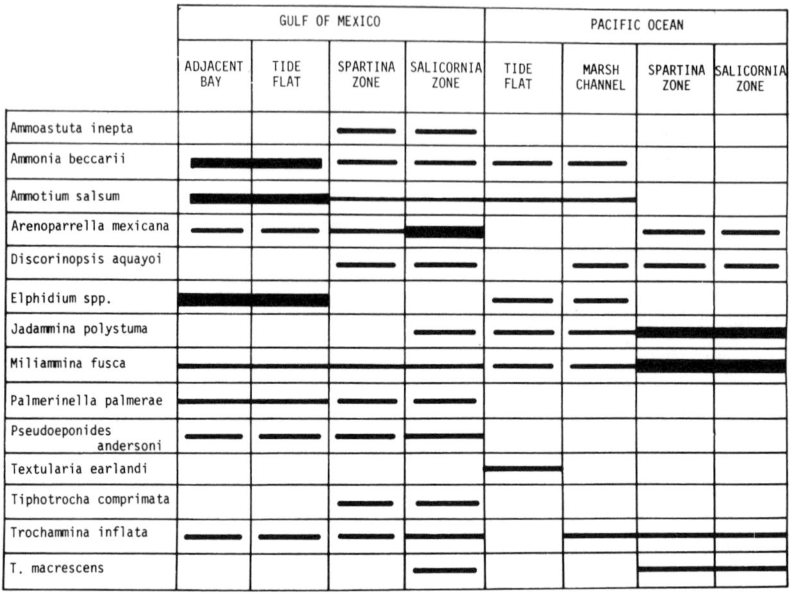

	GULF OF MEXICO				PACIFIC OCEAN			
	ADJACENT BAY	TIDE FLAT	SPARTINA ZONE	SALICORNIA ZONE	TIDE FLAT	MARSH CHANNEL	SPARTINA ZONE	SALICORNIA ZONE
Ammoastuta inepta			▬	▬				
Ammonia beccarii	▬▬	▬▬	▬	▬	▬	▬		
Ammotium salsum	▬▬	▬▬						
Arenoparrella mexicana	▬	▬		▬▬			▬	▬
Discorinopsis aquayoi			▬	▬		▬	▬	▬
Elphidium spp.	▬▬	▬▬			▬	▬		
Jadammina polystuma			▬	▬			▬▬	
Miliammina fusca					▬	▬	▬▬	▬
Palmerinella palmerae	▬		▬					
Pseudoeponides andersoni	▬	▬	▬					
Textularia earlandi					▬▬			
Tiphotrocha comprimata			▬	▬				
Trochammina inflata	▬	▬	▬				▬	▬
T. macrescens				▬			▬▬	▬

Figure 2.1.   Generalized distributions of marsh Foraminifera in the northwest Gulf of Mexico and Pacific Coast of North America. (Figure 1 from Phleger and Bradshaw, 1966, by permission of the editor, *Science*.)

stations in Barnstable Harbor was presumed related to the magnitude of tidal scour.

Phleger and Walton (1950) called attention to the role of environmental parameters affecting Foraminifera distributions, including diurnal tidal action, nature and movement of bottom materials, presence of marsh grass, and relative organic production. These authors explored two possible reasons for the large Foraminifera populations on the high marsh of Barnstable Harbor: (1) the environment could support a large population, or (2) Foraminifera are washed in. They noted the high organic concentration in these marsh sediments and proposed that large accumulations of grass provide shelter and organic matter as food. They found little evidence for Foraminifera being washed into the marsh since the high marsh was not subjected to frequent flooding and strong currents and there were few broken tests.

While the small intertidal populations are characteristic of Barnstable Harbor Foraminifera (Phleger and Walton, 1950), it is evident this is not a universal feature in relation to the extent of tidal inundation. Work done on the Gulf of Mexico marshes (Phleger, 1970) displayed differences between the low *Spartina* and high *Salicornia* marsh (Figure 2.1). Standing stocks were generally large but varied between 10–1500/10 millimeter surface sediment one centimeter thick. Samples from tidal flats had twice the average stock of the low marsh and four times the population of the high marsh. Not only were there larger populations on the intertidal flats but there were more species.

In contrast, the marshes of the Pacific coast of North America (Phleger, 1970) are similar to those of Barnstable Harbor in that the tidal flat and marsh channel assemblages differed from the marsh Foraminifera fauna and low- and high-marsh stocks tended to be larger on the high marsh than on the tidal flats although highly variable.

It is evident from the above that marsh height and vegetation zonation have an impact on Foraminifera distributions. Exposure during the tidal cycle and surface drainage also have an effect. *Ammobaculites dilatatus* was present at every station examined in Poponesset Bay, Massachusetts, but was most common at those stations exposed during part of the tidal cycle. *Miliammina fusca* was also found in greater numbers at those stations periodically exposed because of tidal action (Parker and Athearn, 1959). Murray (1973b) alluded to this when he wrote that *Miliammina fusca, Ammonia beccarii, Protelphidium anglicum,* and *Elphidium articulatum* were common forms found at the margins of an estuary.

Phleger (1970) discussed the impact of drainage in his examination of the abundance of agglutinated tests. The shells of marsh Foraminifera range from agglutinated sand, or silt particles, to entirely calcareous tests. Low marshes in many places contain a fauna dominated by calcareous tests with a few agglutinated ones. Areas such as Mission Bay, California, and Guerrero Negro Lagoon, Mexico, that receive undiluted sea water and have no run-off possess a marsh fauna with calcareous tests. In contrast, the marsh Foraminifera of the Pacific coast of North America have agglutinated tests. This is an area of high run-off where undiluted seawater containing calcareous species does not invade the marshes.

Fewer Foraminifera species have been recorded from areas of high run-off which is probably due to the exclusion of marine water. Such places typically have 10–11 species in contrast to a much more diverse fauna in the absence of run-off: 25 species in a Baja California hypersaline marsh and more than 50 species in a temperate hypersaline lagoon and marsh in Coorong, South Australia. The low diversity in two subarctic marshes may be due to low temperature or high run-off or a combination of the two (Phleger, 1970).

Up to now Foraminifera distributions have been considered on a broad habitat basis. Phleger and Bradshaw (1966) recognized at least three zones (identified by foraminiferal assemblages) for the Gulf of Mexico and Pacific coast marshes (Figure 2.1). Phleger (1965) has suggested there is some evi-

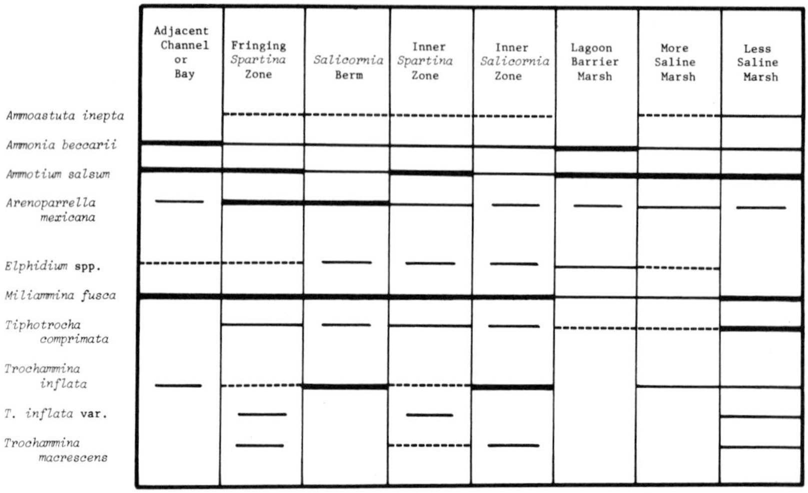

	Adjacent Channel or Bay	Fringing *Spartina* Zone	*Salicornia* Berm	Inner *Spartina* Zone	Inner *Salicornia* Zone	Lagoon Barrier Marsh	More Saline Marsh	Less Saline Marsh
Ammoastuta inepta		--					--------	
Ammonia beccarii								
Ammotium salsum								
Arenoparrella mexicana	—					—	—	—
Elphidium spp.	--------		—	—	—		--------	
Miliammina fusca								
Tiphotrocha comprimata						--------		
Trochammina inflata	—	--------						
T. inflata var.		—		—				
Trochammina macrescens		—	--------					

Figure 2.2. Generalized distribution of principal marsh species of Foraminifera in Galveston Bay areas arranged according to apparent environments. (From Phleger, 1965, by permission of the editor, *Limnology and Oceanography*.)

dence that microenvironments within each zone could have an effect on distributions within the zone (Figure 2.2). Numbers varied greatly which may reflect unevenness in environmental parameters. Matera and Lee (1972) examined such distributions on a finer scale, observing that within the broad limits of tidal excursion Foraminifera have very patchy distributions. There were fewer species but larger standing crops in the sediments than in the epiphytic communities associated with a Southampton, Long Island salt marsh. Within the epiphytic community the Foraminifera were very patchy; 2.6 percent of the total samples accounted for 56.4 percent of the total numbers collected. The epiphytic communities associated with *Enteromorpha intestinalis, Polysiphonia* sp., *Ulva lactuca,* and *Zannichellia palustris* had the most Foraminifera. Species of *Codium* and *Fucus* were never substrates for Foraminifera. Drainage patterns generated by the small rivulets flowing through the marsh at low tide determined the distribution patterns in the epiphytic communities by establishing small changes in temperature, salinity, and grain size of the sediment. The ebb and flood of the tides did not cause foraminiferal migrations in the sediments.

Meiofauna

Meiobenthos, a term coined by Mare (1942) refers to small benthic organisms, including nematodes, harpacticoid copepods, amphipods, polychaetes, oligochaetes, kinorhynchs, turbellareans, and ostracods but excludes the protozoa. Mare (1942) included the Foraminifera among the meiobenthos. Coull and Bell (1979) provided an excellent review of this newly burgeoning aspect of marine ecology.

These various organisms make up over 90 percent of the meiobenthos (numbers/m^2) in a Louisiana marsh (Day *et al.* 1973). Using ATP as a measure of biomass or living carbon Sikora *et al.* (1977) found that over the annual cycle nematodes contributed 92 and 78 percent of the living biomass within intertidal and subtidal sediments respectively. However, Gerlach (1978) considered these figures to be extremely high and atypical. It was his contention, after reviewing the literature, that the meiofauna and Foraminifera contribute 30 and 12 percent respectively, to the living biomass of surface sediments and collectively 20 percent of the food of the deposit-feeding subsurface macrofauna. Sikora *et al.* (1977) found the caloric content to be the same (6.1174 $\pm$ 0.3112 k cal g^{-1} ash-free dry weight or 11.543 k cal g^{-1} of organic carbon) for the meiofauna of the intertidal and subtidal zones. On the basis of such information they concluded that the meiofauna, especially the nematodes, must be considered in evaluating the partitioning of benthic sedimentary systems. In spite of their apparent importance the nematodes may have to share the limelight. Coull and Vernberg (1970) suggested the harpacticoid copepods may play an important role in meiobenthic metabolism. On a weight-for-weight basis, these copepods were found to respire significantly more than the much more numerous nematodes. The nematodes, copepods, and polychaete worms were ranked in decreasing density in a South Carolina salt marsh with values of 73, 15.3, and 7.7 percent, respectively (Bell *et al.,* 1978; Bell, 1979).

There were two polychaetes present in the high marsh. *Manayunkia aestuarina* was dominant and present all year. *Streblospio benedicti* was present in the fall. Spring densities were caused by *M. aestuarina* while fall densities were created by the combined effects of both *M. aestuarina* and the young *S. benedicti* (Bell, 1979).

Four harpacticoid copepods comprised 78 percent of the copepod assemblage in this South Carolina high marsh: *Stenhelia* (D) *bifidia* (48 percent), *Schizopera knabeni* (11.1 percent), *Microarthridion littorale* (9.8 percent), and *Enhydrosoma propinquum* (9.1 percent). *S.* (D) *bifidia* had maximum densities in the fall while the others displayed variable seasonal patterns of abundance (Bell, 1979). In spite of these various species patterns, it was noted that the percent composition of the total meiofauna was constant over time with only minor exceptions. Total meiofauna densities peaked in late fall-early winter and declined in early spring and late summer (Bell *et al.,* 1978; Bell, 1979).

Coull and Bell (1979) gave 10^{6}m^2 and 1 to 2 gm^2 for average densities and biomass, respectively, which appears rather low. From a mud flat in the estuary of the River Lynher, Cornwall, Warwick and Price (1979) found the lowest numbers of nematodes in late fall-early winter ranging between 8 and $9 \times 10^6/m^2$ between October and January gradually increasing to a peak of 22.9×10^6 in May and declining to winter lows. The average for the year was $12.46 \times 10^6/m^2$. The overwintering biomass ranged between 1.4 and 1.6 gm/m^2 dry weight while the peak in May was 3.4 gm/m^2 dry weight and the annual average was 1.97 gm/m^2. Earlier, Teal and Wieser (1966) reported numerical densities of nematodes in a Sapelo Island, Georgia marsh as great as $16 \times 10^6/m^2$ and weighing 7.6 gm/m^2. Densities were reported to be ten times greater than those at Woods Hole, Massachusetts, where Wieser and Kanwisher (1961) found patchy distributions with some densities ranging from 1.4 to $2.1 \times 10^6 m^2$. The biomass of the Sapelo Island samples was small reflecting the small size of the dominant species. This biomass more closely resembled the sublittoral zone of the Woods Hole area than that of the salt marsh. Teal and Wieser (1966) found Sapelo Island nematodes generally more abundant and with the greatest vertical distribution at sites closest to the water.

There are differences in the vertical distribution of the meiofauna within the marsh soils. Wieser and Kanwisher (1961) found most of the nematode population concentrated in the upper four centimeters with a maximum penetration of eight centimeters. They inferred such vertical distributions was related to the reduction of available space caused by the mat of *Spartina* roots. A similar observation has been made by Bell *et al.* (1978) and Coull and Bell (1979) who found the majority of the meiofauna in the top 1.0 centimeter of sediment and a negative correlation with the root masses. In muddy substrates 94 percent of the meiofauna were in this topmost centimeter while the organisms had a deeper penetration in sandy substrate. Bell *et al.* (1978) found significantly more total meiofauna, nematodes, and copepods in the top 0.5 centimeter fraction taken "between" plants than in cores from "around" plants. The data of Wieser and Kanwisher (1961) and Bell *et al.* (1978) contradicts Teal and Wieser (1966) who found greater nematode concentrations with the increased root material, suggesting the nematodes exploited a micro-oxygenated zone in an anaerobic habitat.

Food supply has been suggested as an important factor in establishing the patchy distribution and level of abundance; the low tide area receives the greatest amount of detritus and algae (by way of chlorophyll concentrations) and microbial biomass is higher in the upper sediment layers (Mare, 1942; Teal and Wieser, 1966; Gerlach, 1978; Bell *et al.*, 1978; Coull and Bell, 1979). Bell *et al.* (1978) found significantly more nematodes and total meiofauna from "around" *Uca* burrows while copepod numbers were significantly greater in nonburrow areas. They attributed the reduced numbers of copepods around *Uca* burrows to the reworking of the sediments by the fiddler crabs, while the increase in nematodes may reflect the absence of copepods and an increase in the number of fecal pellets and associated microbial activity around the burrow sites.

While it is evident the various meiobenthic species display a stratification within a vertical soil orientation and a patchiness in horizontal distribution "among" and "between" plants, there has been some evidence of horizontal zonation (Teal and Wieser, 1966). This has now been more firmly established by Coull *et al.* (1979) who demonstrated a zonation of epibenthic or burrowing harpacticoid copepods in a South Carolina salt marsh. Of the five sites examined only the low- and high-marsh zones were covered with vegetation. The sediment of the rest of the sites was composed primarily of *S. alterniflora* detritus. The degree of exposure was identified as a major variable over the gradient although the presence of vegetation and bioturbation, primarily by *Uca,* was considered to be of possible importance in copepod distributions. Copepod numbers varied from site to site, being most abundant in the low marsh and with the lowest number in the high marsh (Table 2.1). The dominant species were typical of mud or detrital substrates. Certain species had a broad distribution while others were more restricted (Figure 2.3). Species like *Microarthridion littorale* must be plastic to have had such a cosmopolitan distribution while others had particular habitat tolerance limits. Species like *Nannopus palustris* were restricted (for unknown reasons) to the zone of anoxic "black muds". The high marsh with its greater habitat heterogeneity did not display greater numbers of species, probably because of harsh conditions induced by extended exposure and temperature—salinity fluctuations. The subtidal area did not have the highest densities, probably because there was less habitat heterogeneity.

Mollusca

Pelecypoda. The ribbed mussel, *Geukensia demissa* (Dilwyn, 1817) (=*Modiolus demissus*), is a much more obvious member of the marsh fauna than

Table 2.1. **Densities of adult copepodite benthic copepods at the five sites of the salt marsh gradient. (from Coull *et al.,* 1979, by permission of the editor, *Estuarine Coast. Mar. Sci.*)**

	Creek Bottom	Sub-tidal	Mud Flat	Low Marsh	High Marsh
No. copepods/10 cm^{-2}					
Range	69–97	23–231	9–245	75–620	20–192
Mean	83	107	89	262	73
% copepods of total					
meiofauna	12	11	4	22	16

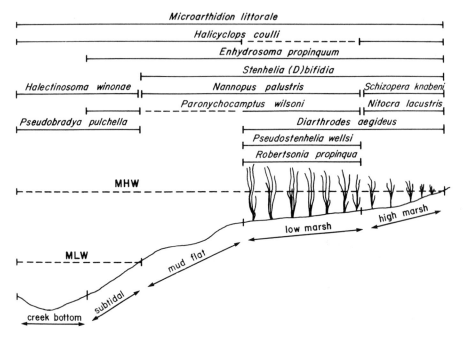

Figure 2.3.   Schematic diagram illustrating the zonation pattern of meiobenthic copepods along a depth gradient in southeastern United States salt marshes. Only those species which comprised >15% of the total copepod fauna in at least one season are illustrated. (From Coull *et al.*, 1979, by permission of the editor, *Estuarine Coast. Mar. Sci.*)

the previously described forms. During 1961, as part of a class exercise in
Canary Creek marsh, Delaware, the average mussel density was found to be
45.5/m^2 within a 1-meter zone bordering drainage ditches. Beyond this the
numbers declined to 6.0/m^2 in the short *Spartina alterniflora* within a 10-
meter distance from the ditches. The mussel has been examined in the Sapelo Island marshes of Georgia where random samples gave an estimated
population density of 7.8/m^2 for the inhabited portions of the marsh. They
were most dense near the heads of small creeks, an average of 52 ani-
mals/m^2 being common in certain marsh types (Table 2.2). The tall *Spartina*
(1–3 meters)—at the creek head, which occupied only 6 percent of the total
marsh area, contained 46 percent of population by weight. The medium
Spartina (0.5–1.0 m) levee had a reported density one-seventh of the tall
Spartina (creek head marsh) but the levee occupied 3.5 times as much area
and contributed the second largest percentage of total weight (Table 2.2)
(Kuenzler, 1961a).

Clumped distributions within uniform marsh areas were a striking fea-

Table 2.2. Population distribution and density of *Geukensia demissa* from the Sapelo Island marshes. (From Kuenzler, 1961, by permission of the editor, *Limnology and Oceanography.*)

No.	Marsh Type Description	% of Total Marsh	$\bar{X}$	Variance	#	Wt.	% Total Population	
			#/0.2m²		Density/m²		% Total	
1	Muddy Creek banks	4	0		0	0	0	0
2	Tall *Spartina* edge	9	0		0	0	0	0
3	Medium *Spartina* levee	21	1.14	12.32	5.7	4.35	17	22
4	Short *Spartina* low elevation	16	1.24	9.29	6.2	3.0	15	12
5	Short *Spartina* high elevation	20	0.08	0.11	0.4	0.15	1	1
6	*Salicornia* spp. *Distichlis spicata*	9	0.23	0.37	1.1	0.40	2	1
7	*Juncus roemerianus*	4	2.64	26.4	13	6.15	9	7
8	Tall *Spartina* creek heads	6	10.4	146	52	31.6	47	46
9	Medium *Spartina* medium elevation	11	1.11	5.72	5.6	4.55	9	12
Total		100					100	100
Mean			1.33		6.66*	4.11		

* The difference in density of 6.66/m² and 7.82/m² reported in the text was due to the mat not being sieved. Mussels less than 25 mg were not recovered but did constitute 18 percent of the total number.

ture of the Sapelo Island mussel populations in that sample variances were larger than the means, indicating nonrandom distributions. Clumps were larger and more numerous in densely populated marsh types such as the creek heads where they often exceeded one meter in diameter or paralleled the creeks for many meters.

Kuenzler reported the vertical distribution to be approximately 200–240 centimeters above mean low water. The center of biomass was situated at 220 centimeters with the maximum density probably at this same level. It was calculated a mussel at the 220 centimeters elevation would be covered by 77 percent of the flood tides or about 18 percent of the time. The greater density by weight at low and medium elevations was thought to be made possible by longer feeding times. When comparing growth rates, it was always greater in the low-marsh types (Short *Spartina,* low elevation; Tall *Spartina,* creek heads) than in higher marsh types (Medium *Spartina,* levee; *Salicornia-Distichlis*; Medium *Spartina,* medium elevation).

Lent (1967a, 1967b, 1968, 1969) elaborated on the significance of intertidal distribution and air-gaping in the ribbed mussel. He compared those mussels typically found in tidal marsh muds with those located on exposed surfaces such as bridge pilings. There was a significant difference in the shell length-height ratios; bridge mussels being longer than marsh mussels. There was no difference between marsh mussels from the different geographic locations of Delaware and Georgia. Lent (1967b) attributed the difference between habitats to the crowding effect of clumping in the marsh.

Kuenzler (1961) and Lent (1967b) found an excellent correlation between shell height and the cube root of the shell-free, dry body weight. However, Lent did not find any relationship between the shell weight-meat weight ratios and intertidal heights. Since the mussel is exposed during part of the tidal cycle and air-gapes during exposure, respiration could be carried on and such exposure would thus not reduce meaty tissue weight as rapidly. Air-gaping by increasing the efficiency of aerial respiration would permit a greater landward penetration of the intertidal zone.

In his 1968 paper, Lent pointed out median survival times in gaseous environments to be proportional to the volume of oxygen present. Lent reported oxygen tension during exposure at 15 millimeter Hg and 110 millimeter Hg while inundated (Figure 6, 1968). Lower rates of respiration in air were explained by these lower oxygen tensions of the mantle cavity fluid in air-gaping mussels. Although the rate was lower in air than when submerged, more oxygen was consumed because of extended exposure (82 percent aerial exposure, Kuenzler, 1961). Mussels survived for long periods of exposure as long as they were protected from desiccation.

Desiccation and temperature changes were environmental parameters with which the exposed mussels were confronted. Lent (1969) considered the mussel to possess a high tolerance to dehydration and a very high enzyme thermostability. Temperature had a significant effect on the rate of desiccation at low but not at high humidity (Lent, 1968). Desiccation resulted from water loss by air-gaping and was a physical phenomenon in which a surface to volume relationship caused small mussels to reach a median lethal weight loss of 36–38 percent more rapidly than large mussels.

Mussels can survive over a temperature range of at least 56 °C with a recorded minimum of −22 °C (Lent, 1969). An upper LD50 for a 10-hour heat stress fell between 36.4 and 37.8 °C with the large mussels more labile to thermal stress than the small animals (Lent, 1968). Such temperature tolerance would explain the geographic distribution ranging from Prince Edward Island in the north to South America.

Salinity limits are wide but not firmly established. The lower limit is at least 3‰. Mussels can survive water losses of 36–38 percent by desiccation and have at least 71 percent of their tissue water frozen (Lent, 1969). Therefore the upper limit must be high.

Mussels living in moist marsh mud occupied a higher intertidal height than those living on exposed bridge pilings. When the intertidal position of bridge mussels was examined as a function of shell size the population fell within an ellipse (Figure 2.4). The intertidal range was greatest for medium size mussels and was reduced for both larger and smaller groups. Lent (1968) considered this ellipse to be a geometric form within which the natural population could live. The upper surface is generated by the physical factors of dessication and thermal stress whereas predation and competition are biotic factors determining the lower surface.

Lent (1969) proposed air-gaping in the mussel to be a significant behavioral adaptation which permits aerial respiration and penetration of the high intertidal zone. In addition, it is physiologically and biochemically adapted in that it is both eurythermal and euryhaline. These two adaptations provide a tolerance toward dessication, salinity variation, thermal stress, and possibly anaerobic conditions. However, there is no obvious morphological adaptation thus the pelecypod body plan precludes further landward penetration.

A recently completed study (Kat, 1978) of another marsh surface bivalve, the Florida marsh clam, *Cyrenoida floridana,* depicted an interesting parallel to the gaping behavior of *G. demissa.* To date, this small bivalve, which gets up to 9 millimeters in length, has a northern range extension limited to southern Delaware, not extending beyond the Great Marsh of Lewes.

The preferred habitat is at 1.36 meters above mean low water in locales where the moisture content is high and the sulfide concentration is low, pri-

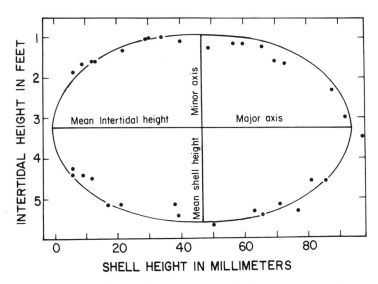

Figure 2.4.   Intertidal height as a function of shell height for 33 mussels on the periphery of the distribution of Canary Creek bridge. (From Lent, 1968, by permission of the editor, *Biol. Bull.*)

marily among the stems of the short *S. alterniflora* and *Distichlis spicata* and secondarily under mats of filamentous algae. At lower elevations the clam is presumably subjected to greater sulfide concentrations and predation. Kat (1978) observed *Fundulus heteroclitus* in the laboratory digging the bivalves out of the substrate and feeding on them. At elevations above 1.36 meters MLW the clam would be subjected to great levels of dessication and reduced feeding times.

C. floridana appears to alternate between air-gaping and keeping the valves closed when exposed to air. Animals that are kept wet gape less frequently. While gaping, air bubbles are taken into the mantle cavity of both juveniles and adults. These bubbles and the abundance of periostracal hairs which increase the shell surface area, give a positive buoyancy to the clam. Because of brood protection provided by the adults, the young might be expected to be clustered about the adults. Dispersion of the juveniles is enhanced by their flotation ability due to trapped air bubbles allowing the young clams to float in the gently flowing water. Whenever the clam comes in contact with an object the active foot expels the air bubbles causing the clam to settle to the substrate.

Kat (1978) found a random distribution of both juveniles and the total population and suggested that environmental heterogeneity is probably responsible for the variations in population density. He proposed that "this site selection, as well as behavioral adaptations such as brood protection, hermaphroditism, and tolerance of wide variations of salinity and temperature, has allowed the bivalve to survive the semi-terrestrial conditions associated with this habitat. Nevertheless, a strong dependence on the aquatic habitat remains for a multitude of functions such as the respiration, excretion, reproduction, and feeding; and adaptation to the high intertidal zone has not occurred on a morphological level." While *C. floridana* may be able to live at slightly higher elevations than the ribbed mussel (Lent, 1968) both possess body plans that would preclude any further landward penetration. It is interesting that two bivalves should employ similar behavioral traits to occupy the same major habitat, a salt marsh.

Gastropoda. The coffee bean snail, *Melampus bidentatus,* is an abundant member of the tidal marsh fauna and has received the attention of numerous workers over the years. Hauseman (1932) found few snails where tides flood the tall marsh grass and where fiddler crabs are common, with snails more numerous above the high tide marsh. According to Holle (1957) *Melampus* can be found only in salt marshes flooded by normal tides and avoids tidal submersion by climbing grass stems or debris. In contrast, Hackney (1944) reported *Melampus* as common on the mud flats of Beaufort, North Carolina.

Dexter, in a series of papers on the marine molluscs of the Cape Ann,

Massachusetts region (1942, 1944, 1945), related *Melampus* distributions to vegetation. In 1942, he often found individuals in small groups under solid objects, occasionally finding the snail in the upper margins of thatch grass or *Spartina glabra* (=*S. alterniflora*) marsh. Small clusters of *Melampus* were found in the *Spartina patens* marshes of Little River (1944). Dexter was of the opinion in his 1945 paper that the high marshes of *Spartina patens*, located for the most part above mean high water, were the only important habitat for *Melampus bidentatus*.

During a 1961 class exercise in Canary Creek marsh where dwarf *S. alterniflora* dominated the vegetation, the mean density of *Melampus* was $645.2/m^2$. The very large standard deviation of 497.2 suggested a very uneven distribution of snails across the marsh surface with numbers tending to decrease toward the marsh borders. It was noted that those sampling sites located in areas devoid of vegetation had very few or no snails. The inference is that the snails crawled up the grass stems to avoid inundation, a pattern of behavior that has been observed many times. Parker (1976) reported similar densities for various marshes bordering both sides of Delaware Bay (Delaware: Canary Creek 693 ± 340; New Jersey: Dras Creek 445 ± 184, Fortesque 420 ± 175).

In his study of the Poropotank River area of Virginia, Kerwin (1972) found the coffee bean snail associated with the brackish water marshes dominated by *S. alterniflora-Scirpus robustus* stage and *Spartina cynosuroides;* and with the salt marshes dominated by *S. alterniflora* (short form), *S. patens* and *Distichlis spicata*. The highest density was $144/m^2$ for the *Distichlis* zone. The percent frequency distribution was *Distichlis*, 87.5 percent; *S. patens*, 75.0 percent; and *S. alterniflora* (short form), 56.3 percent.

Russell-Hunter *et al.* (1972) reported the snail primarily in the *S. patens-Juncus-Distichlis* zone, in the *Distichlis* zone and in the upper levels of the area dominated by the dwarf form of *S. alterniflora*. *Melampus* occurred largely in the upper two-thirds of the zone lying above mean high water of neap tides (MHWN) and below the mean high water of spring tides (MHWS) but was also found in the zone lying between MHWS and the extreme upper limit worked by any tides (Figure 2.5). They described the snail as occupying the upper 12 percent of the intertidal zone which was bathed for only eight of the 354.4 hours (or 2.3 percent) of each semilunar cycle. Apley *et al.* (1967), Apley (1970), and Russell-Hunter *et al.* (1972) described the reproductive cycle of the snail as being synchronized to summertime spring tides.

Arthropoda

Crustacea. There are a number of crustacean species associated with tidal marshes. Fiddler crabs, being among the more apparent forms and being

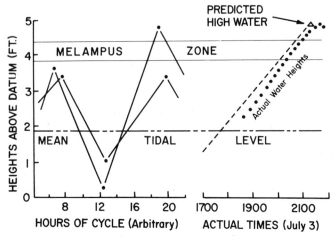

Figure 2.5. The relation of the vertical zone (3.9 to 4.4 feet above datum) occupied by natural populations of *Melampus* at Little Sippewisset, typical ranges of spring (−0.02 to 4.77 feet) and neap (0.9 to 3.28 feet) tides, and the observed time course of actual tidal heights during one high water of springs. Note that the mean level of all tides (MTL) does not necessarily correspond to mean sea level (MSL). (From Figure 8 in Russell-Hunter *et al.*, 1972, by permission of the editor, *Biol. Bull.*)

unique, have generated considerable interest. Until very recently, the less obvious amphipods and isopods have received little attention. In an early report (1905), Smallwood found the salt-marsh amphipod *Orchestia palustris* to be distributed over the entire marsh except in the *Spartina polystachia* (=*Spartina cynosuroides*) zone and the typically fresh water regions. It was abundant in the drift of salt-water plants, under some kind of cover, and in the more saline portions of the marsh. The amphipod, *Orchestia gammarella,* and the isopod, *Paragnathia maxillaris,* have been described by Nichol (1936) as characteristic faunal members of the surface of English marshes.

In a study of *Gammarus palustris* in Great Bay, New Hampshire, Gable and Croker (1977) found the amphipod only in the lower salt marsh with the highest relative abundance most of the year in a narrow zone coinciding with the upper *Spartina* bank, with a shoreward border at about Extreme High Water Neaps (EHWN). The species is thus submerged on essentially every tide. Several microhabitats were identified within the zone, the basal system of *Spartina* culms, the low culm and grass blade junctions, rocks, *Ascophyllum modosum,* and tidal debris. This general pattern was complicated by seasonal changes, animal sizes, and sexes. The upper bank microhabitats, primarily the plant culms, were occupied in the summer, followed by a shoreward shift in early October along with falling temperatures and first frost. At this time rocks on the upper bank were more frequently used. A reverse movement took place in early December and by the end of the month the amphipods were found in that transition between the bank and flat, under fucoid algae. At the onset of ice the amphipods abandoned all microhabitats and sought decaying vegetation, peat depressions, and shallow pools on the lower flat. By May they were back in the transition between the upper bank and lower flat and by June they were occupying the upper bank.

In his study of the thermo-saline tolerances of the isopod *Sphaeroma rugicauda,* Marsden (1973) expected the species to be able to colonize marsh areas infrequently covered by tides. He found that suitable vegetation prevented the penetration of the isopod into a more marine environment.

Fiddler crabs are an obvious scurrying faunal component of tidal marshes. Pearse (1914) identified three characteristics strongly associated with these crabs, having watched 13 species in North and South America and in the Philippines. (1) Fiddler crabs are diurnal, whereas other crabs are nocturnal as well. (2) A substrate specificity was displayed giving rise to zonation in habitat selection. (3) Fiddler crabs feed on tidal flats during low tide with greatest activity on the ebbing flow. Frantic activity by the crabs was reported by Pearse as the tide began to flood. Crabs retreat to their burrows during high tides and prolonged flooding, hastily gathering mud pellets to plug the entrance as the tide floods over the marsh surface. They open their burrows but will remain in them during extended periods of low tides which tend to dry out the tidal flats. Drying tends to inhibit the feeding process for the crabs.

Marsh crabs can be divided into three behavioral groups associated with tidal cycles (Teal, 1959). (1) *Eurytium limosum, Panopeus herbsti,* and *Sesarma reticulatum* are active when the tide is high or when the sky is cloudy and the sun is not shining. When the marsh is uncovered at low tide they are in their burrows, near the top, either exposed to air or in the water. Crichton (1960) described *S. reticulatum* clearing mud from its burrow as the tide receded, depositing it at either side of the entrance where a complete canopy was frequently formed. (2) *Uca pugnax* and *U. minax* are active principally when the tide is out and do feed under water when the tide is high or in tide pools during low tide. (3) *U. pugilator* and *Sesarma cinereum* are active only in the air. *U. pugilator* is in its burrow at high tide while *S. cinereum* climbs above the water level. The first group is found in the low marsh at the low-tide level and the second group occupies an intermediate zone. The third group, with one exception, is located at the high-tide level. Teal found colonies of *U. pugilator* just above the low-tide level on the creek banks of the Georgia marshes. Crabs in the first group build burrows with numerous openings which allow the burrows to fill with water. *Uca pugnax* and *U. minax* dig burrows with single openings but seldom plug them. *U.*

pugilator almost always plugs its burrow entrance at high tide and thus remains in a pocket of air. However, Teal considered the air pocket incidental to the primary need for a hiding place.

Tidal flooding plays a profound role in the lives of these crabs beyond the daily ebb and flow. *U. minax* digs a burrow downward to the point where the chamber is at low-tide water level (Gray, 1942). This species excavates new burrows during prolonged low-water periods or when the burrows are filled with water from extended flooding. In either case, the burrow is dug to a depth to assure flooding of the chamber. Teal (1958) suggested predation may be influential in restricting the distribution of *U. pugnax* at the lower intertidal levels. This species frequently remains outside its burrows, as the tide is flooding while *U. pugilator* almost never does. The former is therefore more subject to predation by aquatic organisms.

While Pearse (1914), Gray (1942), and Teal (1958) pointed out the importance of substrate and tidal flooding in the lives of fiddler crabs, specific associations between crabs and vegetation are also evident. Gray described *U. minax* habitat at Solomons, Maryland, as a high-water sand and mud substrate sparsely covered by *S. cynosuroides* and *Paspalum* sp. *U. minax* was found in association with fifteen species of marsh plants, occurring with five species more than 20 percent of the time in the Poropotank River marshes of Virginia: *S. alterniflora*, 87.8 percent; *S. robustus*, 32.9 percent; *D. spicata*, 31.7 percent; *S. patens*, 24.4 percent; and *S. cynosuroides*, 20.7 percent. High population densities were reported in the tall and short *S. alterniflora* and at the edge of the *D. spicata-S. patens* community with densities ranging from 0–76 burrows/m^2 (Kerwin, 1971).

Schwartz and Safir (1915) described the burrowing of *U. pugnax* where there was dense vegetation cover, while *U. pugilator* burrowed in sparse vegetation or where it was absent. Teal (1958) found *U. pugnax* preferred to burrow where there was vegetation cover and was thus found to be most numerous in the Short marshes wherein the *Spartina* was 10–50 centimeters tall on firm substrate containing varying amounts (40–70 percent) of sand and the Medium marshes where *Spartina* was 1-meter tall on soil that was soft with small amounts of sand (0–10 percent). Gray (1942) and Teal (1958) found *U. minax* in certain of the Short *Spartina* high marshes where the grass was very short (10–20 centimeters) and the sand content was about 30 percent and water tended to stand. *U. pugilator* was found primarily in the *Salicornia-Distichlis* marsh and on the tidal creek banks. The former was high, sandy marsh with sparse vegetation and covered only by spring tides. In both situations, *U. pugilator* seemed to be attracted to sparse or absent vegetation.

The large burrows of the marsh crab, *S. reticulatum*, have been reported within five meters of the tidal water of Canary Creek marsh of Delaware and associated with *S. alterniflora* (Daiber and Crichton, 1967). Crichton (1960) considered this marsh crab responsible for patches of bare mud along the creeks and ditches as it crops the cordgrass and undermines the roots. Frequently these bare areas are swathes separating several feet of lush tall *S. alterniflora* further back on the marsh surface. At other times, they border directly on the bare mud of the stream bank. It is in these swathes that the burrows are the largest and most numerous. The number of burrow openings range from one to ten per square yard with four to five being an average. Crichton considered this burrowing activity to enhance the erosive action of the water and to keep the banks low enough so the tides can flood over the marsh surface.

Insecta. Insects are a common component of the tidal marsh fauna, occupying a variety of habitats. Relatively few families can be classed as pests and those noxious to man are of considerable economic importance and thus have received a great deal of attention. Much work has been devoted to the control of salt-marsh mosquitos, beginning with Smith (1902) who recognized the relationship between mosquito distributions and zonation of salt-marsh vegetation. He advocated filling those depressions on the marsh surface adjoining the uplands where mosquitos breed, or ditching so tidal water could circulate through such areas.

Tidal inundation has been identified as a factor limiting the distribution of *Aedes* species of mosquitos on Delaware salt marshes (Connell, 1940). Young larvae fail to appear in portions of the marshes flooded by tides as frequently as 25 days per lunar month. Abundant breeding can be expected only in portions of *S. alterniflora* marsh where the frequency of tidal inundation is less than eight days per lunar month. Table 2.3 depicts the relationships between vegetation and insect numbers for *Aedes sollicitans* and *Aedes cantator*, wherein most of the mosquitos were taken in the *S. patens* zone. LaSalle and Knight (1974) found the *Juncus* marshes in Carteret County, North Carolina, to be subjected to a higher rate of tidal flooding during the mosquito breeding season than the marshes examined in Pamlico County. Consequently, there was a much lower level of *Aedes* breeding in the former

Table 2.3. Average number of *Aedes* larvae and pupae per dip from the salt marshes of Egg Island, New Jersey. (From Ferrigno, 1958)

| | Average Number of Larvae and Pupae per Dip | | |
	A. cantator	*A. sollicitans*	Total
Spartina patens	0.31	6.95	7.26
S. alterniflora	0.01	0.37	0.38
Mixed	0.29	2.42	2.71

Table 2.4. Mosquito breeding at stations affected by feeding snow geese in New Jersey marshes. (From Ferrigno, 1958)

Station Marker	Description of Eat-Outs		Water Depth in Inches	Number of Larvae-Pupae		Number of Dips
	% Denuded within 70 foot Radius of Station Marker	Vegetation Type		Per Dip	Total	
A	10–30	*S. patens*	0–2	12.71	6607	520
B	10–40	*S. alterniflora*	0–6	1.56	2119	1355
C	50–90	*S. patens-S. alterniflora*	1–8	0.05	25	460
D	50–90	*S. alterniflora*	1–6	0.03	15	490
E	100 (Ponds)	*S. patens-S. alterniflora*	5–24	0.002	3	1401

area than in Pamlico County. The higher flooding frequency in the Carteret County marshes probably accounted for the presence of *Anopheles* and *Culex* mosquitos which were as abundant as, or more so than, *Aedes*. Ferrigno (1958) demonstrated the relationship between flooding and water depth on the success of mosquito breeding caused by snow geese feeding activity (Table 2.4). In addition, the restriction of regular tidal flushing in vegetational zones for agricultural purposes had an impact on the numbers of mosquitos produced (Table 2.5). Diking enhanced the growth of salt hay, *S. patens,* by preventing flooding with salt water. Later reflooding produced great broods of mosquitos, mostly *Culex salinarius* and *A. sollicitans.*

There appears to be some uncertainty from the earlier literature about the relationship between tidal flooding and vegetation zonation on one hand and the distributions of larval greenhead flies (Tabanidae). Hansens (1952) found them in the wetter portions of the salt marsh while Gerry (1950) described development as taking place primarily in the upper marsh reached only by the higher tides. He went on to say evidence indicated that larvae originate in the creeks from which they migrate to thatch piles at the head of the marsh. Wall and Doane (1960) found various species of tabanids well distributed over the surface of various Cape Cod marshes. Bailey (1948a) rarely found *Tabanus nigrovittatus* where there was standing water on the marshes in the vicinity of Newbury, Massachusetts. Jamnback and Wall

Table 2.5. The number of mosquito larvae and pupae sampled from natural and diked salt marshes of the Caldwalder Tract, New Jersey. (A portion of Table 2, Ferrigno, 1959)

| Vegetation Type | Average Number Larvae-Pupae per Dip | | Seasonal totals | |
	Culex salinarius	*Aedes* sollicitans	Dips	Larvae-Pupae
UNDIKED				
S. alterniflora	0	0.001	8280	1
S. patens	0.11	2.74	1080	3293
P. virgatum	0.003	0	600	2
Woodland swamp	0.02	0.01	840	620
DIKED				
S. alterniflora	0.26	4.22	360	1701
S. patens	0.72	3.54	2760	13376
S. cynosuroides	2.94	4.66	240	1988
P. virgatum	0.21	0.75	1320	2219
D. spicata	0	3.52	600	2761
J. gerardi	0	2.86	240	780
Typha	2.01	0.21	120	707

(1959) found the larvae associated with several species of salt-marsh vegetation but most abundant in *S. alterniflora* and *S. patens.* Contrary to Gerry (1950), they believed the larvae can survive in water for a long time. Olkowski (1966) found most larvae among the *S. alterniflora* of Delaware marshes with fewer individuals present as ground elevation increased toward the *S. patens* zone. The mature larvae were presumed to be dispersed to higher ground by tidal action.

More recent work gives additional insights into the distribution of tabanid flies. Dukes *et al.* (1974a) working in Carteret County, North Carolina, and Meany *et al.* (1976) working on Great Sippewissett Marsh, Massachusetts, found *T. nigrovittatus* and *Chrysops fuliginosus* larvae distributed throughout the lower salt marshes occurring in highest densities in areas below mean high tides and dominated by *S. alterniflora.* The preference for low marsh was most marked for *C. fuliginosus* (Tables 2.6 and 2.7). The less abundant *Chrysops atlanticus* were characteristic of low-marsh areas. The abundance of larvae decreased progressively toward slightly higher elevations with concurrent decrease in *S. alterniflora* and increase in the irregularity of flooding. The authors reported areas of *S. cynosuroides, D. spicata,* and *J. roemerianus* had decreasing numbers of larvae, in that order. However, examination of Table 2.6 would suggest the order of *D. spicata* and *J. roemerianus* be reversed. Dukes *et al.* (1974a) did point out that larvae can be found in the high *Juncus* marsh, particularly in interspersed patches of other vegetation, which is indicative of more frequent flooding. In mixed vegetation, as the proportion of *S. alterniflora* decreased, the numbers of tabanid larvae also decreased. Sample sites in two of the marshes where there was no vegetation yielded no tabanid larvae. This concurs with Bailey's (1948a) observation that *T. nigrovittatus* larvae are rarely collected where the marsh peat is devoid of vegetation.

In another paper (Dukes *et al.,* 1974b) the larvae of the sheep fly, *C. fuliginosus* (82 percent), and the greenhead, *T. nigrovittatus* (18 percent), were found widely distributed throughout a Newport River, North Carolina marsh dominated by *S. alterniflora.* A natural drainage ditch had no apparent influence on distributions. The results were not always consistent with earlier work. Sampling methods had varied and Dukes *et al.* (1974b) believed this to be an important factor. However, they proposed surface topography to be equally important. The marsh studied was regularly inundated by the tide with no opportunity to dry out. They considered this contrary to many northern marshes dominated by *S. patens* and the entire Newport River Marsh was portrayed as being equivalent to the ditch margins of the northern *S. patens* marshes.

Various authors have reported ditching increases available breeding areas for the Tabanidae in a tidal marsh (Bailey, 1948a; Hansens, 1949).

Table 2.6. Recovery of tabanid larvae from soil in various plant associations in four salt marshes in Carteret County, N.C., 1972. (Part of Table 3 from Dukes *et al.*, 1974a, by permission of the editor, *Environmental Entomology*.)

	Samples		Larvae	
	Total Number	% with Larvae	Total Number	Average/ Sample
		Newport River		
Spartina alterniflora	179	77.1	521	2.95
Distichlis spicata	27	25.9	12	0.44
Juncus roemerianus	47	26.1	29	0.62
S. cynosuroides	13	53.8	17	1.31
S. alterniflora & D. spicata	15	46.7	14	0.93
J. roemerianus & D. spicata	5	40.0	7	1.40
Totals and overall average	286	44.9	600	1.28
		Hoop Hole Creek		
Spartina alterniflora	11	36.4	6	0.54
Juncus roemerianus	14	7.1	1	0.07
S. alterniflora & D. spicata	5	40.0	3	0.60
S. alterniflora & J. roemerianus	5	40.0	3	0.60
S. alterniflora, D. spicata, & J. roemerianus	5	40.0	2	0.40
None	3	0	0	0
Totals and overall average	43	27.2	15	0.37
		North River		
Juncus roemerianus	16	50.0	14	0.87
S. alterniflora & J. roemerianus	4	50.0	6	1.50
Totals and overall average	20	50.0	20	1.19
		Davis Peninsula		
Spartina alterniflora	10	40.0	5	0.50
Distichlis spicata	6	16.7	1	0.17
Juncus roemerianus	37	16.0	7	0.19
S. alterniflora & D. spicata	4	0.0	0	0.00
S. alterniflora & J. roemerianus	2	50.0	1	0.50
J. roemerianus & D. spicata	14	28.6	7	0.50
S. alterniflora, D. spicata, & J. roemerianus	4	25.0	1	0.25
None	16	0	0	0
Totals and overall average	93	22.0	22	0.26

Wall and Doane (1960) found the greatest numbers of punkies (Ceratopogonidae) along the edges of the bays and drainage ditches where tall *S. alterniflora* was the dominant cover or from the moist mud where other vegetation dominated, but not from dry or hard soil. Rockel (1969a) described the changes in marsh physiography resulting from ditching New Jersey

Table 2.7. Mean numbers of tabanid larvae/m² for the 1972–1973 and 1974 sampling periods for the Great Sippewissett marsh, Massachusetts.
Only the numbers for the control areas are shown, excluding the results from fertilization test plots. *C. atlanticus* was recorded in low numbers from the test plots but not recorded from the control plots. (Modified from Table 1, Meany *et al.*, 1976, by permission of the editor, *J. of Applied Ecology.*)

	1972–73		1974	
	Low Marsh	High Marsh	Low Marsh	High Marsh
Tabanus nigrovittatus	28.4 ± 4.3	22.3 ± 4.6	37.7 ± 8.3	12.5 ± 2.5
T. lineola	5.7 ± 2.7	2.4 ± 1.2	1.2 ± 0.9	1.2 ± 1.2
Chrysops fuliginosus	28.5 ± 4.5	3.8 ± 1.5	35.6 ± 7.7	0
C. atlanticus	0	0	0	0

marshes and the impact on intertidal organisms. Following ditching there was almost a one foot depression of the banks bordering the ditches. With such a soil contour, flooding tides normally covered the marsh to a distance of seven yards from the ditches with plants and animals submerged longer and more frequently than at higher levels. Rockel reported soil drainage to be more complete close to the ditches with the percent soil water increasing at higher elevations. Soil organic matter and surface thatch increased with elevation, the latter tending to reduce evaporation and soil aeration. The salt-water table was closer to the soil surface at higher elevations during ebb tides. There was increasing cordgrass density but decreasing plant height with an increase in elevation. Both greenhead flies, *T. nigrovittatus,* and deer flies, *Chrysops* spp., exhibited population peaks in marsh areas which were about 0.2 feet below mean high water (MHW). Ditching, by producing more surface area below MHW, provided more marsh offering optimum conditions for larvae of the various biting flies. The impact of ditching was emphasized by Rockel (1969a) who stated that 42 percent of a marsh surface is altered with ditches spaced at 100-foot intervals.

Vertical distributions become evident from the literature. Several authors (Bailey, 1948a; Hansens, 1949; Wall and Jamnback, 1957) reported *Tabanus* in the upper strata of marsh soil, usually the topmost one and one half inches. There are apparent species differences in population concentrations. Rockel and Hansens (1970a) found populations of *T. nigrovittatus* and *Chrysops* spp. were highest below mean high-water level on gently sloping banks where the cordgrass was about two feet tall. In their paper of 1970b the deer fly, *C. fuliginosus,* emerged primarily well below mean high water whereas *T. nigrovittatus* emerged from elevations only slightly below MHW. Rockel and Hansens (1970a) found the striped horsefly, *Tabanus lineola,* and the *T. nigrovittatus* variant known as "T sp 3" (and tentatively identified in Freeman and Hansens, 1972, as *T. n. simulans*) mostly at higher elevations where short marsh grass grows. In contrast, Meany *et al.* (1976) found *T. lineola* appeared equally between low- and high-marsh samples. Freeman and Hansens (1972) found the larvae of *T. nigrovittatus* and *T. lineola* in more open marsh areas of short grass with *T. lineola* more abundant in the wetter locations. A greater variance was reported with their finding "T sp 3" more prevalent in the tall grass areas bordering ditches.

Rockel and Hansens (1970a) suggested *Tabanus* females oviposit primarily on vegetation of a certain height which would influence larval distributions. Emergence appeared to be synchronized with the tide because the lowest areas that support vegetation were exposed long enough to allow hardening of the exoskeleton to permit adults to fly or to climb stems before reflooding (1970b). They found no evidence of larval migrations (1970a). This is in sharp contrast to Gerry's (1950) statement where he indicated the flies originated in the open creek and migrated to thatch piles in the higher areas near the marsh edge. Gerry considered that the prevalence of both mosquito and biting fly concentrations in the upper marsh, which is less frequently flooded, could be an asset in terms of control of both species. Since then, Dukes *et al.* (1974a) have cautioned that any control measures directed against the larval stages of tabanids would be inadvisable because such measures would have to be applied to extensive areas with possible adverse impacts on the marsh ecosystem.

Insects in general display an association between the extent of tidal flooding and vegetation zonation. Tide-elevation influences, primarily the length of the hydroperiod, determined the distribution of insect dominants at stations set up within the North Carolina marshes examined by Davis and Gray (1966). The Homoptera were most important and had a more nearly zonal distribution pattern than did species from the other insect orders (Figure 2.6). There were two exceptions. While the preponderance of *Prokelisia marginata* was with *S. alterniflora,* it was taken in all marsh types except *Juncus,* but quite possibly as strays. *Delphacodes detecta* was the most widely distributed homopteran, found during the summer in *S. patens* and *Distichlis* and equally abundant in *S. alterniflora.* Homoptera numbers decreased as other orders increased with the transition from low-marsh to high-marsh elevations.

Evidence for zonation among the Homoptera has been enhanced with the recent work of Foster and Treherne (1975, 1976a). They found the intertidal aphid, *Pemphigus trehernei,* restricted to the roots of the aster, *Aster tripolium,* growing in low marshes near the edges of creeks and salt pans in the marshes of Scolt Head Island, Norfolk. Gray (1971, in Foster and Treherne, 1975) classified salt-marsh communities containing *A. tripolium* into high, mid, and low marshes. High marshes are almost removed from tidal influence while mid-marshes are reached by all high spring tides and can be dis-

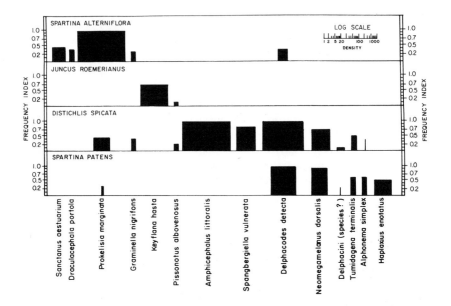

Figure 2.6.   Frequency-density diagram of the principal species of Homoptera from the herbaceous strata of four zones of salt-marsh vegetation. (From Davis and Gray, 1966, by permission of the editor, *Ecol. Monogr.*)

tinguished from the low marshes by the presence of *Plantago maritima.* Low marshes are inundated by high neap and spring tides. Gray was able to distinguish *A. tripolium* plants from one marsh level to other levels by a number of stable characters.

Foster and Treherne (1975) reported a relatively high percent of air space near the creek edges where these root aphids were most abundant (Figure 2.7). Only small aphid populations were found in soils with less than 10 percent air space (Figure 2.8). Adult aphids were about one millimeter in diameter and were associated with cavities of at least that size. These cavities were categorized and arranged in decreasing order of importance:

1. cavities formed by cracking from drying and erosion;
2. cavities formed by decaying roots;
3. cavities formed by burrowing of other animals;
4. cavities formed around mollusc shells and pebbles.

Cavities (1) and (3) were usually confined to edge regions while cavities (2) and (4) were found in all marsh areas and were generally water filled.

First instar aphids penetrated the edge soils of the low marshes considerably earlier than the nonedge areas. In eight trials with twelve aphids at each site, the mean number of aphids floating $\pm$S.E. was 0.88 $\pm$ 0.23 (7.3

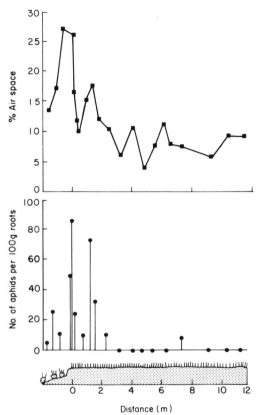

Figure 2.7. Aphid density and % soil air-space along a transect on Missel Marsh East, May 26, 1971. All measurements are of single samples. % air space was measured by the field method. (From Foster and Treherne, 1975, by permission of the editor, *Oecologia*.)

percent) at the edge sites and 6.75 ± 0.59 (56.3 percent) at the nonedge sites, a highly significant difference ($X^2 = 47.8$, $P > 0.001$).

Foster and Treherne found that aphid populations in mid-marsh areas did not show an equivalent edge effect. Such sites did not support high aphid concentrations, the maximum number per core was twenty. The mid-marsh soils were more mature, had a higher organic content, had smaller air spaces, and the large cracks associated with the clay soils did not appear in mid-marsh sites. The small pore size probably limited the aphid populations in the mid-marsh.

Foster and Treherne (1975) suggested that, for a salt-marsh aphid population to maintain itself, there must be appropriate spaces within the soil physically to accommodate these nonburrowing insects, and conditions

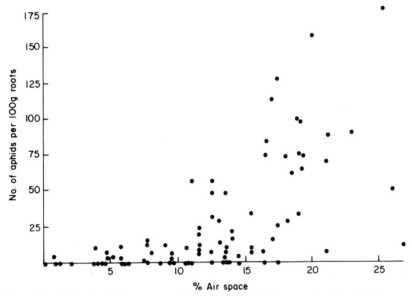

Figure 2.8.   Relationship between aphid density and % air space in the soil. Measurements made in various sites on Scolt Head in 1970 and 1971. % air space measured by field method. Aphid density expressed as numbers per 100 grams fresh weight of aster roots. (From Foster and Treherne, 1975, by permission of the editor, *Oecologia*.)

must be suitable for survival within such spaces. While there is an enormous potential for parasitic exploitation of *A. tripolium* by the aphid, only a small portion of the plant's distribution is available. The edge regions appear more accessible to dispersing aphids through the sheltering effects in the creeks leading to accumulations of aphids along the edges. The greater interplant spacing and larger bare areas may enhance aphid landings along the edges in these low marshes. In addition, the greater number of cavities along the edges would be attractive to these animals.

The Diptera ranked second at most stations set up by Davis and Gray (1966). There was a large and diverse assemblage of flies associated with low marsh *S. alterniflora* and the high marsh *Distichlis*. The Diptera made up a larger proportion of the *S. patens* insect fauna than any other group but there were fewer species than in *Distichlis* or *S. alterniflora*. The fly fauna found in the *Juncus* zone was comprised of strays from other areas. The most common fly species in all given marsh types was the Chloropod *Oscinella infesta* (Figure 2.9).

The Hemiptera seem to have the most restricted distribution as reported by Davis and Gray (1966). There were six abundant species, four of which (*Tytthus vagus, Trigonotylus americanus, Ischnodemus badius,* and

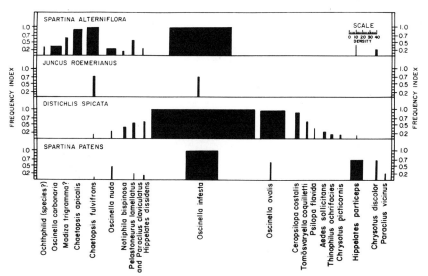

Figure 2.9. Frequency-density diagram of the principal species of Diptera from the herbaceous strata of four zones of salt-marsh vegetation. (From Davis and Gray, 1966, by permission of the editor, *Ecol. Monogr.*)

Rhytidolomia saucia) were each restricted to a single marsh type. A fifth species appeared to have an association with *Spartina* as it was found only with *S. patens* and *S. alterniflora*. The sixth species, *Cymus breviceps*, was widespread but apparently favored the high marsh as it was common in *S. patens* and in the adjoining *Panicum virgatum* (Figure 2.10).

Among the Orthoptera three species were restricted to specific vegetation. *Orchelimum fidicinium* was restricted to *S. alterniflora*. Smalley (1960) reported this to be the only species of grasshopper frequently found in the open marshes of Georgia, being most abundant in the moderately tall dense *S. alterniflora*. *Nemobium sparselsus* and *Paroxua clavuliger* were confined to *Distichlis* and *Juncus* respectively, in the North Carolina marshes. *Clinocephalus elegans* and *Mermiria intertexta* were characteristic members of the high-marsh fauna but the other grasshopper species were not restricted to any one marsh type.

Most common salt-marsh beetles were limited to a single marsh type. All of the common Hymenoptera were ants or belonged to parasitic groups. *Crematogaster clara* was the only ant found in the lower marsh zones; building nests in the upright, dead, hollow stems of *S. alterniflora*. Davis and Gray (1966) found most Hymenoptera frequenting the high ground of the *S. patens* zone. Woodell (1974) described the impact on vegetation found on ant hills located on the border between the landward dune and the marsh at

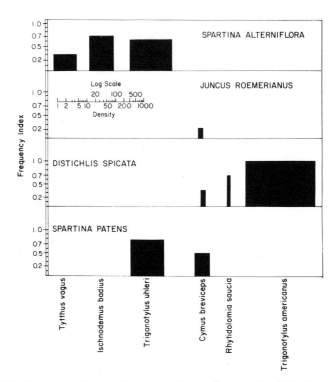

Figure 2.10.   Frequency-density diagram of the principal species of Hemiptera from the herbaceous strata of four zones of salt-marsh vegetation. (From Davis and Gray, 1966, by permission of the editor, *Ecol. Monogr.*)

Scolt Head Island, Norfolk. These ant hills have been present for at least 30 years, flooded by high spring tides and completely inundated on occasion. The ants survive due to the well-drained shingle beneath the shallow marsh soil along with the improved drainage on the ant hills themselves. The grasses, *Puccinellia maritima* and *Festuca rubra,* are present on these ant hills due to their tolerance to rabbit grazing. The dwarf shrub, *Frankenia laevis,* a Mediterranean species at the northern limit of its range, flourishes on the ant habitations due to good drainage. This shrub is found only on the south slopes of the ant hills, indicating ant activity produces profound microclimatic effects.

    Note that Davis and Gray (1966) found considerable variation in average number of insects from station to station, especially within the low marsh zones of *S. alterniflora* and *J. roemerianus.* Of the high-marsh stations, *D. spicata* had a greater insect fauna in numbers and species than *S. patens,* and the average number did not vary greatly from station to station as it did for the low-marsh locations.

There were many more insects in the *Distichlis* zone than for *Juncus* although both have short hydroperiods. The low marsh *S. alterniflora* and the *Spartina-Salicornia-Limonium* zones which were flooded frequently had more insects than did *S. patens* which was flooded only on storm tides. The more frequent branching of *Distichlis* and larger leaf crevices of *S. alterniflora* provide more hiding places. Apparently not many insects even with chewing mouth parts can handle the coarse fibers of *Juncus* for food. Presumably, the Orthoptera which were more evident are better able to cope with these tougher *Juncus* tissues.

The length of the hydroperiod was not believed to limit the total size of the insect aggregations (Davis and Gray, 1966). There was no evidence that any insect in the study allowed itself to be inundated by the tide. They escape by swimming, hopping, walking on the surface film, or by flying. Davis and Gray (1966) concluded that the size of animal assemblages is determined by food and shelter.

In contrast, in his description of the *Spartina* feeding insects of the Poole Harbour, Dorset salt marshes, Payne (1972) portrayed a gradual decline in the numbers of the grasshopper, *Chrothippus albomerginatus,* as the marsh sloped toward the water. *C. albomarginatus* was reported to be a good swimmer but appeared to deposit its eggs at the base of *Spartina* stems where developing nymphs were apt to drown. The grasshopper, *Conocephalus dorsalis,* was associated with the higher *Spartina* plants as it was quite susceptible to drowning. The hemipteran, *Euscelis obsoletus,* presumably not affected by inundation, was found as far as the water's edge.

Other works reported on intertidal insects that are regularly inundated by the flooding tide. As described earlier, Foster and Treherne (1975) found larger populations of aphids living in soil cavities along the edges of tidal creeks and salt pans. Larsen (1951) reported marsh beetle distributions were strongly influenced by soil type and vegetation, changing as vegetation invaded bare areas. Evans *et al.* (1971) described their observations of four species of beetles (*Bledius spectabilis, Heterocerus fenestratus, Dichirotrichus pubescens, and Cillenus lateralis*) which were confined effectively to the upper regions of the banks of the drainage channels of the Scolt Head Island, Norfolk salt marshes, in that region between the anaerobic mud of the lower bank, which was usually covered by a film of algae, and the dense marsh vegetation, mainly *Halimione portulacoides* (Figure 2.11). There were no apparent interspecific differences in beetle distributions within this zone. The beetle area was usually well drained and identified by the castings produced during burrowing. The mud was aerobic and brown with a quantity of organic material. This area differed considerably from the damper muds back from the drainage channels (Figure 2.12). The area is covered intermittently by high tides to a depth of one meter for seven days in every fortnight. Submergence was reported to last about 3–4 hours at the highest tides.

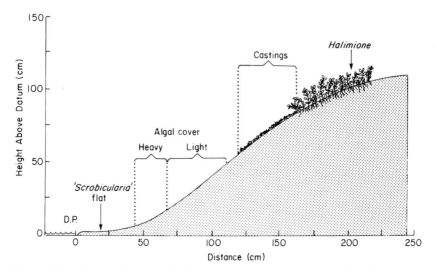

Figure 2.11. Section of the Hut Drain bank, showing region inhabited by *Bledius spectabilis, Heterocerus fenestratus,* and *Cillenus lateralis* (shown by castings). 'DP' marks water level of lowest high tide, August/September 1968. (From Evans *et al.,* 1971, by permission of the editor, *J. Mar. Biol. Ass. U.K.*)

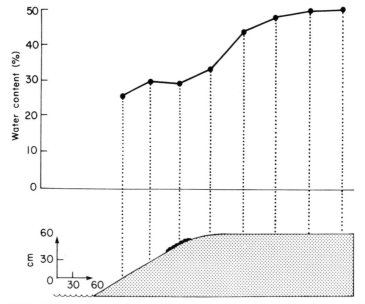

Figure 2.12. Water content in the top 10 cm of mud in a section of Hut Drain bank. The beetle area is represented by casting. (From Evans *et al.,* 1971, Fig. 4, by permission of the editor, *J. Mar. Biol. Ass. U.K.*)

Apparently the behavioral or burrowing activities permit this group of insects to survive and flourish. Evans *et al.* (1971) portrayed burrows of *B. spectabilis* as having been excavated to a maximum depth of 9 centimeters (Figure 2.13). *H. fenestratus* burrowed to a depth of only 1–2 centimeters, while *D. pubescens* did not burrow at all but lived in surface cracks. Evidently *B. spectabilis* could escape direct exposure to seawater by its subterranean mode of life. *D. pubescens* would presumably retreat to higher areas. *H. fenestratus* was considered particularly vulnerable to flooding due to its shallow burrows. Controlled submergence in seawater induced an apparent anoxic condition (Figure 2.14). The onset times of deep anoxia as well as the recovery response varied with species (Figure 2.15).

Subsequent work was done by Treherne and Foster (1977) on another beetle, *Dicheirotrichus gustavi*, which is widespread on the soft shores of the

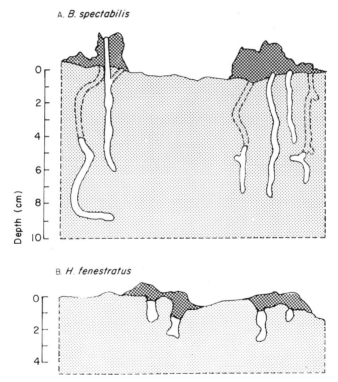

Figure 2.13. Diagram of burrowing activities of (a) *Bledius spectabilis* and (b) *Heterocerus fenestratus,* following introduction of six specimens of each species into 'soil cells.' The solid lines represent open burrows and the broken ones regions at the burrow system previously excavated and subsequently refilled. (From Evans *et al.*, 1971, Fig. 6, by permission of the editor, *J. Mar. Biol. Ass. U.K.*)

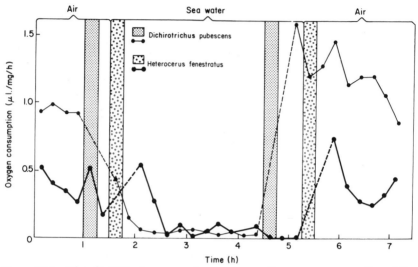

Figure 2.14.   The effect of submergence in seawater on the oxygen consumption of five adult *Dichirotrichus pubescens* and 30 *Heterocerus fenestratus*. The shaded area indicates the equilibrium period allowed on introduction and removal of seawater from the manometer flasks. (Modified from Figs. 12 and 13 in Evans *et al.,* 1971, by permission of the editor, *J. Mar. Biol. Ass. U.K.*)

intertidal zone in the British Isles. In salt marshes, the adult apparently lived in cracks in the mud and did not burrow. During tidal emergence *D. gustavi* exhibited well-defined nocturnal activity. Maximum activity occurred after dusk and decayed exponentially until dawn when it abruptly terminated as individual beetles retreated into soil cavities (Figure 2.16). This circadian activity insured that the majority of the population avoided direct submergence during the first few tidal coverages of the marsh surface of a rising tide sequence. The first tidal coverage, in a sequence of spring tides, occurred shortly before dawn when minimum numbers of adult beetles were exposed to seawater. The second and third critical tides each occurred 12.5 hours later, the second just before dusk while the insects were subterranean (Figure 2.17). Both field and experimental observations indicated that at least two tidal submergences were required to suppress nocturnal activity on the soil surface. This change in behavior did not seem to be related to changed soil character but from direct experience of changed conditions in the cavities of submerged soil. Reversion to nocturnal surface activity followed an absence of two tidal submergences.

Arachnida. The Arachnida have received some intensive attention with Barnes' (1953) study of spider distributions in the nonforest maritime com-

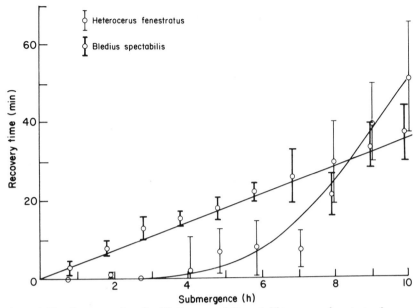

Figure 2.15.   Recovery time for *Bledius spectabilis* and *Heterocerus fenestratus* from an-oxia induced by varying periods of experimental submergence in seawater. (Modified from Figs. 9 and 11, Evans *et al.,* 1971, by permission of editor, *J. Mar. Biol. Ass. U.K.*)

munities in Beaufort, North Carolina and Luxton's (1964, 1967a, 1967b) ex-amination of English salt-marsh acarines. Barnes described closely related populations of spiders for the three estuarine communities: (1) *S. alterni-flora,* (2) *Spartina-Distichlis-Salicornia,* and (3) *J. roemerianus,* with differ-ences being largely variations in densities. The greatest densities and species numbers were found in the first zone and dropped off sharply at the proxim-ity of the high-tide marsh with the *Juncus* zone having a very sparse popula-tion. The low spider densities in the higher two zones may be explained by the structure of the vegetation. The *Spartina-Distichlis-Salicornia* zone was reported by Barnes as often drying out in the summer time, being an area less frequently inundated by the tides. The plants did not grow higher than one and one-half feet, thus there was less space for web building. *Juncus* grew to five feet but the lack of branching reduced the spaces where spiders could build webs. Taxonomic work, distributions, life cycles, and ecology of marsh-inhabiting spiders needs attention.

Acarina zonation is very marked in the horizontal plane (Luxton, 1964). However, the majority of the truly intertidal Acarina do not possess any morphological adaptations that would fully explain their ability to withstand the unstable conditions of salt-marsh turf, especially in the lower

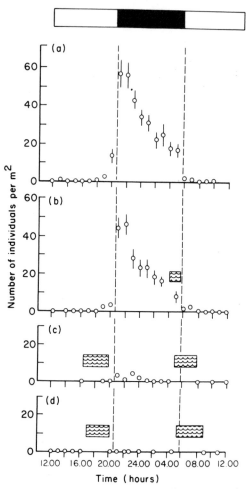

Figure 2.16.   Surface activity of *Dicheirotrichus gustavi*, in twenty experimental plots illustrated in Figure 1, (a) before (31 July 1975) and (b–d) during a period of tidal submergences (horizontal bars) in a sequence of rising tides ((b) 2 September 1975; (c) 3 September 1975; (d) 4 September 1975). The open circles indicate the mean number of individuals on the soil surface and the vertical lines the extent of twice the standard error of the mean. Dawn and dusk are indicated by the broken lines. (From Treherne and Foster, 1977, by permission of the editor, *J. Anim. Ecol.*)

marsh. There are no special respiratory modifications, yet salt-marsh soil oribatids do not seem to suffer unduly from prolonged immersion (up to twelve hours in the laboratory). Salinity gradients did not display the same abrupt changes seen in the sharp demarcations of acarine populations. The

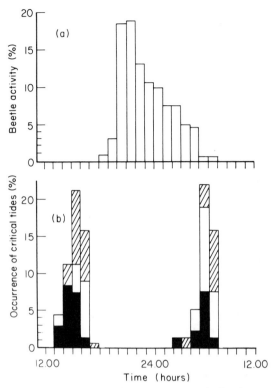

Figure 2.17. Timing of 'critical' tides (first tides to cover the beetle area after a period of emergence) in relation to beetle activity. It is assumed that tides of 20.7 m above Chart Datum just cover the beetle area (as on 3 September 1975). A first 'critical' tide is any tide exceeding 20.7 m which comes after at least three nonflooding tides. The second and third 'critical' tides follow the first at about 12.5 h intervals. (a) Hourly beetle activity in the field. Pooled data from Fig. 2(a), (b) and (c) expressed as a percentage of the total number of beetles observed during this period. (b) Hourly occurrence of 'critical' tides in 1975 and 1976, expressed as a percentage of the total number of 'critical' tides. First 'critical' tide, solid columns; second 'critical' tide, open columns; third 'critical' tide, hatched columns. (Data from Admiralty Tide Tables.) (From Treherne and Foster, 1977, by permission of the editor, *J. Anim. Ecol.*)

only abrupt changes came at the limitations of the various tide levels. Thus tidal effects seem to be of fundamental importance in delimiting distributional patterns. In order to establish populations in a marsh, especially the lower reaches, the Acarina need to possess all or some of the following special features: (1) ability to withstand high osmotic pressures in the soils; (2) ability of the eggs and juveniles in particular to withstand the sudden high salinities of tidal inundations; (3) a means whereby the immature offspring can be protected from the flushing action of tides and rains. Those possessing viviparity have a distinct advantage over egg layers.

Luxton (1967a,b) identified three main site communities, one for each vegetation zone. The acarine community in the *Juncus maritimus* zone is essentially terrestrial in nature and origin. The salt meadow fauna seems to consist of two major components: (1) *Festuca rubra* turf (above HWST mark) which can be considered a transitional community with species able to exploit the salt-meadow niche but not able to deal with the rigorous conditions in the lower marsh, and (2) the *Puccinellia maritima* zone (below HWST mark) which is composed of truly haline species that have developed means to withstand tidal marsh conditions.

Luxton (1967b) suggested the egg-laying microarthropod species are controlled primarily by the mechanical effects of tides. He noted that pH is an important regulating factor (either directly or indirectly) on viviparous oribatids as well as the Mesostigmata and Prostigmata but offered no explanation. There was no significant correlation between tide level, pH, salinity, and soil water content, and the acarine population densities in the *F. rubra* marsh. Possibly the landward region is less rigorous since tides rarely reach it. On the other hand, in the *P. maritima* zone, the acarine populations showed strong correlations with pH and salinity, but most markedly with tide level. The more dense oribatid populations were associated with the highest tide levels while pH had the greatest effect on the Megostigmata and Prostigmata. Luxton reported that correlations between densities of both oribatid and prostigmatid populations and both salinity and tide level were independent of the water content of the soil. *Punctoribates quadrivertex,* an egg-laying mite influenced by the tides, was reported most abundant in the *P. maritima* zone. This suggests the eggs are laid out of harm's way, possibly in the axils of salt-marsh plants. Luxton (1967a) concluded that a combination of the effects of tidal water and precipitation probably controls the fluctuations of microarthropods on salt marshes.

Marsh-Land Ditching and Impoundment. It is apparent from the discussion up to now that the natural flood and ebb of the tides, intertidal heights, and salinity distributions have an effect on plant and animal distributions in a tidal wetland. These environmental parameters have wide fluctuations and relatively few organisms can tolerate such variability in order to live in such a stressful habitat. Man in his ubiquitous fashion has added to the stresses of the marsh ecosystem through his desire to manipulate marsh water levels. Ditching has been carried out to facilitate the removal of water, while diking has been employed to hold water at some level above the natural one or to preclude entry of water. In any case the ecosystem has been altered and many people consider such manipulated tidal wetlands to have been subjected to environmental insults (Bourn and Cottam, 1950).

The history of marsh management and the resulting environmental responses have been reviewed by Daiber (1974). Water level manipulation for agricultural purposes has been carried out for centuries both here and in coastal European countries, with more failures in this country and more successes recorded abroad. The role of mosquitos in disease transmission began to be understood at the turn of the century and, where mosquitos were controlled, diseases such as malaria could be held in check. It has long been recognized that marshes breed mosquitos which detract from the well-being and comfort of both people and livestock and thus hinder the development of the country in such localities (Means, 1903; Wright, 1907).

Smith (1902, 1907) was an early proponent of selective ditching as a means to control mosquitos in those portions of the marsh considered to be good breeding areas. Later work by Connell (1940) demonstrated that ditching *S. alterniflora* marsh was not an effective control of the salt-marsh mosquito. Stearns *et al.* (1940) eliminated mosquito breeding in an experimental ditching study in the Appoquinimink marshes of Delaware and this was substantiated by Catts (1957) and Florschutz (1959). However, Sterns *et al.* (1940) pointed out that ecological side effects may be greater than the original objective. They noted that the water table was lowered by ditching and this was supported by Singh and Nathan (1965) who went on to say the rate of lowering was determined by ditch spacing and soil type. They suggested circulation of water rather than draw down of surface water was important in mosquito control. However, both Headlee (1939) and Travis *et al.* (1954) asserted ditching did not lower the water table and had no adverse effect on vegetation. Stearns *et al.* (1939, 1940), Cottam *et al.* (1938) and Bourn and Cottam (1950) were equally adamant that ditching has a degrading effect on vegetation, changing it from a form useful as food and shelter for various forms of wildlife to a colorful but "useless" expanse of greenery. An attributal direct consequence was a reduction in muskrat populations through reduction in food plants. Another effect was sharp declines in waterfowl abundance, attributed to marked reductions in the marsh pools used as a food source and a resting area, as well as substantial declines in invertebrate populations from the marsh surface.

A recent study by Lesser (1975) suggested a concurrent dredging of the Mispillion River by the United States Army Corps of Engineers rather than ditching alone was responsible for lowering the water table in the marsh studied by Bourne and Cottam (1950). Lesser reported a shift in dominance from *Baccharis* and *Iva* back to *S. alterniflora,* along with an increase in *Melampus* and *Uca* burrows, in a ditched marsh compared to an unditched marsh. Lesser inferred these changes were induced by the cessation of river maintenance dredging and its concomitant effect on the tidal regime. At the same time the ditches were kept clear and in good operating condition.

The inferences that Lesser (1975) made underscore a complex of inter-

actions that are not entirely clear. Lesser attributed a statement (p. 11) to
Rude (1928) wherein dredging can lead to a lowering of the mean low tide
level because of deepening and widening a channel. Zeskind and LeLacheur
(1926, p. 42–44) and Rude (1928, p. 642) reported a decrease in tidal range
in Delaware Bay and River following dredging. They had expected an increase in tidal range with a deepening of the channel and attributed the actual decrease to the channel widening that occurred. However, the decrease
in tidal range was reported only in the Delaware River upstream of Woodland Beach. There should be no change in tidal range following the removal
of some 131,800 cubic yards of sediment from the channel entrance and
river bed of the Mispillion River as reported by Lesser (1975) especially
when the Delaware Bay and nearby Atlantic Ocean are an infinite source of
water relative to the size of the Mispillion River. In addition, the mean low
water level was not lowered following dredging but actually was raised 0.5
foot at Philadelphia and Marcus Hook and 0.9 foot at New Castle (Table 33,
p. 42, Zeskind and LeLacheur, 1926).

While it is uncertain what happened to the tidal range in the Mispillion
River because there is no known data, there is substantial evidence that the
sea level has been rising along the Atlantic Coast (see Kraft, 1971a; Hicks,
1973; Hicks and Crosby, 1974; Belknap, 1975). Lesser (1975) called attention to this when he cited Kraft (1971b) who reported a sea level rise of 15
centimeters (0.5 foot) per century during the past 3000 years with reference
to the Delaware coast. Belknap (1975, p. 50) drew attention to the fact the
average rate or change varies with time. Hicks (1973, p. 3) has calculated a
faster rate of rise since 1903: 0.0155 ft/yr at Sandy Hook, 0.0125 ft/yr at Atlantic City, and 0.0109 ft/yr at Baltimore. Using the Atlantic City value, this
means a sea level rise of 13 centimeters (0.43 foot) for the period 1935–1969.

During the late 1960s the data from Atlantic City showed an average
sea-level rise of approximately 8 centimeters (0.27 foot) over an eight-year
period (Hicks and Crosby, 1974). This is a fantastic increase in sea level for
such a short period of time.

An examination of the tidal curves (Figure 2.18) shows considerable
fluctuation above and below the mean calculated sea level. In spite of such
variation the long-term average clearly displays an upward advance of sea
level. In fact, the lowest yearly sea level recorded at Atlantic City in the
1960s is higher than the highest level recorded during the late 1930s–early
1940s when initial ditching was carried out on the Mispillion marshes.

Belknap (1975), reviewing others, identified a number of minor local or
short-term changes, including seasonal patterns that can modify sea level.
Zeskind and LeLacheur (1926, Table 29, Figure 14) depicted an annual
variation in the plane of mean tide level for Delaware Bay and the lower
river. The tide levels reached their highest points in April–May leveling off

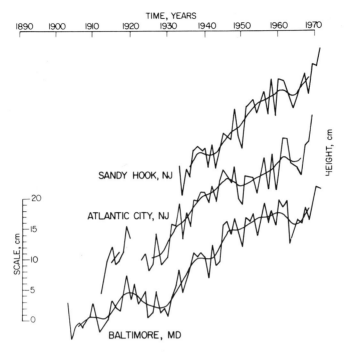

Figure 2.18.   Change in sea level with respect to adjacent land for stations for New Jersey and Maryland. (From Hicks, S. D., 1973)

during the summer and declining in September. These annual variations were attributed by the authors to changing river conditions, presumably fresh-water runoff. These high mean tide levels correspond to the active growing season of marsh plants.

Lesser (1975) reported dredging activity in the Mispillion River (1933–1939) during part of the time (1936–1946) that Bourn and Cottam (1950) were recording drastic changes in vegetation and invertebrates on the marsh surface. Undoubtedly dredging activity suspended great amounts of sediment in the water column.

Auld and Schubel (1974) reported sediment loads of 100 mg/l are uncommon in Chesapeake Bay and rarely exceed such levels except near dredging or spoil deposition sites. In a report dealing with fish migrations in the Delaware River (Anonymous, 1976) the average sediment load in April 1970 was 79 ppm with a variance of 179 ppm and a range of 9 to 904 ppm. A hydraulic suction dredge can produce a sediment concentration of 300 ppm 200–600 yards from the dredge (Proni et al., 1975), while a bucket dredge can generate sediment concentrations as high as 4150 ppm near the opera-

tion and 300 ppm one-half mile away (Masch and Espey, 1967). Citing earlier work Auld and Schubel (1974) reported that on windy days suspended
sediments of 1000 mg/1 were not uncommon and turbidity flows on the
bottom may exceed 20,000 mg/1 as far as 500 m from a dredge. While
dredging will resuspend material, Bohlen et al. (1979) concluded storms increase the total suspended load by nearly an order of magnitude greater
than from dredging. They observed that 1.5–3.0 percent of the sediment volume of each bucket entered the water column with concentrations of suspended material of 200–400 mg/1 which exceeded the background levels by
two orders of magnitude. Downstream of the dredge they found the suspended load was rapidly reduced to concentration approaching background
levels within approximately 700 meters. They concluded such spatial distributions indicate dredge-induced resuspension is primarily a near-field phenomenon producing minor variations as compared to naturally occurring
storm events. Presumably the distance material is transported relates to the
nature of the sediment (silt, clay or sand) and the magnitude of turbulence
and water-borne transport.

Belknap (1975) has calculated the long-term sedimentation rate in the
Delaware marshes to be 14.5 centimeters (0.5 foot) per century with a range
of 3 to 21.6 centimeters (0.1 to 0.7 foot) per century. On a short-term basis it
is possible that, with the peaking of mean tidal level during the summer
months, great amounts of sediment were carried onto the Mispillion marsh
surface and the accretion of the marsh surface during those years
(1933–1939) exceeded the rate of submergence caused by the rising sea level.
The presence of ditches could actually facilitate the greater movement of
sediment laden water onto the marsh surface during flooding tides through
reduced friction.

Ranwell (1964) estimated the mean accretion rate to be about 2 centimeters per year for a marsh at Poole Harbour, Dorset, which has a high
proportion of silt. Another marsh at Bridgwater Bay, Somerset has a high
proportion of sand especially in the lower marsh, and Ranwell estimated a
mean accretion rate at about 4 centimeters per year with maximum values
sometimes reaching 10–12 centimeters per year or even higher. Ranwell
recorded a seasonal pattern of accretion being deposited fairly evenly
throughout the three months of August through October. The monthly data
suggested a tendency for newly deposited silt to move higher from the lower
marsh levels. Ranwell indicated this movement may be associated with the
fact that high tides rise through August and September to the maximum
levels of the autumn equinox.

With the cessation of dredging, the sediment deposition on the Mispillion marsh surface presumably decreased and the rapidly rising sea level in
recent years accounts for the reversion toward a low marsh as reflected in

the great increase in *S. alterniflora* and the corresponding decrease in *Baccharis* and *Iva* (Table 2.8) even though the ditches are open and functioning. All of this seems to infer that an evaluation of the impact of ditching on marsh vegetation and animals is not a simple one-to-one relationship but must take into account other factors; such as annual and seasonal fluctuations in sea level, sediment loads, and accretion rates.

The reduction of invertebrates (reported by Bourn and Cottam, 1950) can be attributed, in part, to the enhanced leaching and oxidation of the marsh soils brought on by a lowering of the water table or raising of the marsh surface. More acid conditions are produced, adversely affecting molluscs and crustacea dependent on alkaline conditions for shell building. Under anaerobic conditions, sulfates in the sea water are reduced to sulfides in the presence of organic matter. In this form these sulfides combine with the iron in the clay to form polysulfides. No further change will occur if the soils remain moist. If they dry out the sulfides are oxidized to form sulfuric acid. This can reduce the pH to 2.5 or less (Neely, 1962) thus making shell development difficult.

As part of the vegetation change induced by increased drainage, *Spartina alterniflora* production can be enhanced by bank slumping through ditching thus increasing the edge effect (Ferrigno, 1961; Rockel, 1969b). This in turn can enhance clapper rail and black duck nesting (Ferrigno, 1961; Stewart, 1951, 1962). As was pointed out earlier (Rockel, 1969b; Dukes *et al.,* 1974b) numbers of tabanid flies can be increased with greater *S. alterniflora* growth along ditch banks. The high density of *Uca* burrows within five meters of the creek and ditch banks for the ditched Mispillion Marsh, and the greater density of *Melampus* beyond the five meters (Lesser, 1975) can be explained by increased intertidal surface for *Uca* brought on by bank slumping (Rockel, 1969) and the zonation of *Melampus* associated with their aerial respiration and spring tides (Russell-Hunter *et al.,* 1972).

The exclusion of water by diking has been done to encourage the production of salt-marsh hay, *S. patens* (Smith, 1907; Ferrigno, 1959). Smith remarked the diked area loses its value for hay production unless the water is completely removed. Ferrigno agrees water removal is necessary to enable machinery to cut and process the hay.

Table 2.8. Changes in the percent composition of plant species on the Mispillion River, 1936–74. (Part of Table 1 from Lesser, 1975)

Plant Species	1936	1938	1939	1941	1946	1974
Spartina alterniflora	62	36	32	36	40	73
S. patens and/or *D. spicata*	31	30	23	18	6	11
Baccharis halimifolia and/or *Iva frutescens*	5	22	39	39	50	14

The retention of water by impounding produces vegetation changes from *S. alterniflora-S. patens* to pond weed *Potamogeton berchtoldi* and *P. pectinatus,* widgeon grass *Ruppia maritima,* and algal mats (during low water principally *Rhizoclonium*). Around the edges a variety of emergent species will appear; three-square *S. americanus,* rose mallow *Hibiscus moscheutos,* cattail *Typha,* reed *Phragmites communis,* and switch grass *Panicum virgatum* (Springer and Darsie, 1956).

This same pattern was noted by Florschutz (1959) and Tindall (1961) in the Assawoman and Little Creek Wildlife areas (Delaware) respectively and by LaSalle and Knight (1974) for Pamlico and Carteret counties, North Carolina. All reported salt-marsh vegetation, *Spartina, Distichlis, Scirpus, Hibiscus, Cladium, Juncus, Baccharis,* and *Iva* were reduced and replaced by open water and emergent types, *Potamogeton* and *Ruppia* beds, *Typha, Echinocloa, Cyperus,* and *Chara.* Florshutz noted *Typha* tended to expand in some places and decrease elsewhere. *S. patens* was greatly reduced on the inner portions of the marsh but flourished along the edge of the impoundment.

Mangold (1962), Shoemaker (1964), Smith (1968), and Harrison (1970) noted the replacement of *S. patens* by *S. alterniflora* during the flooding of low-level impoundments and a champagne pool system. This was particularly true for early flooding. *Distichlis* associated with *S. patens* survived and flourished (Shoemaker) but when associated with *J. gerardi* survived, but not well (Mangold). Flooding caused the disappearance of *Baccharis* and *Iva* while the submergent horned pond weed, *Zannichellia palustris,* increased and flourished. Smith (1968) noted the increase of *Baccharis,* common reed *Phragmites,* poke weed *Phytolacca americana,* and the fox tail grasses *Setaria faberii* and *S. magna* on the higher ground created by the embankments and spoil piles. The poke weed and fox tail grasses provide excellent food and shelter for wildlife. He also noted a decline of widgeon grass in the older impoundments after flourishing in younger pools. As Smith had noted in 1907, impounding a tidal marsh will change the salt-marsh vegetation to that of a fresh-water marsh or that of an upland.

Impounding sharply altered the numbers and species composition of the biting fly populations as compared to a natural tidal marsh (Chapman *et al.,* 1954, 1955; Chapman and Ferrigno, 1956; Catts *et al.,* 1963; Shoemaker, 1964; LaSalle and Knight, 1974). *A. sollicitans* is the most abundant mosquito in natural marsh conditions along the Atlantic and Gulf coasts making up as much as 96 percent by number of immatures dipped (Table 2.9) (Darsie and Springer, 1957; Tindall, 1961). Chapman *et al.* (1954) identified *A. sollicitans* and *A. cantator* along with *Anopheles bradleyi* and *C. salinarius,* the salt-marsh group of mosquitos, as being typical of a natural salt marsh. Essentially *Aedes* spp. can be eliminated from impoundments while breed-

Table 2.9. Mosquito immatures dipped April to October, 1959 and 1960, Little Creek Wildlife Area, Little Creek, Delaware (1959 was the first year of impoundment). (Tindall, 1961)

| | Inside Impoundment | | | | Outside Impoundment | | | |
| | 1959 | | 1960 | | 1959 | | 1960 | |
	No.	%	No.	%	No.	%	No.	%
A. sollicitans	56,137	96.1	76	0.4	1,502	96.5	7,203	99.9
Aedes sp.	62	0.1	10	–	1	–	–	–
TOTAL	56,199	96.2	86	0.4	1,503	96.5	7,203	99.9
A. bradleyi	19	–	677	3.5	1	–	1	–
Anopheles sp.	–	–	161	0.8	–	–	–	–
TOTAL	19	–	838	4.3	1	–	1	–
C. salinarius	2,143	3.7	17,163	88.7	25	1.6	–	–
Culex sp.	69	0.1	743	3.8	27	1.7	–	–
TOTAL	2,212	3.8	17,906	92.5	52	3.3	–	–
Uranotaenia sapphirinia	–	–	512	2.7	–	–	–	–

ing of *Culex* and *Anopheles, Uranotaenia sapphirina,* and *Mansonia perturbans* increased after impoundment but are considered a lesser nuisance (Chapman *et al.,* 1954; Chapman and Ferrigno, 1956; Tindall, 1961; Franz, 1963). *Mansonia* deposits its eggs in sedge tussocks and beneath mats of cattail debris under flooded fresh-water conditions (Hagmann, 1953). Impoundments also can control tabanid flies (Olkowski, 1966; Anderson and Kneen, 1969). Anderson and Kneen also pointed out that populations of *C. fuliginosus* can be decimated when flooding corresponds to the time of larval-pupal and pupal-imaginal molts.

Manipulation of water levels within impoundments seems to control species composition and the magnitude of breeding (Hagmann, 1953; Chapman and Ferrigno, 1956). Springer and Darsie (1956) reported the elimination of *Anopheles* along with the two *Aedes* species. Darsie and Springer (1957) noted many of the permanent water mosquitos are unimportant because of short flight patterns, biting habits, and other behavior. MacNamara (1952) reported constant water levels produced mosquitos while draw-down decreased breeding. Chapman and Ferrigno (1956) noted heaviest breeding for *Aedes* at water depths 5–10 inches below meadow level, slightly below meadow level for *Culex* and slightly above meadow level for *Anopheles.* LaSalle and Knight (1974) found water depths greater than one foot tended to submerge or disperse vegetation and reduced *Anopheles* and *Culex* breeding. Chapman and Ferrigno (1956) reported summer draw-down controls *M. perturbans* but they, along with Darsie and Springer (1957), reported greatly increased *Aedes* broods following rains or reflooding. Catts *et al.* (1963) recommended moderate water levels of 9–12 inches compatible for reduced mosquito production and enhanced waterfowl usage. Tindall (1961) suggested the higher water levels would reduce vegetation and expose the mosquito larvae to wave action and predators.

Diking done to enhance the production of salt hay, *S. patens,* by preventing flooding of tidal marsh land produced great broods of mosquitos, primarily *A. sollicitans* and *C. salinarius* (see Table 2.5, page 27).

Part of the basic premise of water management and mosquito control on these marshes has been to provide a suitable habitat for mosquito-eating fish and the means for these fish to get at the mosquitos. Associated with this, both Mangold (1962) and Shoemaker (1964) believed the attraction of herons, bitterns, terns, etc., to low-level impoundments is due to the increase in fish numbers. *Fundulus* spp. can survive in impoundments and will provide an effective control over mosquito larvae if water levels are high enough to permit the fish to forage amongst the vegetation (Alls, 1969). The numbers of fish species increased and tended to shift toward the fresh water forms following impoundment, including the bullhead *Ictalurus nebulosus,* the pickerel *Esox americanus,* and the sunfish *Lepomis gibbosus.* Bullfrogs, *Rana catesbiana* and the snapping turtle *Chelydra serpentina,* also appeared in impoundments (Darsie and Springer, 1957).

Impoundments have been established and developed for the restoration of wildlife, particular waterfowl and shore birds. Bradbury (1938) reported on this for the Duxbury, Massachusetts marshes while MacNamara (1949) demonstrated the fresh-water impoundments on the Tuckahoe, New Jersey marshes were capable of producing large quantities of desirable waterfowl food by a complete draw-down. Eight inches of water tended to enhance muskrat food instead. MacNamara reported a kill of 1.91 ducks/hunter/day for the 1948 season following impoundment compared to 0.79 ducks/hunter/day in 1947. Following restoration, several uncommon ducks put in an appearance in the area including the red head, ring-neck, surf-scoter, and the shoveller.

Other investigators have reported the increased use of impoundments by birds (Catts, 1957; Darsie and Springer, 1957; Florschutz, 1959; Tindall, 1961; Mangold, 1962; Shoemaker, 1964; Lesser, 1965; Smith, 1968; Provost, 1969). Darsie and Springer identified 86 bird species in contrast to 55 in the area prior to impoundment. Tindall reported a three-fold increase. Smith cited 62 species on the impoundments and 39 on the natural marsh areas. Several of these workers reported increased numbers of broods of young following impoundment, particularly black ducks. These impoundments offered emergent and submergent vegetation as food for ducks, scattered emergent vegetation as important cover for new broods, fish and invertebrates as food for wading birds, and open water for resting areas (Catts *et al.,* 1963).

Some bird species have declined in number with the advent of impoundments. The clapper rail has often disappeared and has been associated with the absence of fiddler crabs (Darsie and Springer, 1957; Mangold, 1962; Shoemaker, 1964). But long-term inundation would also reduce the nesting and feeding areas for this rail. Both Mangold and Shoemaker also noted declines in the small birds: song sparrow, seaside sparrow, sharptail sparrow, and yellow throat warbler, primarily through loss of nesting sites and food. Smith (1968) reported marsh wrens and seaside sparrows relatively abundant, especially where the tide bush grew along ditch or pool margins; however, no comparative quantitative data was given. Provost (1969) indicated the decline in the dusky seaside sparrow following impoundment on Merritt Island, Florida where it preferred the *Distichlis* habitat. Fish-eating birds also declined on Merritt Island, especially the merganser. Provost could give no reason for such declines and went on to say that while 6 species of birds were reduced, there was no apparent effect on 7 species and an increase in number was noted for 22 species.

While most workers have shown enhanced bird usage following flooded impoundment, Ferrigno (1959, 1961) reported a decline in diked "dry" salt hay meadows (Table 2.10).

Evidence of mammals has increased with the creation of impoundments (MacNamara, 1952; Catts, 1957; Darsie and Springer, 1957; Tindall, 1961; Mangold, 1962; Shoemaker, 1964; Smith, 1968). Darsie and Springer noted continued maintenance of high water levels within an impoundment tended to restrict muskrat usage but the recession of water from the vegetated margin during the summer enhanced plants attractive to muskrats and waterfowl. MacNamara and Tindall reported increased numbers of muskrat houses while Mangold found muskrats to have preference for the fresher water impoundments. Smith (1968) noted no direct increase in small mammal populations but increased evidence of predators about the impound-

Table 2.10. Waterfowl and clapper rail usage and mosquito breeding for a New Jersey salt marsh. (Modified from Table 3, Ferrigno, 1959)

Vegetation	Number of birds flushed. 10 censuses of 100 acres in each zone		Annual total larvae & pupae per dip
	Waterfowl	Clapper Rail	
Undiked Marsh			
S. alterniflora, tall form	1742	29	0
S. alterniflora, short form	1239	33	0.0001
S. patens	285	3	3.05
Diked Hay Meadow			
S. patens	111	1	4.13

ments suggested such small mammal populations had indeed expanded. Increased mammal activity was attributed to greater variety of habitat and an increase in prey concentrations due to the edge effect associated with embankments (Florschutz, 1959).

It is evident from the foregoing that water-level manipulation through ditching or impounding may set off unforeseen changes in plant and animal distributions and zonations. The marsh ecosystem is a delicate complex of many interactions. At times the objective of pest control has not been fully achieved whereby numbers of the real pest *A. sollicitans* may have been reduced but other pests may have flourished. As Stearns *et al.* (1940) pointed out forty years ago, the ecological side effects may be greater than the original objective. However, not all such impacts can be classed as detrimental; generalities must be drawn with care.

Pisces

Harrington and Harrington (1961) described the fish feeding activity on a subtropical Florida salt marsh wherein an abrupt tidal-pluvial flooding gave fish sudden access to the marsh surface. Prior to the flooding there had been a prolonged drought driving fish from the marsh and permitting extensive mosquito egg deposition. A mosquito hatch was synchronized with the flooding. Resident marsh fish, the cyprinodontiforms, consumed mosquito larvae and pupae, turning to other things only after the mosquitos were gone. Among the transients (immigrant young of larger species) moving onto the flooded marsh surface, only the mullet, *Mugil cephalus,* fed to some extent upon mosquitos. This work clearly indicates that flooding tidal waters, by permitting access to the marsh surface for marsh fish species, are important in salt-marsh mosquito control.

The fishes associated with tidal marshes have a very wide tolerance to salinities. Harrington and Harrington (1961) called attention to this when they cited references reporting maximum salinity tolerances for the cyprinidontiform fishes at the levels of 80–90 percent. Schmelz (1964), in a study of the mummichog, *Fundulus heteroclitus,* reported salinities up to $40\%_{00}$ from surface pools on Canary Creek marsh in southern Delaware. Later (1970) he described the eggs of the striped killifish, *Fundulus majalis,* as hatching at salinities of $72–73\%_{00}$. However, newly hatched larvae were smaller than those hatched from salinities lower than $35\%_{00}$. Warlen (1964) reported the sheeps-head minnow, *Cyprinodon variegatus,* from marsh surfaces and drainage ditches of southern Delaware with salinities ranging between $14\%_{00}$ and $31\%_{00}$. Zilberberg (1966) found no correlation between species abundance and salinity or fish in a northwest Florida coastal marsh. All of this demonstrates tidal marsh fishes to be euryhaline.

Ichthyoplankton of tidal streams has been examined on a seasonal basis, along a salinity gradient and over several tidal cycles, for Delaware tidal creeks (Daiber, 1962, 1963a, b). A biweekly nighttime midflood sampling program was carried out over 15 months from June 1961 into September 1962. One-half hour collections were made by suspending 12-inch No. 0 mesh nets in the flooding current, surface and bottom. The movement of the tidal front was such that three streams, Canary Creek, Little River, and Appoquinimink Creek, could be sampled successively during a single flooding tide. Another sampling program during the summer of 1962 involved one-half hour collections each hour over periods of 6, 12, 24, and 48 hours using the same nets.

Table 2.11 depicts the numbers of eggs and larvae taken in the three creeks at various dates. The preponderance of eggs and larvae were collected during the summer months and in the higher salinities of Canary Creek and Little River. This, in light of the fact that the Appoquinimink is a much larger stream with a greater velocity of flow, suggested that more spawning occurred in the higher salinities of the lower half of the Bay. Table 2.12 indicates both eggs and larvae were more abundant at the surface during these collections. However, hourly sampling over full tidal cycles showed no consistent pattern. From one hour to the next, or between collection dates, the preponderance of eggs and larvae varied between top and bottom net with a possible tendency for greater numbers in the bottom net. Because of the general turbulence of tidal creeks, any differences between top and bottom may not be as great as it would be in quieter waters.

The several collections of 6-, 12-, 24-, and 48-hours duration showed the Appoquinimink again had a minor role: the greatest numbers of eggs and larvae were taken from the more saline waters of Canary Creek and Little River (Figures 2.19–2.21, note the difference in scale used for three figures). Equal numbers were not necessarily taken at the same time during one collection period, but fluctuated from one creek to the other. This was also evident in the biweekly collections (Table 2.12). This difference in abundance between the two streams suggested that eggs and larvae were "bunched" and entered a creek from the bay only if they were in the immediate vicinity. Even though dispersal undoubtedly occurred, the apparent concentration could result if the eggs and larvae were transported largely within the water mass in which they were spawned or concentrated by eddies and currents.

The eggs and larvae were few in number or even nonexistent in the collections made during daylight hours, late stages of ebb, and early stages of the flooding tide (Figures 2.19–2.22). These reduced numbers during daylight suggested light was a factor in their distribution. Photoperiodism may explain the fluctuation in the numbers of larvae with locomotor capabilities

Table 2.11. Biweekly plankton collections from three tidal creeks in Delaware from June 1961 into September 1962. (From Daiber, 1977, by permission of Elsevier Scientific Publishing Co.)

Date	CANARY CREEK			LITTLE RIVER			APPOQUINIMINK CREEK		
	Salinity	Eggs	Larvae	Salinity	Eggs	Larvae	Salinity	Eggs	Larvae
6/15/61		341	0		0	38		1	1
6/30	15.88	160	24		30	46	3.66	0	2
7/17	26.22	33	15	5.21	40	29	4.60	1	20
7/31	27.63	0	95	12.81	1	72	4.36	0	5
8/14	18.40	8	13	12.00	2	7	4.25	2	7
8/28		3	0	10.72	0	5		0	7
9/13		0	1		2	18		0	11
9/27		0	0		0	1		0	10
10/11		1	0		0	2		0	4
10/25		0	0		0	1		0	1
11/9		0	0		0	0		0	0
11/24		0	0		0	0		0	0
12/9		0	0		0	0		0	0
1/20/62		0	0		0	0		0	0
2/5		0	5		0	1		0	0
2/24		0	0		0	2		0	3
3/23		0	7		0	19		0	7
5/8		7	1		0	53		1	1
5/25	28.40	8	0		5	1081	4.26	0	20
6/8	27.53	168	193	11.98	0	179	4.43	0	6
6/21	28.52	74	14	17.04	1550	65	4.98	0	4
7/6	29.37	36	5	13.60	0	12	6.10	2	2
7/19		7	37	17.76	0	0		0	8
8/6		2	2		0	15		0	18
8/20		0	6		0	30		1	33
9/5		4	0		0	14		0	3
Totals		852	418		1630	1690		8	173

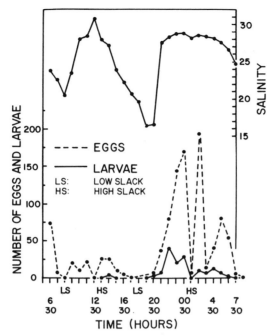

Figure 2.19. Numbers of fish eggs and larvae (average of top and bottom nets) from Canary Creek, Delaware, during a 24-hour period of June 21–22, 1962. (From Daiber, 1977, by permission of Elsevier Scientific Publishing Co.)

but does not clarify the movement of eggs. One explanation suggests the stage of development may affect buoyancy or a change in numbers. Eggs of the sciaenid *Bairdella icistia* fertilized in low salinity water ($15\%_{00}$) were larger and more buoyant than eggs fertilized in high salinities ($33\%_{00}$) (May, 1974). The salinity of the medium during the first five to seven minutes had a lasting effect on egg buoyancy. Subsequent transfer to a different salinity influenced buoyancy but the capacity for adjustment was limited. Predation may be an important factor as demonstrated by Moore (1968) in his studies of *Menidia menidia,* the atlantic silverside, from lower Delaware Bay. He reported this fish to be a daylight feeder with fish larvae making up 4.4 percent and 18.4 percent (by weight) of the stomach contents for June–July and August 1967 collections, respectively. Fish eggs composed less than one percent of the total recorded for both time periods. In addition, many eggs were observed in various ctenophores collected at these times.

Salinity generally reached its highest peak near midflood on the night tide and then leveled off (Figures 2.19–2.22). At the beginning of this salinity plateau, there was a very marked increase in the numbers of eggs and larvae

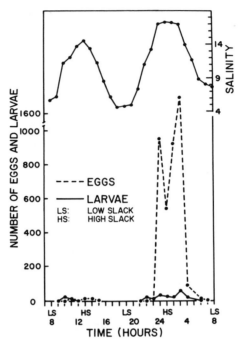

Figure 2.20.   Numbers of fish eggs and larvae (average of top and bottom nets) from Little River, Delaware, during a 24-hour period of June 21–22, 1962. (From Daiber, 1977, by permission of Elsevier Scientific Publishing Co.)

for both the top and bottom nets. At midebb, as the salinity first began to decrease, there was a sharp decline in the numbers of eggs and larvae taken.

The decrease in numbers at slack water before ebb tide was undoubtedly an artificial condition. Water velocity decreases with the approach of slack conditions and the nets hang vertically in the water and do not "fish" well. Thus, there may be no actual decrease in eggs and larvae at this time, as compared to the period prior to and immediately following slack water (Figures 2.19–2.22).

A series of six-hour flooding tide collections spanning a month of time were made during the early evening or after dark. These data suggested that there was not a uniform number of eggs and larvae present. The disparity in numbers is demonstrated in Figures 2.19–2.22 and implies that spawning had certain peaks of intensity.

Since the movement of planktonic stages of fish is primarily dependent on water flow, it should be possible to ascertain the extent of landward dispersion by determining the penetration of high salinity water along the axes of tidal streams. During daylight spring tides, flooding waters penetrated one-half to three-fourths of the 4.4 kilometers length of Canary Creek. In

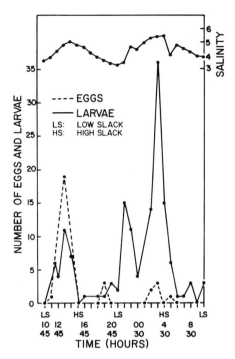

Figure 2.21. Numbers of fish eggs and larvae (average of top and bottom nets) from Appoquinimink Creek, Delaware, during a 24-hour period of June 21–22, 1962. (From Daiber, 1977, by permission of Elsevier Scientific Publishing Co.)

contrast, high salinities frequently existed the full length of the creek during the night flood tides. On the following ebb, the fresher water found at the head of the creek at high slack moved downstream beyond the mouth of the creek out into the bay, substantially flushing the high salinity water from the length of the creek (Daiber, 1963b).

Uniformly distributed high salinity water penetrated larger streams like Broadkill River 4 to 6.4 kilometers; not much farther than the total length of Canary Creek. There was a sharp decline in salinity beyond this point, with the distance and time of penetration being dependent upon wind velocity and direction and the amount of fresh-water runoff. The flushing time for the lower portions of these tidal streams has been calculated to be one-half a tidal cycle (deWitt and Daiber, 1973).

These various observations of Delaware tidal creeks have demonstrated several things. The great majority of the planktonic fish eggs and larvae were present during June and July. Most of them were found in tidal creeks in the lower half of Delaware Bay where salinities are higher. This pelagic phase was not uniformly distributed in space or time: large numbers of eggs

Table 2.12. The vertical distribution of fish eggs and larvae from three Delaware tidal creeks during the midflood stage of tide. (From Daiber, 1977, by permission of Elsevier Scientific Publishing Co.)

| | Canary Creek | | | | Little River | | | | Appoquinimink Creek | | | |
| | Top Net | | Bottom Net | | Top Net | | Bottom Net | | Top Net | | Bottom Net | |
Date	Eggs	Larvae	Eggs	Larvae	Eggs	Larvae	Eggs	Larvae	Eggs	Larvae	Eggs	Larvae
7/17/61	33	10	0	5	1	22	39	7	1	20	0	0
7/31	0	62	0	33	0	64	1	8	0	5	0	0
8/14	3	13	5	0	0	7	2	0	0	7	0	0
8/28	0	0	3	0	0	4	0	1	2	6	0	0
9/13	0	1	0	0	0	6	2	12	0	11	0	0
3/23/62	0	0	6	1	–	–	0	19	0	7	0	0
5/8	2	1	5	0	0	23	0	30	0	5	1	1
5/25	8	0	0	0	5	581	0	500	0	13	0	7
6/8	79	152	89	41	0	58	0	121	0	5	0	1
6/21	67	7	7	7	957	36	593	29	0	4	–	1
7/6	17	0	19	5	0	12	0	0	–	2	1	–
7/19	2	27	5	10	0	0	0	0	1	8	0	0
8/6	0	2	2	0	0	9	0	6	0	18	0	0
8/20	0	6	–	–	0	15	0	15	1	32	0	1
9/5	4	0	0	0	0	3	0	11	0	3	0	0
Totals	215	281	141	102	963	840	637	759	5	146	2	11

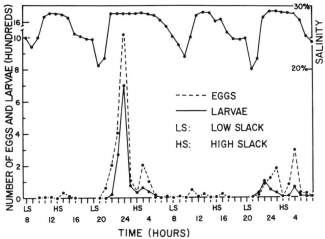

Figure 2.22.   Numbers of fish eggs and larvae (average of top and bottom nets) from Canary Creek, Delaware, during a 48-hour period of June 6–8, 1962. (From Daiber, 1977, by permission of Elsevier Scientific Publishing Co.)

and larvae may enter one creek but not another. It is suggested that little spawning occurred in the creeks. The eggs and larvae remained with the water mass being carried inland to the extent of high salinity intrusion and were on their way out of the creeks by the time the salinity began to decline. Invariably there were fewer eggs and larvae taken on the ebb tide than on the flood.

Aves

There is a definite relationship between bird distributions in a salt marsh and the interplay between vegetational zonation, tidal flooding, and salinity as it affects feeding and reproductive activities. Urner (1935) identified the ava fauna specialized to nest and feed in salt marshes in relation to the marsh wetness, creek and pond depth, salinity, and accessibility of the tides. Both he and Ferrigno (1961) called attention to changes in bird populations following any alterations in these various parameters.

The resident clapper rail, *Rallus longirostris waynei,* of the Georgia salt marshes displayed distinct distributional preferences within the dominant grass, *S. alterniflora* (Oney, 1954). This grass could be divided into three categories. A tall-grass zone was located on the edge of natural drainage ditches, creeks, and rivers with a soft mud substrate and an average plant density of 110/square yard, 4–10 feet tall. The medium-grass zone was found on the gentle level slope away from the creek bank, had a firmer soil with an average plant density of 288/square yard, 2–4 feet tall. The short-grass zone was found in the lowest parts of the Georgia marshes, had a high sand content with an average plant density of 362/square yard, 5 inches to 2 feet tall.

The square back marsh crabs, *Sesarma,* the primary food of the rail, were most abundant in the tall-grass zone. The fiddler crabs, *Uca,* and the periwinkle, *Littorina irrorata,* of secondary and tertiary food value, were found in the medium- and short-grass zones, respectively. However, during his three-year study, Oney found a definite nesting preference for the me-dium-grass zone: of 118 nests measured, 30 were in the tall-grass zone, 87 or 74 percent were in the medium-grass zone and only one nest was recorded for the short-grass zone. Furthermore, his prior studies in 1949 and 1950 in-dicated the bird's preference for the medium-type grass bordering the tall-grass zone along a small ditch or creek. The average distance from a nest to the creek at low tide was 458 feet with a range of 3–1200 feet. The average nest was 20 feet from a change in vegetation zone with a range of 3–80 feet. Earlier, Stewart (1951) had called attention to the importance of the edge between vegetation zones in placement of clapper rail nests. Working in the Eastern Shore marshes of Maryland, he found a high correlation between nest densities and the amount of edge between the tall (and dense) and the short (and sparse) growth form of *S. alterniflora.* Lower correlations were derived from pure stands of short and tall *Spartina.* Stewart recorded nest density in the best edge at 2.5 ± 0.3/acre with nests within 15 feet of the creeks.

Several references called attention to the height of the nest placement and the impact of inundation on hatching success of the rails. In his early work on the life histories of North American marsh birds, Bent (1963) lo-cated the second nestings of the clapper rail, *R. longirostris crepitans,* on higher drier ground covered with only a few inches of water at high tide. He went on to say that most nests were built in small clumps of grass along creek banks in soft wet mud: nest heights varied 8–12 inches above the mud, probably high enough to escape ordinary high tides but not spring tides. King rail nests were usually found in the shallow water portion of the marsh with water depths of 4–24 inches. The nest height above water was depen-dent on water depth; the shallower the water, the lower the nest (Meanley, 1969). Most nests of the resident clapper rail of Georgia were 8–9 inches off the ground with the average distance from the ground to egg level at 14.8 inches with extremes of 9–30 inches. These nests could be covered by as much as 12–19 inches of water and still support a hatch (Oney, 1954). Ear-lier, Stewart (1952) found 1951 hatching success of the first sets of eggs in the Chincogeague, Virginia marshes to be less than 45 percent compared to 94 percent in 1950. Due to high storm tides during the early part of the nesting

Table 2.13. Clapper rail nest census during 1955 and 1956 in Cape May County, New Jersey. (From Table 1, Ferrigno, 1957)

Area	Number of Observed Nests		Number Destroyed (by tides)		Number Hatched Successfully	
	1955	1956	1955	1956	1955	1956
Coney's	29	20	9	4	20	16
Key's	7	10	3	1	4	9
TOTAL	36	30	12	5	24	25

season, production of young was greatly staggered. Ferrigno (1957) clarified the impact of storm tide flooding on hatching success (Table 2.13). On May 10, 1955, there had been a high tide with strong winds but little nest damage since the birds had just begun to nest. High tides of June 8–11 resulted in virtually complete nest destruction. There was subsequent renesting as evidenced by a later hatching peak. There were high lunar tides in 1956 but with no wind. Although 14 percent of the nests were destroyed by a flood tide on June 8, 83 percent of the first nests hatched successfully in that year.

Changes in vegetational cover can affect clapper rail nesting. Ferrigno (1957) reported a decrease in observed nests on the Coney's area but an increase on the Keye's area, both in Cape May County, New Jersey. He attributed the decrease in Coney's to the development of large barren areas which had been formerly covered with *S. alterniflora*. Possible causes given were adverse weather conditions or an overpopulation of fiddler crabs which could have killed the vegetation by burrowing activities.

The clapper rail has been described primarily as a resident of the more saline low marshes (Stewart, 1951; Oney, 1954). In contrast, the king rail, *Rallus elegans*, and Virginia rail, *R. limicola*, are essentially inhabitants of the fresh and brackish marshes whose numbers vary with vegetation (Bent, 1963; Meanley, 1969). They are common in the coastal marshes of Louisiana and abundant in the South Carolina low country fresh and brackish marshes, especially where the giant cut grass, *Zizaniopsis miliacea*, and the fiddler crab, *U. minax*, are present. The grass provides good nesting cover with a nest density as high as one per acre. In the Chesapeake Bay area, the king rail is most abundant where the big cord grass, *S. cynosuroides*, is dominant, providing good cover.

Both rail species occur in transition areas, especially in the lower reaches of brackish marshes where interbreeding sometimes produces hybrids. In Delaware king and clapper rails were taken in the Broadway meadows located between Flemings Landing and Woodland Beach. In that section at Taylors Gut where mixed populations occurred, the dominant vegetation was *S. alterniflora* and *S. robustus* with the salinity range reported at 5.7–7.2‰. Inland at Flemings Landing the dominant vegetation was *S. patens* and *D. spicata* with a salinity range of 3.7–4.4‰ and only the king rail was observed. Only clapper rail were found at Woodland Beach with *S. alterniflora* and *S. robustus* as the dominant vegetation and a salinity range of 7.5–7.6‰.

While both rails can be identified with the low marshes, Bent (1929) described the eastern willet, *Catoptrophorus semipalmatus,* as a decidedly coastal bird, seldom seen far from coastal marshes, beaches and islands. He described the nesting area as being on sand islands overgrown with tall grass or on dry uplands close to marshes. Vogt (1938) was a bit more specific in his observations in the Fortesque, New Jersey marshes. He recorded most nests in the dense *S. patens* of the high marsh, near the ecotone with *S. alterniflora* or *Typha angustifolia.* In addition, Vogt found the willet most abundant where *S. patens* was regularly mowed or burned, presumably making it easier for the birds to feed. This clamorous bird was also found to be abundant where wintering brant or greater snow geese had grazed *S. patens* in the absence of eel-grass, *Zostera marina.* Stewart and Robbins (1958) reported breeding densities of 10.5/100 acres of brackish hay marsh during a 1956 survey of Dorchester County, Maryland. In contrast to earlier observations these workers described the habitat as a strip along the tidal creek 220 yards wide.

The casual visitor to a salt marsh seldom sees the secretive rails as they slip through the vegetation but, during the first half of the summer, a visitor can be announced by the clattering presence of the willet. As the summer progresses, these clamorous calls decline to silence although the bird can still be seen flying over the expanses of grass or walking along a creek bank. Black ducks can be put to flight during the early summer nesting season but waterfowl typically are most obvious during the fall migration flights and over the wintering areas.

Thirteen major types of waterfowl habitat have been categorized by Stewart (1962) in the upper Chesapeake Bay area: six in open tidewater areas, five in marshes and two in the coastal plain interior designated as river bottoms and impoundments. The five marsh habitats were distinguished by salinity distributions which in turn had an influence on vegetational composition. Table 2.14 records those ducks and geese associated with the five tidal marsh types. While Stewart considered the brackish estuarine bays to be the most valuable waterfowl habitat, the marshes bordering such bays had fewer recorded species (10) than the less saline estuarine bay marshes (13) and the estuarine river marshes (12). The three marshes with one or two designated principal species had higher numbers of secondary species. It is evident that nine species were restricted to certain marsh habitats while seven were recorded from all five types. Stewart was

Table 2.14. Principal (P) and secondary (S) waterfowl species associated with various types of upper Chesapeake Bay marshes during 1958–59. (Derived from Stewart, 1962)

	Coastal Embayed Marsh		Salt Estuarine Bay Marsh		Brackish Estuarine Bay Marsh		Fresh Estuarine Bay Marsh		Estuarine River Marsh	
	P	S	P	S	P	S	P	S	P	S
Canada goose	X			X		X	X			X
Black duck	X		X		X		X		X	
Snow goose		X								
Mallard		X	X		X		X	X		
Green-wing teal		X	X	X			X	X		
Blue-wing teal		X	X	X			X	X		
Shoveler		X	X		X		X			
Hooded merganser		X			X					X
Common merganser							X			X
American widgeon		X	X	X			X			X
Ringed-neck duck							X			X
American coot		X					X			X
Pintail		X	X		X		X	X		
Gadwall			X		X		X			
Whistling swan							X			
Wood duck									X	
	2	9	1	8	4	6	2	11	6	6
		11		9		10		13		12

able to develop population distributions for four of the seven species found throughout the marshes and Table 2.15 has been developed from his data. The black duck was the most ubiquitous, being classed as a principal species for all five marsh habitats although even more associated with the open bays or agricultural lands during migration and wintering. In contrast, although the total recorded population was low, the great majority (99 percent) of green-wing teal were found in the tidal marshes. Stewart indicated in his text that the blue-wing teal followed this same pattern.

Vegetation dominance and distributions as well as salinity levels had an influence on waterfowl distributions by providing food and nesting sites. *S. alterniflora* was the predominant plant in the coastal embayed salt marshes located back of the barrier beaches. The black duck was the only species that was common and widely distributed while the Canada goose was numerous along tidal creeks and guts. Canada and snow geese were most numerous on extensive cord grass areas or mud flats. Pintails, shovelers, blue-wing teal, and American widgeon preferred open ponds with poor drainage or stable water levels in artifically created ponds. Scattered pairs of black ducks along with a few mallards and blue-wing teal nested in these marshes.

Table 2.15. Population distribution of waterfowl associated with various types of upper Chesapeake Bay marshes during 1958–1959. (Derived from Stewart, 1962—Tables 44, 45, 76, 84)

Waterfowl	Total Population (X 1000)	Coastal Embayed Marsh	Salt Estuarine Bay Marsh	Brackish Estuarine Bay Marsh	Fresh Estuarine Bay Marsh	Estuarine River Marsh
			Percent of total population*			
		21,000 acres	113,000 acres	47,000 acres	30,000 acres	67,000 acres
Black duck	317	12	10	3	3	5
Canada goose	—					
Mallard	148	6	1	3	5	7
Green-wing teal	10	32	23	13	6	25
Blue-wing teal	—					
American widgeon	196	8	5		4	—
Pintail	—					

* The percentage figures are averaged values derived from five observation periods from October 2, 1958 through March 16, 1959.

The difference between the total percentage figure for each waterfowl species and 100% indicates the birds were observed on the open waters of the adjoining bays and areas other than in the marshes.

They preferred marsh islands rather than shore zone marshes and all nests found by Stewart (1962) were in the drier more elevated areas.

The salt estuarine bay marshes were characterized by a high salinity and narrow tidal fluctuation. Widgeon grass, *R. maritima*, salt grass, *D. spicata*, salt marsh cord grass, *S. alterniflora*, salt meadow cord grass, *S. patens*, the bulrush, *S. robustus*, and black sedge, *J. roemerianus*, were the common plant species. The black duck was the only common and widely distributed waterfowl. All others were scarce.

The brackish estuarine bay marshes comprised a complex mosaic of ponds, creeks, and marshes. The principal plant species were *Ruppia, Distichlis, S. cynosuroides, S. alterniflora, S. patens, S. olneyi,* and *J. roemerianus* depending on the locale. There was a diverse fauna with raccoons and crows as important waterfowl predators. As in the coastal marshes, the black duck and green-wing teal were generally distributed showing a definite preference for tidal creeks and ponds in drainage systems with marginal mud flats exposed at low tide. The American widgeon and gadwalls concentrated on stable ponds with beds of widgeon grass or musk grass (*Chara* sp.). The hooded mergansers were restricted to the larger tidal creeks while Canada geese preferred the larger ponds. Large numbers bred in these marshes with the blue-wing teal restricted almost entirely to the marsh meadow (presumably *S. patens*).

The fresh estuarine bay marshes had next to the smallest total recorded acreage but a much greater diversity of vegetation. Along with this vegetation variety, Stewart recorded the greatest numbers of waterfowl species, though eleven of the thirteen were listed as secondary (Table 2.14) and most of the population was located on the bays adjoining these fresh estuarine bay marshes (Table 2.15) rather than in the marshes themselves. The Canada geese among others, were found on the larger ponds, while the black ducks and teals were found in well-drained areas of creeks and ponds with exposed mud flats.

The vegetation varied with salinity in the estuarine river marshes of the upper Chesapeake. This was an area with a great variety of emergent vegetation and possessed a greater tidal fluctuation than some other marsh types. The greatest concentrations of waterfowl, including many dabbling ducks, were located here between the fresh and brackish water habitats where excellent cover and food were available.

In addition to those birds already described, tidal flooding and marsh elevation influence the distributions and activities of numerous other bird species. The laughing gull, *Larus atricilla,* placed most of its nests where the marsh was elevated from 0 to 0.2 meters above mean high water with *S. alterniflora* taller than 0.6 meters. Some nests were found in shorter vegetation and at lower elevations. The gulls would not nest where the grass had been cut though they had nested at the same site in previous years. They would nest on piles of dead grass brought together by tidal action or by raking (Bongiorno, 1970).

Bent (1937 after Urner, 1925) described three nests of the marsh hawk, *Circus cyaneus hudsonius,* located in a New Jersey salt marsh. One was located on dry sandy ground in a clump of *Iva.* It was only 1–2 inches thick. The other two nests were located on wetter ground in *P. communis* stands. One of these was located some distance from the shore in an area infrequently flooded. The nest was 5–6 inches thick. The other, an enormous structure 15 inches high, three feet long and two feet wide, was located near the creek edge which was frequently flooded.

The magnitude of flooding influenced habitat selection for both the coastal savannah sparrow, *Passerculus sandwichensis alaudinus,* and the eastern sharp-tailed sparrow, *Ammospiza c. caudacuta* (Bent et al., 1968). Both were found at the higher marsh elevations. The former was located in the *Salicornia ambigua* association of California marshes 5–10 feet above mean sea level, behind the more frequently flooded *Spartina foliosa.* The nests, which were on the ground were most often built in the *Salicornia* associes rather than that of *D. spicata.* The sharp-tailed sparrow is found in the drier *S. patens* zone with some nests on the ground but most at varying heights above ground level, presumably above summer high water levels (Bent et al., 1968).

Adequate feeding ground and suitable nesting cover within easy flight of the feeding grounds provided two components of a suitable habitat for both the northern seaside sparrow, *Ammospiza m. maritima* (Bent *et al.,* 1968), and Macgillvrays seaside sparrow, *A. maritima macgillivraii* (Tomkins, 1941). Tidal flooding of the feeding grounds made them unsuitable for nesting sites. Nests were built in a variety of places; a few inches above the mud in *Sporobolus-Paspalum* to three feet in *Spartina* or *Juncus* and up to five feet in *Baccharis.*

Much attention has been focused on the song sparrows *Melospiza melodia* of the salt marshes of the San Francisco Bay region (Marshall, 1948; Johnston, 1956b and c). These investigators discussed habitat, abundance, annual cycles, population structure and maintenance, and concluded that tidal flooding and vegetational zonation were the determining influences. Song sparrow distributions were more circumscribed than vegetation distributions as birds were less tolerant of drying (Marshall, 1948). The birds occupied territories strung out along the tidal sloughs, exercising definite preferences for vegetation types and not dispersing over the marsh surface. Nests were placed off the ground, most commonly in *Salicornia, Grindelia, Distichlis,* or *Spartina.* Any nest less than five inches above the ground would be flooded out. Generally an increase in vegetation height during the growing season enabled the birds to nest at successfully higher levels. Such action paralleled the increased height of tides during the breeding season.

Sibley (1955) described the responses of salt-marsh birds to extreme tides in the San Francisco Bay area at times other than nesting periods. White-crowned, savannah, and song sparrows, and long-billed marsh wrens were concentrated along the levees. When flushed they did not fly out over the flooded marsh. Willets and the least and western sandpipers settled on floating debris. The clapper, sora, and Virginia rails, normally not seen at low or average tidal conditions, were quite evident clinging to *Spartina* stems or huddled in clumps of emergent vegetation. Predators availed themselves of these concentrations; California and ring-billed gulls, marsh hawks, and short-eared owls were reported hunting along the levees and over clumps of emergent vegetation.

Mammalia

A number of small mammals have been associated with the fringes of salt marshes (Paradiso and Handley, 1965). Shure (1970, 1971) found a definite relationship between small mammal distributions and the topographically controlled pattern of barrier beach vegetation of a New Jersey marsh habitat. The meadow mouse, *Microtus pennsylvanicus,* was the most abundant, constituting 97 percent of the captures associated with the dense herbaceous cover of the marshes of the bay shore dominated by *S. patens. Zapus hud-*

sonius, meadow jumping mouse, and *Peromyscus leucopus,* the white-footed mouse, were fairly abundant; the former being most evident in the brackish marshes and upland borders. *Peromyscus,* the masked shrew, *Sorex cinereus,* and the house mouse, *Mus musculus,* were taken occasionally in the salt marsh but primarily at trap sites in the marsh-upland border. There was a change in small mammal distributions during successional stages of a salt marsh (Figure 2.23). Shure (1971) suggested the role of vegetation preference and interspecific relations as contributing factors and seemed to prefer the latter.

Microtus distribution was related to tidal flooding in a study by Shure (1971) who found a significantly greater number of meadow vole in the drier more dense *S. patens* vegetation than in the lower wetter *S. alterniflora.* This distribution was further borne out by the significantly greater number of trap captures from the *S. patens* covered spoil piles bordering drainage ditches than from other marsh locations. Several authors including Harris (1953) and Johnston (1957) have commented on the willingness of *Microtus* to swim. However, Shure (1971) showed a significant restriction of *Microtus* movements caused by the presence of mosquito control ditches that ranged up to one meter in width. This reluctance to swim such a waterway was further substantiated by recordings of significantly smaller recapture distances in a brackish marsh than in a salt-marsh area. The brackish marsh was highly compartmentalized by ditches and most *Microtus* were repeatedly recaptured within the same compartment.

All of these are inconspicuous marsh fringe inhabitants. The muskrat,

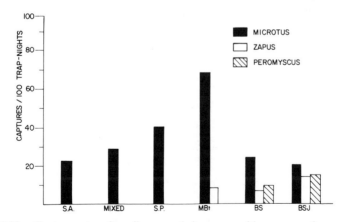

Figure 2.23. Capture rates of small mammals in communities representing seral stages in tidal marsh succession. The initial salt-marsh stage has been divided into mixed and homogeneous areas of *Spartina alterniflora* (SA) and *Spartina patens* (SP). Other seral stages include brackish marsh (MBt) and mixed herb-shrub savannas (BS, BSJ). (From Figure 3, Shure, 1971, by permission of the editor. *Amer. Midl. Natl.*)

Ondatra zibethica, is a much more obvious animal, conspicuous by its houses which dot the marsh surface and its aquatic runs among the vegetation. Much has been written about its activities both in fresh and brackish water marshes. Stearns *et al.* (1939, 1940) reported that ditching for mosquito control, which lowered the water levels, had an adverse effect on vegetation needed for muskrat food and house construction. Important muskrat foods such as *S. olneyi* and *S. cynosuroides* had been replaced by species such as marsh mallow, *Hibiscus oculiroseus,* salt marsh mallow, *Kosteletzkya virginica,* seaside goldenrod, *Solidago remprevirens,* tickseed sunflower, *Bidens trichoxperma,* and New York aster, *Aster novi-belgii,* presenting a brilliant picture but no value to the muskrat (Figure 2.24).

Muskrat food and populations decrease as salinity increases (Harris, 1937; Dozier, 1947; Dozier *et al.,* 1948). The muskrats prefer the less saline types of vegetation such as the three-square sedges, *S. olneyi, S. robustus, S. americanus,* and the cat-tails, *Typha.* Less favored foods are *Spartina cynosuroides, S. alterniflora, S. patens, D. spicata,* and *J. roemerianus.* Dozier *et al.* (1948) reported the heaviest muskrats, with average weights of 2.25 and 2.26 lbs., consuming Group I plants (*S. olneyi, S. americanus, Typha* (salinity 1.1–1.5‰)) and Group II vegetation (*S. olneyi, Typha* (5–11‰)). Those feeding in higher salinity areas on Group IV vegetation (*S. patens, S. alterniflora, S. olneyi,* and *Typha* (15.0–25.0‰)) and Group V plants (*S. patens, S. alterniflora,* and *J. roemerianus* (25.0–43.0‰)) had average weights of 2.16 and 2.20 pounds, respectively. On the surface, this weight differential does not appear significant. However, even casual observation reveals the divergence in plant distributions and numbers of muskrat houses along a

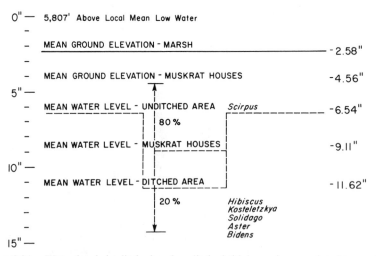

Figure 2.24.   Water levels in ditched and undivided tidal marshes as related to muskrat houses and vegetation. (From Stearns *et al.,* 1939).

salinity gradient. Dozier (1947) made a special point about the impact of salinity on tide water muskrat production. The animals were found in the upper reaches of tidal streams and were abundant where tidal influence was reduced. Diked areas or marshes that were flooded by high salinity water during storms or through evaporation tended to have reduced muskrat populations through loss of food plants and drinking water.

Palmisano (1972) portrayed the interaction between vegetation types, salinity, extent of flooding, and drought on the distribution and abundance of the muskrat in Louisiana coastal marshes. Palmisano recognized four major plant communities: (1) saline marshes adjacent to the Gulf of Mexico dominated by relatively few salt tolerant species; (2) brackish marshes in a broad zone of moderate salinity where plant growth was vigorous; (3) intermediate, slightly brackish marshes; and (4) fresh-water marshes. Muskrats occurred in all the coastal marshes examined; however, population densities varied greatly. Brackish marshes composed of a mixed community of *S. olneyi* and *S. patens* were a preferred habitat (Table 2.16). Although Palmisano recorded approximately equal percentage values for southeastern and southwestern Louisiana, population densities were much higher in the southeast. The saline marshes in the southeast contained populations equal to overall average density. The saline marshes of the southwest were poor muskrat habitat, possibly because of their well-drained nature. The intermediate marshes had below average population densities in general but high or average levels in restricted areas adjacent to the brackish marshes. The fresh-water marshes exhibited the lowest densities of any type; 31.4 percent of the total area examined supported only 4.1 percent of the total houses counted. Populations were recorded at their highest during periods of high precipitation and low salinity. The greatest house counts were recorded in February when water levels were generally high, temperatures low, and the spring breeding season about to begin.

Table 2.16. Acreage of marsh vegetative types of coastal Louisiana, percent of acreage surveyed and percent of houses counted. (Modified from Tables 2, 3, 4, Palmisano, 1972)

| Marsh Type | Southwestern | | | Southeastern | | | Total | | |
| | | Percent Surveyed | | | Percent Surveyed | | | Percent Surveyed | |
	Acreage	Acres	Houses	Acreage	Acres	Houses	Acreage	Acres	Houses
Saline	45,507	2.6	1.0	753,130	22.2	20.8	798,637	12.4	14.2
Brackish	463,938	37.5	70.3	722,202	36.1	70.0	1,186,140	36.8	72.6
Intermediate	368,703	31.5	25.0	283,076	7.2	3.7	651,779	19.4	9.1
Fresh	390,757	28.4	3.7	830,769	34.5	5.5	1,221,526	31.4	4.1
Total	1,268,905	100.0	100.0	2,589,177	100.0	100.0	3,858,082	100.0	100.0

Palmisano reported wide population fluctuations in localized areas with rapid increases for three to four years followed by sharp declines to almost zero in a few months. Such a decline was observed in the brackish marshes in December 1971 following two dry summers. The other marsh types were not as severely affected by the drought with populations actually increasing in a few locations. These marshes served as important reservoirs for musk-rats during periods of stress in the brackish marshes. In December 1971, when populations were below normal, nonbrackish marshes accounted for over 50 percent of the houses recorded. During normal years less than 20 percent were recorded outside the brackish marsh zone.

Mammals respond to storm tides on a salt marsh much as do the birds; Norway rats and meadow mice were often found in the same clumps of grass with birds (Sibley, 1955). Extremely high tides that drove small mam-mals from cover occurred during the winter months in the San Francisco Bay area (Johnston, 1957; Fisler, 1965a; Rudd et al., 1971). At such times only 4–5 inches of vegetation remained exposed, mostly *Grindelia cuneifolia.* Since high ground was some distance from centers of mammal populations, most animals sought safety in emergent vegetation or floating debris. Some were lost and a number of young were drowned in the spring (Johnston, 1957). The shrew, *Sorex vagrans,* normally placed its nests on high ground greater than six feet above mean sea level. Rudd et al. (1971) found the greatest numbers of *Sorex sinuosus* at the interface between the *Salicornia ambigua* marsh and the *Baccharis pilularis* and grasses of the levees. They found no difference in numbers between a dry summer marsh and a flooded winter marsh. The meadow mouse, *Microtus californicus,* although able to swim, preferred to hide in what emergent vegetation existed (Fisler, 1965a). Stark (1963) observed that only those voles with home ranges on higher ground survived several hours of winter storm tide and rain. Later observa-tions by Rudd et al. (1971) depicted a significant decrease in *M. californicus* population from a summer dry marsh to an inundated winter marsh. They suggested the decrease could be explained by drowning, increased predation or exclusion caused by the high numbers of *Peromyscus maniculatus* or *M. musculus.* Harris (1953) could not explain how *M. pennsylvanicus* survived high water in Blackwater Refuge marshes of Maryland. It was not evident whether high tides cause the voles to move from the marsh to muskrat houses or whether the tides restricted the *Microtus* to the vicinity of the houses, thereby concentrating signs of their activity as well as making it eas-ier to take in traps.

Harris considered movement to high ground (landward edge of the marsh, islands in the marsh, or muskrat houses) as means of survival al-though travel of any distance would increase exposure to predation. While he acknowledged ability to swim and dive with ease, he found it difficult to believe *Microtus* could scramble from one *Spartina* culm to the next for any length of time and still survive. Fisler (1965a) found few mice in the *Spartina foliosa*, more in *S. ambigua* and the largest concentrations in the *Grindelia* growing on the levees. This preference for high ground by *M. californicus* agrees with the association between *Microtus pennsylvanicus* and high marsh *S. patens* in New Jersey (Shure, 1970, 1971). However, Johnston (1957) and Rudd et al. (1971) found *Microtus* nests at all levels of the marsh surface, the breeding season occurring during the fewest excessive tides.

The Norway rat, *Rattus norvegicus*, was described by Johnston (1957) as an excellent swimmer and diver but apt to suffer considerable losses of young because its nests were located on the ground. Apparently during the nonbreeding season the Norway rat is better able to survive (Stark, 1963). In contrast, the harvest mouse is a poor swimmer; its fur wets easily and it does not take to the water readily. It normally nests above ground in old sparrow nests and Johnston observed no nests being flooded out. This may explain why Rudd et al. (1971) found only a slight increase in numbers of this species moving from their characteristic *S. ambigua* habitat to the higher levees when the marshes were inundated during winter high and storm tides.

RELATION TO SALINITY AND OSMOTIC PRESSURE

There is a voluminous literature evaluating the effects of salinity on organisms. The reader should turn to works by Lockwood (1962), Kinne (1964), Vernberg and Vernberg (1972), and others for reviews of the subject. A recent synthesis has been made by Gunter et al. (1974). Much of the emphasis of this critique was directed at the animals of the coastal areas and, as the authors pointed out, the salinity reactions of salt-water plants are less well known. Waisel (1972) brought together much of the literature concerned with halophytes.

Kinne (1964) placed the aquatic invertebrates into two major groups: osmoconformers and osmoregulators, with a whole series of gradations in between. The same individual can be a regulator at one point along the salinity range and a conformer at another level of salinity. The oceanic invertebrates tend to be conformers, showing little ability to osmoregulate. The intertidal and semiterrestrial invertebrates have a greater osmo-regulatory capacity with an appreciable tendency toward homoosmosis leading to varying degrees of osmo-stability. According to Kinne, osmoregulation can be subdivided into eurysaline, holoeurysaline, and oligosaline regulators. Eurysaline forms can regulate in varying salinities but require more salt than is available in freshwater. Most invertebrates and some fishes of the tidal marshes would be associated with this category. Holoeurysaline species can live in fresh water as well as salinities as great or greater than normal seawater. The fish *Fundulus heteroclitus* would be an example. Oligosaline osmoregulators can regulate in fresh water but collapse in salinities of a few parts per thousand. Many of the birds and mammals found in the salt marsh would fall into this subdivision. The capacity to osmoregulate varies with temperature, season, stage in the life cycle, sex, and physiological state of the individual (Kinne, 1964).

There are two ways salinity acts on a tidal marsh organism. The first is the direct osmotic effect of being immersed in the water medium; the second is the osmotic problems generated by drinking water. The invertebrates and the lower vertebrates (fishes and amphibians) fall into the former category while the birds and mammals are placed in the latter grouping. Birds and mammals can also be indirectly involved with salinity interaction through the kind of food consumed.

One unique aspect of a salt marsh derives from the fact that it is a meeting place for fresh-water and marine faunas. A specialized fauna has been developed from both sources, much of which has become incapable of living for any length of time in its former environment (Nichol, 1936). The salt marsh contains a mixture of terresterial, brackish water, and marine organisms. As was pointed out in the introduction, salt marsh animals cannot escape the impact of salinity but must tolerate the osmotic effect on body fluids induced by changing salinities.

Macnae (1957b), in his examination of the estuary of the Swartkops River in South Africa with its extensive salt marshes, came to the conclusion that the distribution of animals along that particular estuary was controlled among other things by the almost complete absence of a salinity gradient. This was in sharp contrast to the usual observations related to estuarine systems. Nichol (1936) called attention to the categorization of the fauna associated with marsh surface pools with salinities less than $5\%_{00}$ and those with average salinities of $15\%_{00}$. Lambert (1930) described the reclamation of a marshland for agricultural uses in the Thames estuary. Varying salinities brought on by rainfall and evaporation induced profound faunal changes. Marine species did persist in some ditches, dependent on the extent of replenishment by saline water. Elsewhere the marine fauna was replaced by fresh-water forms as the water becomes fresh. Darsie and Springer (1957), Smith (1968), Dukes et al. (1974c) among others (see Daiber, 1974, for further review) have shown a shift from saline toward fresher water faunas following impoundment, often with increases in the avian fauna in the impoundments and along their borders.

Protozoa

There appears to be some ambiguity about the interactions between Foraminifera distributions and salinity. Phleger (1970) was impressed by the great variation in environmental factors, including salinity, known to affect occurrence and development of foraminiferal populations in a salt marsh. Earlier, Phleger and Bradshaw (1966) and Bradshaw (1968) commented on the greater variability in environmental parameters than had been anticipated in their study in the Mission Bay, San Diego, California marshes. They attributed the salinity variations to tidal flushing and found levels to be much higher than expected on the ebb tide (greater than $5\%_{00}$) and less than $30\%_{00}$ on the flood tide. They attributed such levels to evaporation and plant excretion of salt.

Buzas (1969) felt fairly certain that the importance of temperature, oxygen, and salinity has been established. Gross changes in these factors often affect whole groups of species, yet they still retain niche diversification and define biofacies. Matera and Lee (1972) took another view and said—"it is not yet possible to define the habitat of salt marsh littoral and sublittoral Foraminifera very rigorously on a scale precise enough to characterize their niches." Lee et al. (1975) demonstrated the effects of salinity and temperature on different Foraminifera species (Figures 2.25 and 2.26). In their study of the marshes in Poponesset Bay, Massachusetts, Parker and Athearn (1959) recorded that Arenoparrella mexicana, Haplophragmoides hancocki, Tiphotrocha comprimata, and Trochammina macrescens decreased with salinity. Hadammina polystoma and Trochammina inflata increased along the increasing salinity gradient while other species such as Ammobaculites dilatatus, Ammotium salsu, Miliammina fusca, and Protelphidium tisburyense fluctuated independently of salinity. However, Parker and Athearn were not sure these distributions were directly related to salinity. Phleger (1965) found no information available to explain the observed distributions in highly saline Galveston Bay. Salinity varied with runoff, location in the bay, and the extent of tidal water intrusion. Bradshaw (1968) did not know the effect of continual salinity change on Foraminifera. Citing an earlier paper, Bradshaw reported that constant salinities higher than $45\%_{00}$ decreased the growth rate of Ammonia beccarii. Buzas (1969), using a multiple regression analysis, found the environmental parameters of temperature, salinity, oxygen, and chlorophyll a, b, c to be significant at the 95 percent level for all three species of Foraminifera: Elphidium clavatum, A. beccarii, and Ammobaculities exiguus. However, none of the variables was significant individually. This suggested to Buzas that the various environmental parameters were not independent and the importance of any particular environmental variable was relative to the others. His analysis would explain the vagueness expressed by earlier workers.

While some workers were expressing uncertainty about the influence of salinity on foraminiferal distributions, other investigators were being more explicit. Phleger and Walton (1950) identified two major Foraminifera facies in the Barnstable, Massachusetts area; one found in Barnstable Har-

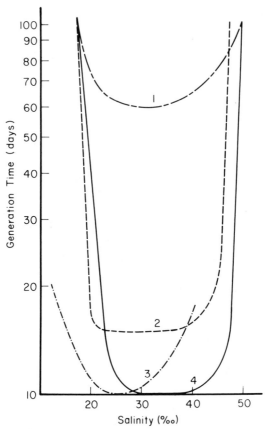

Figure 2.25.   The effect of salinity on the reproduction of four salt-marsh meiofauna at 26 °C: *Rosalina leei, Spiroloculina hyalina, Monhystera denticulata, Allogromia laticollaris.* (From, Lee *et al.,* 1975, by permission of Academic Press.)

bor characterized by *Trochammina inflata* and, the second, an adjacent near-shore Cape Cod facies characterized by *Proteonina atlantica* and *Eggerella advena.* Temperature and salinity variations were given as the cause for separation of these two facies. The salinity range in the harbor area was recorded at 25–31‰ with normal levels at 28–31‰. Channel heads had a range of 20‰ (after heavy precipitation and on the ebb tide) to 31.5 ‰. The near shore bay salinities varied at 31–32‰. In an examination of the highly saline area of Matagorda Bay, Texas, Lehmann (1957) identified salinity as the principal factor determining Foraminifera distributions. He also recognized other influences when he stated that such dispersions resulted from a complex interaction of several factors and not from the variation of a

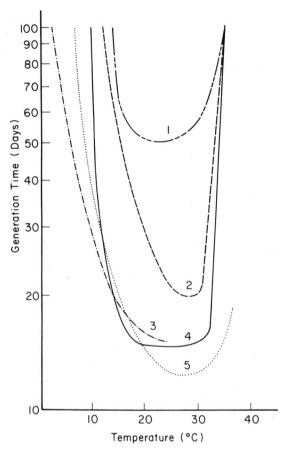

Figure 2.26. The effect of temperature on the reproduction of five salt-marsh meiofauna. Salinity at optimum for each species: *Rosalina leei, Spiroculina hyalina, Monhystera denticulata, Allogromia laticollaris, Rhabditis marina.* (From Lee *et al.,* 1975, by permission of Academic Press.)

single entity. The more important parameters for the Matagorda Bay area were identified as salinity, organic content, extent and nature of water currents, turbulence, and biological competition. Temperature, in contrast to Cape Cod Bay (Phleger and Walton, 1950), along with water depth and turbidity did not appear to be important. Phleger (1970) and Murray (1973a) both identified salinity as an important parameter. For Murray, salinity was a major environmental factor, becoming more variable with passage from the mouth of the estuary to the tidal marshes. He described an estuarine environment with a salinity higher than $30\%_{00}$ and a channel assemblage of moderate diversity (5 to 6). The channel assemblage included *Quinquelocui-lina seminulum* and *Bolivina pseudoplicta*. In midestuary and along the margins, salinity varied from 15–30‰ and the Foraminifera assemblage was less diverse (2 to 4). Common species were *Ammonia beccarii, Protelphidium anglicum, Elphidium articulatum,* and *Miliamminia fusca*. However, *M. fusca* was not found in midestuary. On the tidal marshes salinity was highly variable and the assemblage, while including *E. articulatum* and *M. fusca,* typically consisted of *Jadammina macrescens* and *Trochammina inflata*. Diversity was low (2).

Both Murray (1973b) and Phleger (1970) associated those Foraminfera having calcareous tests with the lower intertidal and subtidal areas while those of the higher tidal marshes possessed a finely agglutinated wall with an organic cement. Phleger (1970) also pointed to the large populations of calcareous species in the hypersaline marshes, the less diverse populations in the high marshes, but an increase in the numbers of species from areas of high runoff. Phleger attributed such distributions to the availability of highly saline marine water. Osmotic effects no doubt play a role in species abundance and distributions but the greater availability of inorganic salts in seawater for shell building would be influential.

It is apparent from the foregoing that there is not a clear-cut view of the role played by salinity. We are confronted by assemblages of Foraminifera that occupy tidal marsh habitats ranging from near-fresh to hypersaline in nature. There is a dynamic range of abiotic and biotic variables that present a multiplicity of interactions which these Foraminifera must face. Thus, as Phleger (1965) concluded, each tidal marsh has its own distinctive Foraminifera assemblage.

Worms

A perusal of Gunter *et al.* (1974) and other reviews would suggest there are varying amounts of information concerning salinity and osmotic effects on flat, round, and segmented worms but little is known about these parameters and the worms which exist in salt marshes. A review of European salt-marsh Turbellaria (den Hartog, 1974) identified three major factors that determine turbellarian distributions and abundance: substrate, hydrology, and salinity. These flatworms have been found on silt, clay, sand, and rocky substrates and these habitats are influenced by fluctuations in water level due to wind velocities and directions and by tidal inundation. den Hartog characterized four groups as determined by a relation to salinity levels: (1) a euryhaline marine group of 17 species with a principal distribution in the marine habitat, (2) a brackish water group of 22 species derived from a marine origin, (3) a typical salt-marsh group of 16 species, all but one derived from a marine origin, and (4) a holoeuryhaline group with one species that was apparently indifferent to salinity levels. Only in the case of the salt-marsh group was den Hartog (1974) able to express any generalities about species groupings and he was uncertain about that degree of reliability since so little was known about the life cycles, preference for and tolerance to environmental factors. It would appear that there are many opportunities for investigation of this little known group of marsh organisms.

Mollusca

The ribbed mussel, *G. demissa,* which is a characteristic bivalve of tidal marshes, can tolerate a wide range of salinity. Wells (1961) recorded the lower limit of salinity at 5‰. Lent (1969) commented on its impressive tolerance to high salinity when he recorded dessicative water losses of 36–38 percent and freezing point dehydration with 71 percent of the water frozen. Lent reported *Guekensia* to be isosmotic between 9‰ and 43‰. Waugh and Garside (1971) reported this mussel to be an osmoconformer at higher salinities but changing to osmoregulation below 10‰.

   Melampus bidentatus also tends to be isosmotic. Russell-Hunter *et al.* (1972) submerged early egg masses in water with salinities of 25–100 percent seawater and found these masses to act like osmometers. Kerwin (1972) recorded *Melampus* densities of $0.23/m^2$ in the Poropotank River, Virginia, brackish marsh where the salinity range was 4.11–9.38‰. In that same marsh where the salinity was higher (9.38–14.72‰) snail densities were $7.24/m^2$. No *Melampus* was recorded in the fresh and slightly brackish marshes with salinities below 4.11‰. Parker (1976) recorded much the same pattern for the Delaware Bay marshes; larger numbers in areas of higher salinities. Parker provided some information on the brackish water snail, *Detracia floridana,* a snail easily confused with *Melampus. Detracia* abundance tended to increase with declining salinities, apparently totally absent in the highly saline marshes.

   Utilizing the aging procedure employed by Apley (1970), Parker (1976) demonstrated a general pattern of increasing length in millimeters within each age class along a decreasing salinity gradient. This was particularly evident in those samples taken from the Broadkill River marshes (Table 2.17). Laboratory observations by Parker clearly portrayed the euryhaline nature of the snail. Larvae were highly active at salinities ranging from 15–40‰, slightly less so at 10‰, and showed a markedly reduced activity at 5‰. Approximately 90 percent of the larvae survived for ten hours in salinities varying from 2.5 to 40‰. None survived in fresh water. Parker reported the adults to be osmoconformers over the salinity range of 8 to 51‰. Above and below these levels osmoregulation might be indicated.

Table 2.17. The mean size ($\pm$ one S.D.) of age classes of *Melampus bidentatus* from the Broadkill River marshes. (Part of Table 3, Parker, 1976) (Station locations and salinities from deWitt and Daiber, 1973)

Station	Salinity	0	I	II	III	Sample Size
			Age Class			
			Length in Millimeters			
1973						
2	26 ± 2.9	1.2 ± .1	4.8 ± .5	6.5 ± .4	7.9 ± .3	151
3	17 ± 8.6	1.5 ± .5	5.2 ± .4	7.6 ± .9	9.5 ± .1	128
4	6 ± 7.4	—	7.0 ± .4	10.4 ± .4	11.8 ± .3	48
1974						
2		2.7 ± .5	5.9 ± .7	8.2 ± .6	9.6 ± .3	369
3		1.8 ± .5	5.7 ± .8	8.0 ± .5	9.7 ± .4	434
4		2.7 ± .4	6.5 ± .8	10.3 ± 1.1	12.5 ± .2	128

However, Parker pointed out that apparent regulation may be merely avoidance reaction as the animals were less active, withdrew into their shells, and there was a copious mucus flow above and below 8–51‰.

Arthropoda

Crustacea. Smallwood (1905) found the amphipod *Orchestia palustris* widely distributed over the entire sale marsh except in the *Spartina cynosuroides* zone and the typically fresh-water areas. It was reported to be more abundant in the more saline portions of the marsh. Heard and Sikora (1972) described a new species of *Corophium* confined to the midintertidal zone of the fresh-water oligohaline portions of Georgia tidal creeks. Bousfield (1973) and Rees (1975) described the amphipod *Gammarus palustris* as being euryhaline (5 to 20‰), being able to survive brief exposures of fresh water at low temperatures and seawater at high temperatures. Experimental work carried out by Marsden (1973) indicated the salt-marsh isopod *Sphaeroma rugicauda* had a greater thermo-saline tolerance than many other intertidal animals with the juveniles having a narrower salinity tolerance than the adults (Table 2.18). Harris (1972) demonstrated the brackish water-salt marsh isopod species of the genus *Sphaeroma* could not survive below 0.7‰ regardless of acclimation. However, the upper limits of survival could be improved by acclimation from 50.1‰ to 65.6‰ for controls and acclimatized individuals respectively. Wilson (1970) noted a hypoosmotic regulatory response by the isopod *Ligua* when immersed in seawater of less than 100 percent concentration. This response maintained a proper water balance at the expense of metabolic work. The hypoosmotic regulatory response in seawater concentrations greater than 100 percent enabled the species to resist water loss.

Table 2.18. Percentage mortalities of *Sphaeroma rugicauda* following exposure to various salinities for 100 hours at various acclimation temperatures. (From Marsden, 1973, by permission of the editor, *Marine Biology*)

Salinity ($^0/_{00}$)	Acclimation Temperature (C_0)			
	5	10	15	20
Adults				
1.7	6.25	5.0	0	21.0
17.0	0	0	10.0	30.0
34.0	0	10.0	30.0	10.0
51.0	0	10.0	50.0	10.0
68.0	10.0	55.0	80.0	57.0
Juveniles				
1.7	48.0		85.0	
34.0	10.0		15.0	
51.0	8.0		20.0	
68.0	30.0		80.0	

Salinity plays some part in fiddler crab distributions. The description of the habitat for *Uca minax* in Solomons Island, Maryland (Gray, 1942) which included *Spartina cynosuroides,* would sugggest this to be a brackish water species. Kerwin (1971) found *U. minax* widely distributed in brackish and salt marshes of the Poropotank River, Virginia, where the salinities were greater than $2\%_{00}$ and less than $16\%_{00}$ (Table 2.19).

Miller and Maurer (1973) reported *Uca pugnax* from high salinities ($21-29\%_{00}$) while *U. minax* was most abundant in lower salinities and even into the fresh waters ($0-12\%_{00}$) of three Delaware tidal streams. An examination of Table 2.20 shows a shift in abundance for the two species between $15\%_{00}$ and $18\%_{00}$ for the Broadkill River. A similar shift in abundance is shown between 23 and $25\%_{00}$ and 18 and $20\%_{00}$ for the Mispillion and Murderkill Rivers respectively. Miller and Maurer displayed a significant (at 0.005) positive correlation between abundance and increasing salinity for *U. pugnax* and a significant negative correlation for *U. minax* in all three rivers. Further examination of Table 2.20 would suggest the points of equal abundance for both species vary between $18-25\%_{00}$, depending on the river examined. The authors speculated that such midpoints may be the areas where neither species is favored by competitive advantage or where both are equally adapted to salinity regardless of competition.

Something other than salinity may be playing a role in such distributions. Students of the present author reported numerous *U. pugnax* and few *U. minax* from one area of the Blackbird Creek marsh in Delaware where the stream salinity was recorded at $4-5\%_{00}$. This is supported by Teal (1958)

Table 2.19. Percent of total samples, mean density per square meter, and the mean salinity range in each marsh in which type *Uca minax* burrows occurred. (Modified slightly from Kerwin, 1971, by permission of the editor, *Ches. Sci.*)

Marsh Type	Frequency %	Density (No./m²)	Salinity (⁰/₀₀)
Fresh	0.0	0.0	0.3– 0.8
Slightly Brackish	0.0	0.0	0.8– 4.1
Brackish	71.4	7.9	4.1– 9.4
Salt	83.8	14.3	9.4–14.7
Total Area	66.7	12.4	0.3–14.7

and Kerwin (1971) who suggested substrate as well as salinity and competition influence fiddler crab distributions. Both Teal (1958) and Miller and Maurer (1973) suggested *U. pugilator* has a preferred salinity range between that of *U. minax* and *U. pugnax*.

Teal (1958) tested the salinity tolerance for the three species of *Uca* by placing them in finger bowls with differing salinities ranging from $0\%_{00}$ to $58\%_{00}$. It was only in the 0 to $7\%_{00}$ salinity that there was a difference in survival. All species survived for three weeks at the higher salinities and in an experiment where the salinity was varied between 0 and $30\%_{00}$ on an alternate day basis. At $0\%_{00}$, 50 percent of *U. minax* had not died at the end of three weeks when the experiment was terminated, 50 percent of *U. pugilator* died at the end of three and one-half days, while 50 percent of *U. pugnax* died within one and one-half days. At $7\%_{00}$, 50 percent mortality of *U. pugnax* occurred at three days while more than 50 percent of the other two species survived over the test time of 10 days.

Teal (1958) also provided these three species with a choice of freshwater or salinity of approximately $30\%_{00}$. Both sexes of *U. minax* showed a statistical preference for fresh water over salt. The males of both *U. pugilator* and *U. pugnax* showed a significant preference for salt over fresh water. The females of both were found more often in salt water but the differences were not statistically significant. In all cases the females showed a less strong preference (Table 2.21).

When working with *U. pugnax* and *U. pugilator* at higher salinities, Green *et al.* (1959) found both species to be hypoosmotic regulators. The sera for those crabs in 100 percent seawater were 12 percent lower in osmotic concentration and 22 percent lower for animals in 175 percent sea water. Lockwood (1962), in a discussion of osmoregulation among the crustacea, considered *U. minax*, *U. pugilator*, and *U. pugnax* to belong to that group of animals wherein the blood is hypoosmotic to the medium in highly saline water and hyperosmotic in low salinities. It is apparent that these three spe-

Table 2.20 Abundance of fiddler crabs in relation to salinity in three Delaware rivers. (From Miller and Maurer, 1973, by permission of the editor, *Ches. Sci.*)

Station	Broadkill River			Mispillion River			Murderkill River		
	No. U. Pugnax	No. U. minax	Salinity ‰	No. U. pugnax	No. U. minax	Salinity ‰	No. U. pugnax	No. U. minax	Salinity ‰
1	0	0	29	30	0	27	30	0	21
2	0	0	29	30	0	26	30	0	21
3	31	0	29	30	0	27	30	0	21
4	25	1	29	30	0	26	30	0	21
5	45	1	29	30	0	26	27	3	21
6	45	2	25	26	4	26	18	12	21
7	37	0	24	29	1	26	23	7	21
8	23	17	23	20	10	25	19	11	21
9	17	7	21	10	20	23	16	14	20
10	16	8	20	8	22	21	6	24	18
11	32	18	18	8	22	15	7	23	11
12	4	13	15	0	0	13	3	27	9
13	3	9	12	0	30	10	6	24	6
14	6	36	9	0	0	5	0	30	5
15	1	35	8	0	0	4	0	30	3
16	0	30	5	0	0	1	0	0	1
17	0	32	1	0	0	0	0	0	0.5
18	0	4	0	0	0	0	0	0	0
19	0	3	0	0	0	0	0	0	0
20	0	2	0	0	0	0	0	0	0

Table 2.21.   Percent of males and females of three species of fiddler crabs which prefer fresh or salt water (30⁰/₀₀) in a 24-hour experiment. (P is probability that results in row are not different.) From Teal, 1958, by permission of the editor, *Ecology*)

| | | Percent Preferring | | |
		Fresh Water	Sea Water	P
U. minax	male	68	32	0.001
	female	60	40	0.024
U. pugilator	male	40	60	0.02
	female	48	52	0.6
U. pugnax	male	20	80	0.001
	female	35	65	0.058

cies have different salinity preferences, wide ranges of tolerance, and differing abilities of adjustment to a salinity range within the framework of hypo- and hyperosmotic regulation.

Insecta-Arachnida. Luxton (1964) considered tidal inundation of fundamental importance in delimiting distributional patterns of salt marsh Acarina (see section on tidal inundation, drainage, vegetation). In order to establish populations in the lower reaches of marshes the Acarina needed to possess, among other things, an ability to withstand high osmotic pressures in the soils. In a later paper (1967b), Luxton found no significant correlation between salinity, pH, etc., and population densities in the landward *Festuca rubra* zone. However, there was a strong correlation between these various components in the lower, seaward *Puccinellia maritima* zone. Such correlation in this lower marsh with salinity and water level was independent of soil water content.

The ubiquitous distributions of salt-marsh mosquitos would suggest that parameters other than salinity, such as tidal inundation, are primary influences on insect distributions in salt marshes. This would be true especially for the air-breathing adult forms. Nichol (1936) observed that animals living permanently on the marsh are of interest in terms of respiration rather than salinity changes. However, the larval forms are subjected to a different set of environmental parameters. Wigglesworth (1972) and Foster and Treherne (1976b) considered salt-marsh insects to have a greater ability to regulate the ionic composition and osmotic pressure of the blood than fresh-water forms. These salt-water insects display varying efficiencies which enable them to adjust to exposure to high and usually fluctuating salinities. Some species such as *Aedes detritus* and *Ephydra riparia* can maintain fairly stable osmotic levels over a wide range of salinity while others such as the trichopteran

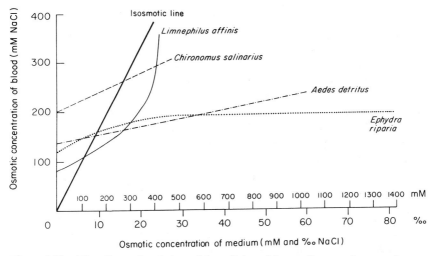

Figure 2.27. The effects of variation of the salinity of the medium on the osmotic concentration of the blood of some representative salt-marsh insects. (From Foster and Treherne, 1976a, by permission of North-Holland Publ. Co.)

Limniphilus affinis and the midge *Chironomus salinarius* can maintain the blood osmotic level below the medium over a limited salinity range (Figure 2.27). How this regulation is carried out has received a great deal of attention over the years with resultant changes of view with time. Earlier work (Beadle, 1939; Ramsey, 1950) reported that salt exchange in the larvae of *A. detritus* took place across the gut. The anterior part of the rectum of this species had an epithelium distinctly different from the rest of the rectum. Although Ramsey reported the larva of the fresh-water *Aedes aegypti* also produced a hypertonic rectal fluid, it did not contain this distinctive rectal epithelium. Phillips and Meredith (1969a) determined that the larvae of *Aedes campestris* produced strongly hypo- or hyperosmotic urine, as expected in this species which can live in varying salinities. While regulation was achieved mainly by the rectum, there was no ultrastructural compartmentalization in this species either.

Stobbart (1965) studied the transport of sodium and chloride and considered the movement of chloride to be important in sodium uptake while chloride uptake could occur independently of sodium influx. Phillips and Meredith (1969b) demonstrated the active transport of both sodium-free solutions respectively. They reported an increase in transport activity across the anal papillae with adaptation to dilute media. They went on to suggest that the direction of transport could be reversed. Treherne (1954) studied the larvae of the fresh-water beetle, *Helodes,* and reported that most of the chloride entered through the gut and anal papillae. He considered the main function of the anal papillae to be salt absorption from the external environment and not respiration.

The larvae of *Aedes taeniorhynchus,* another salt-marsh species, can regulate the osmotic level of the haemolymph by producing hyperosmotic urine through ionic secretion into the lumen of the rectum rather than by water reabsorption (Bradley and Phillips, 1975). The ultrastructural evidence implicates the posterior portion of the rectum in this secretory activity. Further the anterior portion of the rectum is involved in selective reabsorption when the larvae is in hypoosmotic environments. According to the authors the anal papillae may actively secrete chloride ion to the hyperosmotic environment and sodium may be secreted to balance the inward movement of potassium.

Salt-marsh insects often expend considerable energy in the maintenance of osmotic and ionic homeostasis under saline conditions (Figure 2.28). Foster and Treherne (1976b) suggested the invasion of salt marshes by fresh-water and terrestrial insects may be metabolically expensive and thus impose a resistant on the extent of invasion. They felt that such insect species could be put to a competitive disadvantage with other marine forms or be unable to fully utilize some food resources. It is only too evident that, as one is enveloped in a cloud of blood-seeking salt-marsh mosquitos or driven

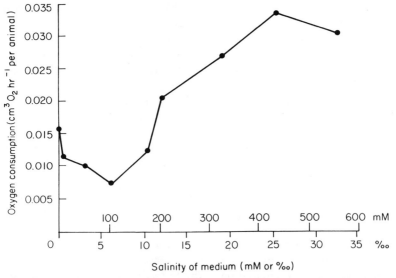

Figure 2.28.   The oxygen consumption of larvae of *Sigara lugubris* (= *stagnalis*), Corixidae) in media of various salinities. (From Foster and Treherne, 1976b, by permission of North-Holland Publ. Co.)

to distraction by voracious tabanid flies, some insects have made highly successful adjustments to life in the salt marsh.

Pisces

The reader should turn to recent reviews (Prosser, 1973; Hill, 1976) for general discussions of osmotic relations among fishes, and a specific review of the literature of marsh fishes in the section on tidal inundation, drainage, and vegetation.

Aves

There appears to be some relationship between avian distributions in tidal marshes and the ability to utilize saline water. Very few terrestrial species of birds can drink sea or estuarine water (Bartholomew and Cade, 1963, p. 518). Bartholomew and associates (Cade and Bartholomew, 1959; Poulson and Bartholomew, 1962; Bartholomew and Cade, 1963) demonstrated subspecific differences in this ability among the savannah sparrows, *Passerculus sandwichensis.* Two west coast subspecies, *P. s. beldingi* and *P. s. rostratus,* are restricted to salt marshes. Three subspecies that have typical avian saltwater responses are migratory and nest in or near fresh-water habitats. The two salt-marsh subspecies have been observed to handle the salt response in different ways; *P. s. rostratus* reduced drinking or went without water for long periods while *P. s. beldingi* drank large quantities of salt water. *P. s. rostratus* had the most clearly defined salt response and was the most sharply distinguishable subspecies. *P. s. beldingi* showed an overlap of response with migratory forms capable of consuming large quantities of distilled water in captivity. Also it maintained a fairly constant salt-water consumption up to a 0.6 M NaCl salinity (100 percent seawater) representing 84–112 percent of body weight. At higher concentrations (0.7 M NaCl) consumption declined to 75 percent body weight. The salt-marsh races of the song sparrow, *M. melodia maxillaris* and *M. m. samuelis,* displayed a similar pattern of consumption but could not maintain their bodyweight on full-strength seawater. Poulson (1969), examining the drinking habits of the salt-marsh form of the sharp-tailed sparrow, *Ammospiza c. caudacuta,* the brackish-freshwater form, *A. c. subvirgata,* and the seaside sparrow, *A. maritima,* noted seasonal differences in both the casual water consumption and the minimum requirements for weight maintenance (Figure 2.29). He also noted differences between races. *A. c. caudacuta* drank more distilled water than *A. m. maritima* in both spring and fall. Both drank less distilled water in the fall than in the spring but both drank more than *A. c. subvirgata.* As salinity increased in the spring *A. m. maritima* regularly drank more. The amount of dilute saline

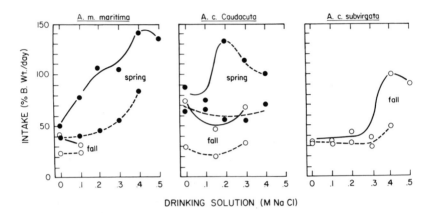

Figure 2.29. Water requirements for *Ammospiza*. Ad libitum drinking (solid lines) and minimum requirements for weight maintenance (broken lines) are shown for fall-caught (open circles) and spring-caught (closed circles) birds. Curves were fitted by eye. (From Poulson, 1969, by permission of the editor, *Auk*.)

water consumed by *A. c. caudacuta* was less than that of distilled water both in spring and fall. When exposed to various salinities, the amount consumed by *A. c. subvirgata* remained constant until the intake suddenly increased to a peak level when the birds drank 0.4 M NaCl. This was in contrast to the other two races.

Poulson (1969) observed that salt-marsh passerines consumed much more distilled water than birds of the same weight from nonsalt-marsh habitats. They also displayed a lower level of libitum drinking of dilute salt solutions than of distilled water or moderately concentrated salt solutions. This response was correlated with the salinity of the available water in the wintering and breeding habitats of these birds. Poulson further observed a slow increase in the amount of increasingly saline water ingested with a peak intake at a salinity below the maximum concentration on which body weight could be maintained. He considered this to be an adaptive response in salt marshes related to the potential for urine concentration. The response of nonsalt-marsh birds did not permit them to achieve their potential for concentrating urine. Poulson summarized a comparison between salt-marsh and nonsalt-marsh passerines in Table 2.22 where the lower numbers in the rankings are associated with the nonsalt-marsh races.

These various authors presumed the salt-marsh subspecies got most of their water needs through water condensing on the marsh vegetation from the coastal fogs and general condensation.

Table 2.22. Ranking of parameters related to salt and water balance for salt-marsh birds and their relatives. (From Poulson, 1969, with permission of the editor, *Auk*)

| | Salinity | | Urine conc | | Drinking dist. H₂O observed-expected | | | | Weight Maint. rate of change of drinking | Ad lib. intake relative to minimum need | Weight loss during acute dehydration | |
| | | | | | Ad libitum | | Minimum | | | | | |
	rank	chlorinity	rank	U/P	rank	%B wt d	rank	%B wt d	rank (Figure 3A)	rank (Figure 3B)	rank	%B wt d
Melospiza melodica cooperi	1	2			1	−4						
Passerculus s. sandwichensis	2	4	4	3.3	2	−3	1	+3	2		4	−3.2
Ammospiza caudacuta nelsoni	3	10	2	2.6	3	+3			1			
P. s. brooksi	4	12	1	2.2	5	+14	4	+14	3	1	3	−3.3
A. c. subvirgata	5	15	3	2.9	4	+7	5	+16	4	2	2	−3.6
M. m. maxillaris	6	17			6	+15						
A. m. maritima	7	23	6	3.5	7	+18	2	+8	5	3	6	−2.9
A. c. caudacuta	8	24	5	3.4	9	+47	3	+11	6	4	1	−3.8
M. m. samuelis	9	25			8	+23						
P. s. beldingi	10	35	7	4.5	10	+75	6	+30	7	5	5	−3.0

The long-billed marsh wren, *Telmatodytes palustris griseus,* is a permanent resident of the marshes from South Carolina to northern Florida (Kale, 1967). During the breeding season, it is found only in the tall *Spartina alterniflora* where fresh water rarely occurs except during a heavy rain. Dew does wet the plants but it is very salty. When birds were supplied with estuarine water, fresh water, or none there was no loss of weight. Instead of adjusting to saline water, the wrens changed food habits by turning to more succulent foods when estuarine water or no water was offered.

The section on tidal inundation, drainage, and vegetation contains discussions concerning the indirect effects of salinity on food preferences of waterfowl.

Mammalia

As with some birds, there appears to be a relationship between small mammal distributions and their ability to utilize salt water in a tidal marsh. There are three possible sources of drinking water for a harvest mouse: (1) dew, (2) juices of succulent plants such as *Salicornia* with a water content of 88 percent, and (3) seawater. The harvest mouse, *Reithrodontomys raviventris,* is restricted to the brackish and salt marshes of San Francisco Bay. One subspecies *R. r. halicoetis* was reported better able to survive higher salt-marsh concentrations and greater dehydration than related forms *R. r. raviventris* and *R. megalotis* but none could survive indefinitely. Food and water consumption were greatly curtailed by drinking seawater (Fisler, 1963). In contrast to Fisler's observations, MacMillen (1964) found *R. megalotis* could readily utilize undiluted seawater for drinking by virtue of an extreme urine concentrating capacity. This mechanism is probably an adaptation for aridity since this species is reported by MacMillen to be primarily distributed inland and thus preadapted for drinking seawater. Haines (1964) found the harvest mouse drank 19 percent of its body weight or 2.4 grams/day. When water was restricted, the animal could get along on 0.8 gram/day and Haines was of the opinion that atmospheric dew could provide that. The vole, *Microtus pennsylvanicus* relies on snow, rain, or dew for water (Getz, 1966) since it is unable to tolerate a salinity above 0.30 M NaCl (50 percent seawater). Getz investigated the water content and salinity of some marsh plants as a possible source of drinking water. He concluded that the voles could get usable water from green *Spartina patens* if other sources were unavailable. *Spartina alterniflora* had a salinity of approximately 0.35 M NaCl which would make its tissue water unsuitable.

The indirect effect of salinity on the muskrat is discussed in the section on tidal inundation, drainage, and vegetation.

OTHER NONBIOTIC FACTORS

There are numerous environmental parameters affecting the distribution and zonation of tidal marsh animals in addition to salinity and inundation. These factors include the normally recognized environmental components such as substrate character, pH, oxygen levels, light, humidity, and temperature as well as less recognized entities such as fire and wind.

Substrate

A number of factors determine the interactions between marsh animals and the substrate with which they are associated. For the most part, discussion will be focused on the marsh soils as a substrate, however, Matera and Lee (1972) did include the epiphytic communities of Foraminifera in their discussions. Soil moisture, grain size, the degree of soil compaction, mechanical obstructions, chemical nature and pH of the soils, and the amount of organic material incorporated in the soil are components that determine the nature of the substrate.

Bilio (1965) found outlines for zonation and formation of the marsh fauna and the vegetation were the same in both the horizontal and vertical direction. Differences between the salt-meadow faunas associated with the clays of the North Sea and the peats of the Baltic coast indicate greater differences than could be detected from the vegetation. These faunal differences between the lower and upper *Puccinellia maritima* community were greater than those between the upper *P. maritima* and the *Juncus gerardi* typicum. In both cases Bilio believed the effects to be caused mainly by differences in the surface layer of soil.

Macnae (1957) attributed animal distributions in the Zwartkops estuary in South Africa partially to the deposition of a thin layer of fine silt on all surfaces and to changes in the configuration of the banks which forced the channel into narrow confines. Macnae found faunal zonation associated with plant zonations but more complex and less precise. Faunal associations varied with the sandy mud, mud, or sand substrates.

The nature of the substrate also plays a role in foraminiferal distributions. Bradshaw (1968) commented on the marked change in the environment when passing from the overlying water through the water-sediment interface into the mud below. Bradshaw and others (Parker and Athearn, 1959; Phleger and Bradshaw, 1966; Phleger, 1970) noted that the pH of the sediments influenced distributions. Low pH tended to retard the formation of calcareous tests and destroy them after death. The nature and movement of particle size along with organic content of the substrate, also determined foraminiferal population sizes and distributions (Phleger and Walton, 1950; Phleger, 1970). Matera and Lee (1972) demonstrated a correlation between abundance and the horizontal and vertical changes in grain size; *Elphidium incertum* distribution clustered around a grain size of 0.1 millimeters while *Trochammina inflata* was clustered around a median grain size of 0.46 millimeters.

In contrast to a depauperate macrofauna, Gerlach (1965) reported a rich and varied microfauna from a Spitzbergen salt marsh although there were fewer species than reported from central and northern European marshes. There were at least 50 species of free-living nematodes with a zonation corresponding to vertical and substrate distributions. Most nematodes were found in the upper four centimeters with some penetrating to eight centimeters. Evidence suggested the dominant species penetrated most deeply into the mud. The greater mixing of the muds near the low tide marsh by larger animals permitted a wider distribution of food and thus nematodes. In contrast, Wieser and Kanwiser (1961) and Teal and Wieser (1966) reported that nematodes tended to be restricted to the surface by root mats and by less stirring of the substrate in the temperate marshes studied by them.

There is general agreement about substrate preferences by fiddler crabs. This specificity gives rise to fiddler crab zones in habitat selection (Pearse, 1914; Gray, 1942; Teal, 1958; Kerwin, 1971). Pearse (1914) described *Uca pugnax* burrows found in mud and Teal (1958) found this species where the sand content was 0 to 10 percent or even greater. He concluded that *U. pugnax* distribution was determined by a preference for a vegetated muddy substrate and salt water. In contrast, *Uca pugilator* preferred sand (Pearse, 1914). Teal (1958) found it dominant in the *Salicornia-Distichlis* marsh where the soil was 80 to 95 percent sand. However, in the short *Spartina* high marsh where the sand content was 40 to 70 percent, Teal reported *U. pugilator* did not burrow to any appreciable extent. In laboratory tests it burrowed in sand above the water level, presumably because such burrows below the water would be more apt to collapse. Teal concluded *U. pugilator* preferred sandy habitats but could not colonize all such habitats because of competition with the other *Uca* species. Both Gray (1942) and Teal (1958) found *U. minax* displaying a preference for sand and mud with the sand content exceeding 30 percent (Teal). The soil had to be wet, although salinity could vary over a wide range. Gray (1942) reported the presence of *Spartina cynosuroides* coincidental with *U. minax* and Teal concluded that the species preferred a mud or variable substrate and fresh water. Miller (1961), when describing the feeding of *U. minax,* commented on the stability of the substrate among the *Spartina* roots and rhizomes as a critical factor limiting burrowing activities. If an obstacle was encountered early in digging, the burrow might be abandoned. If encountered later, however, the crab would change directions more readily than give up digging (Dembrowski, 1926).

U. minax also preferred substrates of high energy value, i.e., high organic content. This appeared to be the case even though such substrates characteristically had the lowest oxygen levels. Substrate oxygen was not considered to be critical to habitat selection as this species could revert to an anaerobic mode of respiration during those times when it was submerged in the water of the burrow (Teal and Carey, 1967). Therefore, organic materials for feeding would be the primary force in habitat selection (Whiting and Moshiri, 1974). Interestingly, Teal (1959) considered *U. minax,* which does not possess any temperature acclimation, has a lower respiratory rate and is more dependent on oxygen concentration, to be greatly limited in distribution in a typical salt marsh. However, as Teal pointed out, competition probably plays an important role in *Uca* distributions.

Other crabs associated with the salt marsh may also be influenced by substrate. Teal (1958) reported *Sesarma reticulatum* and *S. cinereum* along with *Eurytium limosum* (commonly found with *U. pugnax*) in the tall *Spartina* edge marsh and medium *Spartina* levee marsh where the soil was soft with a sand content up to 10 percent. The short *Spartina* low marsh, while having only 10 percent sand, was much firmer than the preceding marsh types due to *Spartina* root mats. As with *Uca, S. cinereum* must respond to influences other than particle size as Teal (1958) reported this marsh crab in locations where the soil was firm with sand content of 80 to 95 percent.

The burrowing activities of various animals can leave a long-term record on the character of the substrate. Allen and Curran (1974) reiterated what has already been said about *Uca* preferences for particle size and salinity distributions and, in addition, described the burrow patterns for these crabs wherein *U. pugnax* had burrows 1–2 centimeters in diameter while *U. minax* formed a simple vertical cavity 2–5 centimeters with a hooded tunnel entrance. The *U. pugilator* burrows were J-shaped and L-shaped, 1–2 centimeter in diameter. Feeding and burrowing activity in the sandy areas preferred by *U. pugilator* was believed to be a major factor in the destruction of primary sedimentary structures. Allen and Curran proposed that biogenic sedimentary structures created by these crabs have a good chance to be preserved and such preservation could be useful as a paleosalinity indicator as well as to evaluate old shore lines of lagoons and estuaries.

Many of the marsh soils have drainage and other characteristics that cannot be attributed to texture or structure alone. Green and Askew (1965), studying the soils of the Romney marsh on the south coast of England, attributed numerous interconnecting pores, holes, and cavities in the subsurface horizons to the activities of plant roots and burrowing by earthworms, ants, and other organisms. These pores were found under a variety of soil conditions and over widespread areas. The earthworms, primarily *Lumbricus terrestris,* and the ants, *Lasius flavus* and *L. niger,* were considered to be primary agents. There was considerable evidence to suggest that the ants moved calcium carbonate from deeper horizons. These pores appeared to be fairly permanent, persisting in buried horizons for hundreds of years. Absence of burrows suggested a lack of colonization rather than burrow collapse, since evidence of the latter would still remain. These pores greatly facilitated the movement of air and water through the soils, enhancing drainage. The recent change of pasturage of these Romney marsh soils to cultivation has destroyed or diminished the agents of pore formation. The authors reasoned that any agent that destroyed or filled these pores would have a deleterious effect, particularly on fine textured soils with 40-or-more percent of clay. This would include deflocculation following surface flooding or by penetration of sea water into the lower layers of the soil profile.

The beetles associated with tidal marshes were behaviorly comparable, replacing each other in successive biotypes (Larsen, 1951). However, Evans *et al.* (1971) found four species effectively confined to the upper regions of the banks of the Scolt Head marsh drainage channels in that region between the anaerobic mud of the lower bank which was usually covered by a film of algae and the dense marsh vegetation. They found no apparent interspecific differences in distribution within this zone. The mud was aerobic and brown with a quantity of organic material. In contrast, Larsen (1951) described beetle distributions to be very restricted, strongly influenced by soil types and vegetation. As soon as conditions changed on those Danish marshes at Skallingen, beetle species distributions changed in accordance with their specific demands. As a rule different communities were kept in pure formations as were the plant communities. However, populations intermingled as an area passed through a transition period. Larsen (1951) established three groupings of beetles based on soil and plant associations.

1. Bare algal clay flats. *Bledius spectabilis* was associated with bare sand with a clay covering and an algal layer covering 20–60 percent, soil water content 20–25 percent, and was most abundant in the tidal zone inundated daily. *Bledius taurus* had much the same substrate requirements but was found with a high soil water content and preferred loose sand outside the tidal zone. *Bledius diota* and *Trogopholuos schneideri* were associated with no vegetation, soil water content 20 percent, and high salinity (30–100‰).

2. Bare humid sand flats. *Bledius arenarius* was found on pure sand, no clay, no algal mats or other vegetation with a salinity of 5–20‰ and a water content of 10–20 percent.

3. Tolerating plant-covered soil. *Bledius trichornis* was found mainly in overgrown biotypes and sandy places with varied salinities, 0–6‰. *Di-*

chirotrichus pubescens was found in sandy places but preferred clay and dense vegetation. *Heterocerus flexuosus* was found in many places except where the sand was pure and bare. It invaded muddy banks with an algal mat and areas of pure sand covered by clay and overgrown with vegetation.

At least three of the beetles described by Evans *et al.* (1971) were found in Larsen's (1951) categories 1 and 3, and still they were confined to a particular zone in the Scolt Head Marsh with no apparent differences within the zone. The divergence probably can be explained by the response of these beetles and the aphids to submergence (Foster and Treherne, 1975, 1976a) as was described in the section on flooding and drainage.

Among the biting flies Wall and Doane (1960) collected from Cape Cod, *Culicoides melleus* was primarily associated with the sand habitat while the others were identified as typical marsh forms with *Culicoides canithorax* the most abundant larvae in the marsh muds. Most larvae were in the upper inch of mud and were found predominantly in the moist muds at the edges of bays and drainage ditches. None were taken where the soil was dry or hard.

Other Factors

Environmental parameters affecting animal zonations other than those already discussed have not received a great deal of direct attention and much is by inference. Parker and Athearn (1959) and Phleger and Bradshaw (1966), among others, mentioned pH as a possibly important parameter influencing Foraminifera distributions through the action on calcareous tests. Bourn and Cottam (1950) inferred marsh drainage would tend to lower the pH and thus have a deleterious influence on the abundance and well being of marsh molluscs and crustacea because of the calcareous nature of the exoskeletons.

Oxygen levels have received some attention. Various authors, including Phleger (1970), inferred that absence of oxygen would produce anaerobic muds with lower pH and decreased abundance of foraminiferal species. Decreased oxygen levels in crab burrows induced anaerobic metabolism among fiddler crabs (Teal and Carey, 1967). Air gaping permitted the ribbed mussel to adapt to the more landward portions of the intertidal zone (Lent, 1968). The inability to withstand prolonged submergence with depleted oxygen levels played a major role in insect distributions (Evans *et al.,* 1971; Payne, 1972; Foster and Treherne, 1975).

Any comparative physiology text such as Prosser (1973) or Hill (1976) can be examined for the direct effects of temperature on various marsh animals. The interaction of water content, temperature, and humidity is illustrated in a variety of ways as affecting marsh animal distributions: Dukes *et al.* (1974c), Wall and Doane (1960) on biting fly distributions; Miller (1961) on the feeding capabilities of fiddler crabs; Lent (1968) on the intertidal distribution of the ribbed mussel; Larsen (1951) on marsh beetles adversely affected by wind desiccation.

A recent paper (Price and Russell-Hunter, 1975) described the behavioral and physiological responses of *Melampus bidentatus* to desiccation. There was a high rate of water loss (6.2 percent wt/hour at 50 percent humidity at 20 °C), inversely proportional to animal size and relative humidity. Under these same conditions water resorption was rapid, 90 percent of water recovered in 40 minutes. The snail could withstand water losses of 75–80 percent of body weight. Under dry field conditions the snails were inactive and positively geotrophic, found under rocks, loose soil, and debris with frequent clumping. Such behavioral responses coupled with extreme desiccation tolerance and rapid dehydration enable the snail to survive in the tidal-marsh habitat.

The wind can cause flooding which can disrupt marsh faunas by drowning (Ranwell, 1974). Gunter and Eleuterius (1971) described windrows of thousands of harvest mice, *Reithrodontomys humulis,* and numerous raccoons on the Gulfport, Mississippi, marsh beaches drowned during Hurricane Betsy in September, 1965. Birds and mammals are also subject to dispersion following flooding due to storm tides as described earlier (Sibley, 1955; Johnston, 1957; Fisler, 1965a).

Fire can have an impact on marsh animal distributions. Cattle will be attracted to the succulent new vegetation following summer burning of marshes in the southern United States and in the process can cause damage by destroying muskrat houses. Summer burns will drive muskrats from a marsh for lack of house-building materials (Lay and O'Neil, 1942; Lynch *et al.,* 1947; Neely, 1962). Blue and snow geese are attracted to portions of the Gulf coast marshes that have been burned two to three weeks before their fall arrival. After such a wet cover burn they find a fresh green area with very little of the old vegetation and are able to easily graze on the plant root systems. Pintails are also attracted to such burned areas but must wait for the geese to grub out small potholes (Hoffpauer, 1968). It was presumed the Eastern willet found easier feeding in New Jersey marshes where mowing or burning occurred (Vogt, 1938).

3
Interaction with Vegetation

INTRODUCTION

There are a variety of plant-animal relationships existing on the tidal marshes. These interactions can take the form of direct or indirect dimensions. Direct effects involve the physical trampling of the vegetation as well as the impact of feeding, reproductive, and residential activities. The outcome of indirect relationships usually becomes evident some time after the plant-animal interaction has taken place. Nutrient cycling and seed dispersal are such categories (Shanholtzer, 1974).

DIRECT RELATIONSHIPS

Grazing

The feeding habitat, as identified by halophyte distributions, varies with seasons, tides, salinity, plant species, and plant heights as well as the numbers, activity, and behavior patterns of grazers. The impact of grazing is generally more evident among the macrophytes: however, Pace *et al.* (1979) described the depressing effect of the mud snail *Nassarius obsoletus* (=*Ilyanassa obsoleta*) on the edaphic algae and total microbial standing stocks on a Georgia salt-marsh mud flat. Removal of the snail resulted in a highly significant increase in algae and total microbial biomass as measured by chlorophyll *a* and ATP respectively. Such a change became evident within three days and was maintained following snail removal. Not only did standing stock levels increase but so did productivity. By agitating the mud surface to simulate snail grazing activity Pace *et al.* concluded the physical disturbance created by the feeding snails did not appear to be a factor in reducing algal biomass or productivity. The natural density of the snails produced a grazing rate exceeding 5–10 percent removal of surface chlorophyll per day and thus such a density must exceed the threshold where grazing stimulates productivity.

Crichton (1960) called attention to the habits of the marsh crab, *Sesarma reticulatum*, for consuming *Spartina alterniflora*. In light of such feeding activity, the present author wonders if this crab does not contribute to the creation of the sporadic bare creek banks, completely denuded of macrophytic vegetation, that can be observed in some of the tidal marshes of southern Delaware. More recently, a graduate student of this writer has observed small grazed areas in the high marsh that became enlarged from day to day. This student also found quantities of grass fragments in these patches and attributed this activity to *Microtus pennsylvanicus.*

Intensive sheep grazing on the Morecambe Bay marshes in England served as a form of management by producing a turf that was particularly attractive to overwintering barnacle geese, *Branta leucopsis,* white-fronted geese, *Anser albifrons,* and widgeon, *Anas penelope* (Gray and Scott, 1977). Cadwalladr *et al.* (1972), studying widgeon populations in England, determined the optimum stocking rate for sheep, beyond which grazing activity became detrimental to both animal species.

Ranwell (1961) discussed the effects of controlled sheep grazing at the upper limits of the seed-bearing *Spartina townsendii* in Bridgwater Bay in southern England. Two study areas were selected; Site 1 was on ungrazed *Spartina* marsh while Site 2 was on grazed *Atriplex-Puccinellia-Spartina* marsh. While he noted that numerous authors have made a passing reference to cattle and sheep grazing on salt marshes, his is alleged to be the first experimental study to assess such an impact on marsh vegetation. Results were obtained employing a point quadrat and biomass sampling procedures. One set of data is portrayed in Table 3.1 using the point quadrat method to record the number of times a species was "hit" out of a possible two hundred. Ranwell observed great fluctuations in the amount of *Spartina* and *Atriplex* from year to year on both ungrazed and grazed plots. He attributed this to variability in seed ripening and germination as well as the density of *Spartina* debris. With large amounts of drift settling at the strand line, the established *Spartina* plants were smothered out and the annual *Atriplex hastata* was favored. The presence of *Spartina* wrack also opened up the dense *Spartina* stands and allowed the rapid spread of *P. communis, S. maritima,* and *P. maritima.* However, Ranwell called attention to the more permanent successional trends engendered by grazing. *Spartina* is an aggressive plant and does well on soft muddy areas. In areas which are less saline and ungrazed, *Phragmites* and *Scirpus* are favored and it is estimated the transition from a *Spartina* marsh would take about eight years. As Yapp (1923) before him, Ranwell noted grazing favors the increase of *Spartina* cover through increased tillering which in turn impedes the establishment of *Atriplex. Puccinellia* is favored by increased grazing due to compaction of the soil. Ten years was the estimated time for a grazed *Spartina* marsh to transform to a *Puccinellia* association.

Grazing seems to have an effect on species presence (Gillham, 1955;

Table 3.1. Presence data for four sheep-grazed *Spartina* plots contrasted with four ungrazed controls, 300 points/plot/annum, June 1955–59. (From Ranwell, 1961, by permission of the editor, *J. Ecol.*)

Ungrazed Plots

Species	1					4					5					8				
	1955	1956	1957	1958	1959	1955	1956	1957	1958	1959	1955	1956	1957	1958	1959	1955	1956	1957	1958	1959
Spartina (mature plants)	95	129	128	105	178	77	49		1	137	109	101			14	71	91	228	51	104
Spartina (seedlings)	54	26	4	120	57	66	9		71	49	32	12	82	44	34	63	30	1	38	
Atriplex hastata	13	183	62	119	22	32	276	86	62	30	9	199		101	66	3	141	58	53	5
Puccinellia maritima						2			11	19	7				22	13	12			
Phragmites communis			1																	
Scirpus maritimus					5				6	63	8	10	68	54	186		17	47	1	28
Aster tripolium											5						4			
Glaux maritima								1	4	2		7					13	12	4	2
Salicornia stricta			2	19				8	5	3			3	2	1			2	2	
Spergularia marginata								1					1	1						
Suaeda maritima			7				1	2	6	4			1	11	4			3		
Bare ground or drift	160	60	129	77	86	149	21	207	160	71	162	52	107	97	24	166	88	34	193	168

Grazed Plots

Species	2					3					6					7				
	1955	1956	1957	1958	1959	1955	1956	1957	1958	1959	1955	1956	1957	1958	1959	1955	1956	1957	1958	1959
Spartina (mature plants)	73	131	258	130	255	64	85	226	81	267	93	108	250	129	252	68	113	241	152	192
Spartina (seedlings)	63	9	4	74	38	67	9	4	66	67	44	8	3	12	2	58	7	2	36	4
Atriplex hastata	10	70	29	50	7	8	63	36	26	2		31	43	6	1		19	49	13	2
Puccinellia maritima		1	1		18		9		1	45	5	36	35	21	78	13	35	46	6	50
Phragmites communis																				
Scirpus maritimus								8							6					3
Aster tripolium																				
Glaux maritima																		1		
Salicornia stricta			1	5					2					2			4	2		
Spergularia marginata																		2		
Suaeda maritima				6	1				3					1			1			
Bare ground or drift	184	124	39	112	26	187	170	64	153	20	174	139	33	146	28	173	138	33	122	93

Ranwell, 1960; Gray, 1972; Shanholtzer, 1974; Reimold *et al.*, 1975b). Succulent plants such as *Plantago maritima* can only survive as an important element in a marsh community when grazing, particularly that of rabbits, is slight or absent (Gillham, 1955). Ranwell recorded thirteen species at Site 1 during his study period and of those *Carex otrubae* and *Triglochin maritima* were found ony in the ungrazed plots. Twelve species were identified for the grazed plots and of those *Hordeum secalinum* was the only species found exclusively in the grazed plots. The restriction of *Limonium vulgare, Limonium humile, Halimione portulacoides, Suaeda maritima* and to some extent *Aster tripolium* to ungrazed areas suggested to Gray that these species are eliminated by grazing. The removal of the *Spartina alterniflora* cover by clipping (simulated grazing) caused a significant decrease in both species diversity (H′) and the numbers of benthic diatom species in Canary Creek marsh, Delaware (Sullivan, 1976). Shanholtzer (1974), Reimold *et al.* (1975b) and Reimold (1976) portrayed *Distichlis spicata* on a grazed and a formerly grazed marsh but absent from an ungrazed one (Figure 3.1 and

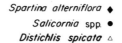

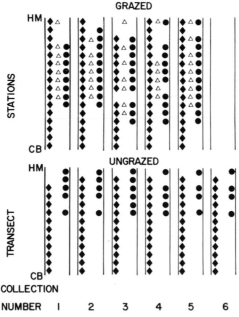

Figure 3.1.   Distribution of marsh plants in six transects of a grazed and an ungrazed marsh. (HM = high marsh, CB = creek bank). (From Shanholtzer, 1974, by permission of the editors, Reimold and Queen, *Ecology of Halophytes,* Academic Press.)

Table 3.2. Average yearly production of plant material per square meter in the three salt-marsh areas considered. N = number of observations. (From Reimold, et al. 1975b, by permission of the editor, Biol. Conserv.)

		g/m²/year	Total	N
Ungrazed	S. alterniflora live	179.2		14
	S. alterniflora dead	131.4		14
	S. virginica	272.8		14
			583.4	
Grazed	S. alterniflora live	92.5		16
	S. alterniflora dead	53.0		16
	S. virginica	36.8		16
	D. spicata live	24.8		16
	D spicata dead	14.8		16
			221.9	
Formerly grazed	S. alterniflora live	99.6		9
	S. alterniflora dead	85.5		9
	S. virginica	67.1		9
	D. spicata live	39.2		9
	D. spicata dead	30.9		9
			322.3	

Table 3.2). Grazing can also affect plant zonation (Shanholtzer, 1974). In two Georgia marshes, grazing seemed to increase the width of the *Spartina alterniflora* zone toward the high marsh areas while *Salicornia* extended toward the creek banks. As was demonstrated by Cadwalladr and Morley (1973), stated by Ranwell (1961) and portrayed by Shanholtzer (1974), grazing can have an affect on the vegetation height as well as plant densities (Tables 3.3 and 3.4). Reimold et al. (1975b) observed no apparent seasonal pattern of stem densities in another Georgia marsh subjected to a lower intensity of grazing but did record a marked increase under simulated heavy grazing conditions (Table 3.5). The very strong implication is that grazing reduces the opportunity for new growth by sexual means through the establishment of inflorescence but enhances new growth by the vegetative process of tillering. Work carried out by A. J. Gray (Gray and Scott, 1975) on *Puccinellia maritima* displayed high within-species variation, much of which was both habitat-correlated and inheritable. *P. maritima* displayed phenotypes in which there is a trend from large tall growing plants with small numbers of tillers associated with ungrazed sward to small, sprawling plants with a large number of tillers on grazed turf (Figure 3.2). Since sexual reproduction did occur, it could be expected that there would be greater genotypic variation on ungrazed marshes where seed production occurs than on grazed marshes where vegetative reproduction would result in greater uniformity (Ranwell, 1972).

Grazing can influence the amount of plant material present on the

Table 3.3. Height of *Spartina alterniflora* at inflorescense. (From Shan-holtzer, 1974, by permission of the editors, Reimold and Queen, *Ecology of Halophytes,* Academic Press.)

Meters from Creek Bank	Mean Height in cm	Sample Size	S. E.
	Grazed Marsh		
300	23.4	2	6.1
260	29.7	9	2.6
100	19.4	9	2.3
80	27.0	12	2.1
60	25.2	7	2.8
	Ungrazed Marsh		
220	61.3	4	3.4
180	38.1	1	—
160	68.2	11	4.1
120	60.1	11	4.4
100	63.6	17	2.9
80	81.5	4	6.5
60	86.4	3	3.7
40	59.5	15	3.3
20	65.2	25	2.4
Creek bank	136.6	2	9.3

Table 3.4. Stem density (stems/m^2) of *Spartina alterniflora.* (From Shanholtzer, 1974, by permission of the editors, Reimold and Queen, *Ecology of Halophytes,* Academic Press.)

Station Location		Grazed Marsh	Ungrazed Marsh
High Marsh	300m	782	—
	280m	118	—
	260m	672	—
	240m	589	—
	220m	980	378
	200m	412	98
	180m	375	208
Middle Marsh	160m	442	321
	140m	509	20
	120m	510	201
	100m	117	287
	80m	274	201
	60m	671	186
	40m	1256	159
	20m	506	158
Creek Bank		172	11

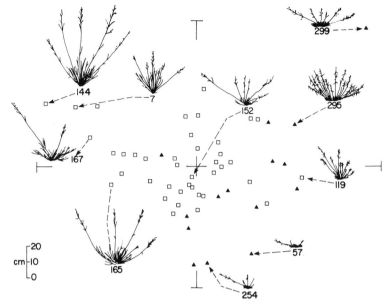

Figure 3.2.   Projection of *Puccinellia maritima* phenotypes onto the first two components of a principal components analysis (using twenty-two growth characteristics). Taken together the two components define a trend from large plants with small numbers of tillers (left) to small plants with high numbers of tillers (right). The plants are to scale; numbers are accession codes. The plants marked by triangle were collected from grazed salt marshes. (From Gray and Scott, 1975.)

marsh surface in that the weight of the individual plant decreases (Figures 3.3 and 3.4) and the physical size of such species as *P. maritima* and *Festuca rubra* are markedly reduced (Gillham, 1955). Reimold *et al.* (1975b) described a 70 percent reduction in primary production in a grazed *S. alterniflora-D. spicata* marsh as compared to an ungrazed one. Where grazing was prohibited for one year, production was doubled (Table 3.2).

When comparing living and dead as well as wet and dry weights of *Spartina alterniflora* and *Salicornia virginica,* the plants in an ungrazed system had a greater percent dry weight biomass than those in a formerly grazed or grazed system (Table 3.6). Further, *Distichlis spicata* which was not present in ungrazed areas had a greater percentage dry weight in the formerly grazed system than the grazed location. In addition, examination of Tables 3.2, 3.5 and 3.6 show the greatest accumulation of dead plant material in an ungrazed marsh and the least accumulation in grazed wetland. All this suggested to Reimold *et al.* (1975b) that the plants in a grazed system are maintained in a younger successional stage due to harvesting by ungulates and are therefore younger and more succulent than in an ungrazed area.

Table 3.5. Comparison of stem densities per square meter, percent dry weight, and dry weight biomass per square meter of living and dead *S. alterniflora* from the simulatively grazed areas, 24 May 1973. $\bar{X}$ = mean, SE = standard error of the mean, CV = coefficient of variation, %DW = percent dry weight, DWB = dry weight biomass. (From Reimold *et al.*, 1975b, by permission of the editor, *Biol. Conserv.*)

1972 Harvest	Living matter									Dead matter					
Day of year	No. of stems			%DW			DWB			%DW			DWB		
	$\bar{X}$	SE	CV	$\bar{X}$	SE	CV	$\bar{X}$	SE	CV	$\bar{X}$	SE	CV	$\bar{X}$	SE	CV
Control (unharvested)	187.6	4.1	4.9	38.7	0.8	4.4	287.3	28.9	22.5	42.2	0.9	10.2	191.7	21.1	24.6
120	198.2	20.0	22.6	36.0	0.9	5.8	327.5	25.5	17.4	40.7	1.2	6.6	271.2	13.2	10.9
180	270.2	57.2	47.0	37.0	1.0	5.9	203.6	28.2	30.9	40.5	1.6	8.6	81.6	6.9	19.0
240	318.0	47.6	33.5	37.3	1.2	7.2	228.2	30.0	29.3	39.2	3.1	7.9	45.8	7.1	34.5

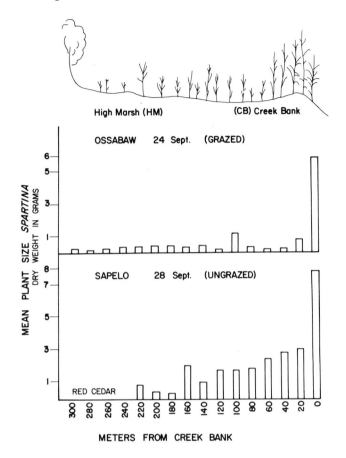

Figure 3.3.   Mean plant size of marsh plants in a grazed and ungrazed salt marsh. (From Shanholtzer, 1974, by permission of the editors, Reimold and Queen, *Ecology of Halophytes,* Academic Press.)

Intensive grazing in a local area for a short period of time can depress production. However, if this happens and the grazers turn to other vegetation, production can be reestablished (Ranwell and Downing, 1959, *Zostera* depletion). Where grazing is intensive and prolonged, a destructive impact on the vegetation can be generated. Both Oliver (1913) and Rowan (1913) portrayed the very destructive habits of the rabbit populations living on Blakeney Point, Norfolk, England. *Salicornia europaea* and *Obione* (=*Halimione*) *portulacoides* were eaten. *Aster tripolium* was a favorite food: there seldom was a plant without nibbled leaves, and a flower stalk was a rarity. This was also true for *Convolvulus soldanella.* Although there was some

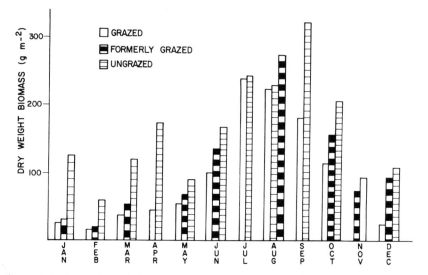

Figure 3.4. Mean dry weight biomass of the aerial portions of live *Spartina alterniflora* in three salt-marsh systems. (From Reimold *et al.,* 1975b, by permission of the editor, *Biol. Conserv.*)

question as to how much *Suaeda fruticosa* was actually consumed, both au-thors remarked upon the great masses of twigs and branches of this halo-phyte that accumulated at the drift line. The depredation of these animals was emphasized by the comparison of grazed vegetation with those plots protected by fencing.

Gillham (1955) made an extensive examination of the impact of grazing on the vegetation of the Pembrokeshire Islands off the Welsh coast. Her study extended inland from the shoreline and included an evaluation of many upland species where the rabbit was found to have the greatest im-pact. Plants could be classified into three groups according to their ability to withstand heavy rabbit grazing. "Rabbit-avoided" species grow well in grazed and ungrazed areas. Since there were other herbivores on the island, a plant that was avoided by rabbits was not necessarily left alone by other browsers. A high percentage of the plants on Skokholm Island belonged in the "rabbit-resistant" category. Many of them were hemicryptophytes which spread by production of new shoots at or below ground level where they are protected from attack. In the case of the grasses, rabbit nibbling of the leaf species stimulated rather than impeded growth. The grasses *Agrostis* and *Festuca* associated with the tidal marshes were the more widespread resis-tant hemicryptophytes. The "non-resistant, palatable" species such as the marsh succulents *Plantago maritima* and *Halimione portulacoides* were un-common on Skokholm Island or restricted to isolated situations (Table 3.7).

Table 3.6. Comparison of living and dead, wet and dry weights, for *Distichlis spicata, Salicornia virginica,* and *Spartina alterniflora.* For the regression equation, Y = dry weight, X = wet weight. All regression equations have a correlation coefficient significant at the 99.9% confidence interval. (From Reimold, *et al.,* 1975b, by permission of the editor, *Biol. Conserv.*)

	Mean wet weight g/m²	Mean dry weight g/m²	Percent dry weight	Regression equation Y a + bX	
Ungrazed					
S. alterniflora (live)	474.4	168.1	35.4	Y	2.05 + 0.35X
S. alterniflora (dead)	326.2	129.5	39.7	Y	8.80 + 0.37X
S. virginica	1080.5	272.8	25.2	Y	13.47 + 0.24X
Grazed					
S. alterniflora (live)	269.7	95.1	35.3	Y	−4.69 + 0.37X
S. alterniflora (dead)	147.1	53.0	36.0	Y	−10.27 + 0.43X
S. virginica	116.4	29.5	25.3	Y	1.57 + 0.24X
D. spicata (live)	55.3	24.8	44.8	Y	1.56 + 0.42X
D. spicata (dead)	35.3	14.8	41.9	Y	2.10 + 0.36X
Formerly grazed					
S. alterniflora (live)	314.5	95.0	30.2	Y	3.79 + 0.29X
S. alterniflora (dead)	353.0	89.6	25.4	Y	15.46 + 0.21X
S. virginica	249.2	62.3	25.0	Y	17.45 + 0.18X
D. spicata (live)	79.8	39.2	49.1	Y	−3.87 + 0.54X
D. spicata (dead)	72.4	30.9	42.7	Y	4.12 + 0.37X

Skokholm Island, which has had grazing mammals since the 14th century with a population estimated at 10,000 on 106 hectares for the years 1940–42, has had the principal communities dominated by "rabbit-resistant" species while no community was dominated by "non-resistant" species. In contrast, Grassholm Island which has had no browsing mammals, displays an overwhelming dominance of long grass Festucetum in which the constituent species had a characteristically "non-resistant" growth habit.

It was noted that in the wind-exposed areas of Skokholm Island the number of species tended to increase. This seemed to arise from a combination of wind exposure and rabbit grazing. Close cropping by rabbits and exposure of bare soil with a greater amount of light facilitated the growth of subordinate species, especially in the more open *Festuca-Agrostis* turf (Figure 3.5). As stated earlier, Skokholm is heavily grazed and Grassholm Island is not grazed at all. Nearby Middleholm is grazed but by a smaller population of rabbits and sheep. The number of species in the *Festuca rubra* community on these three islands portray the impact of grazing (Table 3.8). The number of species present range from 46 on Skokholm through 33 on Middleholm to 8 on Grassholm. The percentage of the ground covered by the dominant *Festuca* varies from 30 to 45 percent on Skokholm through 65 to 80 percent on Middleholm to 80 to 90 percent on Grassholm. The average

Table 3.7. Classification of *Plantago* swards in relation to grazing intensity. (From Gillham, 1955, by permission of the editor, *J. Ecol.*)

Heavy grazing:	*Plantago coronopus* dom., succulent plantains absent	As on Skokholm
Medium grazing:	(a) *P. coronopus* and *P. maritima* co-dom., *P. lanceolata* present	As on Clare Island and St. Kilda
	(b) *P. maritima* dom., *P. coronopus* and *P. lanceolata* present	
No grazing:	Succulent variety of *P. coronopus* locally co-dom. in Festucetum rubrae; nonsucculent plantains absent	As on Grassholm

height of *Festuca* ranged from 1 to 3 centimeters on Skokholm through 3 to 8 centimeters on Middleholm to 20 to 40 centimeters on Grassholm. The same pattern was recorded for the more sheltered *Agrostis* sward. Subsequent observations (Ranwell, 1960; White, 1961) further supported the view that cessation of grazing by rabbits results in a marked increase in the growth and flowering of grasses and sedges and the decline in low-growing dicotyledons.

While certain species such as the widgeon, brent goose, and white-fronted goose, can alter the growth form of the various plants, reduce the amount of plant biomass or alter species composition by their browsing activity, the plants rebound quickly upon reduction or cessation of grazing. Other animals, by way of their feeding habits or numbers, can have a much greater, more lasting or far-reaching impact. This author has observed the Icelandic grey lag goose *Anser anser* feeding on the *Carex* marsh at Gasar on the north coast of Iceland, pulling up the entire plant in order to eat the green leaves. The blue goose *Chen caerulescens*, the lesser snow goose *Chen hyperborea hyperborea*, and the greater snow goose *Chen hyperborea atlantica* as well as the Canada goose *Branta canadensis* feed on the rhizomes of *Spartina alterniflora*, *Spartina cynosuroides*, *Scirpus olneyi*, *Scirpus robustus*, *Scirpus californicus* and *Distichlis spicata*. The underground rhizomes of such plants as *Scirpus americanus* are "puddled out." The flats must be covered with water, making it easier for the birds to get at the roots than when the marsh is exposed at low tide (Griffith, 1940; Lynch *et al.*, 1947). The geese also use their heavy strong bills to pull up these very tough rhizomes and cut them into several pieces before swallowing. Ducks benefit by this puddling activity of the geese by having *Scirpus* seeds made available. Where such grazing is severe, ponds are created that are used by other water fowl. Conversely, such expansive "eat-outs" adversely affect nesting sites

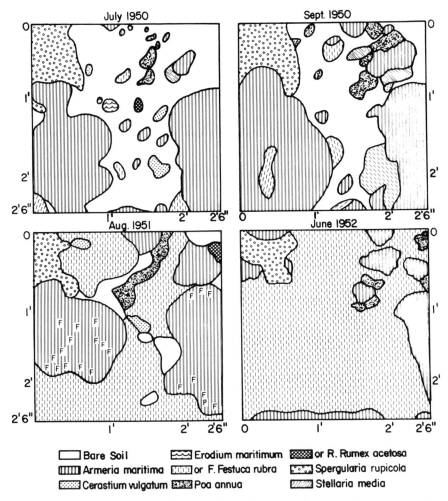

Figure 3.5. Four quadrats of the vegetation within a rabbit-proof enclosure on Skokholm Neck to show the change from an open Armerietum to a closed Festucetum two years after a cessation of grazing. (From Gillham, 1955, by permission of the editor, *J. Ecol.*)

and food supplies reducing the carrying capacity of the marsh for black ducks and other wildlife (Ferrigno, 1976).

Water levels influence where these geese feed. When water is low the geese invade the *Typha* marshes destroying muskrat food. They turn to *Panicum repens* (dog tooth grass) in the Gulf Coast marshes, when these marshes are flooded for longer than normal periods (Lynch *et al.*, 1947).

These geese have prodigious appetites. A flock of 5000 greater snow

Table 3.8. Composition of *Agrostidetum tenius* in relation to grazing intensity. (From Gillham, 1955, by permission of the editor, *J. Ecol.*)

Grazing intensity (estimated by the average number of rabbit pellets per ½ sq.m.)	Number of species in a representative area	Percentage of ground covered by grasses	Percentage of ground covered by two palatable grasses, *Agrostis* and *Festuca*
None	2	100	100
	3	100	96
Very slight (0–10 pellets)	4	100	95
	4	100	75
Medium (5–100 pellets)	21	91	62
	16	75	68
Heavy (300–500 pellets)	23	54	50
	24	56	48

Note. Most of the difference between the two final columns is accounted for by *Holcus lanatus*, the rest by *Poa annua*.

geese *Chen hyperborea atlantica,* feeding extensively on *Spartina alterniflora,* denuded 300 acres in six weeks (Griffith, 1940). In describing the impact of such damage to Gulf Coast marshes, Lynch *et al.* (1947) recorded the lament of a trapper as he watch a flock of approximately 10,000 birds leave their feeding grounds, "That's five acres of my rat marsh you see flying off." These geese apparently feed twice a day and a single meal may involve a double handful of rhizomes. The tops and roots of the plants are discarded. Those plants that are not preferred are pulled up and thrown aside. It has been estimated that these feeding blue and snow geese will pull up and discard as much as ten times the amount they consume. A large flock can denude a marsh in a very short time, a phenomena referred to as an "eat-out" (Lynch *et al.,* 1947).

There is an interesting side effect to such "eat-outs." The marsh surface can be lowered by one or two inches (Griffith, 1940) or the soil may be broken to a depth of five to eight inches (Lynch *et al.,* 1947). Water accumulates in such areas and plant regeneration is inhibited unless a furrow is plowed to prohibit flooding and provide surface drainage (Griffith, 1940). Ferrigno (1958) recorded the impact of such goose activity on mosquito generation (see Table 2.3). Small "eat-outs" produced numbers of mosquitos while large ones tended to form ponds which discouraged *Aedes* breeding and supported populations of *Cyprinodon variegatus,* the sheepshead minnow, and *Fundulus heteroclitus,* the mummichog, giving them access to the mosquito larvae. From this arose the establishment and maintenance of permanent shallow pools in the heavy mosquito breeding areas of salt marshes as a means of mosquito control and waterfowl refuge.

While goose "eat-outs" can have a dismal effect on a marsh, an overpopulation of muskrats, *Ondatra zibethica,* can impart an even greater impact. In fact goose damage may initiate a muskrat "eat-out" (Lynch *et al.,* 1947). Both the geese and the muskrats are attracted to the same food plants. When a muskrat population builds up, exceeding the carrying capacity of the marsh and/or if a wintering concentration of geese utilize the same marsh, damage is inevitable.

As with the geese described earlier, muskrats have great appetites. Not only do they consume large quantities of plant material, but due to their wasteful feeding and digging habits very considerable amounts of vegetation are destroyed (Svihla and Svihla, 1931; O'Neil, 1949). Based on a feeding experiment where captive muskrats were fed various paille-fin grasses (*Panicum hemitomum, Panicum virgatum, Spartina patens*), Svihla and Svihla (1931) found muskrats with an average weight of 30 ounces consumed 10.2 ounces of green vegetation or 33.9 percent of their body weight. The average 1000-gram weight Louisiana muskrat could eat one square foot of *Scirpus olneyi* per day and about two square feet of any other marsh plant. Because of digging and feeding habits, discontinuous stands of *Scirpus olneyi,* open water, the use of *Scirpus olneyi* for housing, and its destruction by runs, it has been estimated that one square mile of *Scirpus olneyi* marsh in Louisiana can support a maximum population of 10,000 muskrats of which 5000 are trappable (O'Neil, 1949). Dozier (1953) suggested two-thirds of the population could be harvested from a good marsh and still maintain a viable population.

Proper harvesting is considered to be the only effective means of controling muskrat populations (Lynch *et al.*, 1947; Dozier, 1953). Under Atlantic coast tidewater conditions, Dozier (1953) recommended that trapping should begin when population densities reach that of one house per acre. A density of 2.5 dwelling houses an acre requires immediate attention to prevent "eat-outs." Dozier suggested "yield per house" to be a much better measure of trapping efficiency than "yield per acre." The harvest of 2.5 muskrats per house would sustain an adequate breeding population. Dozier indicated the best Maryland marshes could maintain a yield of four or five muskrats per acre over an extended period.

Lynch *et al.* (1947) described in considerable detail the ecological consequences to a tidal marsh following goose or muskrat "eat-outs." Such effects are summarized in Figure 3.6. The authors pointed out that some "eat-outs" occurred in spite of control measures. The magnitude of "eat-outs" was influenced by the extent of dominance by climax species. Solid stands of *Scirpus* or *Typha* were more subject to a complete "eat-out" than were mixed stands of secondary and climax plant species. O'Neil (1949) has recorded a direct relationship between muskrat cycles and "eat-outs" in Louisiana; 10–14 year cycles on the better *Scirpus olneyi* marshes and longer on the less productive types such as *Panicum hemitomum* or *Typha* marshes. The alligator grass, *Alternanthera philoxeroides,* had increased its rate of invasion in *Typha* marshes and was, therefore, being eaten more (O'Neil, 1949). Rate of recovery is influenced by many factors including the depth of soil damage, amounts of open water created as well as the quantities of seeds and propagative vegetation parts that survived. The "crevey" or dead marsh that results from an "eat-out" may be attractive to certain wildlife such as some ducks, but is shunned by geese and muskrats until recovery occurs (Lynch *et al.*, 1947).

The destructive effect on a tidal marsh by overpopulation will in turn have a debilitating impact on the muskrat. Many will be driven from the marsh and perish elsewhere (Errington, 1963). For those that remain in the deteriorating marsh, not only is there a decline in numbers but also a decrease in individual weights (Table 3.9). Dozier *et al.* (1948) reported that two of the study areas, Units 18 and 19 (see Table 3.9) had a heavy concentration of 6.05 houses per acre in the spring of 1940 when light trapping harvested only 0.36 muskrats per house. As a result the vegetation was badly

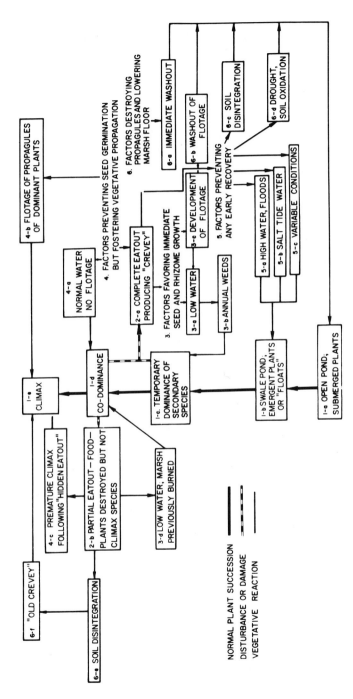

Figure 3.6. Ecological consequences of muskrat and goose damage to marshes. (From Lynch *et al.*, 1947, by permission of the editor, *J. Wildl. Mgmt.*)

113

Table 3.9. Progressive decrease in muskrat density, yield and average weights, as affected by overpopulation, Blackwater National Wildlife Refuge, Maryland. (From Dozier et al., 1948, by permission of the editor, J. Wildl. Mgmt.)

Unit	Marsh	Trapping Season	Houses per Acre	Yield per House	Average Weight
17	Wolf Pit	1941	3.9	1.0	2.13
		1942	1.1	1.8	1.93
		1943	0.7	2.1	1.90
18	Rhode Island	1941	1.8	0.7	2.01
		1942	0.03	3.2	1.97
		1943	0.1	0.7	1.80
19	McGraws Island	1941	0.5	4.3	2.13
		1942	0.2	2.1	1.95
		1943	0.4	0.3	1.83
23	Sunken Island	1941	3.0	0.5	2.36
		1942	0.6	1.4	2.27
		1943	0.6	0.2	2.00

eaten out in the summer, creating open water and mudflats. In the fall of 1940 the population density dropped as low as 0.5 house per acre.

Evans (1970) has reviewed the literature on the nutria, *Myocaster coypus*, including their feeding habits. He and Norris (1967) both reported on the depredations on agricultural crops and water control structures caused by enlarging populations. However, Evans concluded that nutria generated noticeable harm on a marsh only during abnormal conditions such as storms, drought, or marsh burning when the population lost its normal food supply. At such times they mowed down above-water plants or stripped the bottom of underwater roots and tubers. Such damage usually occurs in isolated locations. Normally, they exercise selective cropping. They do not control coon tail, bladderwort, hyacinth, alligator weed, water lily, and water lotus. They can control emergent species such as cattails, rushes, and sedges, creating open water useful to waterfowl. Evans concluded they do not harm the better waterfowl foods such as smartweeds, wild millet, bulrush, Delta duck-potato, widgeon grass, or sago pondweed.

Burning marsh vegetation as a management tool produces interesting plant-animal interactions. Early in the spring, snow and blue geese turn to the new foliage of *Spartina patens* and *Distichlis spicata* on burned Gulf Coast marshes and the vegetation of the bordering coastal cattle pastures (Lynch *et al.*, 1947). Controlled burning makes *Spartina patens* much more available to waterfowl such as Canada and snow geese, the greater yellow legs *Scolopax melanoleuca* (Gmelin), and lesser yellow legs *Scolopax flavipes* (Gmelin), Wilson's snipe *Capella gallinago delicata* (Ord) (Griffith,

1940), and the willet *Catoptrophorus semipalmatus* (Vogt, 1938). In the more brackish coastal marshes of Texas, Lay and O'Neil (1942) and Neely (1962) observed that summer burning, which is useful in providing succulent food for cattle, drives muskrats from the marshes for lack of house-building materials when fall comes. Those rats that remained had to use burned grass fragments and roots for building material and in addition, the cattle destroyed many houses by lying on them. The late summer burns also attracted the fall migrating geese, causing competition for food and thus creating damage to the marsh by "eat-outs." The authors recommended burning marshes in the spring for muskrat food and shelter and burning the adjoining uplands in the summer for cattle and geese grazing. The indirect beneficial effects of burning for muskrats is the control of insects that infest many of the principle food plants such as the widespread and very injurous lepidopterous stem borer, *Arazama obliqua,* and the leaf miners on *Scirpus* that often prevent normal seed setting (Dozier, 1953).

Chabreck (1976) acknowledged that burning has been widely used as a marsh management procedure but questioned much of the value of such efforts. He cited the example whereby burning can give *Scirpus olneyi* an earlier start during the growing season when it is in a mixed stand with the marsh-hay cordgrass, *Spartina patens.* However, he noted that burning alone will not maintain the *Scirpus;* water level maintenance and salinity regulation are still necessary. Chabreck commented that burning makes it easier to walk by removing tangled plant growth but it can also drive animals from a marsh for lack of cover.

Burrowing and Homemaking

The considerable zonational response among birds and mammals relative to plant heights and species distribution has been described in Chapter Two. The appreciable literature pertaining to nest and home sites, distributions and numbers, brood production, etc., will be discussed in Chapter Five. The current discussion will focus on the direct interaction between vegetation and the individual animal. Among the invertebrates, the fiddler crab best demonstrates this relationship. Schwartz and Safir (1915) commented that *Uca* turned aside when it encountered *Spartina* roots and rhizomes during burrowing activity. They also noted that the burrowing activity could disrupt the density, growth, and spreading of *Spartina alterniflora.* Wolf *et al.* (1975) reported an average of 27 *Uca pugnax* burrows per square meter in the tall *Spartina* marsh with $176/m^2$ and $196/m^2$ for the short *Spartina* and medium *Spartina* respectively. Kraeuter and Wolf (1974) suggested the substrate may be too fluid in the tall *Spartina* areas to maintain burrows and the numerous root systems may limit burrowing activity in the dwarf *Spartina* sites. However, the root mat does provide a stabilized sediment layer for such marsh dwellers. The extensive system of burrows beneath the surface has provoked speculation that fiddler crabs may be the earthworms of the marsh.

One of the few known impacts upon marsh vegetation by small animals is that described by Woodell (1974). He reported that ant hills on the marshes of Scolt Head Island, England, drained the substrate and enhanced the growth of a Mediterranean plant species *Frankenia laevis.*

Numerous authors (Stearns *et al.*, 1940; Lay and O'Neil, 1942; Lynch *et al.*, 1947; Dozier *et al.*, 1948; O'Neil, 1949; Palmisano, 1972) have described the relationship between vegetation and muskrat distributions. Svihla and Svihla (1931) and Dozier (1953) described the construction of homes, feeding stations and runways spreading out from the houses, radiating in all directions. The activity of home building and tunnel excavations can have an impact on the vegetation equal to that already described for the feeding habits of this marshland rodent. There is an apparent haphazard piling up of vegetation to create a new dwelling or to enlarge the old one. Such activity is most evident in the fall as cold weather and high tides begin to develop. Feeding shelters, smaller than the lodges, accumulate the debris resulting from numerous meals. In both cases, piles of dead vegetation smother vegetation. This impact, added to the wasteful feeding habits of the muskrat, can have destructive effects on vegetation, especially with high muskrat densities.

Trampling

Trampling is usually considered to be the impact of animal feet upon vegetation. In this discussion, trampling will also include any kind of mechanical disturbance to the soil surface such as turf cutting. The single passage of an animal through marsh vegetation becomes evident by the displacement of vegetation, the breakage of stems, or bruised leaves. When this same animal repeats the passage or others follow behind the trampling effect becomes more obvious. The ultimate result is bare earth, alligator water trails, a quagmire or dry compacted soil. Such impacts are not confined to the large animals, sheep, deer or cattle. The trails of small mammals such as the meadow vole, *Microtus pennsylvanicus,* and the rice rat, *Oryzomys palustris,* can be seen radiating out onto the marsh among the stems of *Spartina alterniflora* in Canary Creek marsh and similar southern Delaware tidal wetlands.

The trampling activity of blue and snow geese is a contributing factor to the severe impact of their feeding habits described earlier.

Whereas such bird activity tends to be localized and seasonal in nature, mammalian activity reflects man's interest in tidal wetlands as pasturage for his domesticated animals. Numerous references discuss grazing and trampling impacts in varying detail (Yapp *et al.*, 1917; Gillham, 1955; Ranwell,

1961; Shanholtzer, 1974; Reimold *et al.*, 1975b; Reimold, 1976). Rabbits can create extensive bare areas about their burrow entrances as the result of close cropping and repeated trampling of the high marsh and adjoining high ground vegetation (Gillham, 1955). The trampling of grazing sheep on the muddy substrate of a *Spartina townsendii* marsh can compact the soil and transform it into a *Puccinellia maritima* marsh over a ten-year period (Ranwell, 1961). In contrast, grazing animals (mostly sheep) can enlarge salt pans in the Upper Solway marshes of western Great Britain by churning up the mud, destroying the marginal vegetation and thus extending the area of the bare pan floor (Marshall, 1962).

Selected human activity may be considered as trampling. It was observed that digging for bait worms in the pans on the Stifkey marshes on the north coast of Norfolk, England, would certainly maintain the open nature of such salt pans. Cutting marsh turf for lawn sodding can create salt pans (Gray, 1972) or, as Cadwalladr and Morley (1974) and Gray and Scott (1977) pointed out, *Puccinellia maritima* and *Agrostis stolonifera* can invade and almost completely cover the bare area in three years after the removal of *Festuca rubra* turf. *Puccinellia* can colonize faster than *Festuca* when the cut areas are wider than 30 centimeters due to the reduction in the number of tillers emanating from the narrow strips of uncut *Festuca*.

Chappell *et al.* (1971) also discussed the effect of trampling on species composition of marshland organisms. Personal observation of the great numbers of sheep hoof prints among the prostrate *Puccinellia phryganodes* in tidal marshes of the Lakselv district of northern Norway presumably would have an influence on such species distributions. *Puccinellia maritima* has been observed to be the last species to persist in the footpaths wandering over the Stifkey marshes of Norfolk. Rabbits have been described as having such an impact on some of the Pembrokeshire Islands off the coast of Wales (Gillham, 1955). Presumably trampling was responsible for the decrease in the numbers of fiddler crabs in grazed marshes in contrast to ungrazed marshes in Georgia (Reimold *et al.* 1975b).

In recent years, human society has become increasingly aware of its surroundings and there have been numerous expressions of concern about environmental depredations. Unfortunately, in our concern, we may be loving our environment to death. In an honest attempt to acquaint more people with the unique and irreplaceable role of tidal marshes to our environment, we have subjected these fragile zones to school groups and adult students in ever expanding numbers. In a marsh so sensitive that the trail of a vole can be identified, the effect of such visitations is as catastrophic as a cattle drive. Repeated excursions produce a quagmire. Destruction of soil structure is known to occur much more quickly under wet conditions, especially on heavy soils (Chappell *et al.*, 1971). In an attempt to side-step muddy areas, people walk along the edges of the path, ever widening the trail, killing the vegetation and making the quagmire deeper. Such has been the case in our southern Delaware marshes and elsewhere. Fortunately, as Reimold *et al.* (1975b) pointed out, salt marshes may recover if grazing (trampling) is kept at a low level. In fact as those authors observed and as has been noted in Delaware, while grazing or trampling has a significant impact on a salt marsh, the turnaround time can be as short as one year, depending upon the magnitude of the imposed environmental insult.

INDIRECT RELATIONSHIPS

Nutrient Cycling

Nutrient enrichment of a marsh via fecal input from animals may be considerable and at present there has been no evident attempt to quantify such input and its significance. In the case of roosting birds and the concentrated nature of their fecal matter, such enrichment may be locally significant (Shanholtzer, 1974).

Kuenzler (1961b) discussed the role of the ribbed mussel, *G. demissa,* in phosphorus cycling. He concluded that the major fractions of the phosphorus are not effectively used by the mussel; the phosphate (dissolved inorganic) only slightly used and the particulate phosphorus largely wasted although it was filtered out of suspension. Since food requirements are satisfied by filtration, phosphorus does not appear to be a limiting factor. The mussels do have an effect in the water over the marsh by removing from suspension one-third of the particulate phosphorus. This material is dropped to the marsh surface in the form of pseudofeces and feces. By acting as a depositional agent, the mussel population may play a greater role in the biogeochemical sense rather than as energy consumers. Such activity presumably would facilitate the feeding process of coprophagus worms and others as well as detritus-ingesting animals.

Reimold *et al.* (1975b) demonstrated a marked decrease in the amount of dead plant tissue from an ungrazed to a grazed marsh (see Table 3.6) with an ensuing decrease in detritus production. It would appear that a major impact of sheep grazing on the *Collembola, Acarina,* enchytraes, and nematodes in a New South Wales pasturage was due to increased removal of herbage by the sheep with an associated reduction in root biomass. Such activity would reduce the amount of living space in the soil and litter mat, shelter and food for the mesofauna (King and Hutchinson, 1976). Reimold *et al.* (1975) attribute the higher nitrogen levels in the ungrazed marsh to detritus conservation. In view of the decrease in fiddler crabs in the grazed marsh ascribed to trampling by cattle, one could presume a comparable effect on other organisms such as the amphipods and isopods.

The estuarine isopod *Cleantis planicauda* has been identified as a major degrader of dead *Spartina* to detritus and, at the same time, amphipods have been considered to play an important role (Gessner and Goos, 1973; May, 1974). These same authors reported large quantities of fungi associated with the dead *Spartina* to which they ascribe the microbial decomposition of the plant tissue. Averill (1976) and Harrison (1977) considered the amphipods to be attracted to the dead grasses by the quantities of bacteria and fungi growing on the moist leaf debris.

Freshly collected amphipods voided recognizable eel grass, *Zostera marina*, fragments in their feces. In the laboratory *Gammarus oceanicus* grazed on untreated dead *Zostera* leaves but not on those leaves that had been scraped or treated with mercuric chloride to remove or kill the epibiota. The rate of decomposition of 100 milligrams of *Zostera* leaf particles was increased 32 percent (5 °C) and 35 percent (21 °C) by two amphipods held in laboratory flasks for 24 days. The amphipods markedly reduced particle size as well as providing additional surface areas for saprovores (Harrison, 1977).

The generation of detritus by *Orchestia grillus* and *O. uhleri* (= *spartinophila*) was brought about by their feeding mechanisms (Averill, 1976). As the amphipods scraped up the fungi, they frequently shaved off a bit of grass from below the fungal layer, ingesting it or letting it fall aside. These grass scrapings were never as thick as the leaf, comprising one or two cells in depth. Having larger mouth parts, *Orchestia grillus* was observed to tear up grass fragments much more frequently than *Orchestia spartinophila*. This appeared to account for the differences in breakdown rates observed for the two amphipod species.

The burrowing activity of fiddler crabs may indirectly facilitate nutrient cycling to *Spartina alterniflora*. This is pure conjecture as there are no known reports directed to the role of such burrows in enhancing the ingress of oxygen and nitrogen to the plant roots. Nor is there any known work evaluating the possible role of nitrogen derived from the crab fecal deposits that might be deposited in the burrows.

Seed Dispersal

Shanholtzer (1974) commented on the role of animal activity in seed dispersal. Birds can scatter seeds about during feeding and it is possible for undigested seeds to pass through the alimentary tract and be dispersed in the fecal droppings. Shanholtzer noted less seed dispersion in an ungrazed marsh and more in a grazed wetland. Lynch *et al.* (1947) ascribed the feeding process of blue and snow geese in "puddling-out" *Scirpus americanus* rhizomes as a dispersion mechanism for *Scirpus* seeds. It is conceivable that the digging activity of muskrats during feeding or runway construction would aid in seed dispersion.

4
Food and Feeding

INTRODUCTION

We have come to recognize that the food and feeding relationships of an animal comprise a whole host of interactions. Feeding sites may be determined or influenced by the home range, the availability of food, the presence of cover, the ability of an organism to move about at the various stages in its life, and by the morphology of the feeding apparatus. Food preferences may be learned from what the parent brings to the young, or by trial and error. Seeming preferences may be no more than expressions of temporal or spatial opportunism. Predator-prey relations may and quite often appear to be manifestations of opportunism. Such relations can also result from some kind of morphological or physiological constraint imposed upon the consumer.

Thienemann (1926) put forth the ecological concept of producers and consumers while Elton (1927) established the principle of the food chain, now recognized as an artificial but convenient device to explain a form of species interaction involving energy transfer. Lindeman (1942) is credited with promulgation of the concept of trophic levels. He, along with Juday (1942) and Bodenheimer (1958), stressed that transfer of energy from one trophic level to the next could be quantified. We now recognize that Lindeman's concept of trophic levels is somewhat artificial in that such levels are not necessarily sharply delineated. An organism can occupy more than one, sometimes two, possibly even three trophic levels brought about by temporal or spatial distinctions, by modifications induced by progression through the animal's life cycle, or changing predator-prey interactions. As E. P. Odum (1971) so aptly pointed out, trophic classification is one of function, not of species.

FEEDING SITES AND THE FEEDING PROCESS

Home range and territory

The location of an animal's home is directly influenced by the availability of adequate food supplies. Given this, the nest or burrow in turn has an influ-

120

ence on feeding sites. This may be highly restricted in passive feeders such as oysters and mussels, limited to a territory close by the burrow opening as in the fiddler crabs, or identified with the defined or extensive home ranges of many of the vertebrates. This author considers a territory to be the defended area, usually smaller and more delineated than the home range. However, such a distinction has not been clearly expressed in some of the literature reviewed.

Fundulus heteroclitus has a home range extending for about 100 feet along the banks of tidal streams during the warm months of the year, seldom wandering from the area even to cross the stream (Lotrich, 1975). By the nature of the ebb and flow of the tide, much of the food is brought to this fish eliminating the need to search for it. It is not known what kind of home range, if any, is established for those mummichog who reside in mosquito control-wildlife refuge impoundments. The rationale for the creation of low-level impoundments and champagne pools with ditches radiating out from the pools has been to facilitate the movement of *Fundulus heteroclitus* out from the pools onto the marsh surface to forage on mosquito larvae and pupae. If indeed such is the case, then the home ranges would have a different configuration from that described by Lotrich.

All feeding activity of the male long-billed marsh wren, *Telmatodytes palustris griseus,* is purported to occur within the established territory (Kale, 1965). The territories of the song sparrow, *Melospiza melodia,* around San Francisco Bay are strung out along the sloughs. The birds are restricted to marsh areas where the tides are unimpeded, using the vegetation as singing perches but dropping to the ground surface to forage as the tides recede (Marshall, 1948; Johnston, 1956b). Food requirements have a stronger influence on habitat selection than nesting sites for the seaside sparrow, *Ammospiza maritima macgillivraii.* The feeding grounds are the wet banks where *Spartina alterniflora* grows the rankest and, because of flooding, such sites are unsuitable nesting locations (Tomkins, 1941). The eastern willet, *Catoptrophorus semipalmatus,* takes most of its food from within its established territory. Some trips are made to the bayshore or uplands and, when the water level is right, the marsh ponds are visited as the birds pick food from the grass blades. The extent of this off-territory feeding appears to be affected by the wind (Vogt, 1938).

The king rail, *Rallus elegans,* establishes territory and places the nest in uniform vegetative stands near the marsh edge (Meanley, 1969). The clapper rail (*Rallus longirostris*) nests are concentrated in the edge between short and tall *Spartina alterniflora* (Stewart, 1951) or in the medium height *Spartina alterniflora* (up to two feet) (Oney, 1954). In neither case is there any evidence that either species confines its feeding to a territory. Instead, they forage in areas adjacent to or in the preferred nesting areas. The king rail often takes advantage of muskrat runs in its search for food. Both rails search along creek banks where the clapper rail finds its preferred food, the marsh crab, *Sesarma,* among the tall *Spartina* or the fiddler crab, *Uca,* in the medium grass zone. The king rail frequently repairs to a favorite feeding site, such as the top of a muskrat house, for dismemberment and ingestion of the food item (Oney, 1954; Meanley, 1969).

Several authors (Harris, 1953; Fisler, 1965b; Rudd *et al.,* 1971) commented on the presence of a home range for *Microtus* in a tidal marsh with Harris identifying the size at one-quarter to one-half acre. Feeding is presumed to occur within that home range and recent observations in Canary Creek marsh on the frequent recaptures of the same individuals and the presence of feeding remains of grass in the same general location would tend to confirm the presence of *Microtus* in a restricted area. Aerial views of muskrat activity tend to display discrete sites for feeding with the house or feeding platform being the focal point. During the fall it is hard from such aerial views to distinguish between feeding activity and harvesting of grass for house construction. Errington (1963) has very ably documented the presence of home range and territorialism among muskrats and in addition has described the increased intraspecific strife induced by continued compression of home range and territory resulting from the expansion of the population. He described instances of animals apparently suffering from malnutrition repeatedly being captured within a limited area degraded by overgrazing. The consequences of such population increases have been described in Chapter Three.

Hoese (1971) has provided an interesting description of unusual fishing behavior of dolphin, *Tursiops truncatus,* in the Duplin Creek marsh of Georgia where they enter the tidal streams. A pair of dolphins swim up a tidal creek during low tide, working below a mud bank in front of a bed of *Spartina* where the bank has a slope less than 25° to 30°. Moving close together, the dolphins rush up the bank, pushing the wave of water in front of them. Small fish carried in this bow wave become entrapped on the bank and are eaten by the dolphins. This feeding behavior is seasonal, limited to a short period in the autumn. Fish may not be common enough to capture without this elaborate rounding up during these seasonal periods. Dolphins are seen in the creek at many tidal stages but this fishing behavior occurs within thirty minutes either side of low tide when the mud bank is more exposed and presumably the fish more concentrated.

Dr. L. Hurd (personal communication) relayed observations of a graduate student wherein the blue crab, *Callinectes sapidus,* displayed similar feeding behavior. When mummichogs, *Fundulus heteroclitus,* or shrimp, *Palaemonetes,* passed between the crab and the bank, the crab made a rush forward, driving the prey into shallow water, and in some instances out of the water.

Food availability and cover

Availability of food can have an influence on species distributions and activity. It is seldom clear whether an organism is ingesting certain kinds of food because the food is simply at hand and abundant or whether the animal is at a specific spot because of the exercise of food preference.

A number of workers have inferred that the quantity and/or the quality of the organic material in the substrate has an influence on Foraminifera (Phleger and Walton, 1950; Lehmann, 1957; Parker and Athearn, 1959; Phleger, 1965; Buzas, 1969; Lee and Muller, 1973) and nematode (Teal and Wieser, 1966) distributions. Presumably such gross factors as tidal flooding will disperse these small, passive animals over the marsh surface after which there may well be minute but discrete sorting out into various microenvironments. However, as Matera and Lee (1972) and Lee *et al.* (1975) commented, there is insufficient information to characterize the niches of these tiny animals in any rigorous fashion.

Salinity and extent of tidal flooding can influence food availability. There are numerous references to muskrat distributions as influenced by food supplies which are determined by salinity and flooding (Stearns *et al.*, 1940; Lay and O'Neil, 1942; Dozier *et al.*, 1948; Palmisano, 1972).

Those red foxes, *Vulpes fulva,* living near tidal marshes restrict their feeding excursions onto the frequently flooded marshes during the winter, tending to stay on the drier uplands. The greater consumption of muskrats in June–July is attributed, in part, to their greater availability in the drier portions of the marshes (Heit, 1944). The feeding ground of Macgillivray's seaside sparrow described earlier is totally unsuitable for nesting but preferred despite the disadvantages of leaving cover.

For other animals the availability of cover has a profound influence on feeding activities. Food and shelter affect the size of insect assemblages; Davis and Gray (1966) found more insects among the *Spartina alterniflora* and *Distichlis spicata* than among *Spartina patens* and *Juncus.* The former provide more crevices for hiding places and at the same time permit the more frequent establishment of spider webs for food capture.

Tabanid fly larvae are reputed to be seldom found where surface water accumulates as they are prone to drowning. Instead they move to thatch piles where they find an abundance of food in the form of crustacea and mollusca. However, in one instance, tabanid fly larvae were reported in a water-logged location, due largely to an abundant supply of tipulid larvae (Gerry, 1950). *Chrysops atlanticus* larvae have been collected in very wet areas bordering ditches (Magnarelli and Anderson, 1978).

The song sparrows, *Melospiza melodia,* of the San Francisco Bay marshes are described as utilizing the tops of the *Grindelia* bushes as avenues of approach as they move through the *Salicornia,* finding concealment under vegetation or overhanging banks where they forage for food (Marshall, 1948). Their territories tend to be smaller where the marsh vegetation is more lush (Johnston, 1956c), suggesting the influence of cover on feeding habits. Both the clapper and king rails tend to be secretive, moving about among the taller vegetation along the stream banks where the most frequently ingested food, *Uca* and *Sesarma,* are most abundant (Oney, 1954; Meanley, 1969).

Morphology of the feeding apparatus

Not unexpectedly, one finds a variety in the functional morphology of the feeding apparatus among animals: mouthparts are adapted for filter feeding, biting and chewing, tearing, scraping, and sucking. Size of ingested material varies from fine particulate matter to large chunks filling the buccal cavity. All of these various forms of feeding devices can be found among tidal marsh animals. The ribbed mussel, a passive feeder, possesses the typical bivalve feeding plan while the snails, *Melampus* and *Littorina,* are equipped with the gastropod radular mechanism for scraping. The marsh hawk, *Circus cyaneus hudsonius,* tears its food apart while the clapper rail and willet can ingest whole organisms or pick larger ones apart. The Canada and snow geese will pick or cut food material and the red fox and racoon tear and cut their food, gulping down larger chunks.

Based on the earlier work of others, Nicholas (1975) placed marine nematodes into four categories based on the correlation between the morphology of the stoma and feeding habits. (1) Selective deposit feeders: without a stoma or with a reduced stomatal cavity. The food must be soft and in suspension, ingested by oesophageal suction. (2) Unselective deposit feeders: the stoma with an unarmored cup-shaped or cylindrical cavity. The oesophageal suction is supplemented by lip and stoma movements. The food must be in suspension. (3) Epigrowth feeders: the stoma armed with teeth, rods, or plates. Food is scraped off the surface or the cell contents sucked out. (4) Predators and omnivores: stoma with a powerful armature of teeth and plates. The prey is swallowed whole or pierced and sucked out. Based on the high percentage of silt common to tidal marshes in general one would expect unselective deposit feeders to be the common nematodes in such habitats. This supposition is borne out by Teal and Wieser's (1966) and Tietjen's (1969) observations of greater numbers of nematodes among the organically rich deposits in the marsh muds.

Water is an important component in the feeding process of fiddler crabs. Two general procedures of feeding are involved: flotation and the coordinated action of the mouth parts. There is a copious use of water from the gill cavities to flood the buccal cavity during feeding and there is always a need for replacement. Thus, to continue feeding, the crab must have access to an external water supply to replenish its respiratory water (Miller, 1961). This would explain Pearse's earlier observation (1914) that feeding activity declined as the mud surface began to dry out on the ebbing tide. Miller (1961) concluded that the inclusion of the flotation process is one major factor keeping *Uca* from living in a terrestrial habitat.

This need for water presumably has an effect on the territoriality of the crabs. *Uca pugnax* has been observed to leave its burrow to feed and, finding insufficient water, to go back to the burrow and a source of respiratory water and then return to the feeding area. This may explain the high degree of territoriality observed for *Uca pugnax*. Such territoriality has not been observed for *Uca minax* which feeds away from the burrow in muddier areas. The need for water for the flotation process for *Uca pugilator,* living in a sandier habitat, has a more pronounced effect on this crab's movements. Because of the greater porosity of the sand, the crab may be forced to feed at the water's edge away from the burrow if the burrow does not hold water during low tide periods (Miller, 1961).

Uca minax has the least modified mouth-part hairs of the three fiddler crabs examined by Miller (*ibid*). The muddy material carried to the mouth is fluid, very fine and little sorting is necessary before ingestion. The presence of flat-tipped hairs on the second maxilliped meropodites is considered to enhance the sorting process and enable *Uca minax* to live in a coarser substrate where food is less available. The modification of the hair tips into a spoon shape on the maxilliped meropodites of *Uca pugnax* enables this crab to feed in coarser substrates. At the same time, the luxuriant fringe of plumose hairs on the outer edges of the second maxillipeds and on the maxillae enables *Uca pugnax* to feed on a muddy substrate. The greatest modification of the hairs of the mouth parts occurs in *Uca pugilator,* greatly increasing the efficiency of the mouth parts to sort out coarse materials. In addition to having to select against coarse mineral material, fiddler crabs are also faced with the greater paucity of food material in a sandy habitat. In *Uca pugilator,* the efficiency of sorting is further enhanced by a cleaning action which involves drawing sand particles over the bristled surface of the first maxilliped basal endites by the second maxillipeds. This cleaning process retains the bulk of food particles which are washed by respiratory water toward the base of the buccal cavity.

The meaning of this is that *Uca minax* cannot efficiently sort out coarse material and must have access to abundant food material on a silty substrate. The more advanced mouth parts of *Uca pugnax* enable it to have a wider distribution including sandy areas of a new marsh. However, *Uca pugnax* is restricted in its ability to sweep sand particles clean of food compared to the efficiency of *Uca pugilator*. The highly modified mouth parts of the latter are most efficient in a psammolittoral habitat; when *Uca pugilator* lives in a marsh, the food-getting efficiency is reduced by its inability to separate out the fine silty material (Miller, 1961).

Dahl (1959) has characterized three different types of Ephydridae, detritus-feeding Diptera living in moist habitats, as far as the morphological adaptation of the species to the structure of the habitat is concerned: (1) species living on the surface of water pools, such as *Ephydra riparia;* (2) flies that may be found in dense, tall vegetation where vertical movement is necessary, such as the *Notiphila* species; and (3) those flies such as *Scatella* species living on the open soil. These adaptations can be recognized by the shape of the legs, female abdomen, eggs, and mouthparts.

By concentrating on the mouthparts of these three morphological categories, Dahl observed the first and third are represented by species with a broad proboscis and the same width of mouth opening and head height. However, those flies living on the water surface have a reduced labellum and pseudotracheae, probably an adaptation to the part of a "plankton net" which is the main function of the proboscis. Those ephydrid flies living among the vegetation have a head height two to three times as great as the mouth opening. Those species such as *Notiphila* living on reed vegetation have a large proboscis while *Hydrellia griseola* and *Psilopia nitidula,* while living among the herb vegetation where surfaces are not as great, have narrow mouth openings with a slender proboscis.

It has been generally accepted that the generation of detritus has been caused by microbial degradation of dead plant material (Burkholder and Bornside, 1957; Odum and de la Cruz, 1967; and others). May (1974) cited references identifying various macroinvertebrates as degraders of mangrove leaves and turtle grass and, from his own studies, concluded that bacteria are few in numbers while fungi are abundant in the *Spartina* culms. The fungi are considered to be the major contributors to microbial decomposition while macroinvertebrates, especially the isopod *Cleantis planicauda,* are major degraders of dead *Spartina* to detritus.

Averill (1976) provided a description of how amphipods contribute to this *Spartina* degradation. Debris that had not been recently grazed had a thick coat of fungi and presumably associated bacteria, protozoa, and other life forms. The fungal coat was commonly thicker than the diameter of the grass itself. Averill observed both *Orchestia grillus* and *Orchestia uhleri* (= *spartinophila*) feeding on this fungal covering by a scraping action of the labra. When the amphipod straddled the leaf during feeding, the amphipod's body was parallel with the leaf. By reaching out with the head and pulling it back, the amphipod scraped up a fragment of the fungal mat which was then pushed into the buccal cavity. This action would be repeated several times and the amphipod would then hitch its body forward to a fresh patch.

Both species of *Orchestia* fed in the same manner. Because of the smaller size of its buccal mass, *Orchestia uhleri* was able to scrape fungi more efficiently. Its labrum could fit in between the longitudinal ribs of the grass leaf while *Orchestia grillus,* with its larger buccal structures, could not. As the amphipods fed, they frequently shaved off a fragment of grass from below the fungal layer, ingesting it or letting it fall to one side. This grass splinter was usually one or two cell layers thick but never as thick as the leaf itself. Averill attributed these inadvertent scrapings of the grass surface to be the source of free grass particles he regularly observed, thereby providing a means by which the amphipods generate detritus from plant debris. *Orchestia grillus,* being larger and more "clumsy" was observed to scrape up grass fragments more frequently than *Orchestia uhleri.* Averill considered this to be the explanation for observed differences in breakdown rates.

FOOD HABITS AND PREDATION

Protozoa

Ciliates have been reported in moderately large numbers from benthic deposits of vascular plant detritus and sediments. The food of these ciliates includes other ciliates, flagellates, diatoms, bacteria and portions of dead metazoa (Odum, W. E., 1971). As part of a nutrient regeneration study, Johannes (1965) isolated bacteria-eating ciliates including *Euplotes crassus* Dujardin, *Euplotes vannus* Muller, and *Euplotes trisculatus* Kahl from the mud flats, tidal creeks, and sand beaches of Sapelo Island, Georgia. Food taken by Foraminifera include algae, bacteria, yeasts, and probably detritus. Bacteria were required for the sustained reproduction of four foraminiferal species described by Muller and Lee (1969).

Meiobenthos

Meiobenthos refers to small benthic organisms, including nematodes, harpacticoid copepods, amphipods, polychaetes, and oligochaetes but excluding the protozoa. Mare (1942) first suggested the densities and distribution of the meiofauna may be correlated with levels of organic matter in the sediments. Subsequent workers (Teal and Wieser, 1966; Giere, 1975; Tenore, 1977; Tietjen and Lee, 1977; Gerlach, 1978) supported this view from direct observations or inferred it from their discussions of food relations among the members of the meiofauna.

Teal (1962) enumerated several annelid species associated with a Georgia salt marsh and examination of gut contents revealed only diatoms, detritus, mud, and sand. He pointed out that two of these annelids, *Capitella capitata* and *Streblospio benedicti,* are generally found in the estuaries thus suggesting these worms had to make little adaptation to marsh life. Further, these worms tended to be most numerous in the most productive portions of the marsh. Production, in this context, presumably referred to concentration of organic matter.

While not restricted to the tidal marsh habitat, the population structure and distribution of littoral oligochaetes can be controlled by food supply (Giere, 1975). Pennate diatoms comprised a large portion of the diet of small interstitial oligochaetes such as *Marionina subterranea.* In a feeding experiment using *Marionina spicula* in a 15 centimeter core of pure sand, a one-centimeter layer of natural detritus was introduced and Giere found the previous uniform distribution changed so that 75 percent of the worms were concentrated in that 20 percent of the sediment encompassing the detritus layer and the two adjacent sand layers. This strongly suggested the attractiveness of detritus to oligochaetes. Upon examination of the gut of *Marionina spicula* Giere (1975) found no detritus but masses of microorganisms scraped from the decaying substrate. He concluded that any detritus that was ingested probably could be considered as an indirect food while the bacteria and fungi constitute the main food source. Gerlach (1978) arrived at the same conclusion but expanded the role of bacteria to that of the main food source for the microfauna as well as the deposit-feeding macrobenthos. Gerlach suggested that, by their activity and excretion of metabolic products, nematodes may "garden," thus creating conditions favorable for sediment bacteria which are in turn fed upon by the nematodes (and one could presume other members of the meiofauna). Many of the oligochaetes, polychaetes, nematodes, and Foraminifera (Giere, 1975; Gerlach, 1978) display special food requirements by selecting particular bacteria or algae and rejecting others.

Particle size may play a role in what can be utilized. *Monhystera denticulata* and *Rhabditis marina* are examples of nonselective deposit feeders that ingest approximately the same weight of algae and bacteria. *Rhabditis marina* has a larger buccal cavity and can ingest more algae than the smaller-mouthed *Monhystera denticulata.* Tietjen and Lee (1977) suggested that selective digestion processes may play a role in selective feeding. Selective ingestion and digestion may be one way to reduce interspecific competition, thus enabling a large number of species to exist in a small area and enable them to utilize diverse food resources. They proposed that such fractionation of resources would also permit high species diversity where food resources are limited.

Giere (1975) and Gerlach (1978) arrived at the conclusion that meiofaunal population size can be limited by the scarcity of proper food supplies despite large quantities of detritus and wrack material in the habitat and that such specific species play a brief but specialized role in sediment food webs. However, there are those nematodes and Foraminifera that can do very well so long as there is enough dead organic material to "garden" in order to provide good environmental conditions for the bacteria on which they graze (Gerlach, 1978).

Giere (1975) speculated on the significance of dissolved organics as a food source and Sikora et al. (1977) suggested fruitful research opportunities in species identification and evaluation of the uptake of dissolved organics for individual meiofaunal species.

Giere (1975) developed a food web focused on the meiofaunal oligochaetes and concluded there was little transfer of energy to the macrofauna. He suggested the larger oligochaete species have to rely on a mixed diet of microorganisms, fresh plant cells and debris in order to acquire the necessary amounts of energy. In reviewing the literature Tenore (1977) decided there was inconclusive evidence about the extent to which the production of the meiobenthos may be important to the productivity of higher trophic levels. He concluded that even if meiofauna were not a direct food source their mechanical activity on detrital material may be a controlling factor in the food chain dynamics of larger deposit-feeding organisms. Because of their small size, Gerlach (1978) suggested the meiofauna can serve only as an additional energy source for the deposit-feeding macrofauna because the macrofauna do not have the ability to select individual meiofauna. Coull and Bell (1979) in reviewing the controversy over the interaction between the meiofauna and higher trophic levels concluded that the meiofauna probably serve as a food source for higher trophic levels in muds more than in sand substrates.

Macroinvertebrates and vertebrates

This large assemblage of organisms is not restricted to tidal marshes, and as Teal (1962) pointed out, many have their centers of distribution outside tidal wetlands. As a further point, their food habits are not uniquely associated with the marsh habitat. They can be classed as filter or deposit feeders, grazers, predators, or omnivores.

Filter and deposit feeders. The bivalve molluscs (oyster species in the lower intertidal zone, ribbed mussel, Geukensia demissa, and marsh clam, Cyrenoida floridana, on the marsh surface) are filter feeders ingesting phytoplankton, smaller members of the zooplankton, detritus, and associated microbial populations only when covered by tidal waters. Most mosquito larvae are filter feeders although some browse algae, fungi, and bacteria from surface films and a few are predacious (Bates, 1949; Clements, 1963).

By their gill raker morphology, the menhaden, Brevoortia tyrannus, and the anchovy, *Anchoa mitchilli,* can be classed as filter feeders. While they are not restricted to the tidal stream habitat, they do appear in tremendous numbers in such locations, especially the anchovy. Being euryhaline, the anchovy has the potential for grazing on the brackish water copepods and other zooplankters swept into the streams on the flooding tide from the bay habitat. Menhaden ingest both phyto- and zooplankton. Menhaden from the marsh environment of Bissel Cove (Nixon and Oviatt, 1973) did not appear to grow during their stay in that marsh. However, young menhaden displayed progressive growth in the stream habitat of Canary Creek marsh, Delaware, during the summer of 1975.

The deposit feeders are a varied lot, ingesting the substrate over which they move or tunnel. Along with the mineral sediments, detritus particles with their microbial populations, protozoa, and the smaller members of the meiobenthos are ingested. The oligochaetes and polychaetes (Giere, 1975), nematodes (Teal and Wieser, 1966; Tietjen, 1967), snails *Ilyanassa obsoleta, Littorina irrorata* (Odum and Smalley, 1959), the fiddler crabs, *Uca* (Teal, 1958; Miller, 1961), mud crabs, *Rhithropanopeus* (Odum and Heald, 1975), grass shrimp, *Palaemonetes pugio* (Welsh, 1975), amphipods, *Orchestia* (Averill, 1976), dolichopodid and ephydrid flies (Davis and Gray, 1966), and the striped mullet *Mugil cephalus* (Odum, 1970) have been identified as deposit feeders.

Levinton (1979), in a review of detritus feeders and resource limitation, identified parameters that affect resource availability for mobile detritus feeders such as the snail *Hydrobia:* (1) fecal pellet breakdown, important since the snail will not ingest newly deposited pellets; (2) the renewal of microbial organisms such as diatoms and bacteria; (3) ample space since the rate of feeding declines with crowding; (4) particle size since there is an inverse relation between feeding rate and particle size. Levinton concluded that a study of deposit feeding organisms must consider the above parameters in a multifactorial design.

In a recent study, wherein changes in the ratios of δ ^{13}C$-$^{12}C associated with marsh vegetation, soil, and fiddler crabs were evaluated, Haines (1976a) displayed a linear relationship between plant and *Uca pugnax* δ ^{13}C distributions. The crabs associated with the low marsh *Spartina alterniflora* possessed δ ^{13}C values (12.3 to 13.7^0/oo) similar to this C$_4$ plant while crabs located in areas with C$_3$ plants like *Salicornia virginica* and *Juncus roemerianus* had δ ^{13}C similar to these particular plants (22.9 to 26^0/oo). The relation between the crab-soil interaction was less clear. The evidence suggested *Uca pugnax* had a preference for C$_4$ plants such as *Spartina alterniflora.* Other work cited by Haines inferred C$_4$ plants decomposed more rapidly and supported a greater microbial biomass than C$_3$ plants, which in turn could provide greater nutritional value for detritivores.

Both the mummichog, *Fundulus heteroclitus* (Schmelz, 1964; Jefferies, 1972), and the sheepshead minnow, *Cyprinodon variegatus* (Warlen, 1964), have been characterized as detritus, thus deposit feeders. However, as will be discussed later, Prinslow *et al.* (1974) and Katz (1975) raised serious doubts about the ability of *Fundulus* to utilize detritus. It is unknown whether or not the same question can be raised about *Cyprinodon*.

Grazers. The marsh grazers are a varied and numerous group ranging from the molluscs to the mammals. Grazing has been used to describe the feeding process of menhaden ingesting a phytoplankton bloom or anchovies consuming a copepod population. Grazing, as used here, denotes herbivores consuming a portion or the whole of an intact plant without any filtering from a volume of water as with the menhaden or anchovies.

The snails *Littorina, Neritina reclivata,* and *Melampus bidentatus* feed on the epidermis of grasses, the ephiphytic film on these plants, and edaphic community consisting of diatoms, the filamentous algae, the small animals associated with this community (Hauseman, 1932; Day *et al.*, 1973) and, at least in the case of *Littorina irrorata* (Odum and Smalley, 1959), the detritus and its associated microbial flora.

Most of the herbivores selectively feed on the stems and leaves of the grasses and other marsh plants while others display preferences for other plant parts (Paviour-Smith, 1956). Many have chewing mouthparts (Orthoptera: Hymenoptera) and others use piercing and sucking mouthparts (Homoptera and Hemiptera) to feed on plant sap while those with sponging mouthparts (largely Diptera) consume plant secretions. *Oscinella* (= *Conioscinella*) *infesta* is a common dipteran in the North Carolina marsh.

Numerous food habit studies have been done on waterfowl. The inland diving ducks (red head *Aythya americana*, ring-neck duck *Aythya collaris,* canvasback *Aythya valisineria,* greater scaup *Aythya marila,* lesser scaup *Aythya affinis* and ruddy *Oxyura jamaicensis jamaicensis*) associated with estuarine and tidal marsh embayments and pot holes are primarily plant feeders and the food of all species is similar in many respects. Cottam (1939) reported relatively few plants to be of particular importance. Most significant were the submerged pond weeds, *Potamogeton* and *Ruppia maritima,* and the naiads, *Najas flexilis* and *Najas quadalupensis.* Other important species were wild celery *Vallisneria spirabilis,* wild rice *Zizania aquatica,* the bulrushes *Scirpus* and the smartweeds *Polygonium.* The sago pondweed, *Potamogeton pectinatus,* because of its tolerance to brackish and relatively fresh water and very wide distribution, was considered to be the single most important duck food plant known. The seeds, tubers, and rhizomes and, to a lesser degree, the green vegetative portions were consumed by many different duck species. Martin and Uhler (1939), after examination of 7998 ducks

Table 4.1. Selected foods of game ducks in the coastal regions of the United States with particular reference to plants associated with tidal marshes. (From Tables 3, 6, and 8, Martin and Uhler, 1939)

Scientific Name	Common Name	Volumetric Percent		
		Atlantic Coast	Gulf Coast	Pacific Coast
Potamogeton	Pondweed	11.73	3.99	12.14
Vallisneria spiralis	Wild celery	6.82	1.06	—
Ruppia maritima	Widgeon grass	6.37	8.47	2.19
Polygonium	Smart weed	4.96	5.94	1.79
Scirpus	Bulrush	4.62	5.39	4.78
Zostera marina	Eelgrass	3.67	—	3.03
Zizania aquatica	Wild rice	2.61	0.42	—
Acnida cannabina	Tide marsh water hemp	2.51	—	—
Najas	Naiad	2.48	1.71	0.47
Echinochloa	Wild millet	1.49	4.11	0.12
Edeocharis	Spikerush	0.95	2.07	2.91
Spartina	Cordgrass	0.45	0.09	—
Cladium	Sawgrass	—	2.99	—
Salicornia	Glasswort	0.09	1.36	—
Distichlis spicata	Saltgrass	—	0.17	2.24
Triglochin maritima	Arrow grass	—	—	2.57
Gastropoda	Snails	11.04	11.62	8.57
Pelecypoda	Bivalves	6.35	1.35	8.48
Crustacea	Crustaceans	6.27	1.06	4.37
Insecta	Insects	1.93	4.43	7.23
Pisces	Fishes	0.98	2.86	—

of 18 species, concluded plant and animal material made up 73 and 27 percent of their diet respectively (Table 4.1).

More recent reports by Stewart (1962) indicated the large consumption of plant material is supplemented by a very substantial quantity of animals (Table 4.2). In fact, the latter often exceed the former and comprise animals typically not associated with the surface of tidal marshes. This should not be too surprising in view of the more open water habits of these diving birds. Table 4.2 also points up the considerable variation in food habits among species of waterfowl occupying different habitats on the Chesapeake Bay marshes. Stewart (*ibid*) attributed these differences to the availability of food, induced by seasonal and habitat changes. He identified widgeon grass, *Ruppia maritima*, as the single most important waterfowl food in the Upper Chesapeake area with clasping leaf pondweed, *Potamogeton perfoliatus*, in second place. Other locally important food plants were wild celery *Vallisneria americana*, eelgrass *Zostera marina*, Olney three-square *Scirpus olneyi*, and dotted smartweed *Polygonum punctatum*. Canada geese, *Branta cana-*

Table 4.2. Fall and winter food of selected waterfowl from tidal marsh areas of the upper Chesapeake region. Derived from Stewart (1962), Tables 39, 61, 62, 67, and 88. Percentage occurrence of foods that made up 5 percent or more of the volume in individual birds. Figures in parentheses show 95 percent confidence limits.

	WATERFOWL				
FOOD ITEM	Canada Goose *Branta canadensis* Fresh and Brackish Marshes 10 Birds	Black Duck *Anas rubripes* Coastal Salt Marshes 6 Birds	Black Duck *Anas rubripes* Estuarine River Marshes 15 Birds	Gadwall *Anas strepera* Brackish Estuarine Bay Marshes 24 Birds	Widgeon *Anas americana* Brackish Estuarine Bay Marshes 50 Birds
ROOT STALKS AND STEMS OF EMERGENT MARSH PLANTS					
Scirpus olneyi	70 (34-94)		7 ($\pm$32)	8 (1-28)	8 (2-20)
S. americana — Three-square	60 (26-88)				
Distichlis spicata — Salt grass	20 (2-56)				4 ($\pm$14)
Spartina alterniflora — Salt marsh cordgrass	10 ($\pm$45)			8 (1-28)	4 ($\pm$14)
LEAVES, STEMS, ROOT STALKS OF SUBMERGED PLANTS					
Ruppia maritima — Widgeon grass	30 (6-66)	17 ($\pm$65)	7 ($\pm$32)	88 (67-98)	90 (78-97)
Potamogeton perfoliatus — Clasping leaf pond weed	30 (6-66)			67 (44-85)	72 (57-84)
Ulva lactuca — Sea lettuce		17 ($\pm$65)		8 (1-28)	
Ceratophyllum demersum — Coon tail			7 ($\pm$32)		
Elodea canadensis — Common water weed			7 ($\pm$32)	4 ($\pm$22)	
Zostera marina — Eel grass				17 (4-38)	
Chara sp. — Musk grass				12 (2-33)	28 (16-43)

Table 4.2. (continued)

		WATERFOWL			
FOOD ITEM	Canada Goose *Branta canadensis* Fresh and Brackish Marshes 10 Birds	Black Duck *Anas rubripes* Coastal Salt Marshes 6 Birds	Black Duck *Anas rubripes* Estuarine River Marshes 15 Birds	Gadwall *Anas strepera* Brackish Estuarine Bay Marshes 24 Birds	Widgeon *Anas americana* Brackish Estuarine Bay Marshes 50 Birds
Potamogeton pusillus Grass leaf pond weed				4 (±22)	
Myriophyllum pinnatum Pinnate water milfoil				4 (±22)	
Filamentous green algae				4 (±22)	2 (±11)
SEEDS					
Zea mays Corn	10 (±45)	33 (4–78)	93 (68–100)	25 (9–47)	8 (2–20)
Triticum aestivum Wheat	10 (±45)				
Scirpus americanus Common 3-square	20 (2–56)		7 (±32)		
Scirpus olneyi Olneyi 3-square	10 (±45)		7 (±32)		
Cladium mariscoides Twigrush	10 (±45)	17 (±65)		8 (1–28)	2 (±11)
Nyssa sylvatica Black gum					2 (±11)
Ruppia maritima Widgeon grass		33 (4–78)		8 (1–28)	2 (±11)
Spartina alterniflora Salt marsh cordgrass		17 (±65)		8 (1–28)	
Distichlis spicata Salt grass		17 (±65)			
Myrica pennsylvanica Bayberry		17 (±65)			6 (1–17)
Polygonum punctatum Dotted smartweed		60 (32–84)			
Polygonum arifolium Halberd-leaf tear thumb			27 (7–56)		

Pontederia cordata	Pickerel weed		20 (4–49)	
Polygonum sagittatum	Arrow-leaf tear thumb		13 (1–41)	
Zizania aquatica	Wild rice		13 (1–41)	
Sparganium americanum	Common burreed		13 (1–41)	
Sparganium eurycarpum	Giant burreed		13 (1–41)	
Peltandria virginica	Arrow arum		13 (1–41)	
Cephalanthus occidentalis	Button bush		7 (±32)	
Hibiscus moscheutos	Rose mallow		7 (±32)	
Ilex verticillata	Winter berry		7 (±32)	
Panicum sp.	Panicum		7 (±32)	
Potamageton perfoliatus	Clasping-leaf pond weed			4 (±22)
Eliocharis palustris	Common spike rush			2 (±11)
	Blackberry		7 (±32)	
	Smartweed		7 (±32)	
	Bulrush		7 (±32)	
ANIMAL FOOD				
Gastropoda	Snail	100(54–100)		4 (±22)
Melampus bidentatus	Coffee bean snail	67(22 –96)	7 (±32)	
		33(4–78)		
Geukensia demissa	Ribbed mussel	17 (±65)		
	Fish	17 (±65)	7 (±32)	4 (±22)
		17 (±65)		
Amphipoda			7 (±32)	
Coleoptera			7 (±32)	
Libelluloidea nymphs			7 (±32)	
Rissoidae			7 (±32)	

Table 4.3. Percentage composition of brent droppings indicating the monthly feeding pattern for 1956–7 and 1957–8 at Scolt Head Island, Norfolk. (T = trace) (From Ranwell and Downing, 1959, by permission of the editor, *Animal Behavior*.)

	Green algae (mainly Enteromorpha)		Puccinellia maritima		Zostera nana		Aster tripolium		Halimione portulacoides		Other dicots. (Mainly *Spergularia marginata, Armeria maritima,* and *Plantago maritima*)	
	1956-7	1957-8	1956-7	1957-8	1956-7	1957-8	1956-7	1957-8	1956-7	1957-8	1956-7	1957-8
November	—	47	—	3	—	32	—	0	—	18	—	T
December	83	95	0	T	17	5	0	T	0	0	T	T
January	87	24	6	38	4	6	3	21	0	T	T	11
February	57	6	10	46	0	0	33	36	0	0	T	12

densis, also ingest quantities of waste corn from the extensive agricultural areas adjacent to fresh and brackish embayments.

Ranwell and Downing (1959) studied feeding habits of the brent goose, *Branta bernicla,* at Scolt Head Island, Norfolk, England and concluded that this species lives mainly on a vegetable diet with traces of animal tissue (Table 4.3 and Figure 4.1). The feeding grounds of the brent goose are typically in the lower intertidal area where the mud surface is characteristically covered by a thin layer of water. There is a seasonality to the occupation of this feeding habitat. During the 1956–57 season, Ranwell and Downing (1959) reported a 30 percent reduction in *Zostera nana* cover and a 75 percent reduction in *Zostera hornemanniana* less than a month after the main flock had arrived. At the same time, *Enteromorpha* increased. By midwinter the *Enteromorpha* had been completely stripped but by spring, regrowth had occurred in the algae and the eel grass. Generally the same pattern was observed for the 1957–58 season except the geese went onto the high marsh in January 1958, nearly two months earlier than in the previous seasons, where they fed on *Puccinellia maritima* and *Aster tripolium.* These various observations led Ranwell and Downing to conclude that the brent goose fed primarily in the *Zostera* zone during the early winter, on *Enteromorpha* in midwinter and turned to the high marsh in early spring. While there was evidence the geese moved to the high marsh because of depleted supplies of *Zostera* and *Enteromorpha,* it was also evident the birds turned to *Enteromorpha* before the *Zostera* resources had been fully used up.

Brant are also common in the large flocks of waterfowl of the Chesapeake Bay marshes and those marshes further south in North Carolina and the Gulf states. While eel grass and widgeon grass are important food sources in the Chesapeake, sea lettuce, *Ulva lactuca,* has largely replaced the depleted eel grass beds in the open coastal areas of the winter feeding grounds.

Owen (1971) reported white-fronted geese were found to be highly selective along the river Severn, preferring the *Agrostis* zone to all others. As the season progressed, the geese moved into the higher zones occupying the *Lolium, Festuca, Hordeum,* and *Juncus* zones in that order. Selection of zones was not absolute; when large numbers of geese were present, all zones were occupied. Owen found some evidence that plants may be selected on the basis of protein, fiber, and carbohydrate content. *Puccinellia maritima* appeared to be preferred by geese over creeping bent grass, *Agrostis stolonifera* and red fescue, *Festuca rubra.* The geese also selected green grass rather than dead. In winter where the turf had 50 percent dead grass, the crops of birds examined contained over 95 percent green grass.

In studies concerned with widgeon conservation and marshland (salting pasture) management of Fenning Island in the Bridgwater Bay National

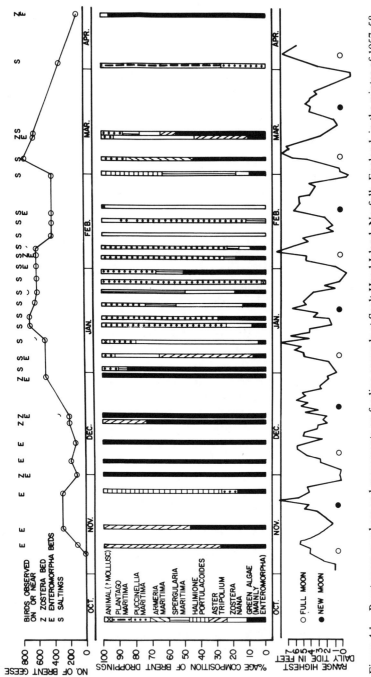

Figure 4.1. Brent geese numbers and movements on feeding grounds at Scolt Head Island, Norfolk, England, in the winter of 1957–58, together with the results of dropping analysis on 28 days. The bottom curve shows the range of highest daily tides recorded at Wells, 5 miles to the east of Scolt. (From Ranwell and Downing, 1959, by permission of the editor, *Animal Behavior*.)

Nature Reserve, Somerset, England, Cadwalladr *et al.* (1972) and Cadwalladr and Morley (1973, 1974) found both widgeon and sheep had a marked preference for the lower intertidal *Puccinellia maritima/Agrostis stolonifera* turf rather than the higher *Festuca rubra* sward. The *Festuca* sod tended to take on a rank, tussocky character which reduced its palatability. Unfortunately, increasing siltation rates favored *Festuca* while decreasing the amount of *Puccinellia/Agrostis* vegetation. The situation became more acute during dry or low-water years when the sheep were able to stay on the marsh well into the fall, thus further reducing the widgeon's winter food resources. However, this could be somewhat alleviated by close mowing the tussocky growth of red fescue which increased its palatability to a degree comparable to that of *Puccinellia/Agrostis.* Although Owen (1971) reported the widgeon used the *Festuca* zone extensively at Slimbridge, he attributed this to wariness since this zone was furthest from various forms of disturbance.

Plant seeds comprise the major portion of late summer-fall foods ingested by the sora rail, *Porzana carolina.* Wild rice, *Zizania aquatica,* made up 94 percent by volume and was found in all stomachs of the rail examined from a fresh tidal marsh in Connecticut while insects constituted 91 percent of the diet of birds taken from a brackish marsh meadow that did not provide the variety or quantity of seeds of the fresher tidal marsh (Webster, 1964). Fifty different food items were found in the stomachs of sora rails from the Patuxent River marshes of Maryland but only twelve made up more than 1 percent. Approximately 80 percent of the stomach volumes consisted of walter millet *Echinochloa walteri,* dotted smartweed *Polygonum punctatum,* halberd-leaf tear thumb *Polygonum arifolium,* and arrow-leaf tear thumb *Polygonum sagattatum.* Insects, mostly Orthoptera, made up 5 percent by volume and 14 percent by frequency (Meanley, 1965).

Meanley (1965) considered the red-wing blackbird, *Agelaius phoeniceus,* to be a serious competitor, limiting some foods for the sora rail. Meanley (1961) examined 130 red-wing blackbird stomachs and found thirteen different plant species with four marsh plants each making up more than one percent by volume. The most important were dotted smartweed, wild rice, walter millet, and halberd-leaf tear thumb, making up 77 percent by volume; corn comprised another 12 percent. These same species had the same frequency of occurrence. Meanley considered the ripening wild rice to reduce the pressure of bird foraging in adjacent corn fields. Insects played a minor role in red-wing blackbird diets in that beetles, grasshoppers and caterpillars made up five percent by volume.

Numerous references attest to the general grazing food habits of the muskrat, *Ondatra zibethica.* While it is primarily a herbivore, O'Neil (1949) and Dozier (1953) reported that the muskrat feeds on animal tissue in a minor and seasonal fashion including crayfish, crabs, mussels, snails, and

Table 4.4. Percent analyses of muskrat stomach contents and marsh plant composition. (From Stearns and Goodwin, 1941, derived from Tables 4 and 5, by permission of the editor, *J. Wildl. Mgmt.*)

Analysis	Muskrat Stomachs	Marsh Plants
Crude protein	9.97%	6.40%
Crude fiber	23.76%	29.74%
Ash	10.31%	6.74%
N-free extract	50.42%	51.78%

minnows. Earlier, Stearns and Goodwin (1941) had compared the percentages of crude protein, crude fiber, and ash content between the plant tops and roots and stomach contents, and inferred that, during the winter months, muskrats got a substantial quantity of protein from other than vegetable sources (Table 4.4). This author has trapped stream-living muskrats in New York State at feeding stations where the middens consisted solely of the empty shells of freshwater clams, Unionidae. Summer food is varied, consisting of leaves and roots of many aquatic plants (Harris, 1937; Dozier, 1953). Several authors (Harris, 1937, 1939; Dozier *et al.*, 1948; O'Neil, 1949) have called attention to food habits changing with salinity. The various species of *Scirpus, Typha* and *Spartina cynosuroides* are primary foods in many of the fresher and brackish marshes. Dozier *et al.* (1948) have reported the heaviest muskrats taken from marshes dominated by these plant species where the salinity range is 0.0–5.0%$_{00}$. In the more saline areas the animals consume *Spartina alterniflora* and, when pressed, turn to *Spartina patens* (Harris, 1939).

In the fresher Louisiana delta marshes, the most important food plants were cattail, *Typha*, 70 percent; alligator grass *Alternanthera philoxeroides* and giant reedgrass *Phragmites communis*, each 5 percent. In the brackish subdelta marshes, *S. olneyi* made up 80 percent, *Spartina patens* 10 percent, and *Spartina cynosuroides* 5 percent while, in the subdelta fresh marshes, the canouche *Panicum hemitomum* composed 70 percent, *Typha* 10 percent, *Phragmites* 10 percent, *Sagittaria, Scirpus californicus* and *Scirpus validus* 5 percent and animal matter 5 percent (O'Neil, 1949).

Relatively little is known about the food habits of other mammals that can be found on the marsh surface. The one exception is the rabbit, and its food habits and impact on English tide-marsh vegetation have already been discussed in the preceding chapter. No obvious work is known in regard to the food habits of North American rabbits on tidal marshes. The meadow vole, *Microtus pennsylvanicus,* is deemed to be herbivorous, feeding on *Spartina* stems whose leaf fragments, with neatly cut ends, have been found at feeding stations adjacent to runways on the marsh surface.

Both quantitative examination and frequency indices displayed seasonal food habit patterns for the Norway rat, *Rattus norvegicus,* on the Bridgwater marsh in England (Drummond, 1960). Seventeen of the 25 common plants and all 17 of the occasional or rare plants (except perhaps *Atriplex patula*) were apparently not eaten by the rats. *Spartina* was eaten all year, mainly the lower parts of the stems, leaving the rest to form a bank of debris along the tide line. Since *Spartina maritima* showed no evidence of damage, it was presumed *Spartina townsendii* was the *Spartina* eaten. Seeds of dicotyledons were eaten in the fall and, as might be expected, insects and crustacea were least evident in the winter period. The rhizomes of *Aster tripolium* were apparently attractive during the winter as this was the only dicotyledon that showed damage. Vertebrate animal tissue in the diet seemed to be confined to dead birds washed ashore. There was little evidence of duck nests (mallard, *Anas platyrhynchos*) being disturbed. The sand hopper, *Orchestia gammarella,* was the most frequently ingested crustacean. Wood lice, particularly *Armadillidium vulgare,* were common but there was no evidence of their being eaten by the rats. The ground beetles, Carabidae, were the most frequently ingested insects. The rat is primarily herbivorous in that it eats *Spartina* throughout the year, supplemented by other foods.

Predators. The predacious arthropods can be divided into two groups: those that feed on solid tissues primarily and those that suck out the body fluids of their prey (Davis and Gray, 1966). In the tidal marsh habitat, the first group includes the dragon flies such as *Erythrodiplax berenice* and *Erythemis simplicicollis.* The malachiid beetle, *Collops nigriceps,* was observed by Davis and Gray to feed on injured flies. The clerid beetles *Isohydnocera tabida* and *I. aegra* (from *S. alterniflora* and *S. patens* marshes respectively) and the coccinellid *Naemia serriata* (from *Distichlis*) were assumed to be predacious as other members of these two families are predacious in other habitats. A more recent study (Meany *et al.,* 1976) demonstrated that the larvae of the greenhead fly, *Tabanus nigrovittatus,* feed on most soft-bodied animals in tidal marsh sod. These larvae were observed to feed on dolichopodid fly larvae, *Chrysops fuliginosus* larvae, hydrophilid beetle larvae as well as the amphipod *Orchestia grillus.* They did not attack the larvae of stratimyiids (Diptera) nor the snail *Melampus bidentatus.* Cannibalism appears to be important in the reduction in numbers and spacing of tabinid larvae in the field; laboratory observed numbers from $80–204/m^2$ to $40–120/m^2$. It was not readily apparent whether or not cannibalism among larval tabanids serves to adjust the population density to the available prey.

The second group of predacious arthropods includes the asilid flies that prey upon grasshoppers, the midges and mosquitos, the reduviids, *Doldina interjungens, Sinea diadema, Zelus cervicalis* and the nabid *Nabis capsil-*

formis. They are widely distributed throughout the high marsh zone but are not abundant (Davis and Gray, 1966). Payne (1972) identified the predacious habits of the damsel bug, *Dolichonabis lineatus* (Hem. Nabidae), which fed on *Euscelis obsoletus* (Hem. Cicadellidae) in the Poole Harbour marsh, Dorset.

Spiders are important arthropod predators in the salt marshes (Barnes, 1953; Marples and Odum, 1964; Davis and Gray, 1966). *Lycosa modesta* was by far the most abundant species in the *Spartina* drift line at Beaufort, North Carolina while the second most important spider *Clubiona nicholsi* was never found outside that particular habitat (Barnes and Barnes, 1954). Davis and Gray observed that spiders usually outnumber carnivorous insects in all types of marshes except *Distichlis*. McMahan *et al.* (1972) noted more spiders in a sewage-treated marsh and attributed this to an increase in herbivorous insects which could result from increased grass growth but whose numbers were held in check by increased spider predation.

Very few fish species are restricted to the tidal marsh habitat. Harrington and Harrington (1961) characterized the cyprinodontiform fishes as being "area" residents, i.e., *Fundulus heteroclitus, F. confluentus, Gambusia affinis, Lucania parva, Cyprinodon variegatus,* etc. Daiber (1962) and Lotrich (1975) found *Fundulus heteroclitus* and *Cyprinodon variegatus* as marsh surface and stream bank residents in Delaware marshes. Various fish species are found in the tidal streams; some come and go with the ebb and flow of the tides while dissimilar ones like *Morone americana* are typical residents during the summer months, moving downstream with cold weather (Daiber, 1962). Others, like the young-of-the-year menhaden, may take up residence in a particular tidal stream such as Canary Creek, Delaware, for one period but not necessarily year after year.

Further south, juvenile tarpon, *Megalops atlantica,* are residents of pools and creeks of Sapelo Island, Georgia marshes. They characteristically feed on *Gambusia affinis* and *Poecilia latipinna* and those over 76 millimeters S.L. ingest *Palaemonetes,* the size of food consumed being directly related to fish size. Typically, a resident population of young tarpon appear in late spring-early summer, grow about 3 centimeters/month, and leave the marshes in October. Rickards (1968) described the outcome of a group of juvenile tarpon that appeared in September 1964, presumably swept ashore by Hurricane Dora. This second group grew half as fast as the first group, apparently because of reduced water temperatures, and the *Gambusia* and *Poecilia* had grown too large to be eaten. This second assemblage succumbed to cold and starvation.

The bay anchovy *Anchoa mitchilli,* Atlantic silverside *Menidia menidia,* and the white perch *Morone americana* have a much greater habitat distribution than tidal marshes, and their food habits reflect such distributions.

The anchovy is a zooplankton feeder (Stevenson, 1958), ingesting such organisms suspended in the water column. One might presume it is more actively feeding during the day since Moore (1968) recorded it would normally be the only species taken with *Menidia menidia* during the daylight hours; at night many more species would be acquired in beach seine collections. Moore observed *M. menidia* to display diurnal feeding activity, judging from the quantity of stomach contents over 24-hour collection periods, with more food ingested during the daylight hours. Moore also perceived *Menidia* to feed on whatever was available, noting seasonal changes in the diet. Horseshoe crab (*Limulus polyphemus*) eggs and larvae were fed on most heavily in June and July; isopods in August; amphipods and *Neomysis americana* in September and October; and by November and December *N. americana* and copepods were dominant.

Neomysis americana ranked first in relative mass and frequency of occurrence for items ingested by the white perch: polychaete worm remains, *Cerebratulus* sp., *Crangon septemspinosus* and *Fundulus heteroclitus* were ranked two through five respectively for relative mass. On the basis of frequency, organic debris, amphipods, polychaete worm remains, and *Cerebratulus* sp. ranked two through five respectively. *F. heteroclitus* was the most frequently recorded fish in the white perch stomachs with a frequency ranking of thirteen. Polychaete worms were frequently observed in the water column at night and this apparently accounted for their abundance in the perch diet. Other items tended to be more sporadic and seasonally abundant, such as horseshoe crab eggs and larvae (Miller, 1963).

An abrupt tidal-pluvial flooding of a drought-stricken tidal wetland along the shore of Indian River, Florida provided Harrington and Harrington (1961) an opportunity to distinguish between the food habits of "area resident" fishes (cyprinodontiforms) and "transients" (immigrant young of large species). Various mosquito species had continued to deposit their eggs on the marsh surface while fish species became progressively excluded from the wetland as the drought intensified. With the sudden flooding of the marsh, there was a simultaneous hatching of mosquito eggs and invasion of fish onto the marsh surface. The pooled gut contents of 2786 fish were by volume: 35.7 percent plant material, 23.8 percent *Aedes* mosquitos, 14.6 percent copepods, 12.5 percent fishes (mostly neonate *Gambusia* and *Mollienesia*), 7.8 percent *Palaemonetes intermedius*. The remaining 5 percent comprised 69 of the 83 categories of food identified.

Based on food volume percentages and frequencies of occurrence, Harrington and Harrington ranked the following fishes as (1) herbivores: *Mollienesia, Mugil, Cyprinodon;* (2) plankton eaters: *Megalops, Diapterus, Lucania, Elops, Mugil;* (3) larvivores: *Fundulus confluentus, Gambusia, Lucania, Cyprinodon, Molliensia, F. grandis;* (4) piscivores: *Centropomus, Elops, Me-*

Table 4.5. Main feeding trends among fishes on the Indian River, Florida marsh. (From Harrington and Harrington, 1961, by permission of the editor, *Ecology*)

STENOPHAGUS	EURYPHAGUS	The Principal Fish Species Invading the Salt Marsh	LARVIVOROUS	HERBIVOROUS	PISCIVOROUS	NON-PISCIVOROUS	PLANKTON-EATING
		AREA RESIDENTS (Common to Abundant)					
—	X	*Lucania parva*	X	—	—	X	X
—	X	*Fundulus confluentus*	X	—	—	—	—
—	X	*Fundulus grandis*	X	—	—	—	—
X	—	*Cyprinodon variegatus*	X	X	—	X	—
—	X	*Gambusia affinis*	X	—	—	—	(X)
X	—	*Mollienesia latipinna*	X	X	—	X	—
		TRANSIENTS (Common)					
X	—	*Elops saurus*	—	—	X	—	X
X	—	*Megalops atlantica*	—	—	X	—	X
X	—	*Mugil cephalus*	(X)	X	—	X	(X)
X	—	*Centropomus undeci-malis*	—	—	X	—	(X)

galops. *Lucania, Cyprinodon, Mollienesia, Mugil,* and *Diapterus* ate no fish. General feeders were *Gambusia, Fundulus confluentus, F. grandis* and *Lucania* while restricted feeders were *Centropomus, Elops, Megalops, Mollienesia, Diapterus, Mugil,* and *Cyprinodon* (Table 4.5).

The "transient" fishes did not avail themselves of the abundant mosquitos as they hatched. Only the juvenile *Mugil* included mosquitos with copepods and plant material, turning to the latter as the mosquitos disappeared. *Elops saurus, Megalops atlantica,* and *Centropomus undecimalis* continued to feed on copepods, fishes, and shrimp with a size-related progression in that order.

The "area residents" turned to other foods only after the departure of the mosquitos. During their abundance, mosquitos contributed to total food volumes as follows: *Fundulus grandis,* 94.8 percent; *F. confluentus,* 85.5 percent; *Gambusia,* 78.7 percent; *Lucania,* 72.8 percent; *Cyprinodon,* 57.3 percent; *Mollienesia,* 52.3 percent. After depletion of the mosquito swarms, *Lucania parva* turned chiefly to copepods, *Cyprinodon variegatus* and *Mollienesia latipinna* turned to plant material while *Gambusia affinis, Fundulus confluentus,* and *F. grandis* consumed a variety of foods.

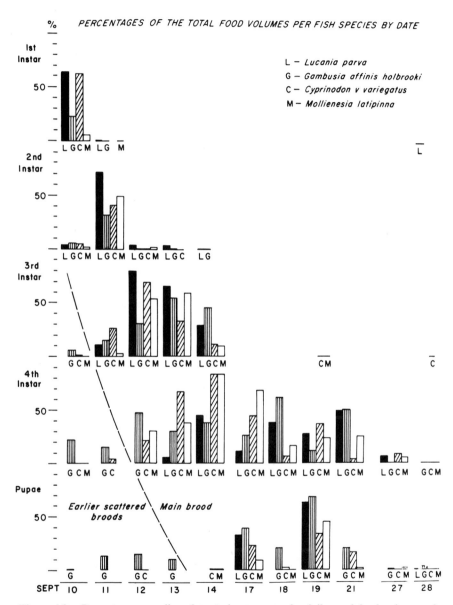

Figure 4.2. Percentages contributed to *Aedes* stages to the daily total food volumes of *Lucania parva* (black bars), *Gambusia affinis* (cross-hatched bars), *Cyprinodon variegatus* (single-hatched bars), and *Mollienesia latipinna* (white bars). (From Harrington and Harrington, 1961, by permission of the editor, *Ecology.*)

Harrington and Harrington (1961) suggested the "area residents" are and must be very responsive, being able to adjust to changes in water level and to exploit newly available food resources. Although these larvivores converged on mosquitos, there was more than enough and the proportions consumed among the various mosquito life stages suggested there was reduced competition among these fishes (Figure 4.2). Once the mosquitos were gone these same fishes turned to other food types, again maintaining a reduced species interaction. The authors also suggested that habitat selections, home range characteristics, and general behavior would also foster larvivore segregation. In contrast, the "transients" had a restricted responsiveness in that they did not exploit a sudden and abundant source of food but continued to ingest their usual food items.

Harrington and Harrington (1961) reported a good correlation between size of mosquito larvae and fish size: small fish ate more instars 1–3 while larger fish consumed more 4th-instar larvae. There was no correlation between fish size and pupae which was more an exercise of species preference (Table 4.6).

A recent study by Vince *et al.* (1976) on the Great Sippewissett marsh, Falmouth, Massachusetts, demonstrated that *Fundulus heteroclitus* predation on *Melampus bidentatus* and *Orchestia grillus* can influence the abundance and size distribution of the prey species. Laboratory feeding trials showed that the maximum size of the prey consumed increased with increasing size of the predator (Table 4.7). The 4–6 centimeter *Fundulus* fed mainly on the smallest amphipods, the 6–8 centimeter fish fed nearly equally on the small and medium *Orchestia* while the largest fish fed on all size classes but to a greater degree on the medium- and large-size amphipods. *Melampus* larger than 7 millimeters in shell height were not consumed and only the largest *Fundulus* fed on the medium size (4–7 millimeters)

Table 4.6. The percentages contributed by each mosquito stage to the pooled food volumes of fish at different length classes regardless of species (includes 400 each of *Lucania, Cyprinodon, Gambusia, Mollienesia*). (From Harrington and Harrington, 1961, by permission of the editor, *Ecology*)

Standard Lengths (mm)	5–15	16–25	26–35	36–45	46–60	5–60
Numbers of Fish	327	761	381	98	33	1600
Instar I	6	6	Trace	Trace	None	2
Instar II	9	4	3	1	Trace	3
Instar III	25	10	9	8	3	9
Instar IV	10	12	23	18	13	18
Pupae	6	9	6	6	1	6
Total *Aedes*	57	41	42	32	17	38

Table 4.7. Percentage of prey consumed ($\pm$ S.E.) by three size-classes of *Fundulus heteroclitus*. (From Vince et al., 1976, by permission of the editor, J. Exp. Mar. Biol. Ecol.)

Fundulus Total Length (cm)	Prey Species	Number of Trials	Prey size Classes		
			Small	Medium	Large
4–6	*Orchestia*	8	75.0 ± 8.2	25.0 ± 12.3	0.0
6–8	*Orchestia*	8	78.6 ± 8.5	83.9 ± 7.1	26.8 ± 8.8
8–10	*Orchestia*	8	67.2 ± 8.5	95.3 ± 4.7	89.1 ± 6.4
4–5	*Melampus*	6	90.0 ± 6.8	0.0	0.0
5–7	*Melampus*	9	92.8 ± 2.5	3.9 ± 2.8	0.0
7–9	*Melampus*	5	92.5 ± 4.6	25.5 ± 6.6	0.0

snails. The authors considered the size of the mouth gape to be an important factor since the prey were ingested whole.

Large, well-spaced plants characteristic of the low marsh and small, closely-spaced plants of the high marsh influenced predator movement. The spatial arrangement of the high marsh reduced the foraging capabilities of *Fundulus* which had been able to move freely among the plants of the low marsh. Vince *et al.* (1976) found only large *Melampus* in the low marsh and large *Orchestia* were more abundant on the high marsh. Only when *Fundulus* was excluded from plots on both the low and high areas were small *Melampus* observed to survive and grow. The natural fencing characteristics of high-marsh vegetation enhanced survival of large amphipods in such a marsh habitat. When excluding *Fundulus,* they noted a greater increase in amphipod density in the low compared to the high marsh as well as differences in amphipod size distributions between the two marsh zones. The authors concluded that *Fundulus* predation was more severe in the low marsh.

There have been varied analyses of the food habits of *F. heteroclitus.* Some authors (Schmelz, 1964; Jeffries, 1972) consider the mummichog to be a detritus feeder. A few (Harrington and Harrington, 1961; Nixon and Oviatt, 1973; Prinslow *et al.,* 1974; Vince *et al.,* 1976) considered it to be a predator consuming a variety of animal foods, including mosquito larvae, snails and amphipods, harpacticoid copepods, *Palaeomonetes,* and juvenile fish from the marsh surface. Jeffries (1972) compared the fatty acid composition of both live and dead marsh-plant tissues to the digestive tract contents and body tissues of *F. heteroclitus, F. majalis,* and the shrimp *Palaemonetes pugio.* He found the plants to have a terrestrial pattern rich in 16–18 carbon fatty acids while the animals were characterized by a marine pattern dominated by longer chain fatty acids (20–22C). On the basis of these observations, Jeffries reasoned that the diet of *F. heteroclitus* and *F. majalis* could consist of a 2.38 to 1 mixture of fatty acids from detritus and *Palaemonetes* or a weight ratio about five parts detritus to one part of invertebrate tissue.

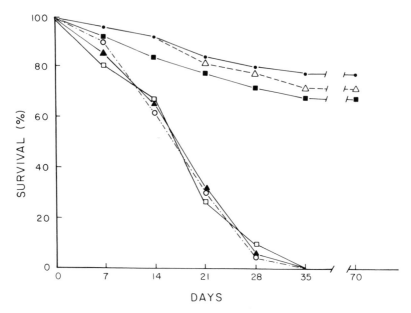

Figure 4.3.   Percent survival of *F. heteroclitus* over 70 days, fed Animal (A) •————•; Plant (P) ▲————▲; Detritus (D) o—·—·o; Animal + Detritus (AD) △-----△; Animal + Plant + Detritus (APD) ■————■; and Starvation control (S) □————□ (From Fig. 1, Katz, 1975.)

He also concluded that this would be a maximum condition to account for the distributions found in the digestive tracts of both fish.

Both Prinslow *et al.* (1974) and Katz (1975) have evaluated the potential contribution of detritus to the growth and maintenance of *F. heteroclitus*. Prinslow *et al.* found no significant effect of additions of detritus on growth rates or conversion efficiencies when more than five times as much detritus (dry weight) was added to a commercial food. However, the addition of detritus to the food did significantly increase the retainment of nitrogen by the fish, suggesting that detritus was an additional source of nitrogen. Further, the greater amount (27.6 percent) of ash in starved fish receiving detritus than those without (22.6 percent) was interpreted as an expression of the inadequacy of detritus in the diet of *F. heteroclitus*.

An examination of Figure 4.3 and Table 4.8 demonstrates the survival value and growth capabilities of an animal diet. Those fish with a full ration of animal tissue had the best survival and specific growth rate per day. When fed the same amount of ration composed of equal amounts of detritus and/or plant material, both survival and growth rate were depressed. Even though they survived the duration of the experiment (70 days), those fish

Table 4.8. Summary of Mean Specific Growth Rates (G) and Production of *F. heteroclitus* fed diets of Animal (A); Plant (P); Detritus (D); Animal + Detritus (AD); Animal + Plant + Detritus (APD) and Starvation Control (S). (From Table 2, Katz, 1975)

Group	Replicate	G_1	# of Fish	G_2	# of Fish	G_3	# of Fish	G_4	# of Fish	G_5	# of Fish	G_T	P(gm)
I (A)	1	1.01	32	-0.04	24	0.5	18	0.94	13	1.13	8	0.73	8.6
	2											0.69	31.7
IV (AD)	1	-0.17	35	0.17	26	0.25	20	0.16	14	0.01	9	0.17	-3.4
	2											0.15	4.0
VI (APD)	1	0	34	-0.36	27	0.05	19	-0.09	12	0.04	6	-0.14	-7.9
	2											-0.16	-1.5
II (P)		-0.881	20	-0.79	4							-0.83	
III (D)		-1.29	25	-0.25	5							-0.77	
V (S)		-1.12	24	-0.47	3							-0.79	

$G_{1,2,3,4,5}$ = Specific growth rate/day $\times$ 100 over individual 2-week periods.
G_T = Specific growth rate/day over total 70-day period.
P = Production in gms over 70-day period.

whose ration was one-third animal tissue had a negative rate of growth (Table 4.8). Feeding plant material or detritus to *F. heteroclitus* was equivalent to starving them. Not only did they not survive beyond 35 days, they also sustained a negative individual growth rate (Katz, 1975). It is evident from the foregoing that *F. heteroclitus* cannot subsist for any length of time on appreciable amounts of detritus. As Harrington and Harrington (1961) and Vince *et al.* (1976) pointed out, the mummichog is an active predator, having to ingest sizable amounts of food to meet metabolic needs. Prinslow *et al.* (1974) and Katz (1975) portrayed moderately low conversion efficiencies with maximum values something less than 10 percent at about 13 °C for the former investigations and 15 percent of body weight/day at 20 °C recorded by Katz.

A similar response has been observed for the glass shrimp *Palaemonetes* wherein neither *P. pugio* or *P. vulgaris* larvae survived a diet of unicellular algae (Broad, 1957a). The larvae of both species lived through molts if fed a diet including animal tissue. The frequency of molts was accelerated from an average of 3.7 days to 2.5 days for *P. pugio* when fed a diet of only animal tissue. When fed living *Artemia* those larvae molted at an average frequency of 2.4 days. *P. vulgaris* followed the same pattern, taking 2.67 days when fed living *Artemia*. Thus the frequency of molts, rate of development, and time to metamorphosis was influenced by the kind of diet: quantities of plant material tending to retard those processes while living animal diet hastened the process.

While there are a few reptiles associated with tidal marshes, there is little literature directed at this group in such a habitat. A few references (Lay and O'Neil, 1942; O'Neil, 1949; Palmisano, 1972) concerned with Gulf of Mexico coastal marshes identify the alligator, *Alligator mississippiensis,* as a muskrat predator with O'Neil ranking it as fourth in this capacity. Presumably the alligator also feeds on fishes living in the pot holes and drainage ditches utilized by this reptile. While the diamondback terrapin, *Malaclemys terrapin,* has become a common sight of some tidal streams, little is known about its life history, movements, and food habits. Recent mark and recapture studies carried out by Dr. L. Hurd of the University of Delaware indicated a large stable population derived from the ingestion of the blue mussel, *Mytilus edulis,* and other invertebrates (personal communication). Lay (1945) identified the water moccasin, *Agkistrodon piscivorus,* as consuming considerable numbers of muskrat during the warm months in Jackson marsh, Texas. One would wonder about the magnitude of such predation when fish would be abundant.

Considerable information is becoming available on the predator food habits of the various birds associated with marshes (Wiese and Smith-Kenneally, 1977). The great blue heron *Ardea herodias,* green heron *Butorides virescens,* great egret *Casmerodins albus,* and snowy egret *Egretta thula* are common sights in the mid-Atlantic marshes and elsewhere. Since much of their diet is fish, and since they stalk their prey in the shallows and the edges of the streams, they will be fishing for the cyprinidontiform fishes such as *Fundulus* and *Cyprinodon.* Bent (1963, after Audubon, 1840) recorded the great blue heron as destroying large numbers of young marsh-hens and rails. He also identified the snowy egret's preference for shrimp along the edges of the more southern marshes as well as fiddler crabs, snails, and aquatic insects.

The food habits for the willet, *Catoptrophorus semipalmatus,* and the clapper rail, *Rallus longirostris,* consist of aquatic insects, marine worms, small crabs and molluscs, fish fry and small fish picked up from the marsh surface among the plant stems of ditch and creek banks (Bent, 1929, 1963). An examination of the northern clapper rail, *Rallus l. longirostris,* and Wayne's clapper rail, *R. l. waynei,* collected from the Georgia coastal marshes revealed that the marsh crabs, *Sesarma cinereum* and *S. reticulatum,* comprised the greatest volume of the gizzards while *Uca* was next most important. All other prey were in lesser amounts (Oney, 1954) (Table 4.9).

Table 4.9. Gizzard content of 284 clapper rail (*Rallus l. longirostris* and *R. l. waynei*) collected in October and November 1947 from the Georgia coastal marshes. (Modified from Oney, 1954)

Organism	Percent Volume	Percent Occurrence
Crabs		
Sesarma cinereum	33	58
Sesarma reticulatum	15	37
Sesarma sp.	6	17
Uca sp.	14	45
Eurytium limosum	3	17
Panopeus herbstii	1	1
Unidentified crabs	2	7
Callinectes sp. and Pinnotheridae	Trace	
Snails		
Littorina irrorata	14	37
Melampus sp., *Nassarius obsoleta, Polygyra*	Traces	
Insects		
Phalaenidae (=Noctuidae)	6	12
Other insects	3	—
Clams, Molulidae, Clam worm *Nereis* sp.	Trace	
Shrimp, *Peneus setiferus* and *Palaemonetes* sp.	Trace	
Spiders, *Lycosa* sp. and *Clubiona* sp.	Trace	
Fish, Poeciliidae and *Fundulus* sp.	Trace	
Plants, *Spartina,* mainly *S. alterniflora*	Trace	
	97%	

The king rail, *Rallus elegans,* and Virginia rail, *R. limicola,* have a more varied diet than the salt-water clapper rail, a reflection of their brackish and fresh-water habitat. While the clapper rail is restricted to saline habitats, the king and Virginia rails have a much more extensive geographic range, extending into midcontinent fresh-water marshes. The diet of the Virginia rail is strictly carnivorous (Bent, 1963). Crustaceans and aquatic insects are the preferred food of the king rail in most areas. Fish, frogs, grasshoppers, crickets, and seeds of aquatic plants are frequently taken. The king rail will ingest greater quantities of vegetable material than the clapper rail; examples are black gum *Nyssa sylvatica,* pine *Pinus* sp., waxmyrtle *Myrica cerifera,* bayberry *Myrica carolinus* seeds, and acorns *Quercus* (Meanley, 1969). Along the Choptank River in Maryland, one bird was observed to feed only on fish while another king rail ingested an assortment including the seeds of arrow-arum, hackberry *Celtis occidentalis,* halberd-leaf tear thumb *Polygonum arifolium,* dogwood *Cornus florida,* grape *Vitis* sp., crayfish, and a snail. Sunfish (Centrarchidae) and yellow perch (Percidae) were important items in 17 birds from Currituck Sound, North Carolina. Examination of six birds from the Patuxent River, Maryland, revealed an assortment including *Fundulus heteroclitus,* crayfish, dragonfly nymphs, snails (*Amnicola* sp.), grasshoppers and crickets, leaves of *Scirpus* and rice-cutgrass, seeds of dotted smartweed, halberd-leaf tear thumb, arrow-leafed tear thumb *Polygonum sagittatum,* burreed *Sparganium eurycarpum,* water parsnip *Sium sauve,* silky dogwood *Cornus amomum,* and wild cherry *Prunus.*

In some parts of its range, particularly in brackish water habitats, the king rail will concentrate on a single food item. Several hundred observations by Meanley (1969) during 1959–61 along Delaware Bay revealed *Uca minax* as the main food item with the clam *Macoma balthica* being the only other food ingested.

Passeriformes associated with coastal marshes included the long-billed marsh wren, *Telmatodytes palustris griseus,* the San Francisco song sparrow, *Melospiza melodia samuelis,* the eastern savannah sparrow, *Passerculus sandwichensis savanna,* the seaside sparrows, *Ammospiza maritima,* and the sharp-tailed sparrows, *Ammospiza caudacuta.* The long-billed wren, the northern seaside sparrow and the eastern sharp-tailed sparrows are identified as being primarily carnivores (Marshall, 1948; Kale, 1965; G. Woolfendin and N. Hill *in* Bent *et al.,* 1968). Hymenoptera and spiders were the most frequent food items for the wren during the breeding season while fulgorid homopterans and ants (Hymenoptera) were most abundant in the winter diet. Fulgorids comprised over 40 percent by volume in winter stomachs while ants and spiders comprised 25 percent by volume of breeding season stomachs (Kalle, 1965).

The sharp-tailed and seaside sparrows are considered to be the salt-marsh representatives of the Fringillidae, being very much restricted to this habitat. The eastern and coastal savannah sparrows are associated with tidal marshes but various subspecies are widely distributed among other habitats. Over 80 percent of the diet of the northern seaside sparrow, *Ammospiza m. maritima,* consists of marine insects, small crabs, and snails. Some plant material is consumed but the conical bill implies a more insectivorous diet (Bent *et al.,* 1968). Kale (1965) characterized the wren feeding on animals living on the *Spatina* stems while the seaside sparrows fed primarily from the ground surface. Animal tissue comprised 80–100 percent of the diet of the eastern sharp-tailed sparrow, *Ammospiza c. caudacuta,* more so than other sparrows. Reviewing earlier observations, Bent *et al.* (1968) recorded Hymenoptera 3 percent, Coleoptera 6 percent, Orthoptera 7 percent, Lepidoptera 14 percent, Hemiptera 12 percent, Diptera 5 percent, miscellaneous insects 8 percent, amphipods, arachnids, small snails 20 percent.

In contrast to the carnivorous diet of the other marsh sparrows, Bent *et al.* (1968) identified the eastern savannah sparrow as having herbivorous food habits, largely grass seeds. A year-round examination from a variety of habitats produced an average of 54 percent plant material and 46 percent animal. In terms of animal food, this sparrow seemed to have a predilection for insects, particularly beetles. Another food study reviewed by Baird (*in* Bent *et al.,* 1968) portrayed insects largely in the summer with plant food at 92 percent in winter, 63 percent in spring, 26 percent in summer, and 84 percent in the fall.

The marsh hawk, *Circus cyaneus hudsonius,* has a very wide geographic distribution and is often seen quartering over open grassy areas including coastal marshes. This hawk displays varied food habits, eating what is readily available in whatever geographic location. Various reviewers (Bent, 1937; Sprunt, 1955; Craighead and Craighead, 1956) have concluded that this bird is generally beneficial. It has been considered to have been an effective control of bobolinks, *Dolichonyx oryzivorus,* in South Carolina rice fields (Sprunt, 1955) and has been recorded as feeding on marsh rabbits, *Sylvilagus palustris,* and cotton rats, *Sigmodon hispidus* (Bent, 1937; Sprunt, 1955). Craighead and Craighead (1956) found small mammals made up 98.4 percent of winter food habits after examining 2311 pellets from 48 birds. The meadow mouse, *Microtus pennsylvanicus,* comprised 93.2 percent of the total. This study was carried out in Superior Township, Michigan, but since the marsh hawk is a frequent sight gliding over coastal marshes and, since *Microtus* is a common small mammal on these marshes (Harris, 1953; Fisler, 1965a; Shure, 1971), one could presume the hawk is feeding on the vole from tidal marshes (see Table 4.10). Lay (1945) identified the marsh hawk as a common winter predator on muskrats in the Jackson marsh of Texas.

An examination of 22 stomachs taken in the fall indicated the rice rat,

Table 4.10. Data and percentage of occurrence of meadow voles, rice rats and unidentified small mammals in Dorchester County, Maryland. Some remains of either rice rats or meadow voles could not be distinguished and they make up much of the unidentified category. (From Table 3, Harris, 1953, by permission of the editor, J. Mamm.)

Species	Material Examined	Source of Data		Habitat	Analysis Percent Material Containing		
		Number Examined	Dates of Collection		Microtus	Oryzomys	Other
Raccoon	Stomach	150	7/49–5/51	Marsh and vicinity	13.3	3.3	8.7
Red fox	Stomach	17	7/49–6/51	Marsh and vicinity	47.1	5.9	5.9
Raccoon	Scat	301	11/49–6/51	Marsh	17.6	4.0	4.3
Red fox	Scat	103	11/49–6/51	Marsh	49.6	4.8	8.7
Barn owl	Pellets	130	2/50–4/51	Marsh and edge	71.5	26.9	6.0
Marsh hawk (?)	Pellets	79	11/49–6/51	Marsh	73.4	15.2	3.8

Table 4.11. Analysis of 95 red fox scats collected on the Blackwater marshes, Dorchester County, Maryland. (From Table 2, Heit, 1944, by permission of the editor, J. Mamm.)

	Occurrences	Percent	Frequency
Mammals	93		97.8
Microtus	47	49.4	
Ondatra zibethica	37	38.9	
Sylvilagus	11	11.5	
Peromyscus	6	6.3	
Oryzomys	1	1.0	
Undetermined small mammals	13	13.6	
Birds	18		18.9
Insects	9		9.4
Seeds	10		10.5

Oryzomys palustris, to be primarily a carnivore, ingesting chiefly insects and small crabs with some plant material. While the numbers of rice rats were not abundant enough to have an impact on the crab and insect populations, Sharp (1967) considered the rats to be an important predator on the eggs and young of the marsh wren. Rats held in captivity showed a preference for animal food, ate more and put on greater weight gains, yet Sharp postulated that rats could utilize grasses as efficiently as animal tissue. Schantz (1943) reported muskrat pelt damage attributed to the rice rat during winter trapping in Delaware.

The meadow vole and rice rat fall prey to a number of predators (Tables 4.10 and 4.11). The higher incidence of rice rats in the barn owl (*Tyto alba*) pellets suggests nocturnal habits of the rice rat.

Heit (1944) noted the vole made up a substantial portion of the red fox diet and were present throughout his study period. Mice varied with time and the availability of muskrats. The latter were more frequently taken in June and July than the field mice. The frequency of occurrence of *Microtus* and *Ondatra,* respectively, for March 10 was 50 and 50 percent; for April 14, 66 and 20 percent; for May 3, 100 and 33 percent; June 7, 43 and 71 percent; July 25, 12 and 64 percent; August 6, 67 and 17 percent. The fox did not travel in the marsh during the winter months, confining food searching to the drier uplands. Heit attributed the greater consumption of muskrats in June-July to a combination of factors: (1) with the drying of the marsh those muskrats in drier areas would become easier prey, and (2) the first litter of muskrats would begin to wander about and would be easier prey than the vole. It was also presumed the fox would find it more efficient to capture one muskrat than expend the energy to capture the equivalent amount of food in

12–15 field mice. The great number of muskrats captured could be a reflection of the foxes taking advantage of a very abundant food supply. The fact that some foxes had dens on islands in the marshes would lend support to this idea (Heit, 1944).

The raccoon is identified as a common predator in tidal marshes (Lay, 1945; Harris, 1953), preying on mice and muskrats. Harris (1953) suggested the muskrat attracts the raccoon, *Procyon lotor,* to occupied houses and, in the process of digging out the muskrat, the vole is encountered in the house wall. O'Neil (1949) ranked raccoon second as a muskrat predator behind the mink, *Mustela vison.* O'Neil deemed muskrats could withstand predation in a good quality *Scirpus olneyi* marsh due to productive capacity but, in poorer quality marshes, predation would be a problem. Day *et al.* (1973, after Bateman, 1965) characterized the raccoon as feeding on a variety of marsh items including rail eggs, with crabs and *Geukensia demissa* being the most important. Varying amounts of plant material are ingested.

Due to the varied food habits of the raccoon, one would expect it to prey on various waterfowl and marsh birds. Stewart (1962) considered it to be an important predator on Chesapeake Bay waterfowl. Raccoon were involved in 39 percent of the waterfowl nests destroyed by predators in a managed marsh bordering western Lake Erie (Urban, 1970).

Fish have been recorded as the main food items for both the mink and the otter, *Lutra canadensis.* In an attempt to assess the role these mammals play as muskrat predators in the marshes of northeast North Carolina, Wilson (1954) recorded the percent frequency of food in mink digestive tracts as fish, 61 percent; mammals, 34 percent; birds, 18 percent; arthropods, 30 percent; amphibians, 11 percent; reptiles, 5 percent. *Fundulus* and *Gambusia* made up the bulk of the fish. Deer mice and meadow mice were found in 49 of 115 stomachs examined while muskrats were found in 16 stomachs. King rails were the more frequently identified bird, found in 8 stomachs. The rice rat was found in only 5 stomachs, a surprise since live trapping indicated a large population. However, examination of the mink scats showed mammals (72 percent) to be the principal food with rice rats showing in 22 of the 53 scats and deer mice appearing in 25 percent of the scats. Muskrat appeared only once in a mink scat. Fish were evident in only seven (13 percent) of the scats, although common in the digestive tract.

In Wilson's examination of 24 digestive tracts and 61 scats of the otter, fish appeared 91 percent of the time with killifish and mosquito fish 9 and 4 percent, respectively. Muskrats made up 1 percent of the food. According to Wilson's (1954) study, muskrats play a minor role in mink and otter predation. However, O'Neil (1949) ranked the mink as number one predator on Louisiana muskrats.

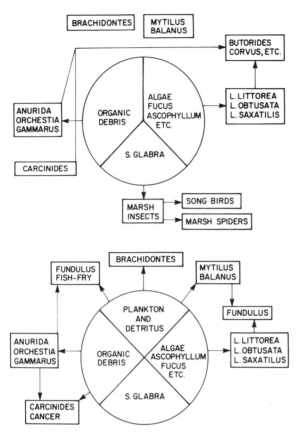

Figure 4.4.   Food coactions of the *Spartina alterniflora-Littorina saxatilis-Geukensia* associes of low marshes. (From Fig. 14, Dexter, 1947, by permission of the editor, *Ecol. Monogr.*)

TROPHIC RELATIONS

Dexter (1947) characterized the various marine communities of a tidal inlet at Cape Ann, Massachusetts and portrayed the feeding interactions in the low marsh as *Spartina glabra* (= *alterniflora*)-*Littorina saxatilis-Brachidontes* (= *Geukensia*) associes, and the high marsh as *Spartina patens-Melampus-Orchestia* associes (Figures 4.4 and 4.5). Paviour-Smith (1956) expanded on the feeding relationships in a salt marsh using the concepts put forth by Lindeman (1942) whereby organisms can be grouped into a series of more or less discrete trophic levels as producers, primary consumers, secondary con-

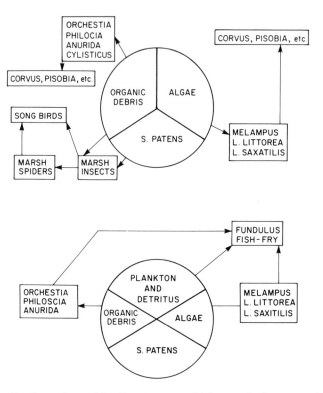

Figure 4.5.   Food coactions of the *Spartina patens-Melampus-Orchestia* associes of high marshes. (From Fig. 17, Dexter, 1947, by permission of the editor, *Ecol. Monogr.*)

sumers, etc., each dependent on the preceding level as a source of energy. She reminded us that green plants, as producers, are directly dependent on sunlight as a source of energy. Her diagram (Figure 4.6) supports a basic consideration that the further an organism is removed from the original energy source the less it will be dependent solely on the preceding energy level. In her discussion, Paviour-Smith brings out several points: (1) animals can feed at more than one level at any one time; (2) animals can occupy different trophic levels at various times during their life cycle; (3) parasites of various marsh animals need be considered and may or may not simultaneously occupy the same trophic levels as their hosts; (4) all material and nutrients are not recycled within the marsh ecosystem. Some may be exported or imported by the movements of animals such as fishes, birds, and mammals and much of their energy in the form of planktonic organisms or detritus is passively moved in and out of the marsh by the ebb and flood of the tides.

This author has followed the scheme laid out by Paviour-Smith to form

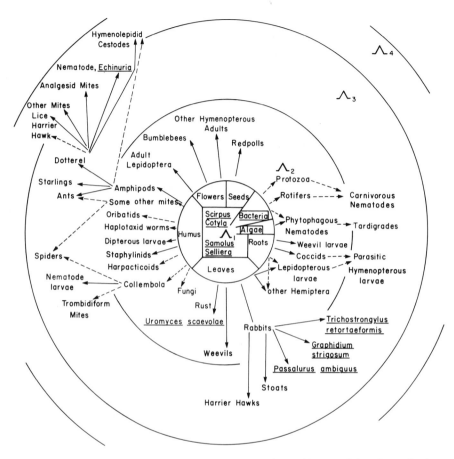

Figure 4.6. Food web of the salt-meadow community at Hoopers Inlet, Otago Peninsula, New Zealand showing trophic levels. The producer organisms are enclosed in boxes, and succeeding trophic levels (T_1, T_2, etc.) are enclosed in succeeding concentric circles. Solid lines represent known relationships and broken lines assumed relationships. (From Fig. 6, Paviour-Smith, 1956, by permission of the editor, *Trans. Roy. Soc. New Zealand*.)

a composite food web for the tidal marshes of the northern hemisphere (Figure 4.7). The primary producers are grouped as (1) rooted plants, (2) algal forms, and (3) detritus, fungi, and bacteria. The primary consumers are grouped adjacent to the producers that are chiefly involved in a particular food chain, i.e., herbivorous or detritus. Thus the same organism may appear in the same trophic position but in different food linkages; for example, *Melampus* and *Littorina* feed on living macrophytic plant epidermis, detritus, fungi and bacteria, as well as algae.

MacNae (1957a and b) recorded the work of early investigators who

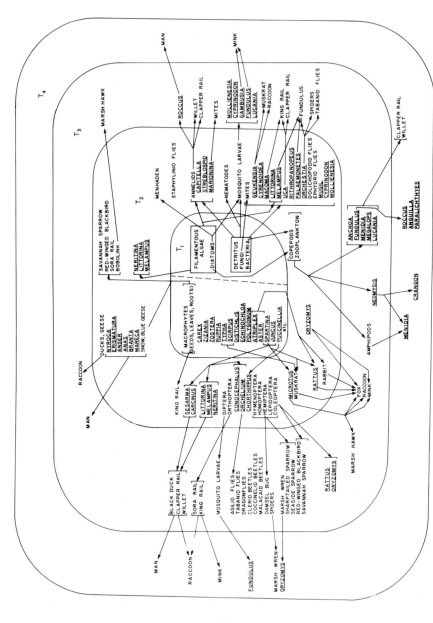

Figure 4.7. A composite food web for tidal marshes in the northern hemisphere derived from the literature. The arrows denote feeding relationships. The absence of arrows infers trophic relationships, at least. Trophic levels are identified by succeeding concentric circles and by the symbols T_1, T_2, etc.

identified the importance of detritus and the edaphic microflora as sources of nutrition in shallow water habitats. Using these sources as well as his own observations in the Zeartkops estuary of South Africa, MacNae characterized the basic food source of estuaries as being derived from three components: (1) inflowing phytoplankton; (2) microflora of bacteria, blue-green algae, diatoms, and flagellates living in the upper few millimeters of the substrate; and (3) detritus derived from plants and other organic sources swept in by the tides and by stream discharge.

The importance of detritus in the tidal marsh ecosystem was early recognized by Paviour-Smith (1956) when she identified humus and bacteria as components of the producers' trophic level and calculated the organic content of marsh soil and total biomass.

Weight of dead organic matter	17,374.4	grams
Weight of organic matter in plants	760.9	grams
Weight of organic matter in animals	25.6	grams
Total organic matter/m^2 of soil	18,160.9	grams
Phytomass—higher plants	1,680	grams
Bacteria	.009	grams
Zoomass	32.4	grams
Approximate total biomass/m^2	1,712.4	grams

Odum and Smalley (1959) more clearly distinguished between the herbivorous and detritus food chains when they examined the feeding relationships between the herbivorous grasshopper *Orchelium fidicinium* and the omnivorous snail *Littorina irrorata* in a Georgia *Spartina* marsh. On the basis of seasonal sampling, respirometry, and calorimetry they demonstrated the interaction between seasonal population growth and food availability. The grasshopper fed solely on the low marsh *Spartina* and the annual cycle persisted for approximately 100 days with numbers peaking in May. There were two periods of mortality which were evident in the population curves identifying numbers, biomass, and energy flow (Figure 4.8). The average weight per animal steadily increased with the most rapid growth among the medium-sized grasshoppers. Odum and Smalley pointed out that numbers overemphasize and biomass underemphasizes the importance of small organisms. They considered a homeostatic condition to exist in the grasshopper population if the energy flow fluctuated two-fold, as determined by population density, mean animal weight, and respiratory rate, while numbers and biomass fluctuated five- to six-fold.

On the other hand, *Littorina* fed on dead *Spartina* and detritus on the high marsh throughout the year. The young put on rapid growth with an associated higher mortality than the adults which also had a lower growth rate. Metabolically the adult snails were more important (Figure 4.9).

Odum and Smalley (1959) calculated these slow-growing, long-lived

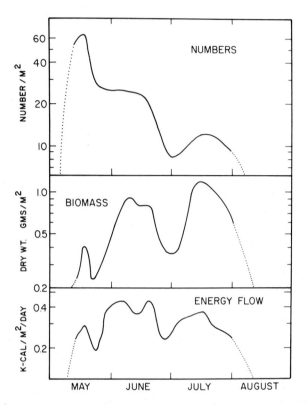

Figure 4.8. Numbers, biomass (dry weight), and energy flow per square meter in a population of salt-marsh grasshoppers (*Orchelium fidicinium*) living in a Georgia low-level *Spartina alterniflora* marsh. (From Odum and Smalley, 1959.)

snails assimilated a large amount of ingested material, with an assimilation efficiency of 45 percent, but their growth efficiency amounted to only 14 percent. In contrast *Orchelium* had a lower assimilation efficiency (36 percent) but a higher growth efficiency (37 percent). Therefore *Littorina* had an energy loss through respiration amounting to 86 percent while the grasshopper energy loss through respiration amounted to 63 percent.

Figure 4.10 depicts the annual pattern of energy flow for both the snail and the grasshopper populations. It is important to recognize the magnitude of this energy flow as related to the availability of food. The grasshopper growth cycle of approximately 100 days (Odum and Smalley, 1959; Smalley, 1960) is intimately associated with the peak net production of *Spartina*. In contrast detritus from decomposing *Spartina* and other marsh plants as well as edaphic algae is available to the snail population throughout the year.

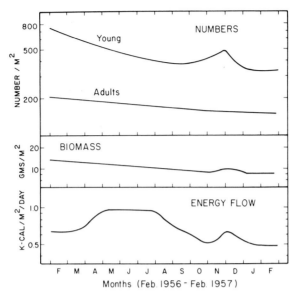

Figure 4.9. Numbers, biomass (dry weight), and energy flow per square meter in a population of snails, *Littorina irrorata* in a Georgia *Spartina* marsh. (From Odum and Smalley, 1959.)

Thus in a sense *Littorina* can "afford" to have a lower growth efficiency. The higher assimilation efficiency is of benefit to the population whose food is produced at a lower but continuous rate, whereas the high growth efficiency is of value to the animal depending on a seasonal "bloom" of primary production.

With reference to the meiofauna, Lee *et al.* (1975) raised numerous questions about ecological efficiencies, such as whether such species grow and reproduce in reaction to specific algal blooms. It is difficult to determine whether a cause and effect or a parallel response to certain environmental parameters produces an apparent synchrony. According to Lee *et al.*, animals that do respond would maximize energy yield by a reduction in hunting effort for each food organism. They would thus display a very high ecological efficiency for a short time but this would be countered by an expense related to the energy of maintenance between such food pulses.

Detritus production in a tidal marsh varies by plant form, some of which have been examined by Reimold *et al.* (1975a). Production flux of detritus was highest in the short-form of *Spartina alterniflora,* 18 mg $g^{-1}day^{-1}$ compared to 7 mg $g^{-1}day^{-1}$ for tall-form *S. alterniflora* and for *Juncus roemerianus.* The average monthly detritus production of tall-form *S. alterniflora* (197.9 g m^{-2}) was reported to be significantly greater than for

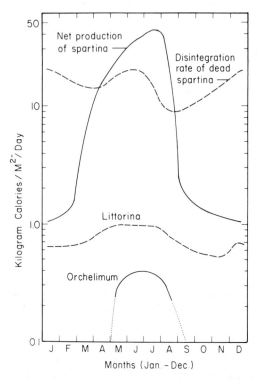

Figure 4.10.   Comparison of the annual pattern of energy flow in *Littorina irrorata* and *Orchelium fidicinium* populations in a Georgia *Spartina alterniflora* marsh. (From Odum and Smalley, 1959.)

short-form *S. alterniflora* (113.6 g m^{-2}). The average monthly *J. roemerianus* detritus production (188.4 g m^{-2}) was significantly greater than that for the short-form but not for the tall-form *S. alterniflora*. The Duplin marsh watershed was calculated to be composed of 23 percent tall-form *S. alterniflora*, 65 percent short-form *S. alterniflora*, and 12 percent *J. roemerianus*. The area weighed mean annual production of detritus was calculated at 1845.8 g m^{-2}year^{-1} with a mean detritus production of 141.9 g m^{-2}month^{-1}. In addition, the authors found the mineral content of the detritus to vary between March and August collections and also between species.

As an interjection, a recent study (Reimold *et al.*, 1975b; Reimold, 1976) portrayed a decrease in detritus availability on Georgia marshes resulting from animal grazing. By taking into account the value of production and processing, the economic worth of a Georgia salt marsh in terms of beef production was computed by Reimold *et al.* (1975b) to be about $6000/ha.

Thus, the marsh and high ground are nearly equal in terms of their value as potential grazing areas for livestock. These workers not only identified a reduction in detritus through grass consumption but a reduction in detritivore populations such as the ribbed mussel, fiddler crabs, and *Littorina* snails by trampling. They proposed that grazing could be permitted during one out of three years in selected marshes without irreversible damage. Such a time sequence would define the limits of asymptotic stability for the marsh with such a grazing perturbation (Hurd and Wolf, 1974). While Reimold *et al.* (1975b) considered grazing to be damaging to a marsh, they inferred that such grazing might be necessary in order to produce an economic basis to protect ecologically valuable marshes from being destroyed through development pressures. This poses an interesting conundrum. Smalley (1960), Teal (1962) and others pointed out that little marsh primary production transfer is by way of the herbivorous food chain, and that the aquatic oriented animals of the marsh are much more valuable because of energy transfer through the detritivore food chain. Yet, Reimold *et al.* (1975b) are proposing that low-level grazing with its concomitant reduction of detritus and detritivore populations may be a way of saving valuable tidal marshes from exploitation by development!

Associated with the continuous annual production of detritus is the presence of a variety of edaphic algae growing on the marsh surface and providing a food source for detritivores such as *Littorina* and *Melampus* and meiofaunal species. These algae make a major contribution to marsh primary production (Pomeroy, 1959). Gallagher (1971) and Gallagher and Daiber (1974) estimated the gross algal production in Canary Creek marsh, Delaware, amounted to about one-third of the net angiosperm production. This algal productivity takes on added importance because much of it occurs during the cold half of the year when grass production is low. Pomeroy (1959) recorded maximum photosynthesis during the summer months when the tide was flooding the marsh but maximum photosynthesis in winter occurred when the tide was at the ebb, exposing the marsh and its algal components. Ranwell (1972, p. 128) called attention to the significance of this wintertime availability of high algal production when he cited an earlier work (Ranwell and Downing, 1959) wherein the brent goose in Norfolk, England, fed on the tidal-flat algae in the winter and on the salt-marsh grasses in the spring.

Teal (1962), among others, identified the detritus food chain as the major energy-flow pathway in the tidal marsh. Smalley (1960) stressed this when he estimated that less than one percent of the *Spartina* is eaten by *Orchelium* in a Georgia marsh, that few animals feed on the growing *Spartina*, and that most of the marsh net primary production is converted to detritus within the marsh or the adjoining waters.

Recent work (Haines, 1976b) suggested the particulate organic carbon (POC) found in the offshore waters of Georgia may not be derived from *Spartina alterniflora* detritus to the extent thought probable by earlier investigators. Haines' inference was based on analyses of changes in the δ ^{13}C-^{12}C ratios between C_4 marsh plants, such as *Spartina alterniflora,* and C_3 marsh plants and the offshore phytoplankton.

Using a radionuclide tracer, Marples (1966) identified three major feeding groups in the Sapelo Island, Georgia marshes. Group I included those species that are primarily grazing herbivores feeding on *Spartina* (Orthoptera—*Orchelium fidicinium,* Homoptera—*Prokelisia marginata,* Hemiptera—*Trigonotylus* sp. and *Ischnodemus badius*). Group II included the *Littorina* snails, the crabs *Uca* and *Sesarma,* and the flies Dolichopodidae and Ephydridae, feeding on detritus. Group III included those arthropods not actively feeding on growing grass or the detritus, and possible predators, since they did not become highly labeled or became labeled only after three to four weeks. This work identified particular food chains and confirmed earlier observations.

Odum and de la Cruz (1967) considered organic detritus to be the main link between primary and secondary production; as the detritus particles decreased in size there was a corresponding increase in protein content, up to 24 percent in dead grass as it entered the water (Figure 4.11). There was the presumption of a microbial population buildup on the surfaces of the detritus which accounted for the enrichment of the decomposing *Spartina.* Earlier, Taschdjian (1954), Burkholder (1956), Burkholder and Burkholder (1956), and Burkholder and Bornside (1957) attributed *Spartina* decomposition to enhanced bacterial activity. Subsequent work by May (1974), Averill (1976), and Harrison (1977) suggested that isopods and amphipods facilitate this decomposition by tearing the grass into particles as they feed on the fungal growth covering the dead grass. It may be that fungal enzymes enhance the breakdown, making it easier for plant disintegration as these crustacea feed. As was pointed out by Odum and de la Cruz (1967), bacterial enrichment occurs, presumably due to an increased surface-area to volume ratio as the detritus particles decrease in size.

Burkholder (1956) and Burkholder and Bornside (1957) stated that the ten essential amino acids required for growth in the rat and man constitute about 15 percent of the *Spartina* protein. This infers that all marine animals cannot directly utilize *Spartina,* and presumably other halophytic plants, as a direct source of energy. This has been borne out by subsequent work with *Fundulus heteroclitus* (Prinslow et al., 1974; Katz, 1975). Burkholder (1956) and Burkholder and Bornside (1957) suggested that microbial conversion facilitates plant protein transformation to a form that can be utilized by

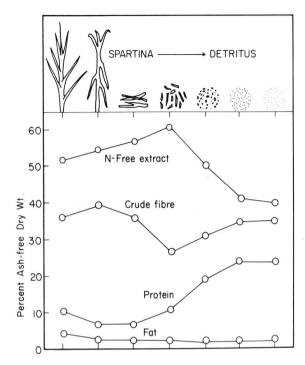

Figure 4.11.   The nutritive composition of successive stages of decomposition of *Spartina* grass, showing an increase in protein and a decrease in carbohydrate with increasing age and decreasing size of detritus particles. (From Odum and de la Cruz, 1967, by permission of *AAAS.*)

those marine fauna identified as detritivores who, in turn, serve as an essential link in various marsh food chains.

Not only are bacteria involved in the detrital food chain by enhancing protein production and its conversion to usable forms by animals, but they are also involved in the synthesis of Vitamin B_{12} (Burkholder and Burkholder, 1956). In addition, bacteria contribute to phosphorus mineralization from detritus. Barsdate *et al.* (1974), using *Carex aquatilus,* demonstrated that decomposition of detritus involves a very rapid cycle of mineral nutrients which, for phosphate, may have a turnover time of about two minutes, and that this mineral cycling may proceed at a rate 100 times faster than the actual release of nutrients from the decomposing plant material. These investigators demonstrated a hot-water extractable, biological phosphorus pool in bacteria, about half of which consisted of inorganic polyphosphates. They also reported the excretion of dissolved organic phosphate by bacteria.

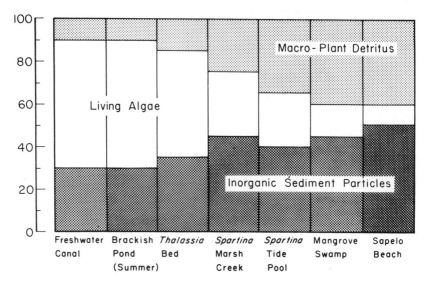

Figure 4.12. Estimated percentages of the three important components occurring in the stomach contents of *M. cephalus* in the seven systems. The value for each system represents over 100 fish which were sampled over a period ranging from 3 to 12 months. (From Odum, 1970, by permission of Oliver & Boyd, Publishers, Edinburgh.)

The presence of ciliated protozoa acting as bacterial grazers greatly enhanced the transfer of phosphorus from detritus through bacteria to solution. Little of the phosphorus was cycled through the protozoa but their grazing kept the bacteria population in the rapid-growth phase which promoted a more rapid assimilation of detrital phosphorus as well as a generally faster circulation of phosphorus. Barsdate *et al.* (1974) reported mean uptakes of 52.11×10^{-7} μg P hr^{-1} and 16.1×10^{-7} μg P hr^{-1} respectively for grazed and ungrazed systems.

Some animals display an ability to utilize two basic estuarine resources, detritus and algae. This is demonstrated by the striped mullet, *Mugil cephalus,* which Odum (1970) classified as a "broad spectrum" herbivore. The percentage of the important portions of the stomach contents from seven habitats is portrayed in Figure 4.12 from which Odum concluded that this fish is able to occupy a position between both food chains, utilizing whichever is easiest to exploit: live-plant material in a fresh-water canal or *Thalassia* bed, or detritus and its associated microorganisms in a mangrove swamp or on the Sapelo Island beach. The mullet apparently exercises food preference when the opportunity presents itself since quantities of detritus were present in the fresh-water canal substrate as well as in the *Thalassia* bed. In both cases, however, greater quantities of living algae were ingested.

Table 4.12. Values of stomach contents from mullet feeding on three diets. Each value represents the mean for the stomach contents from 25 mullet. (From Odum, 1970, by permission of Oliver & Boyd, Publishers, Edinburgh.)

	Algal Diet (*Thalassia* Bed)	Mixed Algal & Detritus (Sapelo marsh)	Detritus Diet (Sapelo Beach)
Plant pigment (mg/g dry wt)	0.465	0.315	0.166
Per cent organic matter (dry wt)	9.81%	6.22%	5.90%
Calorific value (kilocalories per ash-free gram)	5.226	4.552	3.957

Table 4.12 compares the quality of stomach contents from three naturally occurring diets. It is evident that the algal diet has the greatest potential energy source in that there is a greater quantity of plant pigment and organic matter with a higher caloric value. Odum attributed the high caloric content of the algal diet to the epiphytic diatoms which are rich in stored oils and associated with *Thalassia*. Odum also found detritus in all stomachs examined from all habitats. The mullet receives nutrients as well as energy from the complex of bacteria, fungi, and protozoa associated with the detritus, "scrubbing" and returning the detrital particles to the environment to start the cycle over.

In order to obtain the same amount of energy from detritus as from the richer plant material a greater volume of detritus must move through the digestive tract of the mullet. As shown in Figure 4.13, a greater absorptive surface is made available with greater quantities of detritus. The detritus feeders at the Sapelo Island marsh showed a change in ratio of intestine length to fish length from 3.2:1 in 100 millimeter fish to 5.5:1 for 200 millimeter fish, an increase of intestine growth six or seven times greater than the increase in fish length. On the other hand, the fish from the *Thalassia* bed displayed a regression slope slightly greater than one or an almost constant ratio of 3.2:1.

Because the mullet is able to span both food chains, Odum (1970) did not consider food to be limiting. He concluded that such an omnivore, feeding on plentiful and easily obtained food, will have a maximum power output when there is a large and continuous ingestion rate, and a short retention time joined with an assimilation efficiency which, although high for diatoms would be low for the general bulk of ingested organic material.

This low assimilation efficiency for the omnivorous mullet is in direct

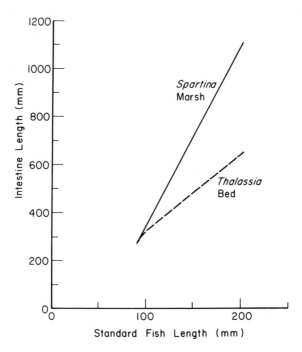

Figure 4.13.   The relationship between the standard fish length and the intestinal length for two populations of mullet: (1) a population from the *Spartina* marsh creek, and (2) a population feeding in the vicinity of the Florida *Thalassia* bed. Each regression line was constructed from measurements made on 50 mullet. (From Odum, 1970, by permission, Oliver and Boyd, Publishers, Edinburgh.)

opposition to the high assimilation efficiency proposed by Odum and Smalley (1959) for the detritus-feeding snail *Littorina*. A possible explanation suggests that, while both the fish and the snail are probably continuous feeders, the sheer volume of material that the fish must ingest will thereby reduce its assimilation efficiency. Odum remarked the fish must filter about 100 grams of sediment just to acquire one gram of material in its digestive tract. The fish's efficiency would fluctuate according to the nature of the ingested material: high assimilation efficiency associated with diatoms but low with detritus and blue-green algae.

Detritus production is considered to be more or less constant throughout the year (Odum and Smalley, 1959; and our own observations in Delaware marshes). Certain fluctuations are dampened as compared to the seasonal pulses of living macrophytic biomass. Some of this dampening effect can be attributed to the feeding activities of the shrimp *Palaemonetes pugio* (Welsh, 1975) and, one might surmise, other detritivores. Welsh described

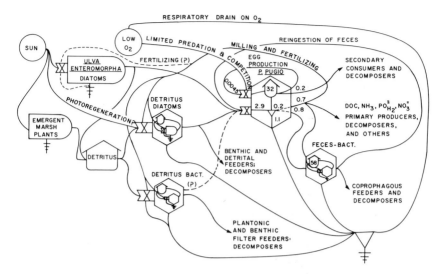

Figure 4.14.   The role of *Palaemonetes pugio* in the tidal marsh ecosystem of Bissel Cove (work circuit symbols of Odum, 1972). Energy flow are in $kcal \cdot m^{-2} \cdot day^{-1}$ and storages are in $kcal/m^2$. Energetic input exceeds expenditures by 0.1 $kcal \cdot m^{-2} \cdot day^{-1}$ because of rounding errors and small numbers of adults persisting through their second winter. Flows to feces and dissolved organics are dashed to avoid differentiation between assimilated and nonassimilated origin. Standing crop, production of biomass, predation, and respiration were measured directly. Ingestion, fecal standing crop, and production and release of dissolved organics were calculated. (From Fig. 19, Welsh, 1975, by permission of the editor, *Ecology*.)

the bursts of organic matter into Bissel Cove, Rhode Island, derived from *Spartina, Ruppia, Ulva,* and *Enteromorpha* at various times of the year. While organic material comprised about 50 percent of the sediments, larger accumulations did not result because of the grazing activity of the large population of *P. pugio* which acts on these periodic pulses. Welsh estimated the total yearly production of tall-form *Spartina* released to Bissel Cove would supply only one-third of the annually ingested energy of the shrimp. The heavy demands of the shrimp during growth and reproduction coincide with the blooms of *Ruppia* and algae. Through the shrimp feeding activity, the production of total consumables (biomass, DOM, and fecal pellets), which amounts to almost 60 percent of the total ingested mass, becomes protein-rich material, which in turn becomes available to several different trophic levels (Figure 4.14). In addition to smoothing out organic pulses, the shrimp process detritus particles in such a way that a substrate is enhanced for the growth of diatoms and bacteria.

Examination of the literature leaves the impression that detritus is an ubiquitous, amorphic mass of organic matter existing somewhere between the structural form of the living organism and the ultimate dissolved inorganic solution ready for uptake by living plants. One can also derive the impression that detritus is omnipresent in the diet of all members of the detritus food chain. However, this does not appear to be a universal truth. Lee and Muller (1973), in their review of the literature, found that within a particular set of gross environmental conditions the Foraminifera have a very patchy distribution. On the basis of field observations and laboratory studies, they, as well as Lee et al. (1975), attributed this uneven dispersion to the selective food habits of many of the meiofauna of the tidal marsh. Apparently these organisms derive different nutritional values from the food they assimilate. Working with three species of Foraminifera, Lee and Muller found populations of *Allogromia laticollaris* and *Spiroloculina hyalina* bloomed when competition was low and the appropriate algal species were present as food. Otherwise their numbers declined to low values. The third species, *Rosalina leei,* appeared to be more of a generalist, feeding on mixtures of algae to meet nutritional requirements. Although great numbers of bacteria were eaten by all three Foraminifera their biomass was negligible compared to the algae, yet only four or five of the twenty-eight algae species made available were ingested in significant quantities.

The distribution of marine oligochaetes among the meiobenthos may be explained by specialized food requirements. Giere (1975) argued that if oligochaetes were to feed nonselectively on detritus and microorganisms, food would presumably be available everywhere and thus not influence oligochaete distributions. Giere's observations described masses of bacteria and diatoms in the guts of these worms but no detritus; apparently the worms scrub these microorganisms from the sand and detritus particles. Not only do they separate the bacteria and algae from their substrate, they also possess a highly developed ability to detect and discriminate between groups of microorganisms. Giere therefore argued that such trophic specialization leads to the possibility that oligochaetes can be limited in distribution by scarcity of adequate food supplies despite quantities of detritus. He also suggested that food selectivity could explain the problematical sympatric occurrence of closely related tubificid species with seemingly identical ecological demands in the same microhabitat. Lee et al. (1975) contended that patchiness is an ecological strategy for meiobenthos that diversifies habitat potential and reduces competition. In an earlier review, McIntyre (1969) asserted that, in salt marshes and other sheltered areas, large populations of deposit-feeding and browsing meiofauna utilize the primary production. He also believed there was little predation by larger organisms, therefore little of this meiofauna tissue would pass upward to higher trophic levels. In contrast, Giere (1975) identified a large group of real or potential predators of

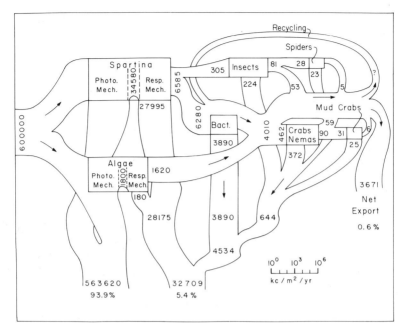

Figure 4.15.   Energy-flow diagram for a Georgia salt marsh. (From Teal, 1962, by permission of the editor, *Ecology.*)

oligochaetes comprising part of the meiofauna. According to McIntyre the main role of the meiofauna in such organically rich habitats is to assist in the recycling of nutrients in a low trophic level.

While Giere (1975) was not specifically concerned with tidal marsh oligochaetes, a very casual examination of Canary Creek, Delaware marsh substrate would suggest oligochaetes could be another very fruitful group of tidal marsh meiobenthos waiting for study.

Various schemes have been put forward to portray food webs and energy flow pathways associated with tidal marshes. Paviour-Smith (1956) (Figure 4.6) was the first to attempt a portrayal of the marsh food web. Teal (1962) (Figure 4.15) is recognized as the first to compile an energy-flow diagram wherein a quantitative evaluation (Table 4.13) was attempted with particular emphasis on the emergent marsh. Since then efforts have been directed at expanding details of energy flow (Figure 4.16 and Table 4.14) or examining the role of a particular organism (grasshopper, Smalley, 1960; ribbed mussel, Kuenzler, 1961; marsh wren, Kale, 1965; shrimp, Welsh, 1975). In keeping with earlier work, Odum and Heald (1975) developed a schematic diagram and conceptual model of the North River, Florida, food

Table 4.13. Summary of salt marsh energetics. (From Teal, 1962, by permission of the editor, *Ecology*)

Input as light	600,000 kcal/m^2/yr
Loss in photosynthesis	563,620 or 93.9%
Gross production	36,380 or 6.1% of light
Producer respiration	28,175 or 77% of gross production
Net Production	8,205 kcal/m^2/yr
Bacterial respiration	3,890 or 47% of net production
1° consumer respiration	596 or 7% of net production
2° consumer respiration	48 or 0.6% of net production
Total energy dissipation by consumers	4,534 or 55% of net production
Export	3,671 or 45% of net production

web (Figure 4.17). While the specifics were directed at the detritus-consuming omnivores of a mangrove community, there is no conceptual reason why the principle cannot be applied to tidal marshes and other intertidal and subtidal areas producing quantities of plant debris. In fact, Odum *et al.* (1973) put forth the principle that there are a few species represented by large numbers in such aquatic habitats that derive much of their nourishment from the ingestion of vascular plant detritus and subsequent reutilization of these detritus particles in the form of fecal pellets. These organisms serve as the critical link between detritus generation and the production of higher consumers in estuarine systems.

There has been an interesting historical evolution in the development of the concepts of food chains and energy transfer between trophic levels. First was the recognition that there is a group of grazers consuming living macrophytes with conversion of solar energy into animal flesh through the procedure of ingesting the end-products of the photosynthesis. While husbandrymen have known this for many millennia, it is only in relatively recent times that it has been stated as an ecological principle (Elton, 1927). More recently, Darnell (1967) brought into focus the nutritive roles of particulate detritus and the microflora. Subsequent workers have elaborated on this theme demonstrating that detritus utilization is the major nutritive pathway in the tidal marsh. The use of dashed lines in Figure 4.16 gives recent recognition to a further elaboration, i.e., dissolved organic material as an energy pathway. Although Juday (1942) portrayed it as the base of the food pyramid, Darnell (1967) identified it as a pathway and Stephens (1967) recognized it as a nutritional source for marine and estuarine invertebrates. Subsequent work (Pomeroy *et al.*, 1976) has shown that a high proportion of the dissolved organic material in marsh waters is refractory and thus not readily available. Further, there is a substantial amount that is labile with a high turnover rate, presumably through microbial activity which appears to be the major sink for these soluble organic materials.

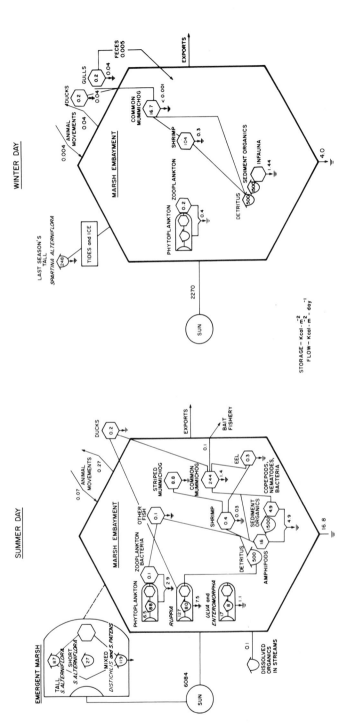

Figure 4.16. Energy-flow diagram for composite winter and summer days in the Bissel Cove marsh. Values were calculated with biomass estimate from the study, the heat of combustion measurements in their Table 14 and an oxycaloric constant of 4 kcal gm⁻¹ oxygen. Symbols from Odum, 1972. (From Nixon and Oviatt, 1973, by permission of the editor, *Ecol. Monogr.*)

175

Table 4.14. Annual energy budget for the Bissel Cove marsh embayment. (From Nixon and Oviatt, 1973, by permission of the editor, *Ecol. Monogr.*)

Item	Kcal m^{-2} yr^{-1}	Kcal yr^{-1}
Production of organic matter within the embayment[a]	9.6×10^3	63.4×10^6
Consumption of organic matter within the embayment[a]	9.8×10^3	64.8×10^6
Excess of consumption over production	2.0×10^2	1.4×10^6
Imports of organic matter from streams[a]	15	1.0×10^5
from net immigration of fish and shrimp[b]	3.5	2.3×10^4
from emergent marsh[c]	2.4×10^2	1.6×10^6
Total imports	2.6×10^2	1.7×10^6
Excess organic matter available for storage and export	60	3.0×10^5

(a) Oxycalorific equivalent of 4 Kcal g^{-1}.
(b) From migration data and calorimetry (3 Kcal g^{-1} for shrimp and 5 Kcal g^{-1} for fish).
(c) Assuming input from 1-m-wide band of tall grass around the perimeter plus total area of the islands and 3.3 Kcal g^{-1}.

While it has been long recognized that bacteria and other saprophytes play a decomposer role, it is only relatively recently that ecologists have begun to perceive the complexity and diverseness of this role. Firstly, these microflora degrade complex plant and animal tissues, changing them into forms that can be recycled and recycled again, thus used by autotrophs as well as a whole series of heterotrophs. In addition, while breaking down these organic substances, the microflora also serve as food and, in the process, release both dissolved organics and inorganics. Thus there is no substantive difference between the three food chains, just the question of emphasis on particular linkages and pathways.

A hypothetical diagram of food chains and trophic levels for European salt marshes has been prepared by Beeftink (1977) (Figure 4.18). The general pathways of energy transfer are well established and there is no reason to believe they differ from those identified from North American tidal marshes. In any case, the number of links in the various food chains as well as the particular pathways will vary from marsh to marsh (examination of Figure 4.7 and the food habit studies earlier in this chapter will give an inkling of this) and, while the principle holds, the particular details will need to be identified for each situation.

Beeftink called attention to the absence of any portrayal of microorganisms as decomposers, saying there is no information on the subject. The

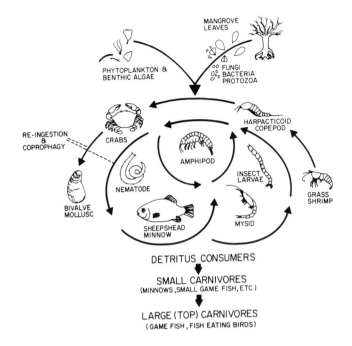

DETRITUS CONSUMERS

↓

SMALL CARNIVORES
(MINNOWS, SMALL GAME FISH, ETC.)

↓

LARGE (TOP) CARNIVORES
(GAME FISH, FISH EATING BIRDS)

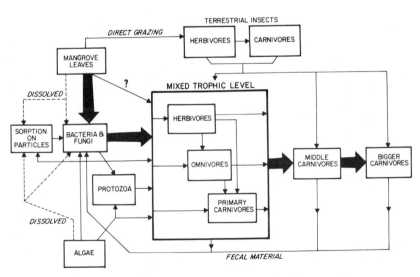

Figure 4.17. A schematic diagram (top) of the detritus-consuming omnivorous organisms and a conceptual model (bottom) of the North River mangrove community food web. The cyclical nature of the diagram depicts the reutilization of detritus particles in the form of fecal material. The most important flow of energy is depicted as a broad arrow, less important food chains as narrow arrows and the pathway of dissolved leaf material as a dotted line. (From Figs. 2 and 3, Odum and Heald, 1975, by permission of Academic Press.)

177

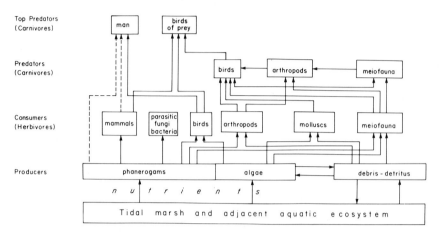

Figure 4.18. Hypothetical diagram of trophic levels and food-chain pathways in the salt-marsh ecosystem. (From Beeftink, 1977, by permission of the Elsevier Scientific Publishing Company.)

subject is identified by the use of the word "nutrients" in Figure 4.18. As Beeftink stated, "there seems to be no reason to suppose that European interrelationships in salt marshes are in principle different from those in North America." Therefore, one can expect some kind of microbial activity associated with detritus production and dissolved organic substances. However, Beeftink considered plant zonations to play a role. He called attention to the downward extension of *Spartina alterniflora* below the midtide level in North America whereas in the Netherlands *Spartina townsendii* agg. reaches to one meter below mean high water or 80–100 centimeters above midtide level. With this in mind, preliminary studies gave a provisional conclusion that the input of detritus and dissolved organics onto the Dutch marshes exceeded the outward transport. No assessment of storm transport was reported possible.

Tidal marshes contribute to the productivity of estuaries: numerous studies (Odum, 1961; Odum and Smalley, 1959; Teal, 1962; Odum, *et al.*, 1973; Nixon and Oviatt, 1973; Heinle *et al.*, 1976) attest to this. High values are placed on marshes by marsh ecologists who are constantly refining techniques in an attempt to produce solid data to support their intuitive judgments. In general, physical studies have shown a net export of water out of coastal plain estuaries, inferring a coincidental outward flow of nutrients from the marshes. While this principle is sound, recent work would suggest restraint in overgeneralizing. Nixon and Oviatt (1973) (Table 4.14) in Rhode Island, drawing upon earlier work done in Georgia (Teal, 1962) (Table 4.13), concluded consumption in Bissel Cove exceeded production by two percent and the difference was made up by contributions from the adjoining marshland. This supports the thesis that marshes are valuable because they contribute to estuarine maintenance processes. However, care should be focused on the fact that extrapolations were made that included differences of several years, latitudinal and growing season differences, as well as extrapolations made from positions that included great gaps of information. All of this leads to a great deal of rounding off and therefore the calculated difference of two percent between consumption and production could very easily fall within the limits of experimental error.

Generally, net nutrient fluxes have been identified as being out of the marsh. With the refinement of analytical procedures, and the nature of the sampling regimes, recent work would suggest this is not always the case. Heinle and Flemer (1976) displayed a net flux of carbon out of a brackish water marsh in Maryland while the net flux of other nutrients was essentially zero. In contrast, Woodwell *et al.* (1977) considered the Flax Pond salt marsh on Long Island as a sink for fixed carbon. Aurand and Daiber (1973) demonstrated a net import of nitrate and nitrite into two Delaware marshes. Preliminary analyses of subsequent work indicates a net outflow of ammonia and an import of nitrate and nitrite into a Delaware marsh. Axelrad (1974) showed an import of nitrate and nitrite into a Virginia marsh but the export of organic nitrogen exceeded the import of inorganic nitrogen, so that the net flow of dissolved nitrogen was outward into the estuary.

New work (Stevenson *et al.,* 1976; Haines *et al.,* 1976) called attention to the various factors of salinity regime, upland sources, stability of the estuarine nutrient flux, successional age of the marsh, the nature and size of the nutrient pools, and the nature and magnitude of microbial activity influencing the nutrient fluxes of tidal marshes. While the old generalities of nutrient fluxes still appear to be valid, they can no longer be accepted quite as readily and, for the present, each marsh must be examined on a case by case basis. Out of this may come a new set of principles of nutrient fluxes and energy transfers, thereby more clearly identifying the roles and value of tidal marshes.

5
Reproduction among Tidal Marsh Animals

INTRODUCTION

There is a considerable variety of animals, ranging from the protozoa to the mammals, associated with the tidal marsh. The distribution of some is restricted to this habitat yet, by their reproductive habits, they display a terrestrial or an aquatic origin, while others are found in a variety of habitats beyond the tidal marsh. In any case there are various morphological, physiological, or behavioral adaptations displayed that permit the species to be successful in this boundary habitat between the aquatic realm and the dry land. For a few of these species the life cycles and reproductive biology have been reasonably well described. Yet, there is a whole host of animals unique to the marsh habitat whose life cycles are unknown or only poorly understood. Because of the nature of this semiaquatic semiterrestrial habitat one could expect to find interesting adaptations to such an environment among these little-known members of the marsh fauna. Inferences can be drawn from related species found in adjoining habitats but, since these are different environments with associated requirements, such speculations must be made with caution. What information is known about the reproductive biology of these animals unique to the tidal marsh has been brought together in this chapter and some speculations will be proffered.

Most of the fishes, some invertebrates such as the blue crab, some bird species, and most mammals that are commonly associated with tidal marshes but are not unique to this habitat, having ubiquitous distributions, will not receive any great amount of attention in this chapter.

PROTOZOA

The order Foraminifera is the only group of protozoa among the salt-marsh fauna to have received any amount of attention and none of the studies examined dealt specifically with reproduction among this group. For this reason any comments directed to the subject will be general in nature.

Species of Foraminifera are dimorphic and reproduction is complex but uniform and involves a definite alternation of asexual and sexual generations (Hyman, 1940; Barnes, 1963; Boltovskoy and Wright, 1976). The asexual stage is the microspheric form, sometimes identified as the agamont or the schizont form. The megalospheric form or gamont gives rise to sexual gametes. In the simpler monothalamous Foraminifera the two forms cannot be morphologically distinguished (Hyman, 1940). Generally, among the polythalamous genera the schizont has a relatively large shell with an initial chamber which is quite small. Typically several nuclei are present, usually of different sizes. At the time of maturity each nucleus gathers some cytoplasm and forms the initial chamber of a new individual. These initial chambers leave the microspheric shell and form new individuals, generally megalospheric. The numbers of young produced vary from species to species and may be a reflection of the size of the parent form (Boltovskoy and Wright, 1976). Small-sized species may produce a few (8–10 to 28–32) while large-sized species may produce several hundred offspring.

The sexual megalospheric or sporozont form usually has a small test and a single nucleus. When mature the nucleus divides into many small nuclei, each with a bit of cytoplasm, which leave the test as flagellated zoospores typically having two flagella of unequal length. It has been estimated that many million gametes can be so produced which are able to survive for up to 24 hours after leaving the test. Two of these gametes fuse to form a zygote, a process called gamogony or the production of the microspheric generation. In their discussion Boltovskoy and Wright (1976) indicated some species display reproductive traits divergent from the general pattern described.

As a general rule the number of microspheric specimens is substantially less than the megalospheric forms. One genus, *Elphidium,* found in salt marshes displayed such a ratio of 1:30. This preponderance of megalospheric forms was observed in repeated generations of asexual reproduction. Reproduction in the microspheric form often produces unrecognizable individuals. While megalospheric forms usually outnumber the microspheric stage, the latter form is usually more abundant when environmental conditions, such as harsh winters and hot summers, become unfavorable.

Knowing the megalospheric:microspheric ratio and the time involved, an estimate of the reproductive rate can be calculated. The duration of the reproductive cycle depends on the species and the environmental conditions. Such a cycle may be only a few days for small-sized species and as much as two years for large species; the cycle for a number of species extends from a few weeks to a year (Boltovskoy and Wright, 1976).

MEIOFAUNA

There has been a steadily increasing interest in the marine meiofauna in recent years. McIntyre's (1969) review of meiofauna cited a number of studies carried out in the intertidal habitat. However, in this zone only six papers were identified with the sheltered soft mud communities of which only two were from salt marshes (Wieser and Kanwisher, 1961; Teal and Wieser, 1966). Since then Coull and Bell (1979) portrayed a markedly higher level of interest in marsh meiofauna. Among other things, they reviewed the controversial literature pertaining to the energy relations between the meiofauna and the higher trophic levels and concluded the meiofauna are an important connecting link with the higher trophic levels when associated with the soft mud substrate. As McIntyre (1969) pointed out, in order to assess the food role of the meiofauna, knowledge of life cycles, rates of reproduction and population fluctuations is needed. Based on their own earlier work (Coull and Fleeger, 1977; Bell, 1979) Coull and Bell (1979) championed the idea that long-term studies are necessary to properly evaluate meiofaunal population dynamics and comprehend the short-term fluctuations in abundance. They also extended a suggestion made earlier that the patchy distribution that has been evident results in part from the presence of pheromones as well as the general absence of a larval dispersal mechanism, and the aggregation of food sources.

Since there appears to be a general lack of information about the salt-marsh meiofauna particularly concerning reproduction, one can only speculate about species composition, population sizes and fluctuations, and life cycles and wonder about the feasibility of information extrapolation from adjoining marine habitats to the salt-marsh meiofauna. One could easily transfer information from such work as Meyers and Hopper (1967) on the fungal development on turtle grass, *Thalassia,* and associated nematode populations to the detritus-generating studies of marsh grasses.

Oligochaeta

No studies have come to light specifically dealing with the reproductive biology of Oligochaeta of tidal marshes. Inferences have been drawn from studies of this case taken from other euryhaline or high organic content habitats. The worms *Lumbricillus lineatus* and *Tubifex costatus* are found in highly euryhaline situations under rotting seaweed, polluted rivers, thick gray mud, and sewage filter beds; all of which are places with high organic content (Reynoldson, 1939; Brinkhurst, 1964).

Brinkhurst (1964) reported that *Tubifex costatus* began to mate in early April, reaching a peak in early May when cocoons first began to appear. The numbers of cocoons dropped sharply by the end of May and by late July large numbers of very small worms appeared. The numbers of large worms fell off sharply after breeding and only immature worms were observed in the fall.

The numbers of eggs per cocoon varied from species to species and within a breeding season. The early cocoons of *T. costatus* contained 2–3 eggs while the later ones enclosed one large egg or one small worm ready to emerge (Brinkhurst, 1964). The cocoons of *Lumbricillus lineatus,* which were ovoid in shape with an average size of 1.1 × 0.75 millimeters, had clearly visible eggs ranging from 1–20 in number with 4–9 being the typical count (Reynoldson, 1939). *Cognettia cognettii* from the moorlands of northern England had an average of 4.5 eggs per worm (Springett, 1970).

Development varied with temperature. Cocoon deposition, rate of development and hatching were adversely affected from *L. lineatus* when temperatures dropped below 6 °C. Hatching took place in 9–11 days with temperatures at 12–14 °C (Reynoldson, 1939). *C. cognettii* and *Cernosvitoviella briganta* had similar incubation periods of 32 ± 2 and 34 ± 3 days respectively while *Marionina clavata* eggs hatched after 48 ± 4 days (Springett, 1970).

Time of maturity varied considerably from species to species ranging from a few months to two years. Springett (1964) observed that most Enchytraeidae from the moors of northern England took several months to mature and had a single generation each year. Size distributions suggested that *T. costatus* took two years to mature, bred once in early summer and died after breeding (Brinkhurst, 1964). Development time was 321 ± 2 days for *C. cognettii,* clearly indicating a one-year cycle. In contrast, the newly hatched larvae collected from the field matured in 54 days, suggesting more than one generation a year. While *Marionina clavata* had eggs hatching in 48 days there appeared to be two types which differed in time needed to reach maturity: 65 ± 3 days and 223 ± 12 days, respectively. This inferred a one- and a two-year life cycle for this species (Springett, 1970), a strategy which calls for an examination of its population dynamics.

Sexual reproduction by fertilized eggs is the general rule among the oligochaetes. However, Springett (1970) reported reproduction by fragmentation in *Cognettia sphagnetorum* and its growth rate suggested there could be 2–3 generations each year.

Nematoda

Nematodes are found everywhere. They are the most numerous of animals and comprise a major portion of the biomass (Nicholas, 1975; Bell *et al.,* 1978). Despite their great numbers there is little information about the life histories, reproductive habits, and ecology of marine species (Hirschmann, 1960; Tietjen *et al.,* 1970; Nicholas, 1975).

Nematodes reproduce entirely by eggs with most species being bisexual, producing cross-fertilized eggs (Nicholas, 1975). There are numerous species that are hermophroditic, but capable of cross-fertilization and, among such species, males tend to be much less common. These hermaphrodites morphologically resemble females, first producing sperm and then eggs in an ovatestis. Parthenogenesis is common and a few species display an unusual form of parthenogenesis, pseudogamy, in which the egg must be fertilized by a spermatozoan before it can develop but the male pronucleus degenerates without fusing with its female counterpart. Such pseudogamy may occur in bisexual or hermaphroditic species. Thus Nicholas (1975) recognized five types of reproduction:

1. bisexual amphimictic (cross-fertilization);
2. bisexual, pseudogamous parthenogenesis;
3. hermaphroditic, usually automictic, with occasional amphimixis;
4. hermaphroditic, pseudogamous parthonogenesis;
5. thelytokous (exclusively female) parthenogenesis, either mitotic or meiotic.

Among certain Rhabditida, old females are unable to discharge eggs; a phenomenon called "endotokia matricida." The larvae hatch in the uterus and after death of the female the larvae consume the body contents of the parent, continuing development after escaping from the parental cuticle (Hirschmann, 1960).

The numbers of eggs and periodicity of egg production vary among species. Tietjen (1967) characterized the gravid marine nematode, *Monhystera filicaudata,* with 8–20 eggs which were released individually but adhered together in packets. The female died following egg deposition. Examining the ecology of the marine species *Rhabditis marina* from a salt-marsh surrounded embayment on Long Island, New York, Tietjen *et al.* (1970) found the average female with 70–100 eggs in clusters or individually. Egg production began generally 4.5 days after hatching, continuing for 3–4 days with about one week elapsing between mating and conclusion of egg deposition. Approximately 60 percent of the females died following completion of egg deposition. A second batch of eggs might be produced by the females that survived with some tendency for ovoviparous development. In reviewing earlier work, Hirschmann (1960) reported aquatic and terrestrial forms produced a few large-sized eggs, 50 or less, while some saprophagus species might lay as many as 200 eggs. Gerlach (1971) characterized 21–36 eggs per female as being typical. Warwick and Price (1979) observed that, for most species on a Cornwall mudflat, the juveniles dominated the population throughout the year making up 60 percent of the population during the fall and winter and 70 percent during the spring and summer. Gravid females were present throughout the year. One species, *Metachromadora vivipara*, with continuous egg production, had a mean number of eggs of 2.75 in January, 5.0 in April, 7.0 in July, and 3.7 in October. Warwick and Price (1979) observed this continuous asynchronous spawning was associated with small-sized nematodes and was typical of what had been found by earlier workers. This pattern was evident not only in temperate areas, but also in the tropics (Govindankutty and Nair, 1972).

Development time seems to vary with the size of the species. *Enoplus communis*, which lives on brown algae and is a very large species, spawns in the spring and reaches maturity in six months (McIntyre, 1969; after Wieser and Kanwisher, 1961). Smaller species, *Monhystera filicaudata*, *Monhystera disjuncta*, and *Diplolaimella schneideri* have life cycles that extend from hatching to egg laying of 24–35 days (20–25 °C), 30 days (0–24 °C), and 40 days (0–24 °C), respectively. For *Rhabditis marina* Tietjen *et al.* (1970) reported a life cycle of 4.5 days on Long Island. Hopper *et al.* (1973) recorded the influence of temperature on the life cycle of nematodes from a red mangrove system. Generation time was as short as 1–3/4 days at 35 °C for *Rhabditis marina* and as long as 112 days for *Haliplectus dorsalis* at 18 °C. The most rapid growth and development for each species was between 24 and 31 °C. Not unexpectedly, lower temperatures tended to extend the life span while temperatures above 31–33 °C interrupted the cycle.

In their evaluation of the interaction of temperature and salinity on *Monhystera denticulata*, Tietjen and Lee (1972) reported generation times, measured as the time elapsed between first egg deposition of consecutive generations, of: 10–12 days at 25 °C and 26‰; 20 days at 25 °C and 13‰; 17 days at 25 °C and 39‰; 18 days at 15 °C and 26‰; 36 days at 15 °C and 13‰ and 34 days at 15 °C and 39‰. This amounts to a doubling of generation time with a decrease in temperature of 10 °C and an increase or decrease in salinity of 13‰. They reported a generation time of 180–197 days at 5 °C. With the assumption of optimal conditions and average generation time, Tietjen and Lee speculated 15 generations could occur for *M. denticulata* at Southampton, New York. They expected the actual number of generations to be less as studies from natural populations would suggest one to four a year. Hopper and Meyers (1966) reported life cycles of approximately one month from laboratory cultures while Gerlach (1971) guessed an average of three generations per year.

Copepoda

It is only in very recent years that those copepods identified as an important component of the meiofauna have received any attention, very largely by Coull and his students in South Carolina.

When examining the reproductive periodicity of subtidal meiobenthic copepods, Coull and Vernberg (1975) noted that, at each station, one species was gravid throughout the year, such as *Microarthridion littorale* for the mud habitat. They noted that, of the other five common species, one had two reproduction peaks and four each had one period of peak reproductive activity. These various reproductive pinnacles alternated and were cyclic. Bell (1979) observed that copepod densities displayed distinct seasonal patterns with a pronounced fall and a lower spring peak in a high marsh habitat of South Carolina. She noted that *Stenhelia* (*Delavalia*) *bifidia* had its maximum densities in the fall and displayed the largest proportion of gravid females in the spring and fall prior to its density peaks. There was no reproductive activity noted during the winter months.

Fleeger (1979) on the other hand, noted a somewhat different pattern for *S.* (*D.*) *bifidia* in a South Carolina low marsh. The density of the naupliar stage was low during the winter months, but suddenly increased in March and then declined to low numbers into midsummer. Fleeger reported a "bloom" of *S.* (*D.*) *bifidia* from mid-June to mid-July with the copepodite stage representing a large proportion of the population. Following this the age structure remained stable until October when naupliar production decreased and adults became more abundant. Altogether, for the period of July–September, 48 percent of the *S.*(*D.*) *bifidia* population was nauplii (Fleeger, 1979).

In the high-marsh habitat, Bell (1979) observed that another common species, *Schizopera knabeni,* displayed a high proportion of gravid females and reproductive activity was evident throughout the sampling period of 20 months. In contrast, *Microarthridion littorale* showed little uniformity and displayed a fluctuating low proportion of gravid females.

Reproductive activity for *M. littorale* in the low marsh began in the early spring (Fleeger, 1979). Nauplii and total numbers increased to a September peak declining as adults became more abundant in October. The naupliar stage dominated from March to October and made up 60 percent of the population.

Fleeger (1979) observed that reproductive activity for *Enhydrosoma propinquum* began in mid-February. Adults were low in number, but made up the bulk of the population at that time and increased in number into March. The quantity of nauplii decreased through the spring after a late-March peak and increased during the fall followed by a decline through November. The nauplii comprised 47 percent of the population from March through October. Adult numbers displayed little variation for the period of March-October, increasing in November.

In an attempt to understand the population dynamics more fully, Fleeger (1979) also compared birth and death rates and brood sizes. He found both rates for *M. littorale* to be high (>0.6/individual/day) and somewhat lower for *S. (D.) bifidia* (0.3/individual/day). Due to spatial variability the values for *S. (D.) bifidia* were subject to fluctuations. The death rate for *S. (D.) bifidia* averaged 24 percent of the population per day for June to September. For *M. littorale* it was 44 percent for March to October. The death rate for *E. propinquum* was 13 percent in the summer and fall and close to zero after October through March. The monthly average brood size was 7–14 eggs per ovigerous female for *M. littorale*. The broods were larger (7–9 eggs) for March–October and less than five from November–February. *S. (D.) bifidia* had monthly averages of 4–8 per clutch with the average brood size increasing during the spring.

Based on these observations, Fleeger (1979) arrived at three generalizations about meiofaunal copepod populations in a South Carolina low-marsh habitat. (1) Reproduction was low and adult survivorship was high for all three species during the winter months. (2) After reproduction began in the spring, approximately one month elapsed between the appearance of the nauplii and the copepodite stage for each species. (3) Because size distributions were stable, constant recruitment occurred for *E. propinquum* from May–September; for *M. littorale,* March–October; for *S. (D.) bifidia,* July–September. Based on an estimate of copepod development time, Fleeger (1979) suggested the number of "generations" during the time of stable age distribution would be nine for *E. propinquum,* twelve for *M. littorale* and five for *S. (D.) bifidia.*

Brood sizes and birth rates were lowest for all three species during the winter, suggesting to Fleeger that food or temperature limited the population at that time. He found no evidence of food limitation for *M. littorale* during the warm half of the year which suggested that predation tended to limit the population. It appeared that food supplies did restrict *S. (D.) bifidia* during the summer since brood size increased and then declined as density increased. While Fleeger (1979) found *E. propinquum* to be the most abundant copepod, he was unable to quantify the birth potential and thus was unable to determine the mechanism of population regulation.

MOLLUSCA

Pelecypoda

Bayne (1976a) provided us with a review of reproduction among the bivalve molluscs indicating that most reproduce by planktonic larval development. All of them have an annual reproductive cycle and most, if not all of their energy goes into gametogenesis, the extent depending on the species. There are few species of bivalves associated with tidal marshes. *Geukensia* (= *Modiolus*) *demissa* and *Cyrenoida floridana* are uniquely related with this habitat; the former having a range extending from Prince Edward Island southward to Florida, while the latter is found from Florida to southern Delaware. Nichol (1936) listed *Mytilus edulis, Macoma balthica,* and *Mya arenaria* from the substrate of pools of a marsh bordering the Firth of Forth. Local observations of *M. edulis* in Delaware have demonstrated that this species can be so abundant at times that it facilitates the development of bars in tidal creeks. MacDonald (1969a, b) portrayed the species as a characteristic member of the tidal creek epifauna of the North American west coast while *Mya arenaria* and species of *Macoma* are associated with the creek infauna. While these bivalve species are present subtidally, none are common in tidal marshes, having centers of distribution in other marine habitats.

In spite of its unique position in the tidal marsh and abundance over an extensive geographic range, there is a paucity of life history information about *G. demissa* (see Chapter 2 for a discussion pertaining to specific environmental parameters and a review of physiological studies by Bayne [1976b]). There is even less information pertaining to the reproductive cycle. Lind (1975) has described the gametogenetic cycle. The inactive stage was characterized by a few small follicles within the connective tissue of the mantle, densely packed with immature oocytes. The average diameter of the oocytes was less than 10 microns. As development proceeded through the spring and early summer, the number of follicles increased in number and size. The follicular walls thickened. Primary oocytes continued to form and develop along the basal membrane. The ripe stage was characterized by a distinct reddish color in the mantle tissue. Examination of the ripe tissue revealed many follicles densely packed with mature unattached ova. The follicles were expanded and the lumen was completely filled. Ripe mussels were found during the midsummer period. A spent individual was characterized by expanded follicles with empty lumina and thickened walls. The remains of unspawned ova which had been cytolized was evident. Primary oogonia and ovocytes were found in the follicular wall as the follicles contracted.

Small indistinct alveoli in the mantle characterized the inactive male during the winter and spring periods. As development proceeded during early summer, the alveolus enlarged with thickened walls due to the development of secondary spermatocytes and spermatids. The ripe stage was characterized in midsummer by dense radiating bands of spermatids and spermatozoa with tails oriented toward the center of the lumen. The entire mantle tissue was packed with filled alveoli. A spent male was identified by

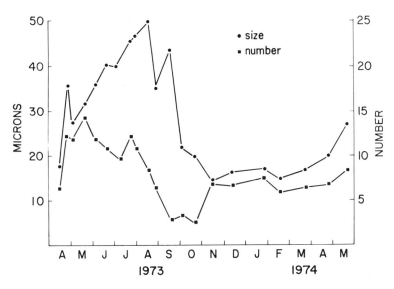

Figure 5.1.   Average egg size and number of *Geukensia demissa*, Rehoboth Bay, Spring 1973–Spring 1974. (From Lind, 1975.)

the absence of radiating bands of spermatozoa and empty alveoli. The alveolus was slightly thickened. Such a condition was seen in late summer and the early fall.

Seed (1976) identified temperature as one factor contributing to mussel spawning, and observed that southern species usually spawn later and have a resticted season progressively northward while northern species spawn earlier and have an extended season southward. This agreed with Lind's (1975) observation that *G. demissa* spawned for a one-month period (Figure 5.1) and did so two weeks earlier in Cape Cod than in Delaware. However, subsequent work (Corbett, 1981) refutes some of Lind's interpretations. Based on gonadal aspect, gonadal index, and the presence of straight-hinge larvae in the plankton, Corbett found continuous low-level spawning from July through December with no concentrated spawning period. Further an individual mussel did not appear to shed all its gametes at once. Maintenance of local populations may be achieved through a prolonged leaking reproductive cycle and passive recruitment of larvae from the larger estuarine population (Corbett).

Sullivan (1948) described *G. demissa* larvae, and recorded their appearance in the plankton when the water around Prince Edward Island reached 20–22 °C in mid–July. She found most larvae appearing in August at temperatures of 22–28 °C. One might presume there would be a progressive wave of spawning moving northward as the temperature extended into the 20 °C levels, beginning in the spring at the lower latitudes. However, Kuenzler (1961a) found small mussels throughout the year in a Georgia marsh which was not expected since ripe adults were found only in the late summer. The largest numbers of recruits to the population were observed in March–April but the larger average size of new arrivals was in September–October. Kuenzler offered a highly variable growth rate as a possible factor; the same variability that Loosanoff and Davis (1963) observed. Another explanation may be provoked by recent studies by Seed (1976) on the duration of the spawning period of *Mytilus edulis:* he reported that the period during which 25 percent of the population spawned along the North Yorkshire coast of England extended over four to six months.

Loosanoff and Davis (1963) described the appearance of the ribbed mussel larvae from two natural spawnings occurring in the laboratory. The straight-hinge stage was reached in 24 hours at room temperature. Most larvae at that time measured 110–115 microns in length and 85–90 microns in width. The smallest was recorded at 105 microns in length. With a temperature of 22 °C and plenty of good food many larvae reached a length of 200 microns by the tenth day. A few developed a prominent "eye" spot and a functional foot. Some larvae completely metamorphosed at 220 microns but most did not lose the velum until 275 microns. While some larvae metamorphosed in 12–14 days after fertilization, many in the same cultures were still free-swimming at 43 days when the experiment was terminated. There was considerable disparity in sizes within a single culture. While there were many 250–295 microns free-swimming larvae, there were also metamorphosed juveniles up to one millimeter in length.

The reproductive biology has recently been described for the Florida marsh clam, *Cyrenoida floridana,* at the known northern limits of its range, extending into southern Delaware (Kat, 1978). *C. floridana* is a functional hermaphrodite and there is simultaneous production of both sexual gametes in paired gonads, by each individual, with male and female elements found in each follicle. A small percentage (11 percent) of those individuals examined by Kat were true males where the oocytes were aborted. The planktonic larval stage had been bypassed.

Four major reproductive stages were recognized in the Florida marsh clam: gametogenic, mature, spawned, and resorbtive. The first was the stage wherein the gonadal follicles contained spermatogenic and/or oogenic cells in various stages of development. The mature stage was recognized by follicles filled with ripe gametes and developing stages absent or reduced in number. The spawned stage was characterized by the discharge of the gametes leaving the follicles more or less empty. Any unspawned gametes were resorbed by phagocytic activity thus constituting the resorptive stage.

These four stages of the reproductive cycle were repeated during the year. The first cycle began in late winter and gametes reached maturity during the early summer. Resorption took place in early fall. The second cycle began in midfall but maturity of the gonads was not achieved. Resorption occurred during late fall-early winter. The only successful spawning took place during the middle of the summer. Follicular walls were generally very thin by late July, indicating a full expansion of the gonad, and by the middle of August all bivalves examined were fully ripe. Kat suggested from the literature, that *C. floridana* probably spawns twice a year in Florida but could do so only once in southern Delaware since the second cycle would be resorbed. Presumably the shorter warm season in Delaware precludes the completion of the second spawning cycle.

Fertilization must have occurred close to the gonoducts since the fertilized eggs were incubated within the brood chambers. There was some evidence that *C. floridana* may reproduce by self-fertilization, but since the incidence of successful fertilization in the population was so low, Kat reasoned that it must be almost completely autosterile.

The first spawned hermaphrodite with trochophore and veliger stages within the demibranches was encountered at the end of July. Juveniles within the brood chambers were found in an advanced stage of development by late August. The spawning period was described by Kat to span a one-month interval from mid-July to the middle of August.

As development proceeded and the larvae reached the juvenile stage (characterized by the loss of the velum, developed organ systems, and the presence of a well-developed foot) they were found in the cloacal chamber whereby they were presumably released through the exhalent siphon. Such fully developed juveniles reached a maximum size of 350 to 400 microns in length which probably was the size at the time of release. Brood protection lasted about one month as Kat collected no bivalves with young in September, yet at the same time some of the young had already grown to a length of 900–1000 microns. There was some evidence the young began to feed prior to leaving the brood pouch.

Brood protection by the marsh clam is of distinct advantage since a pelagic larva would have little chance of returning to the high intertidal zone which is the preferred habitat for this bivalve. At the same time, dispersal ability is reduced during the larval stages by such brood protection. This marsh clam overcomes the problem of dispersion by taking air bubbles into the mantle cavity to become positively buoyant. By such means, the juveniles can float on gentle currents as the flooding tide flows among the grass stems. Kat observed that the foot rapidly extruded air bubbles whenever the floating clam came into contact with an object. A behavioral trait such as flotation would be a substantial aid in dispersion in sheltered waters.

Two bivalves, *G. demissa* and *C. floridana,* have penetrated the high salt marsh. Both have evolved the ability to air gape when not covered by the tide and at the same time occupy an infaunal position to reduce the effects of dessication. *G. demissa* retains the general bivalve plan of releasing planktonic larvae into the water column, thus it must occupy a zone that is frequently covered by the tide. The Florida marsh clam, by adopting a viviparous condition through larval retention in the demibranchs, is able to live at a slightly higher elevation. The same kind of developmental pattern has been suggested for some of the intertidal Gastropoda.

Gastropoda

While there is little known about the reproductive habits of bivalves associated with tidal marshes, the literature dealing with marsh gastropods is more replete. There are extensive reviews by Fretter and Graham (1962) dealing with prosobranch snails and by Hyman (1967) covering that group as well as the pulmonate snails, the two groups that comprise the major component of the gastropod fauna of the tidal marsh.

The common genera of prosobranch snails associated with tidal marshes, though not restricted to the habitat, include *Ilyanassa, Littorina* and *Hydrobia,* all belonging to the order Monotocardia. The diversity of the type of reproduction may be as great within a genus as that of species from unrelated families. Fretter and Graham (1962) recognized three main types of reproduction in the genus *Littorina*: those with pelagic egg capsules and planktonic larvae, those with benthic egg masses and lecithotrophic larvae, and viviparous species.

The egg capsules range from soft gelatinous to hard in consistency and assume a variety of shapes. The common *Littorina littorea,* found on both sides of the Atlantic, produces planktonic capsules one millimeter in diameter, gelatinous disks, pinkish in color with a central domelike expansion, generally hold one to five, or up to nine eggs (Fretter and Graham, 1962, p. 387; Hyman, 1967, p. 303). Fish (1972) recorded an egg diameter of 0.13–0.15 millimeters. Summarizing earlier work, Fretter and Graham described capsules being released one to two hours after copulation and intermittently for a month, the single copulation sufficing. Hatching, usually after six days in normal seawater, is brought about by increased osmotic pressure within the capsule which ruptures the wall. Salinites below $20\%_{00}$ tend to retard development.

A recent study (Fish, 1972) depicted some interesting variations in the breeding cycle of an open coast and an estuarine population of *L. littorea* from the coast of Wales. The estuarine population matured and spawned earlier in the year with maximum spawning in January compared to late February–March for the open coast form. Egg capsules were common in the

Table 5.1. Percentage of specimens of *Littorina littorea* in each developmental state at selected times from an open coast and an estuarine population from the coast of Wales. (From Fish, 1972, by permission of the editor, *J. Mar. Biol. Assoc.*)

	11 XII 68		30 VI 69		6 XI 69		4 XII 69		17 VIII 70		17 XII 70		23 VI 71	
	OC	E	OC	E	OC	E	OC	E	OC	E	OC	E	OC	E
Maturing/ Spawning	16	82	4	0	0	21	13	43	3	0	29	89	0	0
Recovering	80	18	0	0	48	71	80	51	0	0	60	8	12	0
Partially spent	0	0	69	12	0	0	0	3	30	0	0	3	60	15
Spent	4	0	27	88	52	8	7	3	67	100	11	0	27	85

OC = open coast population
E = estuarine population

estuary during early December. Earlier work had displayed egg maturation occurring at low temperatures with spawning taking place with a rise in temperature. However, for this estuarine population, maturity and spawning occurred with falling temperatures. Fish attributed the early maturation and spawning of the estuarine population to the higher nutritional level available in contrast to that found in the open coast habitat. The establishment of new broods in the estuary in March was significantly earlier than June–July on the open coast. The fully spent condition was reached at least a month earlier in the estuarine population (Table 5.1 and Figure 5.2).

The pelagic capsules liberated by the estuarine population would be expected to leave the estuary on ebb tides. Despite extensive sampling, however, egg capsules were not found from open coast deposits. In addition, there were many uncapsulated eggs and free-swimming larvae associated with *Spartina* beds, undergoing full development in the moist detritus. Since the egg capsules were only slightly more dense than seawater, it was postulated that they could sink in the lower specific gravity of the estuarine water and thus be retained in the system. All estuarine individuals spawned during their second winter, whereas earlier work reviewed by Fish (1972) noted open coast forms began to spawn during the second winter but a significant proportion did not spawn until the third winter. This could have important implications in recruitment and maintenance of these open coast and estuarine populations.

Other members of the Littorinidae which produce pelagic capsules include *Littorina scutulata* from the high intertidal rocky coast of the Pacific northwest (Buckland-Nicks and Fu-Shiang Chia, 1973), *L. irrorata* from a salt marsh on the Gulf coast of Florida (Bingham, 1972) and *L. melanostoma* from Malayan mangrove swamps (Berry and Chew, 1973).

Egg laying for *L. scutulata* was observed during the morning and evening between the hours of six and eight in the summer months, suggesting

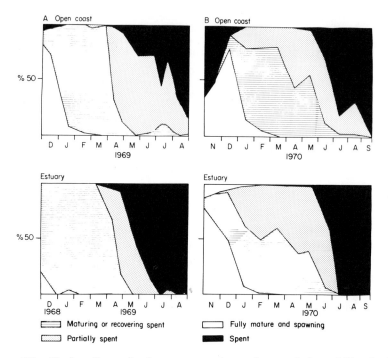

Figure 5.2.   The breeding cycle of open coast and estuarine populations of *Littorina lit-torea* from the coast of Wales. (From Fish, 1972, by permission of the editor, *J. Mar. Biol. Assoc.*)

the influence of changing light intensity on a diurnal basis. The egg capsule was like an inverted saucer with a diameter of 840 microns, containing 1–6 eggs. The eggs were yellow-orange in color and approximately 100 microns in diameter. Three females were observed to produce 896, 1034, and 1398 capsules respectively within a fourteen-day period, stopping production on the fourteenth day. Egg production was four or more during the first week, reduced to three eggs during the last four days. Development through hatching took seven to eight days at 10–14 °C and three days at 22 °C. Just before hatching the egg membrane diameter expanded about one-third, presumably due to osmotic pressure, thus undoubtedly weakening the membrane. This, along with vigorous movement of the veliger, ruptured the membrane freeing the larva. Shortly after this, the capsular lid opened releasing the well-developed larvae into the plankton where they immediately began to feed. These larvae remained planktonic for about three weeks when they achieved a 300–360 micron length of shell. By this time they had settled onto the substrate (Buckland-Nicks and Fu-Shiang Chia, 1973).

Like *L. scutulata*, *Littorina irrorata* mated during the May-July period

(Bingham, 1972). In contrast, *L. melanostoma* tended to produce eggs throughout the year (Berry and Chew, 1973) similar to *L. littorea* (Fretter and Graham, 1962). Bingham observed *L. irrorata* mating on clear sunny days, ceasing on cloudy, cooler days. High temperature was considered to be a stimulus for mating which occurred in a sunlit pan and in a pan in an oven with the temperature at 35 °C. No mating was observed after late September through March. Spawning took place at the time of the next high tide after mating, regardless of time of day. Most spawnings took place at the air-water interface, a few in the submerged positon. The egg cases were expelled continuously at a rate of 4–5 per second for a period of 2–4 hours. Two snails were observed to produce an estimated 43,000 to 85,000 eggs. *L. irrorata* produced clear, planktonic, disk-shaped egg capsules, measuring 250–280 microns in diameter, each holding a single gray egg. The capsules tended to be negatively buoyant in $26\%_{00}$ seawater (Bingham, 1972).

Earlier work, reviewed by Lenderking (1954), suggested an association between intertidal position and the type of reproduction among littorinid snails. *Littorina littorea*, exposed only at very low water, produces single unattached planktonic capsules while *L. littoralis*, exposed at low water, produces attached egg masses. In contrast, *L. saxatilis* and *L. neritoides* live in the upper intertidal area which is seldom covered with water. The former is viviparous but *L. neritoides* is not. A transition from oviparous to viviparous has been suggested for the *Littorina* in this order: *L. littoralis* with eggs hatching as adults (no free-swimming larvae); *L. littorea* and *L. neritoides* with eggs hatching as veligers; *L. angulifera* producing first planktonic eggs followed by veligers in each spawning; and finally the viviparous *L. saxatalis* and *L. scabra*. However, Lenderking concluded that association with zonation is not as simplistic as once believed.

Littorina angulifera, associated with mangroves of southern Florida, displayed bilunar periodicity (Lenderking, 1954). Spawning occurred at least ten months of the year with peaks in April-May and October-November, apparently related to rainfall in excess of one inch. *L. angulifera* began shedding eggs sometime between the quarter phase of the moon and the new or full moon. At the time of the new or full moon only veliger larvae were shed. The peak number occurred at this time with diminishing numbers until the next cycle began. Any one female could spawn up to seven times during a ten-month period (or eight times if spawning also occurred in the months of January and February) since no one female spawned in two successive spawning periods. During such an interval, the actual frequency was influenced by the amount of precipitation.

Berry and Chew (1973) also noted a bilunar periodicity in spawning behavior of *Littorina melanostoma* in Malayan mangroves. This snail, found high in the intertidal zone, moved up and down the stems keeping just ahead of the rising spring tides. Smaller individuals tended to be at lower levels but

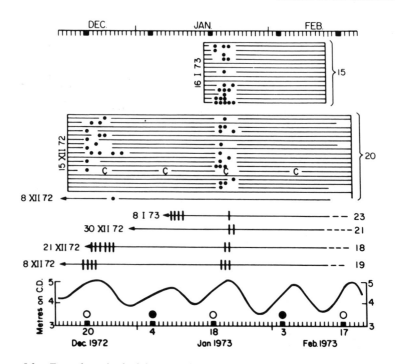

Figure 5.3. Egg-release in the laboratory by *L. melanostoma*: observations of December 1972–February 1973. Dates of full and new moon are given at bottom. Levels reached by highest daily tides only are plotted in meters above chart datum. Thin horizontal lines represent individual females (two groups above) or entire groups of females (four groups below). Heavy dots indicate egg-release by individuals. Short vertical bars indicate egg-release by groups. "C" (on line near center) indicates shedding of cercaria larvae by one female. Dates of collection are at left, numbers of females at right. (From Berry and Chew, 1973, by permission of the editor, *J. Zoology.*)

not on the ground. Maximal egg release was associated with the highest tides of the full moon but not necessarily on the day of the full moon (Figure 5.3). Rarely were eggs found during the new moon or other phases. Eggs were produced throughout the year with considerable variation in numbers but no seasonal pattern was evident. There was no evidence of a relationship between egg release and time of day or night. Nor was there any evidence of an endogenous rhythm of egg release related to times of high tide. Any tidal rhythmicity of egg release during full-moon periods was directly determined by the need for water in which to spawn rather than by true rhythms of oviposition.

Not all females released eggs every full moon. Many released eggs during two successive full moons but slightly more than half released eggs only during one of two such time periods. Some released eggs over two, three, or four days in several sessions of oviposition. The numbers of eggs released were greater where there were several periods of spawning than when there was a single egg deposition. Single releases were estimated at 850–4200 eggs with most ranging between 1500–2500. Multiple releases varied between 8000–14,000 with the first release having the largest number, normally decreasing with subsequent bouts. Where there were multiple releases during one full-moon period there usually was, at best, a single weak release in the succeeding full-moon phase (Berry and Chew, 1973).

The eggs of *L. melanostoma* were released into the water in pelagic egg capsules. Each capsule typically contained a single egg 120–140 micrometers in diameter. The outer capsule was a symmetrical biconcave disc 290–310 micrometers in diameter. Berry and Chew (1973) inferred that species that produce big pelagic egg capsules produce fewer eggs than those species with small capsules. *L. angulifera* produced 760,000 eggs in capsules only 71 micrometers in diameter (Lenderking, 1954). As noted earlier, Bingham (1972) recorded up to 85,000 eggs for *L. irrorata* with a capsule diameter of 250–280 micrometers.

A second mode of reproduction among the littorinid snails is the production of benthic egg masses encapsulated in a gelatinous material. Buckland-Nicks and Fu-Shiang Chia (1973) reported that *Littorina sitkana* produced such eggs about 175 microns in diameter with spawning occurring between six and nine, morning and evening. As with *L. scutulata* this suggested the influence of changing light intensity. The egg capsule was rigid with a maximum diameter of one millimeter. Egg masses were found throughout the year but there were distinct spawning peaks in April and in October (Figure 5.4). The velum formed about the sixth day at which time the veliger larva ruptured the fertilization membrane and began to consume the supply of albumen. By ciliar action the veliger dispersed and consumed the albumen layer, becoming lodged between the albumen and the outer capsule. This took about ten days during which the larval shell began to take on color causing the entire egg mass to shift from pale yellow, through pink to dark brown.

By this time the albumen was exhausted, the velum was reabsorbed and the snail began to move about within the capsule. Such activity began to disrupt the capsular wall which ruptured allowing the foot to be extruded through the hole. Continued foot action enlarged the hole permitting the much larger shell to pass through. Buckland-Nicks and Fu-Shiang Chia (1973) observed hatching in the laboratory to occur 30 days after egg laying at 10–11 °C. The first snails to hatch began to feed on the jelly of the egg mass and the adhering diatoms. Such activity thinned the gelatinous mass facilitating the hatching of those snails deeper in the mass. *L. sitkana* was

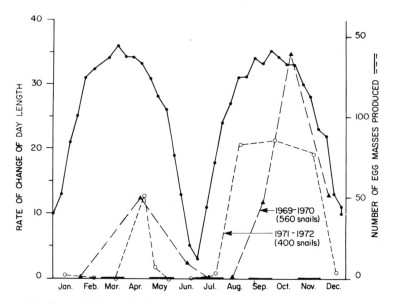

Figure 5.4.   Seasonal fluctuation in egg production of cages *L. sitkana,* from two separate studies (1969–1970; 1971–1972), versus the rate of day length changes during the year. (From Buckland-Nicks and Fu-Shiang Chia, 1973, by permission of the editor, *Can. J. Zool.*)

about 575 microns high on hatching, grew rapidly for the first couple of months, slowed perceptibly, reaching a height of 1 centimeter at one year and attained a maximum height of 2.5 centimeters during a life span of two years.

The reproductive biology of the European marsh snail, *Hydrobia ulvae,* has been described by Fretter and Graham (1962) and by Anderson (1971) and Fish and Fish (1974). This species produces benthic egg masses which are usually fixed to the shells of other live *Hydrobia* but may be deposited on sand grains, dead shells, or green algae. Over 90 percent of the snail shells may have egg masses attached, numbering from 1–22 and a single egg capsule may contain 3–7 eggs (Lebour, 1938) or 5–18 eggs (Fretter and Graham, 1962). From the Ythan estuary in Aberdeenshire, Scotland, Anderson (1971) recorded variable numbers of eggs up to 40 in a capsule with an average of 7.8 (S.D. ± 3.2). Fish and Fish recorded similar numbers with a peak (8.9 ± 3.5 S.D.) in August and a maximum number in July.

The egg capsule is lens-shaped, about 0.6 millimeters in diameter, covered with sand grains and attached to the shell by its flattened base. The egg is covered by a thin membrane and floats within the capsular albumen. Each female may produce 300 eggs during a spawning season, the timing of which

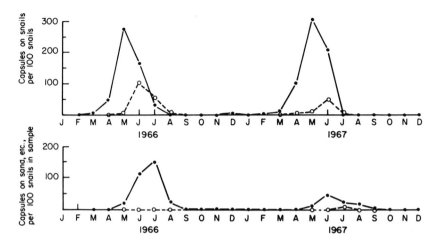

Figure 5.5.   Production of *Hydrobia* egg-capsules, in zone 1 (●) and zone 3 (○). (Zone 1 is higher in the littoral zone, Zone 3 is low intertidal.) (From Anderson, 1971, by permission of the Cambridge University Press.)

displays considerable variability. Spawning may be in May and June at one site or in the fall at another site, extending into the spring and summer. Fish and Fish (1974) reported mature females throughout the year from the Dovey estuary, Wales. Anderson found capsules with eggs every month in the Ythan estuary but the main spawning period was April–June with a peak in May. Fish and Fish noted two peaks of spawning, in May and August of one year, but in June and September of another. Anderson noted that older, larger snails bred earlier and higher in the littoral zone, while Fish and Fish recorded that females matured at a larger size at the higher, muddier site. As the numbers of capsules on live shells decreased after May, the numbers on sand grains and other objects increased (Figure 5.5), suggesting that snails bred a second time (Anderson, 1971). Veliger larvae emerged in about three weeks (Fretter and Graham, 1962) or 8–10 days (Anderson). Fretter and Graham stated that the planktonic stage could last a month or more but was sometimes much shorter, even suppressed. Anderson recorded conflicting views about the time during which the larva was mobile, considering it to be relatively short or nonexistent. Free-swimming larvae in large numbers were found in the Ythan estuary only in June. Veliger larvae were never abundant and were recorded only for July, August, and September, yet young snails with a shell height of 0.25 millimeters and larger were present in the intertidal sediments from June onward (Fish and Fish, 1974). Anderson considered the planktonic stage to be a distinct disadvantage in a fast-moving estuary: limited mobility would enable the larvae to retreat downward to a less exposed habitat. With the loss of the velum the small one-millimeter snails settled to the substrate and were dispersed by the tides. Fretter and Graham recorded earlier estimates of 10 percent survival of the eggs to the small snail stage which was considered to be a high survival compared to bivalves. Earlier work recorded by Anderson (1971) suggested that *H. ulvae* matured in twelve months or two years. Observations in the Ythan estuary suggested attainment of sexual maturity during the third summer, when *Hydrobia* was almost two years old.

Other hydrobiads associated with the tidal marshes of the British Isles include *Assiminea grayana* which spawns in the late spring and summer producing egg capsules containing a single egg which are deposited singly in the mud as the snail crawls about. At times a number of these capsules may be packed together by the foot. A free-swimming larva has been recorded. Another snail, *Truncatella subcylindrica,* restricted to the marshes on the south coast of England, lives at the high tide mark among the *Suaeda maritima* and *Halimione portulacoides* plants. Presumably egg capsules are deposited among the plants. The larval stage has been reported as suppressed (Fretter and Graham, 1962).

The mud snail, *Ilyanassa obsoleta* (= *Nassarius obsoletus*), found in dense concentrations on muddy intertidal flats and in the bottoms of drainage ditches within the tidal marshes of the North American east coast, displays substrate selection by the larva, a characteristic shared by other benthic invertebrates, particularly detritus feeders. Scheltema (1961) considered this ability a decisive factor in benthic population stability.

Egg capsules were abundant at the height of the spawning season, attached to any solid surface. The capsules tended to be irregular, spiny, sessile, straw-colored and about 2.7 millimeters in height. Capsules produced by each female were unique, formed by the pedal gland of the individual. Each capsule contained 40–150 eggs, usually about 100; the egg diameter was approximately 160 microns. At 20 °C larvae were fully differentiated by six or seven days but often remained in the capsule for some time. Water temperatures of 11–13 °C inhibited the rate of larval development within the capsule. Scheltema (1962) concluded that temperatures at the time of capsule deposition probably had little effect on survival of developing embryos. At the time of hatching, larvae were about 275 microns long. When cultured in the laboratory at 20–25 °C, the creeping-swimming stage was reached in 12–16 days at which time the velum was cast off and the planktonic stage was terminated. By this time the larvae were about 630 microns high and they began an alternating creeping-swimming search of the substrate (Scheltema, 1962). Little further growth took place until metamorphosis. The larvae could metamorphose as early as 12–16 days after emergence from the egg capsule but, in the absence of a suitable substrate, planktonic existence could be continued for as long as 20 days after the creeping-swimming stage had been reached. The shell darkened a few days after metamorphosis and the adult character became evident.

The third type of reproduction, viviparity, is associated with prosobranch snails typified by *Littorina saxatilis*. While this species is typically associated with rocky surfaces (Berry, 1961), Dexter (1947) characterized it as a dominant in the lower *Spartina* zone at Cape Ann, Massachusetts, the southern limit of its geographic range in the western Atlantic.

L. saxatilis breeds throughout the year, perhaps interrupted in May through July (Berry, 1961). When egg production was in progress the ovary was distended with eggs 90–300 microns at their greatest diameter. The number of embryos increased through the spring until May. Their numbers declined sharply during June and July and by August the ovary had recovered. Eggs formed the bulk of the ovary during early autumn, replaced by advanced embryos and young by early June. The intertidal position influenced the numbers of eggs and embryos: those snails at higher intertidal levels contained many more eggs and embryos, and thus presumably more favorable environmental conditions existed at higher levels. Male sexual activity followed the same pattern, being least active during June through August. While the sex ratio was essentially even during the year, the numbers of males declined during the summer months. Associated with the summer decline of sexual activity was an increase in trematode infestation.

Mating took place whenever the exposed shore was wet, but with reduced frequency during the summer. Evidence indicated fertilization usually took place within five hours of copulation and Berry observed eggs being introduced into the brood pouch 17 hours after mating. Berry also observed all stages of egg development and, since isolated eggs were observed to develop into unshelled veligers within three days, he speculated that ovulation must be a continuous process with no discrete batches.

L. saxatilis grew at a faster rate at the higher intertidal stations, reaching a shell height of 8 millimeters in ten months, while those at lower stations achieved a height of 7.2 millimeters. Males became sexually mature at 6 millimeters. Females carried eggs in the brood pouch at 7–7.2 millimeters, hence those in the higher zone matured at about eight months while those in the lower zone took 9–10 months (Berry, 1961).

The tidal rhythmicity associated with egg release and hatching of the simultaneous hermaphroditic pulmonate ellobiid salt-marsh snail, *Melampus bidentatus*, unlike that of *Littorina melanostoma* (Berry and Chew, 1973), is obligate with a direct need for water to carry out the reproductive cycle (Russell-Hunter *et al.*, 1972). While the snail is an air breather and cannot be submerged for long periods it still possesses a free-swimming planktonic veliger stage. The eggs must be kept moist and the veliger must

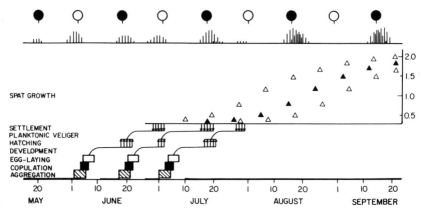

Figure 5.6. Semilunar periodicity in reproduction and early life cycles of *Melampus* at Little Sippewisset. The diagram is based on the actual timings and observations of the "three-cycle" reproductive period of summer 1966, except for the spat growth which is interpolated from the more extensive spat data of 1970. At the top of the figure lunar phases are shown conventionally, with below them a record of those high tides which exceeded a vertical height of 4.4 feet (the height of the top of the *Melampus* zone). At the bottom of the figure, the thicker portions of the base-line indicate times when the population of *Melampus* was dispersed. Three cycles of aggregation, copulation, and egg-laying occur at semilunar intervals. Hatching and settlement also show semilunar synchronization. Three kinds of triangles are used to distinguish successive modal sizes for the three cohorts of spat which result from the three cycles of egg-laying in this reproductive period, and the vertical scale at the right indicates the maximum shell dimension of those spat in millimeters. For further explanation and discussion, see text. (From Russell-Hunter, Apley and Hunter, 1972, by permission of the editor, *Biol. Bulletin.*)

also have water. The species occupies the upper 12 percent of the intertidal zone, and egg release, hatching, and spat setting occur only during the 2–4 percent (approximately eight hours) of the month when that portion of the intertidal zone is flooded by the full- and new-moon spring tides (Figure 5.6). The annual reproductive period extends from late May–early June into early July, usually with three, sometimes four, egg-laying cycles. The onset of reproduction is determined by changing day length in conjunction with conditioning temperature and individual snail biomass. Each cycle has a definite semilunar interval with egg laying restricted to four days in phase with the spring tide. Taking full or new moon as day zero (0) the behavioral sequence involves aggregation (day-1), copulation (+ 1), egg laying (+ 2 through + 6) and dispersion (+ 6 through + 8). Egg production, from an examination of 244 snails, amounted to an estimated 33,150 eggs/female/year (Apley *et al.*, 1967). An individual snail would produce about 39 egg masses during the breeding season with an average of 840 eggs per mass (range 539–1240) (Russell-Hunter *et al.*, 1972). The egg masses were gelatinous with no capsules, and were irregular hemispheres 1–2 millimeters in diameter and 0.5 millimeters thick at the center. The eggs were about 170 microns long and laid in a single continuous strand. These masses were covered with a fine layer of silt and detritus by the flooding spring tide thus preventing dessication.

Hatching in the field occurred about 13 days after egg deposition, was confined to about four days and was synchronized with the spring flood tides at which time tremendous numbers of veligers were collected. These larvae were about 127 microns long. Synchronization with the tides at hatching was more flexible than at egg laying yet synchronization was maintained to permit the future setting of the spat at the appropriate intertidal position on the marsh surface during a subsequent spring tide. Hatched larvae remained inactive unless there was sufficient water for swimming and feeding. Under natural circumstances they swam actively and were carried out to sea on the ebb tide and became a part of the inshore plankton.

Russell-Hunter *et al.* (1972) deduced that the veligers of *Melampus* were a part of the plankton for about fourteen days. Settlement was also synchronized with the spring tides and the bulk of the spat returned to the same zone occupied by the adults. Because of differences induced by varying flow rates many spat settled about the base of *Spartina* stems or in the shallow depressions within the *Melampus* zone. Newly settled spat were about 383 microns in length and four weeks later they were 675 microns long (Apley, 1970).

ARTHROPODA

Crustacea

Isopoda. Kaestner *et al.* (1970, pp. 423–429) have given a general description of the isopod reproductive system. Most isopods are dioecious while a few parasitic forms are protandric hermaphrodites and parthenogenesis has been recognized in one genus. Sexual differences tend to be small. Among some isopods mating can occur only between the molting of the anterior and posterior parts of the female. For others, the female undergoes a partial molt only after mating. The numbers of eggs vary among different species and temperature may have an influence. For species such as *Sphaeroma*, the female releases eggs into the brood pouch two to ten hours after mating. The female circulates respiratory water through the brood pouch and, by use of capillary action, retains water within the pouch and thus can be independent of external water. Only a few isopods are viviparous and in all cases the young remain in the marsupium for a time after hatching with some molts occurring before emergence from the brood pouch.

Dexter (1947) and Averill (1976) recorded high densities of *Philoscia vittata* in the upper portions of the intertidal zone of marshes at Cape Ann, Massachusetts and Lewes, Delaware, respectively. While *P. vittata* was listed as abundant and as a subdominant in the marsh community, there appears to be little information known about its life history.

Nichol (1936) identified two isopods, *Jaera marina* and *Sphaeroma rugicauda* from a Scottish marsh, while Harvey (1969) outlined the breeding cycle of *Sphaeroma rugicauda* from a Welsh marsh. The young *S. rugicauda* were released from the brood pouch in August when they achieved an average 1.9 millimeters in length. They reached an average size of 3.1 millimeters by October, wintering over with a maximum growth rate of 0.47 millimeters per month. Harvey found one female with eggs in January and half the female population was carrying eggs by April (Figure 5.7). Most females carried eggs and embryos in May-July and some females had empty brood pouches in October. Those adults that spawned in the fall wintered over, dying out by spring, and were replaced by their offspring. Thus the life span was identified as 12–18 months for *S. rugicauda*.

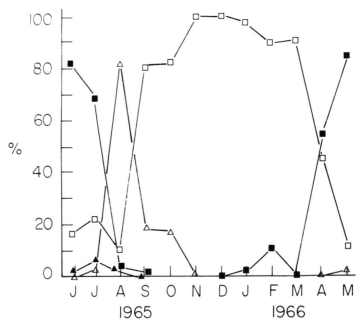

Figure 5.7. Reproductive condition of females as percentatges of the total females of *Sphaeroma rugicauda*. □, with oostigite precursors; ■, with eggs; △, with empty brood pouches; ▲, with embryos. (From Harvey, 1969, by permission of the editor, *J. Anim. Ecol.*)

Considerable attention has been given to the anthurid isopod *Cyanthura polita* which is widely distributed in the estuaries and tidal marshes along the Atlantic and Gulf coasts of the United States (Burbanck, 1961, 1962, ecology and distribution; Miller and Burbanck, 1961, systematics and distribution; Frankenberg and Burbanck, 1963, osmotic relations; Burbanck and Burbanck, 1974, sex reversal; Stromberg, 1972, embryology). However, it is only recently (Kruczynski and Subrahmanyam, 1978) that the reproductive cycle has been fully examined. A review of the literature (Burbanck, 1959, 1962; Stromberg, 1972) identified a spring-summer reproductive period through the range of the species. Stromberg found eggs in the brood pouches at essentially the same stage of development and surmised that reproduction was synchronized in the population. He also suggested that females carried a second brood within the same season. Kruczynski and Subrahmanyam reported that males mature first and comprise 100 percent of the sexually mature population in a north Florida *Juncus roemarianus* marsh during the winter months (November–January). Females with oostigites began to appear from February into May but no young were observed in the brood pouches during February–March. Reproduction occurred primarily from April through June with most gravid females evident in April, being 9–10 millimeters in length. A few gravid females, 10 millimeters in length, were observed in August and one female with oostigites but no eggs in the brood pouch was recorded in October.

A two-year life cycle has been suggested for *Cyathura polita* for northern Florida (Kruczynski and Subrahmanyam, 1978) where males were common in the winter and early spring (Figure 5.8). Some of the large males could have been protogynous hermaphrodites, having functioned as females the preceding spring. Sexual maturity was reached at 9–10 millimeters in length and males were inclined to mature earlier than females. Following the reproductive period in April–June both sexes reverted to a nonreproductive stage and continued to grow. Males and females were recorded in the size range of 12–14 millimeters and a few nonreproductive individuals achieved lengths of 14–15 millimeters (Kruczynski and Subrahmanyam, 1978). Since both sexes reached sexual maturity at 9–10 millimeters in length and this was accomplished in the spring–summer period following their emergence from the brood pouch, the presence of these larger individuals lent credence to the notion that this species lived through a second winter, completing a two-year cycle. The large males tended to disappear in March.

Nothing seems to be known about the numbers of eggs carried in the brood pouch of female *C. polita,* development times or the numbers of broods. For a species with such an extended latitudinal range and restricted range of movement for individuals, one might expect some differences in the

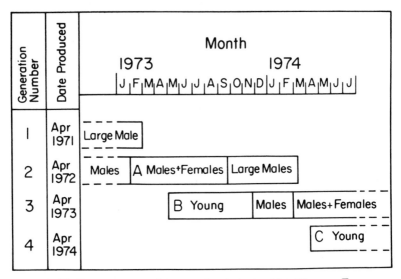

A B C correspond to peaks labeled in Figure 3.

Figure 5.8.   Schematic of life cycle of *Cyathura polita* from a north Florida *Juncus* marsh. Cohort (A) produces young (B) which grow and produce young (C) one year later. Some individuals end life cycle as large males. (From Kruczynski and Subrahmanyam, 1978, by permission of the editor, *Estuaries*.)

various phases of the reproductive cycle. It is not known whether the number of eggs declines in the brood pouch as was reported for *Jaera marina* (Kaestner *et al.*, 1970) where only 3–4 young developed from the 15–16 eggs deposited in the pouch.

Amphipoda. Sexes usually differ in size and, for most gammarideans, the males are larger. The male usually rides on the back of the female for several days prior to the parturial molt with mating taking place immediately following the molt as sperm are transferred to the female gonopores. Some 1.5–4 hours after molting, but while still mating, the female places eggs into the marsupium where they are fertilized. The number and size of the eggs increase with the age of the female. The young may molt first in the marsupium, leave a few days after hatching, and resemble the adults in form (Bousfield, 1973; Kaestner *et al.*, 1970).

The life cycles of two genera of tidal marsh amphipods recently have received attention: *Gammarus palustris* (Rees, 1975; Gable and Croker, 1977; Van Dolah, 1978); and *Orchestia spartinophila* and *O. grillus* (Phillips, 1978).

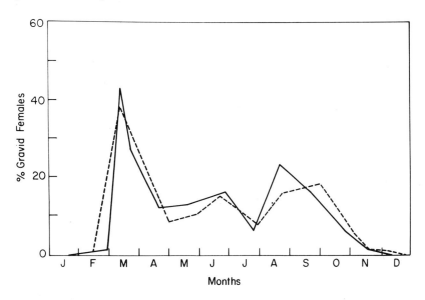

Figure 5.9.   The reproductive activity of *Gammarus palustris* during January 1972 to December 1973, —————, 1972; -----------, 1973. (From Rees, 1975, by permission of the editor, *Estuarine Coast. Mar. Sci.*)

G. palustris is restricted to the lower reaches of marshes and appears to be primarily associated with *S. alterniflora* culms in a narrow band with a shoreward border of extreme high-water neaps (Gable and Croker, 1977) or from approximately midtide level to mean high-water neaps (Bousfield, 1973). Averill (1976) found this amphipod in the very wet areas of Canary Creek marsh, Delaware, usually in more than one centimeter of water and only in the spring and fall, when tides were higher and there was more of the wet habitat to be exploited.

Along the lower Patuxent River, Maryland, the overwintering population of *G. palustris* in December was composed almost entirely of adults with an average female:male ratio of 1:3. Eggs first began to appear in February with a maximum output in March (Figure 5.9). Correspondingly the first young began to appear in March with the greatest numbers in April or May when they made up 79 and 82 percent of the collections for 1972 and 1973 respectively (Figure 5.10). The overwintering population of adults commenced dying off in April and was completely gone by late June–early July. The spring crop of young began to mature by late May and many were mature by late June. They reproduced through the summer into September, ceasing such activity after October (Rees, 1975; Van Dolah, 1978).

There was a gradual, though fluctuating, increase in abundance from

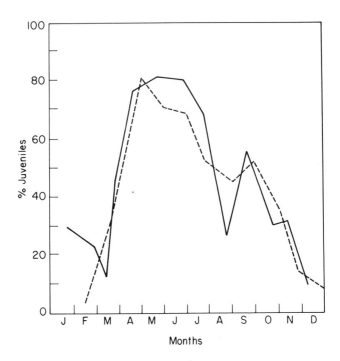

Figure 5.10. Seasonal changes in the juvenile portion of the total population of *Gammarus palustris* during January 1972 to December 1973, ————, 1972; ------------, 1973. (From Rees, 1975, by permission of the editor, *Estuarine and Coast, Mar. Sci.*)

March to October with population lows appearing in midwinter. Van Dolah (1978) attributed these low winter densities in the marsh to a subtidal migration beginning in November and continuing through March. Such a movement occurred over only a short distance to the base of the intertidal shelf: few amphipods were taken in offshore nets. Rees (1975) observed a peak of reproduction in March, produced by the overwintering generation, and a peak in August–September caused by those young produced by the overwintering group. Rees (1975) suggested this overwintering generation might produce only one or two broods while the summer generation might yield several broods. He surmised that young from the earliest summer generation might reach maturity soon enough to create a brood prior to overwintering. At the same time, some of the juveniles produced in September and October overwintered as immatures, enhancing the breeding population the following spring.

Working in the same general area, Van Dolah (1978) observed evidence of a peak of reproductive activity during the spring and the fall in the Patuxent River as did Rees (1975). However, the population of *G. palustris* in the Rhode River displayed increasing numbers of ovigerous females during June and July followed by a steady decline during the rest of the year. Van Dolah attributed the seasonal pattern of population abundance, as well as the difference between the Patuxent and Rhode Rivers, to physical factors during winter months; biological factors were of prime importance for the rest of the year. He found a direct relationship between gammarid densities and *S. alterniflora* stem densities. When culm densities were low there was evidence of intraspecific competition in that the adults displaced the juveniles. Under conditions of low stem density, predation by *Fundulus heteroclitus* was high with a marked preference for larger amphipods. Predation by *Rhithropanopeus harrisii* and *Palaemonetes pugio* was also a factor although not equal to the intensity displayed by the mummichog (Rees, 1975; Van Dolah, 1978).

The sex ratio of *G. palustris* in the Patuxent River marshes varied from 0.24 to 3.45 for females to males, with the ratio reaching a value of 3.5 in April (Rees). Van Dolah observed a preponderance of females in both rivers. Rees speculated that the males might grow faster and die earlier or temperature might determine sex and that males were born earlier in the fall than females. In any case, the greater number of females in the spring enhances production. The change in the ratio during the summer months was attributed to higher temperatures, favoring production of males, or to predation. Evidence suggested a faster growth rate as well as selective predation for the males.

While Rees (1975) and Van Dolah (1978) characterized *G. palustris* in Maryland with one or two broods from the overwintering population and an uncertain number of overlapping broods for the summer generation, Gable and Croker (1977) explicitly identified up to three broods per breeding period for this species at its northern limits in southern New Hampshire. Gable and Croker found the overwintering population to consist of males and immature females. Ovigerous females appeared in April and the first recruitment of young in May. Two generations were present in June and July and the overwintering population was gone by August while the summer generation continued to recruit young into October.

Gable and Croker (1977) found *G. palustris* females carried from 3 to 58 eggs depending on female size and time of year. Reproductive potential reached a peak in May. The overwintering females were larger and carried more eggs than did those from the summer generation (Figure 5.11). Laboratory observations indicated the overwintering females had a minimum of 9–11 weeks of reproductive activity while the summer generation had a

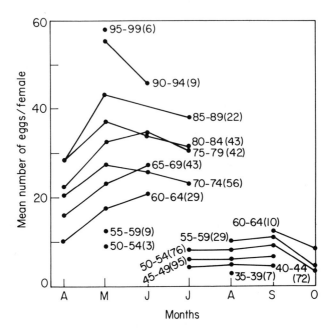

Figure 5.11.   Numbers of eggs per female *G. palustris*. Length range in mm of females is given next to each curve. Spring breeders on left; summer breeders on right. (From Gable and Croker, 1977, by permission of the editor, *Estuarine and Coast. Mar. Sci.*)

minimum of 6–7 weeks of activity. Recently hatched *G. palustris* averaged 1.3 millimeters (range 1.2–1.5) and the young fed and remained in the marsupium two to four days, regardless of temperature.

The talitrid amphipods *Orchestia spartinophila* and *O. grillus* are found to inhabit higher portions of the intertidal zone of a marsh than does *G. palustris*. Phillips (1978) found little overlap in the distributions of *O. spartinophila* and *O. grillus*. The former was found exclusively in low marsh areas characterized by pure stands of *S. alterniflora* or mixed *Distichlis spicata-S. alterniflora* stands but were not uniformly distributed in such habitats. Low numbers were found on higher, sandier areas and individuals were not present on hummocks, even though high densities were often present within the distance of a meter. *Orchestia grillus* was predominantly found among high marsh vegetation, including *S. patens* and *D. spicata*. Individuals were found in *S. alterniflora* adjacent to high marsh vegetation and on hummocks.

The reproductive dynamics of *Orchestia* differ from those described for *Gammarus palustris*. One summer brood was produced for *O. spartinophila* and a second peak of activity was evident in the short *S. alterniflora* community. The spring generation was essentially absent during the fall. Two sum-

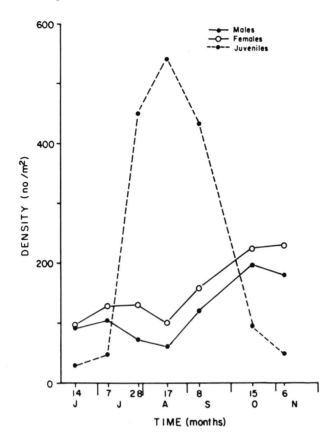

Figure 5.12. Changes in density (number of individuals/m²) of *Orchestia spartinophila* males, females, and juveniles collected in short *S. alterniflora* in the Canary Creek marsh, Lewes, Delaware over the study period. (From Phillips, 1978.)

mer broods were released for *O. grillus,* the second being larger. To produce the size-class structures noted in June for both species, reproductive activity would have to begin in March or April. In 1977, *O. spartinophila* egg laying began in the last week in April. In Canary Creek marsh reproductive activity for both species ceased in September (Phillips, 1978).

The rise in density of *O. spartinophila* at the short *S. alterniflora* site examined in July by Phillips was due to the emergence of juveniles. Adult densities declined to a low of 160/m² in August and at the same time juvenile numbers exceeded 500/m² (Figure 5.12). All three life forms were at approximately 300/m² in June at a mixed *D. spicata-S. alterniflora* site, declin-

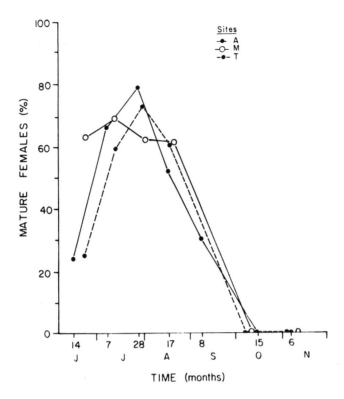

Figure 5.13. Changes in the percent of mature females for *Orchestia spartinophila* collected at three sites in the Canary Creek marsh, Lewes, Delaware over the study period. Site vegetation: A—short *S. alterniflora;* M—mixed short *S. alterniflora-D. spicata;* T—intermediate height *S. alterniflora.* (From Phillips, 1978.)

ing in July but assuming the same density patterns for the remainder of the season. Densities were more variable at an intermediate height *S. alterniflora* site, but followed overall density patterns.

The number of mature females peaked during July (Figure 5.13). This percentage declined by September when summer unsexed juveniles could be identified as immature females. No mature females were found in October or November. The percentage of mature males was highest during June–July showing a similar decline to less than 10 percent by October–November.

Tables 5.2, 5.3 and 5.4 summarize the population characteristics of *O. spartinophila* from the three study sites within the Canary Creek marsh. These data and the information in Figures 5.12 and 5.13 suggested to Phillips (1978) that varying sequences of events occurred at these three sites. In June, densities of the spring generation were much greater at the mixed grass site than at the short *S. alterniflora* site: the spring generation was probably produced in a prolonged period of reproductive activity or in two short periods at the mixed grass site. Greater survival was suggested for the overwintering generation at the mixed grass site. Spring generation adults were producing young about two weeks earlier than the first reproductive peak at the short *S. alterniflora* site. Likewise, a second peak in terms of gravidity and a leveling off of the decline in brood size came in early August, some 2–3 weeks earlier than at the short *Spartina* site.

The major difference between the environment at the sites was the frequency of inundation (Phillips, 1978). In winter, the higher mixed grass site may have been less frequently ice-covered, improving chances of survival. In summer, the frequency of inundation could be reflected in the dryness of the summer. There may be an advantage to synchronizing reproductive activity with the tides wherein juvenile survival could be enhanced if broods were released during spring tide periods.

The intermediate height *S. alterniflora* site consistently had fewer juveniles even though a peak of egg production was evident in July and August. This reduction may be attributed to varying causes: greater dessication stress due to a large surface to volume ratio; migration to higher, wetter, areas; being washed out because of less contact area with crevice walls; or greater predation for the same reason (Phillips, 1978).

Population characteristics of *Orchestia grillus* are summarized in Table 5.5. The sex ratio probably did not differ from 1:1 despite the 4:1 ratio reported for October. Reproductive activity, as expressed as gravidity, percent maturity and brood size, reached a peak in August. Egg density was relatively high (80 to 85/m^2) in late July–mid-August corresponding to the release of the two summer broods. A large number of potential juveniles never appeared in the population (Phillips, 1978).

Decapoda. The grass shrimp genus *Palaemonetes* is widely distributed in both fresh water and saline habitats. A few species such as *P. pugio* and *P. vulgaris* are associated with tidal marshes and related streams. *P. vulgaris* is associated with larger tidal rivers having salinities of 15–35‰ while *P. pugio* is found in smaller tidal creeks, tidal guts, and ditches with lower salinities (Knowlton and Williams, 1970; Hoffman, 1980). The complete life cycles of these species are not known, only bits and pieces. Larval development has been described for *P. pugio* from the North Carolina coast (Broad, 1957a). The nature of the diet had a profound influence on survival, frequency of larval molting and rate of development for both *P. pugio* and *P. vulgaris.*

Table 5.2. Population characteristics of *Orchestia spartinophila* collected in short *Spartina alterniflora* (Site A) in the Canary Creek marsh, Lewes, Delaware over the study period. Categorical data for adjacent dates in boxes not statistically different at 0.05 probability level (less than 5 per category not tested). (From Phillips, 1978)

Characteristic	6/14	7/7	7/28	8/17	9/8	10/15	11/6
				Date			
Number Collected	152	255	542	417	561	438	178
Sex ratio (m/f)	0.94	0.81	0.55	0.59	0.76	0.88	0.79
% mature females	24	66	79	52	30	—	0
% gravid females	88	77	44	77	76	—	—
No. eggs/gravid female	7.38	5.66	3.63	5.17	4.38	—	—
No. eggs/m^2	128	356	147	209	145	—	—
% mature males	81	87	78	24	11	—	—
% juveniles	13	17	69	78	61	19	11

Table 5.3. Population characteristics of *Orchestia spartinophila* collected in a mixed stand of *Spartina alterniflora* and *Distichlis spicata* (site M) in the Canary Creek marsh, Lewes, Delaware over the study period. Categorical data in boxes for adjacent dates not statistically different at 0.05 probability level (less than 5 per category not tested). (From Phillips, 1978)

Characteristic	6/23	7/12	8/2	8/21	10/21	11/11
			Date			
Number collected	204	407	818	350	288	94
Sex ratio (m/f)	0.96	0.74	0.58	0.81	0.92	1.02
% mature females	63	69	62	61	0	0
% gravid females	84	64	84	61	—	—
No. eggs/gravid female	6.39	4.31	3.87	3.29	—	—
No. eggs/m^2	920	420	256	60	0	0
% mature males	78	77	51	31	—	—
% juveniles	35	35	47	75	13	7

Table 5.4. Population characteristics of *Orchestia spartinophila* collected in intermediate height *Spartina alterniflora* (sites T and T') in the Canary Creek marsh, Lewes, Delaware over the study period. Categorical data in boxes for adjacent dates not statistically different at 0.05 level (less than 5 per category not tested). (From Phillips 1978)

Category	Date					
	6/22	7/13	7/31	8/19	10/7	11/4
Number collected	33	72	104	87	96	63
Sex ratio (m/f)	1.37	0.51	0.76	0.61	0.67	0.51
% mature females	25	59	73	61	0	0
% gravid females	50	75	70	90	—	—
No. eggs/gravid female	9.00	5.50	4.84	4.94	—	—
No. eggs/m^2	90	211	294	285	0	0
% mature males	73	57	79	50	13	5
% juveniles	42	43	38	39	17	11

Table 5.5. Population characteristics of *Orchestia grillus* collected in *S. patens* and *D. spicata* (sites D and P, respectively) in the Canary Creek marsh, Lewes, Delaware over the study period. (From Table 4, Phillips, 1978)

Characteristic	Date						
	6/16	7/10	7/29	8/19	9/10	10/14	11/5
Number collected	45	60	60	59	57	31	17
Sex ratio (m/f)	1.83	1.46	0.88	0.94	0.88	4.00	0.60
% mature females	17	38	48	53	38	0	0
% gravid females	100	80	58	67	33	—	—
No. eggs/gravid female	41	12.8	15.0	16.7	10.0	—	—
% mature males	100	100	95	88	71	94	100
% juveniles	54	45	27	46	75	38	19

215

Larvae did not survive beyond the first molt when fed unicellular algae. They molted and developed more rapidly on a diet of animal tissue than on a mixture of plant and animal food (Broad, 1957b).

Both *P. pugio* and *P. vulgaris* have a wide geographic range. Wood (1967), Welsh (1975), and Hoffman (1980) reported a life span of one year for animals from Texas, Rhode Island, and Delaware, respectively. Welsh reported a few adult *P. pugio* passed through a second winter but without additional growth; none survived beyond early April. Female *P. pugio* tended to be larger than the males by 5–7 millimeters (Wood, 1967; Welsh, 1975). The average male was 23.5 millimeters, nonovigerous females 26.2 millimeters, and egg-bearing females 30.0 millimeters (Wood, 1967). Welsh observed that females increased in size over the males by 14 to 30 percent during the summer. Much of the year the sex ratio was 1:1 but males dominated females from May to July by 3:1. Welsh suggested the change was due to greater predation by *Fundulus heteroclitus* on the larger females.

Spawning appears to be related to temperature and salinity. Wood observed males and ovigerous females of *P. pugio* to be most abundant when the water temperatures were $\geq$ 30 °C while nonovigerous females were not plentiful in water temperatures of 14–21.9 °C. Hoffman (1980), while describing work by earlier investigators, reported the best survival for *P. vulgaris* at 25 °C instead of 20 °C or 30 °C. Egg-bearing females and males were most evident with increasing salinity, the reverse for nonovigerous females (Wood ibid.).

The onset of reproductive activity in *Palaemonetes* varies over its broad range, beginning as early as March in Galveston Bay, Texas and in May in Delaware and Rhode Island (Table 5.6). The pattern for reproduction in Delaware was intermediate between that found in Rhode Island and North Carolina. Spawning and recruitment began in Delaware at the same time as in Rhode Island while late summer reproduction followed the southern pattern (Hoffman, 1980). Differences in the length of the spawning season were attributed to seasonal temperature differences found at various latitudes (Wood, 1967).

Both *P. pugio* and *P. vulgaris* are annual species (Hoffman, 1980) and during the breeding season they produce eggs continuously. Welsh (1975) reported maturation times of 15–20 days with eggs being redeposited 1–2 days after hatching of a previous brood (Knowlton and Williams, 1970). Hoffman observed that less than half of the adult females carried eggs except during the breeding peak early in the season. An individual shrimp in Rhode Island (Welsh, 1975) bred throughout a single mating season which terminated in July. The British grass shrimp, *P. varians,* spawned once in early summer (Gurney, 1923; Lofts, 1956). Shrimp from southern populations had a longer breeding season with multiple peaks as in Texas (Wood,

Table 5.6. Breeding seasons for *P. pugio* and *P. vulgaris* (from Hoffman, 1980)

	Rhode Island *P. p.*	Delaware *P. p.*	Delaware *P. v.*	North Carolina *P. p.* & *P. v.*	Texas *P. p.*
Ovary Development				February	
Egg Deposition Begins	May	mid-May	late May	early April	March
Zoea in Plankton				May 1	
Peak Breeding	July	mid-June	mid-June	May 1	April (June and October)
Juveniles Appear	mid-July	early July	early August	early June	April
Age Class 0 Females Spawn	None	late July or early August	early September	late Summer	August
Hatching Stops	late July	early September	early September	mid-October	late October
Age Class 1 Females Disappear	early April of 2nd year	mid-August to early October	mid-August to early October	end of August	
Source	Welsh, 1975	Hoffman, 1980	Hoffman, 1980	Knowlton and Williams, 1970	Wood, 1967

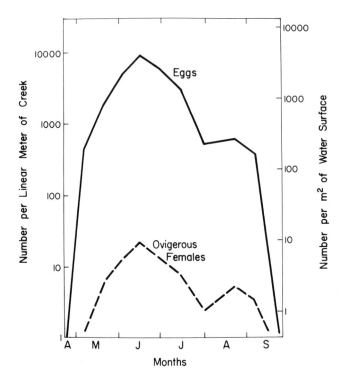

Figure 5.14.   Estimated egg production of *P. pugio* in Canary Creek Marsh, 1977 (from Hoffman, 1980.)

1967) and Delaware (Hoffman, 1980). The evidence for two spawning peaks was based on the bimodal distribution of egg numbers and numbers of ovigerous females (Figure 5.14) (Wood, 1967; Welsh, 1975; Hoffman, 1980). The early spawning gave a chance for some females to begin breeding the same year they were hatched, as well as after overwintering (Table 5.7). This would be especially true for *P. pugio* since the onset of reproduction in *P. vulgaris* lagged two to three weeks behind *P. pugio* in Delaware (Table 5.6). Therefore, few *P. vulgaris* bred during the same year they were hatched. Knowlton and Williams (1970) noted no difference in the breeding seasons of *P. pugio* and *P. vulgaris* in North Carolina.

The size of ovigerous females is largest early in the season with an overall decline with time. For both species of *Palaemonetes,* Hoffman (1980) noted that numbers of eggs, weight of the clutch, and mean weight of a single egg increased with the size of the female. At the same time, clutch size, the weight of a single egg, and the size of ovigerous females declined over the breeding season in Delaware. Wood (1967) demonstrated a linear relation-

Table 5.7. Spawning cycle of *P. pugio* in the Galveston Bay system. (From Wood, 1967, by permission of the editor, *Contrib. Mar. Sci.*)

March-July		August-October		October-March		March-July
A_0 and/or	—	A_1' but with	—	$A_1' + A_2'$	—	A_0' and/or
$A_1 + A_2$		some A_2		(Approx. equal)		$A_1' + A_2'$

A_0 = parent generation

A_1 = generation spawned in spring of previous year

A_2 = generation in fall of previous year

A_1' = generation spawned in spring of present year

A_2' = generation spawned in fall of present year

A_0' = parent generation of the following or future year

ship between female size and the number of eggs carried. In Texas, only the largest (32–38 millimeters) *P. pugio* produced eggs in March to June, gradually being replaced by smaller (20–31 millimeters) egg-bearing females during August and September and reverting to larger females toward the end of the breeding season. Wood also observed fewer ovigerous females in June (23 percent) than in September (28 percent) but noted higher production in June with a calculated average egg number of 372 in contrast to 198 in September. Welsh (1975) recorded 486 eggs per female in early June and 454 eggs in mid-July. Hoffman (1980) noted the females in Delaware carried much smaller clutches than in the Texas or Rhode Island populations but attributed no significance to such a variance.

The Delaware *P. pugio* eggs were larger than *P. vulgaris* eggs with average dry weights of 0.065 milligrams and 0.045 milligrams respectively. Hoffman observed that when the time of the year was taken into account, the clutch weights of *P. pugio* and *P. vulgaris* for a given size female were equivalent. Thus, *P. vulgaris* carried many more eggs per clutch. Hoffman went on to demonstrate that, during the 1977 breeding season, each breeding female *P. pugio* produced an average of 920 eggs. Since it was estimated that only about 10 percent was produced by Age Class 0 females, the Age Class I females must have produced three or more clutches over the breeding season. *P. vulgaris* females produced an average of 750 eggs per female during the breeding season. Therefore, it appeared that most individuals of this species produced no more than two clutches of eggs over the breeding season. Hoffman also noted that clutch size might decrease with the season, independent of female size for both *P. pugio* and *P. vulgaris*. This agreed with Welsh's (1975) observation that second clutches tended to be smaller.

Fiddler crabs of the genus *Uca* are found on estuarine intertidal shores in tropical, subtropical, and warm temperate regions of the world. Their movements between the water's edge and their burrows and the activity of the displaying males are a characteristic and yet unique facet of the tidal marsh scene. Since they are associated with warm climates, activity in temperate zones is confined to the warmest months. Gray (1942) found *Uca minax* overwintering in burrows below the frost line in a state of torpor in the Solomons, Maryland area from October into late April. Surface activity was fully resumed in May.

Crane (1975) provided us with a detailed statement on the reproductive behavior of fiddler crabs. She admonished us to exercise caution in attributing any display component to normal courtship. Displaying individuals are usually reacting toward neighbors and nearby wanderers of both sexes. Conflict and displacement behavior are sometimes prevalent, thus difficulties arise in interpretation.

The burrow becomes the center of a defended territory. Zucker (1974) observed that males, under certain circumstances, build "shelters" over the burrow entrance. It was noted that males without such shelters defend a territory 360° around the burrow. Those males with shelters defend a larger area in front of the shelter and less behind, thus producing an oval-shaped territory. In this way, it was postulated, the territories would be slightly smaller with less overlap, resulting in less aggression between neighboring crabs. Such shelters were more evident in densely populated areas. It appears that high population density would be of distinct advantage to displaying males, providing direct courtship stimulation by neighboring males. In addition females, which may have to be stimulated by many males before becoming receptive, would tend to mate more rapidly. In the majority of species a burrow-holding male increases the tempo of display whether he is threatening another male or directing activities toward a particular female. Display motions not only increase in tempo but become more accentuated. This implies that waving is a threat posture toward other males, but it is not clear that such is necessarily the case. All of the signs of high-intensity display change little or not at all when unequivocal courtship is underway. Only certain components of waving display appear to be restricted to courtship. Curtsy is the only widespread example among several species. Quivering, vibration of the stiffened ambulatories on the major side, and a display toward the rear are courtship displays evident among various species.

Sound, as a definite part of the final stages of courtship has been substantiated among a few species including *U. pugnax* and *U. pugilator*. Salmon (1965) proposed that sound production and nocturnal courtship is an adaptation of temperate zone species which enables faster completion of reproductive activities during the brief time when climatic conditions are favorable for survival of the young. For *U. pugnax,* much of the sound production is done at night by stamping the ambulatories. Salmon (1965) noted that *U. pugilator* produced sounds almost continuously at night when the tide was low. The number of sound-producing crabs increased while the tide was receding and reached a maximum on the incoming tide. The transition from waving to sound production was observed when low tides coincided with sunset: waving ceased within 30 minutes after sunset (Table 5.8). Salmon recorded (Table 5.9) the number of sounds produced by 30 male *U. pugilator* 15 seconds before and during introduction of conspecific males and females into their burrows. The test males did not produce sounds before the introductions during the day but at night all the males were rapping before the introductions. The average rate of sounds during the night time introductions was significantly greater than the rate before introductions.

Among three of the subgenera of *Uca* and possibly a fourth (all in the Indo-Pacific), copulation takes place on the surface. Amid the remaining subgenera, circumstantial evidence suggests mating takes place below ground in the male's burrow after the female has been attracted by the waving display, or in some instances by sound (Crane, 1975). Christy's (1978) report would strongly suggest that mating takes place underground for *U. pugilator* on the west coast of Florida. By observing individually marked crabs he noted that, when a courting male attracted a female into his burrow, he would close the burrow with a plug of sand and remain underground with his mate for one to three days. Females remained in the burrow in which they mated while the egg clutch was incubating, emerging on the night the eggs hatched.

Nocturnal copulation at the surface appears to be common among eastern United States populations of *U. pugilator* and *U. pugnax*. Nocturnal breeding behavior is well developed with acoustical components, and sometimes special acoustical behavior followed by surface copulation takes place by day among species that also mate underground in localities where the vision of individuals is obscured by dense vegetation.

The behavioral role of females in courtship is largely unknown. The most obvious and prevalent form of female courtship behavior is the wandering stage of receptive females. This does not seem to exist among the Indo-Pacific species as the female is much less active, wandering is minimal or absent, and the male approaches the female and mates on the surface. Among the other species it is always the wandering female that is responsible for the male courtship display (Crane, 1975). Herrnkind (1968) observed *U. pugilator* females occasionally stopping near a male which may or may not have been waving his major cheliped during periods of low external activity. Crane characterized such wandering females as traveling in a short jerky fashion, perambulating in spurts with the body low to the ground, and

Table 5.8. The number of male *Uca pugilator* in a screen pen exhibiting waving behavior or sound production at the burrow entrance during various times of the day. (From Salmon, 1965 [part of Table 16], by permission of the editor, *Zoologica*)

I. June 22, 1962: 8 males

Time	1615	1630	1700	1810	1840	1910	1945	2015	2100	2130	2200
Waving	1	1	1	6	2	4	1	0	0	0	*
Sound Production	0	0	0	0	0	0	2	5	3	2	*

* High water mark near to or over crabs which have gone into their burrows.

Table 5.9. The number of sounds produced by 30 male *Uca pugilator* 15 seconds before and during introduction of conspecific males and females into their burrows. (From Salmon, 1965, Table 9, by permission of the editor, *Zoologica*)

Sex of Introduced Crab	Time of Introduction	Before Introduction	After Introduction	t-value
Female	Day	Mean 0.0	10.7	
		S.D.	5.5	
Male	Day	Mean 0.0	10.6	
		S.D.	6.9	
Female	Night	Mean 5.9	10.2	5.51*
		S.D. 2.4	3.4	
Male	Night	Mean 5.0	8.8	4.28*
		S.D. 2.1	4.3	

* Mean number of sounds during introduction is significantly greater than mean before introduction at 0.01 level.

legs little extended. Her nonreceptive posture is one of body raised high and legs spread stiffly. Crane stated that nothing is known of the requirements to initiate receptive behavior in the female.

Based on surface observations, the copulation position assumed appears to be identical throughout the genus. Once the sexes make contact, the male climbs the carapace of the female from the rear. When receptive the female assumes a more or less horizontal rest position with legs bent and close to the body which is in contact with or close to the ground. After varying times of plucking, stroking, tapping with the minor chela, the male turns the quiescent female upside down (Crane, 1975). During mating, the male *U. pugilator* lightly strokes the female on the edge of the carapace with the tips of the ambulatory legs at the beginning of the copulatory act and intermittently every few minutes (Herrnkind, 1968). At the time of copulation the male holds the female with his ambulatory legs. The abdominal flaps of both sexes are extended from the sterna and the tips of the gonopods are inserted in the gonopore. Crane reported that during surface matings the crabs remain in contact for up to an hour or more. Herrnkind (1968) observed that the mating union for *U. pugilator* extends from two to sixteen minutes. The spermatophores in the female appear to be carried largely or entirely internally.

Male fiddler crabs display strong tidal and semilunar rhythms in their social activities (Crane, 1958, 1975; Zucker, 1974). The semilunar rhythms depend on a favorable juxtaposition of time of day with local hours of low tide. Such activity seems to be concentrated during the morning hours. Zucker found that the courtship phase for *U. terpsichores* (= *U. musica terpsichore* [Crane, 1975]) occurs between 1000–1400 hours and peaks during the spring tides, which lag behind the new and full moon by several days. The number of "shelters" also increased at this time. Crane (1975) reported this as a general pattern of maximum social behavior which becomes accentuated during those periods when biweekly morning low tides coincide with changes in light intensity. A second minor peak of activity occurs about sunset with minimum movement in the early afternoon. As was pointed out earlier (Salmon, 1965), visual displays are replaced by acoustical manifestations after sunset among some species.

Uca pugilator females display a different pattern (Christy, 1978). By observing the mating and feeding behavior of individually marked crabs, Christy indicated males cycled through periods of reproductive activity separated by sessions of feeding. During late summer, peaks of courtship and burrow defense occurred on 22 July and on 4 and 5 August (Figure 5.15). The mean length of absence from the feeding aggregation for females known to have mated was 14.5 ± 0.64 days with a range of 11 to 17 days. It was presumed that any female not seen feeding for 11 to 17 days reproduced in that period. An estimation of the temporal distribution of both the number of receptive females and the number of females releasing larvae could be made by direct observation of reproductive activity and absence of individual females from the feeding aggregation. The distribution of the number of females that entered and remained in the burrows of courting males showed two peaks, each about five days before one of the spring tides (Figure 5.15). Christy noted 60 percent of the females mated before the new moon spring tides and 4 percent before the full moon spring tides. Thus the females mated at most, once each lunar month. This was in contrast to the semi-monthly reproductive activity of the males. Twelve days after each peak in mating, there was an increase in the number of females relinquishing newly hatched larvae. These releases took place during neap tide periods seven days before spring tides. On the other hand, Wheeler (1978) observed a different pattern to the 15-day hatching peaks for *Uca pugnax*. The sudden warming of tidal creeks in southern Delaware after a cool spring in 1976 seemed to produce a burst of unsynchronized spawning, thus the hatching pattern was not well defined. During July and August, however, larvae hatched in synchrony with the lunar cycle with peaks occurring at the time of full and new moon (Figure 5.16). Lambert (1978), working subsequently on the same tidal system as Wheeler, found most zoeae sampled to be Stage I. In contrast to Wheeler, Lambert observed that continuous spawning seemed to occur from the middle of June through August with little correlation to lunar phases: 84 percent of the larvae were taken during the spring tides of 21–25 June, 1975, and 16 percent during the neap tide periods of July 2 and 18. This would suggest that some environmental parameter or be-

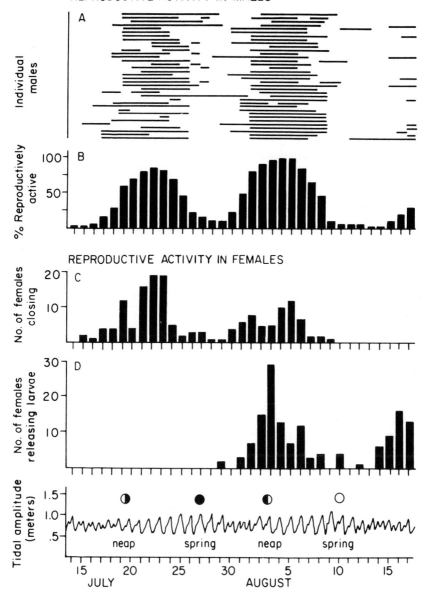

Figure 5.15.   Reproductive activity of male and female *Uca pugilator* in relation to tide cycles. (A) Horizontal bars indicate the days on which reproductive activity was observed or presumed to occur in individual males. (B) Temporal distribution of the percentage of reproductively active males. (C) Temporal distribution of the number of females seen or presumed to have closed to mate in a male's burrow. (D) Temporal distribution of the number of females releasing their larvae. Tide height was recorded with a gauge adjacent to the study beach. ●, ◑, ○, ◐,: new moon, first quarter, full moon, last quarter, respectively. (From Christy, 1978, by permission of the editor, *Science*.)

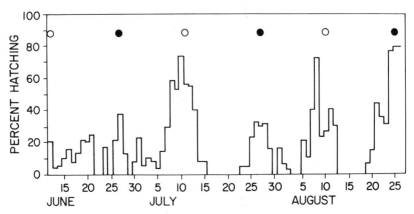

Figure 5.16.   Percent of laboratory population of ovigerous *Uca pugnax* releasing larvae
on a given day. Open circles represent full moon, dark circles represent new moon. (From
Wheeler, 1978, by permission of the editor, *Estuaries*.)

havioral activity was superimposed on the spawning periodicity associated
with the lunar cycle.

A comparison of the distribution of closure times with the dispersion of
larval releases suggests that females either delay or hasten copulation or
oviposition depending on when in the tidal cycle they close. Significant correlations were established between the length of time from closure to hatching and the date of closure during both mating periods, suggesting that females closing early in the cycle delay reproduction so that larval releases
take place over a short period of time. Such adjustments in the duration of
the breeding sequence and the timing of larval release may be behavioral
adaptations related to the semimonthly tidal cycle and the dispersal of the
larvae (Christy, 1978).

There is an exponential relationship between crab size and clutch size:
an 11-millimeter wide female produced 10,000 eggs, a 28-millimeter wide
female produced 302,000 eggs and a female of average width (20 millimeters) produced 200,000 eggs (Gray, 1942). The newly extruded eggs of
Uca are purple-black to black, becoming lighter and distinctly purple to a
dirty gray at the time of hatching (Hyman, 1920; Herrnkind, 1968). Such egg
masses were evident in a laboratory population of *U. pugilator* in the Miami,
Florida area from late April to late September while egg-bearing females
were collected in the field throughout October (Herrnkind, 1968). Gray
(1942) found no *U. minax* sponge crabs during May or June or after the first
week of September at Solomons, Maryland. On June 12, 1976, Wheeler
(1978) found most female *U. pugnax* in Canary Creek marsh, Delaware,

were gravid, and by the end of August less than three percent of the females examined in the field carried eggs.

The larvae of *U. pugilator, U. pugnax* and *U. minax* hatch from the sponge during the evening hours near high tide when the females move to the water's edge, releasing the young into the water (Hyman, 1920; Gray, 1942; Christy, 1978; Lambert, 1978). Gray reported that zoea of *U. minax* were in the plankton from early July to early September at Solomons, Maryland, being most abundant at a water temperature of 25 °C and on an ebbing tide. Lambert (1978), and Epifanio and Dittel (1981), while sampling the Broadkill River and the mouth of Delaware Bay, collected *Uca* spp. larvae from late June through September with a distinct peak in July when 71 percent were taken.

The first three zoeal stages of *Uca* sp. were abundant in surface tows at Beaufort, North Carolina while the fourth and fifth zoeal stages were more evident in the bottom tows (Hyman, 1920). The first molt took place after 4 days, the second molt in 4–5 days. The third molt was less well defined while the fourth occurred in 7 days. The fifth molt to the megalops stage took place in 7–10 days and lasted 3–4 weeks.

The early megalopa stage has been collected in large numbers in surface tows at the mouth of inlets and tidal streams (Hyman, 1920; Herrnkind, 1968; Lambert, 1978). Later it seeks shelter in the intertidal area in the crevices of old boards, under oyster shells, and on the back of pilings where molting to the first crab stage takes place. In three days there is a molt to the second crab stage after which a second crab molt takes place in 4–5 days. Following this second molt the young crab at about two millimeters emerges from the water and begins to burrow (Hyman, 1920; Herrnkind, 1968). On this basis the time from hatching to digging the first burrow is something in excess of fifty days.

The more recent laboratory observations of Wheeler (1978) shortened the time for the zoeal and megalops stages of *U. pugnax* (Table 5.10). The sum of the average duration of zoeal stages I–V was 15.2 days. The length of the megalops stage was variable: 7–18 with an average of 12.5 days or a total of 27.7 days to the first crab stage. Wheeler presumed the duration of larval stages in the laboratory under controlled conditions (T = 25 °C, S = $25^0/oo$, diet = the branchiopod *Artemia salina* and the rotifer *Branchionus plicatalus*) to approximate that of the natural environment. With such a presumption the results implied that, in conjunction with releases during a series of high tides at new and full moon, the molt to megalops would occur during the next spring tides and metamorphosis to the first crab stage would take place approximately one complete lunar cycle after hatching.

While describing the duration of the various larval stages of *Uca,*

Table 5.10. Duration of larval stages of *Uca pugnax* in the laboratory. Zoeal data was obtained from one group of larvae reared to the megalops stage. Length of megalops stage was obtained from a second larval group. Approximately the same number of broods were represented in both groups. (From Wheeler, 1978, by permission of the editor, *Estuaries*)

Larval Stage	n	Mean Duration in Days	S.D.
Zoea I	108	2.1	0.3
Zoea II	105	2.9	0.6
Zoea III	99	3.2	1.1
Zoea IV	82	3.3	1.1
Zoea V	68	3.7	1.2
Zoeal Total		15.2	
Megalopa	14	12.5	3.0
Total		27.7	

Hyman (1920) called attention to their vertical movements in the water column. DeCoursey (1976) observed a major peak in numbers of Stage I *Uca* zoea in predawn samples with a minor concentration late in the afternoon. She observed a distinct tidal rhythm of vertical movement. Wheeler and Epifanio (1978) observed a response to pressure changes for all zoeal stages of *Rhithropanopeus harrisii.* The ability to orient in darkness and swim upward when stimulated by small increments of pressure suggests that oriented movement is important to survival of these larvae. Wheeler postulated that such behavior could enable larvae either to concentrate near the level of no net motion in an estuarine system or to utilize flood tide transport. She reasoned that if larvae were stimulated to move upward by pressure and light, but negative phototaxis was induced whenever they passed through the salinity discontinuity, the larval population would be concentrated just below this level. Such a response could occur in a large estuarine system where a two-layer phenomenon could develop. However, in tidal streams the phenomenon tends to be transient, forming only in the lower reaches of the stream and at the beginning of the flood tide. For the rest of the time the salinity is vertically homogeneous (deWitt and Daiber, 1973).

Earlier, Gray (1942) reported *Uca minax* larvae being abundant on the ebb tide and Hyman (1920) found the megalops stage in the ocean surface waters outside the inlet at Beaufort, North Carolina. Lambert (1978) found higher numbers of *Uca* sp. and *Rhithropanopeus harrisii* during ebb tide than during flood tide periods. Diurnal sampling by Lambert indicated *Uca* sp. Stage I zoeae were flushed from the Broadkill River after two tidal cycles following spawning: the fact that the advanced stages (II–V) accounted for less than one percent of the total *Uca* larvae taken in weekly tows would suggest that little zoeal development occurred in the river. On the other hand, large numbers of *Uca* megalops were collected in evening diurnal samplings at the mouth of the stream. All of this suggests that *Uca* zoeae are carried out of the system, that development occurs in the bay beyond the marsh creeks, and that the megalops stage, while still in the water column, finds its way back to the mouths of these tidal rivers to be transported back and forth by the tides before settling to the bottom prior to molting to the first crab stage. The megalops of *Uca* is a major factor in the repopulation of the adult habitat. In contrast, Lambert found *R. harrisii* zoeal development within the river, suggesting these larvae have a behavioral pattern that changes their vertical distribution so that they are not carried out of a tidal creek by the ebbing tide. This vertical migratory pattern in synchrony with the tides has been further substantiated by Cronin and Forward (1979).

Relatively little is known about the reproductive biology of the marsh crab, *Sesarma reticulatum*. In southern Delaware marshes, from June into August, females can be found carrying sponges containing 8,000 to 10,000 eggs. As the eggs develop, the sponge changes from purple to a greenish color at which time the zoeae hatch into the water. The larvae are positively phototropic and stay near the surface (Crichton, 1960). Nothing appears to be known about the movements and behavior patterns of the various larval stages. Are they swept out of the tidal streams or does their behavior pattern permit them to move vertically in the water column and remain within a tidal stream? Three zoeal stages and one megalops stage have been described. The molting frequency of all three zoeal stages of *S. reticulatum* was similar for both natural and experimental light conditions. The first molt normally occurred on days 3–5. The megalops stage (Molt III) happened by days 8–11. Metamorphosis to the first crab took place in the laboratory between 15–30 days after hatching, displaying considerable variability (Costlow and Bookout, 1962). The comparable time for *S. cinereum* in the laboratory was 25–30 days for four zoeal stages (Costlow et al., 1960).

Seiple (1979), in describing the habitat preference for these two species of marsh crabs, found *S. cinereum* at or above the main high-water spring tides in a high sand (91.4 percent) situation with the high salinity ($\bar{x} = 27.9^0/oo$) and low moisture (18.4 percent) content of Beaufort, North Carolina marshes where stands of *Spartina* and *Salicornia* were dense. *S. reticulatum* was found at lower elevations 2.5–4 meters above mean low-water neap tides, near or at the edge of the *Spartina* zone where silts and clays were more abundant (76.2 percent sand), the water was brackish ($\bar{x} = 16.2^0/oo$) and the moisture content was higher (37.9 percent).

Such habitat distributions appear to be related to reproductive strategies of these two crabs. Egg-bearing females were present from mid-April to mid-September. Seiple (1979) found the numbers of gravid female *S. cinereum* correlated to the lunar cycle with peaks at full moon periods from April to June. Later such an association broke down during July and August. There was evidence of lunar influence on *S. reticulatum*, but the period length was longer. Seiple recorded peaks at new moon periods for this latter species. He postulated the lunar cycle could be an advantage for *S. cinereum*. Because of their position in the intertidal zone, the females would be covered by the highest tides with the subsequent release of young from the egg mass. Synchrony would be less important for *S. reticulatum* since it is lower in the intertidal zone and covered by every high tide.

There was a gradual increase in the size of the gravid females of both species from April until late July–August when the size decreased, presumably as newly matured females entered the population. Seiple (1979) found female *S. cinereum* tended to be smaller with a midpoint at approximately 14 millimeters from April–June, 15 millimeters in July and less than 13 millimeters in August. The smallest gravid female *S. cinereum* was 9.2 millimeters and the largest had a carapace width of 20.2 millimeters. The midpoint for gravid female *S. reticulatum* was about 19 millimeters, carapace width, increasing to almost 20 millimeters in June, and decreasing to slightly less than 18 millimeters in August. The smallest gravid female *S. reticulatum* had a 13.2 millimeter carapace width and the largest width was 23.6 millimeters. Since there was a difference in size at maturity, does *S. reticulatum* grow at a faster rate between molts or mature at an older age? This point was not resolved by Seiple. *S. cinereum* produced an average of 4–6 broods per year while *S. reticulatum* carried 2–3 broods. The *S. cinereum* eggs were small and were carried for 28 days in contrast to the larger eggs of *S. reticulatum* which were carried for 45 days. The shorter carrying period and longer planktonic stage may be associated with more plentiful food or reduced predation. Seiple postulated that this would provide a greater chance for dispersal into suitable habitats. This should be especially important for *S. cinereum* which can be placed in its typical habitat on only the highest spring tides. These kinds of observations should be investigated for both species in other latitudes.

Insecta

There are a number of orders and families of insects represented in tidal marsh faunas (Davis and Gray, 1966; Cameron, 1972). A recent review (Cheng, 1976) of the marine insects identified a wide spectrum of insect species associated with the intertidal marsh habitat, yet it is clear that little or nothing is known about the life cycles of the majority of these species. Only those species of medical or economic importance: the mosquitos, biting midges, horse and deer flies have received any appreciable attention. An examination of O'Meara (1976), Linley (1976), and Axtell (1976) demonstrated only a few species among those blood-sucking flies that are well known and for the majority great gaps of information exist relative to their life cycles and reproduction.

Diptera. Culicidae. Mosquitos have two distinct methods of laying eggs: singly as is the case with most aedine and anopheline mosquitos or in rafts as is the general case with *Culex, Mansonia*, and *Culiseta* (= *Theobaldia*). *Aedes* eggs are generally deposited among debris or leaves or on the moist ground. If covered by water, the eggs seldom float. *Aedes* females seek out regions darker than the general surroundings with patches of darkness rather than water itself attracting the female. Such action facilitates laying eggs in places liable to flooding. The eggs of *Aedes* are laid singly on the soil surface (or other substrate) by the female walking along the water's edge or over a damp zone just above the water's edge. Numerous females may deposit eggs in such a locale. The eggs are cigar-shaped and without floats. At first the eggs are white: they swell to full size shortly after deposition and start to darken, beginning at the future head end. *Aedes* eggs are generally resistant to dessication. Eggs from a single batch will hatch in installments rather than all at once although, as will be shown, this is not always the case.

Anopheles eggs are deposited singly on the water surface, normally floating at the water-air interface. They are boat-shaped and pointed and often have upturned ends. Each is equipped with lateral floats and each egg has its own positive meniscus, gravitating toward other positive menisci such as stems and other eggs. These eggs have little resistance to dessication, heat or cold. *Anopheles* larvae are specific in choice of developmental sites. The menisci around emergent objects are requisite sites for favorable larval development. If there are emergent stems then the water level must remain constant. Species that can stand fluctuations in water level are associated with floating algal mats or other floating objects that provide the intersection line. Such larvae live close to the surface and the temperature of the surface film has an important influence on rate of development. Presumably this last point is equally important for the culicine mosquitos that deposit their eggs in rafts.

The eggs of *Culex* are laid in such a raft with each egg standing on its end, perpendicular to the water surface. The eggs are laid with the future heads of the larvae downward so the larvae will emerge into the water. The eggs adhere, one to another, but are not cemented together. Gillette (1972) and O'Meara (1976) disagreed on this last point; O'Meara stated that eggs are glued together. The whole raft of 100 eggs or more takes on the floating feature, in that flotation devices are absent on individual eggs. During egg laying *Culex* females place the first egg on the water surface, the second egg is laid immediately adjacent to the first and thus pushes the first egg backward from the female by a distance equal to its own diameter. The process is repeated, putting down a row of eggs. A second row is formed in a staggered pattern to the first as the abdomen of the mosquito moves backward. The behavior of the individual *Culex* species determines the shape of the raft.

Most tidal marsh species of mosquitos are multivoltine, i.e., they produce several generations each year with the number being determined by rainfall patterns, frequency of flooding, and overall duration of the breeding season. *Culex salinarius* does not appear until mid-May but breeds into late October, overwintering as adults. The numerous broods of *Aedes cantator* depend on the weather. When marshes become egg-covered every heavy rain or extra tide produces a brood. The early broods hatching in March are slow and irregular with adults appearing in early April. A second series seldom occurs before early June and is mature by late June. Thereafter every larval stage is found in every pool. *Aedes sollicitans* has 5–8 broods in New Jersey from April–May to November (with each female laying up to 200 eggs) but produces continuously in the southern part of its range, as is the case for *A. taeniorhynchus* (Headlee, 1945; Horsfall, 1955; Lake, 1965; Woodward *et al.*, 1968). Such species as *Aedes taeniorhynchus* and *A. sollicitans* exhibit a facultative type of embryonic diapause whereby overwintering eggs do not hatch when submerged (O'Meara, 1976). The results given in Table 5.11 were presented by Woodward *et al.* (1968) to explain the almost continuous breeding of *A. sollicitans* in southwest Louisiana. Only rarely were eggs of *A. sollicitans* found in a state of diapause, while *Psorophora columbiae*, a nontidal species, displayed the lowest level of hatchibility for the fall eggs. Certain females, particularly *P. confinnis*, produced egg batches in which some or all eggs were in a state of diapause, thus more resistant to hatching stimuli.

Among mosquitos and those insects with complete metamorphosis there is a close relation between oviposition habits of the adult and the phys-

Table 5.11. Summary of egg hatching of *Aedes sollicitans*, *A. taeniorhynchus* and *Psorophora confinnis* during the spring and fall of 1966 and 1967. (From Table 2, Woodward *et al.*, 1968)

| Species | Average Percent of Hatch of Eggs | | | | | |
| | 1966 | | 1967 | | Both Years | |
	Spring	Fall	Spring	Fall	Spring	Fall
Psorophora confinnis	73	19	93	24	87	22
Aedes taeniorhynchus	99	83	99	60	90	71
Aedes sollicitans	93	93	99	99	97	97

iological requirements of the larvae. The natural distribution of a species is not necessarily caused by peculiar requirements on the part of the larvae but due to adult oviposition behavior (Bates, 1949). Mosquito species respond to a variety of substances in determining oviposition sites. O'Meara (1976), in reviewing earlier works, called attention to conflicting results of attraction and repulsion. *Aedes taeniorhynchus* was reported to respond positively to sulfate salts, especially when the humidity was below 80 percent (McGaughey, 1968). In other examples the kind and concentration of salts could attract or repel oviposition. Since they remained after boiling, it was presumed that nonvolatile substances in water containing pupae, exuviae and emerging adults served as attractants. Among other species including *A. taeniorhynchus,* volatile, ether-extractable substances induced positive responses. These substances were species specific and in some cases acted as repellants for females of other species.

Both *Aedes sollicitans* and *A. taeniorhynchus* have been reported to select soils for oviposition with moisture contents above 70 percent of the "saturation moisture content" (defined as the maximum amount of water held in the puddled soil without free water collecting in a depression made in the soil mass) (Knight and Baker, 1962). Such soil moistures along with a layer of organic matter produce high relative humidities. Laboratory evidence indicated both species survive best at relative humidities of 85–95 percent. Evidence further suggested that gravid females must get into a physiological "egg-laying state" and only then will they be attracted to a wet surface. Prior to this state females will not oviposit when presented with such a moist surface. According to Knight and Baker the selection of highly moist soils is a reaction by the ovipositing females to the moist atmosphere rather than because these places favor the survival of eggs and larvae. This would suggest a de-emphasis of the positive correlation between adult behavior and larval requirements to which Bates (1949) called attention. However, Knight and Baker (1962) went on to say, in reference to egg deposition by *A. sollicitans* and *A. taeniorhynchus,* that until the eggs blacken, they lose water more readily than they regain it. If the substrate dries out between the time of oviposition and waterproofing of the eggs, the eggs will collapse. While multiple broods occur, submergence of the eggs induces hatching. Drying of the substrate causes more erratic emergence while alternate drying and flooding enhances hatching (Horsfall, 1955). A damp substrate is more likely to be reflooded than an adjacent drier area, a situation that insures subsequent hatching and larval development.

Isolated bits of information on habits and habitats and inferences drawn from related species largely constitute what is known about the majority of the tidal marsh mosquitos. *Anopheles bradleyi* larvae are found in pools of brackish water over a wide range of salinities and usually occur where emergent vegetation is present, preferably the algae *Chara* (Carpenter and LaCasse, 1955) or *Distichlis* but not *S. alterniflora* (Horsfall, 1955).

Aedes detritus is reportedly found in Egypt in salinities ranging from $8.3\%_{00}$ to $52\%_{00}$. In Great Britain eggs were laid among the vegetation of coastal marshes and were able to remain dry for at least a year. As many as 260 eggs were laid, a high value for most *Aedes* (Clements, 1963). In contrast to earlier work, Service (1968) portrayed the optimum oviposition sites for *A. detritus* in the Poole Harbour, England marshes as edges of exposed muddy spots and areas colonized by *Spartina townsendii* and *Juncus maritimus* that were regularly flooded with a relatively large volume of water (Table 5.12). There were few eggs in the middle of the marsh. There was no relationship between egg distributions and the chlorinity or moisture content of the mud. Eggs did not all hatch on the first inundation (Table 5.12) with 80 percent of the larvae emerging during the first six soakings. Service (1971) considered such a differential hatch to be an advantage for species in small habitats subject to repeated dessication. He found eggs to hatch throughout the year but those eggs with a deeper diapause or laid late in the season would winter over.

Service (1971) found desiccation to be the main cause for mortality while neither chlorinity nor maximum temperature were important for larval survival. Fourth instar larvae were collected in all months except November and December but, since pupae did not appear until April, pupation must be delayed during the winter months. Adults appeared from April–May into November. In the laboratory larval development time was 14 ± 3.1 days and time for pupation was 4 ± 0.8 days at 16–18 °C. Fourth instar larvae and pupae were found in the field ten days after hatching in July and August. In January, fourth instar larvae were evident 91 days after the appearance of the first instar. The larvae of *A. detritus* were not randomly distributed but aggregated near the water's edge. The intensity of aggregation varied with the life stage. The first two instars and the pupae were concentrated at the water's edge while the third and fourth instars had a less restricted distribution, being found in the open marsh as well.

For another species, *Aedes caspius*, two broods were recognized. Eggs were deposited in algal filled pools in Denmark during late July and hatched in late August. The second brood was deposited in similar pools probably in September. These hatched early the following June. The resting stage was passed as the egg in both the summer and the winter broods (Natvig, 1948).

Aedes sollicitans and *A. taeniorhynchus* are classed as being particularly pestiforous insects. This is especially so for *A. sollicitans* not only because of its great numbers but for its wide ranging abilities. It has a distribution from Vera Cruz, Mexico along the Gulf and Atlantic coasts of North America to

Table 5.12. Distributions of *A. detritus* eggs in salt marsh and differential hatch. (From Service, 1968, by permission of the editor, *J. Appl. Ecol.*)

Sampling Area	Number of Mud Samples	Mean Numbers of Eggs/Sample Hatching on Successive Soakings						Mean Total Hatch and Percentage (in parentheses) of Total Hatch from All Areas
		1	2	3	4	5	6	
Bare mud	10	17.3	26.7	32.2	30.9	29.5	13.5	150.1 (44.7)
Spartina/Juncus	11	13.9	24.8	36.7	36.1	38.3	16.2	166.1 (48.4)
Spartina/Juncus/Agropyron	5	2.6	2.6	2.2	3.6	1.6	0	12.6 (3.7)
Agropyron	3	0	0	0	0	0	0	0
Phragmites/Spartina	2	4.0	2.0	1.5	0.5	3.5	0	11.0 (3.2)
Phragmites	2	0	2.5	0	1.0	0	0	3.5 (1.0)
All areas combined (% hatch)	33	11.0	17.0	21.0	20.8	21.2	8.6	

235

New Brunswick, Nova Scotia and Prince Edward Island in Canada as well as being found on the islands of Cuba, Puerto Rico, Jamaica, and the Bahamas. While it is primarily associated with coastal areas, it can be found in numerous inland situations in the United States (Lake, 1965). *A. taeniorhynchus* is also found far inland but, with rare exceptions, breeds in a narrow zone along the coast (Nielsen and Nielsen, 1953). Its geographic range extends along the Atlantic coast from Brazil to New England and it is known to occur on the Pacific coast from Peru to California (Carpenter and La-Casse, 1955).

Both species have prolonged breeding seasons. Lake (1965) found *A. sollicitans* eggs present in Delaware tidal marshes throughout the year: larvae and pupae from late March–early April until October; adults from April to November. The eggs laid in the fall provide the overwintering stage and up to 200 eggs may be laid by a female in the course of her lifetime. *A. taeniorhynchus* broods are present throughout the year in the southern portion of its range (Horsfall, 1955).

Most eggs of both species are collected in the higher, drier portions of the marshes. *A. sollicitans* is usually associated with *Distichlis spicata* and *Spartina patens* in Delaware where the marsh is generally flooded less than eight days per month. Few eggs are found in the wetter areas where *S. alterniflora* dominates. This same pattern is evident elsewhere with the eggs deposited above the daily high tide zone. Lake (1965) suggested the eggs of *A. sollicitans* are not deposited on the bare mud of the marsh but in conjunction with vegetation (Table 5.13).

These results would suggest that some other factor or factors are determining oviposition sites. Scotton and Axtell (1979) suggested that the age of dredge spoil sites may be important since they found few eggs on the month-old sites, but numerous eggs on three-year-old sites. In addition, they

Table 5.13. Numbers of *A. sollicitans* eggs from different plant covers and open mud at Port Mahon, Delaware, 1962.* (From Lake, 1965)

Plant Types	Total Number of Samples	Number of Samples With Eggs Present	Mean Number of Eggs Including Empty Shells and Nonviable Eggs
Open mud	5	0	0
S. patens dominant	13	8	27.1
S. patens, D. spicata intermixed	2	2	3.1
D. spicata dominant	13	8	34.9
S. alterniflora	8	7	15.6
S. patens, S. alterniflora mixed	4	1	0
D. spicata, S. alterniflora mixed	5	3	0.4

* Eggs were collected with Horsfall Egg Separator; sample size 6″ × 6″.

found both *A. sollicitans* and *A. taeniorhynchus* displayed a site preference for egg deposition. Eggs were least numerous on the bare mud with increasing densities from the shrub zone at the highest elevation to the old *Aster subulatus* zone. There was a marked preference for the new *Aster* zone immediately adjacent to the bare mud at the lowest elevation within the dredge site inside the dike. Within the *Aster* zone 77 percent of the *A. sollicitans* eggs were associated with the surface root mat of the new *Aster* zone and 49 percent of *A. taeniochynchus* eggs were found in the same microhabitat. The second most important deposition site was the cracks in the soil with 8 and 21 percent for *A. sollicitans* and *A. taeniochynchus,* respectively. When algae was present on the crack walls in the new *Aster* zone, egg deposition was reduced. The soil cracks apparently were more important for larval survival than for providing a deposition site. Egg densities of both species were found to be inversely related to rainfall and the level of standing water: density increased during the season from March to September with the greatest numbers just after the *Aster* bloomed in September.

Nayar and Sauerman (1975) reported a direct relationship between fecundity of female *A. taeniorhynchus* and the abundance of plant nectar. This may also apply to *A. sollicitans* (Scotton and Axtell, 1979).

Smith (1905) reported that *A. sollicitans* eggs must dry or not be covered with water for at least 24 hours after being laid or they will not hatch. However, Travis (1953) stated that *A. sollicitans* and *A. taeniorhynchus* eggs hatched without a period of drying and after being submerged in rain, tap, and distilled water within 24 hours of being laid. The *A. sollicitans* eggs hatched when so treated with seawater but *A. taeniorhynchus* eggs did not hatch. Travis also found *A. sollicitans* eggs were less damaged by drying than *A. taeniorhynchus* while *Psorophora confinnis* eggs were most resistant.

When the eggs of various marsh mosquitos were flooded repeatedly with untreated water the highest percentage (62.8 percent) of *A. sollicitans* hatched with the first flooding while the greatest percentage of *A. taeniorhynchus* (84.3 percent) and *Psorophora confinnis* (71.4 percent) hatched with the third flooding (Table 5.14). When the eggs were subjected to infusions from leaves of marsh plants nearly all the *Aedes* eggs hatched on the first submergence. Flooding of soil samples showed as much as 98 percent of the *Aedes* eggs that did hatch, did so on the first inundation. From their field observations, Nielsen and Nielsen (1953) inferred that all the *A. taeniorhynchus* eggs present in an area hatch at the first inundation. In their study area adjacent to Fort Pierce, Florida, egg hatching depended solely on rain which came largely in thunder showers which tend to be erratic.

As might be expected *A. sollicitans* larvae are most often found in pools in the higher portion of the tidal marshes in Delaware. The spring tides tend to scatter the larvae into other parts of the marshes where they could be ex-

Table 5.14. Percentage of eggs hatching with each flooding of untreated water (120 10-egg samples for all species and 20 additional 50-egg samples for *Aedes taeniorhynchus*). (From Travis, 1953)

Flooding	Aedes taeniorhynchus	Aedes sollicitans	Psorophora confinnis
1	0.3	62.8	0.3
2	12.6	29.7	13.2
3	84.3	6.5	71.4
4	2.5	0	7.9
5	0.3	0	1.0
6	0	—	4.5
7	0	—	1.7

posed to a variety of salinities. Various data from Delaware marshes have recorded *A. sollicitans* larvae in salinities of 0.4^0/oo to 27^0/oo although they are reputed to be able to tolerate an even greater range of salinity, from fresh water to three times that of seawater (Lake, 1965). Nielsen and Nielsen (1953) reported that *A. taeniorhynchus* larval development can take place in any salinity from completely fresh to ocean water.

Based on observations from natural collections of larvae as well as laboratory collection of eggs, nine days is an approximate time for *A. sollicitans* to pass through the four instars and pupae from hatching to adult (Table 5.15). Nielsen and Nielsen (1953) reported some *A. taeniorhynchus* larvae reaching the second instar within 24 hours. They also reported that other workers have tabulated 5–7 days for the entire aquatic stage (hatch to emergence). Their own observations in Florida showed a much longer period, viz., 12–15 days in February and 9–12 and 9–11 days in mid-April and late May, respectively.

The temperature of the natural habitat of *A. sollicitans* larvae fluctuates daily; as much as 33 °F noted in one instance. No significant difference in

Table 5.15. Development rate in terms of 50% ecdysis for larvae and pupae of *A. sollicitans* at Woodland Beach, Delaware, 1964.* (From Lake, 1965)

Instar or Stage	Mean Water Temp. °F	Median in Hours	Range in Hours
1	74.2	41	37–45
2	76.2	34	22–56
3	75.6	33	17–34
4	72.7	72	68–76
Pupa	79.7	50	45–55

* Data collected from four pools.

Table 5.16. Percentage of *A. sollicitans* larvae completing development, reared under near-constant and fluctuating temperature. (Lake, 1965)

Treatment	Test No.	Temperature	Percentage of Larvae Completing Development
Constant temperature	I	27	45.4
	II	25–27	61.8
	III	24–27	73.0
	IV	30–31	100.0
	V	28	33.3
	VI	28	98.0
Fluctuating temperature	I	21–36	80.0
	II	21–37	51.8
	III	23–37	47.0
	IV	21–34	71.4
	V	23–31	95.2
	VI	22–32	94.0

percent of hatching was recorded for eggs subjected to near-constant temperatures versus those exposed to fluctuating temperatures (Table 5.16). Nor was any marked difference observed in time from eclosion of larvae to first emergence of adults during laboratory studies rearing larvae in near-constant versus fluctuating temperatures (Lake, 1965).

Desiccation of the aquatic stage after hatching can have a marked impact on subsequent adult numbers. Smith (1904) reported half-grown *A. sollicitans* larvae can survive for a few hours on moist mud while pupae can remain alive up to 24 hours. Lake (1965) found large larvae and pupae alive after a rain in a pool site that had dried for about 40 hours to soft mud. The inference from Nielsen and Nielsen (1953) is that *A. taeniorhynchus* is less resistant to desiccation. In one instance they found no larvae in a rain-filled pool site after it had dried out for possibly 10–12 hours. In another case, they found large fourth instar larvae among newly hatched larvae in rain-filled pool sites after they had been dry for several days. The supposition was that the large larvae survived among the numerous crab burrows.

Male swarming is a behavioral trait that appears to have no direct association with mating in some mosquito species. Neither Lake (1965) nor Nielsen and Nielsen (1953) observed any mating by swarming males with females of *A. sollicitans* and *A. taeniorhynchus,* respectively. On the other hand, Lake cited earlier work stating that females rise up from the vegetation into the swarm with mating taking place. It is presumed, at least for *A. taeniorhynchus,* that mating occurs in the early adult stage prior to swarming. This species swarms at dusk and early morning from the age of four days: the swarming takes place above small trees and bushes. Lake found *A.*

sollicitans swarming only in the evening and over the general marsh vegetation. The swarming of an individual male *A. taeniorhynchus* lasted about 1½ minutes while the duration of the swarm may last 12–27 minutes.

Nielsen and Nielsen (1953) described the flight of egg-filled females who began to swarm around pools when it was quite dark, rising from the ground to a height of 7–8 meters. The flight of the individual female was slow, graceful, majestic, probably due to the heavily egg-laden abdomen. These females were not sensitive to light, in sharp contrast to newly emerged or biting females. Many of these females settled to the ground, seemingly to rest. Some resumed flight, but after a half hour, more and more came to rest with the number of flying females greatly diminished. Although most settled close to the water's edge of the various pools no egg laying was observed. This special flight was on a 5-day cycle when the females were 7, 12, and 17 days old and followed a 5-day biting cycle, which was most intense when the mosquitos were 4, 9, and 14 days old. This would suggest that females are capable of laying eggs one week after emergence and at approximate weekly intervals thereafter. Headlee (1945) suggested the same for *A. sollicitans.*

Diptera. Tabanidae. The members of this family are commonly called horseflies and deerflies. While most members of the family are associated with upland habitats, there are a number found in the coastal areas. Most of the horseflies of the coastal zone belong to the genus *Tabanus* and are called greenheads. The genus *Tabanus* is world-wide in distribution with 94 species in North America north of Mexico, 139 species south of the United States, and 48 species in Europe. *Tabanus nigrovittatus* and *T. lineola* are the common salt-marsh greenheads of North America. The deerflies include the large genus *Chrysops,* world-wide in distribution. There have been 68 species listed for the Americas south of the United States and 75 species north of Mexico. *C. fuliginosus, C. flavidus,* and *C. atlanticus* are the major coastal species in eastern North America. Since most of these tabanid flies are large, strong fliers and bite man and animals with voracious appetites they are of considerable economic importance. They are capable of disease transmission primarily by mechanical means (Jones and Anthony, 1964; Axtell, 1976; Krinsky, 1976). Magnarelli (1976) suggested it is quite possible for female tabanids to acquire blood meals from more than one host before enough food is taken in to mature a full complement of oocytes. The implications of disease transmission resulting from such interrupted feeding is obvious.

All tabanids have the same general life histories (Jones and Anthony, 1964; Axtell, 1976). The female deposits eggs in clusters on vegetation close to moist or wet substrate (many over water). These sites may be leaves and stems of marsh grasses, emergent vegetation, or the leaves and stems of trees and shrubs overhanging water. The eggs are 1–3 millimeters long, creamy white when first deposited but later they turn brown or brown-black. The eggs are laid in masses of 100–800 arranged in a single layer as in most Chrysopini or several layers, usually two, as in the Tabanini. For those species whose eggs have been identified these eggs hatch in a few days. The first instar drops to the moist soil or into the substrate where development is completed. A high moisture content is required for larval development of most species which go through several molts (6–10) extending from many months up to two years. The larvae feed as predators or as omnivores on organic matter. In the temperate regions they overwinter as larvae. The last larval instar migrates to or near the surface. Pupation lasts a few days to 2–3 weeks, depending on species and temperature. Adult males tend to emerge slightly before the females. Generally different species have distinct periods of emergence, often with a single peak of abundance. Mating may take place soon after emergence. A blood meal is usually necessary for the development of each batch of eggs, although species are autogenous, i.e., producing the initial batch of eggs without a previous blood meal. However, for subsequent batches of eggs produced, usually one or two, the female must seek a blood meal to complete egg development. Females typically oviposit two or three egg clusters in a life time. Egg masses have not been identified for some species and few species have been reared in the laboratory from egg to adult. Even for those few species where extensive information exists there are still wide gaps in the details of the life cycles (Axtell, 1976).

The most abundant salt-marsh greenhead, *Tabanus nigrovittatus,* is distributed through the coastal marshes of the eastern and southern states from Massachusetts to Florida west to Texas and has been reported from Nova Scotia (Jones and Anthony, 1964). It is postulated that the males, in at least New Jersey, emerge three days before the females and mature before the females (Bosler and Hansens, 1974) and have a slightly shorter life span than the females (Rockel and Hansens, 1970b). Generally, similar numbers of males and females emerge with the greatest numbers evident during the third week of July: the range of emergence extends from late June–early July to mid- to late August. Dukes *et al.* (1974b) stated the larvae are widely distributed over the surface of southern marshes in association with *S. alterniflora* but are more restricted to the *S. alterniflora* zone bordering the ditches of northern marshes. However, Magnarelli and Anderson (1978) found larvae widely dispersed through a Connecticut marsh without any apparent relation to soil characters. They found large numbers associated with sediments containing sizable accumulations of wet matted vegetation. Most *T. nigrovittatus* emerge from soil slightly below mean high-water level. Since the larvae are found at this elevation, it appears the larvae do not migrate prior to pupation. Adult female *T. nigrovittatus* aggregate at the marsh edge flying about 1–2 feet off the ground while hunting a blood meal. The direction of wind has a marked effect on fly movements and, since sea breezes predominate during the day, the flies are pushed toward high ground. However, the transition zone of vegetation serves as a barrier since decreasing numbers of flies are taken at successively greater distances from the marsh (Rockel and Hansens, 1970b).

A predominantly male trait is hovering and it may be a courtship phenomenon. Hovering generally occurs on bright, mild, calm midsummer days and any passing clouds will cause a cessation. Hovering begins soon after sun-up and is usually terminated by 10:00 or 11:00 A.M. The flies hover some 6–12 inches above *S. alterniflora*. The males will dart forward toward another fly passing by. Such excited darting may be brought on by a male attempting to seize a female passing through. Mating occurs with both sexes resting on a leaf of grass although they sometimes fly in union if disturbed. The females tend to be more active but it is suggested that the male may control the duration of the mating process since he seems to fly off first when disturbed (Bailey, 1948). Jamnback and Wall (1959) reported that the female *T. nigrovittatus* deposited an egg mass (7.28 millimeters long and 3.4 millimeters wide) on *S. alterniflora* leaf blades about 30 centimeters above the marsh surface where the plant blade was 5–6 millimeters wide. The egg mass was light brown in color and the eggs were arranged in two tiers. Individual eggs were 1.8 millimeters long and 0.38 millimeters wide at the widest point. However, Axtell (1976) pointed out that other investigators have not been able to find egg masses even in the presence of high densities of adults. These earlier observations have thus not been confirmed. Presumably the eggs hatch in a few days and the larvae drop to the marsh surface. Larval development time and the number of molts is unknown. The pattern of large larvae and pupae and the emergence time of the adults suggested to Axtell (1976) a larval development time of 9–10 months. Conversely, Magnarelli and Anderson (1978) concluded that many larvae require two or more years to complete the life cycle, based on winter collections yielding only small-sized larvae. Mature larvae are about 24 millimeters long and pale amber in color, while the pupae are 13–18 millimeters long with a dark brown head and thorax and a yellowish brown abdomen (Axtell, 1976).

Tabanus lineola is found in eastern United States to Louisiana and Kansas, and in Ontario and Quebec. In New Jersey it is the second most abundant salt-marsh greenhead, making up 5–10 percent of the population (Orminati and Hansens, 1974). Likewise, in Florida, while it is not as numerous it is still a severe pest because of its continual presence from early spring until late fall with the heaviest concentrations from May through August (Jones and Anthony, 1964). Like *T. nigrovittatus*, *T. lineola* in New Jersey has a peak emergence during the third week in July but emergence

Table 5.17. Relation of the number of instars to the sex of emerging *T. lineola* adults. (From Orminati and Hansens, 1974, by permission of the editor, *Ann. Ent. Soc. Amer.*)

Number of Instars to Pupation	Number Males	Percentage Males	Number Females	Percentage Females
8	30	78	8	22
9	33	41	47	59
10	9	30	21	70

extends from late June–early July to mid- to late August (Rockel and Hansens, 1970).

One can only surmise about adult activity after emergence as there does not appear to be any record. Orminati and Hansens (1974) found egg masses on the tips of the blades of *S. alterniflora* (181 masses) and *Distichlis spicata* (9 masses) in late July through August. These masses were deposited on grass 14–46 centimeters above the marsh surface, thus not where the tall *S. alterniflora* grows. The two-tiered egg masses were long and narrow (14–15 millimeters long, 1–2 millimeters wide) and contained an average of 208 eggs with a range of 27–416. Each egg was 1.5–1.7 millimeters long, 0.25 millimeters wide, spindle-shaped and turned dark gray a few hours after deposition. Most eggs hatched about the same time after 4–5 days so that masses of larvae dropped to the marsh surface. The larvae were about 2 millimeters long at hatching and 20–24 millimeters at pupation. The duration of each instar varied as did the number of instars to pupation. The frequency of feeding as well as the amount ingested played a major role in the length of the larval instars. The larvae that became males generally pupated earlier with one fewer instars (Table 5.17).

The prepupal stage began after a period of larval inactivity of 1–5 weeks and lasted 24–28 hours. The pupae were 11–19 millimeters long with the males being slightly smaller. Pupation lasted 7–16 days with an average of 10.3 days in New Jersey (Orminati and Hansens, 1974) while in Florida, Jones and Anthony (1964) recorded an average pupal period of 8 days with a range of 4–12 days. Emergence was very rapid lasting about five minutes and flight occurred about an hour later. In the laboratory males and females lived an average of 5.3 and 6 days respectively (Orminati and Hansens, 1974).

When larvae were reared at room temperature the average total elapsed time through instar 10 was 209.6 days with a range of 66–585 days (Table 5.18). Presumably the average time in the field would be longer. This implies that *T. lineola* had one generation a year in the New Jersey marshes. The results from Florida (Jones and Anthony, 1964) suggested the possibility of

Table 5.18. Larval development of *T. l. lineola* reared in 1966–1968. (From Orminati and Hansens, 1974, by permission of the editor, *Ann. Ent. Soc. Amer.*)

Instar	Number Larvae	Range in Days	Average Days
1	94	7–39	14.0
2	90	3–31	12.9
3	122	3–38	11.2
4	171	3–37	14.8
5	155	5–39	15.2
6	156	6–70	18.6
7	156	7–87	23.5
8	153	10–104	32.2
9	115	11–81	35.4
10	35	11–59	31.8
11	5	7–45	27.0
12	2	19–22	20.5
13	1	26	26

more than a single generation a year; eggs deposited in early spring quite probably developed to adults by late fall. It is apparent much is still to be learned about the life cycles of these two common salt-marsh greenheaded flies.

The deerfly, *Chrysops fuliginosus*, is found along the Atlantic and Gulf coasts from Nova Scotia to Mississippi and is considered to be a salt-marsh species (Jones and Anthony, 1964). The larvae of this fly dominates (82 percent of tabanid larvae) North Carolina marshes and is widely distributed where *S. alterniflora* is most evident (Dukes *et al.*, 1974b): emergence in New Jersey salt-marsh areas is primarily from *S. alterniflora* lined ditch banks well below mean high-water level. However, while *C. fuliginosus* is taken from *S. alterniflora* sites, it is usually associated with vegetation indicative of fresh-water influence (Rockel and Hansens, 1970).

A later paper by Magnarelli and Anderson (1979a) reported on egg masses collected from the field or produced in the laboratory. Most females (63.3 percent) deposited eggs in one mass in contrast to two or three. Individual eggs were 2.0 millimeters long and 0.4 millimeters wide. The number of eggs ranged from 72–209 and 73 percent or more of these eggs hatched in 7–10 days after deposition.

Until Magnarelli and Anderson (1978) nothing had been known about larval development. They reported that *C. fuliginosus* tolerated a wide range of soil conditions. Larvae were found in a salinity range of 0.6 to $12^0/oo$, a pH of 5.8 to 7.1 and an organic content ranging from <10 to 40.9 percent. There were no significant correlations between numbers of larvae collected and those parameters, but there was a significant negative correlation between numbers of larvae and distance from drainage ditches. Relatively large numbers occurred within six meters of ditch banks. This is in contrast to Dukes *et al.* (1974) who found larvae widely distributed throughout the marsh. Although the larval abundance of *C. fuliginosus, C. atlanticus,* and *T. nigrovittatus* could not be correlated directly to soil characters, Magnarelli and Anderson (1978) concluded that distributions probably resulted from a number of interacting factors including physical soil features, larval needs, larval dispersal, behavior, and adult oviposition behavior.

Mature larvae are about 14 millimeters long and pupate in the upper strata of the marsh soil. Axtell (1976) presumed the life cycle to take one year since there was a single peak of emergence during late May or early June to late June in New Jersey (Rockel and Hansens, 1970) and a seasonal occurrence from early March to early July in Florida (Jones and Anthony, 1964). In contrast, Magnarelli and Anderson (1978) found that *C. fuliginosus* larvae brought into the laboratory during the spring prior to pupation did not pupate when lengths were less than six millimeters. Since they also found only small larvae in the field during the winter and spring, they concluded that many larvae needed at least two years to mature and that at least a portion of the population had a multiyear life cycle. Like early workers they found pupation to occur during the single time interval of early June with a range from mid-May through early July. It is apparent that duration of the life cycle for this species has not been fully established. This raises the possibility that there may be differing proportions of adults emerging after one or two years in various marsh locations.

The flight season for *C. fuliginosus* is related to the time of emergence. Catts and Olkowski (1972) determined that flight activities peaked in early June with a range from late May to late June. Early in the season, both sexes were in the marsh, but at the peak of activity both sexes shifted to the uplands with males dominant in the marsh. By late June only a few females remained in the uplands. Rockel (1969a) identified two behavioral patterns which sharply segregated the flies spatially because of their physiological state. Those flies on the marsh were considered to be satiated because few attempted to bite and their ovaries were well developed. The upland population consisted of avid biters with poorly developed ovaries.

There is a direct relationship between flight activity of tabanids and environmental factors. Dale and Axtell (1975) found the highest numbers of *T. nigrovittatus* active at intermediate light levels (40,000 lux), a temperature of 25 °C and no wind. The greatest activity for *C. atlanticus* was at low light (5000 lux) and a temperature of 30 °C. *C. fuliginosus* was most active at high light intensities (100,000 lux). The frequency and intensity of flight activity for *C. fuliginosus* increased with increasing morning air temperature (Catts and Olkowski, 1972). Flight activity occurred between 18–24 °C. As the season progressed, males usually began their pursuant activities earlier in the day and terminated sooner. Catts and Olkowski also noted that the darker males began activity earlier in the day than the lighter gray females.

According to Catts and Olkowski (1972) the posturing of the flies indicated their readiness to fly and mate. The females ascended the grass stems and took flight with the males in pursuit. The pair settled into the grass facing in opposite directions with only their caudal parts in contact. When mating ended, the pair quickly separated with the male flying away while the female groomed herself.

Host hunting by females increased as mating terminated. Both Catts and Olkowski (1972) and Anderson (1973) observed that *C. fuliginosus* and *C. atlanticus* sought out the higher portions of the host body. *C. atlanticus* had a biphasic feeding behavior. The peak of feeding activity began shortly after sunrise and lasted for three hours. The second period occurred two hours just prior to sunset. *C. fuliginosus* had a single feeding period with the peak in late morning—continuing for about three hours (Anderson, 1973): this followed the time of mating activity observed by Catts and Olkowski (1972).

Chrysops atlanticus has been recorded from Massachusetts to Florida. Larvae have been collected from short *S. alterniflora* marshes, from wooded islands in the marsh, and from the wooded upland perimeter. While the species seems to be associated with the salt-marsh habitat, upland fresh-water areas should not be overlooked (Jones and Anthony, 1964; Axtell, 1976). A recent paper by Magnarelli and Anderson (1978) reported a highly significant correlation between larval occurrences, salinity, and percentage organic matter. There was no significant relation between numbers of larvae and pH or distance from drainage ditches. Larvae were usually collected from depressions with standing water which had higher salinities than surrounding sediments. These depressions were filled with very black sediments largely composed of silt and clay with a strong H_2S odor. While salinity in the depressions was higher, this particular Connecticut marsh had lower salinities than other coastal marshes due to the proximity of the Housatonic River. Such *C. atlanticus* distributions would tend to be related to the observation noted above by Jones and Anthony (1964), and Hansens and Robinson (1973).

The life cycle parallels that reported for *C. fuliginosus*. A single yearly generation is again suggested (Axtell, 1976) as the adults emerge from late May–early June to late July in New Jersey (Rockel and Hansens, 1970) while the season recorded for Florida extends from late April to mid-August (Jones and Anthony, 1964). Anderson (1971) found only nonaggressive virgin females with well-developed ovaries in a Connecticut salt marsh resting on the tips of *S. alterniflora* leaves after having emerged from the marsh soil. These females were caught only on the marsh, and early in the morning and the evening when the humidity was high. Mating took place only in the morning. The males hovered three to four feet off the ground but below the tops of the plants in open areas created by lodged *S. alterniflora.* They rested, and mated with the females on the tips of the leaves of *Spartina* plants surrounding the openings. Autogeny appears to be the general rule (Anderson, 1971; Magnarelli and Anderson, 1979b). Prior to their first oviposition, the females are not active fliers but following this oviposition they become active and move to the woodland parimeter to aggressively seek a blood meal. They return to the marsh to deposit the second batch of eggs.

Female *C. atlanticus* carried an average of 145 (66–239) eggs (Anderson, 1971) while Magnarelli and Anderson (1979b) recorded an average of 147.5 in the laboratory and 167.6 ± 49.6 SD from field-collected egg masses. Individual eggs were 1.5 millimeters long and 0.3 millimeters wide (Jamnback and Wall, 1959). These egg masses are 13–32 millimeters long and 2 millimeters wide (Jamnback and Wall, 1959; Magnarelli and Anderson, 1979b). They are deposited about 10 centimeters from the leaf tip and about 30 centimeters from the soil. About 78 percent of the eggs hatched within seven days after being collected from the field (Magnarelli and Anderson, 1979b).

Diptera. Ceratopogonidae. The family is large and worldwide in distribution. The genus *Culicoides* with 19 subgenera comprises one quarter of the species in the family and is the most widespread and abundant genus (Kettle, 1977). This family is represented in most habitats where damp or wet substrates are available for larval development. Such substrates always include moisture, not truly aquatic nor terrestrial situations but saturated sites like stream banks, mangrove swamps, salt marshes, bogs, lake shores, dung, rotting fruit, tree holes, and fungi. The members of the family are small to very small flies and the feeding habits of the adults are of considerable economic importance as well as scientific interest. Some species such as *Culicoides furens* and *C. hollensis* have a wide host range showing no preference for birds or mammals (Koch and Axtell, 1979b). Species associated with the marine habitat are especially important as pests to the extent of adversely affecting regional economies in coastal areas. Linley (1976) identified three genera, *Culicoides, Leptoconops,* and *Dasyhelea* associated with the marine habitat. The first two are almost exclusively hematophagous and *Culicoides* is the most important economically.

One of the common pestiforous ceratopogonids is *Culicoides melleus* which is distributed along the east coast of the United States from Maine to Florida. It is associated with nonvegetated, sheltered, sandy, intertidal areas and is virtually confined between high and low tide levels. It is distinctive from some other ceratopogonids in that mating takes place on the ground without a male swarming flight (Linley and Adams, 1972a,b; Kline and Axtell, 1975).

Wet mud in mangrove swamps and salt marshes, rich in organic matter, provides a major breeding site for some of the economically most important *Culicoides*. Linley (1976) recorded the distribution of a number of species from Nearctic and Palaearctic salt marshes as well as mangrove habitats. He considered *C. furens* to be probably the world's number one pest. It ranges along the east coast of the United States, through Central America and the West Indies to Brazil, and it has been reported in Baja California. *C. furens* is characteristically found in mangrove swamp mud (Linley, 1966a) but, in reviewing earlier work, Linley (1976) reported the larvae to be associated with unshaded intertidal mud, the borders of saline pools and ditches, and very rarely in fresh-water habitats. Along the east coast of the United States it is a characteristic member of the fauna of *S. alterniflora* dominated salt marshes.

Culicoides furens and *C. hollensis* were found throughout a North Carolina marsh. *C. hollensis* was most abundant in the tall *S. alterniflora* along large drainage ditches and stream banks while *C. furens* was most abundant in short *S. alterniflora* areas that have a low frequency of flooding (Kline and Axtell, 1976). Both species were equally abundant among the intermediate size *S. alterniflora* (Tables 5.19 and 5.20). Emergence trap data (Table 5.19) displayed a *C. hollensis: C. furens* ratio of about 4:1 in tall form *S. alterniflora* and about 1.5:1 in intermediate *S. alterniflora*. Neither species was abundant in the *Juncus roemerianus* and marsh-shrub sites. Based on emergence traps and larvae from soil samples (Table 5.20) *C. bermudensis* was found restricted to areas covered by *D. spicata*, *D. spicata*-short *S. alterniflora* mixtures and *J. roemerianus*. Those areas were flooded only 6–11 percent of the time (Kline and Axtell, 1977).

While Kline and Axtell (1977) associated *C. furens* emergence with areas with a low frequency of flooding in North Carolina marshes, Bidlingmayer (1957) found ten times as many larvae from shore zone areas of ditches and ponds than from higher areas occupied by *Avicennia* and *Batis* in Florida. These larvae tended to disappear as the marsh dried out but could be found at deeper depths probably using crab burrows. Most of the larvae were found between the high- and low-tide marshes of the larger drainage ditches. The larvae of *C. furens* followed fluctuating water level by horizontal migration in Jamaican mangroves (Linley, 1966a) with the greatest concentrations at the water line or just above. As time for pupation approached the larvae moved vertically as most pupae were found at 15–45

Table 5.19. Number and percentage (in parentheses) of *Culicoides hollensis* and *C. furens* caught in emergence traps in various plant zones in a North Carolina salt marsh. (From Kline and Axtell, 1977, by permission of the editor, *J. Med. Ent.*)

| | Mean No. Adults/Trap/Week* | | | |
| | C. hollensis | | C. furens | |
	1972	1973	1972	1973
Tall *S. alterniflora*, man-made ditch	28.6	25.8a	0.7	4.2d
	(33.1)	(31.9)	(1.9)	(4.4)
Tall *S. alterniflora*, natural ditch	6.5	7.2cd	3.9	8.6d
	(7.5)	(8.9)	(10.7)	(9.0)
Tall *S. alterniflora*, river margin	15.9	17.2b	3.5	13.5c
	(18.4)	(21.2)	(9.6)	(14.1)
Intermediate *S. alterniflora*	16.0	9.5c	4.6	18.1b
	(18.5)	(11.8)	(12.4)	(19.1)
Short *S. alterniflora*	7.6	9.4c	12.2	33.9a
	(8.8)	(11.6)	(32.8)	(35.8)
Distichlis spicata	7.9	6.9cd	8.3	7.7c
	(9.2)	(8.5)	(22.2)	(8.1)
Juncus roemerianus	3.2	3.6cd	1.4	4.5d
	(3.7)	(4.4)	(3.7)	(4.8)
Marsh shrubs	0.7	1.4d	2.5	4.4d
	(0.8)	(1.7)	(6.8)	(4.7)

* Within each species the means with a common letter are not significantly different at the 0.05 level (Duncan's multiple range test). There were 2–4 traps per plant zone for varying portions of 1972 and 4 traps per plant zone in 1973.

centimeters above the water line in drier areas. This suggests the larvae respond to the degree of wetness or inundation. The larvae of *C. furens* have to make contact with air in order to pupate as they cannot do so under water while *C. melleus* can pupate under water but emergence of the adult cannot take place under water. However, emergence for *C. furens* is not influenced if flooding occurs after pupation is completed (Bidlingmayer, 1957; Lindley, 1966b, 1976; Linley and Adams, 1972a).

The eggs of *Culicoides* are about 0.25 millimeters long and banana-shaped with rounded ends. The eggs are white when newly laid, quickly changing to dark brown when exposed to the air. The mean number of eggs laid by autogenous females in the laboratory were: *C. furens* 39.9 ($\pm$ 23.5), *C. hollensus* 54.0 ($\pm$ 38.2), and *C. melleus* 54.5 ($\pm$ 21.8). The percent hatch was 45.5, 77.7 and 90.4, respectively (Koch and Axtell, 1978). Fertilization takes place at oviposition and embryonic development proceeds immediately and is directly related to temperature. Hatching usually occurs immediately upon completion of embryonic development. Most ceratopogonid eggs show little resistance to adverse environmental conditions. Exposure of

Table 5.20. Recover of *Culicoides* larvae from soil in various plant zones in a salt march (1973). (From Kline and Axtell, 1977, by permission of the editor, *J. Med. Ent.*)

Vegetation	% Time Flooded	Number of Samples	Average Number Larvae/ Sample	Number of Larvae Held for Emergence	No. adults emerged/larvae held		
					C. bermudensis	*C. hollensis*	*C. furens*
Tall *S. alterniflora* river margin	19* (8–35)	48	45.3	1559	0.00	0.46	0.15
Tall *S. alterniflora* man-made ditch	36 (26–46)	38	29.2	653	0.00	0.57	0.13
Intermediate *S. alterniflora* man-made ditch	15 (5–32)	34	25.6	641	0.00	0.37	0.13
Intermediate *S. alterniflora* interior marsh	15 (5–25)	48	20.3	659	0.00	0.33	0.26
Short *S. alterniflora*	13 (5–21)	49	14.7	475	0.00	0.20	0.27
D. spicata and short *S. alterniflora*	11 (0–26)	49	18.0	528	0.41	0.14	0.31
Distichlis spicata	6 (0–19)	48	10.9	263	0.99	0.17	0.27
Juncus roemarianus	8 (0–21)	48	7.7	180	0.72	0.23	0.27
Shrubs, ditch spoil pile	12 (3–27)	94	8.6	611	0.00	0.26	0.16

* Average percentage of time covered with water during the year. Values in parentheses are ranges of averages of percentage of time per week during this study (March–December).

C. furens or *C. barbosai* to humidities of 60–80 percent will cause the eggs to collapse. Free water around the eggs of *C. furens* is required for successful hatching (Linley, 1976).

The larvae of *Culicoides* are elongate and cylindrical. They are about 1 millimeter long and transparent at the time of hatching and grow through four instars to a length of 5–7 millimeters and are a white or cream color with yellowish head capsules when mature. The pupae are 2–4 millimeters long with a small head, a humped mesothorax, and an elongated flexible abdomen (Linley, 1976).

At hatching, the larvae possess very small food reserves and must begin to feed immediately. Older larvae are able to withstand starvation for 2–3 weeks. Generally food intake is indiscriminate and many are detritus feeders. Some, like *C. furens* and *C. melleus,* ingest live food such as protozoa, nematodes, annelids, and other small invertebrates, and motile algae.

Larval development is influenced by food supply, competition, and temperature. *C. melleus* development to pupa can be as rapid as nine days at 27 °C; *C. furens* takes 20–34 days from egg to adult, including three days in the pupal stage at constant temperature in the laboratory. From field studies in Florida, the generation time for *C. furens* is 4–6 weeks with the larval stage probably lasting 3–5 weeks. During cooler periods development is slower and the larvae grow to larger size storing reserves which yield adults capable of producing greater numbers of eggs autogeneously. The pupal stage lasts only a few days and emergence is more synchronous on quantitatively richer diets. Males emerge slightly ahead of the females but there is much overlap. Emergence is very rapid; occurring in minutes during the daylight period with 97 percent of *C. furens* emerging between 0700–1500 hours. A similar cycle has been reported for *C. melleus* (Bidlingmayer, 1957; Linley, 1966a, 1976).

The season of emergence varies among species. *C. hollensis* is common in spring and the fall while *C. furens* is abundant from late spring to early fall (Kline and Axtell, 1976). Patterns of emergence are determined largely by temperature. In tropical areas emergence is probably continuous with population overgaps. In reviewing earlier work Linley (1976) deduced a probability of six generations a year in Florida while in Louisiana the season from April to November might produce five generations. He suggested the Connecticut season, extending from mid-June to mid-September, might limit production to three generations.

Upon emergence the males feed only on sugars. The females ingest sugars but also require a protein meal. Some females carry enough food reserves from the larval stage to produce autogeneous eggs in the first batch. Following such an egg deposition, a blood meal is needed to produce a second batch of eggs.

Most *Culicoides* have a crepuscular pattern of daily activity. Bidling-mayer (1961) and Linley (1976) reported that *C. barbosai* and *C. furens* had a larger peak of activity at sunrise than at sunset. They identified female *C. barbosai* as having a low level of activity all night while *C. furens* showed two nocturnal peaks, one in the early evening and again after midnight. However, Koch and Axtell (1979a) found that the largest activity peak for *C. furens* occurred immediately after sunset and continued to midnight with a rapid decline. There was a secondary peak at sunrise with a gradual de-cline throughout the day with a minimum at midafternoon. In contrast, *C. hollensis,* found in the same marshes as *C. furens,* was active during the day with a major peak 3–4 hours after sunrise and another at sunset (Bidling-mayer, 1961; Linley, 1976; Koch and Axtell, 1979a). Such activity was cor-related with wind velocity for *C. furens* while wind direction and tempera-ture determined flight movements of *C. hollensis* (Koch and Axtell, 1979a).

Parthenogenesis is known to occur among only two species; both are *Culicoides* and *C. bermudensis* is one of these. Typically mating among the ceratopogonids takes place as females approach male swarms. The position of such swarms is maintained by visual markers. Males perceive the females' approach by the use of antennae acting as auditory direction finders: mating may occur for only a few seconds or last several minutes (Linley and Adams, 1972b). The duration of the gonotrophic cycle (from feeding to the appear-ance of mature eggs in the ovary) at 20°, 25°, 29°, and 33 °C was 156, 104, 82, and 72 hours respectively for *C. barbosai* and 102, 59, 42, and 36 hours for *C. furens.* The number of eggs produced generally depends on tempera-ture and varies with species. Temperature did not affect the numbers of eggs for *C. barbosai* but at 25 °C, *C. furens* produced an average of 99 eggs (range 21–112) which was more than the numbers produced at 29° or 33 °C. The duration of the egg stage varies with species and with temperature. It is longer in *C. barbosai* at 20, 25, 29, and 33 °C where most eggs hatched in 12, 6–7, 5–6, and 5 days respectively while, for *C. furens,* eggs hatched at the three higher temperatures at 4, 3, and 2 days, respectively. Autogenous fe-males are produced in both species but the proportions vary greatly with dif-ferent populations. There is a greater degree of gonotrophic harmony, with ovaries all in the same stage of development, following a blood meal. This is particularly true for *C. furens* but less so for *C. barbosai* which takes a smaller blood meal. Such autogenous females tend to have well-developed ovaries at the time of emergence from the pupae (Linley, 1966b, 1976).

Dipteran Autogeny. These three families of biting flies are characterized by the fact that many species require a blood meal for the development of the eggs. However, there are a number of species that are autogenous, i.e., pro-ducing the initial batch of eggs without a blood meal. For the production of subsequent batches of eggs, the females must seek a blood meal to complete egg development. The proportion of autogenous females varies greatly among various populations (Lea and Lum, 1959; Linley, 1966b; O'Meara, 1976). It is reported as rare in *A. sollicitans,* unreported for *T. lineola* but common among populations of *A. taeniorhynchus, T. nigrovittatus,* and *C. fuliginosus* and reported among several species of marine *Culicoides* including *C. furens, C. hollensis* and *C. melleus* as well as other ceratopogonids (Rockel, 1969a; Anderson, 1971; Bosler and Hansens, 1974; Linley, 1976; O'Meara, 1976; Kettle, 1977; Magnarelli and Anderson, 1977; Koch and Axtell, 1978). The behavior of the females also varies. Autogenous female deerflies are docile and on the marsh, while those seeking a blood meal display very aggressive behavior and tend to be found on the adjoining uplands (Rockel, 1969a; Anderson, 1971). The ovaries of autogenous females are in an advanced stage of development prior to depositing the first batch of eggs and, at least among the tabanids *T. nigrovittatus* and *C. fuliginosus,* the fat bodies from the larval stage are depleted. Those females with ovaries in earlier stages of ovarian development possess larger fat bodies. Those biting flies captured in the uplands adjoining a tidal marsh have already deposited a batch of eggs, have ovaries in a very early stage of development, have very small fat bodies, and are acquiring a blood meal by feeding aggressively (Linley, 1966b; Rockel, 1969a; Anderson, 1971; Bosler and Hansens, 1974).

While it may be of some comfort to the hosts of these haematophagous flies that autogenous individuals do not need a blood meal to produce the first batch of eggs, these autogenous individuals may pay a price. Thomas (1972) suggested that anautogenous species are capable of more gonotrophic cycles than autogenous species. A comparison between autogenous and anautogenous uniparous (one gonotrophic cycle) and biparous (two gonotrophic cycles) species showed anautogenous species have a greater survival between gonotrophic cycles than do autogenous species. Presumably, the ability to develop and lay eggs without having had a blood meal leaves the insect so weak that it may be unable to obtain a blood meal. The blood meal obtained by anautogenous species allows for egg development and oviposition. Thomas also suggested this blood meal may supply some energy thus eliminating the need to find a carbohydrate source by feeding on plants. As Bosler and Hansens (1974) pointed out, fat bodies are depleted during the first ovarian cycle among autogenous individuals so that, by the time of oviposition, virtually all are exhausted. This would suggest there are no energy stores for subsequent activity. Along with this, Bosler and Hansens observed that about half of the trapped flies living on the marsh obtain carbohydrates in the form of plant nectar while the remaining flies may seek a blood meal for carbohydrates as well as for proteins and lipids essential for subsequent ovarian development. This observation is supported by Magnarelli and Anderson (1977) who considered the sugar from plant nectars to be a main source of nutrient for females following the deposition of the first, autogenous, eggs. In addition to the sugars, the amino acids and proteins acquired from the plant pollen and nectar may be nutritionally important to both sexes (Magnarelli *et al.,* 1979).

It is suggested the quantity of food available during larval development plays a significant part in determining whether or not a particular adult female will be autogenous (Nayar, 1967; Linley, 1976; O'Meara, 1976). According to O'Meara, all mosquitos emerge with their ovaries in Stage I with little or no yolk present in the follicles. The rate of ovarian development in the absence of a blood meal varies between species and within a species. *A. taeniorhynchus* displays both obligate and faculative autogeny. Egg development in the former is completed by the fifth day after emergence while egg development can be extended to the twelfth day among facultatively autogenous females. O'Meara also reviewed earlier work pointing out that the occurrence of autogeny and the size of the egg batch are genetically controlled, and among anautogenous *A. taeniorhynchus,* a blood meal is necessary for the release of egg-development hormone which is not the case for autogenous females. Based on the variability of autogeny reported within species of the tabanids and ceratopogonids one might expect to find genetic and hormonal control of autogeny within species of these two families as well as other mosquitos although such control is only inferred, at best, in the reviews by Axtell (1976) and Linley (1976).

CHORDATA

Pisces

The species within the family Cyprinodontidae are the predominant fishes of the tidal marshes (Gunter, 1945; Simpson and Gunter, 1956; and Harrington and Harrington, 1961). Various other species enter the tidal creeks as ichthyoplankton, juveniles or adults, and move over the surface of the marshes but are not considered to be characteristic members of the marsh fauna (Harrington and Harrington, 1961; Daiber, 1962, 1963a, 1977).

While a large body of literature has accumulated about these cyprinodontid marsh inhabitants there is still much to be known about their life cycles and ecology as witness the continuing flow of papers. The literature has been summarized very ably by Hardy (1978) and the following species accounts will be drawn primarily from his work.

Fundulus heteroclitus. The mummichog has received the greatest attention among biologists. This common name is of Indian derivation and signifies "going in crowds" (Nichols and Breder, 1927). *F. heteroclitus* has a range from Newfoundland to northeast Florida. It is a schooling species with a ubiquitous choice of salinities ranging from fresh water to ocean. The fish is found in a variety of habitats but seems to prefer muddy substrates. It has a summer home range along the banks of tidal creeks of approximately 30 meters (Lotrich, 1975) but the extent of a home range in pools or impoundments is unknown. It is characteristically found close to shore.

The spawning season is a protracted one and varies with location. In North Carolina Brummett (1966) reported spawning from early May to late August while Kneib and Stiven (1978) reported spawning beginning in March and extending through August with a maximum level early in the season (April–May) and a secondary peak in July (Figure 5.17). The go-

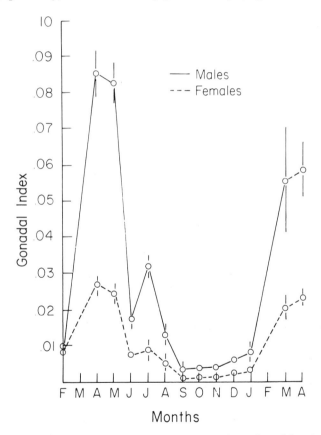

Figure 5.17.   Seasonal changes in gonadal index ±2 S.E. for male and female *F. hetero-clitus*: gonadal index dry gonad weight/total dry body weight. (From Kneib and Stiven, 1978, by permission of the editor, *J. Exp. Mar. Biol. Ecol.*)

nadal index rose sharply in March, prefacing the first spawning peak, and reached a minimum in September signifying the end of the spawning season (Matthews, 1938; Kneib and Stiven, 1978). The spawning season has been recorded for: Virginia, early May to early September; Chesapeake Bay, April to August; Delaware Bay, April through August; New Jersey, April to late August with a peak in late May; New York, mid-May to early August; Connecticut, May to July; Rhode Island, June to July; Massachusetts, mid-May to early August with a peak in June and July; Gulf of Maine, June to early August. It is evident that there is considerable latitudinal variability as well as variance in reported observations within a geographic area.

The laboratory work of Harrington (1959a) on *Fundulus confluentus* led him to hypothesize that, because of the retardation of early ovogenesis by high temperature reinforced by long days, either or both the amplitude of ovoposition and the number of spawners may be greater toward each end of the spawning period when temperatures are lower and days' lengths are shorter. Both Brummett (1966) and Kneib and Stiven (1978) suggested that temperature may be the stimulus determining the timing of reproductive activity for *F. heteroclitus*. Several of the spawning periods cited above from Hardy (1978) identify peaks in the earlier portions of the individual species spawning interval.

Spawning is a relatively short-lived affair as described by Newman (1907). Rivalry was noted to be very intense among the males and the one in the most brilliant "spawning plumage" would drive away other males that encroached upon his territory. Size seemed to be less important than the intensity of coloration. The male took the more active and aggressive part in courtship, but the female frequently acted in ways to attract the male. Females with very ripe eggs frequently turned on their sides near the bottom to flash their white undersides. Whatever courtship there was took place shortly before the spawning act. The fish would pair and swim quietly with the female above and the male below and slightly behind. Gradually the male became more excited in his movements and courtship merged into spawning behavior which would induce the female to seek a secluded spot at the bottom. At this time the male would become so excited it would spawn with any female.

Spawning was characterized by the male grasping the female behind her dorsal and anal fins using his dorsal and anal fins. The corresponding ventral fins were locked together. The female was forced against some solid object at which time she assumed an S-shaped posture. In such position, both fish vibrated, releasing eggs and sperm. Newman was of the opinion that the female initiated the vibratory quivering. If a male was not readily available, the female would assume the S-shaped posture characteristic of the spawning act and vibrate her body. However, no eggs would be released.

Spawning sites are diverse. Newman (1907) observed eggs being deposited in shallow pits in the bottom and covered by silt stirred up by the vibrating anal fin of the female which was in contact with the bottom. Eggs have been found in empty ribbed mussel, *Geukensia demissa,* shells (Able and Castagna, 1975; Kneib and Stiven, 1978) with an approximate shell gape of 2 millimeters. Such shells may contain up to 700 or more eggs in various stages of development. In a Delaware marsh, the eggs have been found on the inner surface of the older, dying, primary leaves of *Spartina alterniflora* (Taylor *et al.,* 1977). As many as 30 eggs (usually 10–25) all in the same stage of development, were found in a single plant. Those eggs were situated 5–10 centimeters above the marsh surface. None were found on the surface or among the plant roots. They were distributed in a narrow zone high on the banks of ditches and creeks at a level exposed at low tide. The eggs have been found 85–90 centimeters above the low water of a spring tide series with daylight highs at 88 centimeters and night high tides at 99 centimeters. All the eggs were covered by the night high tide. The marsh site examined by Taylor *et al.* (1977) was normally not flooded by every tide while the site examined by Kneib and Stiven (1978) was flooded every day. The placement of eggs within ribbed mussel shells, the leaf sheath of marsh plants, and under mats of filamentous algae (Pearcy and Richards, 1962) would provide some protection against desiccation and predation in the intertidal zone.

The placement of eggs in such situations poses interesting questions. How and why do these fish sometimes select a particular site in contrast to the apparent broadcasting of eggs under other circumstances? How do the fish deposit the eggs and fertilize them through the relatively narrow opening provided by the dead mussel shell or leaf sheath? How does the female determine the spatial association to place the eggs just below the position reached by the highest spring tides?

Taylor *et al.* (1979) have examined the problem of timing and found a semilunar periodicity in the spawning cycle. They found the gonadosomatic indices (GSI) for both sexes were significantly higher during the spring tide (Figure 5.18). Spawning readiness (percent ripe fish) was nearly 100 percent in both sexes at gonadal peaks and less than 50 percent between peaks. This spawning rhythm was also apparent in the size distributions of the fry collected from the marsh surface pools during the spawning season. Taylor and DiMichele (1980) found a parallel to this lunar spawning rhythm in the periodicity of oocyte maturation. There were cyclic changes in ovarian hydration, egg size, and yolk content, and follicular development that reached a maxima in synchrony with the peak of spring tide spawning activity. The changes were smaller for the males; the maximum gonad size was reached several days before that of the females, and the male GSIs declined more gradually after the peak.

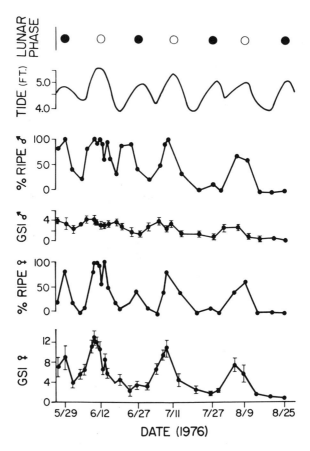

Figure 5.18.   Spawning readiness (% ripe) and Gonadosomatic Index (GSI) of *F. hetero-clitus* in the field. The data presented are means of 9–10 animals (5 animals on 5/24, 5/29, 6/1, and 8/15) sampled at night high tide. Vertical bars delineate ± 1 S.E. Ripeness data are percent of group examined from which gametes could be released by light pressure. Dates given are those of new (dark circle) or full moon (open circle). Tide heights are NOAA Tide Table predictions of the highest high tide on a given day at Roosevelt Inlet, approximately 1500 m from the study site. (From Taylor *et al.,* 1979, by permission of the editor, *Copeia.*)

The gonadosomatic index shows a progressive decline in the relative size of the gonads in both sexes during the spawning season. The mean GSI for females examined at the low points between spawning peaks was 3.93 ± 0.82 on June 1 and declined to 0.91 ± 0.09 by August 20. The mean GSI for males declined from 2.12 ± 0.44 to 0.75 ± 0.12 for the same period. These data indicate a decline in the numbers of fish capable of spawning as well as a decline in the relative gonad weight in the spawning population. Female fish with a GSI less than 1.0 typically had ovaries in a regressed state.

Peaks of spawning readiness and GSI for both sexes were evident on the night high tides for over 80 percent of both sexes on four of the five days defined as the spring tide peak (Figure 5.19). The GSI for females averaged 11.91 ± 0.58 (N=40) at night high tides and it dropped to 7.46 ± 0.43 (N=30) at early morning low tide as compared to 4.25 ± 0.24 (N=164) between lunar peaks. High and low tide means for male GSI were 3.91 ± 0.91 (N=40) and 3.30 ± 0.20 (N=30) respectively. Variation between the means, as determined by ANOVA, was significant at P <0.01 for both sexes (Males, F=3.33; females, F=6.56). Ovaries examined on night tides were filled with

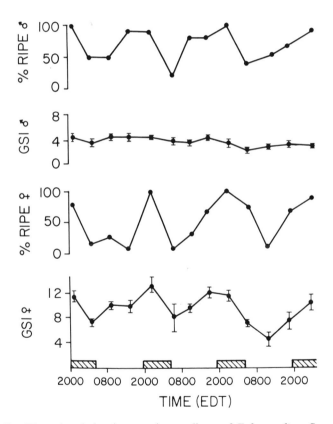

Figure 5.19. Diurnal variation in spawning readiness of *F. heteroclitus*. Samples were taken at slack high and low tide on 9–12 June 1976. Dark period (hatched bars on abscissa) was 1930-0430 EDT. Each point represents the mean of 10 fish. Vertical bars are ± 1 S.E. (From Taylor *et al.,* 1979, by permission of the editor, *Copeia*.)

many mature eggs of which 100 or more were regularly found in the posterior portion while, during the day, the eggs were uniformly dispersed
throughout the ovary. This suggests that ovulation occurred daily, prior to
each night's spawning activity.

Kneib and Stiven (1978) identified three groups of oocytes from fish in
North Carolina. Group I constituted recruitment oocytes that were small
and soft and present throughout the year. Group II comprised soft ripe oocytes 2 millimeters in diameter that were usually in the lumen of the ovary
ready to be shed. Group III was composed of atretic oocytes in follicles
where maturation had ceased and the oocytes were hard, opaque spheres
with flattened sides. The largest number of ripe oocytes in a single female
(72 millimeters SL) was 102. Kneib and Stiven found it difficult to determine fecundity because up to 50 percent of the oocytes were atretic even
early in the season. In contrast, Taylor and DiMichele (1980) found only 1.4
percent of the eggs to be atretic in mature ovaries. By counting the total ova
from mature ovaries Fritz and Garside (1975) found significant differences
in fecundity between salt water and brackish $(0.6-15.5^0/oo)$ populations. The
former population at Petpeswick Inlet, Nova Scotia had spawning females
with a mean length of 65 millimeters, and an average of 243 ova. The
brackish water population of Porter Lake had spawning females with an average length of 61 millimeters and a mean number of 161 ova.

Stripped unfertilized eggs are about 2 millimeters in diameter, amber or
yellow in color, transparent, and demersal. Varying amounts of adhesive filaments on the chorion range from a thick mat to complete absence. There is
evidence of geographic variation in the amount of these filaments (Pearcy
and Richards, 1962; Brummett, 1966). The adhesiveness tends to disappear
upon exposure to seawater. Oil globules are small, numerous, and opaque.
The smaller fish tend to produce smaller eggs. Development time at 20 °C
has been recorded at 228 hours (9.5 days) in the laboratory; about 40 days in
the field at 18 °C; and 11–13 days at 23 °C. Incubation varies with both
temperature and oxygen concentration and tends to be slower when the eggs
are crowded. It has been suggested that the eggs may need aerial exposure
since they appear to develop more rapidly out of water; however, they will
not hatch unless submerged. Able and Castagna (1975) observed hatching to
take place within 14–18 days under natural conditions in a mussel shell.
Taylor et al. (1977) reported that incubation time for air-incubated eggs
from Spartina leaves was 7–8 days with the immediate temperature on the
marsh surface ranging between 22 °–34 °C. It is not known whether the temperature variation within such a cluster of eggs would be less extreme than
that of the marsh surface (Dr. Taylor, personal communication). The development patterns were the same in the air or water up to the time of hatching
(Taylor et al., 1977). Embryos held in the air past the normal hatching time

(Stage 34 of Armstrong and Child, 1965) continued to develop but at a slower rate. The hatching process began within seconds after placing the air-incubated eggs in water. The eggs swelled almost instantly, embryos began to move within five minutes and hatching occurred in 15–20 minutes. The stimulus for hatching was apparently a sudden decrease in oxygen availability. Respiratory movements initiated immediately after immersion were associated with the release of a chorionase from secretory tissue in the mouth (DiMichele, 1980).

The hatching length of the yolk sac larvae ranges from about 4.0 millimeters to 7.7 millimeters with an average of 5.0 millimeters. The yolk can be retained for an extended period after hatching and seems to be a reflection of the stage at which the embryo hatched (Stockard, 1907; Nichols and Breder, 1927; Armstrong and Child, 1965; Brummett, 1966; Schmelz, 1970; Able and Castagna, 1975; Tay and Garside, 1975; Taylor *et al.,* 1977; Hardy, 1978).

Some individuals may mature and spawn in August of their first summer at a length of 38 and 25 millimeters SL for females and males respectively (Hildebrand and Schroeder, 1928). Kneib and Stiven (1978) measured the smallest female with mature or atretic eggs at 31 millimeters. Hardy (1978) reported that most *F. heteroclitus* mature during their second year.

Other Cyprinodonts. Spawning sites. The life cycles of other cyprinodonts associated with tidal marshes appear to be similar to that of *F. heteroclitus.* However, the details remain to be worked out. Spawning generally is associated with shallow waters over muddy bottoms and among vegetation and varying salinities. The specific sites seem to be unknown for *Fundulus luciae, F. grandis,* and *Lucania parva* (Simpson and Gunter, 1956; Hardy, 1978). *F. luciae* spawned in aquaria with salinities of 0.1, 3.9, and 16.9⁰/oo at water temperatures of 20–25 °C and exposed to natural day light. Eggs were deposited on spawning mops, adhering firmly to the mop strands. Most were deposited singly where the strands were densest. Others were scattered throughout the mops in groups of two to four. During the spawning season the same salinity-temperature-photoperiod conditions were observed in the natural habitat but no eggs were found on spawning mops placed in the habitat nor were eggs found on natural substrates (Byrne, 1978). Spawning activity of *F. similis* was associated with soft sandy-silt bottoms and open beaches free of attached sea grasses (Martin and Finucane, 1969). *F. confluentus* deposited its eggs among vegetation in rain-filled swales that had only intermittent access to tidal waters and often dried up (Harrington, 1959b) or at the fluctuating margins of brackish tidal water (Hardy, 1978). *F. majalis* usually spawned in still, shallow water close to shore and presumably in shallow pools (Hardy, 1978). *Cyprinodon variegatus* spawned in the shallow waters of small bays, tidal pools, mangrove lagoons, and in pools of slowly flowing streams, over sandy or mud bottoms (Hardy, 1978), avoiding vegetated areas (Kilby, 1955).

Spawning season. The spawning season is variable in time and extent, dependent on species and latitude. *F. luciae* has been reported to spawn over a time extending from March to October but most references identified a period from late spring to early summer (April–July) (Hardy, 1978). Byrne (1978) found the season in Virginia to extend from mid-April to mid-August based on the presence of mature and maturing ova (>1.6 millimeters diameter). Gunter (1945) recorded ripe male and female *F. grandis* from Copano and Aransas Bays, Texas from March to June while eggs were stripped from mature females in Texas waters during October (Simpson and Gunter, 1956). The presence of all sizes, from less than 20 millimeters to greater than 100 millimeters, at stations along the west coast of Florida suggested a continuous spawning season to Kilby (1955). This also appeared to be the case for *F. similis* (Kilby, ibid.) and *F. confluentus* in Florida waters with a 10- and possibly 12-month period reported in Texas (Harrington, 1959a, b; Hardy, 1978). de Vlaming *et al.* (1978) suggested that *F. similis* spawned during all months except November, December, and January in Florida and Texas. Martin and Finucane (1969) inferred that *F. similis* spawned year-round in the Tampa Bay area of Florida with peaks in the spring and late fall and reductions from July through September. Water temperatures above 30 °C may depress spawning. *F. majalis* spawned from April to September in Chesapeake Bay (Hildebrand and Schroeder, 1928) and June, July, and August from New Jersey northward (Nichols and Breder, 1927; Hardy, 1978). Gravid fish were collected in Delaware during summer spring-tide periods in 1968 and approximately one week after spring tides in 1969 (Schmelz, 1970). *Lucania parva* has a progressively protracted spawning season toward the lower latitudes: April through July in Chesapeake Bay (Hildebrand and Schroeder, 1928); mid-April to mid-August in North Carolina (Kuntz, 1916). The presence of small fish at nearly all seasons suggested a long breeding season in Texas and Florida (Gunter, 1945; Kilby, 1955). *Cyprinodon variegatus* also has an extended spawning season. Warlen (1964) reported a spring peak in early May and a second peak in mid-July with spawning ceasing in mid-August in Delaware. Nichols and Breder (1927) recorded spawning taking place in the vicinity of New York City in June and July but observed ripe fish from early May through August. This same spring and summer spawning pattern was reported for the Chesapeake Bay area (Hildebrand, 1917). Spawning has been observed in December and in the summer in Florida (Raney *et al.,* 1953; Hardy, 1978). Kilby (1955) and de Vlaming *et al.* (1978) suggested a year-round spawning season in Florida and Texas. In the higher latitudes, the season in New York extended from early May through August and from June through July in Massachusetts (Nichols and Breder, 1927). The evidence also suggests that most if not all of these species spawn more than once during a season.

Spawning behavior. Relatively little is known about the spawning behavior of these various species. Itzkowitz (1974) provided us with a detailed account of the role of interference in the spawning behavior of *Cyprinodon variegatus*. With the advent of warm weather the population moved to shallow waters where males set up territories about 0.5 meters in diameter, typically in water depths of 5 centimeters. With increased population densities, males established territories in depths less than 5 centimeters and up to 25 centimeters. The intraspecific interaction caused by high densities served as an attractant to males. Males often selected some topographic feature such as a depression or an algal clump as a part of the territory. The behavior of nonspawning males consisted of patrolling, chasing, boundary fighting, and feeding. Territorial boundaries were constantly violated by both intra- and interspecific intruders. While abundant, *Gambusia* and *Fundulus* were not chased as much as their numbers would imply since they occupied the water column or chose deeper depths. *Lucania parva* received more attention as it was abundant and occupied the same zone near the substrate.

The female *Cyprinodon* tended to be nomadic, ignoring boundaries. Spawning began shortly after she entered a territory with an average of four spawns occurring in less than 20 seconds, after which she left the territory. One of the major reasons for terminating a spawning was an interruption by an intruding fish, usually a neighboring male. Such intrusions were more common if the spawning pair ventured close to the boundary. Spawnings were so brief that in many cases the sequence was completed and the female had left before the neighboring territorial male could interfere.

Byrne (1978) divided courting behavior for *F. luciae* into three phases: approach, pursuit, and spawning. Approach consisted of movement by a male toward a slow-swimming or stationary female. This was usually made in the same plane as the female, from the side or behind but never from a head-on position. The female usually responded by swimming slowly away. If she did not move, the male would butt or brush against her. A male might approach repeatedly and then ignore the female but more often he moved into the active pursuit stage. Repeated short retreats by the female became longer and longer with the male rapidly following. The pair swam side by side with the male positioned so that his eye was opposite her operculum. The male often rubbed and butted his head against the side and belly of the female. His median fin was bent toward or around the female's body. Pursuit was observed by Byrne to last for 60 minutes for one mating pair before culminating in the spawning act. During spawning activity the side bars and ocellus and yellowish-orange underparts of the male were vivid but the drab gray-green of the female was unchanged.

Male territorial behavior for *F. luciae* was centered around the courtship of the female. Since males were promiscuous they frequently switched their attention from one female to another. Antagonistic behavior was sometimes observed between two males pursuing the same female. The more aggressive male would drive off the other by nipping at him.

Eggs. Hardy (1978) had compiled much of the general information available. The eggs are demersal for all of these species, opaque to translucent, amber to yellowish in color, or colorless, and the chorion tends to be adhesive with varying amounts of fibrils covering the surface of the egg. *Cyprinodon variegatus* produces about 140 eggs, half of which are nearly mature. The fertilized eggs are 1.0–1.73 millimeters in diameter. Nothing seems to be known about the fecundity of *F. confluentus* but its egg diameter is 0.8–1.5 millimeters. *F. luciae* females may have 9–16 mature eggs which, when fertilized, are 1.76–2.18 millimeters in diameter with a mean of 1.96 millimeters. The eggs are spherical to slightly elliptical and are characterized by a polar aggregate of oil globules and papillary ornamentation of the chorion. Adhesive gelatinous threads are evident on freshly spawned eggs (Byrne, 1978). The diameter of *F. majalis* eggs is about 2 millimeters and females may produce 200–800 eggs with the large fish producing more than the small fish. The eggs of *F. grandis* are about 2 millimeters in diameter but fecundity appears to be unknown. *F. similis* produces eggs that are 2.8 to 2.9 millimeters in diameter but are somewhat flattened at the poles and possess yolks that are oily and nongranular. *Lucania parva* females produced 7–46 ova with an average size of 1.23 (1.1–1.3) millimeters. The numbers of eggs reported for these various species reflect two methods of counting: stripped eggs from a ripe female or yolked eggs from a preserved ovary.

Development. Development time for *C. variegatus* varied with temperature with a range of 4–8 days (Kuntz, 1916; Hubbs and Drewry, 1959; Hardy, 1978). As the time of hatching approached, the yolk mass might be reduced to half its original volume. The embryo was well developed but short; its length seldom exceeding the circumference of the egg. At the time of hatching the embryo was about 4 millimeters (Kuntz, 1916) or 3.7–4.3 millimeters (Hardy, 1978) in length and had a relatively large yolk sac. After five days the larvae were about 5 millimeters long and the yolk sac was exhausted (Kuntz, 1916). The incubation period for *F. confluentus* has been recorded from 10–14 days up to 28 days (Hardy, ibid.). When exposed to aerial incubation hatching can be retarded for up to 95 days and when immersed in water hatching has taken place in 15–30 minutes (Harrington, 1959b). The embryo was 4–5.6 millimeters in length at hatching (Hardy, 1978). Hubbs and Drewry (1959) recorded hatching times of 9–13 and 14 days for *F. grandis* and *F. similis* respectively at a temperature of 28 °C and a salinity of 30⁰/₀₀. Later Martin and Finucane (1969) reported the first *F. similis* embryo hatched at 258–260 hours (10.7 days) while all but two hatched at 282–310 hours (11.7–12.9 days) at water temperatures of 24–26.9 °C. The last two eggs hatched at 482–484 hours. Salinity as well as temperature influence development of *F. luciae* and *F. majalis*. Byrne (1978) recorded an incubation period for *F. luciae* of 12–16 days at low salinities (0.1 and 3.9 °) and 33 days for 13 eggs and 43 days for one egg at 16.9⁰/₀₀ and temperatures of 20–25 °C. Those hatching in 12–16 days were 5.3–6.0 millimeters TL with large yolk sacs and rayless fin folds. Those hatching at the higher salinity were larger with smaller yolk sacs and fin folds with partially developed anal rays.

No *Fundulus majalis* eggs hatched at 15 °C in the laboratory (Schmelz, 1970; Daiber and Schmelz, 1971) and no hatching took place at 16.5 °C in tap water although some development took place. Hatching did occur at 16.5 °C in salinities of 35‰ and 75‰ with 43 percent and 2.5 percent hatching respectively. At 20 °, 30 °, and 34.5 °C hatching took place in all experimental solutions and in each instance hatching success was greatest in 35‰ and generally least in 75‰ (Figure 5.20). Tay and Garside (1975) produced similar results for *Fundulus heteroclitus*. Embryonic development was accelerated with increasing temperature. Development was retarded at the highest salinity (60‰) and this retardation was accentuated with increasing temperature. Figure 5.21 portrays the incubation time, hatching intervals, and general shape of the hatching frequency curves for *F. majalis* raised under each temperature-salinity combination. In 35‰ at 16.5 °C the incubation period to initial hatching lasted 32 days and the duration of the hatching period extended over 28 days. Throughout the hatching period, emergence occurred at irregular intervals and no more than two embryos hatched in any 24-hour time span. Consequently, the hatching frequency curve for this temperature and salinity has a platykurtic appearance which would be expected at incubation temperatures near biological zero. Two few individuals developed at 75‰ and 16.5 °C to establish an accurate picture of the hatching frequency curve. Those that did hatch appeared to follow the same pattern as individuals incubated in 35‰, although the incubation period to initial hatching was extended to 39 days.

Embryos raised at 20 °C had a bell-shaped hatching frequency curve with an incubation period to initial hatching of approximately 16 days in tap water and 35‰. Embryonic development in 75‰ was retarded and the incubation period to initial hatching extended to 22 days.

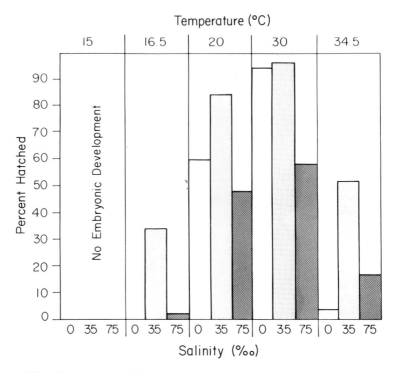

Figure 5.20.   Percent survival of striped killifish embryos incubated at different temperatures and salinities. (From Schmelz, 1970.)

Raising the incubation temperature to 30 °C caused another change in the shape of the hatching frequency curves as well as a reduction of the incubation period. In all salinities the curves were skewed to the left, and for fish raised in tap water and 35‰ the incubation period to initial hatching was reduced to seven days. As at 20 °C, embryonic development in 75‰ was retarded. The difference between the three salinities, however, was not as great as it was at the previous temperature, and only a 48-hour gap was noted in initial hatching time.

The incubation time and shape of the hatching frequency curves at 34.5 °C remained the same for fish reared in tap water and 35‰. The hatching frequency curves resumed a bell-shaped appearance at 75‰ although no change in initial hatching time was evident (Schmelz, 1970; Daiber and Schmelz, 1971). As part of an experiment concerned with the fixation time of vertebral number Fahy (1976) subjected *F. majalis* eggs to a salinity of 33‰ and three different temperature ranges: at 16–20 °C, first hatch occurred at 34 days, 50 percent hatched by 41 days; at 22–26 °C, first hatch oc-

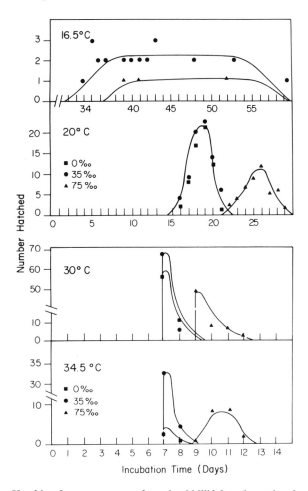

Figure 5.21. Hatching frequency curves for striped killifish embryos incubated at different temperatures and salinities. (From Schmelz, 1970.)

curred at 14 days, 50 percent hatched by 17 days; at 28–32 °C, first hatch took place at 10 days, 50 percent hatched by 12 days.

F. majalis reached their greatest hatching size at 20 °C (Table 5.21) and salinities of 0‰ and 35‰. Over the temperature range of 16.5 to 30 °C there was a gradual increase in the dry weight (including unused yolk) of the embryos in all salinities as well as a decline in the amount of yolk utilized (Table 5.22). There was a decline in embryo weight at 34.5 °C. These data demonstrated that, as the incubation temperature increased for any given salinity, the point at which hatching took place occurred at an earlier stage

Table 5.21. Mean hatching sizes (total length in mm) of *F. majalis* embryos incubated at different temperatures and salinities. N = number of embryos, X = mean length, s = standard deviation. (From Daiber and Schmelz, 1971.)

Salinity ‰		Temperature °C			
		16.5	20	30	34.5
0	N =	0	48	72	4
	X =	0	8.41	7.83	7.72
	s =	0	0.29	0.17	0.02
35	N =	26	74	78	32
	X =	8.05	8.40	7.53	7.22
	s =	0.38	0.18	0.13	0.24
75	N =	3	42	46	17
	X =	6.99	8.33	7.53	7.07
	s =	0.72	0.21	0.28	0.46

in embryonic development. Thus the lower the incubation temperature, the longer the fish remained in the egg and continued to develop. Conversely, increasing the temperature not only caused accelerated development but also premature hatching which forced the embryo to continue development outside the protection of the egg (Schmelz, 1970; Daiber and Schmelz, 1971). The same kind of pattern was noted for salinity by Byrne (1978) for *F. luciae.*

Table 5.22. Dry weights (mg) of newly hatched *F. majalis* embryos incubated at different temperatures and salinities as well as the quantities of yolk utilized in metabolism. (Based on the average weight of a striped, unfertilized ripe egg weighing 1.69 ± 0.06 mg [10 batches of 10 eggs each], the average chorion = 0.25 mg [N = 14], and the average yolk mass available = 1.44 mg.) (From Daiber and Schmelz, 1971.)

Incubation salinity (‰)		Incubation Temperature (°C)			
		16.5	20	30	34.5
0	Y	—	0.32	0.24	0.33
	E	—	1.12	1.20	1.11
35	Y	0.47	0.31	0.20	0.29
	E	0.97	1.13	1.24	1.15
75	Y	0.66	0.46	0.27	0.47
	E	0.78	0.98	1.17	0.97

Y = weight of yolk utilized in metabolism
E = weight of embryo plus unused yolk

At laboratory temperatures *Lucania parva* eggs hatched after 7–14 days (Kuntz, 1916; Hardy, 1978). Hubbs and Drewry (1959) reported a term of 6–9 days at a temperature of 28 °C and a salinity of 30‰. The newly hatched larvae were 4.5–5 millimeters long with a large yolk sac. By seven days after hatching the larvae were approximately 6 millimeters long and the yolk supply was absorbed (Kuntz, 1916).

Size at maturity. The average length in millimeters at which maturity is achieved is summarized as follows: *Cyprinodon variegatus,* males 24–25 mm, females 27–28 mm; *Fundulus confluentus,* 26–40 mm; *F. majalis,* males 63 mm, females, 76 mm; *Lucania parva,* 25 mm; *F. luciae,* males 24–27 mm, females 28–30 mm (Hardy, 1978). Byrne (1978) suggested *F. luciae* had a life span that would not extend beyond one year. Most males were recorded at 28–35 mm TL and most females ranged between 30–40 mm with the largest male and female recorded at 40 and 47 mm TL, respectively.

Reptilia

The diamondback terrapin, *Malaclemys terrapin,* is the only reptile restricted to brackish water and saline tidal marshes in the United States and has a distribution from southern New England to Mexico. Until recently very little has been known about its life history in the wild (Carr, 1952).

Recent publications have concentrated on facets of the reproductive biology. The egg-laying season extends from the second week in June into the third week of July with the greatest number of turtles evident for the month from mid-June to mid-July (Reid, 1955; Burger and Montevecchi, 1975; Burger, 1977a). No eggs are laid before sunrise or after sunset and, while there is no correlation between the time of day and the numbers of turtles searching for a nest site or laying eggs, there is a positive correlation between the height of the tide and the numbers of turtles in the nesting area (Burger and Montevecchi, 1975; Burger, 1977a). Just before high tide turtles move landward into the dunes from the marsh creeks to deposit their eggs. After the occurrence of high tide, turtles are seen walking toward the water (Figure 5.22). Burger and Montevecchi (1975) did not observe any turtles in the dunes during prolonged rains, even at high tide. However, if rain stopped just before high tide and the sun shone, the numbers of turtles were often greater than for those sunny days when it was not raining prior to high tide. Few turtles were observed on cloudy days.

Burger and Montevecchi (1975) found little evidence of turtle activity on sparsely vegetated dunes or on those dunes exposed to the sea whether they were heavily vegetated or not. Turtles showed a preference for the high

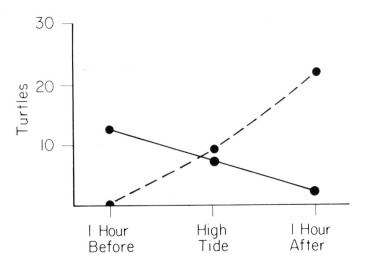

Figure 5.22. Direction of movement of turtles entering and leaving the study area as a function of tide time. The solid line represents the turtles facing inward, and the dotted line represents turtles facing the cove. (From Burger and Montevecchi, 1975, by permission of the editor, *Copeia*.)

dunes. From a daily census involving observation of 200 turtles, 70 percent of the animals were found searching for nest sites, depositing eggs, or leaving the high dunes and 88 percent of the nests were found in these high dunes even though half the area was in low dunes and sand flats. Within the high-dune habitat, they selected relatively flat areas. Random spots among the high dunes had an average slope of 18.1 ± 9.8 degrees while the mean slope of turtle nests was 7.2 ± 6.0 degrees and the mean slope of the entire area was 11.7 ± 8 degrees (Figure 5.23) (Burger and Montevecchi, 1975).

There was no evidence that the terrapins selected particular species of vegetation for nesting sites. They did select sites with less than 20 percent cover and a mean of 8.2 ± 6.4 percent (Figure 5.24) yet at positions typically less than 20 centimeters from vegetation with a mean distance of 11.2 ± 8.3 centimeters (Figure 5.25).

Burger and Montevecchi (1975) explained this turtle behavior as follows. Beaching at high tide decreases turtle exposure to predation, thermal stress, and desiccation; walking distance to the water is decreased and there is insurance that eggs are being laid beyond high tide. Nesting in a vegetated area provides a stable substrate, while digging a short distance from plants reduces the involvement with the roots. Nesting on low slopes reduces the problems of digging on a steep slope and erosion around the nest that might uncover or further bury the eggs.

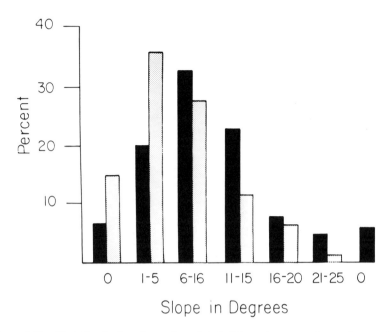

Figure 5.23. Variation in slope in random plots (solid area) compared to turtle nest sites (hatched area). (From Burger and Montevecchi, 1975, by permission of the editor, *Copeia*.)

The nest is dug through the dry top soil into the moist subsoil. Reid (1955) described one nest as being roughly triangular, 10.2 centimeters on one side and 7.6 centimeters on the other two sides with a parapet thrown up on the two short sides about 3.8 centimeters high. The turtle occupied the wide side of the triangle. Burger (1977a) also observed the preparation of a nest. The hole was dug at first with the front feet to about 10.5 centimeters wide, 17.5 centimeters long, and 5 centimeters deep at which time the female advanced over the hole to complete the digging with the hind feet. Females are easily disturbed while hunting a nest site, digging the hole, and during the early stages of egg laying. If the female is disturbed she abandons the nest, leaving the eggs uncovered and subject to immediate predation. Disturbed females tend to lay eggs elsewhere, usually within two hours. However, if a female is disturbed after the fourth egg is laid, she will continue to lay all eggs, covering them before she leaves. The number and distance between rejected nests varies and most are rejected immediately after a rain.

Egg laying is carried out with the head bobbing every 5–10 seconds. Burger (1977a) recorded one instance of a nest being filled with eight eggs laid in one minute and 45 seconds, after which dirt was pulled in by one foot

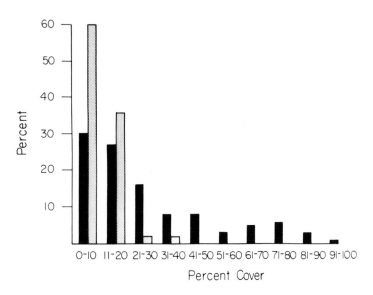

Percent Cover

Figure 5.24.   Cover of random plots (solid areas) compared to turtle nest sites (hatched areas). (From Burger and Montevecchi, 1975, by permission of the editor, *Copeia.*)

then the other, and tamped down with both feet. The location of the nest was obliterated by motion of the feet pulling in and spreading sand. The cover up pattern was generally triangular in shape with a mean width and length of 38.1 and 52.1 centimeters respectively. The nest was usually located in the center of the large base end of the triangle (Burger, 1977a).

After each egg was laid a bit of dirt was pushed into the hole. Of seven eggs in one nest, Reid (1955) found one buried at 17 centimeters, two at 17.8 centimeters, and four at 19 centimeters. On the average the egg compartment was wider than it was deep (Table 5.23, Figure 5.26).

The eggs are pinkish-white, dimpled, leathery-shelled and symmetrical. There is a greater variability between clutches than within clutches for length and breadth. Based on 40 complete clutches, the mean clutch size was recorded at 9.7 ± 2.6 with a range of 4–18 eggs. The mean clutch weight for 30 clutches with a mean average of 9.5 eggs each was 71.8 ± 17.7 grams (Table 5.24). The weight of the clutch was found to be highly correlated with clutch size and larger females tended to lay larger clutches. Egg size tended to decrease as the laying season advanced, a conditon not reported for other reptiles. Montevecchi and Burger (1975) noted that a review of earlier work suggested that the clutch size increased with a more temperate climate. However, their own observations, as well as those of Burger (1977a), reported an average of 8.5 eggs from Louisiana, 5.3 from North Carolina, and

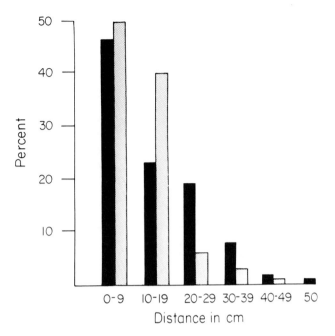

Figure 5.25. Distance to the nearest vegetation of random plots (solid areas) compared to turtle nest sites (hatched areas). (From Burger and Montevecchi, 1975, by permission of the editor, *Copeia.*)

9.7 and 8.7 for 1973 and 1974 respectively from New Jersey. Their review of the work concerned with captive terrapins led them to speculate that there may be more than one clutch laid per female; Burger (1977a) saw no evidence of this from her work in southern New Jersey.

Development time varied, presumably influenced by temperature levels of the sand. Burger (1976a) found nest temperature lagged behind surface temperatures: the daily variation was 2–9 °C with the smallest occurring at 0600 hours and the greatest at 1500 hours. Rainy periods depressed both

Table 5.23. Nest dimensions (cm) of *Malaclemys t. terrapin.* (From Montevecchi and Burger, 1975, by permission of the editor, *Amer. Midl. Nat.*)

Measurement	N	Mean	S D	Range
Nest depth (A)	43	15.0	2.1	10.8–20.3
Depth to top egg (B)	32	10.6	2.2	5.1–14.6
Egg compartment depth (C)	28	4.7	1.8	2.2– 8.9
Egg compartment width (D)	32	7.3	1.4	4.4–10.1

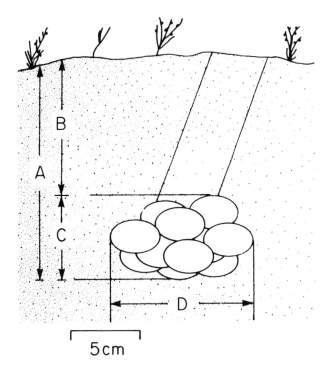

Figure 5.26. Scaled nest diagram. Measurements: (A) nest depth; (B) depth to top egg; (C) egg compartment depth = A–B; (D) egg compartment width. (From Montevecchi and Burger, 1975, by permission of the editor, *Amer. Midl. Nat.*)

surface and nest temperatures. The direction of the slope also influenced temperatures. Nests on a north-facing slope had mean daily temperatures about 1 °C lower than nests on south-facing slopes. The mean hatching time for 10 nests on a south-facing slope was 71 days as opposed to a mean of 79 days for 10 nests on a north-facing slope. Burger noted that nests produced metabolic heat. She found no difference in temperature between a nest with

Table 5.24. Egg characteristics of *Malaclemys t. terrapin.* (From Monte-vecchi and Burger, 1975, by permission of the editor, *Amer. Midl. Nat.*).

Measurement	N	Mean	S D	Range	Coefficient of Variation
Length	336	31.6 mm	1.8 mm	26.3–36.5 mm	5.7
Breadth	336	19.8 mm	1.1 mm	15.9–21.9 mm	5.4
Elongation	336	1.6	0.1	1.4– 2.1	5.7
Weight	300	7.7 gm	1.1 gm	5.0–11.0 gm	14.3
Volume	54	6.4 ml	1.2 ml	4.0– 9.5 ml	19.0

newly laid eggs and an empty nest. The mean difference in nest temperatures and sand temperature at the same depth was 2–12 °C per day. There was a positive correlation between nest depth and the incubation period of the first turtle to hatch. Shallow nests would be exposed to higher temperatures, which apparently affects proper egg development, and eggs in very deep nests may experience low temperature stress. Burger found that in five nests with a mean depth of 14.3 ± 1.3 centimeters the top eggs did not hatch and in eleven nests with a mean depth of 18.7 ± 2 centimeters the bottom eggs did not hatch. Since air temperatures influence rates of embryo development and because monthly temperatures differ, Burger found that nests initiated in June had a significantly shorter incubation period ($\bar{x} = 74.5 \pm 3.4$ days) than nests started in July ($\bar{x} = 86.0 \pm 15.2$ days). The mean nest depths were not significantly different for the two periods. Burger (1977a) reported eggs from a site in southern New Jersey hatching from 20 August through 12 October, 61–104 days after deposition. After observing 36 nests Burger recorded the mean development time for the first egg to hatch at 74.5 ± 3.4 days and the mean development time for all eggs to hatch was 76.2 ± 4.5 days. Hatching time within a nest ranged from one to four days with a mean of 2.0 ± 0.9 days (Burger, 1976a). This was longer than Reid's (1955) observation of four eggs in the laboratory hatching within a two-hour period on the 69th day.

Burger (1977a) found larger hatchlings emerged from larger eggs and had a shorter incubation period. The mean carapace length of hatchlings emerging from 36 nests was 27.5 ± 1.1 millimeters with a range of 25.0–30.7 millimeters. The same mean length was determined from Reid's (1955) data.

Hatching success is greatly influenced by the magnitude of predation. Burger (1977a) reported that in 1973 some eggs in 84 percent of the nests hatched, and in 1974 some eggs hatched in only 25 percent of the nests. The percent of eggs that hatched was 39 and 18 percent in 1973 and 1974, respectively. Fifty-one percent of the eggs were preyed upon in 1973 and 71 percent in 1974. The percentage of eggs that did not develop was essentially the same for both years (Table 5.25).

The main predators recorded by Burger (1977a) were the red fox *Vulpes fulva* (34 percent), laughing gull *Larus atricilla* (8 percent), crow *Corvus brachyrhynchos* (6 percent), and others (4 percent). The birds were responsible for daylight predation while the mammals raided nests at night. The number of gulls circling over the area was directly related to the number of turtles seen digging. Gulls would land behind a turtle while the eggs were being laid and raid the nest before the eggs were buried. The eggs had to be visible for gull predation, but the crows would dig up buried eggs. During nocturnal raids, the raccoons, *Procyon lotor,* often left eggs or hatchlings in the nest which were preyed upon by the gulls as soon as it became light. Avian pre-

Table 5.25. Fate of eggs in nests of *M. terrapin* in 1973 and 1974. (From Burger, 1977a, by permission of the editor, *Amer. Midl. Nat.*)

| | 1973 | | 1974 | |
	Number	Percent	Number	Percent
Number of nests	37		200	
Number of eggs	360		1746	
Mean clutch size	9.7		8.7	
Number of nests in				
which eggs hatched	31	84	51	25
Fate of eggs				
Undeveloped	28	8	190	11
Hatched	141	39	307	18
Died while hatching	5	2	4	—
Preyed upon	186	51	1245	71

dation was more evident in the open areas while mammalian predation was more intense at sheltered sites.

Early nesting turtles had a higher hatching rate and a lower predation rate than late nesters. Predation increased as a function of time. This was borne out by the makeup of the predators. Gulls and crows preyed during egg laying while mammalian predators dug up nests and hatchlings (Figure 5.27): 75 percent of the nests were preyed upon between 60–90 days after egg laying. The hatching period had a maximum of four days per nest with a predation rate of 14 percent, or approximately 3 percent per day. The predation rate during the mean incubation period was 60 percent or about 1 percent per day. Emergence from the nest lasted 4–10 days with a predation rate of 22 percent (Burger, 1977a).

The time between hatching and emergence appears to be related to temperature. The mean air temperature was 25 ± 1 °C on the day of hatching with the hatchlings emerging on the same day. The mean air temperature was 19 ± 2.2 °C during the days from hatching to emergence for those nests in which the hatchlings did not emerge on the first or second day after hatching. Later in the season (September) when the mean daily temperature dropped to 18 °C, the mean number of days between hatching and emergence was six days for nine nests. The young emerged as a group or individually over several days during the daylight hours. Ninety-four percent emerged between 0700–1900 hours and 82 percent emerged between 1200–1700 hours (Burger, 1976b).

Young emerging on flat areas spread in all directions, in the absence of vegetation, extending over a radius of two meters. For those emerging on a slope, most went downhill, a few went up but none were observed to go laterally. With the slope greater than 10 degrees the young did not radiate over

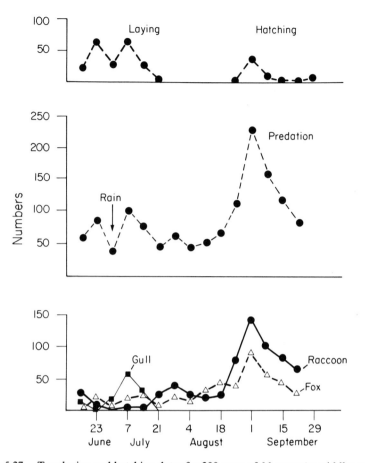

Figure 5.27.   Top: laying and hatching dates for 200 nests of *M. terrapin;* middle: predation in the study area as a function of season. Note that the rainy last week of June depressed both the number laying and the number of nests preyed upon; bottom: predation
as a function of date. (From Burger, 1977a, by permission of the editor, *Amer. Midl. Nat.*)

30 degrees while, with slopes less than 10 degrees hatchlings radiated over
75 degrees. When the vegetation was closer than two meters, the hatchlings
usually went to the nearest plant regardless of the direction of slope. The
young are preyed upon by laughing gulls, black-crowned night herons,
Nycticorax nycticorax, and raccoons. Since the young turtles emerge during
the daylight hours it could be an adaptative advantage to emerge rapidly
and head for the nearest vegetation until nightfall. This is supported by
Burger's (1976b) observation that few were seen on the open dunes during
the day.

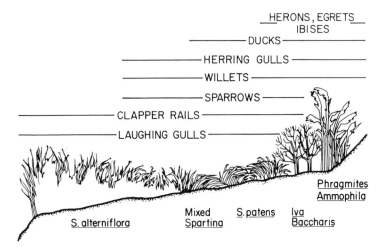

Figure 5.28.   Locations of common bird groups nesting in New Jersey salt marshes. (From Burger, Shisler, Lesser, 1978.)

Aves

Figure 5.28 portrays the major avian groups associated with tidal marshes and their respective nesting habitats as a function of vegetation and thus marsh elevation. It is evident that there is spatial zonation in that all species do not occupy all areas of the marsh (Burger *et al.*, 1978). The rails, laughing gulls, and long-billed marsh wren use the low marsh but extend through the high marsh. Depending on the species, the sparrows reside throughout the marsh while the herring gulls, willets, and ducks utilize the high-marsh areas and extend into the adjoining high ground. The red-winged blackbirds, herons, egrets, and ibises are found on the borders of the marsh; the *Baccharus-Iva* zone and landward (Meanley and Webb, 1963; Kale, 1965; Burger *et al.*, 1978).

Anseriformes. Anatidae. While tidal marshes are extensively used by migrating and wintering ducks and geese, very few birds use them as breeding areas. The vast majority breed inland in fresh-water marsh habitats. The American scoter, *Odemia nigra,* is the only waterfowl that Forbush (1925) specifically mentions as nesting in salt as well as fresh-water marshes.

Stewart (1962) described the black duck, *Anas rubripes,* as being the only common and widespread species in the tidal marshes of the Chesapeake Bay region. Stotts and Davis (1960) described the breeding behavior and reproductive biology of this species for the same region. While it feeds extensively in these tidal marshes (Stewart, ibid) it nests on drier land (Stotts and Davis, ibid; Reed, 1975), most extensively in the woodlands, much less in the meadows and marshes. Burger (1979) noted that when nesting in the marsh, the nests are always near the upland border in the highest areas of *Spartina patens,* least susceptible to flooding. Greenhalgh (1971), in a study of the Lancashire marshes of England, identified one component of the bird community as those birds such as the shelduck, mallard, teal, shoveler, and moorhen that hatch their eggs away from the marsh but bring the young onto the marsh to be reared. In so doing they avoid flooding and minimize predation.

Shorelines covered with dune vegetation, steep banks, and those exposed to wave action are avoided by the black duck. Loafing spots used by the males are situated in protected areas with easy access to the water. Usually the nearest point of water to the nest is the male's loafing spot used while the female incubates the eggs.

Pairing begins to form in late summer with a peak in early April (Stotts and Davis, 1960). The males defend a small territory; a separate one for each clutch of eggs. The frequency of territorial defense is quite low considering the population density of 0.6 to 15.2 nests per acre, depending on availability of cover. The males tend to be promiscuous. The females build nests of material that is immediately at hand and the males gradually desert the females during incubation. Females renest one or more times. Stotts and Davis (1960) reported that dates of first egg laying range from early to late March with a nesting peak during the third week of April. The first hatching was in early April and the last in early August. The average number of eggs in a clutch decline from 10.9 to 7.5 during the season and young females had smaller clutches (9.2) than adults (9.7). Primary clutches were larger (9.1) than secondary clutches (8.1) for some females. The incubation period averaged 26.2 days and about 5.6 percent did not hatch. During the six years of observation, 38 percent of the nests hatched at least one egg, 11.5 percent were abandoned and 50 percent were destroyed (34 percent by crows). The greatest amount of destruction (51.8 percent) took place during the first week of incubation.

Gruiformes. Rallidae. The clapper rail, *Rallus longirostris,* breeds in salt marshes from the San Francisco Bay area southward to northwestern Peru, and from Connecticut south through the West Indies and Mexico to northern South America. The king rail, *Rallus elegans,* is found in brackish and tidal fresh water from the eastern half of the United States and southern Ontario southward into Mexico as well as marshes inland. The Virginia rail, *Rallus limicola,* is typically found in fresh-water marshes of much of North America and most of South America. The sora rail, *Porzana carolina,* is found in fresh-water marshes of most of North America into Mexico (A.O.U., 1957). However, Sprunt and Chamberlain (1949) associated both the Virginia and sora rails with salt marshes as well.

During late February in Georgia, Oney (1954) observed the clapper rail, *Rallus longirostris waynei,* beginning to court. The first nests were observed in 1948, 1949, and 1950 on April 13, 20, and 24 respectively. Forbush (1929) recorded the breeding season for the clapper rail in Virginia as covering the period of April 27–June 1, July 1–20 usually with one brood but possibly double broods in the southern states. Bent (1913) found nests in late June but considered them to be second nestings. Bent (ibid) reported nests mostly built in small clumps of grass growing along creek banks in soft wet mud. During 1948 Oney (1954) found 68.5 percent of the nesting attempts in the medium *Spartina alterniflora,* a zone situated on the gentle slope of the levee away from the creek where the soil was firmer, plants achieved a density average of 288 stems/m^2 and height of 0.6–1.3 meters. Oney concluded that there was a preference for nest sites in the medium grass which borders the tall grass (plant density 100 stems/m^2, 1.3–3 meters tall) along a small ditch or creek. Oney did not consider the short grass zone (plant density 362/m^2, 12.7 centimeters to 0.6 meters tall) to be an important nesting area for the clapper rail. During a three-year study Oney examined 118 nests; 30 in the tall grass, 87 in the medium grass and one in the short grass zone. The average nest was six meters (range 1–24 meters) away from a change in cover. In contrast, Burger (1979) cited a paper by Mangold (1974) which reported clapper rails in New Jersey to prefer short *Spartina alterniflora* (both natural and ditched marshes) followed by tall *Spartina alterniflora,* and finally *Spartina patens.* However, her own observations showed that this species nested in the lowest areas of the marsh.

The height of the nests off the marsh surface varies. Bent (1963) observed 20–30 centimeters while Oney (1954) recorded an average of 37.6 centimeters to egg level with a range of 23–76 centimeters. It was not indicated but this variation in height off the mud surface may be a reflection of the extent of tide height at each nest site. Bent suggested the nests were high enough to escape ordinary high tides but not storm tides. Later Burger (1979) observed the initial nest heights were higher than those of other marsh-nesting birds and because most nests were destroyed by storm tides (Burger, 1979; after Mangold, 1974), she considered the rails' ability to build high nests and to rapidly repair damaged nests to be very important for egg survival. Burger considered the height of the initial nest and the degree of responsiveness to nest repair a reflection of the extent of adaptation to nesting in tidal marshes. The nests were made of grass forming an inverted cone jammed down into the surrounding grass, with or without an overhanging canopy. The outside diameter varied between 18–25 centimeters and the nest cups are well formed with an inside diameter of 12–15 centimeters (Bent, 1963).

Oney (1954) observed the average clutch to be 8.2 eggs with a range of 5–14 and no decrease in clutch size toward the end of the nesting season. In contrast Blandin (1963) reported that first nests had an average of 7.9 eggs, a renest had 6.7 eggs, and a second nest contained an average of 6.2 eggs. Forbush (1929) noted a range of 8–13.

Hatching success varies tremendously and seems to be related to the timing and intensity of storm tides. Oney (1954) recorded hatching success in Georgia on a 20-acre site as 93.3 percent (1948), 48.7 percent (1949), and 48 percent (1950). In 1949 and 1950 when the study site was enlarged to 40 acres, hatching success was 50.8 percent (1949) and 36.7 percent (1950). Stewart (1952, 1953) recorded the hatching success in the Chincoteague marshes of Virginia to be as high as 94 percent in 1950 and 1952 and less than 45 percent in 1951. He postulated that losses in 1951 were due to successive high tides, possibly aggravated by greater vulnerability of the nests from lack of cover. The inference is that predation of the eggs may have played an important role.

Working in South Carolina, Blandin (1963) observed that nests built later in the season are as well built and concealed as the earlier ones. Renesting intervals are shortest when the nest is destroyed late in the incubation period. The choice of site for a renest depends on cover, concealment, and support for the nest. If a site near the old nest exists it will be used for the renest. The clapper rail will renest more than once, persistence varying with the individual bird. Renests represent an appreciable amount of nesting attempts, 14 and 24 percent in the Albergotte Creek and Chowan Creek areas, respectively and such nesting can go on to mid-June (Stewart, 1952). Blandin noted that multiple broods occur, but second nests are fewer than first nests or renests. These second nests tend to be near the first nests. Clutch size of these second nests tends to be smaller and less variable in number than first nests or renests.

While Blandin (1963) ascribed renesting as due to egg and nest losses and Stewart (1952) attributed poor hatching success to successive highstorm tides, Oney (1954) stated that eggs can be covered with 12–19 inches of water and still hatch successfully. One could surmise that the frequency and duration of flooding could have a profound influence on hatching success.

The incubation period for the clapper rail has been noted by Johnston (1956a) to be 23 days, and Nice (1954) estimated incubation to cover 21–23 days. Hatching time was observed at something less than 24 hours by Johnston and 24–48 hours by Nice. Stewart (1952) reported that young birds attained full growth and development in about 50 days. The young remained with the adults until about half grown. His analysis of tagging returns pointed out that all age groups displayed highly restricted local movements.

The California clapper rail, *Rallus longirostris obsoletus* (= *R. obsoletus*), is a permanent resident of the California salt marshes, primarily in the San Francisco Bay area (A.O.U., 1957; Bent, 1963). It is considered to be an endangered subspecies due to its greatly restricted habitat (Wilbur and Tomlinson, 1976). The nest is usually 3–4 inches off the ground at the head of a slough, hidden under the shrub, *Grindelia cuneifolia,* or among the pickleweed, *Salicornia ambigua,* or salt grass. The eggs range in number from 5–14 but usually 8–10.

Another species of rail whose numbers are greatly reduced is the California black rail, *Laterallus jamaicensis,* which is found along the California coast, extending eastward to Connecticut and southward to Peru and Chile (A.O.U., 1957). There is great concern about the status of the species due to loss of wetlands, especially in the San Diego Bay area where 86 percent of the marshes have been destroyed by dredging or other man-induced activities. These marshes have been considered prime nesting areas for this rail.

The nest is loosely made, deeply cupped, and almost concealed by surrounding vegetation. It may be placed at ground surface or raised up to 15 inches above the ground. Nests are rebuilt following dislodgement by high tides. Nest abandonment is high if the birds are disturbed before egg laying is complete. Eggs hatch one at a time and one adult keeps the chicks together until all eggs are hatched (Wilbur, 1974).

The king rail, *Rallus elegans,* is the largest of the North American rails and is abundant in the fresh and brackish tidal marshes of the Atlantic and Gulf coastal plains (Meanley, 1969). He estimated the average number of breeding birds to be 25 pairs per 100 acres. He indicated that giant cut grass, *Zizaniopsis miliacea,* provides good nest cover with as much as one pair of birds per acre.

The king rails establish territories, and some birds return to the same territory in consecutive years. It is conceivable that the first arrivals would claim larger territories but as more birds arrive these territories would be reduced in size depending on the number of birds in a particular habitat. There is both an inter- and intraspecific defense of territories. Females are attracted by simplistic mating calls, displays, and courtship feeding. As the nesting season approaches, a repertoire of mostly soft, subdued calls increases.

The nesting period varies with latitude. It is longer and starts earlier in the southern part of its range, extending from January to mid-July in Florida, and March into September in Louisiana. Such an extended period of 7–8 months should result in a greater chance for renesting and second broods, although Meanley saw no specific evidence to support the idea of double broods. The nesting season in the mid-Atlantic area lasts for about four months. Most clutches in Maryland are laid between 15 May and 30 June. Checks in mid-May suggested nesting was begun in April while downy young have been observed in Delaware in early August (Meanley, 1969).

The nest may be located in a variety of vegetation; the giant cutgrass *Zizaniopais miliacea,* spike rush *Eleocharis palustris,* smartweed *Polygonum* sp., cattail *Typha latifolia, Spartina patens, Scirpus olneyi* or *Juncus* sp. Nests are usually placed in uniform stands of vegetation and are well concealed. There is usually a canopy over the nest and the shape of it sometimes disrupts the uniform pattern of the vegetation thus revealing its location. The nest is usually placed in the shallow water portion of a marsh over water 4–24 inches in depth. The shallower the water the lower the nest. In tidal marshes along the Savannah River, South Carolina the eggs were about two feet above the low-tide mark and one foot above high-tide level. The completed nest is a round elevated platform having a saucer-shaped depression with a round or cone-shaped canopy and a ramp. The average exterior diameter of 11 nests in Arkansas measured by Meanley was 28 centimeters with an inside depth of 1.5 centimeters. The nest is not always completed before the first egg is laid and new material is added to the outside as each new egg is laid.

The number of eggs in the clutch varies from 8–14, with an average of 10.6, reported by Meanley (1969) or 6–16 as recorded by Forbush (1929). Meanley viewed three clutches in Maryland with six eggs each and suggested a smaller clutch may represent a replacement nest, depending on when it occurs. Incubation periods have been reported for 21–23 days. Both sexes assist in the incubation and the birds do not readily flush from the nest: as hatching time approaches they become more tenacious. Hatching occurs over a 24–28 hour period.

The adult king rails may stay with the brood for a month or longer. Survival varies: of 16 nests in Arkansas, 12 hatched one or more eggs with an average of 9.9. Of a total of 147 eggs in all 16 nests, 119 (81 percent) hatched. Meanley (1969) observed ten broods about two weeks after hatching and the number of chicks varied from 2–9 with an average of five for a 50 percent survival rate until two weeks of age.

Charadriiformes. Scolopacidae. The willet, *Catoptrophorus semipalmatus,* breeds from eastern Oregon and southern Canada south to northern California, east to eastern South Dakota and along the Atlantic and Gulf coasts (A.O.U., 1957). The eastern or coastal form *C. s. semipalmatus* breeds in southwestern Nova Scotia and from southern New Jersey and Delaware south along the coast to Florida and from western Florida to southern Texas, and locally in the West Indies (A.O.U., 1957; Tomkins, 1965). It is seldom seen far from coastal marshes, beaches, and islands. There appears to be some divergence of opinion regarding nest site preferences. Bent (1929), Tomkins (1965), and Burger and Shisler (1978c) observed that the birds prefer sandy islands overgrown with tall grass thick enough to conceal the nests on dry uplands adjacent to marshes. Vogt (1938), when observing birds on the New Jersey side of Delaware Bay, found most nests in dense *Spartina patens* near *Spartina alterniflora* or *Typha angustifolia.* The nests were hard to find because of the thick grass canopy. On the other hand Stout (1967) observed the nests in natural hollows where the vegetation was sparse and low.

The feeding habitat is distinct from the nesting habitat: feeding occurs on the mud flats and at the edges of the salt marshes (Bent, 1929; Tomkins, 1965). Vogt (1938) observed a preference for the dense *Spartina patens* that had been mowed or burned.

The willet is a semicolonial species gathering on the breeding grounds in the spring and early summer. About three weeks after arrival, courtship is carried on by the flock in open spaces in the marsh. The early arrivals are usually paired and go to a nest site occupied the previous year but, at times, such pairs join the flock on the courting ground. There appears to be two opposing tendencies in balance. The flocking or gregarious tendency is effective all year, while territorial space is evident during the breeding season and is centrifugal in nature. The willets select nesting sites around the parimeter of the courtship area which is not in itself suitable for nesting. Tomkins (1965) and Burger and Shisler (1978c) observed that the breeding population was not spread evenly over the available nesting habitat but consisted of a series of flock groupings, centered on particular courtship areas: the rest of the area was vacant or thinly populated. Within a clump the birds were more widely dispersed than by random; most of them were 37 to 53 and up to 67 meters apart. The clumping presumably provides increased social stimulation for breeding whereas the spacing is related to predation pressures (Burger and Shisler, 1978c).

The birds are monogamous and usually stay together. Territory for the male willet has three aspects: (1) during the prenesting time it is on the nesting site or in the wetter marsh wherever the female is; (2) during incubation it is limited to the nesting ground where the female is; and (3) in the postnesting period it is in the grass where the young are although this is somewhat a flock reaction. The female shares in the latter two and the male assists in the incubation and early raising of the young (Tomkins, 1965; Stout, 1967).

The male physically defends against other males and by clamor against other intruders (Tomkins). There is a high incidence and visibility of wing displays as a part of this territorial defense. Howe (1974) suggested that, since the natural habitat of the willet lacks conspicuous perches, the more complex repertoire of wing displays and a more striking wing pattern may be mechanisms for enhancing visibility. This parental pair-bond appears to dissolve about the time the young birds are developing in the marsh.

Apparently the female selects the nest site, in contrast to the male bird of other species. The nests are on the ground and many are concealed by the short thick grass with a mat of dead grass forming a dome. Others are only partly concealed and even completely exposed (Bent, 1929; Tomkins, 1965). The nests tend to be placed on higher elevations as the eggs apparently cannot withstand tidal submergence. In one study (Burger and Shisler, 1978c) the birds showed a significant preference for spoil piles in a ditched marsh. Those willets did not nest near bushes but nested randomly with respect to vegetational characteristics, species of vegetation, distance to bushes, and distance to water. The birds nesting on the spoil piles presumably were older, more experienced birds as they laid larger eggs. Nesting on such spoil piles conferred some advantages. Since they were the highest areas, they were drier and provided more visible areas for courtship and territorial displays. The piles also provided grass cover for nest construction and concealment similar to that provided in natural areas.

Egg laying begins in early April in the southern portion of the willet's range, reaching a peak late in the month. In the north most clutches are finished by the end of May (Stout, 1967). The willet is a determinate species, laying a certain number of eggs and no more. Four eggs are normally laid, seldom five and rarely up to six since four is about all a bird can cover while incubating. Rarely is a second clutch of eggs laid if the first clutch is destroyed. Incubation varies between 22–29 days. Hatching success is low. Of 16 nests containing 56 eggs, Tomkins (1965) observed that only 11 young hatched. Raccoon, otter, mink, and snakes are predators. Under such conditions, it is little wonder that the adults attempt to move the young into the protection of the marsh soon after hatching.

Charadriiformes. Laridae. Gulls. Herring gulls, *Larus argentatus,* found throughout much of the Northern Hemisphere (A.O.U., 1957), nest typically in colonies on islands in both fresh-water and marine habitats. The nests are placed on the ground on bare stony shoals, sand, rocks, cliffs, or sometimes thick vegetation. The nest is often made of marsh grasses, weeds, sticks, sea moss, shells or may be a simple depression among the pebbles and cobblestones. The laughing gull, *Larus atricilla,* which also nests in colonies, breeds along the coast from Nova Scotia south into Venezuela, southern California, and northwest Mexico (A.O.U., 1957). The nests are placed on the ground, sometimes a mere hollow in the sand, but usually well built of grasses, seaweeds, or sticks more or less concealed among thick vegetation (Forbush, 1929).

When the laughing gull nesting was observed in tidal marshes, the selected sites were in low areas dominated by *Spartina alterniflora;* locations that were particularly vulnerable to flooding by high and storm tides (Bongiorno, 1970; Burger and Shisler, 1978a). However, in North Carolina, laughing gulls nested primarily in the low swales between the sand dunes of coastal islands and in the dense *Spartina patens* along the edges of the islands. The birds did not overlap into a herring gull colony but did extend their nesting sites further up the dunes when herring gulls were absent (Parnell and Soots, 1975).

In New Jersey both Bongiorno (1970) and Burger and Shisler (1978a) found that laughing gulls selected higher elevations in the *Spartina alterniflora* marshes; 0.0 to 0.2 meters above mean high water with *Spartina alterniflora* taller than 0.6 meters (Bongiorno). Using an arbitrary elevation in the marsh as zero Burger and Shisler sighted laughing gull nests within a range of elevations of 7–30 centimeters.

Montevecchi (1975) found no differences between nest sites and randomly chosen sites. However, Burger and Shisler (1978a) reported that early- (9–15 May) and mid-nesting (16–21 May) arrivals select significantly higher nest site elevations than late (22–30 May) entrants. They found an inverse relationship between marsh elevation and the height of the nest: gulls nesting at lower marsh levels built higher nests. This was considered to be a direct response to tidal influences. This was corroborated when Burger (1979) determined that laughing gulls are capable of perceiving and responding to environmental changes in their nests. The birds did not respond when Burger simply wet the nest as in the case of rain storms. They did respond significantly to simulated flooding when water stood in the nest cup, by actual nest inundation, and when nests were damaged. They responded by quickly building the nests higher. Burger also submerged eggs for 15, 30, and 120 minutes. There was a significant decrease in hatching when eggs were submerged for 120 minutes during the first week of incubation, and a significant decrease when the eggs were submerged for all three time periods during the third week of incubation. The laughing gull's quick response to nest flooding and damage and the ability of the eggs to withstand some submergence, suggested the species is as well-adapted to nesting in low marsh areas as is the clapper rail.

Laughing gulls tended to nest close together ($\bar{x} = 2.9 \pm 1.8$ meters—nearest neighbor distance) and, in spite of potential flooding, closer (4.5 ± 4.3 meters) to pools, pans, or creeks than randomly chosen sites (8.1 ± 5.7 meters). They also chose sites that had significantly less dead grass but more live grass than randomly chosen sites. The explanation proffered by Burger and Shisler (1978a) stated that, by the time the eggs hatch, the grass would be taller and would provide the chicks with further protection from predators and adverse climatic factors. The taller grass also provided shelter by impeding water movement during flooding tides. However, the tall grass could hamper courtship and escape.

The significance of the role of tall *Spartina alterniflora* in the life of the laughing gull has been born out by Bongiorno's (1970) work. The gulls reused rather precisely the same discrete areas of a marsh from season to season with a marked preference for tall grass. Birds did not nest where the grass had been cut although they had nested there in previous years. *Spartina alterniflora,* taller than 0.8 meters, when growing on higher elevations, provided sites for high nest survival during storms. When the cord grass was shorter, growing in lower areas or associated with *Spartina patens,* nest survival was reduced by storms.

Bongiorno (1970) noted that laughing gulls showed a marked preference for nesting wherever the debris of dead cord grass collected. The birds also nested on cut grass that had been raked into windrows. In describing the nest-repairing behavior of the laughing gull, Moore (1975) observed that nests were first built on a platform, usually of dry *Spartina* grass. She noted that *Spartina* mats, formed by tidal action, were frequently used, providing an extensive platform capable of floating at high tide. On this mat a simple concavity was formed by the gull working from inside the nest. Typically the rim was built up gradually and essentially uniformly. This nest building behavior of laughing gulls was directed by feedback from the state of the nest even during incubation.

While Bongiorno (1970) and Moore (1975) indicated that *Spartina* mats are used as nesting sites, Burger and Beer (1975) identified such sites as courtship areas for laughing gulls, especially during peak activity in mornings and evenings. During the midday periods these same mats were used for loafing and resting by even more birds. Unmated birds were observed to display on the mats and paired birds moved to new growth *Spartina* areas away from the mats. Burger's and Beer's suggestion that the use of these *Spartina* mats as pairing territories and not as nesting territories is supported by the following factors. (1) The mats provide maximum visibility for displaying birds seeking mates. (2) The mats are less desirable as nesting areas because they are harder to defend from birds gathering nest materials. Sizable mats up to two meters across can be dismantled in 2–3 days. (3) Nests and eggs in the growing *Spartina* are less visible to predators. One could wonder if the differences in reported uses for these *Spartina* mats could reflect different behavioral adaptations of individuals to different local habitats within *Spartina* marshes.

In their comparative study of the nesting characteristics of laughing gulls and herring gulls on Clam Island in Barnegat Bay, New Jersey, Burger and Shisler (1978a) noted the surface of the four subislands was dominated (51 percent) by *Spartina alterniflora.* Ponds covered 25 percent of the island and four percent of it was covered by *Iva frutescens* and *Baccharis halimifolia,* distributed along the higher edges of the subislands. In spite of the relatively small amounts of brush 82 percent of the herring gulls nested under the bushes, showing preference for an area where the bushes made up 27 percent of the cover. Since there was 100 percent bush cover nearby, it is apparent herring gulls selected nest sites with some, rather than complete, brush cover. This same pattern was made evident in another study (Burger and Shisler, 1978b) where herring gulls moved from one-half an island where the density of bushes and *Spartina patens* had changed from 20 to 84 percent coverage in five years. They moved to a site where *Spartina patens* and bushes were scattered. There was also a temporal utilization of bush cover. Ninety-five percent of the early-nesting gulls, 68 percent of the mid-nesting, and 10 percent of the late-nesting pairs placed nests under the bushes. The late-nesting birds attempted to nest under such cover but were driven off by early nesting pairs. When the herring gulls selected sites in grass areas the grass stems were less dense but taller than randomly selected sites. The herring gulls space their nests further apart ($\bar{x} = 4.6 \pm 2.3$ meters) than the laughing gulls and those herring gulls who utilized the sparse cover (40 percent) produced significantly larger eggs than those birds nesting in dense (41 percent) cover (Burger and Shisler, 1978a).

The herring gulls' choice of nest sites appears to be a compromise of selection and defense of territory with protection from predators (Burger, 1977c). Visibility determines the direction of the closest nest and is directly related to the nearest-neighbor distance. Gulls react most vigorously to the most visible intruder. Size of territory can also be influenced by the degree

Table 5.26. Comparison of characteristics of habitat, gull nests, and eggs as a function of their location on spoil piles or in a natural situation. Given are means $\pm$ 1 S.D. (from Burger and Shisler, 1978b, by permission of the editor, *Amer. Midl. Nat.*)

Characteristic	Spoil Pile	Nonspoil
Percent bush cover	34 ± 32	18 ± 25
Percent vegetation cover	88 ± 21	95 ± 11
Nest depth (cm)	18 ± 8	12 ± 6
Nest width (cm)	52 ± 5	51 ± 4
Clutch size	2.89 ± 0.5	2.5 ± 0.4
Egg size (length × diameter)	183.96	172.86

of neighbor visibility. Burger (1977c) also noted that nesting under or near bushes or on spoil piles offers certain advantages: (1) bushes that grow on the higher elevations, and nests on spoil piles are less apt to be flooded; (2) bushes provide shelter against rain, sun, hail, or heat; (3) bushes provide shelter from predators, including cannabalistic gulls. Nests on spoil piles were more widely dispersed ($\bar{x} = 39.4 \pm 25$ meters) than those nests not situated on spoil piles ($\bar{x} = 17.9 \pm 8.9$ meters) and were also less subject to marauding gulls. The early nesters were observed to select territories under bushes adjacent to open *Spartina patens* swards where courting displays took place. Herring gulls with such an edge territory would be able to escape more easily than from dense bushy areas where they might become entangled during escape attempts. Gulls with territories in sparse brush and on spoil piles were the early nesters, the older more experienced birds who produced larger eggs (Table 5.26) (Burger and Shisler 1978a, b).

Citing earlier works, Burger (1977b) indicated that the geographic range and abundance of the herring gull has been expanding. Furthermore, gulls have moved into previously unused salt marshes. They now nest at lower elevations in the *Spartina alterniflora* zone when the bushes are occupied by earlier nesting gulls or herons. Burger classified nests on Islajo, Big Heron, and Little Gull islands in the Absecon Island–Little Egg Harbor area of New Jersey as dry, wet-dry, and wet habitats depending on the number of times water reached an area during high tides. (1) Dry areas did not get wet during high or storm tides; (2) wet-dry areas were covered by high tides half of the time; (3) wet areas were covered by half or more of the high tides (Figure 5.29). Egg laying was observed to start earlier in the dry habitat and last

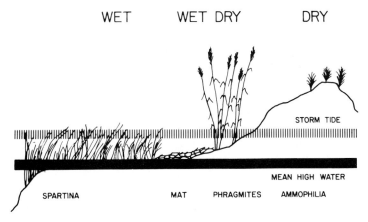

Figure 5.29. Schematic profile of Islajo showing vegetation and location of herring gull nesting habitats. (From Burger, 1977b, by permission of the editor, *Condor*.)

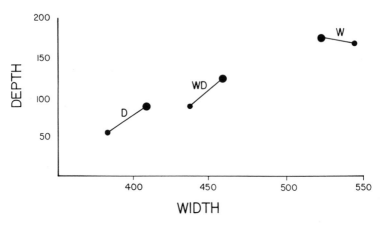

Figure 5.30.   Nest depth and width (in mm) as a function of habitat type. D = dry area, WD = wet-dry area, and W = wet area. The small dot is the mean size during the first week of incubation, and the large dot is the mean from these same nests 10 days later. (From Burger, 1977b, by permission of the editor, *Condor*.)

a shorter period of time, again a reflection of selection by older experienced birds. Late nesters, moving outward from the brush, demonstrated changes in adaptive behavior by constructing nests with significant increases in width and depth as the habitat became wetter (Figure 5.30). During an exceptional tide all the nests in the lower wet *Spartina* area were destroyed or missing. Nests elsewhere in the wet *Spartina* at slightly higher elevations survived the storm tide. No nests in the dry area were damaged. Only those nests at the edge of the mat in the wet-dry area were destroyed, reflecting the use of a floating platform. Following this tide, all nests on the mat were enlarged and deepened. Burger (1977b) conducted experiments on nest depth and width by damaging occupied nests at all sites. While there was no significant difference in nest depth following repair of nests in the dry and wet-dry habitats, there was a significant difference for those repaired in the wet habitat (Figure 5.31, exp. 1). Thus a simulated tidal erosion of nest material in the wet habitat provoked a more thorough repair, reinforcing and raising the nest to a higher level. Experimental removal of one side of the nest resulted in some repair in the wet habitat (Figure 5.31, exp. 2).

This responsive behavior pattern was further explored by Burger (1979) on Clam Island when she simply wet the nest or filled the nest cup with water to simulate a high tide or removed a portion of the nest. As expected no significant repair was made to nests that had been only wetted.

Herring gulls did react to nest damage and to actual tidal inundation, substantiating the earlier observations. However, they did not respond to the simulated tidal flooding as anticipated. Burger explained this contradiction by suggesting this species, unlike the laughing gulls, is not yet fully adapted

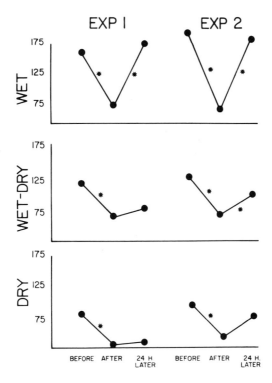

Figure 5.31.   In experiment 1, material was removed from the entire circumference of the nest, while in experiment 2, it was removed from only one side of the nest. The first dot shows the mean nest depth (in mm) before treatment, the second dot the mean after treatment, and the third dot the mean 24 h later. A star indicates a significant difference. (From Burger, 1977b, by permission of the editor, *Condor*.)

to the tidal marsh as a nesting site. This point of view is supported by hatching records cited in the 1977 studies. Hatching success was highest in the dry areas, lowest in the wet areas, and varied in the wet-dry areas (Table 5.27). Tidal influence determined hatching success directly by destroying nests and indirectly by causing rotten eggs and increasing rates of predation (Table 5.28).

While intraspecific predation has been recorded among the herring gulls, they prey largely on laughing gulls nesting in tidal marshes. The fish crow *Corvus osifragus,* the common crow *Corvus b. brachyrhynchus,* and raptors such as the barn owl *Tyto alba* and the great horned owl *Bubo virginianus* also preyed on the laughing gull colony observed by Montevecchi (1977). Most egg predation occurred early in the nesting cycle before incubation behavior was fully developed and when crow and herring gull intrusions were at a maximum. About 4.4 percent (63/1421) of the eggs were

Table 5.27. Herring gull habitats studied in New Jersey. (Burger, 1977b, by permission of the editor, *Condor*)

Location	Habitat	Vegetation	Percent of Nests having at least one egg hatch (total nests)	
Islajo	Dry	*Ammophilia-Phragmites*	100	(15)
Island	Wet-Dry	edge of *Spartina*	45	(42)
		Spartina mat (dead grass)	79	(42)
	Wet	live *Spartina* (low marsh)	0	(25)
Big Heron	Wet-Dry	live *Spartina* (high marsh)	83	(6)
Island		edge of areas of *Ammophila* grass and *Phragmites*	88	(32)
	Dry	*Phragmites*	95	(20)
Little Gull Island	Wet-Dry	*Spartina* (high marsh)	70	(20)

preyed upon. Predation was lower (2.9 percent, 8/273) in the peripheral nesting ground than in the central one (4.8 percent, 55/1138). Predation success of crows increased as a functon of prey density. According to Montevecchi, central nesting does not serve the antipredator function as in other gulls because the laughing gull has a less intense antipredator reaction. This would certainly account for the greater predator response. Herring gull activity was greater in the post hatch period when they preyed on laughing gull chicks: crows did not. Intraspecific attacks by adults accounted for a major portion of laughing gull chick mortality.

Table 5.28. Nesting characteristics on Islajo Island. (Burger, 1977b, by permission of the editor, *Condor*)

	Dry	Wet-Dry		Wet
		Edge of Spartina	Spartina mat	
Number of nests	15	42	42	25
x̄ clutch size	2.83	2.71	2.66	2.38
SD clutch size	0.39	0.40	0.64	0.79
Number of eggs	42	114	112	60
Fate of eggs (%)				
Hatched	95	40	75	0
Predated*	0	10	3	25
Lost in flood	0	45	7	75
Rotten	0	3	10	0
Unknown	5	2	5	0

* Predation by other herring gulls during high tides.

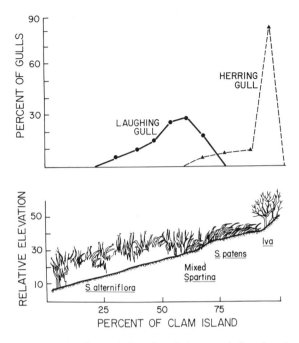

Figure 5.32. Location of gull populations in relation to relative elevation and vegetational distributions on Clam Island. (From Burger, 1977b, by permission of the editor, *Auk*.)

It is apparent that the spread of herring gulls is being enhanced, in part by predation on and successful competition with the laughing gulls (Burger and Shisler 1978a). Where they nest together the peak of laughing gull nesting activity occurs very near the beginning of the elevations used by the herring gulls (Figure 5.32). Presumably if the herring gulls are not present the laughing gulls would nest at higher elevations which would be less apt to be flooded (Parnell and Soots, 1975). Thus the foreshortening of the laughing gull nesting sites eliminates those nests most apt to be successful. Laughing gulls are at a disadvantage in this competition for two reasons: (1) they are smaller and (2) they arrive later. The study by Burger and Shisler (1978a) indicated that herring gull nests were well formed by 11 April. Egg laying began by 14 April with the peak of egg laying between 20 April–10 May and the last eggs were laid by 30 May. The laughing gull began egg laying by 9 May–2 June with 75 percent of the eggs laid from 12–21 May. With the expansion of the herring gulls into lower marsh areas it is likely that they will replace the laughing gulls.

The great black-backed gull, *Larus marinus,* breeds throughout much of the northern portion of the northern hemisphere (A.O.U., 1957). It is also expanding its range southward and has taken to nesting with the herring gull on marsh islands (Burger, 1978). Typically it has nested under *Iva* bushes in the center of the densest area of herring gulls. The individual nests were spaced 500–800 meters apart, distributed as if solitary with respect to conspecifics but colonially with respect to herring gulls. Egg laying took place in all colonies between 7–18 April 1976, during the earliest period of herring gull egg laying. All nests observed contained three eggs. Hatching success was high (95 percent) due to nesting synchrony and an absence of mammalian predators: both gull species established territories at the same time thus reducing a disruptive effect. The black-backed gulls fledged a high number of young (2–3 per nest with a mean of 2.4) which Burger (1978) attributed to a good food supply, low predation, and experienced parents.

Charadriiformes. Laridae. Terns. Other aquatic birds have moved to marsh habitats for nesting sites because of human disturbances on the beaches which have been their natural breeding sites. Frohling (1965) reported finding oyster catchers, *Haematopus palliatus,* and black skimmers, *Rynchops nigra,* nesting on the drift line of dead grass situated atop *Spartina* grasses on a marsh island located in Little Egg Harbor, New Jersey. Stone (1937) commented on the disturbance caused by humans and dogs to the common tern, *Sterna hirundo,* nesting on New Jersey beaches which caused the birds to seek quieter sites elsewhere. Greenhalgh (1974) and Burger and Lesser (1978) described the establishment of tern colonies in the marshes of the west coast of England and New Jersey, respectively. The English colony showed an annual increase of 19.3 percent from 1954 through 1974. In 1974 the ternery covered 115 hectares with a nest density of 7.4 pairs per hectare. In contrast, due to the cohabitation of herring gulls on some of the New Jersey marsh islands used by terns, Burger and Lesser expressed concern about the future success of these colonies. The tern nested on 34 of the 259 salt-marsh islands with less than 12 percent windrows of dead vegetation (Burger and Lesser, 1978). The selection of the islands seemed to be a response to vegetation, island size, distance to the nearest island, distance to the nearest shore, and exposure to open water. All these New Jersey marsh islands selected by the terns faced at least two miles of open water from at least one direction.

Most of the nests in the English ternery were concentrated in a strip across the marsh with an irregular placement in subcolonies, often with more than 100 meters separating subcolonies. This great scatter was reported to be due to the larger area available in the marsh as well as some disturbance due to egg collecting and trampling by cattle. Most subcolonies occupied areas of thicker vegetation, mainly *Atriplex littorales, A. hastata* and *Suaeda maritima,* all of which tend to occur on marsh islands and channel ridges (Greenhalgh, 1974).

In contrast, the New Jersey colonies were much more narrowly confined in a linear arrangement. Eighty percent of the nests were situated on windrows of dead vegetation laid down by storm tides and which occupied a mean of 4.6 percent of an island's surface area. Further, the birds tended to utilize those windrows deposited earlier in the year. The partially decayed, flattened windrows of the previous year were rejected. Only 18 percent of the terns nested in the *Spartina* although *Spartina* covered 88 percent of the islands (Burger and Lesser, 1978).

The selection of nest sites is a compromise between flooding and predation (Burger and Lesser, 1978). The nests in the English colony tended to be located on raised areas in the marsh, presumably affording some protection from spring tide flooding as well as providing visible warning against predators (Greenhalgh, 1974). Flooding by exceptional tides destroyed more nests in the *Spartina* than on the windrows of the New Jersey terneries. Terns nesting on windrows often formed only a cup in the dry material while those nesting in *Spartina alterniflora* and *Spartina patens* built nests on the ground but raised them 40–150 millimeters ($\bar{x}$ = 90 millimeters) in *Spartina alterniflora* and 30–180 millimeters ($\bar{x}$ = 107 millimeters) in *Spartina patens.* Those nests in the *Spartina* that did survive flooding were deeper with a higher rim (Burger and Lesser, 1978). Burger (1979) found the common tern repaired nest height under tidal conditons and when the nests were damaged. They also extended the width of the nest when the nests were wetted by rain or experimentally. They repaired damage so that the eggs were maintained well above the marsh level. The most successful nests were those situated on the highest part of the mat and were built higher than the surrounding nests. Burger surmised that the response of terns nesting in the marsh reflected their adaptation to nesting on the sandy beaches which were subjected to high flood tides.

Predation was carried out by the oyster catchers, skimmers, laughing gulls and herring gulls. Where the herring gulls nested on the same New Jersey islands predation exceeded 10 percent. Burger and Lesser (1978) noted the nests located on the windrows were more subject to predation than those nests in the *Spartina.* The grass also provided more protection from the rain and the sun. However, nesting in the *Spartina* could be accomplished only when the plants were small. Later it became difficult to build nests between the stems. The presence of the grass stems also hampered landing at the nest site and reduced social interaction as a result of reduced visibility.

At one point Greenhalgh (1974) reported the tern mean clutch size at 2.42 eggs. However, when noting the impact of renesting on clutch size, he observed the mean size of the first clutch to be 2.77 eggs for 43 nests and 2.56 eggs for 37 replacement nests. Burger and Lesser (1978) reported a significant difference in clutch size from nests on the windrows ($\bar{x} = 2.86 \pm 0.09$ eggs) and those nests in the *Spartina* ($\bar{x} = 2.63 \pm 0.21$).

Passeriformes. Trogloydtidae. The various races that comprise the long-billed marsh wren, *Telmatodytes palustris,* breed from the Gulf of Mexico to southern Canada and from the Atlantic to the Pacific. *T. palustris* breeds in coastal and estuarine marshes from Rhode Island to Virginia. *T. palustris waynei* breeds in the coastal marshes of Virginia and North Carolina while *T. palustris griseus* breeds in South Carolina to northern Florida. *T. palustris marianae* and *T. palustris thryophilus* are found in the coastal marshes of the Gulf of Mexico (A.O.U.,1957). *T. palustris palustris* frequents the shores of tidal creeks, salt and brackish marshes, and the marshy borders of sluggish rivers. The habitat requirements of the long-billed marsh wren restrict it to such environments and these areas must be extensive. Small isolated tracts do not suffice. The species does not leave the marsh unless flooded out (Forbush, 1929; Todd, 1940; Sprunt and Chamberlin, 1949).

Todd (1940) records the spring arrival of *Telmatodytes palustris* in western Pennsylvania in late April–early May while Forbush (1929) noted its appearance in Massachusetts in mid-May. Upon arrival singing and nest building commence. Kale (1965) noted in Georgia all breeding activity of *T. palustris griseus,* such as nest building, feeding, and care of the young took place in a territory established and defended by the male. The mean territory size was $100m^2$ (range 30–242 m^2) and was delinated by the male who sang everywhere in the territory: in the dense grass or near the tops of dead grass stalks. Kale noted that singing reached a peak in late April–early May and remained high from May to July.

The species is gregarious, nesting in loose colonies (Warren, 1890; Forbush, 1929; Sprunt and Chamberlain, 1949). The density varied little from year to year and Kale expressed it in a variety of ways. (1) Crude density was calculated at approximately 0.5 pairs per hectare (0.2 pairs/acre) of total marsh. (2) Ecological density was estimated at 45–56 pairs per hectare (18–23 pairs/acre) of suitable nesting area. (3) Utilized area density amounted to 98–109 pairs per hectare (42–45 pairs/acre) of territorial area actually occupied. Kale considered territoriality as the principal control of population size. By limiting the area occupied by breeding wrens to about one-half the potential habitat the colonial behavior reduced predation pressure upon the food supplies in the unoccupied areas.

The long-billed marsh wren has the curious behavior of building a number of nests but only using one. The use of the dummy nests is uncertain. They may draw attention away from the nest with the eggs, be used by the male as a resting place, or provide an outlet for the superabundance of the male's energy. Forbush (1929) noted the nest with the eggs appeared old and weather worn while the dummy nests were made of fresh material. The nest is a globular structure made of coarse grass leaves. It is suspended on marsh grass stems 30–120 centimeters above the water with the leaves woven into the nest. The entrance is on the side and the nest is well concealed. It is lined with fine material: feathers, fine grass, leaves, or cattail down. The dummy nests are not lined (Warren, 1890; Forbush, 1929; Todd, 1940; Sprunt and Chamberlain, 1949).

The number of eggs varies from four to ten; each is very small and typically dark chocolate in color (citations above). Kale (1965) observed egg laying from early April to mid-August for *T. palustris griseus* with normally no more than two broods per female and very little polygamy. For the same subspecies Sprunt and Chamberlain (1949) noted three broods per year. The mean clutch size was recorded by Kale as 4.6 eggs during the early part of the season while later clutches had a mean of 3.8 eggs. Fifty-nine percent of the breeding nests contained five eggs; 32 percent had four eggs and 9 percent had three eggs per clutch (Kale, ibid). The incubation time was approximately 13 days.

Nests, eggs, and young losses among *T. palustris griseus* result from spring high tides, tropical storms, and mice. Sprunt and Chamberlain put emphasis on flooding and storms while Kale stressed losses due to predation. Mortalities recorded by Kale for eggs and young for 1958–1961 were 58.4, 79.6, 93.2, and 85.2 percent, respectively with predation responsible for the greater part (39.3, 66.9, 66.8, and 80.8 percent, respectively). Large mammals such as raccoon and mink not only robbed but destroyed the nests. If the nest was left intact the rice rat, *Oryzomys palustris*, was implicated. Infertility, addling, and some desertion contributed to low levels of mortality. Kale observed an unusual cause of mortality created when dolphins flattened tracts of grass while driving fish up onto the creek banks. Nesting success varied during 1958–1961 at 42, 20, 6.8, and 14.8 percent, respectively.

Passeriformes. Icteridae. The red-winged blackbird, *Agelaius phoeniceus,* is the most abundant and widely distributed breeding bird of the Chesapeake Bay region. It occurs in virtually all marsh habitats but is usually commonest in marshes with such emergents as *Typha, Hibiscus moscheutos, Baccharis halimifolia,* and *Iva frutescens* (Meanley and Webb, 1963). Forbush (1927) considered it to be a typical marsh bird while Sprunt and Chamberlain (1949) found spring arrivals on the back beaches of barrier islands, salt marshes, and inland stream edges as well as river and willow swamps.

Meanley and Webb (1963) and A.O.U. (1957) identified its range throughout the United States and most provinces of North America. As might be expected, most reproductive biology studies have been conducted on inland populations (see Meanley and Webb).

The species is gregarious, nesting in colonies of various sizes. In the Chesapeake Bay region the males establish territories during March with the earliest arrivals appearing in late February while the females arrive in early April. Territories are defended until early August. The nesting season is similar throughout its range extending from late April to mid-August but dropping off sharply after mid-July (Meanley and Webb, 1963). In the coastal area of South Carolina most eggs were laid during the first two weeks of May with the earliest and latest records being in late April and late June respectively (Sprunt and Chamberlain, 1949). Forbush (1927) showed a progressive delay in the breeding season in the higher latitudes.

The nest is usually placed among the reeds, flags, rushes, and grasses above the mud and water or in bushes over or near water. High tide bush is frequently used along the coast. The nest is rarely placed on the ground and even less often at any appreciable height. Most of the time the nests are about 30 centimeters above the ground or water. The nests are made of grasses, deeply cupped, and securely fastened to the stems or branches (Forbush, 1927; Sprunt and Chamberlain, 1949). Forbush (1927) noted the red-winged blackbird to be polygamous, the males mating with 2–3 females who nested near each other with the male showing concern for the whole group. Meanley and Webb (1963) noted a ratio of males to females of 1:1.96: yearling females often breed whereas yearling males seldom or never do.

The eggs are pale blue or blue-green with dark scrawled lines. During four nesting seasons Meanley and Webb recorded a mean number of 3.3 eggs for 537 clutches. The mean clutch size decreased as the nesting season progressed: from 3.5 (N = 255 clutches) in May to 3.2 (N = 177 clutches) in June to 3.0 (N = 105 clutches) in July.

Both Forbush (1927) and Sprunt and Chamberlain (1949) declared that only one brood is produced yearly, unless the nest is destroyed. Meanley and Webb (1963) recorded an average yearly production of 4.2 fledglings per female or 8.1 per male. Since the average clutch size was determined to be 3.3 eggs, females must average more than one brood per year and this was confirmed from four marked females. Such a condition may stem from the extended nesting season in the Chesapeake Bay region.

Nesting success of 675 active nests was 57 percent with a range from 38 percent in the salt bay colonies to 69 percent in the brackish tidal river colonies. The lower success in the first instance stemmed from livestock trampling and a lack of nest-supporting plants. Avian predators were also more evident.

Robust plants that held constant form through the nesting season supported 95 percent of the nests: *Baccharis* and *Iva* made up 78 percent. Nesting success was high at 58 percent for such plants. In contrast, nonrobust plants supported only 5 percent of the nests and success of nesting was only 26 percent.

Nesting success varied with plant height; 45 percent for nests less than 60 centimeters above the ground; 55 percent for nests 60–120 centimeters above the ground, and 62 percent for nest heights greater than 120 centimeters. Nest heights varied from 15 centimeters in the salt marsh to 285 centimeters in high tide bushes.

The red-winged blackbird can be classed as a successful nester. The huge flocks seen in the fall attest to this. About 90 percent of the completed nests received eggs. Nestlings hatched in 63 percent of the nests with eggs and young fledged in more than 90 percent of the nests with nestlings. Fifty-seven percent of the active nests produced one or more young who reached the flying stage (Meanley and Webb, 1963).

Passeriformes. Fringillidae. The members of the sparrow family Fringillidae tend to live in open grassy areas: several are especially associated with the coastal zone. The song sparrow, *Melospiza melodia,* is prevalent in low, wet areas where bushes grow in profusion. This species has a coast-to-coast distribution with the subspecies *M. melodia atlantica* associated with east coast salt and brackish marshes while *M. melodia maxillaris, M. melodia pussilula* and *M. melodia samuelis* are found in west coast brackish and salt marshes, especially in the San Francisco Bay area. The savannah sparrow, *Passerculus sandwichensis,* likewise has an extensive distribution with the subspecies *P. sandwichensis savanna* associated with the coastal areas in the sand dunes and grassy flats bordering tidal marshes and grassy expanses that are not wooded in southeastern Canada and the northeastern United States (A.O.U., 1957). Another subspecies, the Ipswich sparrow, *P. sandwichensis princeps* (= *P. princeps*), has a very limited habitat restricted to the coast dunes above the high-water mark among the beach grasses behind the front dunes. It breeds on Sable Island off Nova Scotia and winters along the coast from Massachusetts to southern Georgia (A.O.U., 1957). The swamp sparrow, *Melospiza georgiana,* has an extensive range over much of Canada and the United States east of the Rockies and is found at the edges of tidal marshes. The sharp-tailed sparrows, *Ammospiza caudacuta,* include subspecies that nest in Canadian fresh-water marshes but spend their winters in coastal tidal marshes. The subspecies *A. caudacuta subvirgata* breeds coastwise from southeastern Quebec and Nova Scotia, south to southern Maine. *A. caudacuta caudacuta* breeds in the Atlantic coastal marshes from southern Maine south to New Jersey. The southern sharp-tailed sparrow, *A.*

caudacuta diversa, nests from the coastal marshes of Delaware southward into North Carolina. These various subspecies winter from North Carolina into Florida westward to Texas (A.O.U., 1957).

The seaside sparrows, *Ammospiza maritima,* are restricted to the coastal marshes from Massachusetts southward to Florida and westward to Texas. The subspecies *A. maritima maritima* breeds from Massachusetts to northeastern North Carolina. Macgillivrays seaside sparrow, *A. maritima macgillivaraii,* is found from North Carolina into northern Florida. Various other subspecies are found on both coasts of Florida in the northern half of the state westward to Texas. The Cape Sable seaside sparrow, *Ammospiza mirabilis,* is indigenous to the Cape Sable area of southwestern Florida. It and the dusky seaside sparrow, *Ammospiza nigrescens,* found in the marshes of Indian River have the most restricted ranges of North American birds (Forbush, 1929; Sprunt and Chamberlain, 1949).

The sharp-tailed sparrows and seaside sparrows are the only members of the family Fringillidae restricted to coastal tidal marshes. While the sharp-tails are coastal they do penetrate inland along the narrow fringes of marshes flanking tidal creeks and guts wherever salt water penetration enables *Spartina patens* to become established (Montagna, 1942; Bent *et al.,* 1968).

The sharp-tailed sparrows prefer the higher drier portions of the marsh that are only occasionally submerged. They place their nests in tussocks of grass or on slightly elevated islands typically covered with *Spartina patens* or *Distichlis spicata* when the surrounding marsh is covered with *Scirpus* or *Juncus gerardi,* or under dead *Spartina alterniflora,* or the "cow licks" of *Spartina patens.* They tend to nest along the edge of a marsh toward the water or alongside tidal pools close to the main body of water. Some nests are placed on the ground but most are at varying heights (12 to 30 centimeters) above the ground, apparently above high water. The nest is located where dead and fallen grasses are the thickest. These dead stems and leaves are interwoven among the standing stems forming a crude outer nest. Within this is placed the nest proper, an extremely neat, well rounded, and deeply cupped structure, composed uniformly of very fine grasses. The outside diameter varies between 7.6–10.8 centimeters with a mean of 8.6 centimeters (Forbush, 1929; Montagna, 1942; Woolfenden, 1956; Bent *et al.,* 1968; Murray, 1969; Post, 1970a, b).

The northern seaside sparrow, *Ammospiza m. maritima,* nests in the wetter portions of the marsh where *Juncus gerardi* and *Spartina alterniflora* are dominant. The nests are concealed and may be placed in fine grass, often under patches of dead drift grass, in bushes above the usual high tide, or suspended from *Spartina alterniflora* over water. The way the grass is bent determines the direction from which the nest can be entered. Spoil piles from ditching for mosquito control enable the birds to nest in the *Iva* on such piles. The nests have a mean outside diameter of 9.9 centimeters with a range of 7.6–11.4 centimeters. The nests are made with dead grass and lined with finer grass (Woolfenden, 1956; Bent *et al.*, 1968; Post, 1970a, b).

Some differences in nesting characteristics have been noted for the more southern subspecies of seaside sparrows. Macgillivray's seaside sparrow may place its nest a few inches above the mud in *Sporobolus paspalum* to a height of three feet in *Spartina* or *Juncus*, or up to five feet in *Baccharis*. A preference has been displayed for nest sites in fairly thick grass with an order of preference as follows: *Sporobolus paspalum*, *Spartina alterniflora*, *Juncus*, *Baccharis*. A few nests have been found in mangroves, a number in *Salicornia*, but none on the ground. Nests are not built in shrubbery unless no other suitable plants are near or a suitable height above the tides. The nests are so situated that the entrance is below the top level of the grasses or just below the leaf canopy of *Baccharis* but not among the base branches. The nests that are not covered by natural foliage are canopied. The dusky seaside sparrow prefers dry places or moist ground with some preference for dry locations. Their nests have also been found 30–40 centimeters above ground in dense stands of *Salicornia*, isolated patches of switch grass, or *Juncus*. The nests in the switch grass are made of the same grass and attached to the stems. It has been observed that the dusky seaside sparrow tends to have more canopied nests than Macgillivray's seaside sparrow. The Cape Sable sparrow also nests in the switch grass about 40 centimeters off the ground, where the grass covers the nest for concealment but it is not an arched nest. The bird also nests in the short salt grass a few centimeters off the ground, building the nest of the same material and lining it with fine grass (Nicholson, 1928; Tomkins, 1941).

The breeding season extends through May and June into July for both species. Forbush (1929) recorded breeding dates of 15–24 May for the sharp-tail in Virginia and 24 May–14 July in southern New England. Montagna (1940) observed the sharp-tail singing through the breeding season as late as 25 July at Popham Beach, Maine. Woolfenden (1956), citing earlier workers, recorded egg laying from 19 May to 4 August with the possibility of two broods. Murray (1969) observed the sharp-tails arriving on the New Jersey coast on 5 May in 1955 and they were most numerous during the second and third weeks. Post (1970a) observed them in Suffolk County, Long Island on 1 May.

Forbush (1929) recorded the breeding period for seaside sparrows in Virginia as 20 May–7 June and later in southern New England (8 June–17 July). Woolfenden (1956) found the breeding activity concentrated in early June with the extremes from 23 May to 2 July in Ocean County, New Jersey.

Tomkins (1941) has recorded a long breeding season for Macgillivray's seaside sparrow in South Carolina and Georgia with incomplete sets of eggs in late April and partially fledged birds in late August: the greatest number of nests were seen in June but almost as many were present in May.

The sharp-tailed sparrows produce only one brood in New England but two broods have been recorded for New Jersey with 4–5 eggs per brood. Only one brood is typically recorded for the seaside sparrows although Post (1970a) observed those that successfully nested in June renested in July. One pair with repeated failures renested four times with the last egg found on 29 July. Only the females of both species incubate the eggs. The female sharp-tailed sparrow is more secretive and the evidence suggests the male does not know the location of the nest. In contrast, the male seaside sparrow sings close by while the female incubates the eggs. Both parents feed the nestlings. This is compatible with the monogamous habits of the seaside sparrow in contrast to the promiscuous behavior of the sharp-tailed. The young of both species stay in the nest for 9–10 days (Forbush, 1929; Woolfenden, 1956; Bent *et al.,* 1968).

Substantial losses occur for both species. The typical clutch size is four eggs with a range of 3–6 (Forbush, 1929; Woolfenden, 1956). Post (1970a) recorded 106 seaside sparrow nests at Oak Beach, Long Island and 67 had eggs. The rest were practice nests or failures. Seventy-four young, or an estimated 28 percent of the young that hatched, left the nest. Four sharp-tailed sparrow nests, on the periphery of the area densely occupied by seaside sparrows, had 14 eggs and ten young left the nest. On another occasion in Nassau County, Long Island Post (1970b) located five seaside nests and only two produced four and three young respectively. Five sharp-tailed sparrow nests were located—none produced any young—three of which were destroyed by predators.

The sharp-tailed sparrows are not territorial in the usual sense but are colonial or at least occur in groups and there is the suggestion that there may be selection for aggregations. The birds do restrict themselves to a breeding home range, an area where an individual confines itself during one nesting attempt. There can be considerable overlap of such breeding home ranges for individual males. Such ranges are 3–4 acres in size for the males while the female sharp-tailed sparrows confine themselves to smaller areas about one acre in size. The birds feed throughout these home ranges. Woolfenden (1956) suggested the female may be territorial as well as secretive. As a consequence the males do not participate in rearing the young.

The male sharp-tailed sparrow sings only while engaged in fighting and singing is considered to be an expression of sexual excitement. The males are promiscuous, attempting to mate with any bird, including seaside sparrows (Woolfenden, 1956; Murray, 1969). After an aerial display by the male two birds were observed by Montagna (1940) to copulate following a short flight along a drainage ditch. Such sparse displays by the sharp-tailed sparrows reflect their simple social organization (Post, 1974). Singing is much more evident in the morning, becoming quiet and inconspicuous during the afternoon, but persisting throughout the length of the breeding season. Montagna (1942) and Murray (1969) commented that the coastal sharp-tailed sparrow, *Ammospiza caudacuta subvirgata,* sings frequently and loudly from a perch or in flight while birds further south have a much weaker and infrequent song.

The seaside sparrows are monogamous and territorial. The seaside sparrows advertise and defend the nest area by singing and chasing. In contrast to the sharp-tailed sparrows, advertisement of intolerance is the primary purpose of seaside sparrow song. The chase is not vigorous but Woolfenden observed the intruders gave way in all cases and there was no physical fighting (Woolfenden, 1956; Bent *et al.,* 1968; Post and Greenlaw, 1975).

The size and nature of the seaside sparrow territory appears to be determined by population density and configuration of the marsh. The work by Tomkins (1941) and Woolfenden (1956) clearly indicated that a suitable habitat for seaside sparrows must consist of a nesting area in thick vegetation and a separate feeding ground located in the more frequently flooded open mud flats bordering the edges and not the interior of the marshes. Tomkins considered food requirements to be much more important in determining habitat limitations. He observed small groups of birds feeding together and considered the subspecies *Ammospiza maritima macgillivrai* at least, to be communal in nature. On the other hand Woolfenden (1956) reported no communal feeding. He considered the flyways between feeding and nesting areas of different pairs of birds to be mutually exclusive. The evidence suggested to Woolfenden that the males defend the feeding sites and flyways as part of their territories by advertisement through use of the areas.

More recent work (Post, 1974; Post and Greenlaw, 1975) displayed two dispersion patterns: territories and group territories. Group territories were found in unaltered Long Island marshes where the vegetation was dominated by *Spartina alterniflora.* These grouped territories were small activity spaces from which the birds made distant foraging flights. The population density of seaside sparrows was an average 24.8 pairs/hectare in the un-ditched marsh. The altered marsh was transected by mosquito control ditches. The territories were large, all-purpose activity spaces and bird density was an average of one pair per hectare.

For birds nesting in unaltered habitat availability of nest sites appeared to be most important in determining the spacing pattern of the population.

The birds were forced to nest close together because of a lack of suitable cover. The territorial (solitary) tendency of birds in the altered marsh suggested to Post that those birds nesting in grouped territories in an unaltered marsh were not voluntarily gregarious. The data presented by Post implies that such spacing patterns were the result of rather than the determinants of population density, and therefore there appeared to be no upper limit to population size that could be accommodated in a given area.

Post (1974) noted that birds in grouped territories, while feeding communally some distance away from the nest site, were able to deliver food equally well to the nest as compared to the solitary birds feeding in the general-purpose territory. Such behavior coincides with Tomkins's (1941) observation but is at variance with Woolfenden (1956). Post concluded that food availability in the unaltered marsh did not inhibit reproductive success. Birds in the grouped territories tended to remain silent when foraging away from their defended activity spaces, probably because they were attacked when they sang. This seems to be at variance with Woolfenden's (1956) earlier observation that the feeding sites for bird pairs were mutually exclusive. Post and Greenlaw (1975) observed that visual displays and fighting in sparse populations was largely confined to a nest-centered area about 47 percent of the size of the singing activity space (Table 5.29). Such birds often sang as they foraged probably because they had few neighbors and were thus free from attack.

Post and Greenlaw (1975) noted no difference between populations in the amount of singing (Table 5.30). Before the female seaside sparrows arrived the males spend a great deal of time singing, with peaks of activity in the early morning and late afternoon. When the males were feeding the young, singing was greatly reduced (4.9 percent in the dense population in the unaltered marsh, 2.7 percent in the sparse population in the ditched marsh). The singing space was always larger than the defended territories in the ditched marsh where visual display and fighting took place. In the dense populations of an unditched marsh the singing spaces were often smaller than the defended territory.

Seaside sparrows in grouped territories spent more time engaged in visual displays than did the birds in sparse populations (Post and Greenlaw, 1975). Presumably such visual displays are more effective in the close quarters of the grouped territories while vocal displays would be less effective in dense populations because of noise interference. On the other hand, vocal displays would be more effective in the sparse population density of a ditched marsh as the song would carry over longer distances.

Because of the structural simplicity of the marsh there is a greater incidence of interspecific aggression by seaside sparrows toward the sharp-tailed sparrows. The latter invariably flee before the former, possibly because of

Table 5.29. Sizes of activity spaces (m^2) of seaside sparrows. (From Post and Greenlaw, 1975, by permission of the editor, *Auk*)

		Dense Population Unaltered Marsh				Sparse Populations Ditch Marsh		
	N	Mean	SE(S$\bar{x}$)	Range	N	Mean	SE(S$\bar{x}$)	Range
Total Activity Space	25	1203	240	160–6190	13	8781	2435	810–17640
Forging Activity Space	21	1039	238	170–5135	11	8121	2448	520–17510
Singing Activity Space	21	484	111	88–2590	11	4669	1408	505–9000
Defended Activity Space	19	393	90	35–1296	5	2183	976	430–3250

Table 5.30. Percent of daylight period that male seaside sparrows engaged in primary song and visual display. (From Post and Greenlaw, 1975, by permission of the editor, *Auk*)

Diurnal Interval	Dense Population Before Arrival of Female (n = 88)[1]		(Unaltered Marsh) After Arrival of Female and Incubation (n = 101)		Sparse Population Before Arrival of Female (n = 49)		(Ditch Marsh) After Arrival of Female and Incubation (n = 66)	
	Primary Song	Visual Display	Primary Song	Visual Display	Primary Song	Visual Display	Primary Song	Visual Display
1	59.6	2.9	17.6	8.1	42.3	0.2	53.1	0.4
2	30.1	11.5	14.1	13.6	47.4	2.8	26.1	5.2
3	25.8	11.8	17.2	12.3	36.3	0	32.7	2.4
4	41.4	4.3	18.3	9.5	16.0	7.3	17.7	2.3
(1300)								
5	15.4	0.2	27.1	0.4	14.9	0	22.9	2.4
6	12.3	14.5	28.2	1.7	25.6	0	19.5	0
7	19.3	2.4	27.0	7.9	32.4	2.3	18.6	3.1
8	43.8	4.4	28.5	15.1	44.2	0	33.3	0.7
Mean	32.1	6.5[2]	22.3	8.6[2]	32.4	1.6[2]	30.0	2.1[2]

1. Mean of 30 minute observation periods.
2. Males in dense populations spent a greater amount of time engaged in visual displays than males in sparse populations (P o.d.; F = 23.3). There was no difference in the amount of time engaged in primary song.

misdirected intraspecific territorality. The monogamous seaside sparrows may consider the promiscuous sharp-tailed sparrows as potential competitors for female seaside sparrows or space (Post and Greenlaw, 1975).

The song sparrow, *Melospiza melodia,* is characteristically found associated with brushy vegetation growing in wet places throughout North America from Alaska and eastern Canada south to central Mexico. The species is highly variable: Marshall (1948) indicated there are thirty geographic races while the American Ornithological Union (1957) lists thirty-one. At least four of these are associated with tidal marshes. *M. melodia atlantica* is found in the Atlantic coast marshes while three races inhabit the tidal marshes in the San Francisco Bay region. *M. melodia maxillaris* is related to the brackish water habitat while *M. melodia pusillula* and *M. melodia samuelis* are linked with the salt-water marshes. A fourth race, *M. melodia gouldii,* of the bay region is associated with the upland fresh-water marshes.

Marshall (1948) recognized eight different song sparrow habitats. Moisture and light played an important role with the birds showing less tolerance for dry conditions than the plants of the fresh-water marsh. The birds were also restricted to those portions of the fresh-water marsh where there were bare areas for foraging. Marshall observed no interruption in the linear continuity of song-sparrow territories in the transition zone from one type of vegetation to the other. In some situations where the line of demarcation between fresh- and salt-water marsh vegetation was fairly abrupt, neither habitat was large enough to support song sparrows and the birds fed in both types of vegetation. Both in the fresh-water marshes and the streamside habitats pairs of song sparrows were further apart where the vegetational zones were narrow. Bird pairs were about 30 meters apart where the vegetational zone width was 40 meters, and about 80 meters apart where the zone was 10–15 meters.

Brackish-water marshes with plant dominants of *Scirpus acutus* and *Typha latifolia* make up a large part of the marshes of the San Francisco Bay region. The growth composed of *Scirpus californicus* and *Typha* extends upstream beyond tidal flow while seaward, the salt tolerant *Scirpus acutus* extends the equivalent growth form into the *Spartina* marshes. There was no interruption of linear sequence of breeding song sparrows through these transitions and the birds did not sort out according to plant associations. Here again the width of the zone influenced the spacing of breeding pairs. Where the vegetational zone was broad the pairs were about 48 meters apart at the bay shores and were separated by 52–70 meters along the sloughs, depending on the width of the plant fringe, 15–5 meters, respectively. The birds only occupied territories where there was a patch of *Scirpus acutus* standing above the surrounding vegetation. Such a patch is apparently essential as a song perch. A suitable territory must also contain bare patches of mud as foraging sites. The birds avoided any situation where there was no tidal flow and there was standing water, even though bushy vegetation such as *Grindelia* grew in such situations. The birds visited such vegetation on levees but territory headquarters were always at slough margins.

Salt-marsh vegetation in the San Francisco Bay area is dominated by *Spartina foliosa, Salicornia ambigua,* and *Grindelia cuneifolia* with *Spartina* at the lowest altitude while *Salicornia* is covered only by the highest tides. *Grindelia* is found on the elevated margins of the sloughs. Between the sloughs there is a dense interlocking stand of *Salicornia* bushes that are seldom occupied (Marshall, 1948; Johnston, 1956c). Song sparrow pairs in the *Spartina* portions of the marsh were spaced at 76 meters single file along the bank of each slough where the average width of the territory was 10 meters and a great deal of mud was exposed as a foraging area (Marshall, 1948; Johnston, 1956c). On the *Salicornia-Grindelia* marsh pairs of birds were 30–100 meters apart, closer together where the *Grindelia* zone was wider. The birds forage in the territory along the exposed mud banks of the sloughs and only at high tide did they forage more than 30 meters from the slough.

The birds were limited by the height of the vegetation. They were not found where the *Spartina* was less than 46 centimeters high or in areas where the *Salicornia* was less than 30 centimeters tall. Pairs were about 100 meters apart where the *Spartina* was two-thirds to one meter high.

The average size of the territory of inland song sparrows has been calculated at 2700 m^2 (two-thirds of an acre) (Nice, 1943, p. 152). Using data cited above the average territory along a tidal slough had an area of 760 m^2. Johnston (1956c) estimated actual densities to be eight to ten pairs per acre during periods of high numbers in the San Pablo marshes of the San Francisco Bay region. This would indicate a very high density. Johnston observed that territories were larger in the *Spartina* zone than in the *Salicornia* habitat. At the heads of sloughs where the height of vegetation was reduced, especially that of *Grindelia,* the territories were larger than in the mud marsh with its lusher vegetation. Changes in density reflect levels of nestling production of the previous year.

From the foregoing, Marshall (1948) concluded that song sparrows, in at least the San Francisco Bay region, were limited in distribution by the moisture levels, the height and spacing of vegetation, the amount of light pentrating the vegetation, and the availability of open mud flats for foraging.

It is also evident from Marshall's discussion that the song sparrows of the marsh habitat move about very little and do so only at high tide periods to a distance up to 30 meters. Johnston (1955), while commenting on the influence of winter high tides on song sparrow populations in the Bay region, remarked that most birds did not move out of their winter territories. He observed one exception where a bird moved 150 meters, settled on vegetation, was driven out by the territory holder and returned to its own territory. Most birds did not move more than 10–20 meters during high tides. Most adult song sparrows of the San Pablo marshes remained for life in or near the territory they took up in the fall of their first year and Johnston (1955) presumed they did so elsewhere. Males set up territories through the late fall and winter and were completely territorial by late February. Territorial defense was lacking from July to September when adults molt. Adult birds seldom shifted territory from one breeding season to the next and those that did moved an average distance of 16 meters from center to center. Dispersal of the juveniles occurred in the late spring and summer and halted in late August and September when territorial activity began. Those aspects of population structure that favor isolation, high density of populations, and the existence of habitat selection by the birds enhanced the maintenance of the integrity and distinctness of song sparrow populations in the San Francisco Bay region (Johnston 1956c).

The breeding season for the various west coast races is shorter and starts later in the year at higher latitudes than at lower latitudes (Johnston, 1954). For the two races found in salt marshes, *Melospiza melodia pusillula* and *M. melodia sameulis,* the season starts in late February–early March and for *M. melodia samuelis* extends into late June. For *M. melodia pusillula* the season ends in early June. *M. melodia pusillula* displays three distinct peaks, early March, late March–early April and late April. *M. melodia samuelis* exhibits a single peak in late March–early April with a steady decline thereafter in the frequency of completed clutches. The peaks for both races are earlier by two weeks than those upland races at the same latitude. This may be an adaptation to salt-marsh conditions as the peaks coincide with the neap tide periods of late March and April. With the bulk of the population nesting during these low tides, the birds which do nest close to the ground surface lose a smaller percentage of eggs and young to flooding tidal waters. It has been shown that it is not the absolute height of the tides that govern egg and nestling mortality but whether or not the birds can nest early enough to escape the high run of tides in April to June. When they breed late there is a higher mortality caused by high tides.

Nests are placed off the ground, most commonly in stands of *Salicornia, Grindelia, Distichlis* or *Spartina.* Any nest less than 13 centimeters above the ground would be flooded out. The average nest height has been 24 centimeters over the entire marsh and 30 centimeters in the lower marsh. Generally with the increase in the height of the vegetation during the growing season it becomes possible for the song sparrows to nest at successively higher levels. This also parallels the increased height of the tides during the

Table 5.31. Clutch size in song sparrows of the Pacific coast. (Part of Table 2, Johnston, 1954, by permission of the editor, *Condor*)

	First Clutch	Second Clutch	Third Clutch
San Francisco Bay salt marsh			
Melospiza melodia pusillula	3.25	3.40	3.31
San Francisco Bay salt marsh			
Melospiza melodia samuelis	3.10	3.40	3.28

season. Predators may exert some selective pressure on nest height since the higher nests could be more evident to avian predators. No nest is used more than once and the nests of the season are scattered about in the territory (Johnston, 1956c).

The clutch size of the song sparrow eggs increases with increasing latitude, increasing altitude and decreasing longitude for western North America (Johnston, 1954). Nice (1937, p. 136) gave a five-year average of 4.05 eggs per clutch for inland birds. For the two salt-marsh races on the west coast the average clutch size was smaller but there was an increase from the first to the second clutch (Table 5.31). For the only race for which he had information, Johnston (1954) noted clutch size was smaller at the beginning and end of the season and larger in the middle: 3.1 from start of the season to 5 April, 3.4 from 6 April–15 May, and 3.1 from 16 May to the end of the season.

Natality rates varied from 7.5 to 9.1 total eggs and 2.0 to 5.0 fledglings per pair of song sparrows per season. Mortality rates varied from 56 percent in the first three weeks to 80–85 percent from the third to fifty-second weeks and, adult birds, 43 percent per year. Predation, primarily by the Norway rat, tidal floods, and desertion caused about 80 percent of the total mortality for the eggs and nestlings (Johnston, 1956c).

Marsh management and bird nesting. Tidal marshes have been subjected to some form of management for extensive periods of time; and most common have been diking, ditching, grazing, or fire. All too often there have been conflicts among users in the application of management procedures (see a review of this by Daiber, 1974).

Diking to exclude tidal action to create pasturage for livestock or for salt hay production can have an adverse impact on certain species, such as the clapper rail and black duck, by reducing their food supplies and at the same time can increase mosquito production (Ferrigno, 1959, 1961; Ferrigno and Jobbins, 1966). Greenhalgh (1971) noted that, when salt marshes are embanked, the halophyte vegetation is replaced by farmland plants;

Glue (1971) observed that the floral state is determined by the age of the dike. The natural avian community of the salt marsh disappears and passerine birds become more abundant on these wet pastures. If poorly drained, the bird species of fens and ponds become abundant. If pools remain behind the dike, along with a high water table, a rich bird community can develop. When the land is drained and ploughed, all species leave except for a poor farmland bird community (Greenhalgh, 1971). Glue (1971) noted that each stage is dominated by a different bird species: the salt-marsh and brackish pools by the meadow pipit; the soft mud pans by the reed bunting; the hard mud pans by the yellow wagtail; and the grasslands by the skylark. In addition, Glue observed that enclosed salt-marsh and grassland stages hold the greatest variety and density of breeding birds; 15 species, 107 pairs/km^2 and 16 species, 157 pairs/km^2, respectively. Such numbers could reflect the size and heterogeneity of these particular habitats, a condition that was pointed out by Moller (1975). Glue (1971) also noted an association between the loss of tidal mud flats and salt marsh, along with an increase in suitable roosting areas and a peripheral ditch system, and the changes in the incidence and absolute numbers of certain waders. Four species decreased, nine increased, and four showed no change.

Diking to impound water will naturally exclude clapper rails, willets, and other bird species such as the seaside and sharp-tailed sparrows that do not nest in flooded areas (Darsie and Springer, 1957; Mangold, 1962; Shoemaker, 1964; Provost, 1969). At the same time there will be an increase in a variety of birds including water fowl and wading birds. These impoundments provide a variety of foods, open water resting areas, and flooded cover for nesting sites (Darsie and Springer, 1957; Tindall, 1961; Mangold, 1962; Chabreck, 1963; Shoemaker, 1964; Lesser, 1965).

Grazing by both livestock and waterfowl can have not only an impact on the vegetation of a tidal marsh but on an interaction between the grazers (see a discussion on feeding relationships in Chapter 3, Interaction with Vegetation). Grazing or mowing tends to produce a more uniform environment (Larsson, 1969; Cadwalladr and Morley, 1963; Moller, 1975; Gray and Scott, 1977) and the bird fauna inclines to be more varied in an ungrazed habitat (Larsson, 1969, 1976; Moller, 1975). However, the natural ground irregularities can be emphasized by cattle trampling thus intensifying heterogeneity (Larsson, 1976) and at the same time trampling can enhance the dispersion of nesting birds, at least for colonial species like the common tern (Greenhalgh, 1974). Bird habitat requirements include foraging for food adjacent to the nest site, sites for singing, and look-out posts, as well as shelter for the young. All of these are more easily met in ungrazed areas (Larsson, 1969). On the other hand, wading birds find a more suitable habitat where grazing and trampling keep the vegetation lower, reduce the height of tussocks, and create muddy patches for feeding. Such an interaction appears to be related to suitable look-out sites against predators and reduced hampering of movements among newly hatched young (Larsson, 1969, 1976; Moller, 1975). If management plans are directed toward wading birds, the seashore meadows should be manipulated by grazing or mowing to keep the tussocks low and reduce the height of the vegetation. At the same time such management policies will have a detrimental effect on other kinds of birds that prefer taller vegetation. A well-managed area should provide feeding, nesting, and hiding places for various bird species.

Ditching of tidal marshes to control mosquitos has been the subject of greater argument than any other form of marsh management. Much of the discussion stems from the grid system of ditches wherein ditches traverse the full width of the marsh and cross various zones of vegetation whether or not heavy mosquito breeding sites are intersected. In the process of digging the ditches the spoil has been piled in a row paralleling the ditch. Such spoil piles supposedly impede the flow of tidal waters moving across the surface of the marsh and permit the invasion of the marsh by the high tide bushes, *Baccharis* and *Iva,* and other drier ground species. The ditches are purported to lower the water table which would dry out the marsh permitting species of higher elevations to invade and reducing the invertebrate populations which are used as a food resource by the avian population which in turn would be reduced (Ferrigno, 1959; Shisler, 1973; Burger and Shisler, 1978c; Bourn and Cottam, 1950; and the discussion in Chapter 2 on Zonation regarding subsequent interpretation of events in the Mispillion marshes to which Bourn and Cottam refer).

Presumably a natural unditched marsh is relatively level. Following ditching there is almost a one-foot slumping of the banks bordering the ditches. Soil elevation gradually increases further from the ditches so that a zone about 7 meters wide develops on each side of the ditch where the low marsh tall form of *Spartina alterniflora* is enhanced. Rockel (1969b) estimated about 42 percent of the marsh would be so altered with ditches about 30 meters apart. Earlier, Stewart (1951) found a high correlation between the density of clapper rail nests and the amount of edge between the tall and the short form of *Spartina alterniflora.* The best correlation existed where the edge consisted of 20 meters of short *Spartina alterniflora* and 10 meters of the tall form. Obviously Stewart's 10 meters is not much different from Rockel's 7 meters of tall marsh grass. Stewart recommended the clapper rail management include increasing the edge effect by constructing ditches or creeks with sloping banks. Subsequent observations suggest there can be some variance from this recommendation. Shisler and Shulze (1976) noted from earlier workers that tidal range can have an effect on the growth of

Spartina alterniflora, and where the tidal range is small (0.5 meters) the construction of ditches may not always provide the nesting niche for clapper rails. Under such conditions, Shisler and Schulz inferred that spoil piles colonized by *Spartina patens* and/or *Spartina alterniflora* may serve as nest sites for clapper rails which would not normally be found in such marsh habitats. The willet shows a decided preference for nesting on spoil piles in a heavily ditched marsh rather than in an unditched marsh (Burger and Shisler, 1978c).

The seaside sparrow normally is located in the wetter portions of the marsh and frequently nests along the ditches. It has also been observed to nest on or near the spoil piles on which *Iva* grows (Woolfenden, 1956; Bent *et al.,* 1968; Post, 1970b). However, Post (1974) found fewer birds (1 pair/hectare) in a ditched marsh than in an unditched marsh (24.8 pairs/hectare) and in some way ditching presumably had a pronounced effect on the birds' behavior (see earlier discussion on the sparrows). Ditches open to tidal flow can have a detrimental effect on the nesting site of herring gulls. After such ditching there was a marked change in vegetation from 20 percent to 84 percent bushes over a five-year period (Burger and Shisler, 1978b). This caused the birds to abandon that portion of the marsh for areas less densely covered with bushes. This was confirmed elsewhere (Burger and Shisler, 1978a) when herring gulls nested under *Baccharis* and *Iva* bushes where the bushes made up 27 percent of the cover but avoided nearby sites with 100 percent bush cover.

It is evident from the foregoing presentation that the relationship between various forms of marsh management and nesting birds is not a simple straightforward interaction. Whatever is done will enhance the populations of certain species at the expense of others. Management practices will induce changes in the habitat which in turn will cause changes in the species composition, density, and distribution of the avian fauna. It is apparent that species such as the willet and herring gull, which typically nest on higher ground, can adapt by moving out into the marsh taking advantage of grass- or bush-covered spoil piles. At the same time, the herring gull can survive from flooding in the lower marsh without spoil piles. Under certain circumstances the clapper rail, which normally nests in the lower marsh, can modify its nesting behavior to utilize spoil piles. Yet these various birds would presumably have fewer nesting sites if the sods are smashed down or the spoil spread as a mulch over the marsh as advocated by a number of authors (Ferrigno, 1958; Ferrigno *et al.,* 1967; Ferrigno and Jobbins, 1968; Ferrigno *et al.,* 1969; Ferrigno *et al.,* 1976). Ditching may lower the water table, permitting the invasion of high tide bushes, which should favor herring gulls. However, these birds will leave if the bush cover becomes too dense. On the other hand, ditching is supposed to cause portions to revert to a lower, wetter

marsh conducive to seaside sparrows, yet there were fewer sparrows associated with a ditched marsh. It is apparent that we are still lacking enough
information about the biology and behavior of these marsh animals to determine whether we are making management decisions that will have the
least detrimental impact on the marsh fauna.

Mammalia

Harris (1953), Johnston (1957), Paradiso and Handley (1965), Shure (1970),
and Jones (1978) are some of the authors who have enumerated the mammals found on various tidal marshes. However, no mammals appear unique
to tidal marshes since all are distributed extensively in or along fresh-water
inland marshes or along the borders of ponds, lakes, or streams and into the
upland area. The raccoon *Procyon lotor,* mink *Mustela vison,* and otter *Lutra
canadensis* are typical mammalian predators who invade the tidal marshes
looking for various kinds of food including: voles, rats, mice, muskrats, nutria, rabbits and shrews. Of these, the muskrat *Ondatra zibethica,* marsh
rabbit *Sylvilagus palustris,* swamp rabbit *Sylvilagus aquaticus,* harvest mouse
Reithrodontomys, nutria *Myocaster coypus,* and the shrew *Sorex vagrans halicoetes* may be considered marsh animals.

When associated with a tidal marsh, the deer mouse *Peromyscus leucopus,* the jumping mouse *Zapus hudsonius,* the cotton rat *Sigmodon hispidus,* and the least shrew *Cryptosis parva* are characteristically found along
the high land borders of the marsh out of reach of normal tide waters
(Svihla, 1930; Shure, 1970; Jones, 1978). Therefore they will not be included
in this discussion.

Insectivora. Soricidae. The salt-marsh shrew, *Sorex vagrans halicoetes,* is a
common inhabitant of the San Francisco Bay salt marshes, making up 10
percent of the mammalian fauna. It inhabits areas of dense cover which
provide nesting material, fairly continuous ground moisture, and plenty of
invertebrates for food. The shrew is found in medium high grass 6–8 feet
above sea level, extending into lower areas not regularly flooded by tides.
Nesting and resting areas are provided by driftwood and plant material including *Spartina foliosa* litter and *Salicornia.* The high marsh which is devoid of cover and the lower zone of *Spartina* which is regularly flooded are
devoid of shrews (Johnston and Rudd, 1957).

There are two kinds of nests: one to hold litters, probably made by the
female, and a second or resting nest which is probably used by both sexes.
Johnston and Rudd (1957) reported that shrews built breeding nests of variable shape depending on the size of the plank they selected for a cover. Pre-

sumably the nests would be situated under logs, branches, or other material when man-made planks were not available. The nest itself was made of dead plant fragments: *Spartina* leaves and stems, *Distichlis,* and *Salicornia.* Paper was frequently incorporated into the top part of the nest which was usually domed. The mass of the nest might be 8–24 × 6–12 centimeters across and 4–6 centimeters deep. The central cup was 3 × 3 or 4 × 4 centimeters across and 2–3 centimeters deep. The dome of the nest frequently filled a cavity on the underside of the covering structure. As the young grew, the cup was enlarged and the dome lost. The cup was not open to view until the young were 2–3 weeks old. Runways entered from the side or from below. Resting nests were smaller: 2–3 × 3–4 centimeters and with shallow cups only. They were raised above the ground surface in the depressed *Salicornia.*

The principal breeding season extends from late February to early June. The peak of parturition is late April and more than half of the litters are born in April. Breeding adults are not common through the summer and the small amount of breeding which occurs in September is probably attributable to the young of the year born early in the season.

The gestation period lasted 20 days. The average litter size was 5.2 with a range of 2–9. Uterine litters averaged 5.5; in the nests the mean was 4.7. They were born naked and with eyes closed. They were furred dorsally and the eyes opened at two weeks. By three weeks they were totally furred and the teeth were fully erupted. The female began to wean the young at about 16 days and they were completely weaned by 25 days. The young stayed in the nest until the fifth week. No social grouping behavior was evident outside of litter mates.

At birth the young weighed 0.5 grams and growth was rapid at a consistent rate to one month when they weighed 5–6 grams followed by a decline to 4–5 grams until December–January. At the onset of breeding the maximum weight for the males was 8.4 grams and for females, 7.7 grams (Johnston and Rudd, 1957).

There were no specific causes of mortality in the nest, some no doubt drown during tidal flooding and rat predation may have been a factor. Mortality from conception to seven days after birth was not less than 15 percent with survival to three weeks amounting to 55–60 percent. Litter size had no influence on mortality (Johnston and Rudd, 1957).

The masked shrew, *Sorex cinereus,* has a distribution and choice of habitat greater than any other American mammal, ranging from salt marshes to the high slopes of the mountains above timberline. A subspecies, *S. c. nigriculus* may be restricted to the salt marshes of New Jersey (Hamilton, 1943; Hall and Kelson, 1959). A small fine nest composed of leaves and grass is typically found under a log or stump or in a shallow burrow. The young are born from spring to early fall. Three litters are typical and each litter consists of 4–10. These are remarkable numbers for such a small mammal.

Rodentia. Cricetidae. Muskrat. There is an extensive literature covering the muskrat, *Ondatra zibethica,* and most of it pertains to those populations associated with inland fresh-water marshes. Much of this work has been brought together by Errington (1963) and reflects his own very extensive efforts. *O. zibethica* and its subspecies is found over most of North America north of Mexico. The Louisiana muskrat *O. z. rivalicus* is found in the coastal marshes from Texas to Mississippi while the Virginia muskrat *O. z. macrodon* is found on the Delmarva peninsula south through the coastal marshes of Virginia and North Carolina (Hall and Kelson, 1959).

The beginning of the breeding season and arrival of the young are denoted by the presence of freshly worked vegetation and newly plastered mud on old houses or the creation of new houses (Svihla and Svihla, 1931; O'Neil, 1949; Dozier, 1953). The essential purpose of the house is to provide the muskrat with a comparatively dry nest with an even temperature. Houses are situated above normal high tides and are made of the local vegetation; the most substantial ones are constructed of *Scirpus* stems in the brackish marshes. A new house can be created in a few hours by heaping vegetation into a pile, boring a hole from underneath and rounding out a nest 20–25 centimeters in diameter some 25–38 centimeters above the water level. The nest is lined with fine grass stems. Such a house, the plunge hole, and deep underground runs are usually all done by the time the young are born. While the first litter is still feeding, the male lives in a separate nest in the house. As the house increases in size so do the number of nests. The second litter is deposited in a new nest about the time the first litter is weaned. Each new litter is deposited in its own nest. During the spring and fall the young are born in the grasslined nests, but during the summer the litters are born in more open situations such as cattail rafts, brush piles, or among debris thrown up just out of reach of high tides (Dozier, 1953). Both the adults and kits take part in maintaining the house. Those muskrats that establish dens in banks and levees nest in the same way as those living in marshes (Svihla and Svihla, 1931; O'Neil, 1949).

Territories exist but they are not as rigid as those of some bird species nor are they as rigidly defended. The adult female shows the greatest intolerance to intrusion especially during the breeding season (Errington, 1963). Males do not display the same level of territorial intolerance and are safer company for weaned young. The place defended may be considerably larger than the near vicinity of the litter and the size of the territory can vary tremendously from a hundred to thousands of square meters in sparse populations or 20–40 square meters at high population densities. Differences in territorial tolerance may result from opportunities, individual dispositions, the impact of physiological and environmental variations, social conditioning, and unknown tensions. There is a tendency for equalization of distances between territories in prime habitat and such territorial spacing increasingly becomes a matter of compromise as densities increase (Errington, 1963).

Home ranges vary with the age of the muskrat. While weaned young have unimpeded movement within an area 60–80 meters in diameter, adults may range up to one-half mile when living along underpopulated shores or central bodies of water. With high densities and the associated territories of intolerant females, the home ranges are smaller and more circumscribed. Under such circumstances home ranges of residents are almost the same as territories so far as any wandering strangers are concerned. Adjustments in both territories and home ranges readily take place in response to environmental pressures so long as the animals are able to move without effective hindrance to new suitable habitat. However, where family groups cannot move because of physical barriers or other occupied territories, they will remain in place despite increased losses. Some individuals may break free as wanderers to die or live elsewhere as they can amid the hazards of wandering (Errington, 1963).

The sex ratio favors the males. At birth 61.2 percent of 147 newborn young were males and as adults the general sex ratio was 55 percent males: 45 percent females (Errington, 1963). Although muskrats pair off they are not monogomous. At times the males may be very polygamous causing much fighting as one rat invades another's territory looking for a mate (Dozier, 1953).

From earlier investigations Errington noted that breeding can take place every month of the year. In the southern part of the range winter breeding is more common. In Iowa, Errington (1963) observed a marked increase in gonadal size by December. Donohoe (1966) found corpora lutea present from July through August and collected pregnant females from February through August in the Lake Erie marshes of northwest Ohio. Errington reported that the breeding season in Iowa extended from March to October with the greatest percent of births occurring early in the season: 30.6 percent in May and 28.6 percent in June. Dozier (1953) observed that the first young were usually born in the Maryland marshes between 27 April and 5 May and noted this to be the period of greatest productivity in total numbers born and the highest rate of survival of the young. Donohoe (1966) suggested sexual activity decreased among Ohio animals during the latter part of the breeding season, April through August.

The gestation period is approximately one month (Errington, 1963) or 28–29 days (Dozier, 1953). The vagueness stems from the uncertainty of the actual time the ova are implanted (Errington, 1963).

The litter size, as well as the number of litters per female, varies with race, latitude, and the quality and quantity of food (Dozier *et al.*, 1948; Gashwiler, 1950; Dozier, 1953; Errington, 1963; Palmisano, 1972). Data from Louisiana, Texas, and Mississippi showed a mean litter size of 3.7 (Errington) and 3.8 (Gashwiler, Dozier) for *O. z. rivalicus*. The Virginia race, *O. z. macrodon*, averaged 4.4 per litter (Gashwiler, Dozier). The common muskrat *O. z. zibethica* tended to have more young. In Iowa, Errington (1963) recorded a mean of 6.8 young from 188 litters and 7.50 ± 0.06 from 279 litters. In Maine, Gashwiler found an average of 7.1 embryos from 45 pregnant females and cited another case where there was an average of 5.4 from 62 litters. The Maine muskrats bore 2.7 more embryos than the Maryland-Virginia animals and 3.3 more embryos than those from Louisiana. Errington (1963) studied older females in northern Canada and recorded an average of 5.0 for the first litter and 5.6 for the second.

While the number per litter tended to increase in a northward progression, the number of litters per female per year tended to decrease. Among the southern race, *O. z. rivalicus*, there were 4–5 litters per year (Dozier, 1953) with a potential for 7–8 (Errington, 1963). In Iowa, among 76 females, Errington found 17 (22.4 percent) had one litter, 43 (56.6 percent) had two litters, 14 (18.4 percent) had three litters, and 2 (2.6 percent) had four litters per year. On the evidence of 824 Iowa females with traceable breeding histories, the average number of litters per female life span was 2.87. In Maine the number of litters per year was two with possibly a few instances of three. In northern Canada there was only one litter, mainly in late June, for yearling muskrats, while older females had two litters, in June and again in July (Errington, 1963).

These newborn young, with an average weight of 21 grams, are very hardy. They are able to withstand severe chilling, bites, trampling, and lack of food for several days. The hardiness gradually decreases as tissues become more differentiated and by four weeks there is a markedly lower tolerance to chilling than in the newborn individuals. The young are covered with a coarse gray pelage by the end of the first week. The eyes open in 14–16 days with a range of 12–20 days. The young can swim and climb out of the water while still blind. They begin to feed on grass before they are weaned at four weeks. There is an accelerated growth about the twentieth day when they begin to forage for themselves. The rate of growth is influenced by the quality as well as the quantity of food, water conditions, and racial characters. As they grow the young are very active in the general territory of the parents. They become active burrowers, living in old lodges, brush piles, and mats of debris and are subjected to considerable predation. Those young born early in the spring can breed the spring following their birth if not earlier (Dozier, 1953; Errington, 1963). O'Neil (1949) indicated that the southern race of females may breed any time after the age of four weeks. O'Neil also suggested the female may become reimpregnated two weeks after giving birth.

Rodentia. Cricetidae. Meadow Vole. Throughout most of Canada and the United States where there is good grass cover members of the genus *Microtus* are likely to be found. They range from tide water, moist fields, tundra stream banks, dry slopes, moist rocky woodlands to above the timber line. Their presence may be detected by the narrow runways 2–5 centimeters wide through the grass as well as small piles of brown droppings. The evidence of short pieces of grass stems are further clues to their presence (Hall and Kelson, 1959).

Microtus pennsylvanicus has the widest distribution, being found throughout Canada and the northern United States including East Coast tidal marshes (Harris, 1953; Hall and Kelson, 1959; Shure, 1970; Jones, 1978). There is a voluminous literature covering the species. *Microtus californicus* is essentially restricted to the state of California ranging from salt- and fresh-water marshes to wet meadows as well as dry hillsides. Thaeler (1961) presented an extensive analysis of the population of *Microtus californicus* inhabiting the salt marshes of the San Francisco Bay region. Harris (1953) and Fisler (1965a) found both species to be capable swimmers when associated with tidal marshes.

Both *Microtus pennsylvanicus* and *Microtus californicus* are polyestrous, breeding throughout the year, and females will accept attention from any male (Bailey, 1924). The mean breeding season for *Microtus californicus* is in the late winter and spring months with a minor peak in the fall. During the rest of the year sporadic pregnancies occur (Greenwald, 1956). During the late estival pause no males are in breeding condition. After the first winter rains the larger males greater than 40 grams are first in breeding condition. Winter temperatures and the amount of green food may determine the extent of the major breeding peak (Hoffman, 1958). Harris (1953) found voles breeding most of the winter in the Maryland marshes with females and young in December and January extending into at least the summer (Table 5.32).

Bailey (1924) reported the typical female *Microtus californicus* became sexually mature at an age of 41 days and a weight of 35 grams. Since males matured at the later age of 45 days, he maintained that inbreeding within the litter was not a factor. Hatfield (1935) found female *Microtus californicus* beginning to breed at 21–22 days, and, when fed in the lab-

Table 5.32. The presence and average number of embryos for meadow voles and rice rats in a tidal marsh habitat. (From Harris 1953, by permission of the editor, *J. Mammal.*)

	Meadow Voles			Rice Rats		
Month	# Examined	% With Embryos	Aver # Embryos	# Examined	% With Embryos	Aver # Embryos
March	14	71	4.3	1	0	—
May	10*	40	4.3	10	20	5.5
June	5	60	3.0	1	100	6.0
July	5	40	3.0	4	100	5.5

* Four without embryos showed evidence of suckling.

oratory, they would produce three litters in two months. Greenwald (1956), reporting on 1952 research, first judged sexual maturity at 30 grams and 29 days. However, studies of laboratory reared animals in 1953 further reduced that weight to 15.1 grams and an age equivalence of 14 days. He also observed that a wild female weighing 15 grams had sperm in the uteri and had two-celled tubal ova. The smallest female, at 10 grams, had an open vagina and the ovary contained medium-sized follicles. Greenwald considered these to be exceptions and that most of such early matings would represent sterile breeding cycles at puberty. Even more recently, Greenwald (1957) and Hoffman (1958) have concluded that sexual maturity for *Microtus californicus* is attained at 25–35 grams for females and 35–46 grams for males.

Bailey (1924) found that well-fed *Microtus pennsylvanicus* began to breed when half grown at 25 days and to have young at 45 days. Greenwald (1956, after Hamilton 1941) observed that *Microtus pennsylvanicus* began to mate when four weeks old. Once begun, breeding was continuous; immediately after birth of the young the females would mate again. Breeding activity could be depressed, however, by cold weather, lack of cover, low food supplies, and a high population density (Bailey, 1924).

Mating of *Microtus californicus* may take place with little precopulatory behavior or after several minutes to a half hour of courtship. Often there were several acts of copulation with 1.5–3.5 minutes between acts (Hatfield, 1935). *Microtus californicus* is an induced ovulator with ovulation taking place less than 15 hours after mating. Greenwald (1956) considered induced ovulation to be of importance in mammals that experience marked cyclic fluctuations since it would greatly enhance the possibility of a male encountering an estrous female.

The number of corpora lutea increased with the season. At the same time there was a seasonal distribution of corpora lutea in the ovary corresponding to the peaks of the breeding season (Greenwald, 1956; Hoffman,

1958). Conceivably the same pattern exists for *Microtus pennsylvanicus.* Hoffman (*ibid*) found the mean litter size for 73 female *Microtus californicus* to be 4.9 with a range of 1–10. This is somewhat larger than that reported by Greenwald (1956): 4.2 per litter for 154 pregnancies. Based on both embryo and placental scar counts, the litter size increased from three at the beginning of the breeding season in November to a peak of about six in April, followed by a decline to three or four. Hatfield (1935), Greenwald (1956), and Hoffman (1958) found young first-bred females tended to have smaller litters (4.6 ± 0.25) than multiparous females (5.19 ± 0.34). The larger litter size later in the season has been attributed to older multiparous females, however, Hoffman found primiparous females also had larger litters at that time. Bailey (1924) had noted the same pattern for *Microtus pennsylvanicus.* Young females usually produce four in a litter while older females when full grown, usually after the first or second litter, would produce 6–8 young at a birth. In contrast, however, information shown in Table 5.32 indicates that Harris (1953) noted a decrease in litter size within the small samples of voles he examined.

A new nest for each litter is placed on the ground among the matted grass stems. Constructed of fine grasses, it contains thicker walls during colder periods (Bailey, 1924). The female begins to build the nest at 15–18 days of pregnancy, assisted by the male (Hatfield, 1935). Harris (1953) noted that voles built globular nests of fine grasses in the walls of muskrat houses. Both voles and rice rats were taken at houses occupied and unoccupied by muskrats. On the basis of a short-term trapping interval, the percent of houses used by voles and rats varied between 11 and 34. On a long-term basis 48 percent were so occupied. Such use of houses provides protection for voles and rice rats but has no obvious advantage for the muskrat; nor is there evidence of disadvantage except the muskrat may be disturbed by raccoons digging for voles.

The female keeps the young covered and leaves them for only a few moments. While pregnant the female will drive off any male and will drive off any intruder after the young are born. If the nest is disturbed she will immediately move the young (Bailey, 1924).

The gestation period for both species of voles is 21 days (Bailey, 1924; Hatfield, 1935). Hatfield proffered the suggestion that lack of exercise seems to prolong gestation while exertion seems to shorten it. When born the young are hairless, blind, and weigh about three grams. The body is covered with fur by the sixth day and the eyes and ears are open on the eighth day. *Microtus pennsylvanicus* are weaned at the twelfth day while young *Microtus californicus* will suckle up to 21 days if allowed although they can eat solid food before that. The young will stay together with the mother until she deserts them to build a new nest for her next family.

The litter is soon dispersed as the young females reach maturity, followed later by the males who then wander in search of one mate after another. The sex ratio for adult *Microtus pennsylvanicus* was noted to be 49.1 percent male: 51.9 percent female (Harris, 1953). Greenwald (1957) recorded a value for *Microtus californicus* of 49.6 percent male embryos and newborn, declining to 42.6 percent for postnatal voles but varying seasonally.

Rodentia. Cricetidae. Rice Rat. *Oryzomys palustris* is subtropical in origin and is found in marshy areas throughout the southeastern United States extending into southern New Jersey and westward to eastern Missouri, Oklahoma, and Texas (Hall and Kelson, 1959). These rats are usually found along the higher drier portions of the marshes (Svihla, 1931). Harris (1953) found them associated with voles in muskrat houses while Jones (1978) saw them frequenting mosquito drainage ditches in southern Delaware.

There appear to be irregularities and uncertainties in the breeding season of the rice rat. Svihla (1931) and Worth (1950) observed the season to extend from mid-February to early October. Both sets of observations were made from captive animals with very irregular litter production. Negus *et al.* (1961) found the breeding season to be variable for wild animals along the Gulf coast. It might cease during the winter and early spring or it may extend throughout the year. Harris (1953) recorded the breeding season for a Maryland marsh population to span from March to November.

The time for attainment of sexual maturity is also variable: Svihla (1931) recorded 50 days; Conaway (1954) observed 50–60 days for captive animals; Negus *et al.* (1961) noted 40–45 days for a wild population still in the subadult pelage. Svihla (1931) reported a first litter born at 75 days, giving a gestation period of 25 days.

Litter size is also variable. Svihla (1931) noted a range of one to five with an average of three from eastern Texas. Negus *et al.* (1961) noted that 20 adult females from the same general area produced an average of 4.8. Negus *et al.* further noted a direct influence of population densities: high density paralleled small litters (2.7, range 2–5); low density correlated with greater numbers (6.0, range 4–7). Svihla (1931) noted older females tended to produce larger litters, averaging one more than younger females. Harris (1953) compared a mean of 5.5 for a wild population in Maryland with that of 5 (range 4–6) for ten litters held in captivity.

The estrous cycle was observed to be 7.6 days with a range of 6–9 (Conaway, 1954) and females go into estrous immediately after birth of a litter (Svihla, 1931). One captive female produced six litters totaling 20 young and Svihla considered nine litters to be the maximum possible. He estimated the average longevity to be seven months with a few living longer than a year. Negus *et al.* (1961) assumed an average female has at most six months of reproductive activity during her life span and the maximum numbers of litters would be five to six. The actual number may be considerably less due to food shortages, inclement weather, and population density. This would suggest a maximum number per female of 24–27 young, depending on latitude and habitat. Harris (1953) recorded an excess (63.6 percent) of males in the adult population.

The young are naked at birth with an average weight of 3.14 grams. The eyes are open and the body covered with fur by the sixth day and most are weaned by 11 days (Svihla, 1931) although some still nursed up to 20 days (Worth, 1950). Worth noted some cannibalism but most females took great care of the young.

Rodentia. Cricetidae. Harvest Mice. The genus *Reithrodontomys* consists of small brown mice resembling house mice and are characterized by a distinct groove running length-wise down the front of each upper incisor. The eastern harvest mouse, *Reithrodontomys humulis,* is associated with old fields, marshes, and wet meadows of the southeastern United States and, while the type locality is Charleston, South Carolina (Howell, 1914), it has not specifically been identified with tidal marshes. *Reithrodontomys fulvescens,* the fulvous harvest mouse, is found in grasslands and weedy fields of Louisiana and Texas, extending into arid regions of northern Mexico and the subspecies *R. fulvescens aurantus* has been collected from the fringes of marshes in Louisiana and Texas. The western harvest mouse, *Reithrodontomys megalotis,* occupies the grasslands and deserts, in dense vegetation near water over much of the western United States. One subspecies, *R. megalotis longicaudus,* is found in the coastal areas of northern California. The salt-marsh harvest mouse, *R. raviventris,* has two subspecies *R. raviventris raviventris* and *R. raviventris halicoetes* which are found only in the marshes of the San Francisco Bay area (Howell, 1914; Hall and Kelson, 1959). Zetterquist (1977) considered it to be an endangered species where marginal habitats are being used and populations are small. Not a great deal has been done on the life histories of these salt-marsh inhabiting forms. MacMillen (1964) has examined salt-water tolerance in *Reithrodontomys megalotis* while Fisler (1965b) has described the adaptations and speciation among the three forms of harvest mice in the marshes of the San Francisco Bay region.

Svihla (1930) and Johnston (1957) described the harvest mice nests as being several feet off the ground, often utilizing old song sparrow nests (Johnston) or well concealed in the rank vegetation (Svihla). The nests of *R. fulvescens aurantus* were made of finely shredded leaves of marsh grasses such as *Phragmites communis, Spartina patens,* and *Panicum hemitomum.* Such nests were compact, the size of a baseball. Nest building by *R. megalotis* and *R. raviventris raviventris* is similar. *R. megalotis* nests in the field were grassy balls 3–4 inches in diameter with 1–3 entrances at the ground surface or at the base of the nest. Citing earlier workers Fisler (1965b) stated that *R. megalotis* built open cuplike nests placed on the ground in shallow depressions, underground in shallow burrows, or above ground in low bushes like *Baccharis.* Fisler observed that most nests regardless of construction were placed on the ground in the San Francisco area. A few nests were made from roofed-over bird nests but they were not common. The nests of *Reithrodontomys raviventris halicoetes* were built of dry grasses and sedges and were placed on the ground or in the hummocks common to the marshes. This subspecies seldom puts its nests in the *Baccharis* or *Grindelia* bushes. Such nests could be rebuilt in half a night if destroyed by flooding. Harvest mice generally utilize several nests in an area and do not establish one as a home.

Breeding females of *Reithrodontomys megalotis* kept the nests in good repair and in a very sanitary condition. *R. raviventris halicoetes* nests often contained several individuals and, because such communal nests had thinner walls, they broke down and became more easily fouled than one containing several *R. megalotis. R. raviventris raviventris* did not build a nest but burrowed into a pile of debris and shouldered out a space, or perched on top of the pile of vegetation. Such nests were soon broken down and soon fouled. This subspecies is also reputed to use old song sparrow nests (Fisler, 1965b).

Fisler (1971) determined the age structure of populations of *R. megalotis longicaudus, R. raviventris raviventris,* and *R. raviventris halicoetes* to be similar throughout the year. There was observed an essentially complete yearly turnover of individuals in the population with few mice reaching the age of twelve months. This turnover was gradual throughout the year with no massive die-off of old individuals. He found males to be most active from April through September and delineated an association between the size of the testes and the degree of aggressiveness. *R. megalotis longicaudus* had the largest testes and was most aggressive while *R. raviventris raviventris* was the least aggressive with the smallest testes. *R. raviventris halacoetes* was intermediate for both characters.

The breeding season for the females of all three taxa extended primarily from March to November. For any single year it could vary depending on local conditions. Breeding *R. raviventris halicoetes* females appeared to have a very low reproductive rate in the field possibly only one litter per year in spite of the fact that several litters could be produced in the laboratory. There was a higher incidence of pregnancies for *R. megalotis longicaudus* and *R. r. raviventris* for March through August. In his earlier work (1965b) Fisler observed some differences in that the percent of pregnancies for *R. megalotis longicaudus* ranged from a high of 75 in May to a low of 14.3 percent in April. Values for *R. raviventris raviventris* were somewhat lower varying from 27–53 percent for the period of March through November. The number of embryos in litters for *R. megalotis longicaudus* and *R. raviventris raviventris* was essentially the same while litter size was slightly higher for *R. raviventris halicoetes* (Table 5.33).

The gestation period for another subspecies, *R. megalotis megalotis,* was recorded by Svihla (1930) at 23–24 days; two mice at 23 days and another two at 24 days, as measured by the time the male was placed with the female. Females did not go into estrous immediately after birth of the young. Litter size varied between 1–7; seven litters with one, six with two, five with three, six with four, and one with seven young. Newly born young were naked and blind and weighed 1.5 grams. They were covered with hair at 11 days and the eyes were open at 12 days. When the eyes opened the young began to take solid food, gradually becoming weaned. They became independent of the adults by at least 19 days. Svihla noted the youngest sexually mature *R. megalotis megalotis* bred at 128 days and the most prolific female produced seven litters with 17 young in one year with no further breeding.

Rodentia. Capromyidae. The nutria, *Myocaster coypus,* is a South American rodent introduced into the European continent, England, and Louisiana during the early 1930s for its pelt. Since then by deliberate stocking or inadvertent escapes it has become established in a number of places. It is a semiaquatic animal confined to the vicinity of marshes and waterways. The nutria tends to live in fresh-water marshes in Louisiana and there is a considerable overlap, perhaps up to 90 percent (personal communication, Dr. R. Chabreck), with the muskrat which is more abundant in brackish-water marshes. Where they occur together, nutria tend to restrict the natural population growth of the muskrat (Newson, 1966; Evans, 1970) by resting on the rat beds during high water (Chabreck, *ibid*).

The nutria breeds all year. Virtually all adult females are pregnant, lactating, or both throughout the year with 78 percent of the lactating females being pregnant (Atwood, 1950; Newson, 1966; Brown, 1975). Drawing upon earlier work Brown (1975) identified the main breeding season to be December–January with a major secondary effort in June–July for animals found in natural Louisiana marshes. Both Newson (1966) and Evans (1970) noted that breeding was interrupted by climatic disturbances such as hurricanes, droughts, or cold weather, followed by a higher incidence of conceptions. Newson found many animals were killed in English marshes by cold snaps thus reducing animal density.

Sexual maturity is variable but is usually achieved at a body weight of 1.5–2.5 kilograms while growth can continue to eight kilograms and beyond (Newson, 1966). Physical maturity is achieved at age 30 months at about the

Table 5.33. Litter size in three forms of *Reithrodontomys*. (From Fisler, 1965b, by permission of the editor, *Univ. Calif. Publ. Zool.*)

	Number of embryos in utero (excluding litters with resorbing embryos)								Number litters	Average in utero	Litters with resorbing embryos	total number litters	Average resorbed	Average litter size
	1	2	3	4	5	6	7	8						
R. m. longicaudus	0	1	18	11	8	3	0	0	41	3.85	4	45	0.11	3.82
R. r. raviventris	1	3	6	9	7	0	0	1	27	3.85	5	32	0.29	3.72
R. r. halicoetes	0	0	0	11	3	0	0	0	14	4.21	0	14	0.00	4.21

time of parturition of the sixth litter, however less than 10 percent of the females survive to such an age (Atwood, 1950). Atwood's findings indicated that when food supplies are good animals can mature in four months; when supplies are insufficient it can take 5–6 months. However, Evans (1970) observed that most animals do not mature until eight months. Age of sexual maturity varies with the time of the year; 3–4 months for animals born in the summer to 6–7 months for animals born in the fall (Newson, 1966). Young males born in the early summer can reach sexual maturity in 4–6 months while those born in early winter require 7–8 months. Females reach sexual maturity at 4–6 months during the summer and mild winters but take 5–7 months during severe winters (Evans, 1970).

Females are polyestrus with a sexual cycle of 24–26 days but which may vary from a few days to six weeks and up to 60 days. There is a postpartum heat period 48 hours after the birth of the young and ovulation is induced by copulation. Courtship is common before the female comes into estrus. There is calling, chasing and biting, both in and out of the water. Once the female comes into estrus courtship is generally disregarded or very brief. Both sexes are promiscuous, breeding in and out of the water. Inbreeding is common, especially in marshes where nutria form colonies (Wilson and Dewees, 1962; Newson, 1966; Evans, 1970; Brown, 1975).

While Evans noted that over 85 percent of the females examined in Louisiana and Texas were pregnant, the number of miscarriages of whole litters averaged 32 percent over a four-year period and reached a high of 45 percent in one year. Miscarriage of part of the litter reached another eight percent. It was thus estimated that only 60 percent of the embryos survived to be born (Evans). In contrast, Newson (1966) estimated the loss of implanted embryos before birth from all causes to be 50–60 percent for English nutria.

The litter size seems to vary. Evans (1970) gave a mean of 4.5 with a range of 1–9 in the Gulf States while Newson (1966) presented an annual mean size of 5.3 for English nutria and Brown (1975) observed a mean of 5.7 ± 1.5 with a range of 3–12 for animals in Florida. The first litters tend to be smaller (Atwood, 1950; Evans, 1970) with values given by Newson (1966) for first and subsequent litters at 5.1 ± 0.1 and 5.6 ± 0.1 with ranges of 1–9 and 1–13 respectively. The number of still-births was lower (5.7 percent) in first litters than in later litters (9.4 percent). Newson observed an apparent excess of corpora lutea for the number of embryos. The mean number of implantation sites was 5.4 ± 0.1 for the first litter and 6.2 ± 0.1 for other litters. Losses of dead embryos of 0.3 and 0.6 were in first and subsequent litters or 5.7 and 9.4 percent respectively. He also observed the mean number of implantation sites declined to 4.9 during the winter and had a maximum of 6.7 in July.

Atwood (1950) found that the litter size increased with size and age of the female but decreased from the second to the third and from the fourth to the fifth litter. The increase in litter size from the first to second, third to the fourth, and fifth to sixth was related to size increase of healthy females. Atwood stated that serious food shortages would break up this pattern. A decrease in litter size was primarily related to prenatal mortality which in turn was largely influenced by the food supply. This was illustrated by his observations on a series of 35 females from an area which was 5 percent overgrazed where the mean fetus number was 5.6 (2–11) with evidence of embryo reabsorption at one percent. When 10 percent of the area was over-cropped the mean fetus number for 26 females showed a highly significant decrease to 4.2 (1–9) with a 3.5 percent embryo absorption. Brown (1975) substantiated this view from observation of a population of nutria inhabiting dairy waste holding ponds in the Tampa, Florida area. The mean litter size in the presence of a copious food supply was the largest reported, 5.7 ± 1.1. This suggested to Brown that, under continual breeding in a nonlimiting habitat, the nutria could produce 2.7 litters annually which represents a total maximum annual reproductive potential of 15.5 young per female.

The gestation period is approximately 130 days with a range of 127–139 days (Newson, 1966; Evans, 1970; Brown, 1975). This is approximately the same length of time it takes for the young to become sexually mature, thus bringing them into phase with their mothers and enhancing any periodicity of young being produced (Newson). The eyes are open at birth and the young are fully furred, active, and have an average weight of 234 grams. They ingest solid food immediately or within 24 hours. They can survive if weaned at five days, are normally weaned at five weeks but will suckle for a few weeks longer (Atwood, 1950; Newson, 1966; Evans, 1970).

Lagomorpha. Leporidae. The marsh rabbit, *Sylvilagus palustris,* is found in' the coastal marshes of the Southeastern United States (Hall and Kelson, 1959). It is common in the brackish-water marshes of the Savannah and Altamaha Rivers and occurs in lesser numbers to the fall line. As salinity increases numbers decrease despite a continuous edge cover of *Spartina alterniflora.* It is particularly common where there is sufficient high ground to offer protection during higher tides although its normal habitat is the wet marsh. Although a strong swimmer, it shows a marked reluctance to enter the water. It is nocturnal in its habits, becoming active an hour before dark (Tomkins, 1935, 1955; Blair, 1936).

Blair (1936) considered this rabbit to have a limited home range of 100 to 300 meters in extent. The form or resting space was little more than a bare spot, well hidden and just large enough for the rabbit. It was generally oval in shape with the smaller end accommodating the forefeet.

Blair (1936) recognized that there was a definite breeding season but was unclear about its extent for Florida animals. Females were carrying 3–5 embryos during March, April, and May but no pregnant rabbits were observed from October to mid-March. Tomkins (1935) found the breeding season for Georgia animals to extend from late February into early November. On the other hand Holler (1973) found pregnant females throughout the year in Florida but with a definite cycle. July through November was a period of declining or low reproduction with increasing productivity from December through June.

Holler (1973) observed anestrous females throughout the year. The mean ovulation rate was 3.1 with preimplantation losses of 0.2 ova per litter. Partial litter resorption had a mean of 0.1 embryos per litter with an implantation rate of 2.8 embryos per female. Litter losses were very low (only two females) despite the fact the study area was subjected to considerable habitat disruption during the sugar cane harvest. Tomkins (1935) found 3–5 young were produced and deposited in a nest made of soft grass and rabbit fur fourteen inches across and eight inches deep.

The testicular cycle of *S. palustris* males was similar to but preceded the female breeding cycle by about one month with spermatogenesis evident in at least 60 percent of the males in all months. Juvenile females that became parous showed lower levels of activity than older females: mean ovulation = 2.7; ova loss mean = 0.4; and the implantation rate mean = 2.4. Juvenile males had smaller testes than the adults but the majority of the younger males were sexually active during December through May (Holler, 1973).

The swamp rabbit, *Sylvilagus aquaticus,* is abundant in the flood plains and bottom lands of the Piedmont and Appalachian valley of Georgia as well as the coastal marshes and heavily wooded bottom lands of south central United States (Hall and Kelson, 1959). In the coastal marshes it is abundant where *Phragmites communis, Panicum hemitomum, Spartina patens, Spartina cynosuroides, Scirpus robustus, Typha latifolia,* and *Typha angustifolia* are common. This rabbit is found throughout the marsh, under dense vegetation and briar patches, wherever too much water does not prevent easy travel. It frequently uses the cheniers or wooded ridges that extend out into the Louisiana marshes where its resting places or forms and runways are dry and intruders can be more easily observed. Many old nests of grass and rabbit fur have been found in the marsh, especially evident after the marsh has been burned. Like the marsh rabbit, *Sylvilagus aquaticus* takes to the water reluctantly, swimming slowly but strongly. It prefers to hide under a bush or amid debris with only its nose out of the water (Svihla, 1929; Lowe, 1958; Lowery, 1974).

The home range of the swamp rabbit appears to be considerably larger than that proposed for the marsh rabbit. Furthermore, it appears to vary in size depending on the measuring criteria (Table 5.34). Toll *et al.* (1960) also suggested some behavioral differences between the sexes as reflected in the consistently smaller home ranges for the males (Table 5.34). Lowe (1958) recorded the average size of seven home ranges to be 18.9 acres with a density of 5.6 rabbits per 100 acres of bottom land. Low numbers were attributed to the trampling and grazing by cattle.

Young are born every month of the year (Lowery, 1974) but most reproduction is from late January to the end of September. Hunt (1959) found gravid females every month except September, October, and December. However the appearance of the uteri of females taken during these three months suggested they had been pregnant within the preceding ten days. He recorded the peak of the breeding season to be in late February and March. Working with confined rabbits in Missouri, Sorensen *et al.* (1968) found the earliest litters in mid-February to mid-March. Most final litters were born from late-June to mid-July but few were born into early September. This time span concurs with the observations of Svihla (1929), Lowe (1958), and Toll *et al.* (1960) who reported young from January through September. Toll *et al.* observed that males have a longer breeding season than females with some capable of breeding throughout the year. Sorensen *et al.* (1968) referring to earlier work, suggested that the breeding season may start sooner and last longer among more southern populations. Hunt (1959) suggested the duration of green vegetation in the fall probably is an important factor in the length of the rabbits reproductive activity. Hunt also presented some evidence that the extension of the breeding season into the fall may result from pregnancies among rabbits born earlier in the season. Sorensen *et al.* (1968) observed that under favorable conditions some females can breed when only 23–30 weeks old but most breed after one year of age.

Breeding synchrony is evident and is enhanced by the postparturition estrus which usually lasts less than an hour following birth of the litter. Behavioral stimuli also appear to be important in maintaining such synchrony. Sorensen *et al.* (1968) stated that the gestation period ranges from 35–39 days with 36 and 37 being the most common, while Hunt (1959) using artificial insemination procedures recorded gestation periods of 39–40 days.

Table 5.34. Size of the home range of the swamp rabbit. (Compiled from Toll *et al.*, 1960.)

	Size in Acres	
	Female	Male
Beagle hound round-up	4.1	2.0
"Trap squares"	5.9	4.6
"Minimum home range"	2.1	1.8

Table 5.35. Sizes of swamp rabbit nestling litters, Missouri. Sample size in parentheses. (From Sorensen et al., 1968, by permission of the editor, J. Wildl. Mgmt.)

Litter Sequence Number 1965	Yearling Parent		Other Parent		Mean
	Mean	SE	Mean	SE	
1st	3.25(4)*	0.48	2.33(6)⁺	0.33	2.70(10)
2nd	5.00(3)*⁺	0.58	3.67(6)*⁺	0.42	4.11(9)
3rd	3.00(4)⁺	0.41	2.50(2)*	0.50	2.83(6)
4th	2.50(2)	0.50	2.00(1)	—	2.34(3)
5th	—	—	3.00(1)	—	3.00(1)
1966					
1st	2.00(3)	0.58	3.33(6)	0.33	2.89(9)

* Within each column, paired means not significantly different (t-test, P0.05).
⁺ Within each column, paired means significantly different (t-test, P0.05).

Litter size varies: Svihla (1929) reported 3–5 with an average of 2.7; Lowe (1958) recorded an average of 2.6; Hunt (1959) found a range of 1–5 with a mean of 2.8; Sorensen et al. (1968) established a mode at three. They also determined that second litters were larger than first or subsequent litters (Table 5.35).

Toll et al. (1960) cautioned that the potential litter size can vary depending on how numbers of embryo are counted. A maximum number was achieved by counting corpora lutea of 46 females; average litter size was 3.7 (range 2–6). By counting embryos, 14 pregnant females had an average litter size of 2.8 (range 1–4). In this instance Toll et al. counted only larger embryos in order to eliminate the chances of including resorption of any small embryos. When all embryos of 24 females were counted the average litter count was three. By counting placental scars in seven rabbits the average litter size was 3.7 (range 3–4). Toll et al. suggested that this particular method may give an overestimate of litter size due to inability to distinguish between scars from resorbed embryos and term embryos.

Hunt (1959) suggested that average litter size is highest during the peak of the breeding season and lowest just before the period of least fertility. He also suggested litter size declines with female reserves, the quality and quantity of food supplies, and that females born early in the season who achieve a breeding condition in that same season will produce small litters. Sharp changes in the physical environment can have an impact on the number of embryos carried and subsequent litter size. Conaway et al. (1960) noted a high incidence (twelve out of eighteen) of total litter resorption following a sudden and persistent flooding which resulted in population crowding. There was no evidence of litter resorption before flooding nor in the following year when flooding of the habitat did not occur.

The breeding potential of the swamp rabbit varies considerably; the number of litters per female that survive the breeding season ranged from two to five. Of the females examined by Sorensen *et al.* (1968) eleven (27 percent) had two litters, 46 percent had three litters, 18 percent had four, and 9 percent had five litters. Yearlings averaged more litters (3.5) than older females (2.8).

The young are born furred and blind. Eighteen young weighed 61.4 grams the morning after birth with little variation in size. The eyes open between 5–8 days. They leave the nest permanently between 10–17 days. They nurse after leaving the nest but are completely weaned before the next litter is born (Sorensen *et al.*, 1968).

6
The Tidal Marsh Community

INTRODUCTION

The tidal marsh community is an unusual phenomenon and is therefore a very interesting one. It is found in sheltered areas, in that boundary zone between land and water, situated primarily along the temperate zone coasts throughout the world. The tidal marsh may be flooded at every high tide, or only during extreme conditions such as storms. It may be a fringing marsh a few feet wide or it may be a broad marsh several miles across. Such marshes may be dominated by a single plant species or comprised of many species. Like sand bars and beaches, tidal marshes occur in changeable environments, yet they maintain an integrity both spatially and temporally which clearly differentiates them from other habitats (see Chapter 2 for detailed discussions). Offshore geologic data have revealed the presence of salt-marsh deposits remaining from marshes formed along now submerged coastlines (Dawson, 1855; Mudge, 1858; Shaler, 1886; Kraft, 1971a, 1976; Kraft and Belknap, 1975; Allen, 1978). The assemblages of organisms associated with these deposits are the same or similar to those found in the present day tidal marsh community.

One of the most characteristic features of marshes is the vegetation. Plants growing in the tidal marsh must be able to tolerate daily fluctuations in tidal inundation, salinity, temperature, wetting and drying, and much more. Such environmental characteristics limit the vegetation which can survive in this changeable habitat. Plant species that live in the salt marsh are not necessarily existing under optimal conditions. In fact, many tidal marsh plants grow better under fresh-water conditions. However, because of competition they are found only in the salt-marsh environment. This leads to an assemblage of grasses which is dominated by one or two species in the most saline marshes and an increasingly varied vegetation as the salinity decreases.

The saline marshes of the coastal plain of the eastern United States are characterized by the cord grass, *Spartina alterniflora,* and large expanses of marsh are essentially monospecific stands of this grass. As the elevation increases, *S. alterniflora* gives way to *Distichlis spicata* and *Spartina patens* or *Juncus roemerianus* or *Juncus gerardi*. Other marsh species are rare or only locally abundant. On the west coast *Spartina foliosa* and *Salicornia* sp. are dominants. *S. foliosa* occurs in pure stands on the lower marsh while *Salicornia* is characteristic of higher marsh elevations. In Europe the low marshes are dominated by *Spartina anglica* while *Puccinellia maritima* and *Festuca rubra* are associated with the high marshes. In the arctic *Puccinellia phryganodes* and *Hippuris tetrafolia* dominate the low-marsh areas while various *Carex* spp. are found on the higher marsh elevations.

Salt-marsh vegetation is frequently portrayed as having a zonal distribution of dominant species (Daiber, 1974; Zedler, 1977). However, Zedler found little support for the concept of zones when she examined the composition and structure of southern California salt-marsh vegetation in relation to a one-meter elevation gradient which was correlated with a salinity and inundation gradient. With the exception of *S. foliosa* each species was positively associated with the next, but few species had the same list of positive associates, so that discrete groups were not identified. Zedler's data displayed a progression of dominants in an order of increasing elevation. *Spartina* was the only species that formed a zone and even it graded into dominance by *Salicornia virginica*, *Batis maritima*, and *Salicornia bigelovii*. The evidence indicated that vegetational change was gradual with considerable overlap in species distribution and little evidence of zonation. This is in marked contrast to earlier views as portrayed in Daiber (1974) and should be a subject for reexamination.

The examination of the development, organization, and maintenance of the community has comprised an important component of ecology for many years. Part of this effort during the recent past has focused on the development and use of a variety of diversity indices as a means to better understand community organization and to evaluate the influence of various types of stress on the structure and function of communities. Several forms of species diversity, species richness, equitability or evenness of species distributions, measures of dominance as well as indices of homogeneity and similarity have been developed to assist in these community organization analyses. At times their uses have been misused as statistical tools. The publications of Hulbert, 1971; Hurd and Wolf, 1974; Peet, 1974, 1975; and Pielou, 1977 are suggested to the reader who would seek an evaluation of such indices. An examination of Peet (1975) would suggest that the use of any one of several indices could produce the same results but, as Peet pointed out, a very minor change in sample composition could have a very pronounced impact on the direction the indices would move.

EDAPHIC MICROBIOTIC AND MEIOFAUNAL COMMUNITIES

Microbiotic Community

Grasses are not the only primary producers on the marsh, although they do comprise the bulk of the tidal marsh vegetation. Edaphic algae may be found throughout the marsh with specific algal assemblages associated with the various vegetational zones with distributions, in some cases, related to tidal inundation. However, the principal factors affecting the distribution of edaphic algae are humidity and light (Sullivan, 1974, 1976). At the marsh surface, these parameters are largely regulated by the dominant vegetational cover (Blum, 1968). Other parameters such as temperature, salinity, blue light energy, elevation, and soil moisture can be important in determining the structural organization of edaphic diatom communities (Sullivan, 1977). Therefore it can be expected that edaphic algal assemblages would show variations between different vegetative zones on a tidal marsh.

Sullivan (1971, 1975) found the edaphic diatom community of a tidal marsh to consist of an organization of almost exclusively small pennate diatoms in the upper (less than 3 millimeters) oxygenated layer of the marsh surface. While this generalization is true, the diatom communities of the five habitats sampled (tall *S. alterniflora,* short *S. alterniflora, D. spicata,* bare creek bank, and panne) were quite distinct with regard to community structure. An analysis of variance showed that the mean species diversity and the number of species were greatest for the diatom communities associated with the short *S. alterniflora* and *D. spicata* habitats, intermediate for the bare bank and tall *S. alterniflora,* and lowest for the panne (Table 6.1). These last three communities were significantly different from each other in regard to both parameters of community structure, mean species diversity, and numbers of species over the course of a full year. An analysis of the similarity index (SIMI) for community pairs showed the communities to possess a high degree of dissimilarity (Table 6.2). All but one value is less than 0.5. The lack of similarity is especially pronounced when the panne habitat is included. The highest value of SIMI (0.619) was recorded for a comparison of the short *S. alterniflora* and bare bank habitats. Except for the abundance of *Navicula cincta* and *Navicula salinicola* these communities had little in common. Each community was characterized by different dominant species and a significant proportion of these taxa are restricted species. Those species that were found in more than one community generally had a greater relative abundance in one or more of the communities than others. Sullivan noted that examination of one of the ninety slides prepared could easily identify the habitat sampled by the association of the dominants. It was

Table 6.1. The mean species diversity (H' = bits per individual), number of species (S), and marsh surface salinity (%ₒₒ), and their standard errors (S.E.), and minimum and maximum values for each habitat of Canary Creek salt marsh, Delaware. (From Sullivan, 1975, by permission of the editor, *J. Phycol.*)

	Marsh Habitat				
	TS	DS	D	BB	P
H′					
$\bar{x}$ ± S.E.	4.034 ± .149	4.646 ± .092	4.688 ± .091	3.604 ± .239	2.648 ± .231
minimum–maximum	2.119–4.676	3.923–5.221	3.537–5.196	0.998–4.850	0.466–3.811
S					
$\bar{x}$ ± S.E.	42.5 ± 1.9	48.2 ± 1.9	52.1 ± 1.6	29.8 ± 2.3	22.5 ± 1.7
minimum–maximum	23–53	35–69	43–67	10–46	12–37
Salinity $\bar{x}$ ± S.E.	30.1 ± 1.1	34.1 ± 2.0	32.6 ± 1.2	48.9 ± 7.1	58.8 ± 9.8
minimum–maximum	22–41	16–53	26–44	18–135	30–185

TS = tall *S. alterniflora*; DS = short *S. alterniflora*; D = *D. spicata*; BB = bare bank; P = panne.

Table 6.2. A matrix of similarity values (SIMI) for comparisons of eda-phic diatom communities on a yearly basis from Canary Creek salt marsh, Delaware. All values × 10³. (From Sullivan, 1975, by permission of the editor, *J. Phycol.*)

| | Marsh Habitat (a) | | | |
	DS	D	BB	P
TS	257	238	243	85
DS		477	619	140
D			340	91
BB				192

(a) See Table 6.1 for explanation of code.

concluded that each of the five habitats sampled established an environment that created a particular and easily recognizable edaphic diatom community over an annual cycle.

A multiple regression analysis of the data in this particular study (Sullivan, 1975) signified that the structural differences between the five communities were closely related to differences in temperature and elevation, to an interaction between the edaphic diatoms, and to the presence or absence and kinds of filamentous algae (Table 6.3). However, the analysis also suggested that each variable had approximately the same effect in producing the observed differences in community structure. There was a high degree of correlation between variables suggesting that any discussion of the effect of a single variable must be treated with caution. This same characterization of multiple interactions between environmental parameters, rather than identification of an individual variable in determining community organization, has been expressed by Gray and Bunce (1972) in their analysis of soils determining vegetational groupings.

In a subsequent study Sullivan (1977) examined the structure of the diatom communities associated with short *S. alterniflora* and *S. patens* in the Great Bay marsh near Tuckerton, New Jersey. Both grass species are associated with higher marsh levels with, in this case, *S. patens* at slightly higher elevations. The diatom community associated with *S. patens* was characterized by higher values for the various components of community structure (Table 6.4). Species diversity, numbers of species, and evenness were all higher in the community associated with *S. patens*. The SIMI value of 75 percent indicated these two edaphic diatom communities were fairly similar. The same three taxa were among the five most dominant species in each community. The extent of dissimilarity between the two communities apparently stemmed from the greater number of species associated with the *S. patens* habitat which, in turn, showed a highly significant correlation with the lower surface salinities of that zone.

Table 6.3. Physical and biological characteristics of each habitat in Canary Creek salt marsh, Delaware (24 July 1969–21 July 1970). (From Sullivan, 1975, by permission of the editor, *J. Phycol.*)

	Marsh Habitat				
	TS	DS	D	BB	P
Average T(C), marsh surface, N = 18	13.5	16.2	16.6	16.8	19.9
Average illuminance (klx) reaching marsh surface N = 12	9.2	14.5	10.3	56.8	56.8
Average pH, marsh surface, N = 16	7.66	6.87	7.24	7.43	7.61
% collections with standing water on marsh surface, N = 17	100	70.7	94.2	0.0	64.8
Depth (cm) standing water, 25 August 1969	63.5	21.6	21.9	34.3	9.9
Presence of filamentous algae	Never	blue-greens dominant in summer; greens dominate in winter		Never	blue-greens dominate year round

Table 6.4. The mean species diversity (H'—bits per individual), number of taxa (S), evenness (J') and marsh surface salinity ($^{0}/_{00}$), and their
standard errors (S.E.) and minimum and maximum values, for the edaphic diatom communities associated with dwarf *Spartina alterniflora*
and *S. patens* in Great Bay salt marsh, New Jersey. (From Sullivan, 1977,
by permission of the editor, *Hydrobiologia*)

		S. alterniflora	*S. patens*
H'	$\bar{x} \pm$ S.E.	3.955 ± 0.064	4.825 ± 0.081
	min-max	3.464 − 4.289	4.424 − 5.206
S	$\bar{x} \pm$ S.E.	42.6 ± 2.3	66.4 ± 3.6
	min-max	29 − 52	45 − 85
J'	$\bar{x} \pm$ S.E.	0.729 ± 0.007	0.799 ± 0.008
	min-max	0.687 − 0.767	0.759 − 0.847
Salinity	$\bar{x} \pm$ S.E.	31.2 ± 3.1	11.2 ± 2.7
	min-max	18 − 48	0 − 26

Of the 91 diatom taxa that Sullivan (1977) found, eight were restricted
to the dwarf *S. alterniflora* habitat, 42 were restricted to the *S. patens* locale
and 41 were common to both. Sullivan also observed that the number of
species associated with *S. patens* varied over the year. During the first half of
the year, from January to June, the number of species varied between 64
and 85 with an average of 75.7. For this same period the salinity never rose
above $4^{0}/_{00}$. In the period from July through December, the number of species ranged from 45 to 71 with an average of 57.2 and the salinity never
dropped below $12^{0}/_{00}$. It was during the period of sustained low salinities
that most of the 42 restricted species appeared in the *S. patens* habitat. Sullivan considered them to be opportunistic species, responding to low salinities and quite possibly to the absence of filamentous algae. In reviewing his
earlier work Sullivan (1975) concluded that *S. patens* provides an environment quite different from the other grassy habitats investigated and that reduced salinities enhance the number of diatom taxa which was not seen in
any other grassy environment of salt marsh.

Sullivan (1978) attempted to explain the similarities and divergences
encountered in the community organization of the diatom flora of several
geographically distinct salt marshes. Such comparisons were derived from
work described above and more recent work in Graveline Bay Marsh, Mississippi (Sullivan, 1978). A total of 119 taxa were recognized as comprising
the edaphic diatom flora associated with five pure stands of spermatophytes
located in this particular marsh: *S. alternifora, S. patens, Scirpus olneyi, D.
spicata,* and *J. roemerianus.* Diatom taxa restricted to a specific spermatophyte habitat numbered seven; and five of these were associated with the
sediments beneath *D. spicata,* accounting for 17.2 percent of all the

individuals counted. One species each was restricted to *S. patens* and *J. roemerianus*. The single most abundant diatom was *Navicula tripunctata,* which accounted for 21.5 percent of all individuals counted in this study. Community diversity (H′) and number of taxa in a sample (S) were highest in the *D. spicata* and *S. patens* habitats, lowest under the *S. alterniflora* and *J. roemerianus* canopies and intermediate under the *S. olneyi* screen. H′ ranged from 3.348 to 4.246 and S varied from 35.3 to 43.5. SIMI values for community comparisons ranged from 0.242 to 0.976. Twenty-seven of the 40 SIMI values were greater than 0.500 indicating that in general these communities were more similar than divergent. Sullivan decided the community pairs structurally most similar were *S. olneyi* and *J. roemerianus,* and *S. olneyi* and *S. alterniflora;* while the most dissimilar were *D. spicata* and *S. alterniflora, D. spicata* and *S. patens,* and *J. roemerianus* and *S. patens.* Structural differences among the diatom communities associated with the five spermatophyte stands were significantly related to far red light energy, soil moisture, ammonia nitrogen, elevation, and the seasons. The height of the canopy may also play a significant role in determining the structure of the diatom community.

As is apparent from the above presentations, Sullivan (1978) found structural differences and similarities among the diatom communities within and between salt marshes. While Sullivan identified 119 taxa in the Mississippi marsh against the 104 and 91 taxa encountered in the Delaware and New Jersey marshes respectively (Sullivan, 1975; 1977) he attributed the differences to the number of grassy habitats sampled (i.e., five in Mississippi, three in Delaware and two in New Jersey). He considered the numbers of taxa to be low compared to fresh-water habitats and attributed such numbers to the more variable conditions found in tidal salt marshes. This is emphasized as one recalls that the increase in the average number of taxa rose from 57.2 to 75.2 when the salinity declined from above $12^0/_{00}$ to below $4^0/_{00}$ under the *S. patens* canopy in New Jersey (Sullivan, 1977).

The greater majority of the dominant taxa have a well developed raphe and Sullivan considered this locomotor system to be important in a habitat where sediment accumulation is continuous and where microhabitats may exist. This was used to explain the dominance of the genera *Navicula* and *Nitzschia* in salt marshes. The dominant taxa were common to the various marshes examined and in fact, 100 of the 119 taxa collected in Mississippi were common to Delaware and/or New Jersey marshes.

In each assemblage, the most common genus of diatoms was far more common than any others. The relative abundance of these diatoms suggests there are a few dominant genera and a few subordinate genera which are adapted to a special portion of the environment. Such distributions are characteristic of a rigorous environment (Whittaker, 1965). This suggested to Sullivan there may be a single basic edaphic diatom community native to Atlantic and Gulf coast salt marshes and that certain diatom taxa may be common to all tidal salt marshes. On the other hand, the presence of restricted species, those species associated with a single spermatophyte cover, indicates there are significant differences among the edaphic habitats under the various grassy canopies within a particular marsh.

While there were statistical differences displayed within each of the diversity indices H' and S, the values were relatively high and there was considerable overlap in those values for the Delaware, New Jersey, and Mississippi marshes. The latter marsh tended to be slightly less diverse than those of the Atlantic coast. In addition the diatom communities under the *D. spicata* and *S. patens* canopies were consistently more diverse in a particular marsh. Sullivan posed an interesting question when he called attention to the fact that the edaphic marsh diatoms had a relatively high diversity which was in sharp contrast to the low diversity of the spermatophyte cover. He suggested that the marsh sediments do not present a stressful environment to well-adapted edaphic diatoms, and that the highly dynamic nature of the marsh sediments probably creates heterogeneous sediment conditions where various microniches can become established. This is supported by data indicating that various environmental parameters have a significant influence on the diatom community structure. This could preclude any one diatom species from completely dominating the community, thus producing relatively high H' values. Such diversity values and associated taxonomic data along with variable SIMI values for Mississippi, Delaware, and New Jersey marshes establish the notion that no two edaphic diatom communities have a statistically identical structure. The presence of marked similarities and dissimilarities among diatom communities within and between marshes suggested to Sullivan that we have only a preliminary understanding of the biotic and abiotic components of the salt-marsh system.

Any man-induced changes to the surface of the marsh can cause a depression of diatom community diversity as well as a reduction in the number of species. The addition of nitrogen fertilizer in the form of sewage sludge or urea after one summer to a Cape Cod, Massachusetts marsh lowered the species diversity from that of control plots, and fewer species made up a greater proportion of the total algal population. One diatom, *Navicula salinarum,* encompassed over 40 percent of the population in the plot receiving a high level of fertilization (25.2 $gm/m^2/wk$ of sewage sludge containing 10% N) as compared to 10 percent in the control. The pattern was the same after three years of fertilizer additions: there were fewer rare species or decreased species richness, and a decreased evenness with the presence of unusually

Table 6.5. The Shannon-Weaver index of diversity, H′ ($\bar{x} \pm$ S.E.) of benthic algae in replicate plots treated with a high level (HF) and a low level (LF) of sewage sludge and urea (U) inside and outside of the fertilized plots. The differences in H′ between treatment and controls is statistically significant (P = 0.01). (From Van Raalte *et al.*, 1976, by permission of the editor, *Water Research*)

Treatment	Inside	Outside
HF	3.14 ± 0.11	4.08 ± 0.18
LF	3.35 ± 0.10	3.82 ± 0.01
U	3.39 ± 0.06	3.83 ± 0.16

abundant species (Table 6.5). *N. salinarum* was still the most abundant species comprising about 20 percent of the individuals in the treated plots but only 5 percent in the controls (Van Raalte *et al.*, 1976).

Sullivan (1976) examined the long-term effects of manipulating nutrient enrichment and light intensity on the diatom community associated with a pure stand of dwarf *S. alterniflora* in the Canary Creek marsh, Delaware. The experimental design called for four levels of light intensity in conjunction with three nutrient conditions for a total of twelve treatments. The four areas were maintained as follows: (1) *Spartina* was clipped regularly, exposing the marsh surface to full light intensity; (2) appropriate screening was suspended above the *Spartina* to reduce light intensity by 30 percent; (3) shading was increased to 60 percent; (4) no manipulation. Each light treatment was paired with three separate nutrient conditions defined as follows: (1) nitrogen as NH_4NO_3 at the rate of 20 gms $N/m^2/month$; (2) phosphorus as super phosphate $(CaH_4(PO_4)_2)$ at the rate of 3 gms $P/m^2/month$; (3) no nutrient additions.

Sullivan found that clipping or light reduction by 30 percent irrespective of nutrient conditions reduced species diversity and the numbers of species. Clipping had the greatest negative effect. Phosphorus additions to the natural marsh caused a decrease in both diversity and the number of species while nitrogen enrichment significantly reduced the number of taxa. A total of 105 taxa were enumerated and 95 were more or less common to all twelve study plots. Ten had restricted distributions and eight were found only in the clipped areas. Five of those eight were normally found in the algal mats associated with the salt pannes (Sullivan, 1975).

When Sullivan (1976) examined the relative abundances of the 19 most common diatom taxa, he found each taxon responded to certain experimental designs at certain times. He could not group those taxa into similar response groups due to the statistical significance of interaction terms. One of those abundant species was *N. salinarum* which was present in all five habitats sampled (Sullivan, 1975). It reacted positively to both nitrogen and

Table 6.6. Matrix of similarity values (SIMI) comparing edaphic diatom communities established in response to the light intensity gradient on a yearly basis (N-0 = natural marsh; 30-0 = 30% shaded; 60-0 = 60% shaded; C-0 = clipped marsh; -0 = no nutrient additions). Values $\times 10^3$. (From Sullivan, 1976, by permission of the editor, *J. Phycol.*)

	30-0	60-0	C-0
N–0	922	887	837
30–0		982	734
60–0			689

phosphorus enrichment at various times and the greatest response was at the highest light intensities found in the clipped areas.

Table 6.6 gives the SIMI values for the four diatom communities established in response to light intensity without any nutrient manipulation. The two shaded communities had the highest similarity (0.982) while the greatest dissimilarity existed between the two communities with the greatest difference in light intensity. When Sullivan compared the similarity responses of these experimental plots to his earlier work (Table 6.7), he found the similarity values for comparisons with the tall *S. alterniflora* and *D. spicata* to be almost the same, especially when the natural marsh, 30–0 and 60–0 sites were compared. Sullivan interpreted this to mean that shading did not produce a shift in edaphic diatom community structure towards that associated with the diatom communities found under the *D. spicata* or tall *S. alterniflora* cover. However, the values related to the panne habitat indicated that, by clipping the short *S. alterniflora*, there was a shift in the diatom community toward that found with the algal mats of salt pannes.

From these marsh surface manipulations Sullivan (1976) concluded

Table 6.7. Matrix of similarity values (SIMI) comparing edaphic diatom communities established in response to the light intensity gradient in the present study with those of Sullivan (1975) on a yearly basis (abbreviations as in Table 6.6). Values $\times 10^3$. (From Sullivan, 1976, by permission of the editor, *J. Phycol.*)

	1969–1970	1971–1972			
	D.S.[1]	N-0	30-0	60-0	C-0
Dwarf *Spartina*	1000	789	825	862	645
Distichlis	477	527	527	511	416
Tall *Spartina*	257	272	247	239	233
Panne	140	179	144	149	323

1. D.S. = 1969–70 dwarf *Spartina* edaphic diatom community.

that regulation of light intensity by the dominant grasses of Canary Creek marsh was not responsible for the differences he had observed earlier (1975) in their associated diatom communities. On the other hand, exposing the diatom community to full sunlight by clipping away the grass canopy caused a shift toward the diatom community associated with the salt panne (Sullivan, 1976, 1979) resulting in a decrease in species diversity (H') and the number of taxa (S) in all seasons except winter. Few species displayed an even distribution as expressed by the niche breadth statistic. The high number of low niche values suggested the treatments had significant spatial and temporal effects on the distribution of the majority of the taxa. Such a shift was apparently caused by the great stimulatory effect of light on the filamentous green and blue-green algae in such exposed pannes in a Delaware marsh where short *S. alterniflora* had been clipped (Sullivan, 1976). However, when the *D. spicata* canopy was removed by clipping in a Mississippi marsh, there was no corresponding increase in filamentous algae, a factor that Sullivan (1979) was not able to explain. He postulated that factors other than light intensity and nitrogen supplies were limiting the development of filamentous algae on this particular Mississippi marsh. Preliminary observations by Lee *et al.* (1975) demonstrated changes in experimental laboratory diatom community structure affected by the presence of various metallic ions. A second explanation for such a shift might be increased salinity caused by greater dessication rates resulting from loss of the protective grass canopy.

Nitrogen enrichment in the Mississippi marsh had more positive than negative impacts on community organization as expressed by H' and S, and there was no elimination of taxa from the community (Sullivan, 1979). These results were just the opposite from earlier observations reported by Sullivan (1976) and Van Raalte *et al.* (1976). Sullivan (1979) noted that many diatom species responded to clipping and nitrogen enrichment as in his earlier work. However, a number of species such as *Navicula salinicola, N. binodulosa,* and *N. tripunctata* did not give consistent results when comparing their responses to clipping and nitrogen enrichment in a Delaware and a Mississippi marsh. This suggested these diatom species respond to some other environmental parameters.

Both Sullivan (1976, 1979) and Van Raalte *et al.* (1976) commented that the depression of the diatom community structure associated with the marsh surface could be used as an indicator of marsh eutrophication. Sullivan (1979) identified *Nitzschia gandersheimiensis* and *Nitzschia perversa* as having the potential as bioindicator organisms in the Mississippi marsh. Natural light intensity and nitrogen enrichment greatly stimulated the growth of *N. perversa* in the spring and summer while high light intensity caused by clipping, in conjunction with nitrogen enrichment, markedly increased the relative abundance of *N. gandersheimiensis* from fall through the spring. Sullivan did add the caution that monitoring would have to be done on a continuing basis to evaluate changes. This would be especially true for communities where the species have short life spans. Hedgepeth (1973) and Lee *et al.* (1975) warned that, as a single index of a coupled system, species diversity has merit only if cautiously interpreted or used with other indices. Gannon and Stemberger (1978) observed that valuable information may be lost when using simple indices such as species diversity where various species involved become unimportant, and they advocated approaches designed to retain maximal information about species by regarding community composition as the relative abundance of species within the community. In another context, while examining a community with several trophic levels, Hurd and Wolf (1974) suggested it may be more appropriate to examine trophic complexity more closely on the basis of known feeding relationships within a community rather than to use biotic diversity as a predictive index of stability.

Sullivan (1979) noted that low niche breadth values were characteristic of a number of diatom species. Dr. Lee and associates (Lee, 1974; Lee *et al.,* 1972; Lee *et al.,* 1975) called attention to the patchy distribution of foraminiferal species. Patchiness was considered to be the result of diversified habitats which reduced competition. These workers noted that species diversity of Foraminifera was found to be closely correlated to temperature differences caused by the flow patterns of small rivulets on the marsh surface.

Lee and associates (loc. cit.) identified a pronounced linkage between species of Foraminifera and algal and bacterial populations. Lee *et al.* (1969) observed that patches of decaying *Enteromorpha* had the greatest standing crop of Foraminifera and a low species diversity (0.58) while young green growth of *Enteromorpha* had a higher diversity (0.94). Lee and Muller (1973) and Lee (1974), while describing their tracer feeding studies, reported Foraminifera to be quite selective in their feeding habits. In general, selected species of diatoms, bacteria, and chlorophytes were eaten in great quantities while most species of bacteria, cyanophytes, dinoflagellates, and chyrsophytes were not consumed. No doubt such feeding habits coupled with abiotic factors would enhance the patchy distribution of the Foraminifera and the pronounced occurrence of blooms.

Lee *et al.* (1972) noted that approximately 50 percent of samples collected during the summers of 1966–1968 had some Foraminifera: the 30 bloom samples of 1966 and 1968 contained 60 percent of all the Foraminifera collected for the year; those collected during the 1967 season comprised 80 percent. Blooms accounted for 97–98 percent of the total Foraminifera collected throughout the year. Species diversity values for such blooms ranged from 0.38 to 1.12. *Ammonia beccarii* was dominate in 18 of these blooms with *Allogromia laticollaris, Protelphidium tisburyense,* and *Elphi-dium incertum* each dominant in three blooms. These data support the contention that low diversity is a characteristic feature of foraminiferal assemblages of all tidal marshes. In hyposaline and normal marine marshes the index of diversity was generally well below a value of 2. The index was usually below 3 with an occasional value above 4 and 5 for hypersaline marshes (Murray, 1973). This apparent trend is opposite to that portrayed earlier.

While species diversity is low for tidal marsh foraminiferal assemblages such diversity is purported to provide stability and enhance a high level of productivity in the microbial and microfaunal assemblages of the tidal marsh. This is presumably made possible by the opportunistic nature of these assemblages and their high level of adaptability to the very rapidly changing food webs in the marsh edaphic community (Lee and Muller, 1973). This relation between stability and productivity runs counter to the traditional theory that states there is an inverse relation between the two (Margalef, 1963; Odum, 1969). However, Hurd *et al.* (1971) found such a negative relation to hold only for the producer trophic level.

Meiofaunal Community

The organization and structure of the meiofaunal community of the salt marsh has only very recently begun to receive attention and most of this effort has been directed toward the copepods. Coull and Vernberg (1975) and Coull and Fleeger (1977) have reported that the Copepoda associated with a South Carolina subtidal sand habitat were primarily interstitial forms while those found at mud sites were largely burrowing species. Coull and Vernberg (1975) found only 1–3 percent of the copepod fauna to be similar for the two habitats. Those that were similar were more mobile taxa: semipelagic or associated with free-floating algae. Coull and Fleeger (1977) and Fleeger (1980) found only one species common to both sand and mud habitats. Three species, *Microarthridion littorale, Enhydrosoma propinquum,* and *Diarthrodes aedigeus* were common to both the subtidal mud and low-marsh mud habitats. The intertidal mud station samples examined by Coull and Fleeger contained four distinct groups: winter (January–March), spring (March–June), summer (July–September), and fall (September–December). The mud fauna had a varying community abundance and diversity which did not significantly vary over the three-year study period. Diversity was controlled by a marked seasonal cycling which was evident on a regular basis throughout the study. In contrast, the sand community was much less distinct with no cyclic, repeatable pattern. Diversity in the sand community decreased significantly with time and was correlated to an increasing abundance trend. Seasonality was put forward by Coull and Fleeger (1977) to explain many of the differences between the two sites.

Species persistence and community persistence can be used to evaluate community organization. Although there was a great deal of seasonality in the abundance of individual species at the mud station, the sand habitat was less persistent in terms of species fluctuations over the three years of study. This was attributed by Coull and Fleeger (1977) to the cyclic stability of the species groups at the mud station from year to year. When compared over the three years both sites had approximately the same level of community persistence. This was attributed to the yearly repeatable cycling of species at the mud site which would tend to raise similarity values while the irregular community fluctuations at the sand site would lower similarity values.

Coull and Fleeger (1977) had not expected to find diversity equivalence in such different habitats. The fact that values were the same was attributed to varying affects of parameters such as substrate and seasonality of reproductive activity among the various species. For these reasons they cautioned against considering only diversity indices to provide insights into community dynamics. There is continued need to know the biology of the various species involved and their interactions with each other.

In a nearby South Carolina low-marsh site associated with *S. alterniflora,* Fleeger (1980) found copepod numbers ranged from 75 to 620/10 cm^2 throughout the year. Densities were lowest in the winter-early spring with a maximum in the fall and a secondary peak for adults in April. The nauplii showed similar trends but with a peak in March. Fleeger found 21 species, eight of which made up 97 percent of the copepod fauna.

There were two patterns of abundance: *E. propinquum, M. littorale, Stenhelia(D.) bifidia,* and *Pseudostenhelia wellsi* peaked in September (*E. propinquum* was present in high numbers all year except January and February); the other four species *D. aedigeus, Robertsonia propinqua, Cletocamptus* sp., and *Paronychocamptus wilsoni* had their lowest numbers in the summer, June-September (Fleeger, 1980). At an adjacent high-marsh site Bell (1979) found that four harpacticoid copepods comprised 78 percent of the copepod assemblage: *S.(D.) bifidia* (48 percent), *Schizopera knabeni* (11.1 percent), *M. littorale* (9.8 percent), and *E. propinquum* (9.1 percent). Bell found *S.(D.) bifidia* had its maximum density in the fall while the other three displayed variable seasonal patterns of abundance.

In contrast to the four groupings noted by Coull and Fleeger (1977) at an intertidal marsh mud site Fleeger (1980) observed three distinct temporal groupings at a low-marsh site. The winter collection consisted of four dominant species comprising 70 percent of the copepod fauna. *D. aedigeus* was most common while *E. propinquum* had its lowest densities. It was a time of the lowest level of dominance with the highest levels of H' and J' for the year. A second group of spring and late-fall collections displayed peaks in numbers of *Cletocamptus* sp., *P. wilsoni,* and *R. propinqua. E. propinquum* dominated the collections making up 53.9 percent of the copepods. Diversity values were intermediate, ranging from 1.2–1.6. Evenness was also intermediate. The third group of *M. littorale, E. propinquum,* and *S.(D.) bifidia* made up 91 percent of the copepod fauna in July through September and 83 percent for the whole year. H' and J' values were highest in July for this group when numbers for each species were nearly equal. H' and J' declined in September when *M. littorale* became numerically dominant. The monthly means over the year for H', J' and numbers of species were 1.50, 0.63, and 11.2 respectively. Examining earlier work Fleeger (1980) found no significant differences for H', J' and numbers of species for the low marsh he worked on and the subtidal sand and mud sites of prior investigations.

Bell (1979), in her high-marsh site, found seasonal fluctuations in copepod community diversity values with H' lowest in September and highest values in the winter similar to Fleeger (1980). Her yearly average was slightly higher at 1.61. At this high-marsh site J' values strongly reflected the dominance of *S.(D.) bifidia* with the lowest values in the fall and a yearly average of 0.66 similar to the low marsh. Bell found no consistent seasonal trends for numbers of species, observing an average of 11.5.

Fleeger (1980) found strong evidence of horizontal positioning among the species during the summer and fall. *M. littorale* had a near random distribution, *E. propinquum* was slightly aggregated and the aggregation decreased when densities were highest. *S. (D.) bifidia* was the most aggregated species among the three dominants and aggregations were enhanced with increased densities. Fleeger made a number of suggestions to explain this horizontal partitioning of species, but there was no strong evidence to support any one. He considered predation and distribution to be the most probable reasons.

MACROMETAZOAN INVERTEBRATE COMMUNITIES

Christian *et al.* (1978) suggested the soil microbial community is relatively "unlinked" to the macrophytic plant growth. This "unlinking" is alleged to be responsible for the observed resistance to change by the microbial community when the marsh is subjected to disarrangement. The evidence suggests that such microbial communities are limited less by nutrition than by some physiochemical space limitation.

A number of the components of the tidal marsh community appear to be markedly influenced by abiotic factors. Phleger (1970) called attention to the great variation in parameters known to affect the occurrence and development of foraminiferal populations. Luxton (1967b) suggested that egg-laying species of Acarina are controlled primarily by the mechanical effects of the tides while pH is an important regulating factor for viviparous species. The distribution of fiddler crabs is largely influenced by the mechanical nature of the substrate (Teal, 1958). Dexter (1947) described a rhythmical change in the composition and the dynamics of marine communities associated with a tidal inlet. He observed the organization and interactions between intertidal communities to be very different at low and high periods with the transformation taking place gradually with the ebb and flow of the tide. He also noted that narrow ecotones exist between the major communities with an overlapping of characteristic species at the position of spring low-water or spring high-water margins. An intermingling of communities results from the uneven distribution of various kinds of substrate.

Insecta

The assemblage of insects among the various vegetational zones of the marsh is determined largely by the nature and amount of shelter available as well as by the food supply. The length of submergence of the vegetation does not limit the total size of the insect aggregations. Davis and Gray (1966) found both *Distichlis* and *Juncus* had short hydroperiods but many more insects were associated with *Distichlis. S. alterniflora* and *Spartina-Salicornia-Limonium,* which are frequently flooded, have more insects than *S. patens* which is flooded only during spring or storm tides. A greater variety of insects is associated with vegetation possessing a greater structural variation.

The analysis of salt marsh insect trophic diversity by Cameron (1972) called attention to two factors that can enhance species diversity in a tidal marsh: food partitioning and omnivory, and allogenic parameters. Various workers (Odum and Smalley, 1959; Odum and Heald, 1975; also see Chapter 4, Food and Feeding) have described the temporal partitioning of the same source of primary production by herbivores and detritivores. Chapter 2 on Zonation and Distribution is devoted to a discussion of allogenic or forcing factors that mold and direct the components of the salt-marsh community.

By working with the *Spartina foliosa* and *Salicornia pacifica* communities of a California salt-marsh community, Cameron (1972) has demonstrated a distinct seasonal pattern to the trophic diversity of both communities, although the amplitude was slightly greater in the *Salicornia* community. The total annual insect diversity was mirrored by the herbivore diversity. There was a peak in herbivore diversity during the summer and a low in the winter with a corresponding positive correlation with above-ground primary production. Herbivore diversity increased following spring productional increases with a 2–3 week lag. A similar lag in decreasing diversity followed decreases in production at the end of the growing season. A lag was also noted between litter accumulations and saprovore diversity changes with a peak in diversity occurring during the winter months. The abundance of predacious species was considerably lower in the *Salicornia* than among the *Spartina* plants. There was no significant correlation between predator trophic diversity and saprovore diversity in both communities and herbivore trophic diversity in the *Salicornia* community. There was a significant correlation between predator diversity and saprovore-herbivore diversity which was attributed to the presence of noninsect predators. Cameron (1972) found spiders to be abundant throughout the year with numbers increasing with the spring herbivore and winter saprovore diversity increases.

Cameron (1972) noted that the seasonal changes in herbivore and saprovore diversities was not due to changes in abundance of individuals per species but to an addition or subtraction of species in response to resource availability. Predacious species diversity was, in part, due to changes in species richness but also to changes in numbers of individuals per species or prey abundance, suggesting that they are host-specific.

Resource availability plays a role in two ways. First, as primary production develops in the spring, there is an increase in plant structural complexity. This is especially true for *Spartina* where more of the plant is edible and there is an enhancement of growth of stems, long flat leaves that intertwine with the leaves of adjoining plants, and terminal flower clusters. All of these increase the number of places for various insect species to reside (Davis and Gray, 1966; Cameron, 1972). In contrast, Cameron observed that *Salicornia* has a succulent, jointed stem with reduced leaves and flowers, providing fewer microhabitats. Structural complexity influences the numbers of insect species associated with various plant species. This same kind of pattern was identified for spider distributions wherein Barnes (1953) recorded an increase in the number of spider species in a progression from the *Spartina* marsh to the adjoining maritime forest community.

Primary production in the spring with its concomitant increase in biomass has a positive and significant correlation with herbivore diversity and later with an increase in saprovore diversity. Two kinds of species are involved in these changes in diversity. Cameron (1972) identified persistent species as those species that are present as adults in the salt marsh during the entire year. Their abundance fluctuates seasonally: herbivores are most evident during the growing season while saprovores are most evident with litter accumulation. Seasonal species are evident as adult herbivores only during the growing season or as adult saprovores during periods of litter accentuation. These seasonal species are responsible for the increase in diversity or richness with an expansion of the resource. Such species do not emigrate from other habitats but originate within the marsh.

Cameron (1972) suggested and discussed several strategies that would accommodate the coexistence of persistent and seasonal species. One strategy involved overlapping niches wherein the persistent species would have generalized food requirements and the seasonal species would have generalized or specialized food habits. Cameron reasoned that such a pattern would cause an overlap of food requirements during the productive season which in turn would enhance competition and lead to a lower diversity. However, just the opposite, a higher trophic diversity, was observed.

A second strategy suggested that seasonal species would have physiological requirements along some environmental gradient. Such gradients would be most evident during the growing season and would have the greatest effect on the herbivores. A corollary to this would be that the gradient would be at a minimum when the vegetation was dead and litter was accumulating. However, Cameron argued that such gradients could not exist readily and would be overwhelmed by the regular tidal inundation.

Cameron concluded that the only strategy which appeared feasible is that both persistent and seasonal species have specialized food requirements resulting in resource partitioning. He supported this by indirect evidence that identified both persistent and seasonal species having feeding specialization imposed by feeding appendage morphology. He found the seasonal herbivores in the upper portions of the plants and the persistent herbivores only in the lower one-third of the plants. He argued that such spatial separation was cause enough to reject the overlapping niche strategy. Cameron also found that 30–40 percent of the seasonal herbivores were evident during a nine-week period of flowering when structural complexity would be at its greatest.

Allogenic factors appear to work at two levels in determining species distribution and richness. Cameron (1972) found a positive correlation between the standing crop of green plant parts and temperature. There was a positive correlation between herbivore diversity and vapor pressure deficit. In contrast, saprovores responded negatively to temperature, and to vapor pressure deficits. It is, however, conceivable that these saprovores may have responded to accumulated quantities of litter during the winter months rather than declining temperatures. Temperature-vapor pressure gradients would be enhanced during the growing season and would be related to increased biomass and structural complexity.

Tidal inundation has an effect on vertical zonation of vegetation while salinity and osmotic problems have an influence across a marsh surface due to evaporation in the summer and the interaction between tidal inundation and rain fall. Such parameters will determine plant zonations which in turn have a profound influence on animal distributions (See Chapter 2, Zonation and Distribution).

Other Invertebrates

MacDonald (1969b) examined the molluscan fauna associated with the *Spartina-Salicornia* salt marshes and related tidal creeks of the North American Pacific coast. He found each to have a distinctive community organization with one or two widely distributed and very abundant species. The remaining species were represented by small numbers of patchily distributed individuals. This organization remained fairly uniform between different sites within a faunal province, based on the identity and numbers of species present and their relative abundance and size frequency. The creek faunas contained more species and had a more variable species composition than did the marsh faunas. This may reflect a greater opportunity for the creek faunas to be enhanced by immigration of species from elsewhere as well as species habits and relation to sediments. The marsh species all had the same feeding type (i.e., raspers, feeding on algae and detritus), while the creek types included ciliary suspension feeders, deposit feeders, and predators in addition to the rasping type of feeder. The marsh species were all epifaunal in distribution and thus independent of the substrate. These marsh faunal groups were very uniform; five species made up 96.9 percent of the samples. The remaining 3.1 percent were frequently found in the marsh creeks. The creek faunas included a number (83.4 percent) of infaunal species and thus reacted to sediment type. Within the creek environment, MacDonald (1969b) found the number of types of niches occupied by the molluscan fauna did not change with latitude, although the specific types did (infaunal and epifaunal species, feeding types). The median value of 0.53 for species diversity as derived by MacDonald's use of the Simpson diversity index and the overlap between the 95 percent confidence levels suggested that in most cases the faunal diversity did not differ significantly between sites. Along with this the numbers of mollusc species found in the faunas of successively larger salt marshes or tidal creeks were not significantly different. This suggested to MacDonald that increases in species diversity obtained from increasingly larger regional samples could reflect an increase in the variety of habitats within the region rather than an enrichment of faunas.

Working on a much smaller geographic scale, Subrahmanyam *et al.* (1976) described the community organization of the macroinvertebrates of two *Juncus roemerianus* marshes of the Gulf coast of northern Florida. They found the pooled mean density, from samples taken from both high- and low-marsh stations in these two marshes, showed a bimodal distribution with a large peak from February through April and a second smaller peak in September. These density peaks in the early spring and fall may have been due to more species and the increased density of a few. The greatest density ($578/m^2$) occurred in the late winter and the lowest ($375/m^2$) in the summer. The low-marsh zones had higher densities than the high marsh but the mean densities were not significantly different.

Species that contributed the most to the elevated densities were different in the two marsh zones at each locality. Forty-eight species were collected. Of these, 40 were collected at St. Mark's and 63 percent were common to the upper and lower marsh. Forty-three species were taken at Wakulla and 53 percent were common to the upper and lower marsh. At both locations the lower marsh had significantly more species than upper marsh sites. Subrahmanyam *et al.* (1976) attributed this to the proximity of the low marsh to tidal creeks and the estuary and to tidal flooding. They also recognized species adaptability to changing conditions as a factor. The fact that the monthly densities did not fluctuate markedly suggested there was a fairly stable population throughout the year. Grazing by various fish species was proffered as an explanation for lower summer densities.

The Homogeneity Index (HI) denotes a measure of the numerical abundance of species in percentages of common species between two samples and considers the relative density of species in the compared samples. Even though some species are common to two sites their relative abundance must be similar to produce a high HI. A low HI is a reflection of a low number of common species and a low density of common species in one zone. Subrahmanyam *et al.* (1976) found the HI varied within 33–38 percent between marsh zones indicating that one-third of the densities at any two zones was made up of the same species. The HI for the low-marsh zone was highest (49 percent) in the summer and lowest (22 percent) in the winter. High-marsh zones had a low homogeneity (16 percent) in the winter and a maximum (43 percent) in the fall. Even though the upper and lower marsh zones of the two areas were physically similar, species homogeneity was low. Based on this index, all four marsh zones had a different community structure with reference to common species and their relative densities each month.

Species diversity (H') showed significant seasonal variations with peaks in the spring and the fall. Such diversity levels coincided with peaks in density and were significantly different between marsh zones. The overall H' of 2.49 was reported by Subrahmanyam *et al.* (1976) to be higher than earlier work they had reviewed. The H' value was higher in the low-marsh zone indicating a richer and more diverse community which they attributed to an easier access to tidal flooding.

The Biological Index (BI) is a function of the frequency of occurrence and relative density of species in each sample. Species that occur in reasonable numbers through a major part of the year will have a high rank while sporadic species will have a lower rank. By using the BI to evaluate biological importance, Subrahmanyam *et al.* (1976) found the snail, *Littorina irrorata,* and the isopod, *Cyathura polita,* to be the two top ranked species in both zones of both marshes. A polychaete, *Scoloplos fragilis,* also ranked high while the remaining species and their rank varied in each zone and locality (Table 6.8). Using biomass instead of density Subrahmanyam *et al.* found little difference in species rank (Table 6.9). *Littorina* made up 81 percent of the biomass, therefore total seasonal biomass reflected changes in the biomass of *Littorina.* Peak biomass levels occurred from May through September when the mean density was the lowest. There was a conspicuous pattern to the seasonal succession of organism densities for a few species of the marsh fauna. Polychaetes were the most abundant resident species and successional changes were the most evident. *S. fragilis* was most common in all zones but was replaced by *Meanthes succinea* in the low marshes in the fall. Other species replaced *S. fragilis* during the summer in the upper marsh zones.

By evaluating the biological importance through a ranking of relative abundance and frequency of occurrence, Subrahmanyam *et al.* (1976) characterized those species associated with North Florida *Juncus* marshes as abundant, scarce, or rare (Table 6.10). By such a ranking and the use of the BI they identified such marshes as *Littorina-Cyathura*-tanaidacean communities with increasing emphasis on molluscs as one proceeded from the water's edge toward the upland (Figure 6.1). They concluded that such a community structure is continually shaped by the appearance of species through immigration or by redistribution within the marsh to seek better ecological conditions, as well as by the increased density of resident species as a function of breeding activities and recruitment.

The recent interest in the use of dredge spoil material for marsh development and reclamation (Seneca, 1974; Garbisch *et al.,* 1975; Seneca *et al.,* 1975) has provided an opportunity to evaluate community development on a marsh surface. One such opportunity has been explored by Cammen (1976) who compared the macroinvertebrate community on two separate spoil piles each of which had an adjacent natural marsh.

The first (Drum Inlet, N.C.) was a high salinity site which had been planted with *S. alterniflora* for approximately one year: the second (Snow's Cut) was a brackish area on which *Spartina* had been planted approximately two years earlier.

Cammen found the Bare (unplanted) and Planted spoil sites at Drum Inlet to be quite similar in three of the four community attributes measured (biomass, number of taxa per sample, and species diversity). This suggested

Table 6.8. Rankings (R), frequency of occurrence (F/12), and Biological Index values (BI), of the 10 most important species of macroinvertebrates in the two marsh zones of St. Marks and Wakulla based on densities/m² in trap samples. (From Subrahmanyam et al., 1976, by permission of the editor, *Bull. Mar. Sci.*)

Species	WLM R	F/12	BI	SLM R	F/12	BI	WUM R	F/12	BI	SUM R	F/12	BI
Littorina irrorata	1	12	96	1	12	104	1	10	89	2	12	92
Cyathura polita	2	10	86	2	11	81	2	9	75	1	11	101
Apseudes sp.	3	8	70	7	5	41	7	4	33	—	—	—
Scoloplos fragilis	4	6	57	4	8	57	6	5	39	4	8	63
Sesarma reticulatum	5	8	37	—	—	—	9	5	26	—	—	—
Modiolus demissus	6	6	36	5	8	51	4	6	42	—	—	—
Neanthes succinea	7	6	36	8	5	34	3	6	48	3	11	81
Leptochelia sp.	8	6	33	—	—	—	—	—	—	—	—	—
Insect larvae	9	5	33	10	5	30	—	—	—	9	6	32
Uca spp.	10	3	24	3	8	65	—	—	—	7	5	39
Heleobops sp.	—	—	—	6	10	47	—	—	—	8	5	34
Cyrenoida floridana	—	—	—	9	5	31	—	—	—	6	7	40
Amphicteis gunneri	—	—	—	—	—	—	—	—	—	5	8	59
Laeonereis culveri	—	—	—	—	—	—	5	6	41	—	—	—
Polymesoda caroliniana	—	—	—	—	—	—	8	5	30	—	—	—
Cerithidea scalariformis	—	—	—	—	—	—	10	4	20	—	—	—
Melampus bidentatus	—	—	—	—	—	—	—	—	—	10	5	30

* WLM = Wakulla low marsh, SLM = St. Marks low marsh, WUM = Wakulla upper marsh, SUM = St. Marks upper marsh.

Table 6.9. Rankings (R), frequency of occurrence (F/12), and Biological Index values (BI) of the five most important species of macroinvertebrates in the two marsh zones of St. Marks and Wakulla based on biomass/m² in trap samples. (From Subrahmanyam et al., 1976, by permission of the editor, *Bull. Mar. Sci.*)

| | Marsh Zones* | | | | | | | | | | | |
| | WLM | | | SLM | | | WUM | | | SUM | | |
Species	R	F/12	BI	R	F/12	BI	R	F/12	BI	R	F/12	BI
Littorina irrorata	1	12	120	1	12	120	1	10	95	1	12	120
Cyathura polita	2	10	64	2	11	75	2	9	63	2	11	83
Modiolus demissus	3	6	47	3	8	61	3	6	51	—	—	—
Scoloplos fragilis	4	6	40	—	—	—	—	—	—	3	8	50
Sesarma reticulatum	5	8	38	—	—	—	—	—	—	—	—	—
Neanthes succinea	—	—	—	4	8	47	5	7	42	—	—	—
Cyrenoida floridana	—	—	—	5	8	41	—	—	—	—	—	—
Polymesoda caroliniana	—	—	—	—	—	—	4	5	47	—	—	—
Uca spp.	—	—	—	—	—	—	—	—	—	4	6	46
Leptochelia sp.	—	—	—	—	—	—	—	—	—	5	8	34

* Abbreviations for marsh zones are the same as for Table 6.8.

Table 6.10. Horizontal distribution and relative abundance of macroinvertebrates of two *Juncus* marshes. Abundant species occurred in at least three seasons at densities greater than $3/m^2$, scarce species in at least two seasons at densities greater than $1/m^2$, and rare species in one or two seasons at densities less than $1/m^2$. (* denotes species found only in transect samples). LM = lower marsh, UM = upper marsh, HM = high marsh. (From Subrahmanyam et al., 1976, by permission of the editor, *Bull. Mar. Sci.*)

Abundance	LM (0–100 m)	LM & UM (0–300 m)	UM (200–300 m)	UM & HM (200–500 m)	HM (400–500 m)	Ubiquitous (0–500 m)
		L. irrorata			*M. bidentatus*	*C. floridana*
		C. polita				
		Apseudes sp.				
		Leptochelia sp.				
		S. fragilis				
		L. culveri				
Abundant		*N. succinea*				
		A. gunneri				
		M. demissus				
		S. reticulatum				
		G. bonnieroides				
		Uca spp.				
		N. abiuma				

357

Table 6.10. (continued)

Abundance	LM (0–100 m)	LM & UM (0–300 m)	UM (200–300 m)	UM & HM (200–500 m)	HM (400–500 m)	Ubiquitous (0–500 m)
Scarce	S. quadridentatum	G. mucronatus	M. nitida	N. reclivata	C. scalariformis	Insect larvae
	E. limnosum	U. longisignalis		P. caroliniana		Ogligochaetes
	L. palustris	U. speciosa		U. pugilator		L. pontica*
		O. grilhus				
		Talitrid				
	T. bowmani	C. louisianum	S. cinereum	P. floridana		
	M. almyra	P. herbstii	L. hyalina			
	P. pugio	E. rupicolum				
	C. fragilis					
Rare	M. corono					
	H. succinea					
	A. papyria					
	T. plebius					
	E. heteropoda*					
	M. sanguinea*					
	C. capitata					
	Notomastis sp.					

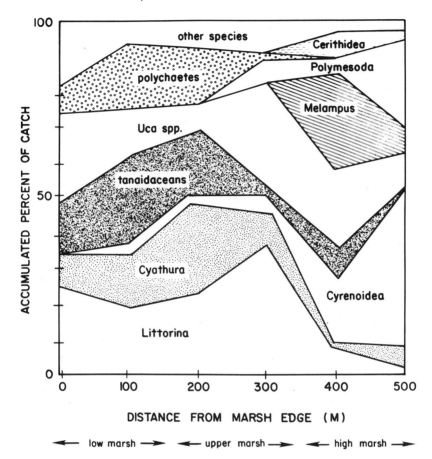

Figure 6.1.   Horizontal distribution of macroinvertbrates in St. Marks and Wakulla tidal marshes based on transect sampling. (From Subrahmanyam *et al.,* 1976, by permission of the editor, *Bull. Mar. Sci.*)

to Cammen that the *Spartina* plantings had no apparent effect on community structure. The natural marsh at Drum Inlet displayed a greater biomass, more taxa per sample, and a higher species diversity than the spoil plots early in the season (June), but these differences had disappeared by August. Species diversity (H') for all three sites tended to fluctuate around 0.5. Only in June did H' for the natural marsh exceed a value of one.

The Bare and Planted spoil sites at Snow's Cut were markedly different in all community characteristics and faunal affinity was very low. Most of the differences in numbers and biomass were due to the absence of the polychaete, *Laeonereis culveri,* from the Planted site and its abundance in the

Bare spoil site. Samples appear to have been taken only in November from the natural marsh at Snow's Cut and evinced greater number of species, an intermediate biomass, and a lower diversity than at the two spoil sites. There were no significant differences between the natural marsh and the two spoil sites. Cammen postulated that *Spartina* probably had a major impact on the fauna of the spoil plots.

Because of the divergence in the results from the two study areas, Cammen suggested that *Spartina* was not playing a direct role in the community organization of the study sites. There appeared to be a strong relationship between elevation and the similarity of the faunas. According to Cammen this was made evident in two ways. At Drum Inlet the elevation of the two spoil sites was the same and the faunas were similar. At Snow's Cut the elevation of the Bare site was lower than that of the Planted site. The polychaete, *L. culveri*, was abundant at the Bare site and absent at the Planted site.

The species diversity was much lower (overall H' approximated 0.5) at the North Carolina sites (Cammen, 1976) in contrast to higher values from northern Florida (H' = 2.49) (Subrahmanyam *et al.*, 1976). Although the numbers of individuals and biomass values for these two studies cannot be compared directly, the evidence suggests the North Carolina study area had a more depauperate and less diverse fauna than the Florida marsh sites. One could suggest this to be a reflection of newly planted spoil deposition sites in contrast to a well established marsh. Even though the above ground *Spartina* biomass of the spoil sites approached or even exceeded that of the natural marsh, the below ground biomass was less than half that of the natural marsh. One could argue that spoil sites do not represent a true tidal marsh with its associated macroinvertebrate fauna. The low diversity values bear this out. However, it is also clear in this particular case that the natural marsh sites did not fare any better so far as a diverse invertebrate community is concerned. Cammen's (1976) study was carried out in 1973. It would be interesting to reexamine these same North Carolina sites for changes in community structure. Spoil sites rehabilitated into marshes and natural marsh sites at other locations and latitudes could provide further insights into tidal marsh community organization.

VERTEBRATE COMMUNITY

Both physical and biological parameters have an influence on community structure. In regard to the estuarine fish community, Dahlberg and Odum (1970) identified the following eleven factors that may regulate species, individuals, and average size of fish: (1) variety of niches; (2) size of niche or niche overlap; (3) stability of environment; (4) rigorousness of environment;

(5) succession of geologic time; (6) productivity; (7) biomass accumulation; (8) competition; (9) space; (10) length of food chain; and (11) body size. The use of such indices can be useful in evaluating the well-being of a community especially when dealing with some kind of perturbation (Dahlberg and Odum, 1970; McErlean *et al.,* 1973; Cain and Dean, 1976) and is considered to be more sensitive than the use of an individual "indicator." The divergence of views about the use of indices, as discussed earlier, would suggest the need for continued experimental work.

Pisces

Seasonal variation has been demonstrated for numbers of species, numbers of individuals, and for several diversity indices (Dahlberg and Odum, 1970; McErlean *et al.,* 1973; Subrahmanyam and Drake, 1975; Cain and Dean, 1976). During their examination of three Georgia coastal habitats (open sound, large, and small tidal creeks) where they collected 31,637 individual fish of 70 species representing 37 families, and where 12 species made up 90 percent of the individuals, Dahlberg and Odum (1970) noted significant seasonal differences in numbers of species and individuals, and in all but species richness (D) among the indices. There were no differences between the three habitats (Table 6.11). While the kinds of species changed seasonally it was the evenness component (J') and not species richness (D) that influenced the seasonal variation in the Shannon-Weaver (H') index. The species richness did not change because the numbers of species and individuals changed simultaneously. This was not the case for the Florida collections made by Subrahmanyam and Drake (1975) (Table 6.12). They reported significant

Table 6.11. **Analysis of variance of effect of zones and seasons on composition and diversity of fish in trawl samples from Georgia estuaries. (From Dahlberg and Odum, 1970, by permission of the editor, *Amer. Midl. Nat.*)**

	Zones F values	Seasons F values	Interaction (Z and S) F values
No. species	1.069	3.073*	0.334
No. specimens	0.551	10.908**	1.170
H'	2.032	2.986*	0.734
D	0.638	1.926	0.535
J'	2.153	5.226**	0.467
S'/S	1.986	5.521**	0.480

* significant 95% level
** significant 99% level

Table 6.12.   F values in the two-way classification of analyses of variance for different statistics of catch data, and various community diversity indices (degrees of freedom are 3/33 for tides, 11/33 for seasons, and 3/11 for interactions). (From Subrahmanyam and Drake, 1975, by permission of the editor, *Bull. Mar. Sci.*)

Parameter	Tides F values	Seasons F values	Interaction (T and S) F values
No. species	4.934***	9.509***	0.518
Numbers/catch	2.681*	1.424	1.883
Biomass (g)/catch	0.553	3.000***	0.422
Species diversity H'	1.079	3.736***	0.288
Species richness D	0.753	4.302***	0.175
Evenness index J'	0.428	1.529	0.280
Equitability index E	1.048	2.144**	0.488

* Significant at P 0.10 level
** Significant at P 0.05 level
*** Significant at P 0.01 Level

changes in the seasonal species richness but found no significant difference in the evenness index (J') which they attributed to the large numbers of one or two species. Higher values in the summer were attributed to an increase in the numbers of individuals of more species in the warmer season.

Cain and Dean (1976) found the numbers of fish collected were primarily influenced by the numbers of *Fundulus heteroclitus, Leiostomus xanthurus,* and *Menidia menidia,* but numbers did not vary significantly with the season. The index of diversity (H'), species richness (D), and species evenness (J') were significantly influenced by season. H' peaked in August with a high of 2.3 and dipped in February with a low of 0.42 (Figure 6.2). The significant values for D and J' indicate they influenced changes in the index (H'). Season also significantly influenced the numbers of species.

These studies (Dahlberg and Odum, 1970; McErlean et al., 1973; Subrahmanyam and Drake, 1975; Cain and Dean, 1976) all identified the seasonal pattern of various fish communities. Three of them examined one annual cycle, for the most part at monthly intervals: McErlean et al. sampled over a four-year period at quarterly intervals. This group noted that all the parameters examined had a regular sine wave characteristic which might be useful for predictive purposes. On the other hand Cain and Dean (1976) observed that species diversity (H') varied between 1.47 and 2.0 during four consecutive days, suggesting diversity in a tidal creek is not normally constant from day to day. Shenker and Dean (1979) examined this theory by setting up a time-series of samples at an interval of approximately every 2.5 hours and sampling every third tide over a thirteen-day period. They found

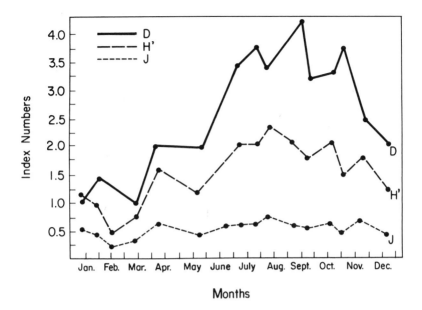

Figure 6.2.   Annual cycles of species diversity indices, Clambank Causeway Creek from June, 1971 to May, 1972. (From Cain and Dean, 1976, by permission of the editor, *Mar. Biol.*)

the catch size, species diversity (H'), species richness (D), and evenness (J') varied widely between samples. Although the variance was large, there was no significant difference for larval and juvenile fish. When adults were included there was a significant difference between day and night samples with higher values for the night samples (Figure 6.3). Their work indicated day-to-day variations as well as day-night differences in catch which could influence relative abundance, diversity indices, and movement patterns. While they found no diurnal-nocturnal pattern for the spot *L. xanthurus,* mullet *Mugil* spp., pinfish *Lagodon rhomboides,* and croaker *Micropogon undulatus,* the leptocephali of the speckled eel, *Myrophis punctatus,* were taken when the flood tides occurred during the daylight hours. The larvae and juveniles of the flounders, *Paralichthys* spp., were taken when flood tides occurred at night. Shenker and Dean suggested that any one sample could give a biased interpretation and monthly day and night samples could only give a broad view of fish community structure.

The variation in day-to-day and day-night samples, attributed to the presence of adults, no doubt resulted from the greater mobility of the adults. This suggested the idea that the use of diversity indices may be more suitable for communities where horizontal movement is minimal. It is also pos

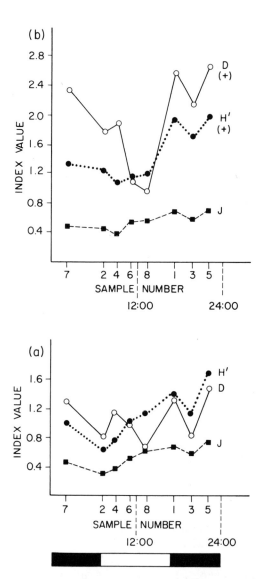

Figure 6.3. Diversity values, arranged on a 24-hour scale, as discussed in text (a) larval and juvenile fishes only; (b) all fishes; H′ = Shannon-Weaver diversity index; J′ = evenness; D = species richness; (+) = signficant difference between day and night samples, as evaluated by the Mann-Whitney U-Test with α = 0.05. (From Shenker and Dean, 1979, by permission of the editor, *Estuaries.*)

sible to arrive at different conclusions regarding trends in abundance and various indices depending on the time period selected and its duration (Coull and Fleeger, 1977). These authors also pointed out the need for more biological information from individual species, cautioning against the sole reliance on diversity indices for analysis of community structure.

The fluctuations in the various parameters of fish community structure associated with estuarine and tidal creek habitats is markedly influenced by the nursery role played by such habitats and the migratory movements of some fish species (Dahlberg and Odum, 1970; McErlean *et al.*, 1973; Subrahmanyam and Drake, 1975; Cain and Dean, 1976; Shenker and Dean, 1979). Subrahmanyam and Drake grouped fish species into permanent residents, species using the marsh as a nursery, foraging species coming in on high tide, and sporadic species. They characterized seven species of cyprinodonts as permanent residents. These plus four other species (*Menidia beryllina, L. xanthurus, Eucinostomus argenteus,* and *Anchoa mitchilli*) made up most of the juveniles using the marsh as a nursery. Eight species were classed as foragers and one was characterized as sporadic.

Community parameters are influenced by size of habitat available, breeding activity, and proximity to larger estuarine habitats. McErlean *et al.* (1973) noted fish species were more uniformly distributed during the warm season, but concentrated in deeper channel areas and upstream in shallow water during the winter months. Subrahmanyam and Drake noted the variation in the Homogeneity Index (HI) was probably due to the availability of the marsh surface. A higher index might result if the species could spread out evenly throughout the marsh. Another factor influencing HI would be the proximity of open bay water. They noted a higher seasonal species similarity at Wakulla which they attributed to closer proximity of that marsh to the open Apalachee Bay. Dahlberg and Odum observed a tendency for the various indices to be higher in the small creeks in contrast to large creeks and sounds. They attributed this difference to the more equitable distribution of species or the lack of dominance by one or two species in the smaller habitat.

Feeding migrations, recruitment of juveniles, and the movements of resident species contribute to the temporal variation in the community structure of the marsh ichthyofauna. While many of these species have no commercial importance they provide an important link in the transfer of energy from the marsh to the estuarine and coastal environment (Subrahmanyam and Drake, 1975). This energy transfer is largely by way of the detritus food chain which is derived primarily from the production of *S. alterniflora* and other marsh grasses. Although many of the young fish found in tidal streams are not detritivores, they derive benefit from such productivity as secondary consumers (Shenker and Dean, 1979). However, the marsh species with the greatest annual biomass and absolute numbers are detritivores, omnivores or primary consumers. All of these appear to have the ability to move from one trophic level to another, shifting their behavior accordingly as food supplies change. This ability to exploit various food sources in both a temporal and spatial configuration may lend stability to the community structure. The results obtained by McErlean *et al.* (1973) caused them to express concern about shifts in community structure of the fish populations in the Patuxent Estuary. Regression lines fitted to the cyclic-trend patterns for the various diversity indices all showed decreasing functions with time. The trend data for evenness (J') suggested that the amplitude of the seasonal cycle was increasing with time and that this trend was due to lower cold weather values. McErlean *et al.* considered such dominance shifts to favor the resident species but not at the expense of the seasonal migrants. What they found alarming was the downward trend in the numbers of species, species richness (D), species diversity (H'), and evenness. Such downward trends could indicate the loss of species and/or dominance shifts; both of which would result in simpler population structures. The outcome would be the shunting of energy to the dominant species with a corresponding reduction in the number of food-web linkages. Thus the buffering capacity within the community would be reduced and the system could be more susceptible to crashes and booms.

Aves

There appear to be few studies concerned with community organization among the higher vertebrates associated with tidal marshes. To date research has focused on various aspects of the biology of single species (seaside sparrow, muskrat, etc.). A few papers have focused on the modifications in the avian fauna following changes in marsh usage (See Marsh Management and Bird Nesting, Chapter 5).

   Greenhalgh (1971) identified four components of the bird community structure in natural marshes. (1) Aquatic birds such as the shelduck *Tadorna tadorna,* mallard *Anas platyrhynchos,* teal *A. crecca,* shoveler *Spatula clypeata,* and moorhen *Gallinula chloropus* hatch their eggs off the marsh and bring the young to the marsh to be reared. Thus they avoid tidal flooding and minimize predation. (2) The perching birds, skylark *Alauda arvensis,* yellow wagtail *Motacilla flava,* grasshopper warbler *Locustella naevia,* and reed bunting *Emberiza schoeniclus* nest in the drier inner marsh where they are subject to predation as well as disturbance and destruction of their nests by grazing cattle. They have more than one brood a year which helps compensate for losses. (3) Shore birds such as the oyster catcher *Haematopus ostralegus,* redshank *Tringa totanus,* dunlin *Calidris alpina,* and the meadow pipit *Anthus pratensis* are dispersed throughout the marsh, nesting in tussocks which can be flooded at times. Predation is low due to nest dispersion and concealment. (4) The colonial gulls and terns nest on the outer part of the marsh which predators cannot reach. The mobbing tactics of such colonial species also reduce predation. Species composition as well as abundance varies as marsh drainage and vegetation changes due to diking, ditching, mowing, or grazing (Larsson, 1969, 1976; Glue, 1971; Greenhalgh, 1971; Moller, 1975). Glue (1971) noted that each breeding bird community was dominated by a different species: the salt marsh and brackish pools by the meadow pipit; soft mud pans by the reed bunting; hard mud pans by the yellow wagtail; and the grasslands by the skylark. The dunlin, black-tailed godwit *Limosa limosa*, redshank, and yellow wagtail prefer grazed areas; their numbers can be reduced by drainage, diking, or cessation of grazing in areas close to the shore. Other species like the grasshopper warbler, reed warbler *Acrocephalus scirpaceus*, reed bunting, sedge warbler *Acrocephalus schoenobaenus*, great crested grebe *Podiceps cristatus*, water rail *Rallus aquaticus*, moorhen, and coot, *Fulica atra* increase in numbers when moist areas become revegetated following cessation of grazing (Larsson, 1969).

A paper by Moller (1975) discussed changes in the vegetation of the Danish Tipperne peninsula over the past several decades. There has been a shift from short halophytes toward a mixed reed swamp and *Carex nigra* community. Cattle grazing decreased in the 1950s. Hay production declined in the period from 1940 to 1970. The water table level dropped about 0.2 meters since 1932 and regular flooding has been reduced. The creeks and ditches gradually became clogged due to *Phragmites communis* and *Scirpus maritimus*. There was an increase in terrestrial predators, primarily the fox, *Vulpes vulpes*.

Moller characterized four plots on the basis of vegetational composition and extent of usage and related this to avian community organization. Plot A was intensively grazed by cattle. The vegetation was short and uniform and dominated by grasses. The plot was periodically fertilized and about 25 percent was drained by ditches. Plot B was similar to Plot A but was less intensively grazed by cattle. The vegetation was about 10 centimeters high with tussocks of higher grass left untouched by the cattle. There was no drainage. Plot C had not been subjected to cattle grazing for 10 years but was resumed with no apparent effect. There was some sheep grazing in the winter. Hay harvesting had been reduced from 75 to 25 percent of the area in 10 years and then stopped in 1972. Reeds formed dense stands, especially in the creeks and ponds. About one-half of the area covered by reeds was harvested each winter. Plot C had the most complex vegetation with open and closed ponds and a herb layer of varying density and height. Plot D had received the least human interference during the preceding twenty years with no cattle grazing since 1955 and no hay production during 1950–1960. There was some light sheep grazing in the winter. The original salt-marsh community had been altered greatly. There was a mixture of low shrub, *Nardus* heath, and *Carex nigra* depressions along with dense stands of grasses, *Deschampsia caespitosa* and *P. communis*. A reed swamp was rich in plant species and the ponds and creeks were filled with *P. communis* and *S. maritimus*.

Moller (1975) used three criteria to characterize the avian community structure associated with the four study plots: (1) an index of dominance $c = \Sigma(\eta i/N)^2$ where c = concentration of dominance, ηi = number of individuals in i^{th} species and N = total individuals; (2) the Shannon-Weaver index of diversity (H'); (3) equitability or evenness (J'). Dominance was found to be highest in the exploited Plot A and lowest in Plot C which had the most complex vegetational organization. These results mean the tendency of a few species to dominate the breeding bird community was most pronounced in A, least in C, with Plots B and D occupying an intermediate position (Table 6.13). The skylark *A. arvensis,* was overwhelmingly the dominant species, making up 35–58 percent of the whole population.

Plot C, with the most complex vegetational organization, had the highest bird diversity. The least disturbed plot, D, had a higher diversity than the exploited plots A and B with A having the lowest diversity, an association with the high dominance value. Moller observed no correlation between bird species diversity and vegetation height but he did find a strong correlation between density of territories and the average height of the vegetation. The difference in evenness values follows the same pattern for diversity (Table 6.13).

The changes in diversity appear to be related to changes in vegetation (Moller, 1975). The highest value in Plot C is related to the greater heterogeneity of the habitat. The increase in height of vegetation in Plot D caused the gulls and ducks to leave due to a decrease in habitat heterogeneity and the impact of increased numbers of predators who could now find a place to hide in the taller vegetation. The social gulls and terns were the first to go,

Table 6.13. Indices of dominance (C) bird species diversity (H') and equitability (J) for all plots A, B, C for 1972–73. (From Moller, 1975, part of Table 3, by permission of the editor, *Ornis Scand.*)

Index	A72	A73	B72	B73	A+B72	A+B73	C72	C73	D73
Dominance (C)	0.44	0.37	0.23	0.37	—	—	0.13	0.17	0.25
Equitability (J')	0.61	0.65	0.77	0.67	0.54	0.52	0.81	0.78	0.74
Diversity (H')	1.73	2.17	2.85	2.15			3.58	3.29	2.45
Mean H' (1972 and 1973 combined)	1.95		2.50				3.44		2.56

followed by the waders, as the vegetation became more dense and taller and forage areas at the shore declined because of development of the reed swamp. As Plot D matured there was a shift from breeding ducks and waders to a few passerine species that bred in higher densities in Plot D.

Moller concluded that, in order to maintain a high species diversity with many nesting waders, ducks, gulls, terns, and passerine birds, a variety of habitat niches must be maintained by marsh management procedures including hay production, reed harvesting, and grazing. If grazing is employed, the cattle (and presumably sheep) should not be put on the meadow until after the breeding season. Larsson (1976) suggested controlled burning or the use of a tiller to help where grazing cannot keep tussock growth down.

SYNTHESIS

The tidal marsh can be identified as a community in that it comprises an assemblage of populations living in a habitat dominated by particular physical parameters including periodic tidal inundation and a salinity gradient. There is an organization to these assemblages, in part derived from the characteristics of lower levels of organization yet, at the same time, possessing attributes in addition to those of the individual organism and the population. It is a functional unit identified by the flow of energy along particular pathways and by possessing a characteristic trophic structure. Not only is there a functional unity but there is a compositional unity in that there is a particular taxonomic composition along with a fairly uniform appearance. There is some level of probability that certain species will occur together (Odum, 1971, p. 140; Sullivan, 1975, 1977, 1978). Associated with this view is the perception that, while some communities are sharply defined with distinct boundaries, many communities blend gradually into each other with indistinct boundaries (Odum, 1971).

Elton (1966) talked about patterns as a characteristic of communities which could be identified as "the repetition of certain component shapes to form a connected or interspersed design." The community according to Elton, is an intricately dynamic system influenced by common factors from one situation to another, yet there is an orderliness to these dynamic processes. Elton stressed the fact that this pattern is a repetition of component parts, but not a replication of identical constituents, nor at exact time intervals. Each pattern has some degree of difference from other patterns yet there is some level of sameness which signifies the inherent complexity and stability of communities. Elton suggested these two charcteristics go hand in hand. The converse of this would suggest that simple communities, those communities with few species, could be unstable and vulnerable. Such communities could be vulnerable to invasion because they would lack compensatory capabilities due to a reduction or lack of multiple food chains and flexible food habits, and the behavior of the many species which are characteristic of highly organized communities.

Elton (1966) characterized community stability by two criteria: species composition remains stable although populations may fluctuate; and herbivores do not increase to the point where they destroy the vegetational component or other features of the habitat. According to Hurd *et al.* (1971) and Horn (1974), stability can be measured by the degree of resistance to disturbance or the ability of a community to return to an equilibrium state after a temporary disturbance. The more rapid the return and the lesser the fluctuations the more stable the community. If these alterations make no essential difference, then the community is by definition more stable (Conrad, 1972). MacArthur (1955) stated that, in a harsh environment with only a few species, stability would be hard to achieve. He was talking about an arctic habitat but the analog could be the tidal marsh. Usually, high diversity is associated with stability.

According to some of the arguments presented in this discussion, tidal marshes would be unstable and liable to drastic change at the slightest disturbance. McErlean *et al.* (1973) raised this concern in their discussion of declines in the indices of the estuarine fish community of the Patuxent River. The marsh does seem to fit into the category of habitat described by Pimentel (1961) and Root (1973): essentially a collection of vegetational monocultures in a progressive zonation from low to high marsh. These spermatophyte zones demonstrate a high level of dominance with relatively few species and characterize a direct, relatively uncomplicated food web. Why, then, do they persist? This evaluation applies to the marsh spermatophyte cover, but not to the edaphic diatom communities in the same tidal marsh (Sullivan, 1975, 1977, 1978). Such an enigma needs further attention.

According to Elton's (1966) characterization, marsh communities would be stable since geologic coring of earlier tidal marshes show that species composition does not change. Typically, herbivores do not destroy the vegetational organization of the marsh. An exception would be the goose or muskrat "eat-outs" (See Chapter 3, Interaction with Vegetation). The degree and rate of return to an equilibrium state following such grazing impacts would be influenced by the intensity and duration of feeding by a large population in a relatively restricted area.

MacArthur (1955) asserted that community stability may be achieved in two ways. Many species with restricted diets will form a stable community, or a few species with broad diets can also provide stability. While the former is more efficient and probably selected for in climax communities, the salt marsh fits into the latter category. There are only a few species of plants responsible for the bulk of the primary production. There is not enough variety for a large number of specialists. Therefore, diversity is low.

Species diversity appears to be maintained at lower levels in communities that are regulated by physical parameters while diversity increases when community structure is determined by biotic regulation. Kushlan (1976) noted that, under fluctuating water level conditions in an Everglades marsh, the diversity of small omnivorous fishes which dominate the community in biomass and numbers decreased. When water levels were maintained at consistent levels, species diversity and numbers of species increased while biomass diversity decreased. According to Kushlan this demonstrated a functional shift within the fish community toward the dominance of large carnivorous fish along with small carnivorous forms at the expense of small omnivorous species.

An examination of the food and feeding relationships (Chapter 4, Food and Feeding) indicated that many marsh animals have broad food habits. They are primary consumers, detritivores, or omnivores. They can occupy different trophic levels, either at various stages in their life cycles or at any one time. If one food is in short supply they have recourse to other food sources. McErlean et al. (1973), in their concern about the progressive decline in community indices, speculated that the increased dominance by fewer species could lead to the loss of various links in the food web which could lead to protracted crashes and booms in the populations. Such a suggestion would need to be examined carefully since, at the least, the primary consumer trophic level would be involved and no doubt the secondary consumer levels as well. These have been traditionally viewed as those able to exploit more varied food resources.

One of the ways an ecological system can react to variations in the quantity of total energy entering the system is by organizing itself in such a way as to take advantage of compensating variations in sources of energy or in conditions affecting the use of these sources. Such a process is possible if species can use more sources of energy or have fewer requirements. In both cases, species differentiate between energy sources becoming less specialized. The possibility for taking advantage of such compensating variations increases with the number of sources of energy for each species (Conrad, 1972). Thus the stability of the tidal marsh community may be enhanced by the presence of both the grazing and detritus food webs even though diversity tends to be low.

In closing, it is apparent that most of the work dealing with community structure has been descriptive in nature. This is as it should be. It is also apparent that more groups of species are becoming evident as we examine the milieu of the tidal marsh. Present and future investigators now have the opportunities, even the need, to carry out experimental designs directed at an understanding of the biological components of community structure. But to be effective, it will be necessary to further explore the life cycles and organization of individual species, before turning to more extensive examination of interactions between coexisting species within the community.

7
Opportunities for the Future

The tidal marsh is a unique habitat serving as a boundary area between the aquatic and upland environments. Future management and conservation of such areas will depend upon the availability of sufficient information with which to make wise decisions. At present, this information is incomplete and sporadic.

It is evident that we know much about some of the animals living in the marsh. As examples, numerous investigators have studied the familiar fiddler crabs and yet there is minimal information regarding larval behavior and distributions and their relations to tidal hydrodynamics. The biting flies have been the focus of a voluminous literature. However, there are still great gaps in information about the life cycles of most of these pests.

It is also evident that we have learned much about the ecological requirements, biological processes, and life cycles of a few organisms. However, these organisms enjoy a wide geographic distribution and much of our findings has been restricted to very limited study sites. One cannot safely extrapolate these data to form generalized statements without further investigation. Thirdly, it is clear that we have only superficial knowledge regarding a large section of the marsh community. It is very possible that some animal groups are yet to be characterized as members of the marsh fauna. Certainly, some species are yet to be identified. While considerable attention has been given to the Foraminifera, little is known of other Protozoa associated with the edaphic habitat or occurring on the grass stems. The Oligochaeta, Polychaeta, Turbellaria, Nematoda, Amphipoda, Isopoda, nonbiting members of the Insecta, and Arachnida all need attention. Once identified, the distributional patterns, biology, and role in the marsh community provide opportunities for study.

I would like to suggest some areas for future investigation categorized under varying disciplines. These include reproductive biology and life cycles; physiological and behavioral problems; feeding relationships and energy transfer; population dynamics; species interactions; community organizations; taxonomy and zoogeography. This will be recognized as an oversimplified and somewhat artificial classification which does not completely

373

represent the overlap and interwoven structure of the tide marsh. It is not meant to be a complete list or to be organized in any priority rating. Rather it is proferred solely to stimulate ideas for expanding our knowledge of this ecosystem.

Reproductive biology and life cycle studies. There are opportunities to gather important intraspecific information on this aspect for all marsh species—spawning seasons; age at maturity; numbers of spawnings; fecundity and development of eggs; numbers and growth rates of the young; length of cycles; activity peaks; care of young. Careful work in this area has been done for relatively few marsh species and usually for a particular location under very specific circumstances. The work on the isopod, *Cyathura polita* (Kruczynski and Subrahmanyam, 1978) and the fish, *Fundulus heteroclitus* (Kneib and Stiven, 1978; Taylor *et al.,* 1979) are such examples. Can this information be considered representative of the species throughout its geographic range and habitat distributions?

Physiological and behavioral problems. Studies are needed on the physiological reaction to salinity, temperature, oxygen tensions, and ionic responses on egg, larva, juvenile, adult, and spawner. Functional aspects of feeding, spawning, and other life processes must be clarified. Some of these factors have been explored in research on *Cyrenoida floridana* (Kat, 1978); on *Gammarus palustris* (Rees, 1975; Gable and Croker, 1977); and on *Fundulus heteroclitus* (Matthews, 1938; Brummett, 1966; Kneib and Stiven, 1978; Taylor *et al.,* 1979). Interactions among various environmental entities and their effects on the above are unclear. Behavioral responses should be examined within the same contexts. Such information would help explain species distribution along latitudinal gradients, which is imperative to any understanding of the impact of marsh manipulation. Examples of such relationships already include these research efforts: latitude and the number of spawnings of *Cyrenoida floridana* (Kat, 1978); moisture and the distribution of the amphipod genus *Orchestia* (Phillips, 1978); habitat preferences and spawning among *Sesarma reticulatum* and *Sesarma cinereum* (Seiple, 1979).

Another interesting area of investigation is that of the comparative needs, reactions, and behavioral responses for species that live both in the tidal marsh and in fresh-water marshes and/or in upland areas. Along this vein, some comparisons have been made with respect to water needs among savannah, seaside, and sharp-tailed sparrows (Cade and Bartholomew, 1959; Bartholomew and Cade, 1963; Poulson, 1969).

Feeding relationships and energy transfer. Food requirements in terms of individual metabolic needs or reproductive cycles should be examined with regard to rate and amount of material ingested, as well as quality and chemical composition of this material. Feeding habits relative to the stage in the life cycle and the size and age of an organism may be different. Do those animals with extended ranges ingest the same prey species from one area to another, or are there ecological equivalents with respect to food quality and metabolic needs? Temporal distributions should also be explored. Is the presence of food items synchronized with the appearance of the feeder? Is food selection based on preference or availability? Are preferences the result of metabolic need or palatability? Do these change with age of the animal? Research in this general category include studies on the white-fronted goose and widgeon by Owen (1971) and Cadwalladr et al. (1972, 1973, 1974), and the mud snail, *Ilyanassa obsoleta* (Curtis and Hurd, 1979).

Population dynamics. As components of any ecosystem analysis, we need to know more about specific populations within and between marshes. This would include birth and mortality rates as well as age structure and turnover rate of a population. To date, there have been very few such analyses. Those that come to mind include studies on: *Fundulus heteroclitus* (Valiela et al., 1977; Meredith and Lotrich, 1979); *Microtus pennsylvanicus* (Jones, 1978); *Malaclemys terrapin* (Hurd et al., 1979). Other marsh species, especially those whose life cycles exceed one year, need similar attention. What population assessments we do have are restricted to specific sites and need to be tested in other marsh locations.

Species interactions. Mutualism and parasitism in the tide marsh are subtle relationships about which we know nothing. Inter- and intraspecific competition is an important determinant in the success or failure of any population. We need to know what form this competition takes. Predator-prey interactions affect the structure and function of the community. Recognition and understanding of these interactions has been initiated by the rather extensive literature dealing with food studies. However, little is known about the impact of predator-prey interaction on either predator or prey populations. Vince et al. (1976) discussed such interactions between *Fundulus heteroclitus* and the amphipod *Orchestia* and the snail, *Melampus bidentatus*. Nothing is known about behavioral patterns or the timing of environmental parameters that bring such interacting species together.

Community organization. Animal distributions are usually influenced by plant zonations. This has been delineated in varying degrees for many of the obvious macrofauna. The enormous void of information concerning the meiofauna provide opportunities for investigators of differing fields of interest. In addition, only after we have garnered more information about organismal-environmental interactions as well as population fluctuations and temporal interspecific relations and predator-prey interplay, can we assign biological significance to the statistics of diversity, species richness, and evenness as applied to the tidal marsh community.

Zoogeography. Since the tide marsh is subjected to periodic inundation, its animal populations should be examined in the context of zonal or successional changes related to fluctuations in sea level. Such work has begun for the Foraminifera (Phleger, 1970) and some of the west coast molluscs (Mac-Donald, 1969). Many marsh species have extensive latitudinal distributions and are subjected to different environmental pressures. Dispersion and local movements would be fruitful areas of endeavor. The snail genus *Littorina,* the bivalve *Cyrenoida floridana,* the isopod *Cyathura polita,* and the rice rat *Oryzomys palustris* are interesting examples for such inquiries.

References

Able, K. W., and M. Castagna. 1975. Aspects of an undescribed reproductive behavior in *Fundulus heteroclitus* (Pisces: Cyprinodontidae) from Virginia. *Ches. Sci.* **16**(4):282–284.

Adams, D. A. 1963. Factors influencing vascular plant zonation in North Carolina salt marshes. *Ecol.* **44**(3):445–456.

Allen, Elizabeth A. 1978. Petrology and stratigraphy of holocene coastal-marsh deposits along the western shore of Delaware Bay. Ph.D. dissertation. Univ. Delaware. 287 pp.

Allen, Elizabeth A., and H. A. Curran. 1974. Biogenic sedimentary structures produced by crabs in lagoon margin and salt marsh environments near Beaufort, N. C. *J. Sed. Petrol.* **44**(2):538–548.

Alls, R. T. 1969. Killifish predation of mosquitos in low level impounded Delaware salt marshes. Master's thesis. Univ. Delaware. 73 pp.

Anderson, A. 1971. Intertidal activity, breeding and the floating habit of a *Hydrobia ulvae* in the Ythan estuary. *J. Mar. Biol. Assoc. U.K.* **51**(2):423–437.

Anderson, J. F. 1971. Autogeny and mating and their relationship to biting in the salt-marsh deer fly, *Chrysops atlanticus* (Diptera: Tabanidae). *Ann. Ent. Soc. Amer.* **64**(6):1421–1424.

Anderson, J. F. 1973. Biting behavior of salt marsh deerflies (Diptera: Tabanidae). *Ann. Ent. Soc. Amer.* **66**(1):21–23.

Anderson, J. F., and F. R. Kneen. 1969. The temporary impoundment of salt marshes for the control of coastal deerflies. *Mosq. News* **29**(2):239–243.

Anonymous. 1976. Monitoring fish migration in the Delaware River. Draft final report. Prepared for Dept. of the Army, Corps of Engineers. Martin Marietta Corp., Baltimore, Md.

A.O.U. 1957. Check-list of North American Birds, 5th Ed. *Amer. Ornith. Union.* 691 pp.

Apley, M. L. 1970. Field studies on life history, gonadal cycle and reproductive periodicity in *Melampus bidentatus* (Pulmonate: Ellobiidae). *Malacol.* **10**(2):381–397.

Apley, M. L., W. D. Russell-Hunter, and R. J. Avolizi. 1967. Annual reproductive turnover in the salt marsh pulmonate snail, *Melampus bidentatus* (Abstract). *Biol. Bull.* **133**(2):455–456.

Armstrong, P. B., and J. S. Child. 1965. Stages in the development of *Fundulus heteroclitus. Biol. Bull.* **128**:143–168.

Atwood, E. L. 1950. Life history studies of nutria, or coypu in coastal Louisiana. *J. Wildl. Mgmt.* **14**(3):249–265.

Auld, A., and J. Schubel. 1974. Effects of suspended sediment on fish eggs. Johns Hopkins Univ., C.B.I. Spec. Rept. 40. 61 pp.

Aurand, D., and F. C. Daiber. 1973. Nitrate and nitrite in the surface waters of two Delaware salt marshes. *Ches. Sci.* **14**(2):105–111.

Averill, P. H. 1976. The role of Orchestid amphipods in the breakdown of tidal marsh grasses. Master's thesis. Univ. Delaware. 83 pp.

Axelrad, D. M. 1974. Nutrient flux through the salt marsh ecosystem. Ph.D. dissertation. College of William and Mary. 80 pp.

Axtell, R. C. 1976. Horseflies and deerflies (Diptera: Tabanidae). *In:* L. Cheng, ed. *Marine Insects.* North-Holland Publ. Co., Amsterdam, Netherlands. pp. 415–445.

Bailey, N. S. 1948a. A mass collection and population technique for larvae of Tabanidae (Diptera). *Bull. Brooklyn Ent. Soc.* **43**:22–29.

Bailey, N. S. 1948b. The hovering and mating of Tabanidae: a review of the literature with some original observations. *Ann. Ent. Soc. Amer.* **41**(4):403–412.

Bailey, V. 1924. Breeding, feeding, and other life habits of meadow mice (*Microtus*). *J. Agric. Res.* **27**(8):523–536.

Barnes, B. M., and R. D. Barnes. 1954. The ecology of the spiders of maritime drift lines. *Ecol.* **35**(1):25–35.

Barnes, R. D. 1953. The ecological distribution of spiders in non-forest maritime communities at Beaufort, North Carolina. *Ecol. Monogr.* **23**(4):315–337.

Barnes, R. D. 1963. *Invertebrate Zoology.* W. B. Saunders Co., Philadelphia. p. 26.

Barsdate, R. J., R. T. Prentki, and T. Fenchel. 1974. Phosphorus cycle of model ecosystems: significance for decomposer food chains and effect on bacterial grazers. *Oikos* **25**(3):239–251.

Barske, P. 1961. Wildlife on the coastal marshes. *Conn. Arboretum Bull.* **12**:13–15.

Bartholomew, G. A., and T. J. Cade. 1963. The water economy of land birds. *Auk* **80**:504–539.

Bates, M. 1949. *The Natural History of Mosquitos.* Macmillan Co., N.Y. 379 pp.

Bayne, B. L. 1976a. Aspects of reproduction in bivalve molluscs. *In* Wiley, M., ed. *Estuarine Processes.* Vol. 1. Academic Press, N.Y. pp. 432–448.

Bayne, B. L. 1976b. *Marine Mussels: Their Ecology and Physiology.* Cambridge Univ. Press, Cambridge, U.K. 506 pp.

Beadle, L. C. 1939. Regulation of the haemolymph in the saline water mosquito larvae *Aedes detritus* Edw. *J. Exp. Biol.* **16**(3):346–362.

Beeftink, W. G. 1977. The coastal salt marshes of western and northern Europe: an ecological and phytosociological approach. *In:* V. J. Chapman, ed. *Wet Coastal Ecosystems.* Elsevier Sci. Publ. Co., Amsterdam, Netherlands. pp. 109–155.

Belknap, D. F. 1975. Dating of late Pleistocene and Holocene relative sea levels in coastal Delaware. Master's thesis. Univ. Delaware. 95 pp.

Bell, Susan S. 1979. Short- and long-term variation in the high marsh meiofauna community. *Estuarine Coast. Mar. Sci.* **9**(3):331–350.

Bell, Susan S., Mary C. Watzin, and B. C. Coull. 1978. Biogenic structure and its effect on the spatial heterogeneity of the meiofauna in a salt marsh. *J. Exp. Mar. Biol.* **35**(2):99–107.

Bent, A. C. 1929. Life histories of North American shore birds. *U.S. Nat. Mus. Bull.* **146**:412 pp.

Bent, A. C. 1937. Life histories of North American birds of prey. *U.S. Nat. Mus. Bull.* **167**:398 pp.

Bent, A. C. 1963. Life histories of North American marsh birds. *U.S. Nat. Mus. Bull.* **235**: 392 pp.

Bent, A. C., and collaborators. Compiled and edited by O. L. Austin, Jr. 1968. Life histories of North American cardinals, grosbeaks, buntings, towhees, finches, sparrows, and allies. *U.S. Nat. Mus. Bull.* **237**. 1889 pp.

Berry, A. J. 1961. Some factors affecting the distribution of *Littorina saxatilis* (Olivi). *J. Anim. Ecol.* **30**(1):27–45.

Berry, A. J., and E. Chew. 1973. Reproductive systems and cyclic release of eggs in *Lit-*

torina melanostoma from Malayan mangrove swamps (Mollusca: Gastropoda). *J. Zool. London* 171(3):333–344.

Bidlingmayer, W. L. 1957. Studies on *Culicoides furens* (Poly) at Vero Beach. *Mosq. News* 17(4):292–294.

Bidlingmayer, W. L. 1961. Field activity studies of adult *Culicoides furens. Ann. Ent. Soc. Amer.* 54:149–156.

Bilio, M. 1965. Die verteilung der aquatischen bodenfauna und die Gliederung der vegetation im strandbereich der Deutschen Nordound Osteekuste. (With English summary). *Proc. 5th Mar. Biol. Symp. Acta Univ. Goteborg* III:25–42.

Bingham, F. O. 1972. Several aspects of the reproductive biology of *Littorina irrorata* (Gastropoda). *Nautilus* 86(1):8–10.

Blair, W. F. 1936. The Florida marsh rabbit. *J. Mammal.* 17(3):197–207.

Blandin, W. W. 1963. Renesting and multiple brooding studies of marked clapper rails. Proc. Ann. Conf. Southeastern Assoc. Game and Fish Comm. 17:60–68.

Blum, J. L. 1968. Salt marsh *Spartinas* and associated algae. *Ecol. Monogr.* 38(3):199–222.

Bodenheimer, F. S. 1958. Animal ecology today. *In:* F. S. Bodenheimer and W. W. Weisbach, eds. *Monographiae Biologicae,* Vol. VI. Uitgeverij Dr. W. Junk, The Hague, Netherlands. 276 pp.

Bohlen, W. F., D. F. Cundy, and J. M. Tramontano. 1979. Suspended material distributions in the wake of estuarine channel dredging operations. *Estuarine Coast. Mar. Sci.* 9(6):699–711.

Boltovskoy, E., and R. Wright. 1976. *Recent Foraminifera.* Uitgeverij Dr. W. Junk, The Hague, Netherlands. 515 pp.

Bongiorno, S. F. 1970. Nest-site selection by adult laughing gulls (*Larus atricilla*). *Anim. Behav.* 18:434–444.

Boon, J. D. 1975. Tidal discharge asymmetry in a salt marsh drainage system. *Limnol. Oceanogr.* 20(1):71–80.

Borror, A. C. 1965. New and little-known tidal marsh ciliates. *Trans. Amer. Microscop. Soc.* 84(4):550–565.

Bosler, E. M., and E. J. Hansens. 1974. Natural feeding behavior of adult salt marsh greenheads and its relation to oogensis. *Ann. Ent. Soc. Amer.* 67:321–324.

Bourn, W. S., and C. Cottam. 1950. Some biological effects of ditching tidewater marshes. Res. Rept. 19, Fish and Wildl. Serv., U.S. Dept. Interior. 17 pp.

Bousfield, E. L. 1973. *Shallow-water Gammaridean Amphipoda of New England.* Cornell Univ. Press, Ithaca, N.Y. 312 pp.

Bradbury, H. M. 1938. Mosquito control operations on tide marshes in Massachusetts and their effect on shore birds and waterfowl. *J. Wildl. Mgmt.* 2(2):49–52.

Bradley, T. J., and J. E. Phillips. 1975. The secretion of hyperosmotic fluid by the rectum of a saline-water mosquito larva, *Aedes taeneorhynchus. J. Exp. Biol.* 63(2):331–342.

Bradshaw, J. S. 1968. Environmental parameters and marsh Foraminifera. *Limnol. Oceanogr.* 13:26–38.

Brinkhurst, R. O. 1964. Observations on the biology of the marine oligochaete *Tubifex costatus. J. Mar. Biol. Assoc. U. K.* 44(1):11–16.

Broad, A. C. 1957a. The relationship between diet and larval development of *Palaemonetes. Biol. Bull.* 112:162–170.

Broad, A. C. 1957b. Larval development of *Palaemontes pugio* Holthius. *Biol. Bull.* 112:144–161.

Brown, L. N. 1975. Ecological relationships and breeding biology of the nutria (*Myocastor coypus*) in the Tampa, Florida area. *J. Mammal.* 56(4):928–930.

Brummett, A. R. 1966. Observations on the eggs and breeding season of *Fundulus heteroclitus* at Beaufort, North Carolina. *Copeia* 1966:616–620.

Buckland-Nicks, J., and Fu-Shiang Chia. 1973. Oviposition and development of two intertidal snails, *Littorina sitkana* and *Littorina scutulata*. *Canad. J. Zool.* **51**(3):359–365.

Burbanck, W. D. 1959. The distribution of the estuarine isopod *Cyathura* sp. along the
eastern coast of the United States. *Ecol.* **40**:507–511.

Burbanck, W. D. 1961. The distribution and ecology of *Cyathura polita* (Stimpson) in
tidal marshes of Cape Cod, Massachusetts, and its vicinity. *ASB Bull.* **8**(2):29.

Burbanck, W. D. 1962. An ecological study of the distribution of the isopod *Cyathura polita* (Stimpson) from brackish waters of Cape Cod, Massachusetts. *Amer. Midl. Nat.*
67(2): 449–476

Burbanck, M. P., and W. D. Burbanck. 1974. Sex reversal of female *Cyathura polita*
(Stimpson, 1855) (Isopoda, Anthuridae). *Crustaceana* **26**(1):110–112.

Burger, Joanna. 1976a. Temperature relationships in nests of the northern diamondback
terrapin, *Malaclemys terrapin terrapin*. *Herpetologica* **32**:412–418.

Burger, Joanna. 1976b. Behavior of hatching diamondback terrapins (*Malaclemys terrapin*) in the field. *Copeia* **1976**(4):742–748.

Burger, Joanna. 1977a. Determinants of hatching success in diamondback terrapin, *Malaclemys terrapin*. *Amer. Midl. Natl.* **97**(2):444–464.

Burger, Joanna. 1977b. Nesting behavior of herring gulls: invasion into *Spartina* salt-
marsh areas of New Jersey. *Condor* **79**:162–169.

Burger, Joanna. 1977c. Role of visibility in nesting behavior of *Larus* gulls. *J. Comp. Physiol. Psychol.* **91**(6):1347–1358.

Burger, Joanna. 1978. Great black-backed gulls breeding in a salt marsh in New Jersey.
Wilson Bull. **90**(2):304–305.

Burger, Joanna. 1979. Nest repair behavior in birds nesting in salt marshes. *J. Comp.
Physiol. Psychol.* **93**(2):189–199.

Burger, Joanna, and C. G. Beer. 1975. Territoriality in the laughing gull (*L. atricilla*). *Behavior* **55**(3–4):301–320.

Burger, Joanna, and F. Lesser. 1978. Selection of colony sites and nest sites by common
terns, *Sterno hirundo* In Ocean County, New Jersey. *Ibis* **120**(4):433–449.

Burger, Joanna, and J. Shisler. 1978a. Nest site selection and competitive interactions of
herring and laughing gulls in New Jersey. *Auk* **95**(2):252–266.

Burger, Joanna, and J. Shisler. 1978b. The effects of ditching a salt marsh on colony and
nest site selection by herring gulls *Larus argentatus*. *Amer. Midl. Nat.* **100**(1):54–63.

Burger, Joanna, and J. Shisler. 1978c. Nest-site selection of willets in a New Jersey salt
marsh. *Wilson Bull.* **90**(4):599–607.

Burger, Joanna, J. Shisler, and F. Lesser. 1978. The effects of ditching salt marshes on
nesting birds. Compiled by W. Southern. Proc. Colonial Water Bird Group Publ. at
Northern Illinois Univ., Dekalb, Ill. pp. 27–37.

Burger, Joanna, and W. A. Montevecchi. 1975. Tidal synchronization and nest selection
in the northern diamondback terrapin, *Malaclemys terrapin terrapin* Scheopff. *Copeia*
1975:113–119.

Burkholder, P. R. 1956. Studies on the nutritive value of *Spartina* grass growing in the
marsh areas of coastal Georgia. *Bull. Torrey Bot. Club* **83**(5):327–334.

Burkholder, P. R., and G. H. Bornside. 1957. Decomposition of marsh grass by aerobic
marine bacteria. *Bull. Torrey Bot. Club* **84**:336–383.

Burkholder, P. R., and L. M. Burkholder. 1956. Vitamin B-12 in suspended solids and
marsh muds collected along the coast of Georgia. *Limnol. Oceanogr.* **1**(3):202–208.

Buzas, M. A. 1969. Foraminiferal species densities and environmental variables in an estuary. *Limnol. Oceanogr.* **14**(3):411–422.

Byrne, D. M. 1978. Life history of the spotfin killifish, *Fundulus luciae* (Pisces: Cyprinodontidae) in Fox Creek Marsh, Virginia. *Estuaries* **1**(4):211–227.

Cade, T. J., and G. A. Bartholomew. 1959. Sea water and salt utilization by savannah sparrows. *Physiol. Zool.* **32**(4):230–238.

Cadwalladr, D. A., and J. V. Morley. 1973. Sheep grazing preferences on a salting at Bridgwater Bay National Nature Reserve, Somerset, and their significance for widgeon (*Anas penelope* L.) conservation. *J. Br. Grassld. Soc.* **28**:235–242.

Cadwalladr, D. A., and J. V. Morley. 1974. Further experiments on the management of saltings pasture for widgeon (*Anas penelope* L.) conservation at Bridgwater Bay National Nature Reserve, Somerset. *J. Appl. Ecol.* **11**(2):461–466.

Cadwalladr, D. A., M. Owen, J. V. Morley, and R. S. Cook. 1972. Widgeon (*Anas penelope* L.) conservation at Bridgwater Bay National Nature Reserve, Somerset. *J. Appl. Ecol.* **9**(2):417–425.

Cain, R. L., and J. M. Dean. 1976. Annual occurrence, abundance and diversity of fish in a South Carolina intertidal creek. *Mar. Biol.* **36**:369–379.

Cameron, G. N. 1972. Analysis of insect trophic diversity in two salt marsh communities. *Ecol.* **53**(1):58–73.

Cammen, L. M. 1976. Macroinvertebrates colonization of *Spartina* marshes artifically established on dredge spoil. *Estuarine Coast. Mar. Sci.* **4**:357–372.

Carpenter, S. J., and W. J. LaCasse. 1955. *Mosquitos of North America.* Univ. Calif. Press, Berkeley, 360 pp.

Carr, A. 1952. *Handbook of Turtles.* Comstock Publ. Ithaca, N.Y. 542 pp.

Catts, E. P., Jr., 1957. Mosquito prevalence on impounded and ditched salt marshes, Assawoman Wildlife Area, Delaware, 1956. Master's thesis. Univ. Delaware. 65 pp.

Catts, E. P., Jr., F. H. Lesser, R. F. Darsie, Jr., O. Florschutz, and E. E. Tindall. 1963. Wildlife usage and mosquito production on impounded tidal marshes in Delaware, 1956–1962. *Trans. 28th N. Amer. Wildl. Nat. Res. Conf.* pp. 125–132.

Catts, E. P., and W. Olkowski. 1972. Biology of Tabanidae (Diptera): mating and feeding behavior of *Chrysops fuliginosus. Environ. Eng.* **1**(4):448–453.

Chabreck, R. H. 1973. Proceedings of the coastal marsh and estuary management symposium. Div. Continuing Ed., La. State Univ., Baton Rouge. 316 pp.

Chabreck, R. H. 1976. Management of wetlands for wildlife habitat improvement. *In:* M. Wiley, ed. *Ecological Processes,* Vol. **1**. Academic Press, N.Y. pp. 226–233.

Chapman, H. C., and F. Ferrigno. 1956. A three-year study of mosquito breeding in natural and impounded salt marsh areas in New Jersey. *Proc. N. J. Mosq. Exterm. Assoc.* **43**:48–65.

Chapman, H. C., P. F. Springer, F. Ferrigno, and R. F. Darsie, Jr. 1955. Studies of mosquito breeding in natural and impounded salt marsh areas in New Jersey and Delaware in 1954. *Proc. N. J. Mosq. Exterm. Assoc.* **42**:92–94.

Chapman, H. C., P. F. Springer, F. Ferrigno, and D. MacCleary. 1954. Studies on mosquito breeding in natural and impounded salt marsh areas in New Jersey and Delaware. *Proc. N. J. Mosq. Exterm. Assoc.* **41**:225–226.

Chapman, V. J. 1960. *Salt Marshes and Salt Deserts of the World.* Intersci. Publ., N.Y. 392 pp.

Chapman, V. J. 1974. *Salt Marshes and Salt Deserts of the World.* 2nd Suppl. reprint ed. Verlag Von. J. Cramer, Bremerhaven, Germany. 102, XVI, 392 pp.

Chapman, V. J., ed. 1977. *Wet Coastal Ecosystems.* Elsevier Scientific Publ. Co. Amsterdam, Netherlands 428 pp.

Chappell, H. G., J. F. Ainsworth, R. A. D. Cameron, and M. Redfern. 1971. The effect of trampling on a chalk grassland ecosystem. *J. Appl. Ecol.* **8**(3):869–882.

Cheng, L., ed. 1976. *Marine insects.* North-Holland Publ. Co., Amsterdam, Netherlands.

Christian, R. R., K. Bancroft, and W. J. Wiebe. 1978. Resistance of the microbial community within salt marsh soils to selected perturbations. *Ecol.* **59**(6):1200–1210.

Christy, J. H. 1978. Adaptive significance of reproductive cycles in the fiddler crab *Uca pugilator:* a hypothesis. *Science* **199**(4327):453–455.

Clements, A. N. 1963. *The Physiology of Mosquitos.* Macmillan Co., N.Y. 393 pp.

Conaway, C. H. 1954. The reproductive cycle of rice rats (*Oryzomys palustris palustris*) in captivity. *J. Mammal.* **35**(2):363–366.

Conaway, C. H., T. S. Baskett, and J. E. Toll. 1960. Embryo resorption in the swamp rabbit. *J. Wildl. Mgmt.* **24**(2):197–202.

Connell, W. A. 1940. Tidal inundation as a factor limiting distribution of Aedes spp. on a Delaware salt marsh. *Proc. N. J. Mosq. Exterm. Assoc.* **27**:166–177.

Conrad, M. 1972. Stability of food webs and its relation to species diversity. *J. Theoret. Biol.* **34**(2):325–335.

Corbett, Kathleen. 1981. Strategy of population maintenance in *Geukensia* (= *Modiolus*) *demissa* (Dillwyn 1817). Masters thesis, Univ. Delaware.

Costlow, J. D., Jr., and C. G. Bookout. 1962. The larval development of *Sesarma reticulatum* Say reared in the laboratory. *Crustaceana* **4**:281–294.

Costlow, J. D., Jr., C. G. Bookout, and R. Monroe. 1960. The effects of salinity and temperature on larval development of *Spartina alterniflora* (Bosc) reared in the laboratory. *Biol. Bull.* **118**:183–202.

Cottam, C. 1939. Food habits of North American diving ducks. U.S. Dept. Agr. Tech. Bull. 643. 139 pp.

Cottam, C., W. S. Bourn, F. C. Bishop, L. L. Williams, Jr., and W. Vogt. 1938. What's wrong with mosquito control? *Trans. N. America. Wildl. Conf.* **3**:81–107.

Coull, B. C., and Susan S. Bell. 1979. Perspectives of marine meiofaunal ecology. *In:* Livingston, R. J., ed. *Ecological Processes in Coastal and Marine Systems.* Marine Science Vol. 10. Plenum Press, N.Y. pp. 189–216.

Coull, B. C., Susan S. Bell, Ardis M. Savory, and Bettye W. Dudley. 1979. Zonation of meiobenthic copepods in a southeastern United States salt marsh. *Estuarine Coast. Mar. Sci.* **9**(2):181–188.

Coull, B. C., and J. W. Fleeger. 1977. Long-term temporal variation and community dynamics of meiobenthic copepods. *Ecol.* **58**(5):1136–1143.

Coull, B. C., and W. B. Vernberg. 1970. Harpacticoid copepod respiration: *Enhydrosoma propinquum* and *Longipedia helgolandica. Mar. Biol.* **5**:341–344.

Coull, B. C., and W. B. Vernberg. 1975. Reproductive periodicity of meiobenthic copepods: seasonal or continuous? *Mar. Biol.* **32**:289–293.

Craighead, J. J., and F. C. Craighead. 1956. *Hawks, Owls and Wildlife.* The Stackpole Co., Harrisburg, Pa. and Wildlife Mgmt. Inst., Washington, D.C. 443 pp.

Crane, J. 1958. Aspects of social behavior in fiddler crabs, with special reference to *Uca maracoani* (Latreille). *Zoologica* **43**(4):113–130.

Crane, J. 1975. *Fiddler Crabs of the World: Oxypodidae: Genus Uca.* Princeton Univ. Press, Princeton, N.J. 736 pp.

Crichton, O. W. 1960. Marsh crab—intertidal tunnel-maker and grass-eater. *Est. Bull.* **5**:3–10.

Cronin, T. W., and R. B. Forward, Jr. 1979. Tidal vertical migration: an endogenous rhythm in estuarine crab larvae. *Science* **205**(4410):1020–1021.

Curtis, L. A., and L. E. Hurd. 1979. On the broad nutritional requirements of the mud snail (*Ilyanassa* (*Nassarius*) *obsoleta*), and its polytrophic role in the food web. *J. Exp. Mar. Biol. Ecol.* **41**:289–297.

Dahl, R. G. 1959. Studies on Scandinavian Ephydridae (Diptera, Brachycera). *Opusc. ent. suppl.* **15**:1–224.

Dahlberg, M. D., and E. P. Odum. 1970. Annual cycle of species occurrence, abundance, and diversity in Georgia estuarine fish population. *Amer. Midl. Nat.* **83**:382–392.

Daiber, F. C. 1959. Tidal marsh; conflicts and interactions. *Est. Bull.* **4**(4):4–16.

Daiber, F. C. 1962. Role of the tide marsh in the lives of salt water fishes. Ann. D-J Rept. F-13-R-3. Del. Bd. Game and Fish Comm. 25 pp. mimeo.

Daiber, F. C. 1963a. The role of the tide marsh in the lives of salt water fishes. Ann. D-J Rept. F-13-R-4. Del. Bd. Game and Fish Comm. 22 pp. mimeo.

Daiber, F. C. 1963b. Tidal creeks and fish eggs. *Est. Bull.* **7**(2, 3):6–13.

Daiber, F. C. 1974. Salt marsh plants and future coastal salt marshes in relation to animals. *In:* R. J. Reimold and W. H. Queen, eds. *Ecology of Halophytes.* Academic Press, N.Y. pp. 475–510.

Daiber, F. C. 1977. Salt marsh animals: distribution related to tidal flooding, salinity and vegetation. *In:* V. J. Chapman, ed. *Ecosystems of the World: I, Wet Coastal Ecosystems.* Elsevier Scientific Publ. Co., Amsterdam, Netherlands. pp. 79–108.

Daiber, F. C., and O. Crichton. 1967. Caloric studies of *Spartina* and the marsh crab *Sesarma reticulatum* (Say). Ann. Pittman-Robertson Rept. Del. Bd. Game and Fish Comm. Proj. W-22-R-2, Job No. 4. 20 pp. mimeo.

Daiber, F. C., and G. W. Schmelz. 1971. Additional studies on the tolerance of the striped killifish, *Fundulus majalis,* embryos to different temperatures and salinity conditions. Suppl. 1969–70 Ann.Dingell-Johnson Rept. Div. Game and Fish, Dept. Nat. Resources Environ. Control, State of Delaware. Project F-13-R-12. 23 pp.

Dale, W. E., and R. C. Axtell. 1975. Flight of the salt marsh Tabanidae (Diptera), *Tabanus nigrovittatus, Chrysops atlanticus* and *C. fuliginosus:* correlation with temperature, light, moisture and wind velocity. *J. Med. Ent.* **12**(5):551–557.

Darnell, R. M. 1967. Organic detritus in relation to the ecosystem. Amer. Assoc. Advan. Sci. Publ. No. 83, *Estuaries:* 376–382.

Darsie, R. J., Jr., and P. F. Springer. 1957. Three-year investigation of mosquito breeding in natural and impounded tidal marshes in Delaware. Univ. Delaware Agr. Exp. Sta. Bull. 320. 65 pp.

Davis, L. V., and I. E. Gray. 1966. Zonal and seasonal distribution of insects in North Carolina salt marshes. *Ecol. Monogr.* **36**(3):275–295.

Dawson, J. W. 1855. *Acadian Geology.* London.

Day, J. W., Jr., W. G. Smith, P. R. Wagner, and W. C. Stowe. 1973. Community structure and carbon budget of a salt marsh and shallow bay estuarine system in Louisiana. Center for Wetlands Res. La. St. Univ. Publ. LSU-SG-72-04. 80 pp.

De Coursey, P. J. 1976. Vertical migration of larval *Uca* in a shallow estuary. *Amer. Zool.* **16**(362):244.

den Hartog, C. 1974. Salt marsh Turbellaria. *In:* N. W. Riser and M. Patricia Morse, eds. *Biology of the Turbellaria.* McGraw-Hill Book Co., N.Y. pp. 229–247.

Dembowski, J. B. 1926. Notes on the behavior of fiddler crabs. *Biol. Bull.* **50**:179–201.

de Vlaming, V. L., A. Kuris, and F. R. Parker, Jr. 1978. Seasonal variations of reproduction and lipid reserves in some subtropical Cyprinodontids. *Trans. Amer. Fish. Soc.* **107**(3):464–472.

deWitt, P., and F. C. Daiber. 1973. The hydrography of the Broadkill River estuary, Delaware. *Ches. Sci.* **14**(1):28–40.

Dexter, R. W. 1942. Notes on the marine mollusks of Cape Ann, Massachusetts. *Nautilus* **56**(2):57–61.

Dexter, R. W. 1944. Annual fluctuations of abundance of some marine mollusks. *Nautilus* **58**(1):20.

Dexter, R. W. 1945. Zonation of the intertidal marine mollusks at Cape Ann, Massachusetts. *Nautilus* **58**(2):56–64.

Dexter, R. W. 1947. The marine communities of a tidal inlet at Cape Ann, Massachusetts: a study in bio-ecology. *Ecol. Monogr.* **17**(3):261–294.

DiMichele, L. 1980. The hatching mechanism of *Fundulus heteroclitus*. Ph.D. Dissertation. Univ. Delaware. 124 pp.

Donohoe, R. W. 1966. Muskrat reproduction in areas of controlled and uncontrolled water-level units. *J. Wildl. Mgmt.* **30**(2):320–326.

Dozier, H. L. 1947. Salinity as a factor in Atlantic Coast tide water muskrat production. *Trans. N. Amer. Wildl. Conf.* **12**:398–420.

Dozier, H. L. 1953. Muskrat production and management. Circ. 18 Fish and Wild. Serv., U.S. Dept. Interior, 42 pp.

Dozier, H. L., M. H. Markley, and L. M. Llewellyn. 1948. Muskrat investigations on the Blackwater National Wildlife Refuge, Maryland, 1941–1945. *J. Wildl. Mgmt.* **12**(2):177–190.

Drummond, D. C. 1960. The food of *Rattus norvegicus* Berk, in the area of seawall, salt marsh and mudflat. *J. Anim.Ecol.* **29**(2):341–347.

Dukes, J. C., R. C. Axtell, and K. L. Knight. 1974a. Additional studies of the effects of salt marsh impoundments on mosquito populations. Water Resources Res. Inst., Univ. North Carolina. Rept. No. 102. 38 pp.

Dukes, J. C., T. D. Edwards, and R. C. Axtell. 1974b. Associations of Tabanidae (Diptera) larvae with plant species in salt marshes, Carteret County, North Carolina. *Environ. Ent.* **3**(2):280–286.

Dukes, J. C., T. D. Edwards, and R. C. Axtell. 1974c. Distribution of larvae Tabanidae (Diptera) in a *Spartina alterniflora* salt marsh. *J. Med. Ent.* **11**(1):79–83.

Elton, C. S. 1927. *Animal Ecology*. Sidgwick and Jackson, Ltd., London. 209 pp.

Elton, C. S. 1966. *The Pattern of Animal Communities*. Methuen & Co., London. 432 pp.

Epifanio, C. E., and Anna Dittell. 1981. Seasonal abundance and vertical distribution of crab larvae in Delaware Bay. *Estuaries*. In press.

Errington, P. L. 1963. *Muskrat Populations*. Iowa State Univ. Press, Ames, Iowa. 665 pp.

Evans, J. 1970. About nutria and their control. Resource Publ., Fish and Wildl. Serv., Dept. Int., No. 86. 65 pp.

Evans, P. D., E. N. E. Ruscoe, and J. E. Treherne. 1971. Observations on the biology and submergence behavior of some littoral beetles. *J. Mar. Biol. Assoc. U.K.* **51**(2):375–386.

Fahy, W. E. 1976. The morphological time of fixation of the total number of vertebrae in *Fundulus majalis* (Walbaum). *J. Cons. Int. Explor. Mer.* **36**(3):243–250.

Ferrigno, F. 1957. Clapper rail study. *In:* J. W. Aldrich, et al. Investigations of woodcock, snipe, and rails in 1956. U.S. Fish and Wildl. Serv., Spec. Sci. Rept., Wildl. **34**:81–85.

Ferrigno, F. 1958. A two-year study of mosquito breeding in the natural and untouched salt marshes of Egg Island. *Proc. N. J. Mosq. Exterm. Assoc.* **45**:132–139.

Ferrigno, F. 1959. Further study on mosquito production on the newly acquired Caldwalder Tract. *Proc. N. J. Mosq. Exterm. Assoc.* **46**:95–102.

Ferrigno, F. 1961. Variations in mosquito-wildlife associations on coastal marshes. *Proc. N. J. Mosq. Exterm. Assoc.* **48**:193–203.

Ferrigno, F. 1976. Snow Goose Management. *New Jersey Outdoors* **3**(5):22–24.

Ferrigno, F., and D. M. Jobbins. 1966. A summary of the nine years of applied mosquito–wildlife research on Cumberland County, N.J. salt marshes. *Proc. N. J. Mosq. Exterm. Assoc.* **53**:97–112.

Ferrigno, F., and D. M. Jobbins. 1968. Open marsh water management. *Proc. N. J. Mosq. Exterm. Assoc.* **55**:104–115.

Ferrigno, F., D. M. Jobbins, and M. P. Shinkle. 1967. Coordinated mosquito control and wildlife management for the Delaware Bay coastal marshes. *Proc. N. J. Mosq. Exterm. Assoc.* **54**:80–94.

Ferrigno, F., L. G. MacNamara, and D. M. Jobbins. 1969. Ecological approach for improved management of coastal meadowlands. *Proc. N. J. Mosq. Exterm. Assoc.* **56:**188–203.

Ferrigno, F., L. Widjeskog, J. Hansen, and P. Slavin. 1976. OMWM—quality mosquito control on cordgrass salt marshes. *Proc. N. E. Fish and Wildl. Conf.* **33:**87–100.

Fish, J. D. 1972. The breeding cycle and growth of an open coast and estuarine populations of *Littorina littorea. J. Mar. Biol. Assoc. U.K.* **52**(4):1011–1019.

Fish, J. D., and S. Fish. 1974. The breeding cycle and growth of *Hydrobia ulvae* in the Dovey estuary. *J. Mar. Biol. Assoc. U.K.* **54:**685–697.

Fisler, G. F. 1963. Effects of salt water on food and water consumption and weight of harvest mice. *Ecol.* **44**(3):604–608.

Fisler, G. F. 1965a. Behavior of salt marsh *Microtus* during winter high tides. *J. Mammal.* **42:**37–43.

Fisler, G. F. 1965b. Adaptation and speciation in harvest mice of the San Francisco Bay. *Univ. Calif. Publ. Zool.* **77:**1–108.

Fisler, G. F. 1971. Age structure and sex ratio in populations of *Reithrodontomys. J. Mammal.* **52**(4):653–662.

Fleeger, J. W. 1979. Population dynamics of three estuarine meiobenthic harpacticoids (Copepoda) in South Carolina. *Mar. Biol.* **52:**147–156.

Fleeger, J. W. 1980. Community structure of an estuarine meiobenthic copepod assemblage. *Estuarine Coast. Mar. Sci.* **10**(1):107–118.

Florschutz, O., Jr. 1959. Mosquito production of wildlife usage in impounded, ditched and unditched tidal marshes in the Assawoman Wildlife Area, Delaware. *Proc. N. J. Mosq. Exterm. Assoc.* **46:**103–111.

Forbush, E. H. 1925. *Birds of Massachusetts and other New England States. Pt. 1. Water birds, Marsh birds and Shore birds.* Mass. Dept. Agr. Norwood Press. Norwood, Mass. Printed by Berwick and Smith Co.

Forbush, E. H. 1927. *Birds of Massachusetts and other New England States. Pt. 2. Land birds from Bob-whites to Grackles.* Mass. Dept. Agr. Norwood, Mass. Printed by Berwick and Smith Co. 461 pp.

Forbush, E. H. 1929. *Birds of Massachusetts and other New England states. Pt. 3. Land Birds from Sparrows and Thrushes.* Mass. Dept. Agr. Norwood Press, Norwood, Mass. Printed by Berwick and Smith Co.

Foster, W. A., and J. E. Treherne. 1975. The distribution of an intertidal aphid, *Pemphigus trehernei* Foster on marine saltmarshes *Oecologia* **21:**141–155.

Foster, W. A., and J. E. Treherne. 1976a. The effects of tidal submergence on an intertidal aphid *Pemphigus trehernei* Foster. *J. Anim. Ecol.* **45**(1):291–301.

Foster, W. A., and J. E. Treherne. 1976b. Insects of marine salt marshes: problems and adaptations. *In* L. cheng, ed. *Marine insects.* Elsevier Sci. Publ. Amsterdam, Netherlands. pp. 5–42.

Frankenberg, D., and W. D. Burbanck. 1963. A comparison of the physiology and ecology of the estuarine isopod *Cyathura polita* in Massachusetts and Georgia. *Biol. Bull.* **125**(1):81–95.

Franz, D. R. 1963. Production and distribution of mosquito larvae on some New Jersey salt marsh impoundments. *Proc. N. J. Mosq. Exterm. Assoc.* **50:**279–285.

Freeman, J. V., and E. J. Hansens. 1972. Collecting larvae of the salt marsh greenhead *Tabanus nigrovittatus* and related species in New Jersey: comparison of methods. *Environ. Ent.* **1:**653–658.

Fretter, V., and A. Graham. 1962. *British Prosobranch Molluscs; Their Functional Anatomy and Ecology.* Roy. Soc. Publ., London. 755 pp.

Fritz, E. S., and E. T. Garside. 1975. Comparison of age composition, growth, and fecundity between two populations each of *Fundulus heteroclitus* and *F. diaphanus* (Pisces: Cyprinodontidae). *Can. J. Zool.* **53**(4):361–369.

Frohling, R. C. 1965. American oyster catcher and black skimmer nesting on salt marsh. *Wilson Bull.* **77**(2):193–194.

Gable, M. F., and R. A. Croker. 1977. The salt marsh amphipod, *Gammarus palustris* Bousfield, 1969 at the northern limit of its distribution. I. Ecology and life cycle. *Est. and Coastal Mar. Sci.* **5**:123–134.

Gallagher, J. L. 1971. Algal productivity and some aspects of the ecological physiology of the edaphic communities of Canary Creek tidal marsh. Ph.D. dissertation. Univ. Delaware. 120 pp.

Gallagher, J. L., and F. C. Daiber. 1974. Primary production of edaphic algae communities in a Delaware salt marsh. *Limnol. Oceanogr.* **19**(3):390–395.

Gannon, J. E., and R. S. Stemberger. 1978. Zooplankton (especially crustaceans and rotifers) as indicators of water quality. *Trans. Amer. Micros. Soc.* **97**(1):16–35.

Garbisch, E. W., P. B. Woller, W. J. Bostian, and R. J. McCallum. 1975. Biotic techniques for shore stabilization. *In* Cronin, L. E., ed. *Estuarine Research,* Vol. **2**, Academic Press, N.Y. pp. 405–426.

Gashwiler, J. S. 1950. A study of the reproductive capacity of Maine muskrats. *J. Mammal.* **31**(2):180–185.

Gerlach, S. A. 1965. Uber die fauna in Gezeiten zone von Spitzbergen. (The fauna of a Spitzbergen salt marsh.) *Proc. 5th Mar. Biol. Symp. Acat. Univ. Goteborg* **III**:81–92.

Gerlach, S. A. 1971. On the importance of marine meiofauna for benthos communities. *Oecologia* **6**:176–190.

Gerlach, S. A. 1978. Food-chain relationships in subtidal silty sand marine sediments and the role of meiofauna in stimulating bacterial productivity. *Oecologia* **33**(1):55–69.

Gerry, B. I. 1950. Salt marsh fly control as an adjunct to mosquito control in Massachusetts. *Proc. N. J. Mosq. Exterm. Assoc.* **37**:189–193.

Gessner, R. V., and R. D. Goos. 1973. Fungi from decomposing *Spartina alterniflora. Can. J. Bot.* **51**:51–55.

Getz, L. L. 1966. Salt tolerance of salt marsh meadow voles. *J. Mammal.* **47**(2):201–207.

Giere, O. 1975. Population structure, food relations and ecological role of marine oligochaetes, with special reference to meiobenthic species. *Mar. Biol.* **31**(2):139–156.

Gillette, J. D. 1972. *Mosquitos.* The World Naturalist. Weidenfeld and Nicolson. London. 274 pp.

Gillham, M. E. 1955. Ecology of the Pembrokeshire Islands, III. The effect of grazing on the vegetation. *J. Ecol.* **43**(1):172–206.

Glue, D. E. 1971. Salt marsh reclamation stages and their associated bird life. *Bird Study* **18**(4):187–198.

Goodwin, R. H. 1961. Connecticut's coastal marshes—a vanishing resource. *Conn. Arbor. Bull.* **12**:1–36.

Govindankutty, A. G., and N. B. Nair. 1972. Observations on the breeding periods of certain interstitial nematodes, gastrotrichs and copepods of the south-west coast of India. *J. Mar. Biol. Assoc. India* **14**:402–406.

Gray, A. J. 1972. The ecology of Morecambe Bay. V. The salt marshes of Morecambe Bay. *J. Appl. Ecol.* **9**(1):207–220.

Gray, A. J., and R. G. H. Bunce. 1972. The ecology of Morecambe Bay. VI. Soils and vegetation of the salt marshes: a multivariate approach. *J. Appl. Ecol.* **9**(1):221–234.

Gray, A. J., and R. Scott. 1975. Genecology of salt marsh plants. Ann. Rept. 1974. Inst. Terr. Ecol. Natural Environ. Res. Council. Her Majesty's Stationery Office, London. pp. 35–36.

Gray, A. J., and R. Scott. 1977. The ecology of Morecambe Bay. VII. The distribution of

Puccinellia maritima, Festuca rubra and *Agrostis stolonifera* in the salt marshes. *J. Appl. Ecol.* **14**(1):229–241.

Gray, E. H. 1942. Ecological and life history aspects of red jointed fiddler crab, *Uca minax* (Le Conte), region of Solomons Island, Maryland. *Md. Bd. Nat. Res., Dept. Res. and Ed. CBL Publ.* **51,** pp. 3–20.

Green, J. W., M. Harsch, L. Barr, and C. L. Prosser. 1959. The regulation of water and salt by the fiddler crabs *Uca pugnax* and *Uca pugilator. Biol. Bull.* **116**(10):76–87.

Green, R. D., and G. P. Askew. 1965. Observations on the biological development of macropores in soils of Romney marsh. *J. Soil Sci.* **16**(2):342–349.

Greenhalgh, M. E. 1971. The breeding bird communities of Lancashire salt marshes. *Bird Study* **18**:199–212.

Greenhalgh, M. E. 1974. Population growth and breeding success in a salt marsh common tern colony. *Naturalist* **931**:121–127.

Greenwald, G. S. 1956. The reproductive cycle of the field mouse *Microtus californicus. J. Mammal.* **37**(2):213–222.

Greenwald, G. S. 1957. Reproduction in a coastal California population of the field mouse *Microtus californicus. Univ. Calif. Publ. Zool.* **54**:421–446.

Griffith, R. E. 1940. Waterfowl management of Atlantic coast refuges. *Trans. N. Amer. Wildl. Conf.* **5**:373–377.

Gunter, G. 1945. Studies on marine fishes of Texas. *Publ. Inst. Mar. Sci.* **1**(1):1–190.

Gunter, G., B. S. Ballard, and A. Venkataramiah. 1974. A review of salinity problems of organisms in the United States coastal areas subject to the effects of engineering works. *Gulf Res. Repts.* **4**(3):380–475.

Gunter, G., and L. N. Eleuterius. 1971. Some effects of hurricanes on terrestrial biota, with special reference to Camille. *Gulf. Res. Repts.* **3**(2):283–289.

Gurney, R. 1923. Some notes on *Leander longirostris* Edwards, and other British prawns. *Proc. Zool. Soc. London* **1**:114–123.

Hackney, A. G. 1944. List of mollusca from around Beaufort, North Carolina, with notes on *Tethys. Nautilus* **58**(2):56–64.

Hagmann, L. E. 1953. Biology of *Mansonia perturbans* (Walker). *Proc. N. J. Mosq. Exterm. Assoc.* **40**:141–147.

Haines, E. B. 1976a. Relation between the stable carbon isotope composition of fiddler crabs, plants, and soils in a salt marsh. *Limnol. Oceanogr.* **21**(6):880–883.

Haines, E. B. 1976b. Stable carbon isotope ratios in the biota, soils and tidal water of a Georgia salt marsh. *Est. Coastal Mar. Sci.* **4**(6):609–616.

Haines, E. B., A. Chalmers, R. Hanson, and B. Sherr. 1976. Nitrogen pools and fluxes in a Georgia salt marsh. *In:* M. Wiley, ed. *Estuarine Processes,* Vol. **2:** Academic Press, N.Y. pp. 241–254.

Haines, H. 1964. Salt tolerance and water requirements in the salt marsh harvest mouse. *Physiol. Zool* **37**(3):266–272.

Hall, E. R., and K. R. Kelson. 1959. *The Mammals of North America.* Ronald Press, N.Y. 1083 pp.

Hamilton, W. J. 1943. *The Mammals of Eastern United States.* Cornell Univ. Press, Ithaca, N.Y. 432 pp.

Hansens, E. J. 1949. The biting fly problem in New Jersey resorts and its relation to mosquito control. *Proc. N. J. Mosq. Exterm. Assoc.* **36**:126–130.

Hansens, E. J. 1952. Some observations on the abundance of salt marsh green-heads. *Proc. N. J. Mosq. Exterm. Assoc.* **39**:93–98.

Hansens, E. J., and J. W. Robinson. 1973. Emergence and movement of the saltmarsh deerflies *Chrysops fuliginosus* and *Chrysops atlanticus. Ann. Ent. Soc. Am.* **66**:1215–1218.

Hardy, J. D., Jr. 1978. *Development of Fishes of the Mid-Atlantic Bight: an Atlas of Egg,*

Larval and Juvenile Stages. Vol. **2.** *Anguillidae through Syngnathidae.* Biol. Serv. Program, Fish & Wildl. Serv. FWS/OBS-78-12. pp. 141–216.

Harrington, R. W., Jr. 1959a. Effects of four combinations of temperature and day length on the ovogenetic cycle of a low-latitude fish, *Fundulus confluentus* Goode & Bean. *Zoologica* **44**(4):149–168.

Harrington, R. W., Jr. 1959b. Delayed hatching in stranded eggs of marsh killfish, *Fundulus confluentus. Ecol.* **40:**430–437.

Harrington, R. W., Jr., and E. S. Harrington. 1961. Food selection among fishes invading a high subtropical salt marsh: from onset of flooding through the progress of a mosquito brood. *Ecol.* **42**(4):646–666.

Harris, E. S. 1937. Muskrat culture and its economic significance in New Jersey. *Proc. N. J. Mosq. Exterm. Assoc.* **24:**20–25.

Harris, E. S. 1939. Plants constituting the food of the muskrat on the New Jersey coastal and inland marshes and the comparative importance of each. *Proc. N. J. Mosq. Exterm. Assoc.* **26:**221–228.

Harris, R. R. 1972. Aspects of sodium regulation in a brackish water and a marine species of isopod genus *Sphaeroma. Mar. Biol.* **12**(1):18–27.

Harris, V. T. 1953. Ecological relationships of meadow voles and rice rats in tidal marshes. *J. Mammal.* **34:**479–487.

Harrison, F. J., Jr. 1970. The use of low-level impoundments for the control of the salt marsh mosquito, *Aedes sollicitans* (Walker). Master's thesis. Univ. Delaware. 66 pp.

Harrison, P. G. 1977. Decomposition of macrophyte detritus in seawater: effects of grazing by amphipods. *Oikos* **28**(2–3):165–169.

Harvey, C. E. 1969. Breeding and distribution of *Sphaeroma* (Crustacea: Isopoda) in Britain. *J. Anim. Ecol.* **38**(2):399–406.

Hatfield, D. M. 1935. A natural history study of *Microtus californicus. J. Mammal.* **16**(4):261–271.

Hauseman, S. A. 1932. A contribution to the ecology of the salt marsh snail, *Melampus bidentatus* Say. *Amer. Natur.* **66:**541–545.

Headlee, T. J. 1939. Relation of mosquito control to wildlife. *Proc. N.J. Mosq. Exterm. Assoc.* **26:**5–12.

Headlee, T. J. 1945. *The Mosquitos of New Jersey and Their Control.* Rutgers Univ. Press. New Brunswick, N.J. 326 pp.

Healey, B. 1975. Fauna of the salt marsh, North Bull Island, Dublin (Eire). *Proc. R. Ir. Acad. Sect.* **B 75**(10):225–234.

Heard, R. W. III, and W. B. Sikora. 1972. A new species of *Corophium* Latreille, 1806 (Crustacea: Amphipoda) from Georgia brackish waters with some ecological notes. *Proc. Biol. Soc. Wash.* **84**(55):467–476.

Hedgepeth, J. W. 1973. Impact of impact studies. *Helgolander wiss. Meeresunters* **24:**436–445.

Heinle, D. R., and D. A. Flemer. 1976. Flows of materials from poorly flooded tidal marshes and an estuary. *Mar. Biol.* **35**(4):359–373.

Heinle, D. R., D. A. Flemer, and J. F. Ustach. 1976. Contribution of tidal marshlands to mid-Atlantic estuarine food chains. *In:* M. Wiley, ed. *Estuarine Processes,* Vol. 2. Academic Press, N.Y. pp. 309–320.

Heit, W. S. 1944. Food habits of red foxes in the Maryland marshes. *J. Mammal.* **25:**55–58.

Herrnkind, W. F. 1968. The breeding of *Uca pugilator* (Bosc) and mass rearing of the larval with comments on the behavior of the larval and early crab stages (Brachyura, Ocypodidae). *Crustaceana.* Suppl. 2. Studies on decapod larval development: 214–224.

Hicks, S. D. 1973. Trends and variability of yearly mean sea level 1893–1971. NOAA Tech. Mem. No. 12. U.S. Dept. Comm. 13 pp.

Hicks, S. D., and J. E. Crosby. 1974. Trends and variability of yearly mean sea level. NOAA Tech. Memo. No. 13. Natl. Ocean. Atmos. Admin./Natl. Ocean Survey. U.S. Dept. Comm. 14 pp.

Hildebrand, S. F. 1917. Notes on the life history of the minnows *Gambusia affinis* and *Cyprinodon variegatus*. Appendix VI, Rep. U.S. Fish Comm., Bureau Fish. Doc. **857**:1–15.

Hildebrand, S. F., and W. C. Schroeder. 1928. *Fishes of Chesapeake Bay. Bull. Bur. Fish.* **43**(1):366 pp.

Hill, R. W. 1976. *Comparative Physiology of Animals.* Harper & Row Publ., N.Y.

Hirschmann, H. 1960. Reproduction of nematodes. *In:* J. N. Sasser and R. W. Jenkins, eds. *Nematology.* Univ. North Carolina Press, Chapel Hill, N.C. pp. 140–167.

Hoese, H. D. 1971. Dolphin feeding out of water in a salt marsh. *J. Mammal.* **52**(1):222–223.

Hoffman, C. P., Jr. 1980. Growth and reproduction of *Palaemonetes pugio* Holthuis and *P. vulgaris* (Say) populations in Canary Creek Marsh, Delaware. Master's thesis, Univ. Delaware. 125 pp.

Hoffman, R. S. 1958. The role of reproduction and mortality in population fluctuations of voles (*Microtus*). *Ecol. Monogr.* **28**(1):79–109.

Hoffpauer, C. M. 1968. Burning for coastal marsh management. *In* Newsom, J. D., ed. *Proc. Marsh and Estuary Management Symposium,* Louisiana State Univ., pp. 134–139.

Holle, P. A. 1957. Life history of the salt marsh snail *Melampus bidentatus* Say. *Nautilus* **70**:90–95.

Holler, N. R. 1973. Reproduction of the marsh rabbit (*Sylvilagus palustris*) in south Florida. Ph.D. dissertation. Univ. Missouri. 121 pp.

Hopkins, C. S., J. G. Gosselink, and R. T. Parrondo. 1978. Above ground production of seven marsh plant species in coastal Louisiana. *Ecol.* **59**(4):760–769.

Hopper, B. E., J. W. Fell, and R. C. Cefalu. 1973. Effect of temperature on life cycles of nematodes associated with the mangrove (*Rhizophora mangle*) detrital system. *Mar. Biol.* **23**:293–296.

Hopper, B. E., and S. P. Meyers. 1966. Aspects of the life cycle of marine nematodes. *Helgolander wiss. Meeresunters* **13**:444–449.

Horn, H. S. 1974. The ecology of secondary succession. *In:* R. E. Johnston, P. W. Frank and C. D. Michener, eds. *Ann. Rev. Ecol. Syst.* **5**:25–37.

Horsfall, W. R. 1955. *Mosquitos: Their Bionomics and Relation to Disease.* Ronald Press, N.Y. 723 pp.

Howe, M. A. 1974. Observations on the terrestrial wing displays of breeding willets. *Wilson Bull.* **86**:286–288.

Howell, A. H. 1914. Revision of the North American harvest mice (Genus *Reithrodontomys*). U.S. Biol. Survey. North American Fauna. No. 36. 97 pp.

Hubbs, C., and G. E. Drewry. 1959. Survival of F. hybrids between cyprinodont fishes, with a discussion of the correction between hybridization and phylogenetic relationship. *Publ. Inst. Mar. Sci.* **6**:81–91.

Hulbert, S. H. 1971. The nonconcept of series diversity: a critique and alternative parameters. *Ecol.* **52**(4):577–586.

Hunt, T. P. 1959. Breeding habits of the swamp rabbit with notes on its life history. *J. Mammal.* **40**(1):82–91.

Hurd, L. E., M. V. Mellinger, L. L. Wolf, and S. J. McNaughton. 1971. Stability and diversity at three trophic levels in terrestrial successional ecosystems. *Science* **173**:1134–1136.

Hurd, L. E., G. W. Smedes, and T. A. Dean. 1979. An ecological study of a natural population of diamondback terrapin (*Malaclemys t. terrapin*) in a Delaware salt marsh. *Estuaries* **2**:28–33.

Hurd, L. E., and L. L. Wolf. 1974. Stability in relation to nutrient enrichment in arthropod consumers of old-field successional ecosystems. *Ecol. Monogr.* **44**(4):465–482.

Hyman, L. H. 1940. *The Invertebrates: Protozoa through Ctenophora*. McGraw-Hill Book Co., N.Y. 733 pp.

Hyman, L. H. 1967. *The Invertebrates: Mollusca I*. McGraw-Hill Book Co., N.Y. 792 pp.

Hyman, O. W. 1920. The development of *Gelasiums* after hatching. *J. Morph.* **33**(2):484–525.

Itzkowitz, M. 1974. The effects of other fish on the reproductive behavior of the male *Cyprinodon variegatus* (Pisces: Cyprinodontidae). *Behavior* **48**(1–2):1–22.

Jamnback, H., and W. J. Wall. 1959. The common salt marsh Tabanidae of Long Island, New York. *Bull. N.Y. State Mus. No. 375*. Albany, N.Y. 77 pp.

Jeffries, H. P. 1972. Fatty-acid ecology of a tidal marsh. *Limnol. Oceanogr.* **17**(3):433–440.

Johannes, R. E. 1965. Influence of marine protozoa on nutrient regeneration. *Limnol. Oceanogr.* **10**(3):434–442.

Johnston, R. F. 1954. Variation in breeding season and clutch size in song sparrows on the Pacific coast. *Condor* **56**(5):268–273.

Johnston, R. F. 1955. Influence of winter high tides on two populations of salt marsh song sparrows. *Condor* **57**(5):308–309.

Johnston, R. F. 1956a. The incubation period of the clapper rail. *Condor* **58**(2):166.

Johnston, R. F. 1956b. Population structure in salt marsh song sparrows. I. Environment and annual cycle. *Condor* **58**:24–44.

Johnston, R. F. 1956c. Population structure in salt marsh song sparrows. II. Density, age structure, and maintenance. *Condor* **58**:254–272.

Johnston, R. F. 1957. Adaptation of salt marsh mammals to high tides. *J. Mammal.* **38**(4):529–531.

Johnston, R. F., and R. L. Rudd. 1957. Breeding of the salt marsh shrew. *J. Mammal.* **38**(2):157–163.

Jones, C. M., and D. W. Anthony. 1964. The Tabanidae of Florida. U.S.D.A. Agric. Res. Ser. Agric. Tech. Bull. No. 1295. 85 pp.

Jones, D. R. 1978. Density, distribution and productivity of small mammals on the Canary Creek marsh, Delaware. Master's thesis. Univ. Delaware.

Juday, C. 1942. The summer standing crop of plants and animals in four Wisconsin lakes. *Trans. Wisconsin Acad. Sci.* **34**:103–135.

Kaestner, A., H. W. Levi, and L. R. Levi. 1970. *Invertebrate Zoology: Crustacea* Vol. 3. Interscience Publ. N.Y. 523 pp.

Kale, H. W., II. 1965. Ecology and bioenergetics of the long-billed marsh wren *Telmatodytes palustris griseus* Brewster in Georgia salt marshes. *Publ. Nuttall Ornithol. Club No. 5.* pp 589–591.

Kale, H. W., II. 1967. Water sources of the long-billed marsh wren in Georgia salt marshes. *Auk* **84**(4):589–591.

Kat, P. W. 1978. The functional morphology and ecology of *Cyrenoida floridana* Dall (Bivalvia: Cyrenoidae). Master's thesis. Univ. Delaware. 180 pp.

Katz, L. M. 1975. Laboratory studies on diet, growth and energy requirements of *Fundulus heteroclitus* (Linnaeus). Ph.D. dissertation. Univ. Delaware. 80 pp.

Kerwin, J. A. 1971. Distribution of the fiddler crab (*Uca minax*) in relation to marsh plants within a Virginia estuary. *Ches. Sci.* **12**(3):180–183.

Kerwin, J. A. 1972. Distribution of salt marsh snail (*Melampus bidentatus* Say) in relation to marsh plants in the Poropotank River area, Virginia. *Ches. Sci.* **13**(2):150–153.

Kettle, D. S. 1977. Biology and bionomics of blood sucking ceratopagonids. *Ann. Rev. Ent.* **22**:35–51.

Kilby, J. D. 1955. The fishes of two Gulf coastal areas of Florida. *Tulane Stud. Zool.* **2**(8):177–247.

King, K. L., and K. J. Hutchinson. 1976. The effects of sheep stocking intensity on the abundance and distribution of mesofauna in pastures. *J. Appl. Ecol.* **13**(1):41–55.

Kinne, O. 1964. The effects of temperature and salinity on marine and brackish water animals. II. Salinity and temperature-salinity combinations. *Oceanogr. Mar. Biol. Ann. Rev.* **2**:281–339.

Kline, D. L., and R. C. Axtell. 1975. *Culicoides melleus* (Coq). (Diptera: Ceratopogonidae): seasonal abundance and emergence from sandy intertidal habitats. *Mosq. News* **35**(3):328–334.

Kline, D. L., and R. C. Axtell. 1976. Salt marsh *Culicoides* (Diptera: Ceratopogonidae): species, seasonal abundance and comparison of trapping methods. *Mosq. News* **36**(1):1–10.

Kline, D. L., and R. C. Axtell. 1977. Distribution of *Culicoides hollensis, C. furens* and *C. bermudensis* in relation to plant cover in North Carolina salt marsh (Diptera: Ceratopogonidae). *J. Med. Ent.* **13**(4–5):545–552.

Kneib, R. T., and A. E. Stiven. 1978. Growth, reproduction and feeding of *Fundulus heteroclitus* (L.) on a North Carolina salt marsh. *J. Exp. Mar. Biol. Ecol.* **31**(2):121–140.

Knight, K. L., and T. E. Baker. 1962. The role of the substrate moisture content in the selection of oviposition sites by *Aedes taeniorhynchus* (Weid.) and *A. sollicitans* (Walk.). *Mosq. News* **22**(3):247–254.

Knowlton, R. E., and A. B. Williams. 1970. Life histories of *Palaemonetes vulgaris* (Say) and *P. pugio* Holthuis in coastal North Carolina. *J. Elisha Mitchell Sci. Soc.* **86**(4):185.

Koch, H. G., and R. C. Axtell. 1978. Autogeny and rearing *Culicoides furens, C. hollensis* and *C. melleus* (Diptera: Ceratopogonidae) from coastal North Carolina. *Mosq. News* **38**(2):240–244.

Koch, H. G., and R. C. Axtell. 1979a. Correlation of hourly trap collections of *Culicoides furens* and *C. hollensis* (Diptera: Ceratopogonidae) with wind, temperature and habitat. *J. Med. Ent.* **15**(5–6):500–505.

Koch, H. G., and R. C. Axtell. 1979b. Attraction of *Culicoides furens* and *C. hollensis* (Diptera: Ceratopogonidae) to animal hosts in a salt marsh habitat. *J. Med. Ent.* **15**(5–6):494–499.

Kraeuter, J. N., and P. L. Wolf. 1974. The relationship of marine macro-invertebrates to salt marsh plants. *In:* R. J. Reimold and W. H. Queen, eds. *Ecology of Halophytes.* Academic Press, N.Y. pp. 449–462.

Kraft, J. C. 1971a. Sedimentary facies patterns and geologic history of a Holocene marine transgression. *Geol. Soc. Amer. Bull.* **82**(8):2131–2158.

Kraft, J. C. 1971b. A guide to the geology of Delaware's coastal environment. Coll. Mar. Std., Univ. Delaware, Newark, Delaware. 220 pp.

Kraft, J. C., ed. 1976. Geological reconstructions of ancient coastal environments in the vicinity of the Island Field archaeological site, Kent County, Delaware. *Trans. Del. Acad. Sci.,* Vol. **VI**. Newark, Delaware.

Kraft, J. C., and D. F. Belknap. 1975. Transgressive and regressive sedimentary lithosomes at the edge of a Late Holocene marine transgression. *Proc. IX Congress Internatl. Assoc. Sedimentologists,* Nice, France. Vol. **Pl**, pp. 87–95.

Krinsky, W. L. 1976. Animal disease agents transmitted by horseflies and deerflies (Diptera: Tabanidae). *J. Med. Ent.* **13**:225–275.

Kruczynski, W. L., and C. B. Subrahmanyam. 1978. Distribution and breeding cycle of

Cyathura polita (Isopoda: Anthuridae) in a *Juncus roemerianus* marsh of northern Florida. *Estuaries* **1**(2):93–100.

Kuenzler, E. J. 1961a. Structure and energy flow of a mussel population in a Georgia salt marsh. *Limnol. Oceanogr.* **6**(2):191–204.

Kuenzler, E. J. 1961b. Phosphorus budget of a mussel population. *Limnol. Oceanogr.* **6**(4):400–415.

Kuntz, A. 1916. Notes on the embryology and larval development of five species of teleostean fishes. *Bull. U.S. Bur. Fish.* **34**(1914):409–429.

Kushlan, J. A. 1976. Environmental stability and fish community diversity. *Ecol.* **57**(4):821–825.

Lake, R. W. 1965. Bionomics of *Aedes sollicitans* (Walker). Master's thesis. Univ. Delaware. 83 pp.

Lambert, F. J. 1930. Animal life in the marsh ditches of the Thames estuary. *Proc. Zool. Soc. London* **1930**(37):801–808.

Lambert, Rose M. 1978. Larval development of *Uca* sp. and *Rhithropanopeus harrisii* (Gould) in the Broadkill River. Master's thesis. Univ. Delaware. 74 pp.

Larsen, E. Bro. 1951. Studies on the soil fauna of Skallingen. *Oikos* **3**(2):166–192.

Larsson, T. 1969. Land use and bird fauna on shores in southern Sweden. *Oikos* **20**(1):136–155.

Larsson, T. 1976. Composition and density of the bird fauna in Swedish shore meadows. *Ornis Scand.* **7**(1):1–12.

LaSalle, R. N., and K. L. Knight. 1974. Effects of salt marsh impoundments on mosquito populations. Water Resources Res. Inst., Univ. North Carolina. Rept. No. 92. 85 pp.

Lay, D. W. 1945. Muskrat investigations in Texas. *J. Wildl. Mgmt.* **9**:56–76.

Lay, D. W., and T. O'Neil. 1942. Muskrats on the Texas coast. *J. Wildl. Mgmt.* **6**(4):301–312.

Lea, A. O., and P. T. M. Lum. 1959. Autogeny in *Aedes taeniorhynchus* (Wied). *J. Econ. Ent.* **52**(2):356–357.

Lebour, M. V. 1938. The eggs and larvae of the British prosobranchs with special reference to those living in the plankton. *J. Mar. Biol. Assoc. U.K.* **22**(10):105–166.

Lee, J. J. 1974. Towards understanding the niche of the Foraminifera. *In:* R. H. Hedley and C. G. Adams, eds. *Foraminifera,* Vol. I. Academic Press, N.Y. pp. 207–260.

Lee, J. J., and W. A. Muller. 1973. Trophic dynamics and niches of salt marsh Foraminifera. *Amer. Zool.* **13**:215–223.

Lee, J. J., W. A. Muller, R. J. Stone, M. E. McEnery, and W. Zucker. 1969. Standing crop of Foraminifera in sublittoral epiphytic communities of a Long Island salt marsh. *Mar. Biol.* **4**(1):44–61.

Lee, J. J., J. H. Tietjen, N. M. Saks, G. G. Ross, H. Rubin, and W. A. Muller. 1975. Inducing and modeling the function relationships within sublittoral salt-marsh aufwuchs communities—inside one of the Black Boxes. *In:* L. E. Cronin, ed. *Estuarine Research,* Vol. I. Academic Press, N.Y. pp. 710–734.

Lee, J. J., J. H. Tietjen, R. J. Stone, W. A. Muller, M. McEnery, N. Saks, C. Mastropaolo, and E. Kennedy. 1972. The effects of environment stress on the community structure, productivity, energy flow and mineral cycling in salt marsh epiphytic communities. *Third Natl. Symp. Radioecology.*

Lehmann, E. P. 1957. Statistical study of Texas Gulf Coast recent foraminiferal facies. *Micropaleontology* **3**:325–356.

Lenderking, R. E. 1954. Some recent observations on the biology of *Littorina angulifera* Lam. of Biscayne and Virginia Keys, Florida. *Bull. Mar. Sci. Gulf Carrib.* **3**(4):273–296.

Lent, C. M. 1967a. Effects and adaptive significance of air-gaping by the ribbed mussel, *Modiolus* (Arcuatula) *demissus* (Dillwyn). Ph.D. dissertation. Univ. Delaware. 77 pp.

Lent, C. M. 1967b. Effect of habitat on growth indices in the ribbed mussel, *Modiolus* (Arcuatula) *demissus*. *Ches. Sci.* **8**(4):221–227.

Lent, C. M. 1968. Air-gaping by the ribbed mussel *Modiolus demissus* (Dillwyn): effects and adaptive significance. *Biol. Bull.* **134**:60–73.

Lent, C. M. 1969. Adaptations of the ribbed mussel *Modiolus demissus* (Dillwyn) to the intertidal habitat. *Amer. Zool.* **9**:283–292.

Lesser, C. R. 1975. Some effects of grid systems mosquito control ditching on salt marsh biota in Delaware. Master's thesis. Univ. Delaware. 24 pp.

Lesser, F. H. 1965. Some environmental considerations of impounded tidal marshes on mosquito and waterbird prevalence, Little Creek Wildlife Area, Delaware. Master's thesis. Univ. Delaware. 121 pp.

Levington, J. S. 1979. Deposit-feeders, their resources, and the study of resource limitations. *In:* R. J. Livingston, ed. *Ecological Processes in Coastal and Marine Systems.* Mar. Sci. Vol. **10**. Plenum Press, N.Y. pp. 117–141.

Lind, H. F. 1975. The effect of temperature on gametogenic development in two marine bivalves, *Mya arenaria* and *Modiolus demissus*. Masters thesis, Univ. Delaware. 86 pp.

Lindeman, R. L. 1942. The trophic-dynamic aspects of ecology. *Ecol.* **23**:399–418.

Linduska, J. P. 1964. *Waterfowl Tomorrow.* U.S. Dept. Int. Fish and Wildl. Serv. 770 pp.

Linley, J. R. 1966a. Field and laboratory observations on the behavior of the immature stages of *Culicoides furens* Poey (Diptera: Ceratopogonidae). *J. Med. Ent.* **2**(4):385–391.

Linley, J. R. 1966b. The ovarian cycle in *Culicoides barbosai* Wirth & Blanton and *C. furens* (Poey) (Diptera: Ceratopogonidae). *Bull. Ent. Res.* **57**(1):1–17.

Linley, J. R. 1976. Biting midges of mangrove swamps and salt marshes (Diptera: Ceratopogonidae). *In:* L. Cheng, ed. *Marine Insects.* North-Holland Publ. Co., Amsterdam, Netherlands. pp. 335–376.

Linley, J. R., and G. M. Adams. 1972a. Ecology and behavior of immature *Culicoides melleus* (Coq.) (Diptera: Ceratopogonidae). *Bull. Ent. Res.* **62**(1):113–127.

Linley, J. R., and G. M. Adams. 1972b. A study of the mating behavior of *Culicoides melleus* (Coquilett) (Diptera: Ceratopogonidae). *Trans. R. Ent. Soc. London* **124**:81–121.

Linthurst, R. A., and R. J. Reimold. 1978. An evaluation of methods for estimating the net aerial primary productivity of estuarine angiosperms. *J. Appl. Ecol.* **15**(3):919–931.

Lockwood, A. P. M. 1962. The osmoregulation of Crustacea. *Biol. Rev.* **37**(2):257–305.

Lofts, B. 1956. Notes on the distribution of the prawn *Palaemonetes varians* (Leach) in a typical area of saltmarsh. *Ann. Mag. Nat. Hist.* **9**(103):521–525.

Loosanoff, V. L., and H. C. Davis. 1963. Rearing of bivalve mollusks. *In:* F. S. Russell, ed. *Advances in Marine Biology,* Vol. **1**. Academic Press, N.Y. pp. 1–136.

Lotrich, V. A. 1975. Summer home range and movements of *Fundulus heteroclitus* (Pisces: Cyprinodontidae) in a tidal creek. *Ecol.* **56**(1):191–198.

Lowe, C. E. 1958. Ecology of the swamp rabbit in Georgia. *J. Mammal.* **39**(1):116–127.

Lowery, G. H., Jr. 1974. *The Mammals of Louisiana and its Adjacent Waters.* Louisiana State Univ. Press. 565 pp.

Luxton, M. 1964. Some aspects of the biology of salt marsh Acarina. *Proc. 1st Internat. Congr. Acarol. 1973 Acarol. 6 Fasc. hors. ser.:* 172–182.

Luxton, M. 1967a. The ecology of salt marsh Acarina. *J. Anim. Ecol.* **36**(2):257–277.

Luxton, M. 1967b. The zonation of salt marsh Acarina. *Pedobiolog.* **7**:55–66.

Lynch, J. J., T. O'Neil, and D. W. Lay. 1947. Management significance of damage by geese and muskrats to Gulf Coast marshes. *J. Wildl. Mgmt.* **11**:50–76.

MacArthur, R. H. 1955. Fluctuations of animal populations, and a measure of community stability. *Ecol.* **36**:533–536.

MacDonald, K. B. 1969a. Molluscan faunas of Pacific coast salt marshes and tidal creeks. *Veliger* **11**:399–405.

MacDonald, K. B. 1969b. Quantitative studies of salt marsh faunas from the North American Pacific coast. *Ecol. Monogr.* **39**(1):33–60.

MacMillen, R. E. 1964. Water economy and salt balance in the western harvest mouse, *Reithrodontomys megalotis*. *Physiol. Zool.* **37**(1):45–46.

Macnae, W. 1957a. The ecology of the plants and animals in the intertidal regions of the Zwartkops estuary near Port Elizabeth, South Africa. Part I. *J. Ecol.* **45**(1):113–131.

Macnae, W. 1957b. The ecology of the plants and animals of the intertidal regions of the Zwartkops estuary near Port Elizabeth, South Africa. Part II. *J. Ecol.* **45**(2):361–387.

MacNamara, L. G. 1949. Salt-marsh development at Tuckahoe, New Jersey. *Trans. N. Amer. Wildl. Conf.* **14**:100–117.

MacNamara, L. G. 1952. Needs for additional research on mosquito control from the standpoint of fish and game management. *Proc. N. J. Mosq. Exterm. Assoc.* **39**:111–116.

Magnarelli, L. A. 1976. Physiological age of Tabanidae (Diptera) in Eastern New York State, U.S.A. *J. Med. Ent.* **12**(6):679–682.

Magnarelli, L. A., and J. F. Anderson. 1977. Follicular development in salt marsh Tabanidae (Diptera) and incidence of nectar feeding with relation to gonotrophic activity. *Ann. Ent. Soc. Amer.* **70**:529–533.

Magnarelli, L. A., and J. F. Anderson. 1978. Distribution and development of immature salt marsh Tabanidae (Diptera). *J. Med. Ent.* **14**(5):573–578.

Magnarelli, L. A., and J. F. Anderson. 1979a. Oviposition, fecundity, and fertility of the salt marsh deerfly, *Chrysops fuliginosus* (Diptera: Tabanidae). *J. Med. Ent.* **15**(2):176–179.

Magnarelli, L. A., and J. F. Anderson. 1979b. Oogenesis and oviposition in *Chrysops atlanticus* (Diptera: Tabanidae). *Ann. Ent. Soc. Amer.* **72**(3):350–352.

Magnarelli, L. A., J. F. Anderson, and J. H. Thorne. 1979. Diurnal nectar-feeding of salt marsh Tabanidae (Diptera). *Environ. Ent.* **8**(3):544–548.

Mangold, R. E. 1962. The role of low-level dike salt impoundments in mosquito control and wildlife utilization. *Proc. N. J. Mosq. Exterm. Assoc.* **49**:117–120.

Mare, Molly F. 1942. A study of a marine benthic community with special reference to the micro-organisms. *J. Mar. Biol. Assoc. UK* **25**(3):517–554.

Margalef, R. 1963. On certain unifying principles in ecology. *Amer. Nat.* **97**:357–374.

Marples, T. 1966. A radionuclide tracer study of arthropod food chains in a *Spartina* salt marsh ecosystem. *Ecol.* **47**(2):270–277.

Marples, T. C., and E. P. Odum. 1964. A radionuclide tracer study of arthropod food chains in a *Spartina alterniflora* salt marsh. (Abstract) *Bull. Ecol. Soc. Amer.* **45**:81.

Marsden, I. D. 1973. The influence of salinity and temperature on the survival and behavior of the Isopod *Sphaeroma rugicauda* from a salt marsh habitat. *Mar. Biol.* **21**(2):75–85.

Marshall, J. R. 1962. The morphology of the Upper Solway salt marshes. *Scot. Geogr. Mag.* **78**:81–99.

Marshall, J. T., Jr. 1948. Ecologic races of song sparrows in the San Francisco Bay region. I. Habitat and abundance. *Condor* **50**:193–215.

Martin, A. C., and F. M. Uhler. 1939. Food of game ducks in the United States and Canada. U.S. Dept. Agr. Tech. Bull. 634. 156 pp.

Martin, R. A., and J. H. Finucane. 1969. Reproduction and ecology of the longnose killifish. *Quart. J. Fla. Acad. Sci.* **31**:101–111.

Masch, F. D., and W. H. Espey. 1967. Shell dredging—a factor in sedimentation in Galveston Bay. Center for Res. Water Resources. Univ. Texas Tech. Rept. No. 7. 168 pp.

Matera, N. J., and J. J. Lee. 1972. Environmental factors affecting the standing crop of

Foraminifera in sublittoral and psammolittoral communities of a Long Island salt marsh. *Mar. Biol.* **14**(2):89–103.

Matthews, S. A. 1938. The seasonal cycle in the gonads of *Fundulus. Biol. Bull.* **75**:66–74.

May, M. S., III. 1974. Probable agents for the formation of detritus from the halophyte, *Spartina alterniflora. In:* R. J. Reimold and W. H. Queen, eds. *Ecology of Halophytes.* Academic Press, N.Y. pp. 429–440.

May, R. C. 1974. Factors affecting buoyancy in the eggs of *Bairdiella icistia* (Pisces: Sciaenidae). *Mar. Biol.* **28**(1):55–59.

McErlean, A. J., Susan G. O'Connor, J. A. Mihursky, and C. I. Gibson. 1973. Abundance, diversity and seasonal patterns of estuarine fish populations. *Estuarine and Coast. Mar. Sci.* **1**(1):19–36.

McGaughey, W. H. 1968. Role of salts in oviposition site selection by the black salt-marsh mosquito, *Aedes taeniorhynchus* (Wiedemann). *Mosq. News* **28**(2):207–217.

McIntyre, A. D. 1969. Ecology of marine benthos. *Biol. Rev.* **44**(2):245–290.

McMahan, E. A., R. L. Knight, and A. R. Camp. 1972. A comparison of microarthropod populations in sewage-exposed and sewage-free *Spartina* salt marshes. *Environ. Ent.* **1**:244–252.

Meanley, B. 1961. Late-summer food of the red-winged blackbirds in a fresh tidal-river marsh. *Wilson Bull* **73**:36–40.

Meanley, B. 1965. Early-fall food and habitat of the sora in the Patuxent River marsh, Maryland. *Ches. Sci.* **6**(4):235–237.

Meanley, B. 1969. Natural history of the king rail. North American fauna. Bur. Sports Fish. and Wildl. Fish and Wildl. Serv., No. 67. 108 pp.

Meanley, B., and J. S. Webb. 1963. Nesting ecology and reproduction of the red-winged blackbird in tidal marshes of the upper Chesapeake Bay region. *Ches. Sci.* **4**(2):90–100.

Means, T. H. 1903. Reclamation of salt marsh lands. U.S. Dept. Agr., Bur. Soils Circ. 8 pp.

Meany, R. A., I. Valiela, and J. M. Teal. 1976. Growth, abundance and distribution of larval tabanids in experimentally fertilized plots on a Massachusetts salt marsh. *J. Appl. Ecol.* **13**(2):323–332.

Meredith, W. H., and V. A. Lotrich. 1979. Production dynamics of a tidal creek population of *Fundulus heteroclitus* (Linnaeus). *Estuarine Coastal Mar. Sci.* **8**:99–118.

Meyers, S. P., and B. E. Hopper. 1967. Studies on marine fungal-nematode associations and plant degradation. *Helgo. wiss. Meeresunters* **15**:270–281.

Miller, D. C. 1961. The feeding mechanisms of fiddler crabs with ecological considerations of feeding adaptations. *Zool.* **46**(8):89–101.

Miller, K. G., and D. Maurer. 1973. Distribution of the fiddler crabs, *Uca pugnax* and *Uca minax,* in relation to salinity in Delaware rivers. *Ches. Sci.* **14**(3):219–221.

Miller, L. W. 1963. Growth, reproduction and food habits of the white perch, *Roccus americanus* (Gmelin) in the Delaware River estuary. Master's thesis. Univ. Delaware. 62 pp.

Miller, M. A., and W. D. Burbanck. 1961. Systematics and distribution of an estuarine isopod crustacean, *Cyathura polita* (Stimpson, 1855), new comb., from the Gulf and Atlantic seaboard of the United States. *Biol. Bull.* **120**(1):62–84.

Moller, H. S. 1975. Danish salt marsh communities of breeding birds in relation to different types of management. *Ornis Scand.* **6**:125–133.

Montagna, W. 1940. The Acadian sharp-tailed sparrows of Popham Beach, Maine. *Wilson Bull.* **52**:191–197.

Montagna, W. 1942. The sharp-tailed sparrows of the Atlantic coast. *Wilson Bull.* **54**:107–120.

Montanari, J. H. and J. A. Kusler. 1978. *Proceedings of the National Wetland Protection Symposium.* Biol. Services, Fish & Wild. Serv. Dept. Interior FWS/OBS-78/97.

Montevecchi, W. A. 1975. Behavioral and ecological factors influencing the reproductive success of a tidal marsh colony of laughing gulls (*Larus atricilla*). Ph.D. dissertation. Rutgers Univ.

Montevecchi, W. A. 1977. Predation in a salt marsh laughing gull colony. *Auk* **94**(3):583–585.

Montevecchi, W. A., and Joanna Burger. 1975. Aspects of the reproductive biology of the northern diamondback terrapin, *Malaclemys terrapin terrapin. Amer. Midl. Nat.* **94**:166–178.

Moore, C. J. 1968. The feeding and food habits of the silversides *Menidia menidia* (Linnaeus). Master's thesis. Univ. Delaware. 65 pp.

Moore, C. L. 1975. Nest repair in laughing gulls. *Wilson Bull.* **87**:271–274.

Mudge, B. F. 1858. The salt marsh formations of Lynn. *Proc. Essex Inst.* **2**:117–119.

Muller, W. A., and J. J. Lee. 1969. Apparent indispensability of bacteria in Foraminifera nutrition. *J. Protozool.* **16**(3):471–478.

Murray, B. G., Jr. 1969. A comparative study of the Le Conte's and sharp-tailed sparrows. *Auk* **86**(2):199–231.

Murray, J. W. 1973a. Recognition of estuarine environments using foraminiferids. *J. Geol. Soc.* **129**(4):456.

Murray, J. W. 1973b. *Distribution and Ecology of Living Benthic Foraminiferids.* Crane, Russak & Co., N.Y. 274 pp.

Natvig, L. R. 1948. *Contributions to the Knowledge of the Danish and Fennoscandian Mosquitos.* Suppl. I. Norsk Entomolgisk Tidsskrift. A. W. Broggers Boktrykkeri A/S Oslo, Norway. 567 pp.

Nayar, J. K. 1967. Effects of larval and pupal environment factors on biological status of adults at emergence in *Aedes taeniorhynchus* (Wied). *Bull. Ent. Res.* **58**:811–827.

Nayar, J. K., and D. M. Sauerman, Jr. 1975. The effects of nutrition on survival and fecundity in Florida mosquitos. Part 3. Utilization of blood and sugar for fecundity. *J. Med. Ent.* **12**:220–225.

Neely, W. W. 1962. Saline soils and brackish waters in management of wildlife, fish and shrimp. *Trans. N. Amer. Wildl. Conf.* **27**:321–334.

Negus, N. C., E. Gould, and R. K. Chipman. 1961. Ecology of the rice rat *Oryzomys palustris* (Harlan), on Breton Island, Gulf of Mexico, with a critique of the social stress theory. *Tulane Stud. Zool.* **8**(4):93–123.

Newman, H. H. 1907. Spawning behavior and sexual dimorphism in *Fundulus heteroclitus* and allied fish. *Biol. Bull.* **12**:314–345.

Newsom, J. D., ed. 1968. Proceedings of the marsh and estuary management symposium. Div. Cont. Educ., La. State Univ. 250 pp.

Newson, R. M. 1966. Reproduction in the feral coypu (*Myocastor coypus*). *In:* J. W. Rowlands (ed.), *Comparative Biology of Reproduction in Mammals. Symp. Zool. Soc. London* **5**:323–334.

Nice, M. M. 1937. Studies in the life history of the song sparrow. A population study of the song sparrow. *Trans. Linn. Soc. N.Y.* Vol. **4**. 246 pp.

Nice, M. M. 1943. Studies in the life history of the song sparrow. The behavior of the song sparrow and other passerines. *Trans. Linn. Soc. N.Y.* Vol. **6**. 328 pp.

Nice, M. M. 1954. Problems of incubation periods in North American birds. *Condor* **56**(4):173–197.

Nichol, E. A. 1936. The ecology of a salt marsh. *J. Mar. Biol. Assoc. U.K.* **20**:203–261.

Nicholas, W. L. 1975. *The Biology of Free-living Nematodes.* Oxford Univ. Press. London. 219 pp.

Nichols, J. T., and C. M. Breder, Jr. 1927. The marine fishes of New York and southern New England. *Zoologica* 9(1):1–192.

Nicholson, D. J. 1928. Nesting habits of the seaside sparrows in Florida. *Wilson Bull.* 49(4):225–237.

Nielsen, E. T., and A. T. Nielsen. 1953. Field observations on the habits of *Aedes taeniorhynchus. Ecol.* 34(1):141–156.

Niering, W. A. 1961. Tidal marshes: their use in scientific research. *Conn. Arboretum Bull.* 12:3–7.

Nixon, S. W., and C. A. Oviatt. 1973. Ecology of a New England salt marsh. *Ecol. Monogr.* 43(4):463–498.

Norris, J. D. 1967. A campaign against feral coypus *Myocaster coypus* Molina in Great Britain. *J. Appl Ecol.* 4:191–199.

Odum, E. P. 1961. The role of tidal marshes in estuarine production. *New York State Conserv.* 16:12–15, 35.

Odum, E. P. 1969. The strategy of ecosystem development. *Science* 164:262–270.

Odum, E. P. 1971. *Fundamentals of Ecology.* 3rd ed. W. B. Sanders Co. Philadelphia. 574 pp.

Odum, E. P., and A. A. de la Cruz. 1967. Particulate organic detritus in a Georgia salt marsh-estuarine ecosystem. *In:* G. H. Lauff, ed. *Estuaries.* AAAS Publ. No. 83, Washington, D.C. pp. 383–388.

Odum, E. P., and A. E. Smalley. 1959. Comparison of population energy flow of a herbivorous and a deposit feeding invertebrate in a salt marsh ecosystem. *Proc. Natl. Acad. Sci.* 45:617–622.

Odum, H. T. 1972. An energy circuit language for ecological and social systems: its physical basis. *In:* B. C. Patten, ed. *Systems Analysis and Simulation in Ecology,* Vol. 2. Academic Press, N.Y. pp. 140–211.

Odum, W. E. 1970. Utilization of the direct grazing and plant detritus food chains by the striped mullet *Mugil cephalus. In:* J. H. Steele, ed. *Marine Food Chains.* Oliver and Boyd, Edinburgh. pp. 222–240.

Odum, W. E. 1971. Pathways of energy flow in a south Florida estuary. Ph.D. dissertation. Univ. Miami. Sea Grant Program Tech. Bull. 7. 162 pp.

Odum, W. E., and E. J. Heald. 1975. The detritus-based food web of an estuarine mangrove community. *In:* L. E. Cronin, ed. *Estuarine Research,* Vol. 1. Academic Press, N.Y. pp. 265–286.

Odum, W. E., and S. S. Skjei. 1974. The issues of wetlands preservation and management: a second view. *Coastal Zone Mgmt. J.* 1(2):151–163.

Odum, W. E., J. C. Zieman, and E. J. Heald. 1973. The importance of vascular plant detritus in estuaries. *In:* R. H. Chabreck, ed. *Proc. Coastal Marsh and Est. Mgmt. Symp., La. State Univ.* pp. 91–114.

Oliver, F. W. 1913. Some remarks on Blakeney Point, Norfolk. *J. Ecol.* 1(1):4–15.

Olkowski, W. 1966. Biological studies of salt marsh tabanids in Delaware. Master's thesis. Univ. Delaware. 116 pp.

O'Meara, G. F. 1976. Saltmarsh mosquitos (Diptera: Culicidae). *In:* L. Cheng, ed. *Marine Insects.* North-Holland Publ. Co., Amsterdam, Netherlands. pp. 303–333.

O'Neil, T. 1949. The muskrat in the Louisiana coastal marshes. Louisiana Dept. Wildl. and Fish. 152 pp.

Oney, J. 1954. Final report: clapper rail survey and investigation study. Georgia Game and Fish Comm. 50 pp.

Orminati, S. A. and E. J. Hansens. 1974. The biology of *Tabanus lineola lineola* F. *Ann. Ent. Soc. Amer.* 67(6):937–939.

Owen, M. 1971. The selection of feeding site by white-fronted geese in winter. *J. Appl. Ecol.* **8**(3):905–917.

Pace, M. L., S. Shimmel, and W. M. Darley. 1979. The effect of grazing by a gastropod, *Nassarius obsoletus,* on the benthic microbial community of saltmarsh mudflat. *Estuarine Coast. Mar. Sci.* **9**(2):121–134.

Palmisano, A. W. 1972. The distribution and abundance of muskrat (*Ondatra zibethica*) in relation to vegetative types in Louisiana coastal marshes. *Proc. Ann. Conf. Southeast. Assoc. Game and Fish Comm.* **26**:1–31.

Paradiso, J. L., and C. O. Handley, Jr. 1965. Checklist of mammals of Assateague Island. *Ches. Sci.* **6**(3):167–171.

Parker, F. L., and W. D. Athearn. 1959. Ecology of marsh Foraminifera in Poponesset Bay, Massachusetts. *J. Paleont.* **33**:333–343.

Parker, N. H. 1976. The distribution, growth and life history of *Melampus bidentatus* (Gastropoda: Pulmonata) in the Delaware Bay region. Master's thesis. Univ. Delaware. 65 pp.

Parnell, J. F., and R. F. Soots. 1975. Herring and great black-backed gulls nesting in North Carolina. *Auk* **92**(1):154–157.

Paviour-Smith, K. 1956. The biotic community of a salt meadow in New Zealand. *Trans. Roy. Soc. N.Z.* **83**(3):525–554.

Payne, K. T. 1972. A survey of the *Spartina* feeding insects in Poole Harbour, Dorset. *Ent. Mon. Mag.* **108**(1295–1297):66–79.

Pearcy, W. G., and S. W. Richards. 1962. Distribution and ecology of fishes of the Mystic River estuary, Connecticut. *Ecol.* **43**:248–259.

Pearse, A. S. 1914. Habits of fiddler crabs. *Ann. Rept. Smith. Inst.* **1913**:415–428.

Peet, R. K. 1974. The measurement of species diversity. *In:* Johnston, R. F., P. W. Frank, and C. D. Michener, eds. *Ann. Rev. Ecol. Syst.* **5**:285–307.

Peet, R. K. 1975. Relative diversity indices. *Ecol.* **56**(2):496–498.

Penfound, W. T. and J. D. Schneidau. 1945. The relation of land reclamation to aquatic wildlife resources in southeastern Louisiana. *Trans. N. Amer. Wildl. Conf.* **10**:308–318.

Phillips, J. E., and J. Meredith. 1969a. Osmotic and ionic regulation in a salt water mosquito larvae (*Aedes campestris*). *Amer. Zool.* **9**(3):588.

Phillips, J. E., and J. Meredith. 1969b. Active sodium chloride transport by and papillae of a salt water mosquito larvae (*Aedes campestris*). *Nature* **222**(5189):168–169.

Phillips, N. 1978. Spatial distribution and population dynamics of *Orchestia* spp. (Amphipoda: Telatridae) in the Canary Creek salt marsh, Delaware. Master's thesis. Univ. Delaware. 151 pp.

Phleger, F. B. 1965. Patterns of marsh Foraminifera, Galveston Bay, Texas. *Limnol. Oceanogr.* **10**:R169–184.

Phleger, F. B. 1970. Foraminifera populations and marine marsh processes. *Limnol. Oceanogr.* **15**:522–534.

Phleger, F. B. and J. S. Bradshaw. 1966. Sedimentary environments in a marine marsh. *Sci.* **154**:1551–1553.

Phleger, F. B., and W. R. Walton. 1950. Ecology of marsh and bay Foraminifera, Barnstable, Massachusetts. *Amer. J. Sci.* **248**(4):274–295.

Pielou, E. C. 1977. *Mathematical Ecology.* John Wiley & Sons, New York. 385 pp.

Pimentel, D. 1961. Species diversity and insect population outbreaks. *Ann. Ent. Soc. Amer.* **54**:76–86.

Pomeroy, L. R. 1959. Algal productivity in salt marshes of Georgia. *Limnol. Oceanogr.* **4**(4):386–397.

Pomeroy, L. R., K. Bancroft, J. Breed, R. R. Christian, D. Frankenberg, J. R. Hull, L. G. Maurer, W. J. Wiebe, R. G. Wiegert, and R. L. Wetzel. 1976. Flux of organic matter through a salt marsh. *In:* M. Wiley, ed. *Estuarine Processes,* Vol. **2.** Academic Press, N.Y. pp. 270–279.

Post, W. 1970a. Salt marsh. *Audubon Field Notes* **24**(6):771–772.

Post, W. 1970b. Ditched salt marsh. *Audubon Field Notes* **24**(6):772–774.

Post, W. 1974. Functional analysis of space-related behavior in the seaside sparrow. *Ecol.* **55**(3):564–574.

Post, W., and J. S. Greenlaw. 1975. Seaside sparrow displays: their function in social organization and habitat. *Auk* **92**(3):461–492.

Pough, R. H. 1961. Valuable vistas: a way to protect them. *Conn. Arboretum Bull.* **12:**28–30.

Poulson, T. L. 1969. Salt and water balance in seaside and sharp-tailed sparrows. *Auk* **86**(3):473–489.

Poulson, T. L., and G. A. Bartholomew. 1962. Salt balance in the savannah sparrow. *Physiol. Zool.* **35:**109–119.

Price, C. H., and W. D. Russell-Hunter. 1975. Behavioral and physiological aspects of water relations in the high littoral snail, *Melampus bidentatus* Say. *Biol. Bull.* **149**(2):442–443.

Prinslow, T. E., I. Valiela, and J. M. Teal. 1974. The effect of detritus and ratio size on the growth of *Fundulus heteroclitus* (L.). *J. Exp. Mar. Biol. Ecol.* **16**(1):1–10.

Proni, J. R., D. C. Rona, C. A. Lauter, and R. L. Sellers. 1975. Acoustic observations of suspended particular matter in the ocean. *Nature* **254:**412–415.

Prosser, C. L. 1973. *Comparative Animal Physiology.* 3rd ed. W. B. Saunders Co., Philadelphia. Vol. **1,** pp. 46–54.

Provost, M. W. 1969. Ecological control of salt marsh mosquitos with side benefits to birds. *Proc. Tall Timbers Conf. on Ecol. Animal Control by Habitat Mgmt.* **1:**193–206.

Ramsey, J. A. 1950. Osmotic regulation in mosquito larvae. *J. Exp. Biol.* **27:**145–157.

Raney, E. C., R. H. Backus, R. W. Crawford, and C. R. Robbins. 1953. Reproductive behavior in *Cyprinodon variegatus* Lacepede, in Florida. *Zoologica* **38**(6):97–104.

Rankin, J. S., Jr. 1961. Salt marshes as a source of food. *Conn. Arboretum Bull.* **12:**8–13.

Ranwell, D. S. 1960. Newborough Warren, Anglesey. III. Changes in the vegetation on parts of the dune system after the loss of rabbits by myxomatosis. *J. Ecol.* **48**(2):385–395.

Ranwell, D. S. 1961. *Spartina* salt marshes in southern England. I. The effects of sheep grazing at the upper limits of *Spartina* marsh in Bridgewater Bay. *J. Ecol.* **49**(2):325–340.

Ranwell, D. S. 1964. *Spartina* salt marshes in southern England. II. Rate and seasonal pattern of sediment accretion. *J. Ecol.* **52**(1):79–94.

Ranwell, D. S. 1972. *Ecology of Salt Marshes and Sand Dunes.* Chapman and Hall, London. 258 pp.

Ranwell, D. S. 1974. The salt marsh tidal woodland transition. *Hydrobiol. Bull., Netherlands Hydrobiol. Soc.* **8**(1/2):139–151.

Ranwell, D. S., and B. M. Downing. 1959. Brent goose (*Branta bernicla* L.) winter feeding pattern and *Zostera* resources at Scolt Head Island, Norfolk. *Anim. Behav.* **7:**42–56.

Reed, A. 1975. Reproductive output of black ducks in the St. Lawrence estuary. *J. Wildl. Mgmt.* **39**(2):243–255.

Rees, C. P. 1975. Life cycle of the amphipod *Gammarus palustris* Bousfield. *Estuarine Coast. Mar. Sci.* **3**(4):413–419.

Reid, G. K., Jr. 1955. Reproduction and development in the northern diamondback terrapin *Malaclemys terrapin terrapin. Copeia* **1955:**310–311.

Reimold, R. J. 1976. Grazing on wetland meadows. *In:* M. Wiley, ed. *Estuarine Processes,* Vol. **1.** Academic Press, N.Y. pp. 219–225.

Reimold, R. J., J. L. Gallagher, R. A. Linthurst, and W. J. Pfeiffer. 1975a. Detritus production in coastal Georgia salt marshes. *In:* L. E. Cronin, ed. *Estuarine Research,* Vol. I. Academic Press, N.Y. pp. 217–228.

Reimold, R. J., R. A. Linthurst, and P. L. Wolf. 1975b. Effects of grazing on a salt marsh. *Biol. Conserv.* **8:**105–125.

Reimold, R. J., and W. H. Queen, eds. 1974. *Ecology of Halophytes.* Academic Press, N.Y.

Reynoldson, T. B. 1939. On the life history and ecology of *Lumbricillus lineatus* Mull. (Oligochaeta). *Ann. Appl. Biol.* **26**(4):782–799.

Rickards, W. L. 1968. Ecology and growth of juvenile tarpon, *Megalops atlanticus,* in a Georgia salt marsh. *Bull. Mar. Sci. Gulf Carib.* **18:**220–239.

Rockel, E. G. 1969a. Autogeny in the deerfly, *Chrysops fuliginosus* (Diptera: Tabanidae). *J. Med. Ent.* **6**(2):140–142.

Rockel, E. G. 1969b. Marsh physiography: influence on distribution of intertidal organisms. *Proc. N. J. Mosq. Exterm. Assoc.* **56:**102–115.

Rockel, E. G., and E. J. Hansens. 1970a. Distribution of larval horseflies and deerflies (Diptera: Tabanidae) of a New Jersey salt marsh. *Ann. Ent. Soc. Amer.* **63:**681–684.

Rockel, E. G., and E. J. Hansens. 1970b. Emergence and flight activity of salt marsh horseflies and deerflies. *Ann. Ent. Soc. Amer.* **63:**27–31.

Root, R. B. 1973. Organization of a plant-arthropod association in simple and diverse habitats: the fauna of collards (*Brassica oleracea*). *Ecol. Monogr.* **43:**95–124.

Rowan, W. 1913. Note on the food plants of rabbits on Blakeney Point, Norfolk. *J. Ecol.* **1**(4):273–274.

Rudd, R. L., H. C. Hadaway, and J. R. Newman. 1971. Differential responses of five species of salt marsh mammals to inundation. *J. Mammal.* **52:**818–820.

Rude, G. T. 1928. Tides and their engineering aspects. *Trans. Amer. Soc. Civil Eng.* **92:**606–716.

Russell-Hunter, W. D., M. L. Apley, and P. D. Hunter. 1972. Early life history of *Melampus* and the significance of semilunar synchrony. *Biol. Bull.* **143**(3):623–656.

Salmon, M. 1965. Waving display and sound production in the courtship behavior of *Uca pugilator,* with comparisons to U. *minax* and U. *pugnax. Zoologica* **50:**123–150.

Sanders, J. E., and C. W. Ellis. 1961. Geological aspects of Connecticut's coastal marshes. *Conn. Arboretum Bull.* **12:**16–20.

Schantz, V. S. 1943. The rice rat, *Oryzomys palustris* in Delaware. *J. Mammal.* **24:**103–104.

Scheltema, R. S. 1961. Metamorphosis of the veliger larvae of *Nassarius obsoletus* (Gastropoda) in response to bottom sediment. *Biol. Bull.* **120**(1):92–109.

Scheltema, R. S. 1962. Pelagic larvae of New England intertidal gastropods. I. *Nassarius obsoletus* Say and *Nassarius vibex* Say. *Trans. Amer. Micros. Soc.* **81**(1):1–11.

Schmelz, G. W. 1964. A natural history of the mummichog, *Fundulus heteroclitus* (Linnaeus) in Canary Creek marsh. Master's thesis. Univ. Delaware. 65 pp.

Schmelz, G. W. 1970. Some effects of temperature and salinity on the life processes of the striped killifish, *Fundulus majalis* (Walbaum). Ph.D. dissertation. Univ. Delaware. 104 pp.

Schwartz, B., and S. R. Safir. 1915. The natural history and behavior of the fiddler crab. *Cold Spring Harbor Monogr.* **8:**1–24.

Scotton, G. L., and R. C. Axtell. 1979. *Aedes taeniorhynchus* and *A. sollicitans* (Diptera: Culicidae) oviposition on coastal dredge spoil. *Mosq. News* **39**(1):97–110.

Seed, R. 1976. Ecology. *In:* B. L. Bayne, ed. *Marine Mussels: Their Ecology and Physiology.* Cambridge Univ. Press, Cambridge, U.K. pp. 19–38.

Seiple, W. 1979. Distribution, habitat preferences and breeding periods in the crustaceans

Sesarma cinereum and *S. reticulatum* (Brachyura: Decapods: Grapsidae). *Mar. Biol.* **52**(1):77–86.

Seneca, E. D. 1974. Stabilization of coastal dredge spoil with *Spartina alterniflora*. *In:* R. J. Reimold and W. H. Queen, eds. *Ecology of Halophytes*. Academic Press, N.Y. pp. 525–530.

Seneca, E. D., W. W. Woodhouse, and S. W. Broome. 1975. Salt-water marsh creation. *In:* L. E. Cronin, ed. *Estuarine Research,* Vol. **II**. Academic Press, N.Y. pp. 427–438.

Service, M. W. 1968. The ecology of the immature stages of *Aedes detritus* (Diptera: Culicidae). *J. Appl. Ecol.* **5**(3):613–630.

Service, M. W. 1971. Conservation and the control of biting flies in temperate regions. *Biol. Conserv.* **3**:113–122.

Shaler, N. S. 1886. Sea coast swamps of the Atlantic coast. *U.S. Geol. Surv.* **6**:353–398.

Shanholtzer, G. G. 1974. Relationship of vertebrates to salt marsh plants. *In:* R. J. Reimold and W. H. Queen, eds. *Ecology of Halophytes*. Academic Press, N.Y. pp. 463–474.

Sharp, H. F., Jr. 1967. Food ecology of the rice rat *Oryzomys palustris* (Harlan) in a Georgia salt marsh. *J. Mammal.* **48**(4):267–278.

Shaw, S. P., and C. G. Fredine. 1956. Wetlands of the United States—their extent and their value to waterfowl and other wildlife. U.S. Dept. Interior, Fish and Wildl. Serv. Circ. 39. 67 pp.

Shenker, J., and J. M. Dean. 1979. The utilization of an intertidal salt marsh creek by larval and juvenile fishes: abundance, diversity and temporal variations. *Estuaries* **2**(3):154–163.

Shisler, J. K. 1973. Pioneer plants on spoil piles associated with mosquito ditching. *Proc. N. J. Mosq. Exterm. Assoc.* **60**:135–141.

Shisler, J. K., and T. L. Schulze. 1976. Some aspects of open marsh water management procedures on clapper rail production. *Proc. N. E. Fish and Wildl. Conf.* **33**:101–104.

Shoemaker, W. E. 1964. A biological control for *Aedes sollicitans* and the resulting effect upon wildlife. *Proc. N.J. Mosq. Exterm. Assoc.* **51**:93–97.

Shure, D. J. 1970. Ecological relationships of small mammals in a New Jersey barrier marsh habitat. *J. Mammal.* **51**:267–278.

Shure, D. J. 1971. Tidal flooding dynamics: its influence on small mammals in barrier beach marshes. *Amer. Midl. Nat.* **85**(1):36–44.

Sibley, C. G. 1955. The responses of salt marsh birds to extremely high tides. *Condor* **57**:241–242.

Sikora, J. P., W. B. Sikora, C. W. Erkenbrecher, and B. C. Coull. 1977. Significance of ATP, carbon and caloric content of meiobenthic nematodes in partitioning benthic biomass. *Mar. Biol.* **44**:7–14.

Simpson, D. G., and G. Gunter. 1956. Notes on habitats, systematic characters and life histories of Texas saltwater cyprinodonts. *Tulane Stud. Zool* **4**(4):115–134.

Singh, P. B., and K. Nathan. 1965. Hydraulic studies of drainage ditches under tidal influence. *Trans. Amer. Soc. Agr. Eng.* **8**:460–463, 469.

Smalley, A. E. 1960. Energy flow of a salt marsh grasshopper population. *Ecol.* **41**:672–677.

Smallwood, M. E. 1905. The salt marsh amphipod: *Orchestia palustris*. Cold Spring Harbor Monogr. **3**:3–21.

Smith, D. H. 1968. Wildlife prevalence on low level impoundments used for mosquito control in Delaware, 1965–1967. Master's thesis. Univ. Delaware. 83 pp.

Smith, J. B. 1902. The salt marsh mosquito, *Culex sollicitans, Walk.* Spec. Bull. N. J. Agr. Exp. Sta. 10 pp.

Smith, J. B. 1904. Report of the New Jersey state agricultural experiment station upon the mosquitos occurring within the state, their habits and life history, etc. MacCrellish and Quigley, Trenton, N.J. 482 pp.

Smith, J. B. 1905. Vitality of mosquito eggs. *Science* **21**(529):266–267.

Smith, J. B. 1907. The New Jersey salt marsh and its improvement. Bull. N. J. Agr. Exp. Sta. No. 207. 24 pp.

Sorensen, M. F., J. P. Robert, and T. S. Baskett. 1968. Reproduction and development in confined swamp rabbits. *J. Wildl. Mgmt.* **32**(3):520–531.

Springer, P. F., and R. F. Darsie, Jr. 1956. Studies on mosquito breeding in natural and impounded coastal salt marshes in Delaware during 1955. *Proc. N. J. Mosq. Exterm. Assoc.* **43**:74–79.

Springett, J. A. 1964. A method for culturing Enchytraeida. *Oikos* **15**:175–177.

Springett, J. A. 1970. The distribution and life histories of some moorland Enchytraeidae (Oligochaeta). *J. Anim. Ecol.* **39**(3):725–737.

Sprunt, A., Jr. 1955. *North American Birds of Prey.* Harper Bros., N.Y. 227 pp.

Sprunt, A., Jr., and E. B. Chamberlain. 1949. *South Carolina Bird Life.* Univ. South Carolina Press, Columbia, S.C. 585 pp.

Stark, H. E. 1963. Nesting habits of the California vole, *Microtus californicus,* and microclimatic factors affecting its nests. *Ecol.* **44**(4):663–669.

Stearns, L. A., and M. W. Goodwin. 1941. Notes on the winter feeding of the muskrat in Delaware. *J. Wildl. Mgmt.* **5**(1):1–12.

Stearns, L. A., D. MacCreary, and F. C. Daigh. 1939. Water and plant requirements of the muskrat in a Delaware tide water marsh. *Proc. N.J. Mosq. Exterm. Assoc.* **26**:212–221.

Stearns, L. A., D. MacCreary, and F. C. Daigh. 1940. Effects of ditching on the muskrat population of a Delaware tide water marsh. Univ. Delaware Agr. Exp. Sta. Bull. **225**:55 pp.

Stephens, G. C. 1967. Dissolved organic material as a nutritional source for marine and estuarine invertebrates. *AAAS Publ. No. 83, Estuaries.* pp. 367–373.

Stevenson, J. C., D. R. Heinle, D. A. Flemer, R. J. Small, R. A. Rowland, and J. F. Ustach. 1976. Nutrient exchanges between brackish water marshes and the estuary. *In:* M. Wiley, ed. *Estuarine Processes,* Vol. **2**. Academic Press, N.Y. pp. 219–240.

Stevenson, R. A., Jr. 1958. The biology of the anchovies *Anchoa mitchilli mitchilli* Cuvier and Valenciennes 1848 and *Anchoa hepsetus hepsetus* Linneaus 1758 in Delaware Bay. Master's Thesis, Univ. Delaware. 56 pp.

Stewart, R. E. 1951. Clapper rail populations of the Middle Atlantic States. *Trans. N. Amer. Wildl. Conf.* **16**:421–430.

Stewart, R. E. 1952. Clapper rail studies. *In:* J. W. Aldrich, *et al.* Investigations of woodcock, snipe and rails in 1951. U.S. Fish and Wildl. Ser. Spec. Sci. Rept., Wildl. **14**:56–58.

Stewart, R. E. 1953. Breeding populations of clapper rail at Chincoteague, Virginia— 1952. *In:* J. W. Aldrich, *et al.* Investigations of woodcock, snipe, and rails in 1952. U.S. Fish and Wildl. Serv. Spec. Sci. Rept. Wildl. **18**:55.

Stewart, R. E. 1962. Waterfowl populations in the upper Chesapeake region. U.S. Fish and Wildl. Serv., Spec. Rept. Wildl. **65**:208 pp.

Stewart, R. E., and C. S. Robbins. 1958. Birds of Maryland and the District of Columbia. North American Fauna No. 62. Bur. Sports Fish and Wildl., Fish and Wildl. Serv. 401 pp.

Stobbart, R. H. 1965. The effect of some anions and cations upon the fluxes and net uptake of sodium in the larva of *Aedes aegypti. J. Exp. Biol.* **42**(1):29–43.

Stockard, C. R. 1907. The influence of external factors, chemical and physical, on the development of *Fundulus heteroclitus. J. Exp. Zool.* **4**(2):165–201.

Stone, W. 1937. *Bird Studies of Old Cape May*. Vol. **2**. Delaware Valley Ornithol. Club, Philadelphia. pp 485–941.

Stotts, V. D., and D. E. Davis. 1960. The black duck in the Chesapeake Bay of Maryland: breeding behavior and biology. *Ches. Sci.* **1**(3):127–154.

Stout, G. D. 1967. *The Shore Birds of North America*. Viking Press, N.Y. pp. 201–206.

Stromberg, J. O. 1972. *Cyathura polita* (Crustacea, Isopoda): some embryological notes. *Bull. Mar. Sci.* **22**:463–482.

Subrahmanyam, C. B., and S. H. Drake. 1975. Studies on the animal communities in two north Florida salt marshes. Part I. Fish communities *Bull Mar. Sci.* **25**:445–465.

Subrahmanyam, C. B., W. L. Kurczynski, and S. H. Drake. 1976. Studies on the animal communities in two north Florida salt marshes. II. Macroinvertebrate communities. *Bull. Mar. Sci.* **26**(2):172–195.

Sullivan, Charlotte M. 1948. Bivalue larvae of Malpeque Bay, *P.E.I. Bull. Fish. Res. Bd., Canada* **77**:1–36.

Sullivan, M. J. 1971. Distribution and ecology of edaphic diatoms in the Canary Creek marsh. Master's thesis. Univ. Delaware. 99 pp.

Sullivan, M. J. 1974. Long-term effects of light intensity and inorganic nitrogen and phosphorus enrichment on the community structure of edaphic salt marsh diatoms and standing crop of soil algae. Ph.D. dissertation. Univ. Delaware. 132 pp.

Sullivan, M. J. 1975. Diatom communities from a Delaware salt marsh. *J. Phycol.* **11**(4):384–390.

Sullivan, M. J. 1976. Long-term effects of manipulating light intensity and nutrient enrichment on the structure of a salt marsh diatom community. *J. Phycol.* **12**(2):205–210.

Sullivan, M. J. 1977. Edaphic diatom communities associated with *Spartina alterniflora* and *S. patens* in New Jersey. *Hydrobiol.* **52**(2–3):207–211.

Sullivan, M. J. 1978. Diatom community structure: taxonomic and statistical analyses of a Mississippi salt marsh. *J. Phycol.* **14**(4):468–475.

Sullivan, M. J. 1979. Effects of ammonia enrichment and high light intensity on a salt marsh diatom community. Water Resources Research Inst. Miss. State Univ. Project No. A–124–Miss. 53 pp.

Svihla, A. 1930. Notes on the golden harvest mouse. *J. Mammal.* **11**(1):53–54.

Svihla, A. 1931. Life history of the Texas rice rat (*Oryzomys palustris texensis*). *J. Mammal.* **12**(3):238–242.

Svihla, A., and R. Svihla. 1931. The Louisiana muskrat. *J. Mammal.* **12**(1):12–28.

Svihla, R. D. 1929. Habits of *Sylvilagus aquaticus littoralis*. *J. Mammal.* **10**(4):315–319.

Taschdjian, E. 1954. A note on *Spartina* protein. *Econ. Bot.* **8**:164–165.

Tay, K. L., and E. T. Garside. 1975. Some embryogenic responses of mummichog, *Fundulus heteroclitus* (L.) (Cyprinodontidae), to continuous incubation in various combinations of temperature and salinity. *Canad. J. Zool.* **53**(7):920–933.

Taylor, M. H., and L. DiMichele. 1980. Ovarian changes during the lunar spawning cycle of *Fundulus heteroclitus*. *Copeia* **1980**(1):118–125.

Taylor, M. H., L. DiMichele, and G. J. Leach. 1977. Egg stranding in the life cycle of the mummichog *Fundulus heteroclitus*. *Copeia* **1977**:397–399.

Taylor, M. H., G. J. Leach, L. DiMichele, W. H. Levitan, and W. F. Jacob. 1979. Lunar spawning cycle in the mummichog, *Fundulus heteroclitus* (Pisces: Cyprinodontidae). *Copeia* **1979**:291–297.

Teal, J. M. 1958. Distribution of fiddler crabs in Georgia salt marshes. *Ecol.* **39**(2):185–193.

Teal, J. M. 1959. Respiration of crabs in Georgia salt marshes and its relation to their ecology. *Physiol. Zool.* **32**(1):1–14.

Teal, J. M. 1962. Energy flow in the salt marsh ecosystem of Georgia. *Ecol.* **43**(4):614–624.

Teal, J. M., and F. G. Carey. 1967. The metabolism of marsh crabs under conditions of reduced oxygen pressure. *Physiol. Zool.* **40**(1):83–91.

Teal, J. M., and W. Wieser. 1966. The distribution and ecology of nematodes in a Georgia salt marsh. *Limnol. Oceanogr.* **11**:217–222.

Tenore, K. R. 1977. Food chain pathways in detrital feeding benthic communities: a review, with new observations on sediment resuspension and detrital recycling. *In:* B. C. Coule, ed. *Ecology of Marine Benthos.* Univ. South Carolina Press. pp. 37–53.

Thaeler, C. S., Jr. 1961. Variations in some salt-marsh populations of *Microtus californicus.* *Univ. Calif. Publ. Zool.* **60**:67–94.

Thienemann, A. 1926. *Limnologie.* Jedermanns Bucherei, Breslau.

Thomas, A. W. 1972. Physiological age structure of adult tabanid populations (Diptera: Tabanidae) in Alberta, Canada. *J. Med. Ent.* **9**(4):295–300.

Tietjen, J. H. 1967. Observations on the ecology of the marine nematode *Monhystera filicaudata* Allgen, 1929. *Trans. Amer. Micros. Soc.* **86**(3):304–306.

Tietjen, J. H. 1969. The ecology of shallow water meiofauna in two New England estuaries. *Oecologia* **2**:251–291.

Tietjen, J. H., and J. J. Lee. 1972. Life cycles of marine nematodes: influence of temperature and salinity on the development of *Monhystera denticulata* Timm. *Oecologia* **10**:167–176.

Tietjen, J. H., and J. J. Lee. 1977. Feeding behavior of marine nematodes. *In* B. C. Coull, ed. *Ecology of Marine Benthos.* Univ. South Carolina Press. pp. 21–35.

Tietjen, J. H., J. J. Lee, J. Rullman, A. Greengart, and J. Trompeter. 1970. Gnotobiotic culture and physiological ecology of the marine nematode *Rhabditis marina* Bastian. *Limnol. Oceanogr.* **15**(4):535–543.

Tindall, E. E. 1961. A two-year study of mosquito breeding and wild-life usage in the Little Creek impounded salt marsh, Little Creek Wildlife area, Delaware, 1959–1960. *Proc. N. J. Mosq. Exterm. Assoc.* **48**:100–105.

Todd, W. E. C. 1940. *Birds of Western Pennsylvania.* Univ. Pittsburgh Press, 710 pp.

Toll, J. E., T. S. Baskett and C. H. Conaway. 1960. Home range, reproduction, and foods of the swamp rabbit in Missouri. *Amer. Midl. Nat.* **63**(2):398–412.

Tomkins, I. R. 1935. The marsh rabbit: an incomplete life history. *J. Mammal.* **16**:201–205.

Tomkins, I. R. 1941. Notes on Macgillivray's seaside sparrow. *Auk* 58:38–51.

Tomkins, I. R. 1955. The distribution of the marsh rabbit in Georgia. *J. Mammal.* **36**(1):144–145.

Tomkins, I. R. 1965. The willets of Georgia and South Carolina. *Wilson Bull.* **77**:151–167.

Travis, B. V. 1953. Laboratory studies on the hatching of marsh-mosquito eggs. *Mosq. News* **13**(3):190–198.

Travis, B. V., G. H. Bradley, and W. C. McDuffie. 1954. The effect of ditching on salt marsh vegetation in Florida. *Proc. N. J. Mosq. Exterm. Assoc.* **41**:235–244.

Treherne, J. E. 1954. Osmotic regulation in the larvae of *Helodes* (Coleoptera: Helodidae). *Trans. Roy. Ent. Soc. London* **105**:117–130.

Treherne, J. E., and W. A. Foster. 1977. Diel activity of an intertidal beetle, *Dicheirotrichus gustavi* Crotch. *J. Anim. Ecol.* **46**(1):127–138.

Urban, D. 1970. Raccoon populations, movement patterns and predation on a managed waterfowl marsh. *J. Wildl. Mgmt.* **34**(2):372–382.

Urner, C. A. 1935. Relation of mosquito control in New Jersey to bird life of the salt marshes. *Proc. N. J. Mosq. Exterm. Assoc.* **22**:130–136.

Valiela, I., J. E. Wright, J. M. Teal, and S. B. Volkmann. 1977. Growth, production and energy transformations in the salt marsh killifish, *Fundulus heteroclitus. Mar. Biol.* **40**(2):135–144.

Van Dolah, R. F. 1978. Factors regulating the distribution and population dynamics of the amphipod *Gammarus palustris* in an intertidal salt community. *Ecol. Monogr.* **48**(2):191–217.

VanRaalte, C. D., I. Valiela, and J. M. Teal. 1976. The effect of fertilization on the species composition of salt marsh diatoms. *Water Res.* **10**:1–4.

Vernberg, W. B., and F. J. Vernberg. 1972. *Environmental Physiology of Marine Animals.* Springer-Verlag, N.Y.

Vince, S., I. E. Valiela, N. Backus, and J. M. Teal. 1976. Predation by the salt marsh killifish *Fundulus heteroclitus* (L.) in relation to prey size and habitat structure: consequences for prey distribution and abundance. *J. Exp. Mar. Biol. Ecol.* **23**:255–266.

Vogt, W. 1938. Preliminary notes on the behavior and ecology of the eastern willet. *Proc. Linn. Soc., N.Y.* **49**:8–42.

Waisel, Y. 1972. *The Biology of Halophytes.* Academic Press, N.Y. 395 pp.

Wall, W. J., Jr., and O. W. Doane, Jr. 1960. A preliminary study of the blood sucking Diptera on Cape Cod, Massachusetts. *Mosq. News* **20**:39–44.

Wall, W. J., Jr., and H. Jamnback. 1957. Sampling methods used in estimating larval reproduction of salt marsh tabanids. *J. Ecol. Ent.* **50**:389–391.

Warlen, S. M. 1964. Some aspects of the life history of *Cyprinodon variegatus* Lacepede 1803, in southern Delaware. Master's thesis. Univ. Delaware. 40 pp.

Warren, B. H. 1890. *Birds of Pennsylvania.* 2nd ed. E. K. Meyers, State Printer. Harrisburg, Pa. 434 pp.

Warren, G. M. 1911. Tidal marshes and their reclamation. Bull. Exp. Sta. U.S.D.A. **240**: 1–99.

Warwick, R. M., and R. Price. 1979. Ecological and metabolic studies on free-living nematodes from an estuarine mud flat. *Estuarine Coast. Mar. Sci.* **9**(3):257–271.

Waugh, D. L., and E. T. Garside. 1971. Upper lethal temperatures in relation to osmotic stress in the ribbed mussel *Modiolus demissus. J. Fish. Res. Bd., Canada* **28**(4):527–532.

Webster, C. G. 1964. Fall foods of soras from two habitats in Connecticut. *J. Wildl. Mgmt.* **28**:163–165.

Wells, H. W. 1961. The fauna of oyster beds with special reference to the salinity factor. *Ecol. Monogr.* **31**:329–366.

Welsh, B. 1975. The role of grass shrimp, *Palaemonetes pugio,* in a tidal marsh system. *Ecol.* **56**(3):513–530.

Wheeler, Diana E. 1978. Semilunar hatching periodicity in the mud fiddler crab *Uca pugnax* (Smith). *Estuaries* **1**:268–269.

Wheeler, Diana E., and C. E. Epifanio. 1978. Behavioral response to hydrostatic pressure in larvae of two species of xanthid crabs. *Mar. Biol.* **46**:167–174.

White, D. J. B. 1961. Some observations on the vegetation of Blakeney Point, Norfolk, following the disappearance of the rabbits in 1954. *J. Ecol.* **49**(1):113–118.

Whiting, N. H., and G. H. Moshiri. 1974. Certain organism-substrate relationships affecting the distribution of *Uca minax. Hydrobiol.* **44**(4):481–493.

Whittaker, R. H. 1965. Dominance and diversity in land plant communities. *Science* **147**:250–260.

Wiese, J. H., and T. Smith-Kenneally. 1977. A heron colony called Pea Patch. *Del. Conserv.* **21**(2):8–15.

Wieser, W., and J. Kanwisher. 1961. Ecological and physiological studies on marine nematodes from a small salt marsh near Woods Hole, Massachusetts. *Limnol. Oceanogr.* **6**:262–270.

Wigglesworth, V. B. 1972. *The Principles of Insect Physiology.* 7th ed. Chapman and Hall, London. pp. 430–433, 514–515.

Wilbur, S. R. 1974. The literature of the California black rail. U.S. Fish and Wildl. Ser. Spec. Sci. Rept. Wildl. 179. 17 pp.

Wilbur, S. R., and R. E. Tomlinson. 1976. The literature of the western clapper rails. U.S. Fish and Wildl. Ser. Spec. Sci. Rept. Wildl. **194:**31 pp.

Wilson, E. D., and A. A. Dewees. 1962. Body weights, adrenal weights and oestrous cycle of nutria. *J. Mammal.* **43:**362–364.

Wilson, K. A. 1954. The role of mink and otter as muskrat predators in northeastern North Carolina. *J. Wildl. Mgmt.* **18**(2):199–207.

Wilson, W. J. 1970. Osmoregulatory capabilities in isopods: *Ligua occidentalis* and *Ligua pallasii. Biol. Bull.* **138**(1):96–108.

Wolf, P. L., S. F. Shanholtzer, and R. J. Reimold. 1975. Population estimates for *Uca pugnax* (Smith, 1870) on the Duplin Estuary marsh, Georgia, U.S.A. (Decapoda: Brachyura: Ocypodidae). *Crustaceana* **29**(1):79–91.

Wood, C. E. 1967. Physioecology of the grass shrimp, *Palaemonetes pugio,* in the Galveston Bay estuarine system. *Contrib. Mar. Sci. Univ. Texas.* **12:**54–79.

Woodell, S. R. J. 1974. Anthill vegetation in a Norfolk salt marsh. *Oecologia* **16**(3):221–225.

Woodhouse, W. W., Jr., E. D. Seneca, and S. W. Broome. 1974. Propagation of *Spartina alterniflora* for substrate stabilization and salt marsh development. Tech. Memo. No. 46. Coastal Eng. Res. Center, U.S. Army Corps of Eng., Fort Belvoir, Va. 155 pp.

Woodward, D. B., H. C. Chapman, and J. J. Peterson. 1968. Laboratory studies on the seasonal hatchability of egg batches of *Aedes sollicitans, A. taeniorhynchus* and *Psorophora confinnis. Mosq. News* **28**(2):143–146.

Woodwell, G. M., and D. E. Whitney. 1977. Flax Pond ecosystem study: exchanges of phosporus between a salt marsh and the coastal waters of Long Island Sound. *Mar. Biol.* **41**(1):1–6.

Woodwell, G. M., D. E. Whitney, C. A. S. Hall, and R. A. Houghton. 1977. The Flax Pond ecosystem study: exchanges of carbon in water between a salt marsh and Long Island Sound. *Limnol. Oceanogr.* **22**(5):833–838.

Woolfenden, G. E. 1956. Comparative breeding behavior of *Ammospiza caudacuta* and *A. maritima. Univ. Kansas Publ. Mus. Nat. Hist.* **10:**47–75.

Worth, C. B. 1950. Observations on the behavior and breeding of captive rice rats and wood rats. *J. Mammal.* **31**(4):421–426.

Wright, J. O. 1907. Reclamation of tidal lands. U.S. Dept. Agr. Off. Exp. Sta. Rept. **1960:**373–397.

Yapp, R. H. 1923. *Spartina townsendii* on the Dovey salt marshes: a correction. *J. Ecol.* **1:**102.

Yapp, R. H., D. Johns, and O. T. Jones. 1917. The salt marshes of the Dovey estuary. Part II. *J. Ecol.* **5**(2):65–103.

Zedler, J. B. 1977. Salt marsh community structure in the Tijuana estuary, California. *Estuarine Coast. Mar. Sci.* **5**(1):39–53.

Zeskind, L. M., and E. A. LeLacheur. 1926. Tides and currents in Delaware Bay and River. U.S. Coast. and Geodetic Sur. Spec. Publ. No. 123. 122 pp.

Zetterquist, D. K. 1977. The salt marsh harvest mouse (*Reithrodontomys raviventris raviventris,* in marginal habitats. *Wasmann J. Biol.* **35**(1):68–76.

Zilberberg, M. H. 1966. Seasonal occurrence of fishes in a coastal marsh of northwest Florida. *Publ. Inst. Mar. Sci., Univ. Texas* **11:**126–134.

Zucker, N. 1974. Shelter building as a means of reducing territory size in the fiddler crab, *Uca terpsichores* (Crustacea: Ocypodidae). *Amer. Midl. Nat.* **91**(1):224–236.

Author Index

Scientific Name Index

Subject Index